Python: Advanced Guide to Artificial Intelligence

Expert machine learning systems and intelligent agents using Python

Giuseppe Bonaccorso
Armando Fandango
Rajalingappaa Shanmugamani

BIRMINGHAM - MUMBAI

Python: Advanced Guide to Artificial Intelligence

First published: December 2018

Production reference: 1191218

Published by Packt Publishing Ltd.
Livery Place
35 Livery Street
Birmingham
B3 2PB, UK.

ISBN 978-1-78995-721-1

www.packtpub.com

Contributors

About the authors

Giuseppe Bonaccorso is an experienced team leader/manager in AI, machine/deep learning solution design, management, and delivery. He got his MScEng in electronics in 2005 from the University of Catania, Italy, and continued his studies at the University of Rome Tor Vergata and the University of Essex, UK. His main interests include machine/deep learning, reinforcement learning, big data, bio-inspired adaptive systems, cryptocurrencies, and NLP.

Armando Fandango is an accomplished technologist with hands-on capabilities and senior executive level experience with startups and large companies globally. Armando is spearheading Epic Engineering and Consulting Group as Chief Data Scientist. His work spans across diverse industries including FinTech, Banking, BioInformatics, Genomics, AdTech, Utilities and Infrastructure, Traffic and Transportation, Energy, Human Resource, and Entertainment.

Armando has worked for more than ten years in projects involving Predictive Analytics, Data Science, Machine Learning, Big Data, Product Engineering and High-Performance Computing. His research interests span across machine learning, deep learning, algorithmic game theory and scientific computing. Armando has authored book titled "Python Data Analysis - Second Edition" and published research in international journals and conferences.

Rajalingappaa Shanmugamani is currently working as a Engineering Manager for a Deep learning team at Kairos. Previously, he worked as a Senior Machine Learning Developer at SAP, Singapore and worked at various startups in developing machine learning products. He has a Masters from Indian Institute of Technology – Madras. He has published articles in peer-reviewed journals and conferences and applied for few patents in the area of machine learning. In his spare time, he coaches programming and machine learning to school students and engineers.

Packt is searching for authors like you

If you're interested in becoming an author for Packt, please visit `authors.packtpub.com` and apply today. We have worked with thousands of developers and tech professionals, just like you, to help them share their insight with the global tech community. You can make a general application, apply for a specific hot topic that we are recruiting an author for, or submit your own idea.

Table of Contents

Preface

This Learning Path is your complete guide to quickly getting to grips with popular machine learning algorithms. You'll be introduced to the most widely used algorithms in supervised, unsupervised, and semi-supervised machine learning, and learn how to use them in the best possible manner. Ranging from Bayesian models to the MCMC algorithm to Hidden Markov models, this Learning Path will teach you how to extract features from your dataset and perform dimensionality reduction by making use of Python-based libraries.

You'll bring the use of TensorFlow and Keras to build deep learning models, using concepts such as transfer learning, generative adversarial networks, and deep reinforcement learning. Next, you'll learn the advanced features of TensorFlow1.x, such as distributed TensorFlow with TF clusters, deploy production models with TensorFlow Serving. You'll implement different techniques related to object classification, object detection, image segmentation, and more.

By the end of this Learning Path, you'll have obtained in-depth knowledge of TensorFlow, making you the go-to person for solving artificial intelligence problems

This Learning Path includes content from the following Packt products:

- Mastering Machine Learning Algorithms by Giuseppe Bonaccorso
- Mastering TensorFlow 1.x by Armando Fandango
- Deep Learning for Computer Vision by Rajalingappaa Shanmugamani

Who this book is for

This Learning Path is for data scientists, machine learning engineers, artificial intelligence engineers who want to delve into complex machine learning algorithms, calibrate models, and improve the predictions of the trained model.

You will encounter the advanced intricacies and complex use cases of deep learning and AI. A basic knowledge of programming in Python and some understanding of machine learning concepts are required to get the best out of this Learning Path.

What this book covers

`Chapter 1`, *Machine Learning Model Fundamentals*, explains the most important theoretical concepts regarding machine learning models, including bias, variance, overfitting, underfitting, data normalization, and cost functions. It can be skipped by those readers with a strong knowledge of these concepts.

`Chapter 2`, *Introduction to Semi-Supervised Learning*, introduces the reader to the main elements of semi-supervised learning, focusing on inductive and transductive learning algorithms.

`Chapter 3`, *Graph-Based Semi-Supervised Learning*, continues the exploration of semisupervised learning algorithms belonging to the families of graph-based and manifold learning models. Label propagation and non-linear dimensionality reduction are analyzed in different contexts, providing some effective solutions that can be immediately exploited using Scikit-Learn functionalities.

`Chapter 4`, *Bayesian Networks and Hidden Markov Models*, introduces the concepts of probabilistic modeling using direct acyclic graphs, Markov chains, and sequential processes.

`Chapter 5`, *EM Algorithm and Applications*, explains the generic structure of the Expectation-Maximization (EM) algorithm. We discuss some common applications, such as Gaussian mixture, Principal Component Analysis, Factor Analysis, and Independent Component Analysis. This chapter requires deep mathematical knowledge; however, the reader can skip the proofs and concentrate on the final results.

`Chapter 6`, *Hebbian Learning and Self-Organizing Maps*, introduces Hebb's rule, which is one of the oldest neuro-scientific concepts and whose applications are incredibly powerful. The chapter explains how a single neuron works and presents two complex models (Sanger network and Rubner-Tavan network) that can perform a Principal Component Analysis without the input covariance matrix.

`Chapter 7`, *Clustering Algorithms*, introduces some common and important unsupervised algorithms, such as k-Nearest Neighbors (based on KD Trees and Ball Trees), K-means (with K-means++ initialization), fuzzy C-means, and spectral clustering. Some important metrics (such as Silhouette score/plots) are also analyzed.

`Chapter 8`, *Advanced Neural Models,* continues the explanation of the most important deep learning methods focusing on convolutional networks, recurrent networks, LSTM, and GRU.

`Chapter 9`, *Classical Machine Learning with TensorFlow,* teaches us to use TensorFlow to implement classical machine learning algorithms, such as linear regression and classification with logistic regression.

`Chapter 10`, *Neural Networks and MLP with TensorFlow and Keras,* introduces the concept of neural networks and shows how to build simple neural network models. We also cover how to build deep neural network models known as MultiLayer Perceptrons.

`Chapter 11`, *RNN with TensorFlow and Keras,* covers how to build Recurrent Neural Networks with TensorFlow and Keras. We cover the internal architecture of RNN, Long Short-Term Networks (LSTM), and Gated Recurrent Units (GRU). We provide a brief overview of the API functions and classes provided by TensorFlow and Keras to implement RNN models.

`Chapter 12`, *CNN with TensorFlow and Keras,* covers CNN models for image data and provides examples in TensorFlow and Keras libraries. We implement the LeNet architecture pattern for our example.

`Chapter 13`, *Autoencoder with TensorFlow and Keras,* illustrates the Autoencoder models for image data and again provides examples in TensorFlow and Keras libraries. We show the implementation of Simple Autoencoder, Denoising Autoencoder, and Variational Autoencoders.

`Chapter 14`, *TensorFlow Models in Production with TF Serving,* teaches us to deploy the models with TensorFlow Serving. We learn how to deploy using TF Serving in Docker containers and Kubernetes clusters.

`Chapter 15`, *Deep Reinforcement Learning,* covers reinforcement learning and the OpenAI gym. We build and train several models using various reinforcement learning strategies, including deep Q networks.

`Chapter 16`, *Generative Adversarial Networks,* shows how to build and train generative adversarial models in TensorFLow and Keras. We provide examples of SimpleGAN and DCGAN.

`Chapter 17`, *Distributed Models with TensorFlow Clusters*, covers distributed training for TensorFLow models using TensorFLow clusters. We provide examples of asynchronous and synchronous update methods for training models in data-parallel fashion.

`Chapter 18`, *Debugging TensorFlow Models*, tells us strategies and techniques to find problem hotspots when the models do not work as expected. We cover TensorFlow debugger, along with other methods.

`Chapter 19`, *Tensor Processing Units*, gives a brief overview of Tensor Processing Units. TPUs are futuristic platforms optimized to train and run TensorFlow models. Although not widely available yet, they are available on the Google Cloud Platform and slated to be available soon outside the GCP.

`Chapter 20`, *Getting Started with Deep Learning*, introduces the basics of deep learning and makes the readers familiar with the vocabulary. The readers will install the software packages necessary to
follow the rest of the chapters.

`Chapter 21`, *Image Classification*, talks about the image classification problem, which is labeling an image as a whole. The readers will learn about image classification techniques and train a deep learning model for pet classification. They will also learn methods to improve accuracy and dive deep into variously advanced architectures.

`Chapter 22`, *Image Retrieval*, covers deep features and image retrieval. The reader will learn about various methods of obtaining model visualization, visual features, inference using TensorFlow, and serving and using visual features for product retrieval.

`Chapter 23`, *Object Detection*, talks about detecting objects in images. The reader will learn about various techniques of object detection and apply them for pedestrian detection. The TensorFlow API for object detection will be utilized in this chapter.

`Chapter 24`, *Semantic Segmentation*, covers segmenting of images pixel-wise. The readers will earn about segmentation techniques and train a model for segmentation of medical images.

`Chapter 25`, *Similarity Learning*, talks about similarity learning. The readers will learn about similarity matching and how to train models for face recognition. A model to train facial landmark is illustrated.

To get the most out of this book

It's important to have basic-intermediate Python knowledge with a specific focus on NumPy.All the examples are based on Python 3.5+. It is suggested to use the Anaconda distribution (`https://www.anaconda.com/download/`), which is probably the most complete and powerful one for scientific projects. A good mathematics background is necessary to fully understand the theoretical part. In particular, basic skills in probability theory, calculus, and linear algebra are required.

To practice the TensorFlow chapter, you will need Docker and Kubernetes installed. It's preferable that the reader has GPU hardware but it's not necessary.

Download the example code files

You can download the example code files for this book from your account at `www.packt.com`. If you purchased this book elsewhere, you can visit `www.packt.com/support` and register to have the files emailed directly to you.

You can download the code files by following these steps:

1. Log in or register at `www.packt.com`.
2. Select the **SUPPORT** tab.
3. Click on **Code Downloads & Errata**.
4. Enter the name of the book in the **Search** box and follow the onscreen instructions.

Once the file is downloaded, please make sure that you unzip or extract the folder using the latest version of:

- WinRAR/7-Zip for Windows
- Zipeg/iZip/UnRarX for Mac
- 7-Zip/PeaZip for Linux

The code bundle for the book is also hosted on GitHub at `https://github.com/PacktPublishing/Python-Advanced-Guide-to-Artificial-Intelligence`. In case there's an update to the code, it will be updated on the existing GitHub repository.

We also have other code bundles from our rich catalog of books and videos available at `https://github.com/PacktPublishing/`. Check them out!

Conventions used

There are a number of text conventions used throughout this book.

`CodeInText`: Indicates code words in text, database table names, folder names, filenames, file extensions, pathnames, dummy URLs, user input, and Twitter handles. Here is an example: "As the optimization algorithm requires a single array, we have stacked all vectors into a horizontal array `theta0` using the `np.hstack()` function."

A block of code is set as follows:

```
from sklearn.model_selection import train_test_split
X_train, X_test, Y_train, Y_test = train_test_split(X, Y,
train_size=0.7,
random_state=1)
```

Any command-line input or output is written as follows:

```
graph = tf.get_default_graph()
```

Bold: Indicates a new term, an important word, or words that you see onscreen. For example, words in menus or dialog boxes appear in the text like this. Here is an example: "If you need something different, click on the **DOWNLOADS** link in the header for all possible downloads: "

Warnings or important notes appear like this.

Tips and tricks appear like this.

Get in touch

Feedback from our readers is always welcome.

General feedback: If you have questions about any aspect of this book, mention the book title in the subject of your message and email us at `customercare@packtpub.com`.

Errata: Although we have taken every care to ensure the accuracy of our content, mistakes do happen. If you have found a mistake in this book, we would be grateful if you would report this to us. Please visit `www.packt.com/submit-errata`, selecting your book, clicking on the Errata Submission Form link, and entering the details.

Piracy: If you come across any illegal copies of our works in any form on the Internet, we would be grateful if you would provide us with the location address or website name. Please contact us at `copyright@packt.com` with a link to the material.

If you are interested in becoming an author: If there is a topic that you have expertise in and you are interested in either writing or contributing to a book, please visit `authors.packtpub.com`.

Reviews

Please leave a review. Once you have read and used this book, why not leave a review on the site that you purchased it from? Potential readers can then see and use your unbiased opinion to make purchase decisions, we at Packt can understand what you think about our products, and our authors can see your feedback on their book. Thank you!

For more information about Packt, please visit `packt.com`.

1
Machine Learning Model Fundamentals

Machine learning models are mathematical systems that share many common features. Even if, sometimes, they have been defined only from a theoretical viewpoint, research advancement allows us to apply several concepts to better understand the behavior of complex systems such as deep neural networks. In this chapter, we're going to introduce and discuss some fundamental elements that some skilled readers may already know, but that, at the same time, offer several possible interpretations and applications.

In particular, in this chapter we're discussing the main elements of:

- Data-generating processes
- Finite datasets
- Training and test split strategies
- Cross-validation
- Capacity, bias, and variance of a model
- Vapnik-Chervonenkis theory
- Cramér-Rao bound
- Underfitting and overfitting
- Loss and cost functions
- Regularization

Models and data

Machine learning algorithms work with data. They create associations, find out relationships, discover patterns, generate new samples, and more, working with well-defined datasets. Unfortunately, sometimes the assumptions or the conditions imposed on them are not clear, and a lengthy training process can result in a complete validation failure. Even if this condition is stronger in deep learning contexts, we can think of a model as a gray box (some transparency is guaranteed by the simplicity of many common algorithms), where a vectorial input $\bar{X}$ is transformed into a vectorial output $\bar{Y}$:

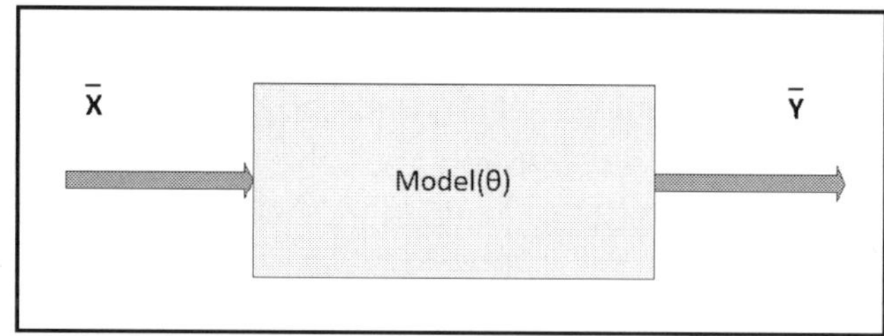

Schema of a generic model parameterized with the vector θ

In the previous diagram, the model has been represented by a pseudo-function that depends on a set of parameters defined by the vector θ. In this section, we are only considering **parametric** models, although there's a family of algorithms that are called **non-parametric**, because they are based only on the structure of the data. We're going to discuss some of them in upcoming chapters.

The task of a parametric learning process is therefore to find the best parameter set that maximizes a target function whose value is proportional to the accuracy (or the error, if we are trying to minimize them) of the model given a specific input X and output Y. This definition is not very rigorous, and it will be improved in the following sections; however, it's useful as a way to understand the context we're working in.

Then, the first question to ask is: What is the nature of X? A machine learning problem is focused on learning abstract relationships that allow a consistent generalization when new samples are provided. More specifically, we can define a stochastic **data generating process** with an associated joint probability distribution:

$$p_{data}(\bar{x}, \bar{y}) = p(\bar{y}|\bar{x})p(\bar{x})$$

Sometimes, it's useful to express the joint probability $p(x, y)$ as a product of the conditional $p(y|x)$, which expresses the probability of a label given a sample, and the marginal probability of the samples $p(x)$. This expression is particularly useful when the prior probability $p(x)$ is known in semi-supervised contexts, or when we are interested in solving problems using the **Expectation Maximization** (**EM**) algorithm. We're going to discuss this approach in upcoming chapters.

In many cases, we are not able to derive a precise distribution; however, when considering a dataset, we always assume that it's drawn from the original data-generating distribution. This condition isn't a purely theoretical assumption, because, as we're going to see, whenever our data points are drawn from different distributions, the accuracy of the model can dramatically decrease.

If we sample N **independent and identically distributed** (**i.i.d.**) values from p_{data}, we can create a finite dataset X made up of k-dimensional real vectors:

$$X = \{\bar{x}_0, \bar{x}_1, \ldots, \bar{x}_N\} \ where \ \bar{x}_i \in \mathbb{R}^k$$

In a supervised scenario, we also need the corresponding labels (with t output values):

$$Y = \{\bar{y}_0, \bar{y}_1, \ldots, \bar{y}_N\} \ where \ \bar{y}_i \in \mathbb{R}^t$$

When the output has more than two classes, there are different possible strategies to manage the problem. In classical machine learning, one of the most common approaches is **One-vs-All**, which is based on training N different binary classifiers where each label is evaluated against all the remaining ones. In this way, $N-1$ is performed to determine the right class. With shallow and deep neural networks, instead, it's preferable to use a **softmax** function to represent the output probability distribution for all classes:

$$\tilde{y}_i = \left(\frac{e^{z_0}}{\sum e^z}, \frac{e^{z_1}}{\sum e^z}, \ldots, \frac{e^{z_N}}{\sum e^z} \right)$$

This kind of output (z_i represents the intermediate values, and the sum of the terms is normalized to 1) can be easily managed using the cross-entropy cost function (see the corresponding paragraph in the *Loss and cost functions* section).

Zero-centering and whitening

Many algorithms show better performances (above all, in terms of training speed) when the dataset is symmetric (with a zero-mean). Therefore, one of the most important preprocessing steps is so-called **zero-centering**, which consists in subtracting the feature-wise mean $E_x[X]$ from all samples:

$$\hat{x}_i = \bar{x}_i - E_x[X]$$

This operation, if necessary, is normally reversible, and doesn't alter relationships both among samples and among components of the same sample. In deep learning scenarios, a zero-centered dataset allows exploiting the symmetry of some activation function, driving to a faster convergence (we're going to discuss these details in the next chapters).

Another very important preprocessing step is called **whitening**, which is the operation of imposing an identity covariance matrix to a zero-centered dataset:

$$E_x[X^T X] = I$$

As the covariance matrix $E_x[X^T X]$ is real and symmetric, it's possible to eigendecompose it without the need to invert the eigenvector matrix:

$$E_x[X^T X] = V \Omega V^T$$

The matrix V contains the eigenvectors (as columns), and the diagonal matrix Ω contains the eigenvalues. To solve the problem, we need to find a matrix A, such that:

$$\hat{x}_i = A\bar{x}_i \;\; and \;\; E_x[\hat{X}^T \hat{X}] = I$$

Using the eigendecomposition previously computed, we get:

$$E_x[\hat{X}^T \hat{X}] = E_x[AX^T X A^T] = AE_x[X^T X]A^T = AV\Omega V^T A^T = I$$

Hence, the matrix A is:

$$AA^T = V\Omega^{-1}V^T \;\Rightarrow\; A = V\Omega^{-\frac{1}{2}}$$

One of the main advantages of whitening is the decorrelation of the dataset, which allows an easier separation of the components. Furthermore, if X is whitened, any orthogonal transformation induced by the matrix P is also whitened:

$$Y = PX \Rightarrow E[Y^T Y] = PE[X^T X]P^T = PP^T = I$$

Moreover, many algorithms that need to estimate parameters that are strictly related to the input covariance matrix can benefit from this condition, because it reduces the actual number of independent variables (in general, these algorithms work with matrices that become symmetric after applying the whitening). Another important advantage in the field of deep learning is that the gradients are often higher around the origin, and decrease in those areas where the activation functions (for example, the hyperbolic tangent or the sigmoid) saturate $(|x| \to \infty)$. That's why the convergence is generally faster for whitened (and zero-centered) datasets.

In the following graph, it's possible to compare an **original dataset**, **zero-centering**, and **whitening**:

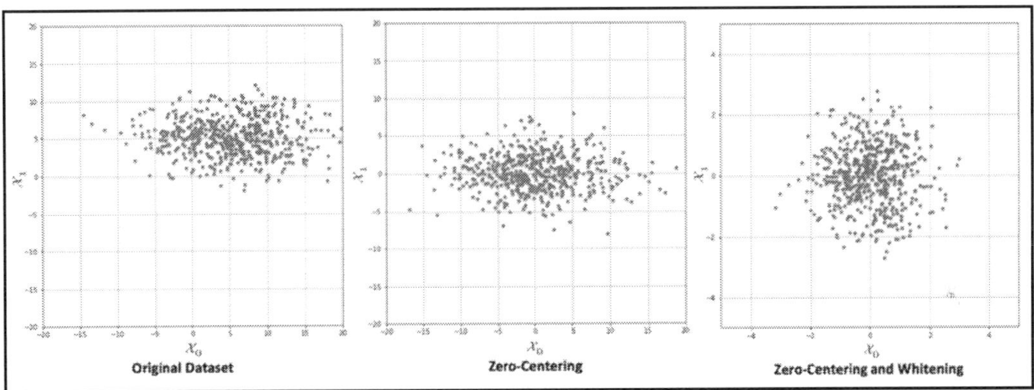

Original dataset (left), centered version (center), whitened version (right)

When a whitening is needed, it's important to consider some important details. The first one is that there's a scale difference between the real sample covariance and the estimation X^TX, often adopted with the **singular value decomposition** (**SVD**). The second one concerns some common classes implemented by many frameworks, like Scikit-Learn's `StandardScaler`. In fact, while zero-centering is a feature-wise operation, a whitening filter needs to be computed considering the whole covariance matrix (`StandardScaler` implements only unit variance, feature-wise scaling).

Luckily, all Scikit-Learn algorithms that benefit from or need a whitening preprocessing step provide a built-in feature, so no further actions are normally required; however, for all readers who want to implement some algorithms directly, I've written two Python functions that can be used both for zero-centering and whitening. They assume a matrix X with a shape ($N_{Samples} \times n$). Moreover, the `whiten()` function accepts the parameter `correct`, which allows us to apply the scaling correction (the default value is `True`):

```
import numpy as np

def zero_center(X):
    return X - np.mean(X, axis=0)

def whiten(X, correct=True):
    Xc = zero_center(X)
    _, L, V = np.linalg.svd(Xc)
    W = np.dot(V.T, np.diag(1.0 / L))
    return np.dot(Xc, W) * np.sqrt(X.shape[0]) if correct else 1.0
```

Training and validation sets

In real problems, the number of samples is limited, and it's usually necessary to split the initial set X (together with Y) into two subsets as follows:

- **Training set** used to train the model
- **Validation set** used to assess the score of the model without any bias, with samples never seen before

According to the nature of the problem, it's possible to choose a split percentage ratio of 70% – 30% (a good practice in machine learning, where the datasets are relatively small), or a higher training percentage (80%, 90%, up to 99%) for deep learning tasks where the number of samples is very high. In both cases, we are assuming that the training set contains all the information required for a consistent generalization. In many simple cases, this is true and can be easily verified; but with more complex datasets, the problem becomes harder. Even if we think to draw all the samples from the same distribution, it can happen that a randomly selected test set contains features that are not present in other training samples. Such a condition can have a very negative impact on global accuracy and, without other methods, it can also be very difficult to identify. This is one of the reasons why, in deep learning, training sets are huge: considering the complexity of the features and structure of the data generating distributions, choosing large test sets can limit the possibility of learning particular associations.

In Scikit-Learn, it's possible to split the original dataset using the `train_test_split()` function, which allows specifying the train/test size, and if we expect to have randomly shuffled sets (default). For example, if we want to split `X` and `Y`, with 70% training and 30% test, we can use:

```
from sklearn.model_selection import train_test_split

X_train, X_test, Y_train, Y_test = train_test_split(X, Y,
train_size=0.7, random_state=1)
```

Shuffling the sets is always a good practice, in order to reduce the correlation between samples. In fact, we have assumed that `X` is made up of i.i.d samples, but several times two subsequent samples have a strong correlation, reducing the training performance. In some cases, it's also useful to re-shuffle the training set after each training epoch; however, in the majority of our examples, we are going to work with the same shuffled dataset throughout the whole process. Shuffling has to be avoided when working with sequences and models with memory: in all those cases, we need to exploit the existing correlation to determine how the future samples are distributed.

When working with NumPy and Scikit-Learn, it's always a good practice to set the random seed to a constant value, so as to allow other people to reproduce the experiment with the same initial conditions. This can be achieved by calling `np.random.seed(...)` and using the `random-state` parameter present in many Scikit-Learn methods.

Cross-validation

A valid method to detect the problem of wrongly selected test sets is provided by the **cross-validation** technique. In particular, we're going to use the **K-Fold** cross-validation approach. The idea is to split the whole dataset X into a moving test set and a training set (the remaining part). The size of the test set is determined by the number of folds so that, during k iterations, the test set covers the whole original dataset.

In the following diagram, we see a schematic representation of the process:

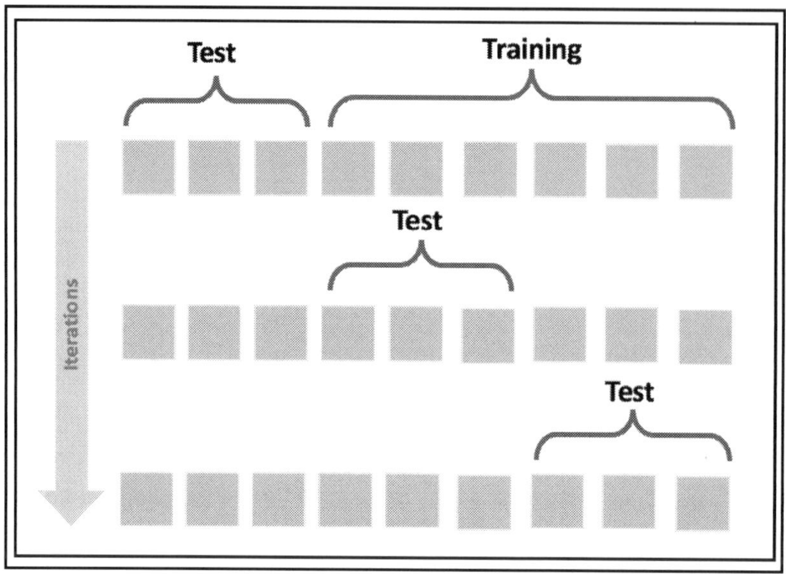

K-Fold cross-validation schema

In this way, it's possible to assess the accuracy of the model using different sampling splits, and the training process can be performed on larger datasets; in particular, on *(k-1)*N* samples. In an ideal scenario, the accuracy should be very similar in all iterations; but in most real cases, the accuracy is quite below average. This means that the training set has been built excluding samples that contain features necessary to let the model fit the separating hypersurface considering the real p_{data}. We're going to discuss these problems later in this chapter; however, if the standard deviation of the accuracies is too high (a threshold must be set according to the nature of the problem/model), that probably means that X hasn't been drawn uniformly from p_{data}, and it's useful to evaluate the impact of the outliers in a preprocessing stage. In the following graph, we see the plot of a 15-fold cross-validation performed on a logistic regression:

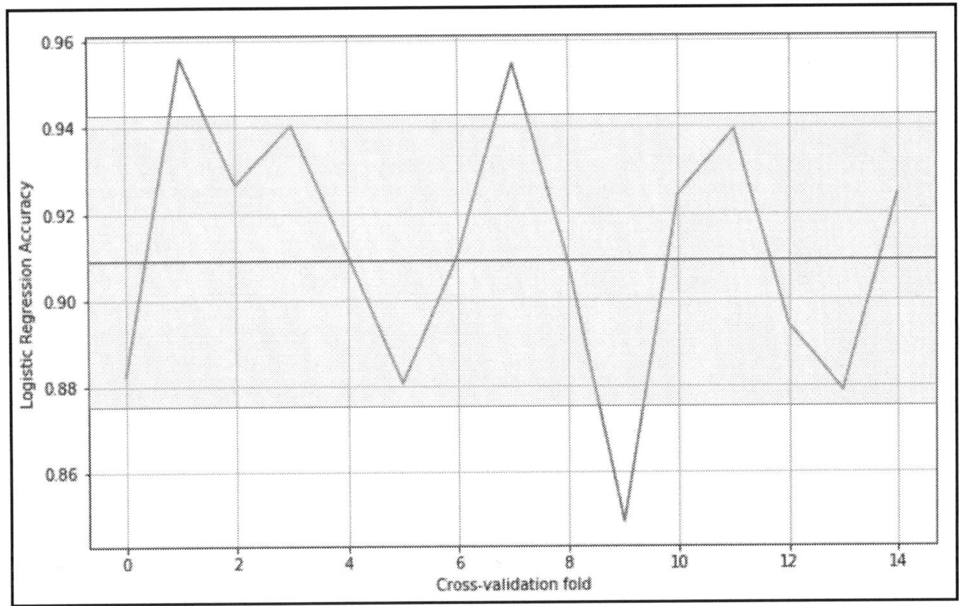

Cross-validation accuracies

The values oscillate from 0.84 to 0.95, with an average (solid horizontal line) of 0.91. In this particular case, considering the initial purpose was to use a linear classifier, we can say that all folds yield high accuracies, confirming that the dataset is linearly separable; however, there are some samples (excluded in the ninth fold) that are necessary to achieve a minimum accuracy of about 0.88.

K-Fold cross-validation has different variants that can be employed to solve specific problems:

- **Stratified K-Fold**: A **Standard K-Fold** approach splits the dataset without considering the probability distribution $p(y|x)$, therefore some folds may theoretically contain only a limited number of labels. Stratified K-Fold, instead, tries to split X so that all the labels are equally represented.

- **Leave-one-out** (**LOO**): This approach is the most drastic because it creates *N* folds, each of them containing *N-1* training samples and only 1 test sample. In this way, the maximum possible number of samples is used for training, and it's quite easy to detect whether the algorithm is able to learn with sufficient accuracy, or if it's better to adopt another strategy. The main drawback of this method is that *N* models must be trained, and when *N* is very large this can cause a performance issue. Moreover, with a large number of samples, the probability that two random values are similar increases, therefore many folds will yield almost identical results. At the same time, LOO limits the possibilities for assessing the generalization ability, because a single test sample is not enough for a reasonable estimation.
- **Leave-P-out** (**LPO**): In this case, the number of test samples is set to *p* (non-disjoint sets), so the number of folds is equal to the binomial coefficient of *n* over *p*. This approach mitigates LOO's drawbacks, and it's a trade-off between K-Fold and LOO. The number of folds can be very high, but it's possible to control it by adjusting the number *p* of test samples; however, if *p* isn't small or big enough, the binomial coefficient can *explode*. In fact, when *p* has about *n/2* samples, the number of folds is maximal:

$$\binom{n}{p} = \frac{n!}{p!(n-p)!} \approx \prod_{t=1}^{p} \frac{n-t}{t} \quad if\ p \approx \frac{n}{2}\ and\ n \gg 1$$

Scikit-Learn implements all those methods (with some other variations), but I suggest always using the `cross_val_score()` function, which is a helper that allows applying the different methods to a specific problem. In the following snippet based on a polynomial **Support Vector Machine** (**SVM**) and the MNIST digits dataset, the function is applied specifying the number of folds (parameter `cv`). In this way, Scikit-Learn will automatically use Stratified K-Fold for categorical classifications, and **Standard K-Fold** for all other cases:

```
from sklearn.datasets import load_digits
from sklearn.model_selection import cross_val_score
from sklearn.svm import SVC

data = load_digits()
svm = SVC(kernel='poly')

skf_scores = cross_val_score(svm, data['data'], data['target'], cv=10)

print(skf_scores)
[ 0.96216216  1.          0.93922652  0.99444444  0.98882682
```

```
0.98882682
  0.99441341  0.99438202  0.96045198  0.96590909]

print(skf_scores.mean())
0.978864325583
```

The accuracy is very high (> 0.9) in every fold, therefore we expect to have even higher accuracy using the LOO method. As we have 1,797 samples, we expect the same number of accuracies:

```
from sklearn.model_selection import cross_val_score, LeaveOneOut

loo_scores = cross_val_score(svm, data['data'], data['target'],
cv=LeaveOneOut())

print(loo_scores[0:100])
[ 1.  1.  1.  1.  1.  0.  1.  1.  1.  1.  1.  1.  1.  1.  1.  1.  1.
1.
  1.  1.  1.  1.  1.  1.  1.  1.  1.  1.  1.  1.  1.  1.  1.  1.  1.
1.
  1.  0.  1.  1.  1.  1.  1.  1.  1.  1.  1.  1.  1.  1.  1.  1.  1.
1.
  1.  1.  1.  1.  1.  1.  1.  1.  1.  1.  1.  1.  1.  1.  1.  0.  1.
1.
  1.  1.  1.  1.  1.  1.  1.  1.  1.  1.  1.  1.  1.  1.  1.  1.  1.
1.
  1.  1.  1.  1.  1.  1.  1.  1.  1.  1.]

print(loo_scores.mean())
0.988870339455
```

As expected, the average score is very high, but there are still samples that are misclassified. As we're going to discuss, this situation could be a potential candidate for overfitting, meaning that the model is learning perfectly how to map the training set, but it's losing its ability to generalize; however, LOO is not a good method to measure this model ability, due to the size of the validation set.

We can now evaluate our algorithm with the LPO technique. Considering what was explained before, we have selected the smaller Iris dataset and a classification based on a logistic regression. As there are *N=150* samples, choosing `p = 3`, we get 551,300 folds:

```
from sklearn.datasets import load_iris
from sklearn.linear_model import LogisticRegression
from sklearn.model_selection import cross_val_score, LeavePOut

data = load_iris()
```

```
p = 3
lr = LogisticRegression()

lpo_scores = cross_val_score(lr, data['data'], data['target'],
cv=LeavePOut(p))

print(lpo_scores[0:100])
[ 1.          1.          1.          1.          1.          1.
1.
  1.          1.          1.          1.          1.          1.
1.
  1.          1.          1.          1.          1.          1.
1.
  1.          1.          1.          1.          1.          1.
1.
  1.          1.          1.          1.          1.          1.
1.
  1.          1.          1.          1.          1.          1.
1.
  1.          1.          1.          1.          1.          1.
1.
  1.          1.          1.          1.          1.          1.
1.
  1.          1.          1.          1.          1.          1.
1.
  1.          0.66666667  ...

print(lpo_scores.mean())
0.955668420098
```

As in the previous example, we have printed only the first 100 accuracies; however, the global trend can be immediately understood with only a few values.

The cross-validation technique is a powerful tool that is particularly useful when the performance cost is not too high. Unfortunately, it's not the best choice for deep learning models, where the datasets are very large and the training processes can take even days to complete. However, as we're going to discuss, in those cases the right choice (the split percentage), together with an accurate analysis of the datasets and the employment of techniques such as normalization and regularization, allows fitting models that show an excellent generalization ability.

Features of a machine learning model

In this section, we're going to consider supervised models, and try to determine how it's possible to measure their theoretical potential accuracy and their ability to generalize correctly over all possible samples drawn from p_{data}. The majority of these concepts were developed before the *deep learning age*, but continue to have an enormous influence on research projects. The idea of *capacity*, for example, is an open-ended question that neuroscientists keep on asking themselves about the human brain. Modern deep learning models with dozens of layers and millions of parameters reopened the theoretical question from a mathematical viewpoint. Together with this, other elements, like the limits for the variance of an estimator, again attracted the limelight because the algorithms are becoming more and more powerful, and performances that once were considered far from any feasible solution are now a reality. Being able to train a model, so as to exploit its full capacity, maximize its generalization ability, and increase the accuracy, overcoming even human performances, is what a deep learning engineer nowadays has to expect from his work.

Capacity of a model

If we consider a supervised model as a set of parameterized functions, we can define **representational capacity** as the intrinsic ability of a certain generic function to map a relatively large number of data distributions. To understand this concept, let's consider a function *f(x)* that admits infinite derivatives, and rewrite it as a Taylor expansion:

$$f(x) = f(x_0) + \frac{f'(x_0)}{1!}(x - x_0) + \frac{f''(x_0)}{2!}(x - x_0)^2 + \ldots = \sum_{n=0}^{\infty} \frac{f^{(n)}(x_0)}{n!}(x - x_0)^n$$

We can decide to take only the first n terms, so to have an n-degree polynomial function. Consider a simple bi-dimensional scenario with six functions (starting from a linear one); we can observe the different behavior with a small set of data points:

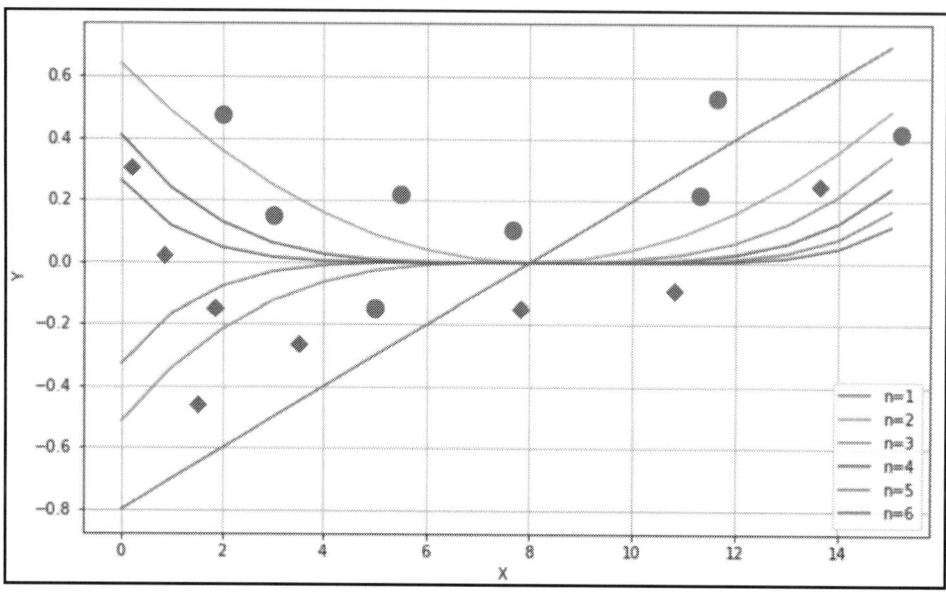

Different behavior produced by six polynomial separating curves

The ability to rapidly change the curvature is proportional to the degree. If we choose a linear classifier, we can only modify its slope (the example is always in a bi-dimensional space) and the intercept. Instead, if we pick a higher-degree function, we have more possibilities to *bend* the curvature when it's necessary. If we consider **n=1** and **n=2** in the plot (on the top-right, they are the first and the second functions), with **n=1**, we can include the dot corresponding to *x=11*, but this choice has a negative impact on the dot at *x=5*.

Only a parameterized non-linear function can solve this problem efficiently, because this simple problem requires a representational capacity higher than the one provided by linear classifiers. Another classical example is the XOR function. For a long time, several researchers opposed perceptrons (linear neural networks), because they weren't able to classify a dataset generated by the XOR function. Fortunately, the introduction of multilayer perceptrons, with non-linear functions, allowed us to overcome this problem, and many whose complexity is beyond the possibilities of any classic machine learning model.

Vapnik-Chervonenkis capacity

A mathematical formalization of the capacity of a classifier is provided by the **Vapnik-Chervonenkis theory**. To introduce the definition, it's first necessary to define the concept of **shattering**. If we have a class of sets *C* and a set *M*, we say that *C* shatters *M* if:

$$\forall m_i \subseteq M \; \exists c_j \in C \Rightarrow m_j = c_i \cap M$$

In other words, given any subset of *M*, it can be obtained as the intersection of a particular instance of *C* (c_j) and *M* itself. If we now consider a model as a parameterized function:

$$C = f(\bar{\theta}) \; where \; \bar{\theta} \in \mathbb{R}^p$$

We want to determine its capacity in relation to a finite dataset *X*:

$$X = \{\bar{x}_0, \bar{x}_1, \ldots, \bar{x}_N\} \; where \; \bar{x}_i \in \mathbb{R}^k$$

According to the Vapnik-Chervonenkis theory, we can say that the model *f* shatters *X* if there are no classification errors for every possible label assignment. Therefore, we can define the **Vapnik-Chervonenkis-capacity** or **VC-capacity** (sometimes called **VC-dimension**) as the maximum cardinality of a subset of *X* so that *f* can shatter it.

For example, if we consider a linear classifier in a bi-dimensional space, the VC-capacity is equal to 3, because it's always possible to label three samples so that f shatters them; however, it's impossible to do it in all situations where $N > 3$. The XOR problem is an example that needs a VC-capacity higher than 3. Let's explore the following plot:

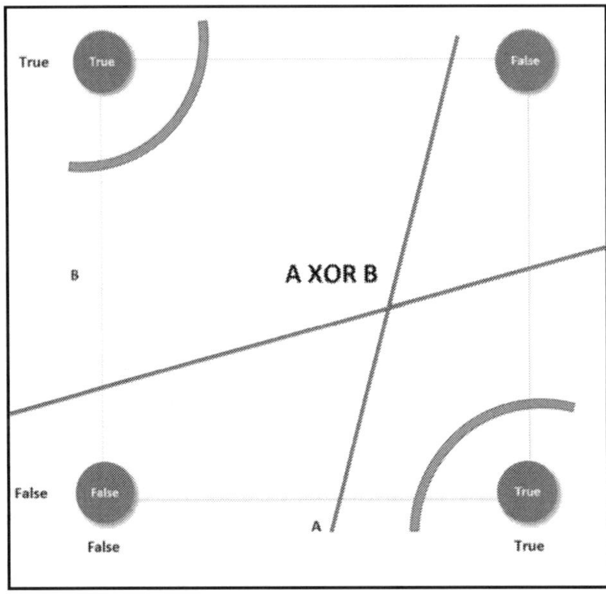

XOR problem with different separating curves

This particular label choice makes the set non-linearly separable. The only way to overcome this problem is to use higher-order functions (or non-linear ones). The curve lines (belonging to a classifier whose VC-capacity is greater than 3) can separate both the upper-left and the lower-right regions from the remaining space, but no straight line can do the same (while it can always separate one point from the other three).

Bias of an estimator

Let's now consider a parameterized model with a single vectorial parameter (this isn't a limitation, but only a didactic choice):

$$p(X; \bar{\theta})$$

The goal of a learning process is to estimate the parameter θ so as, for example, to maximize the accuracy of a classification. We define the **bias of an estimator** (in relation to a parameter θ):

$$Bias\left[\tilde{\theta}\right] = E_{x|\bar{\theta}}\left[\tilde{\theta}\right] - \bar{\theta} = \left(\sum_x \tilde{\theta} p(x|\bar{\theta})\right) - \bar{\theta}$$

In other words, the bias is the difference between the expected value of the estimation and the real parameter value. Remember that the estimation is a function of X, and cannot be considered a constant in the sum.

An estimator is said to be **unbiased** if:

$$Bias\left[\tilde{\theta}\right] = 0 \Rightarrow E\left[\tilde{\theta}\right] = \bar{\theta}$$

Moreover, the estimator is defined as **consistent** if the sequence of estimations converges (at least with probability 1) to the real value when $k \to \infty$:

$$\forall \epsilon > 0 \quad P(|\bar{\theta} - \tilde{\theta}_k| < \epsilon) \to 1 \ \ when \ \ k \to \infty$$

Given a dataset X whose samples are drawn from p_{data}, the accuracy of an estimator is inversely proportional to its bias. Low-bias (or unbiased) estimators are able to map the dataset X with high-precision levels, while high-bias estimators are very likely to have a capacity that isn't high enough for the problem to solve, and therefore their ability to detect the whole dynamic is poor.

Let's now compute the derivative of the bias with respect to the vector θ (it will be useful later):

$$\frac{\partial Bias\left[\tilde{\theta}\right]}{\partial \bar{\theta}} = \frac{\partial}{\partial \bar{\theta}}\left(\left(\sum_x \tilde{\theta} p(x|\bar{\theta})\right) - \bar{\theta}\right) = \left(\sum_x \tilde{\theta} \frac{\partial p(x|\bar{\theta})}{\partial \bar{\theta}}\right) - 1 =$$

$$= \left(\sum_x \tilde{\theta} p(x|\bar{\theta}) \frac{\partial \log p(x|\bar{\theta})}{\partial \bar{\theta}}\right) - 1 = E_{x|\bar{\theta}}\left[\tilde{\theta} \frac{\partial \log p(x|\bar{\theta})}{\partial \bar{\theta}}\right] - 1$$

Consider that the last equation, thanks to the linearity of *E[•]*, holds also if we add a term that doesn't depend on x to the estimation of θ. In fact, in line with the laws of probability, it's easy to verify that:

$$\sum_x (\tilde{\theta} + a)\, p(x|\bar{\theta}) = \sum_x \tilde{\theta} p(x|\bar{\theta}) + a \sum_x p(x|\bar{\theta}) = \sum_x \tilde{\theta} p(x|\bar{\theta})$$

Underfitting

A model with a high bias is likely to underfit the training set. Let's consider the scenario shown in the following graph:

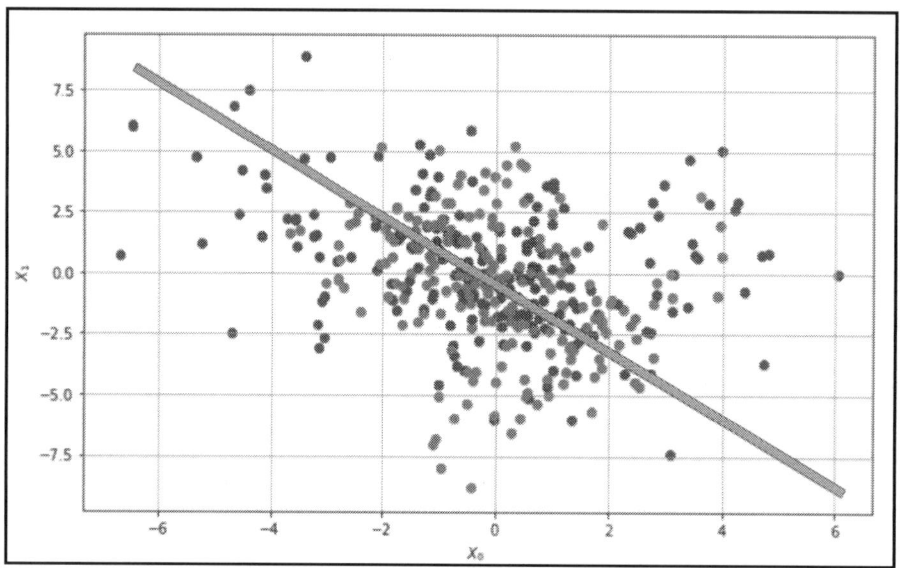

Underfitted classifier: The curve cannot separate correctly the two classes

Even if the problem is very hard, we could try to adopt a linear model and, at the end of the training process, the slope and the intercept of the separating line are about -1 and 0 (as shown in the plot); however, if we measure the accuracy, we discover that it's close to 0! Independently from the number of iterations, this model will never be able to learn the association between X and Y. This condition is called **underfitting**, and its major indicator is a very low training accuracy. Even if some data preprocessing steps can improve the accuracy, when a model is underfitted, the only valid solution is to adopt a higher-capacity model.

In a machine learning task, our goal is to achieve the maximum accuracy, starting from the training set and then moving on to the validation set. More formally, we can say that we want to improve our models so to get as close as possible to **Bayes accuracy**. This is not a well-defined value, but a theoretical upper limit that is possible to achieve using an estimator. In the following diagram, we see a representation of this process:

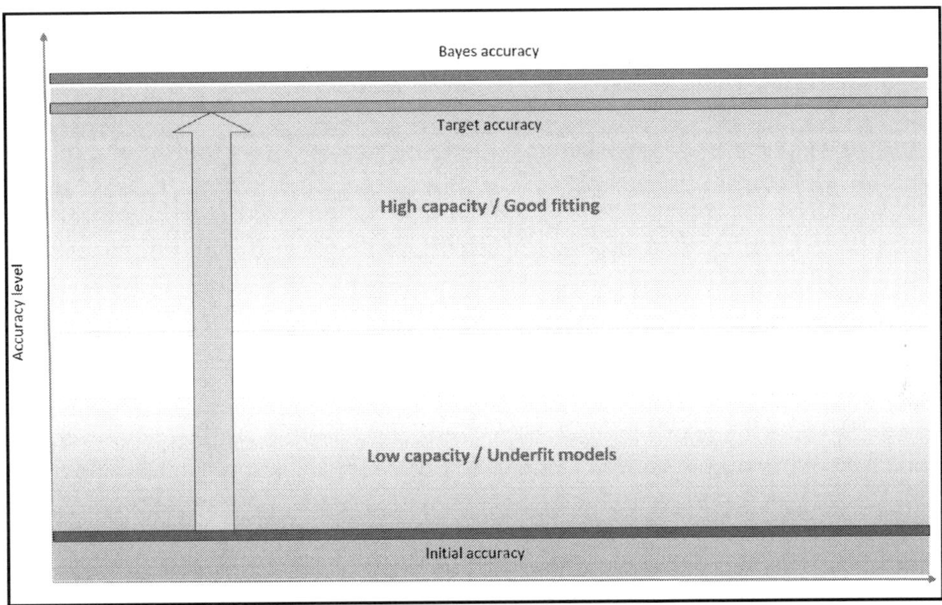

Accuracy level diagram

Bayes accuracy is often a purely theoretical limit and, for many tasks, it's almost impossible to achieve using even biological systems; however, advancements in the field of deep learning allow to create models that have a target accuracy slightly below the Bayes one. In general, there's no closed form for determining the Bayes accuracy, therefore human abilities are considered as a benchmark. In the previous classification example, a human being is immediately able to distinguish among different dot classes, but the problem can be very hard for a limited-capacity classifier. Some of the models we're going to discuss can solve this problem with a very high target accuracy, but at this point, we run another risk that can be understood after defining the concept of variance of an estimator.

Variance of an estimator

At the beginning of this chapter, we have defined the data generating process p_{data}, and we have assumed that our dataset X has been drawn from this distribution; however, we don't want to learn existing relationships limited to X, but we expect our model to be able to generalize correctly to any other subset drawn from p_{data}. A good measure of this ability is provided by the **variance of the estimator**:

$$Var\left[\tilde{\theta}\right] = StdErr\left[\tilde{\theta}\right]^2 = E[(\tilde{\theta} - E[\tilde{\theta}])^2]$$

The variance can be also defined as the square of the standard error (analogously to the standard deviation). A high variance implies dramatic changes in the accuracy when new subsets are selected, because the model has probably reached a very high training accuracy through an over-learning of a limited set of relationships, and it has almost completely lost its ability to generalize.

Overfitting

If underfitting was the consequence of a low capacity and a high bias, **overfitting** is a phenomenon that a high variance can detect. In general, we can observe a very high training accuracy (even close to the Bayes level), but not a poor validation accuracy. This means that the capacity of the model is high enough or even excessive for the task (the higher the capacity, the higher the probability of large variances), and that the training set isn't a good representation of p_{data}. To understand the problem, consider the following classification scenarios:

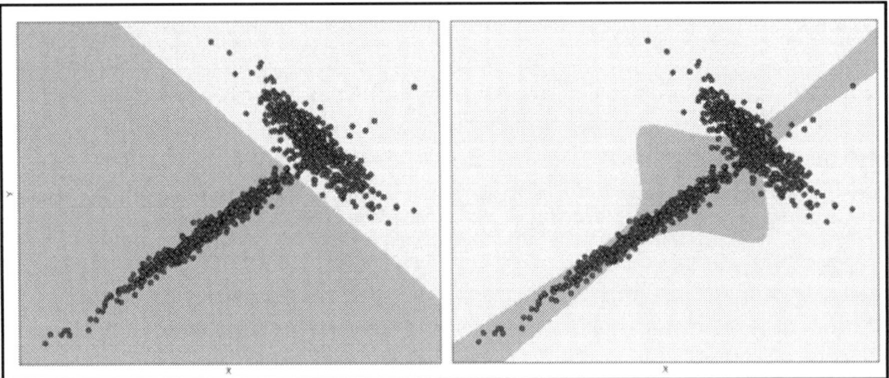

Acceptable fitting (left), overfitted classifier (right)

The left plot has been obtained using logistic regression, while, for the right one, the algorithm is SVM with a sixth-degree polynomial kernel. If we consider the second model, the decision boundaries seem much more precise, with some samples just over them. Considering the shapes of the two subsets, it would be possible to say that a non-linear SVM can better capture the dynamics; however, if we sample another dataset from p_{data} and the diagonal *tail* becomes wider, logistic regression continues to classify the points correctly, while the SVM accuracy decreases dramatically. The second model is very likely to be overfitted, and some corrections are necessary. When the validation accuracy is much lower than the training one, a good strategy is to increase the number of training samples to consider the real p_{data}. In fact, it can happen that a training set is built starting from a hypothetical distribution that doesn't reflect the real one; or the number of samples used for the validation is too high, reducing the amount of information carried by the remaining samples. Cross-validation is a good way to assess the quality of datasets, but it can always happen that we find completely new subsets (for example, generated when the application is deployed in a production environment) that are misclassified, even if they were supposed to belong to p_{data}. If it's not possible to enlarge the training set, data augmentation could be a valid solution, because it allows creating artificial samples (for images, it's possible to mirror, rotate, or blur them) starting from the information stored in the known ones. Other strategies to prevent overfitting are based on a technique called **regularization**, which we're going to discuss in the last part of this chapter. For now, we can say that the effect of regularization is similar to a partial linearization, which implies a capacity reduction with a consequent variance decrease.

The Cramér-Rao bound

If it's theoretically possible to create an unbiased model (even asymptotically), this is not true for variance. To understand this concept, it's necessary to introduce an important definition: the **Fisher information**. If we have a parameterized model and a data-generating process p_{data}, we can define the likelihood function by considering the following parameters:

$$L(\bar{\theta}|X) = p(X|\bar{\theta})$$

This function allows measuring how well the model describes the original data generating process. The shape of the likelihood can vary substantially, from well-defined, peaked curves, to almost flat surfaces. Let's consider the following graph, showing two examples based on a single parameter:

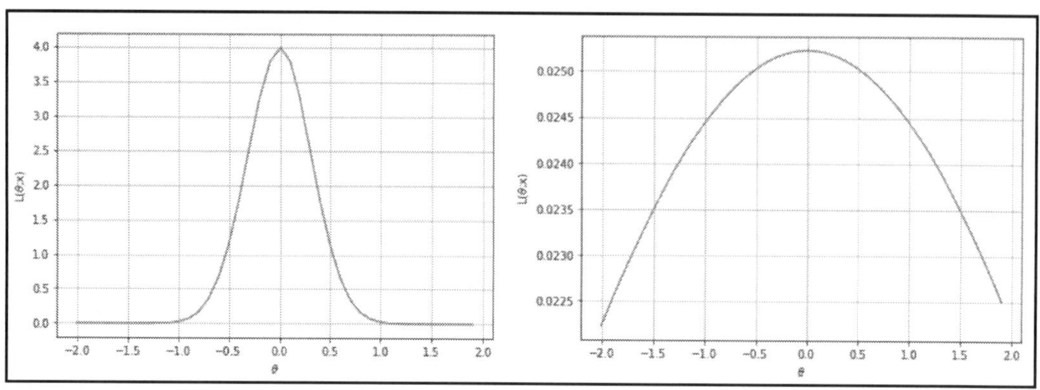

Very peaked likelihood (left), flatter likelihood (right)

We can immediately understand that, in the first case, the maximum likelihood can be easily reached by gradient ascent, because the surface is very peaked. In the second case, instead, the gradient magnitude is smaller, and it's rather easy to stop before reaching the actual maximum because of numerical imprecisions or tolerances. In worst cases, the surface can be almost flat in very large regions, with a corresponding gradient close to zero. Of course, we'd like to always work with very sharp and peaked likelihood functions, because they carry more information about their maximum. More formally, the Fisher information quantifies this value. For a single parameter, it is defined as follows:

$$I(\theta) = E_{\bar{x}|\theta}\left[\left(\frac{\partial}{\partial\theta} log\, p(\bar{x}|\theta)\right)^2\right]$$

The Fisher information is an unbounded non-negative number that is proportional to the amount of information carried by the log-likelihood; the use of logarithm has no impact on the gradient ascent, but it simplifies complex expressions by turning products into sums. This value can be interpreted as the *speed* of the gradient when the function is reaching the maximum; therefore, higher values imply better approximations, while a hypothetical value of zero means that the probability to determine the right parameter estimation is also null.

When working with a set of K parameters, the Fisher information becomes a positive semidefinite matrix:

$$I(\bar{\theta}) = \begin{pmatrix} E_{\bar{x}|\bar{\theta}}\left[\left(\frac{\partial}{\partial\theta_0} log\, p(\bar{x}|\bar{\theta})\right)\left(\frac{\partial}{\partial\theta_0} log\, p(\bar{x}|\bar{\theta})\right)\right] & \cdots & E_{\bar{x}|\bar{\theta}}\left[\left(\frac{\partial}{\partial\theta_0} log\, p(\bar{x}|\bar{\theta})\right)\left(\frac{\partial}{\partial\theta_K} log\, p(\bar{x}|\bar{\theta})\right)\right] \\ \vdots & \ddots & \vdots \\ E_{\bar{x}|\bar{\theta}}\left[\left(\frac{\partial}{\partial\theta_K} log\, p(\bar{x}|\bar{\theta})\right)\left(\frac{\partial}{\partial\theta_0} log\, p(\bar{x}|\bar{\theta})\right)\right] & \cdots & E_{\bar{x}|\bar{\theta}}\left[\left(\frac{\partial}{\partial\theta_K} log\, p(\bar{x}|\bar{\theta})\right)\left(\frac{\partial}{\partial\theta_K} log\, p(\bar{x}|\bar{\theta})\right)\right] \end{pmatrix}$$

This matrix is symmetric, and also has another important property: when a value is zero, it means that the corresponding couple of parameters are orthogonal for the purpose of the maximum likelihood estimation, and they can be considered separately. In many real cases, if a value is close to zero, it determines a very low correlation between parameters and, even if it's not mathematically rigorous, it's possible to decouple them anyway.

At this point, it's possible to introduce the **Cramér-Rao bound**, which states that for every unbiased estimator that adopts x (with probability distribution $p(x; \theta)$) as a measure set, the variance of any estimator of θ is always lower-bounded according to the following inequality:

$$Var\left[\tilde{\theta}\right] \geqslant \frac{1}{I(\theta)}$$

In fact, considering initially a generic estimator and exploiting Cauchy-Schwarz inequality with the variance and the Fisher information (which are both expressed as expected values), we obtain:

$$E_{\bar{x}|\theta}\left[(\tilde{\theta} - E_{\bar{x}|\theta}[\tilde{\theta}])^2\right] E_{\bar{x}|\theta}\left[\left(\frac{\partial\, log\, p(\bar{x}|\theta)}{\partial\theta}\right)^2\right] \geqslant E_{\bar{x}|\theta}\left[(\tilde{\theta} - E_{\bar{x}|\theta}[\tilde{\theta}])\frac{\partial\, log\, p(\bar{x}|\theta)}{\partial\theta}\right]^2$$

Now, if we use the expression for derivatives of the bias with respect to θ, considering that the expected value of the estimation of θ doesn't depend on x, we can rewrite the right side of the inequality as:

$$E_{\bar{x}|\theta}\left[(\tilde{\theta} - E_{\bar{x}|\theta}[\tilde{\theta}])\frac{\partial\, log\, p(\bar{x}|\theta)}{\partial\theta}\right]^2 = \left(\frac{\partial Bias\left[\tilde{\theta}\right]}{\partial\theta} + 1\right)^2$$

If the estimator is unbiased, the derivative on the right side is equal to zero, therefore, we get:

$$Var\left[\tilde{\theta}\right] \cdot I(\theta) \geqslant 1$$

In other words, we can try to reduce the variance, but it will be always lower-bounded by the inverse Fisher information. Therefore, given a dataset and a model, there's always a limit to the ability to generalize. In some cases, this measure is easy to determine; however, its real value is theoretical, because it provides the likelihood function with another fundamental property: it carries all the information needed to estimate the worst case for variance. This is not surprising: when we discussed the capacity of a model, we saw how different functions could drive to higher or lower accuracies. If the training accuracy is high enough, this means that the capacity is appropriate or even excessive for the problem; however, we haven't considered the role of the likelihood $p(X|\theta)$.

High-capacity models, in particular, with small or low-informative datasets, can drive to flat likelihood surfaces with a higher probability than lower-capacity models. Therefore, the Fisher information tends to become smaller, because there are more and more parameter sets that yield similar probabilities, and this, at the end of the day, drives to higher variances and an increased risk of overfitting. To conclude this section, it's useful to consider a general empirical rule derived from the **Occam's razor** principle: whenever a simpler model can explain a phenomenon with enough accuracy, it doesn't make sense to increase its capacity. A simpler model is always preferable (when the performance is good and it represents accurately the specific problem), because it's normally faster both in the training and in the inference phases, and more efficient. When talking about deep neural networks, this principle can be applied in a more precise way, because it's easier to increase or decrease the number of layers and neurons until the desired accuracy has been achieved.

Loss and cost functions

At the beginning of this chapter, we discussed the concept of generic target function so as to optimize in order to solve a machine learning problem. More formally, in a supervised scenario, where we have finite datasets X and Y:

$$X = \{\bar{x}_0, \bar{x}_1, \ldots, \bar{x}_N\} \; where \; \bar{x}_i \in \mathbb{R}^k$$

$$Y = \{\bar{y}_0, \bar{y}_1, \ldots, \bar{y}_N\} \; where \; \bar{y}_i \in \mathbb{R}^t$$

We can define the generic **loss function** for a single sample as:

$$J(\bar{x}_i, \bar{y}_i; \bar{\theta}) = J(f(\bar{x}_i, \bar{\theta}), \bar{y}_i) = J(\tilde{y}_i, \bar{y}_i)$$

J is a function of the whole parameter set, and must be proportional to the error between the true label and the predicted. Another important property is convexity. In many real cases, this is an almost impossible condition; however, it's always useful to look for convex loss functions, because they can be easily optimized through the gradient descent method. It's useful to consider a loss function as an intermediate between our training process and a pure mathematical optimization. The missing link is the complete data. As already discussed, *X* is drawn from p_{data}, so it should represent the true distribution. Therefore, when minimizing the loss function, we're considering a potential subset of points, and never the whole real dataset. In many cases, this isn't a limitation, because, if the bias is null and the variance is small enough, the resulting model will show a good generalization ability (high training and validation accuracy); however, considering the data generating process, it's useful to introduce another measure called **expected risk**:

$$E_{Risk}[f] = \int J(f(\bar{x}, \bar{\theta}), \bar{y})\, p_{data}(\bar{x}, \bar{y})\, d\bar{x} d\bar{y}$$

This value can be interpreted as an average of the loss function over all possible samples drawn from p_{data}. Minimizing the expected risk implies the maximization of the global accuracy. When working with a finite number of training samples, instead, it's common to define a **cost function** (often called a loss function as well, and not to be confused with the log-likelihood):

$$L(X, Y; \bar{\theta}) = \sum_{i=0}^{N} J(\bar{x}_i, \bar{y}_i; \bar{\theta})$$

This is the actual function that we're going to minimize and, divided by the number of samples (a factor that doesn't have any impact), it's also called **empirical risk**, because it's an approximation (based on real data) of the expected risk. In other words, we want to find a set of parameters so that:

$$\bar{\theta}^* = argmax_{\bar{\theta}}\, L(X, Y; \bar{\theta})$$

When the cost function has more than two parameters, it's very difficult and perhaps even impossible to understand its internal structure; however, we can analyze some potential conditions using a bidimensional diagram:

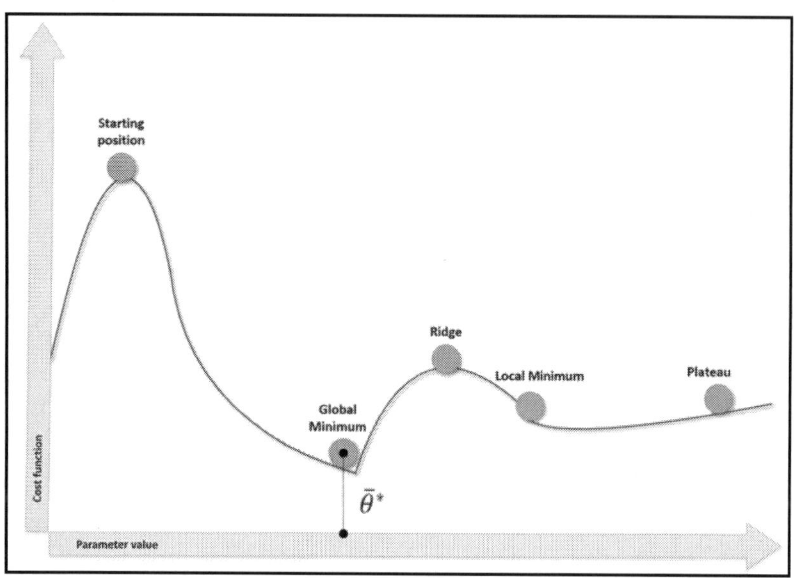

Different kinds of points in a bidimensional scenario

The different situations we can observe are:

- The **starting point**, where the cost function is usually very high due to the error.
- **Local minima**, where the gradient is null (and the second derivative is positive). They are candidates for the optimal parameter set, but unfortunately, if the concavity isn't too deep, an inertial movement or some noise can easily move the point away.
- **Ridges** (or **local maxima**), where the gradient is null, and the second derivative is negative. They are unstable points, because a minimum perturbation allows escaping, reaching lower-cost areas.

- **Plateaus**, or the region where the surface is almost flat and the gradient is close to zero. The only way to escape a plateau is to keep a residual kinetic energy—we're going to discuss this concept when talking about neural optimization algorithms.
- **Global minimum**, the point we want to reach to optimize the cost function.

Even if local minima are likely when the number of parameters is small, they become very unlikely when the model has a large number of parameters. In fact, an n-dimensional point θ^* is a local minimum for a convex function (and here, we're assuming L to be convex) only if:

$$\begin{cases} \nabla_\theta L(x^*) = 0 \\ H_\theta L(\theta^*) \, positive \; semidef. \end{cases}$$

The second condition imposes a positive semi-definite Hessian matrix (equivalently, all principal minors H_n made with the first n rows and n columns must be non-negative), therefore all its eigenvalues $\lambda_0, \lambda_1, ..., \lambda_N$ must be non-negative. This probability decreases with the number of parameters (H is a $n \times n$ square matrix and has n eigenvalues), and becomes close to zero in deep learning models where the number of weights can be in the order of 10,000,000 (or even more). The reader interested in a complete mathematical proof can read *High Dimensional Spaces, Deep Learning and Adversarial Examples, Dube S., arXiv:1801.00634 [cs.CV]*. As a consequence, a more common condition to consider is instead the presence of **saddle points**, where the eigenvalues have different signs and the orthogonal directional derivatives are null, even if the points are neither local maxima nor minima. Consider, for example, the following plot:

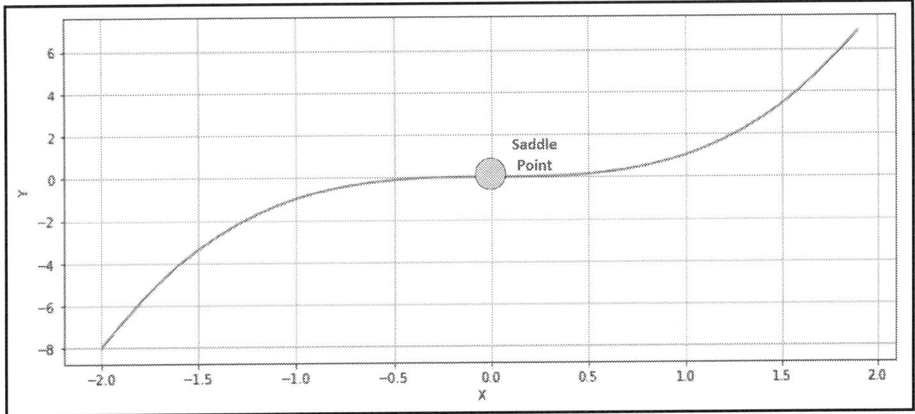

Saddle point in a bidimensional scenario

The function is $y=x3$ whose first and second derivatives are $y'=3x2$ and $y''=6x$. Therefore, $y'(0)=y''(0)=0$. In this case (single-valued function), this point is also called a **point of inflection**, because at $x=0$, the function shows a change in the concavity. In three dimensions, it's easier to understand why a saddle point has been called in this way. Consider, for example, the following plot:

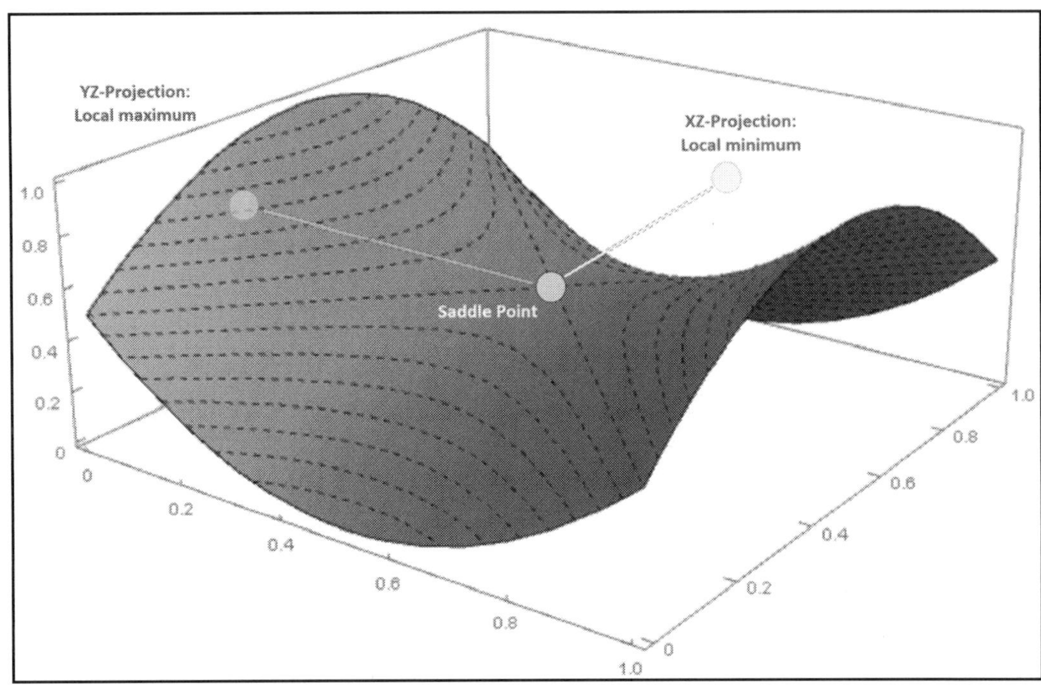

Saddle point in a three-dimensional scenario

The surface is very similar to a horse saddle, and if we project the point on an orthogonal plane, *XZ* is a minimum, while on another plane (*YZ*) it is a maximum. Saddle points are quite dangerous, because many simpler optimization algorithms can slow down and even stop, losing the ability to find the right direction.

Examples of cost functions

In this section, we expose some common **cost functions** that are employed in both classification and regression tasks. Some of them will be extensively adopted in our examples in the next chapters, particularly when discussing training processes in shallow and deep neural networks.

Mean squared error

Mean squared error is one of the most common regression cost functions. Its generic expression is:

$$L\left(X, Y; \bar{\theta}\right) = \frac{1}{N} \sum_{i=0}^{N-1} \left(f\left(\bar{x}_i, \bar{\theta}\right) - y_i\right)^2$$

This function is differentiable at every point of its domain and it's convex, so it can be optimized using the **stochastic gradient descent** (**SGD**) algorithm; however, there's a drawback when employed in regressions where there are outliers. As its value is always quadratic when the distance between the prediction and the actual value (corresponding to an outlier) is large, the relative error is high, and this can lead to an unacceptable correction.

Huber cost function

As explained, mean squared error isn't robust to outliers, because it's always quadratic independently of the distance between actual value and prediction. To overcome this problem, it's possible to employ the **Huber cost function**, which is based on threshold t_H, so that for distances less than t_H, its behavior is quadratic, while for a distance greater than t_H, it becomes linear, reducing the entity of the error and, therefore, the relative importance of the outliers.

The analytical expression is:

$$L\left(X, Y; \bar{\theta}, t_H\right) = \begin{cases} \frac{1}{2} \sum_{i=0}^{N-1} \left(f\left(\bar{x}_i, \bar{\theta}\right) - y_i\right)^2 & if \left|f\left(\bar{x}_i, \bar{\theta}\right) - y_i\right| \leqslant t_H \\ t_H \sum_{i=0}^{N-1} \left|f\left(\bar{x}_i, \bar{\theta}\right) - y_i\right| - \frac{t_H}{2} & if \left|f\left(\bar{x}_i, \bar{\theta}\right) - y_i\right| > t_H \end{cases}$$

Hinge cost function

This cost function is adopted by SVM, where the goal is to maximize the distance between the separation boundaries (where the support vector lies). It's analytic expression is:

$$L(X,Y;\bar{\theta}) = \sum_{i=0}^{N-1} max\left(0, 1 - f\left(\bar{x}_i, \bar{\theta}\right) \cdot y_i\right)$$

Contrary to the other examples, this cost function is not optimized using classic stochastic gradient descent methods, because it's not differentiable at all points where:

$$f\left(\bar{x}_i, \bar{\theta}\right) \cdot y_i = 1 \Rightarrow max(0,0)$$

For this reason, SVM algorithms are optimized using quadratic programming techniques.

Categorical cross-entropy

Categorical cross-entropy is the most diffused classification cost function, adopted by logistic regression and the majority of neural architectures. The generic analytical expression is:

$$L(X,Y;\bar{\theta}) = -\sum_{i=0}^{N-1} y_i \; log\, f\left(\bar{x}_i, \bar{\theta}\right)$$

This cost function is convex and can be easily optimized using stochastic gradient descent techniques; moreover, it has another important interpretation. If we are training a classifier, our goal is to create a model whose distribution is as similar as possible to *pdata*. This condition can be achieved by minimizing the Kullback-Leibler divergence between the two distributions:

$$D_{KL}\left(p_{data} \| \tilde{p}_M\right) = \sum_{i=0}^{N-1} p_{data}\left(\bar{x}_i, y_i\right) log \frac{p_{data}\left(\bar{x}_i, y_i\right)}{\tilde{p}_M\left(\bar{x}_i, y_i; \bar{\theta}\right)}$$

In the previous expression, p_M is the distribution generated by the model. Now, if we rewrite the divergence, we get:

$$D_{KL}\left(p_{data}\|\tilde{p}_M\right) = \sum_{i=0}^{N-1} p_{data}\left(\bar{x}_i, y_i\right) log\, p_{data}\left(\bar{x}_i, y_i\right) - \sum_{i=0}^{N-1} p_{data}\left(\bar{x}_i, y_i\right) log\, \tilde{p}_M\left(\bar{x}_i, y_i; \bar{\theta}\right) =$$
$$= H\left(p_{data}\left(\bar{x}_i, y_i\right)\right) + H\left(p_{data}\left(\bar{x}_i, y_i\right), \tilde{p}_M\left(\bar{x}_i, y_i; \bar{\theta}\right)\right)$$

The first term is the entropy of the data-generating distribution, and it doesn't depend on the model parameters, while the second one is the cross-entropy. Therefore, if we minimize the cross-entropy, we also minimize the Kullback-Leibler divergence, forcing the model to reproduce a distribution that is very similar to p_{data}. This is a very elegant explanation as to why the cross-entropy cost function is an excellent choice for classification problems.

Regularization

When a model is ill-conditioned or prone to overfitting, **regularization** offers some valid tools to mitigate the problems. From a mathematical viewpoint, a regularizer is a penalty added to the cost function, so to impose an extra-condition on the evolution of the parameters:

$$L_R\left(X, Y; \bar{\theta}\right) = L\left(X, Y; \bar{\theta}\right) + \lambda g\left(\bar{\theta}\right)$$

The parameter λ controls the strength of the regularization, which is expressed through the function $g(\theta)$. A fundamental condition on $g(\theta)$ is that it must be differentiable so that the new composite cost function can still be optimized using SGD algorithms. In general, any regular function can be employed; however, we normally need a function that can contrast the indefinite growth of the parameters.

To understand the principle, let's consider the following diagram:

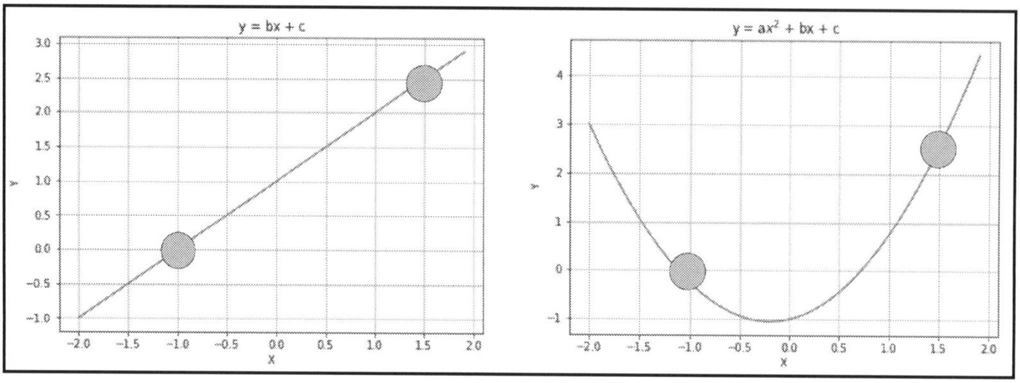

Interpolation with a linear curve (left) and a parabolic one (right)

In the first diagram, the model is linear and has two parameters, while in the second one, it is quadratic and has three parameters. We already know that the second option is more prone to overfitting, but if we apply a regularization term, it's possible to avoid the growth of a (first quadratic parameter), transforming the model into a linearized version. Of course, there's a difference between choosing a lower-capacity model and applying a regularization constraint. In fact, in the first case, we are renouncing the possibility offered by the extra capacity, running the risk of increasing the bias, while with regularization we keep the same model but optimize it so to reduce the variance. Let's now explore the most common regularization techniques.

Ridge

Ridge regularization (also known as **Tikhonov regularization**) is based on the squared L2-norm of the parameter vector:

$$L_R\left(X, Y; \bar{\theta}\right) = L\left(X, Y; \bar{\theta}\right) + \lambda \|\bar{\theta}\|_2^2$$

This penalty avoids an infinite growth of the parameters (for this reason, it's also known as **weight shrinkage**), and it's particularly useful when the model is ill-conditioned, or there is multicollinearity, due to the fact that the samples are completely independent (a relatively common condition).

In the following diagram, we see a schematic representation of the Ridge regularization in a bidimensional scenario:

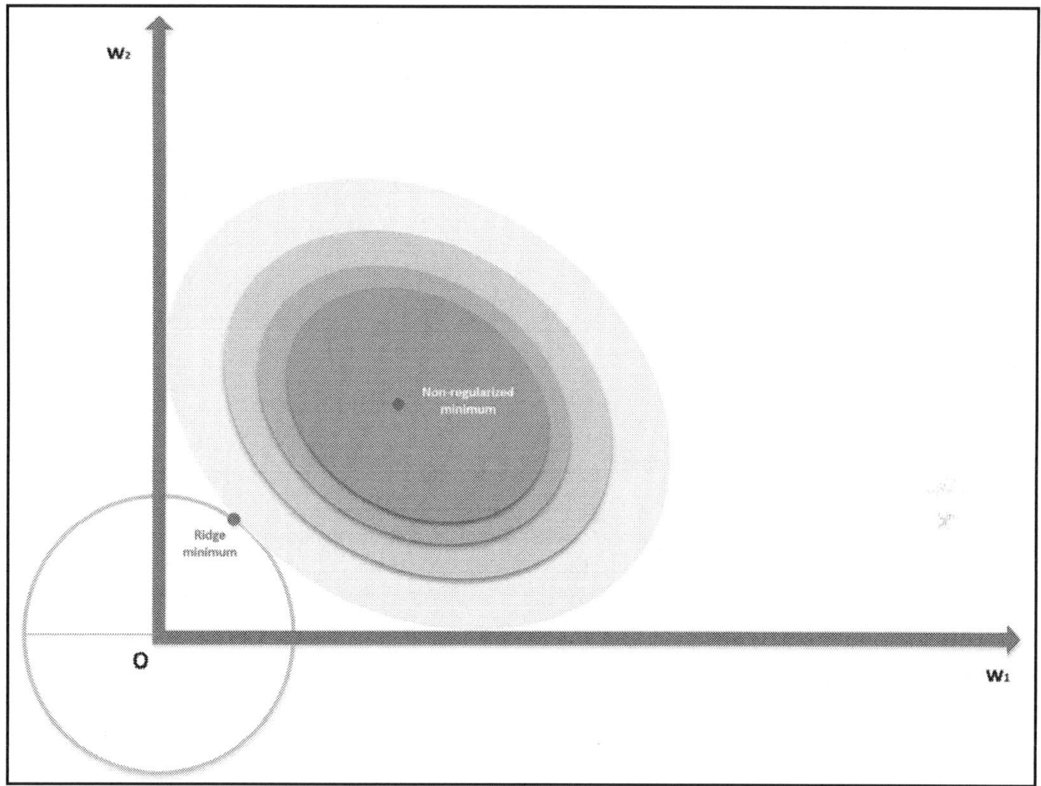

Ridge (L2) regularization

The zero-centered circle represents the Ridge boundary, while the shaded surface is the original cost function. Without regularization, the minimum ($\mathbf{w}_1$, $\mathbf{w}_2$) has a magnitude (for example, the distance from the origin) which is about double the one obtained by applying a Ridge constraint, confirming the expected shrinkage. When applied to regressions solved with the **Ordinary Least Squares** (**OLS**) algorithm, it's possible to prove that there always exists a Ridge coefficient, so that the weights are shrunk with respect the OLS ones. The same result, with some restrictions, can be extended to other cost functions.

Lasso

Lasso regularization is based on the *L1*-norm of the parameter vector:

$$L_R\left(X,Y;\bar{\theta}\right) = L\left(X,Y;\bar{\theta}\right) + \lambda\|\bar{\theta}\|_1$$

Contrary to Ridge, which shrinks all the weights, Lasso can shift the smallest one to zero, creating a sparse parameter vector. The mathematical proof is beyond the scope of this book; however, it's possible to understand it intuitively by considering the following diagram (bidimensional):

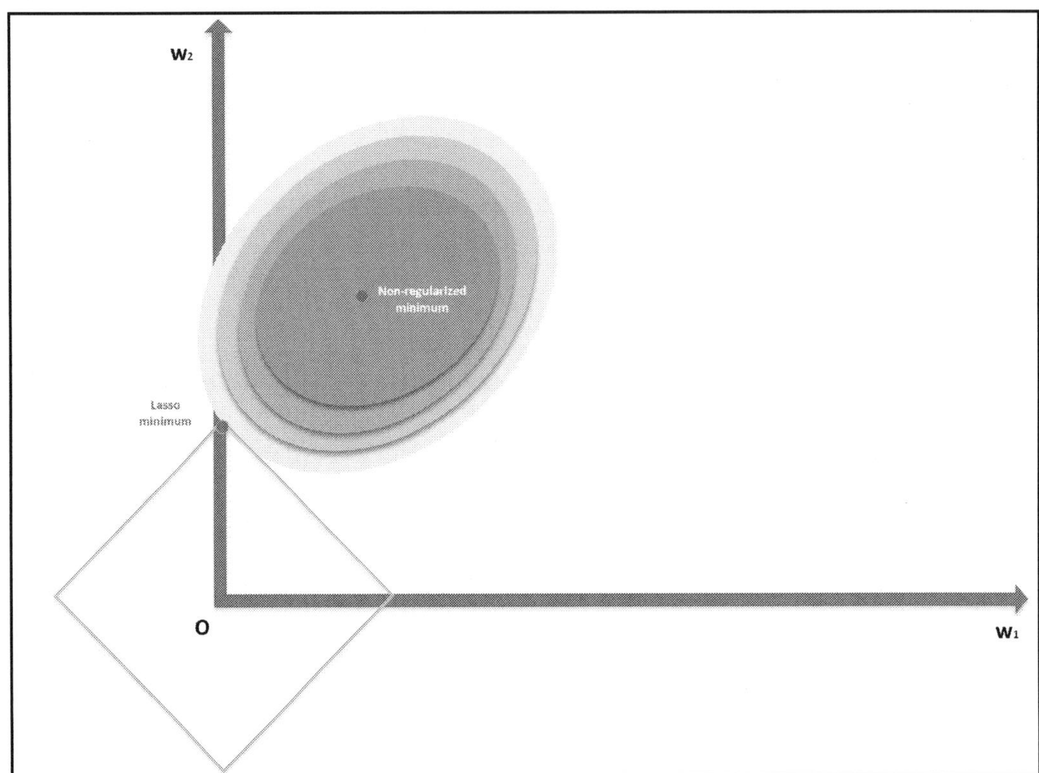

Lasso (L1) regularization

The zero-centered square represents the Lasso boundaries. If we consider a generic line, the probability of being tangential to the square is higher at the corners, where at least one (exactly one in a bidimensional scenario) parameter is null. In general, if we have a vectorial convex function *f(x)* (we provide a definition of convexity in `Chapter 5`, *EM Algorithm and Applications*), we can define:

$$g(\bar{x}) = f(\bar{x}) + \|\bar{x}\|_p$$

As any L_p-norm is convex, as well as the sum of convex functions, *g(x)* is also convex. The regularization term is always non-negative, therefore the minimum corresponds to the norm of the null vector. When minimizing *g(x)*, we need to also consider the contribution of the gradient of the norm in the ball centered in the origin where, however, the partial derivatives don't exist. Increasing the value of *p*, the norm becomes smoothed around the origin, and the partial derivatives approach zero for $|x_i| \rightarrow 0$.

On the other side, with *p=1* (excluding the L_0-norm and all the norms with $p \in]0, 1[$ that allow an even stronger sparsity, but are non-convex), the partial derivatives are always +1 or -1, according to the sign of x_i $(x_i \neq 0)$. Therefore, it's *easier* for the L_1-norm to push the smallest components to zero, because the contribution to the minimization (for example, with a gradient descent) is independent of x_i, while an L_2-norm decreases its *speed* when approaching the origin. This is a non-rigorous explanation of the sparsity achieved using the L_1-norm. In fact, we also need to consider the term *f(x)*, which bounds the value of the global minimum; however, it may help the reader to develop an intuitive understanding of the concept. It's possible to find further and mathematically rigorous details in *Optimization for Machine Learning, (e*dited by) *Sra S., Nowozin S., Wright S. J., The MIT Press.*

Lasso regularization is particularly useful whenever a sparse representation of a dataset is needed. For example, we could be interested in finding the feature vectors corresponding to a group of images. As we expect to have many features but only a subset present in each image, applying the Lasso regularization allows forcing all the smallest coefficients to become null, suppressing the presence of the secondary features. Another potential application is latent semantic analysis, where our goal is to describe the documents belonging to a corpus in terms of a limited number of topics. All these methods can be summarized in a technique called **sparse coding**, where the objective is to reduce the dimensionality of a dataset (also in non-linear scenarios) by extracting the most representative atoms, using different approaches to achieve sparsity.

ElasticNet

In many real cases, it's useful to apply both Ridge and Lasso regularization in order to force weight shrinkage and a global sparsity. It is possible by employing the **ElasticNet** regularization, defined as:

$$L_R\left(X, Y; \bar{\theta}\right) = L\left(X, Y; \bar{\theta}\right) + \lambda_1 \|\bar{\theta}\|_2^2 + \lambda_2 \|\bar{\theta}\|_1$$

The strength of each regularization is controlled by the parameters λ_1 and λ_2. ElasticNet can yield excellent results whenever it's necessary to mitigate overfitting effects while encouraging sparsity. We are going to apply all the regularization techniques when discussing some deep learning architectures.

Early stopping

Even though it's a pure regularization technique, **early stopping** is often considered as a *last resort* when all other approaches to prevent overfitting and maximize validation accuracy fail. In many cases (above all, in deep learning scenarios), it's possible to observe a typical behavior of the training process considering both training and the validation cost functions:

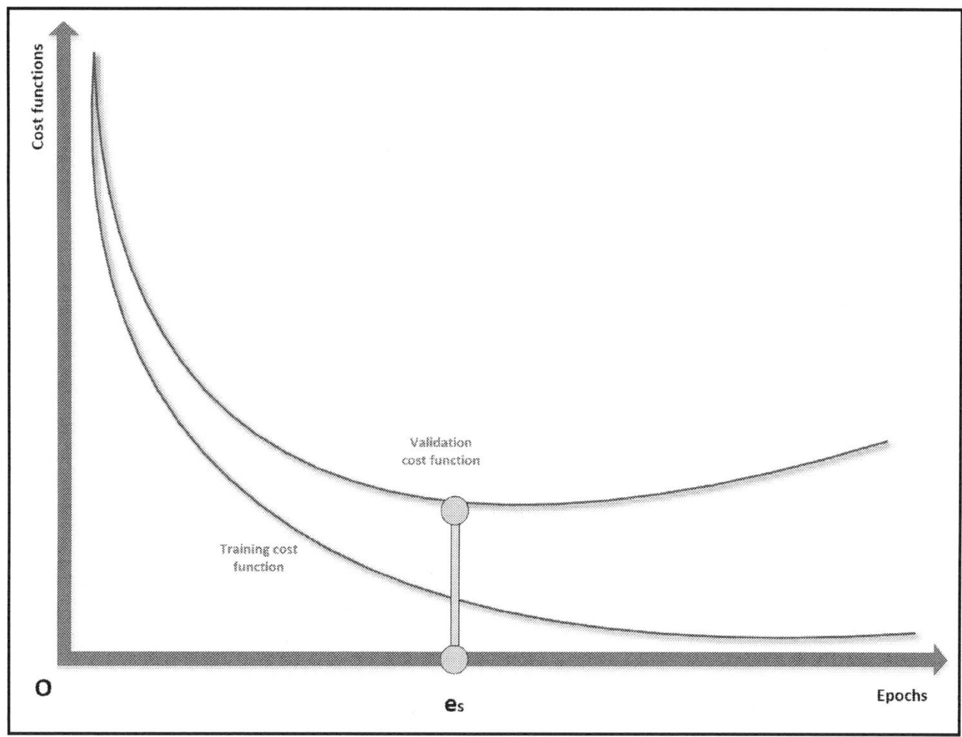

Example of early stopping before the beginning of ascending phase of U-curve

During the first epochs, both costs decrease, but it can happen that after a *threshold* epoch e_s, the validation cost starts increasing. If we continue with the training process, this results in overfitting the training set and increasing the variance. For this reason, when there are no other options, it's possible to prematurely stop the training process. In order to do so, it's necessary to store the last parameter vector before the beginning of a new iteration and, in the case of no improvements or the accuracy worsening, to stop the process and recover the last parameters. As explained, this procedure must never be considered as the best choice, because a better model or an improved dataset could yield higher performances. With early stopping, there's no way to verify alternatives, therefore it must be adopted only at the last stage of the process and never at the beginning. Many deep learning frameworks such as Keras include helpers to implement an early stopping callback; however, it's important to check whether the last parameter vector is the one stored before the last epoch or the one corresponding to e_s. In this case, it could be useful to repeat the training process, stopping it at the epoch previous to e_s (where the minimum validation cost has been achieved).

Summary

In this chapter, we discussed fundamental concepts shared by almost any machine learning model. In the first part, we have introduced the data generating process, as a generalization of a finite dataset. We explained which are the most common strategies to split a finite dataset into a training block and a validation set, and we introduced cross-validation, with some of the most important variants, as one of the best approaches to avoid the limitations of a static split.

In the second part, we discussed the main properties of an estimator: capacity, bias, and variance. We also introduced the Vapnik-Chervonenkis theory, which is a mathematical formalization of the concept of representational capacity, and we analyzed the effects of high biases and high variances. In particular, we discussed effects called underfitting and overfitting, defining the relationship with high bias and high variance.

In the third part, we introduced the loss and cost functions, first as proxies of the expected risk, and then we detailed some common situations that can be experienced during an optimization problem. We also exposed some common cost functions, together with their main features. In the last part, we discussed regularization, explaining how it can mitigate the effects of overfitting.

In the next chapter, `Chapter 2`, *Introduction to Semi-Supervised Learning*, we're going to introduce semi-supervised learning, focusing our attention on the concepts of transductive and inductive learning.

2
Introduction to Semi-Supervised Learning

Semi-supervised learning is a machine learning branch that tries to solve problems with both labeled and unlabeled data with an approach that employs concepts belonging to clustering and classification methods. The high availability of unlabeled samples, in contrast with the difficulty of labeling huge datasets correctly, drove many researchers to investigate the best approaches that allow extending the knowledge provided by the labeled samples to a larger unlabeled population without loss of accuracy. In this chapter, we're going to introduce this branch and, in particular, we will discuss:

- The semi-supervised scenario
- The assumptions needed to efficiently operate in such a scenario
- The different approaches to semi-supervised learning
- Generative Gaussian mixtures algorithm
- Contrastive pessimistic likelihood estimation approach
- **Semi-supervised Support Vector Machines** (S^3VM)
- **Transductive Support Vector Machines** (TSVM)

Semi-supervised scenario

A typical semi-supervised scenario is not very different from a supervised one. Let's suppose we have a data generating process, p_{data}:

$$p_{data}(\bar{x}, \bar{y}) = p(\bar{y}|\bar{x})p(\bar{x})$$

However, contrary to a supervised approach, we have only a limited number N of samples drawn from p_{data} and provided with a label, as follows:

$$\begin{cases} X_l = \{\bar{x}_0^l, \bar{x}_1^l, \dots, \bar{x}_N^l\} & where \;\; \bar{x}_i^l \in \mathbb{R}^p \\ Y_l = \{\bar{y}_0^l, \bar{y}_1^l, \dots, \bar{y}_N^l\} & where \;\; \bar{y}_i^l \in \mathbb{R}^q \end{cases}$$

Instead, we have a larger amount (M) of unlabeled samples drawn from the marginal distribution $p(x)$:

$$X_u = \{\bar{x}_0^u, \bar{x}_1^u, \dots, \bar{x}_M^u\} \;\; where \;\; \bar{x}_i^u \in \mathbb{R}^p$$

In general, there are no restrictions on the values of N and M; however, a semi-supervised problem arises when the number of unlabeled samples is much higher than the number of complete samples. If we can draw $N >> M$ labeled samples from p_{data}, it's probably useless to keep on working with semi-supervised approaches and preferring classical supervised methods is likely to be the best choice. The extra complexity we need is justified by $M >> N$, which is a common condition in all those situations where the amount of available unlabeled data is large, while the number of correctly labeled samples is quite a lot lower. For example, we can easily access millions of free images but detailed labeled datasets are expensive and include only a limited subset of possibilities. However, is it always possible to apply semi-supervised learning to improve our models? The answer to this question is almost obvious: unfortunately no. As a rule of thumb, we can say that if the knowledge of X_u increases our knowledge about the prior distribution $p(x)$, a semi-supervised algorithm is likely to perform better than a purely supervised (and thus limited to X_l) counterpart. On the other hand, if the unlabeled samples are drawn from different distributions, the final result can be quite a lot worse. In real cases, it's not so immediately necessary to decide whether a semi-supervised algorithm is the best choice; therefore, cross-validation and comparisons are the best practices to employ when evaluating a scenario.

Transductive learning

When a semi-supervised model is aimed at finding the labels for the unlabeled samples, the approach is called transductive learning. In this case, we are not interested in modeling the whole distribution $p(x|y)$, which implies determining the density of both datasets, but rather in finding $p(y|x)$ only for the unlabeled points. In many cases, this strategy can be time-saving and it's always preferable when our goal is more oriented at improving our knowledge about the unlabeled dataset.

Inductive learning

Contrary to transductive learning, inductive learning considers all the *X* samples and tries to determine a complete *p(x|y)* or a function *y=f(x)* that can map both labeled and unlabeled points to their corresponding labels. In general, this method is more complex and requires more computational time; therefore, according to *Vapnik's principle*, if not required or necessary, it's always better to pick the most pragmatic solution and, possibly, expand it if the problem requires further details.

Semi-supervised assumptions

As explained in the previous section, semi-supervised learning is not guaranteed to improve a supervised model. A wrong choice could lead to a dramatic worsening in performance; however, it's possible to state some fundamental assumptions which are required for semi-supervised learning to work properly. They are not always mathematically proven theorems, but rather empirical observations that justify the choice of an approach otherwise completely arbitrary.

Smoothness assumption

Let's consider a real-valued function *f(x)* and the corresponding metric spaces *X* and *Y*. Such a function is said to be Lipschitz-continuous if:

$$\exists\, K : \forall\, x_1 \; and \; x_2 \in X \Rightarrow d_Y\left(f(x_1), f(x_2)\right) \leqslant K d_X(x_1, x_2)$$

In other words, if two points x_1 and x_2 are near, the corresponding output values y_1 and y_2 cannot be arbitrarily far from each other. This condition is fundamental in regression problems where a generalization is often required for points that are between training samples. For example, if we need to predict the output for a point $x_t : x_1 < x_t < x_2$ and the regressor is Lipschitz-continuous, we can be sure that y_t will be correctly bounded by y_1 and y_2. This condition is often called general smoothness, but in semi-supervised it's useful to add a restriction (correlated with the cluster assumption): if two points are in a high density region (cluster) and they are close, then the corresponding outputs must be close too. This extra condition is very important because, if two samples are in a low density region they can belong to different clusters and their labels can be very different. This is not always true, but it's useful to include this constraint to allow some further assumptions in many definitions of semi-supervised models.

Cluster assumption

This assumption is strictly linked to the previous one and it's probably easier to accept. It can be expressed with a chain of interdependent conditions. Clusters are high density regions; therefore, if two points are close, they are likely to belong to the same cluster and their labels must be the same. Low density regions are separation spaces; therefore, samples belonging to a low density region are likely to be boundary points and their classes can be different. To better understand this concept, it's useful to think about supervised SVM: only the support vectors should be in low density regions. Let's consider the following bidimensional example:

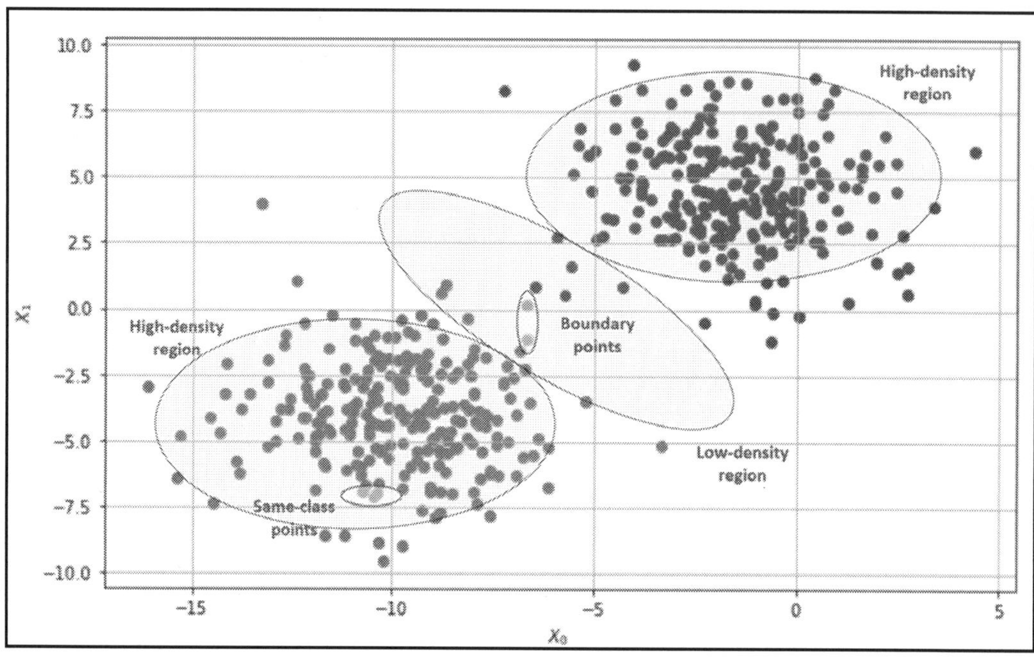

In a semi-supervised scenario, we couldn't know the label of a point belonging to a high density region; however, if it is close enough to a labeled point that it's possible to build a ball where all the points have the same average density, we are allowed to predict the label of our test sample. Instead, if we move to a low-density region, the process becomes harder, because two points can be very close but with different labels. We are going to discuss the semi-supervised, low-density separation problem at the end of this chapter.

Manifold assumption

This is the less intuitive assumption, but it can be extremely useful to reduce the complexity of many problems. First of all, we can provide a non-rigorous definition of a manifold. An *n*-manifold is a topological space that is globally curved, but locally homeomorphic to an *n*-dimensional Euclidean space. In the following diagram, there's an example of a manifold: the surface of a sphere in $\Re^3$:

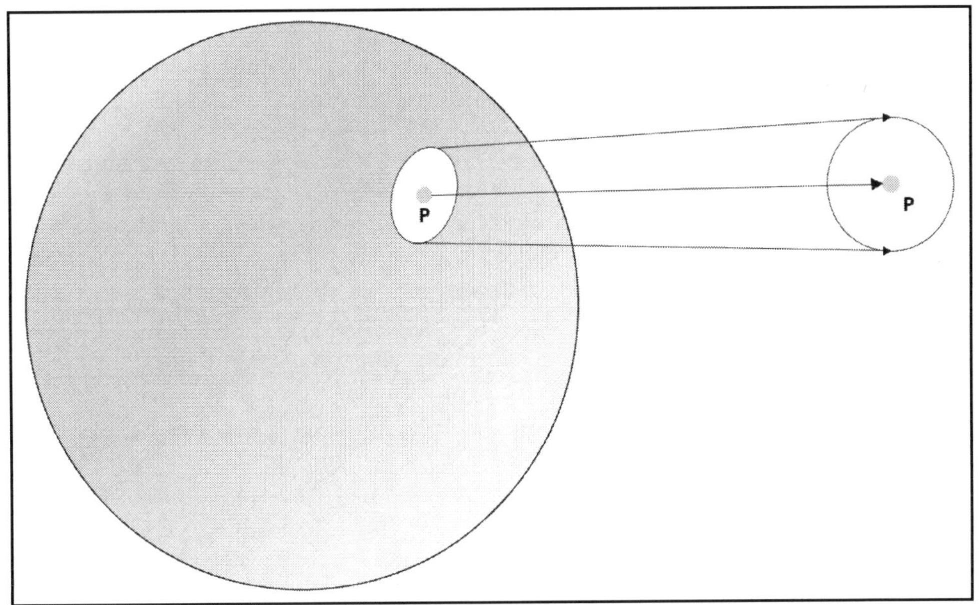

2D manifold obtained from a spherical surface

The small patch around *P* (for $\varepsilon \rightarrow 0$) can be mapped to a flat circular surface. Therefore, the properties of a manifold are locally based on the Euclidean geometry, while, globally, they need a proper mathematical extension which is beyond the scope of this book (further information can be found in *Semi-supervised learning on Riemannian manifolds, Belkin M., Niyogi P., Machine Learning 56, 2004*).

The manifold assumption states that p-dimensional samples (where $p >> 1$) approximately lie on a q-dimensional manifold with $p << q$. Without excessive mathematical rigor, we can say that, for example, if we have N 1000-dimensional bounded vectors, they are enclosed into a 1000-dimensional hypercube with edge-length equal to r. The corresponding n-volume is $r^p = r^{1000}$, therefore, the probability of filling the entire space is very small (and decreases with p). What we observe, instead, is a high density on a lower dimensional manifold. For example, if we look at the Earth from space, we might think that its inhabitants are uniformly distributed over the whole volume. We know that this is false and, in fact, we can create maps and atlases which are represented on two-dimensional manifolds. It doesn't make sense to use three-dimensional vectors to map the position of a human being. It's easier to use a projection and work with latitude and longitude.

This assumption authorizes us to apply dimensionality reduction methods in order to avoid the *Curse of Dimensionality*, theorized by Bellman (in *Dynamic Programming and Markov Process, Ronald A. Howard, The MIT Press*). In the scope of machine learning, the main consequence of such an effect is that when the dimensionality of the samples increases, in order to achieve a high accuracy, it's necessary to use more and more samples. Moreover, Hughes observed (the phenomenon has been named after him and it's presented in the paper *Hughes G. F., On the mean accuracy of statistical pattern recognizers, IEEE Transactions on Information Theory, 1968, 14/1*) that the accuracy of statistical classifiers is inversely proportional to the dimensionality of the samples. This means that whenever it's possible to work on lower dimensional manifolds (in particular in semi-supervised scenarios), two advantages are achieved:

- Less computational time and memory consumption
- Higher classification accuracy

Generative Gaussian mixtures

Generative Gaussian mixtures is an inductive algorithm for semi-supervised clustering. Let's suppose we have a labeled dataset (X_l, Y_l) containing N samples (drawn from p_{data}) and an unlabeled dataset X_u containing $M >> N$ samples (drawn from the marginal distribution $p(x)$). It's not necessary that $M >> N$, but we want to create a real semi-supervised scenario, with only a few labeled samples. Moreover, we are assuming that all unlabeled samples are consistent with p_{data}. This can seem like a vicious cycle, but without this assumption, the procedure does not have a strong mathematical foundation. Our goal is to determine a complete $p(x|y)$ distribution using a generative model. In general, it's possible to use different priors, but we are now employing multivariate Gaussians to model our data:

$$f(\bar{x};\bar{\mu};\Sigma) = \frac{1}{\sqrt{det(2\pi\Sigma)}} e^{-\frac{(\bar{x}-\bar{\mu})^T\Sigma^{-1}(\bar{x}-\bar{\mu})}{2}}$$

Thus, our model parameters are means and covariance matrices for all Gaussians. In other contexts, it's possible to use binomial or multinomial distributions. However, the procedure doesn't change; therefore, let's assume that it's possible to approximate $p(x|y)$ with a parametrized distribution $p(x|y, \theta)$. We can achieve this goal by minimizing the Kullback-Leibler divergence between the two distributions:

$$argmin_{\bar{\theta}} D_{KL}(p(\bar{x}|y)||p(\bar{x}|y,\bar{\theta})) = \sum_i p(\bar{x}_i|y_i) log \frac{p(\bar{x}_i|y_i)}{p(\bar{x}_i|y_i,\bar{\theta})}$$

In Chapter 5, *EM Algorithm and Applications* we are going to show that this is equivalent to maximizing the likelihood of the dataset. To obtain the likelihood, it's necessary to define the number of expected Gaussians (which is known from the labeled samples) and a weight-vector that represents the marginal probability of a specific Gaussian:

$$\bar{w} = (p(y=1), p(y=2), \ldots, p(y=M))$$

Using the Bayes' theorem, we get:

$$p(y_i|\bar{x}_j,\bar{\theta},\bar{w}) \propto w_i p(\bar{x}_j|y_i,\bar{\theta})$$

As we are working with both labeled and unlabeled samples, the previous expression has a double interpretation:

- For unlabeled samples, it is computed by multiplying the ith Gaussian weight times the probability $p(x_j)$ relative to the ith Gaussian distribution.
- For labeled samples, it can be represented by a vector p = [0, 0, ... 1, ... 0, 0] where 1 is the ith element. In this way, we force our model to trust the labeled samples in order to find the best parameter values that maximize the likelihood on the whole dataset.

With this distinction, we can consider a single log-likelihood function where the term $f_w(y_i|x_j)$ has been substituted by a per sample weight:

$$L(\bar{\theta};\bar{w}) = \sum_j log \sum_i f_w(y_i|\bar{x}_j)p(\bar{x}_j|y_i,\bar{\theta}) = \sum_j log \sum_i w_i p(\bar{x}_j|y_i,\bar{\theta})$$

It's possible to maximize the log-likelihood using the EM algorithm (see `Chapter 5`, *EM Algorithm and Applications*). In this context, we provide the steps directly:

- $p(y_i|x_j,\theta,w)$ is computed according to the previously explained method
- The parameters of the Gaussians are updated using these rules:

$$w_i = \frac{\sum_j p(y_i|\bar{x}_j, \bar{\theta}, \bar{w})}{N}$$

$$\bar{\mu}_i = \frac{\sum_j \left(p(y_i|\bar{x}_j, \bar{\theta}, \bar{w})\bar{x}_j\right)}{\sum_j p(y_i|\bar{x}_j, \bar{\theta}, \bar{w})}$$

$$\Sigma_i = \frac{\sum_j \left(p(y_i|\bar{x}_j, \bar{\theta}, \bar{w})(\bar{x}_j - \bar{\mu}_i)(\bar{x}_j - \bar{\mu}_i)^T\right)}{\sum_j p(y_i|\bar{x}_j, \bar{\theta}, \bar{w})}$$

N is the total number of samples. The procedure must be iterated until the parameters stop modifying or the modifications are lower than a fixed threshold.

Example of a generative Gaussian mixture

We can now implement this model in Python using a simple bidimensional dataset, created using the `make_blobs()` function provided by Scikit-Learn:

```
from sklearn.datasets import make_blobs

nb_samples = 1000
nb_unlabeled = 750

X, Y = make_blobs(n_samples=nb_samples, n_features=2, centers=2,
cluster_std=2.5, random_state=100)

unlabeled_idx = np.random.choice(np.arange(0, nb_samples, 1),
replace=False, size=nb_unlabeled)
Y[unlabeled_idx] = -1
```

We have created 1,000 samples belonging to 2 classes. 750 points have then been randomly selected to become our unlabeled dataset (the corresponding class has been set to -1). We can now initialize two Gaussian distributions by defining their mean, covariance, and weight. One possibility is to use random values:

```
import numpy as np

# First Gaussian
m1 = np.random.uniform(-7.5, 10.0, size=2)
c1 = np.random.uniform(5.0, 15.0, size=(2, 2))
c1 = np.dot(c1, c1.T)
q1 = 0.5

# Second Gaussian
m2 = np.random.uniform(-7.5, 10.0, size=2)
c2 = np.random.uniform(5.0, 15.0, size=(2, 2))
c2 = np.dot(c2, c2.T)
q2 = 0.5
```

However, as the covariance matrices must be positive semi definite, it's useful to alter the random values (by multiplying each matrix by the corresponding transpose) or to set hard-coded initial parameters. In this case, we could pick the following example:

```
import numpy as np

# First Gaussian
m1 = np.array([-3.0, -4.5])
c1 = np.array([[25.0, 5.0],
               [5.0, 35.0]])
q1 = 0.5

# Second Gaussian
m2 = np.array([5.0, 10.0])
c2 = np.array([[25.0, -10.0],
               [-10.0, 25.0]])
q2 = 0.5
```

The resulting plot is shown in the following graph, where the small diamonds represent the unlabeled points and the bigger dots, the samples belonging to the known classes:

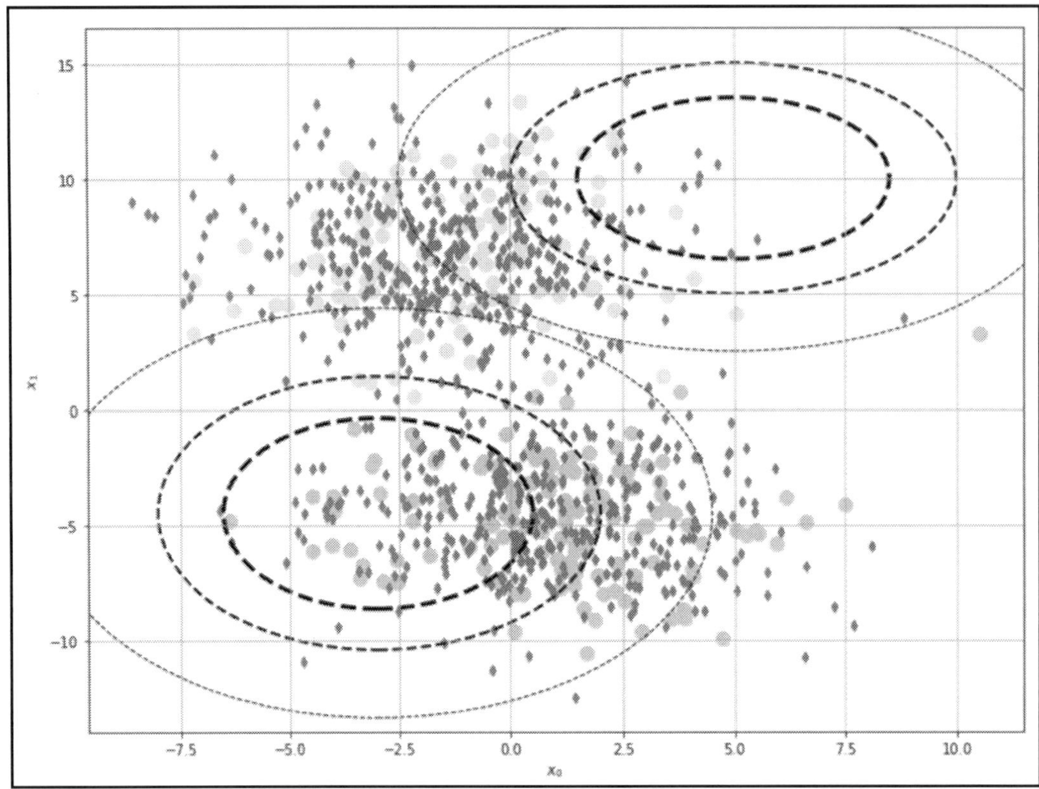

Initial configuration of the Gaussian mixture

The two Gaussians are represented by the concentric ellipses. We can now execute the training procedure. For simplicity, we repeat the update for a fixed number of iterations. The reader can easily modify the code in order to introduce a threshold:

```
from scipy.stats import multivariate_normal

nb_iterations = 5

for i in range(nb_iterations):
    Pij = np.zeros((nb_samples, 2))
    for i in range(nb_samples):
        if Y[i] == -1:
            p1 = multivariate_normal.pdf(X[i], m1, c1,
allow_singular=True) * q1
            p2 = multivariate_normal.pdf(X[i], m2, c2,
allow_singular=True) * q2
            Pij[i] = [p1, p2] / (p1 + p2)
        else:
            Pij[i, :] = [1.0, 0.0] if Y[i] == 0 else [0.0, 1.0]
    n = np.sum(Pij, axis=0)
    m = np.sum(np.dot(Pij.T, X), axis=0)
    m1 = np.dot(Pij[:, 0], X) / n[0]
    m2 = np.dot(Pij[:, 1], X) / n[1]
    q1 = n[0] / float(nb_samples)
    q2 = n[1] / float(nb_samples)
    c1 = np.zeros((2, 2))
    c2 = np.zeros((2, 2))

    for t in range(nb_samples):
        c1 += Pij[t, 0] * np.outer(X[t] - m1, X[t] - m1)
        c2 += Pij[t, 1] * np.outer(X[t] - m2, X[t] - m2)
    c1 /= n[0]
    c2 /= n[1]
```

The first thing at the beginning of each cycle is to initialize the `Pij` matrix that will be used to store the $p(y_i|x_j,\theta,w)$ values. Then, for each sample, we can compute $p(y_i|x_j,\theta,w)$ considering whether it's labeled or not. The Gaussian probability is computed using the SciPy function `multivariate_normal.pdf()`. When the whole P_{ij} matrix has been populated, we can update the parameters (means and covariance matrix) of both Gaussians and the relative weights. The algorithm is very fast; after five iterations, we get the stable state represented in the following graph:

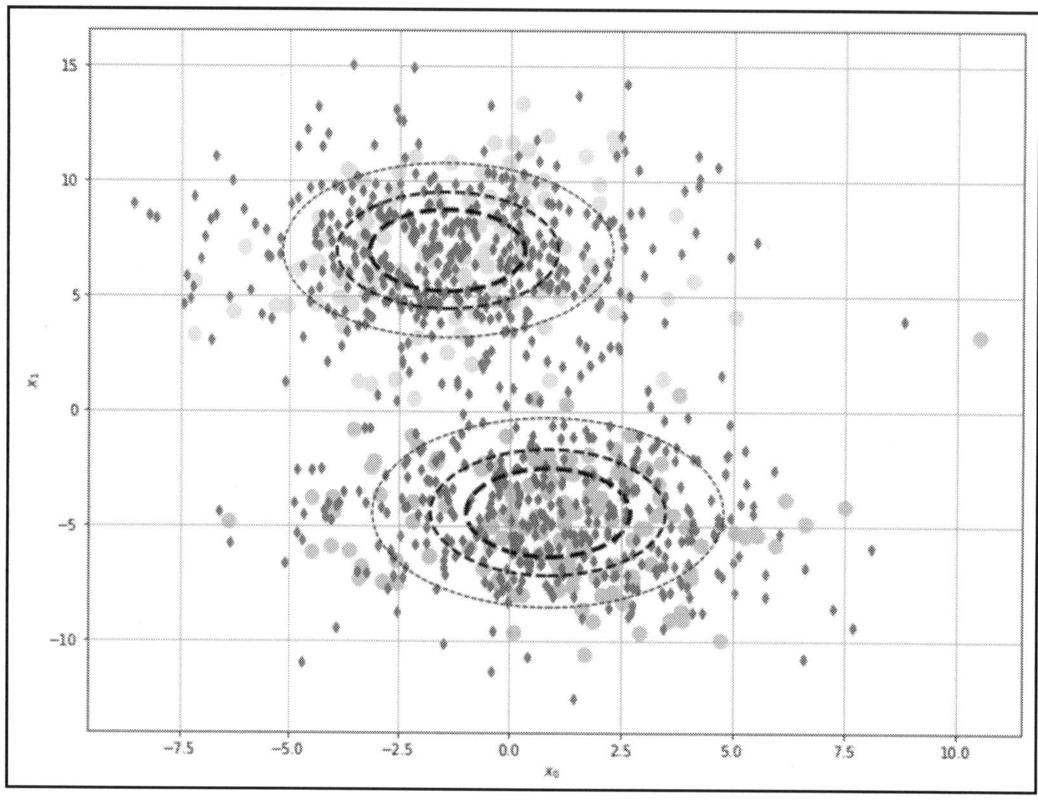

The two Gaussians have perfectly mapped the space by setting their parameters so as to cover the high-density regions. We can check for some unlabeled points, as follows:

```
print(np.round(X[Y==-1][0:10], 3))

[[  1.67    7.204]
 [ -1.347  -5.672]
 [ -2.395  10.952]
 [ -0.261   6.526]
 [  1.053   8.961]
```

```
[ -0.579  -7.431]
[  0.956   9.739]
[ -5.889   5.227]
[ -2.761   8.615]
[ -1.777   4.717]]
```

It's easy to locate them in the previous plot. The corresponding classes can be obtained through the last P_{ij} matrix:

```
print(np.round(Pij[Y==-1][0:10], 3))

[[ 0.002  0.998]
 [ 1.     0.   ]
 [ 0.     1.   ]
 [ 0.003  0.997]
 [ 0.     1.   ]
 [ 1.     0.   ]
 [ 0.     1.   ]
 [ 0.007  0.993]
 [ 0.     1.   ]
 [ 0.02   0.98 ]]
```

This immediately verifies that they have been correctly labeled and assigned to the right cluster. This algorithm is very fast and produces excellent results in terms of density estimation. In `Chapter 5`, *EM Algorithm and Applications*, we are going to discuss a general version of this algorithm, explaining the complete training procedure based on the EM algorithm.

In all the examples that involve random numbers, the seed is set equal to 1,000 (`np.random.seed(1000)`). Other values or subsequent experiments without resetting it can yield slightly different results.

Weighted log-likelihood

In the previous example, we have considered a single log-likelihood for both labeled and unlabeled samples:

$$L(\bar{\theta};\bar{w}) = \sum_j log \sum_i f_w(y_i|\bar{x}_j)p(\bar{x}_j|y_i,\bar{\theta}) = \sum_j log \sum_i w_i p(\bar{x}_j|y_i,\bar{\theta})$$

This is equivalent to saying that we trust the unlabeled points just like the labeled ones. However, in some contexts, this assumption can lead to completely wrong estimations, as shown in the following graph:

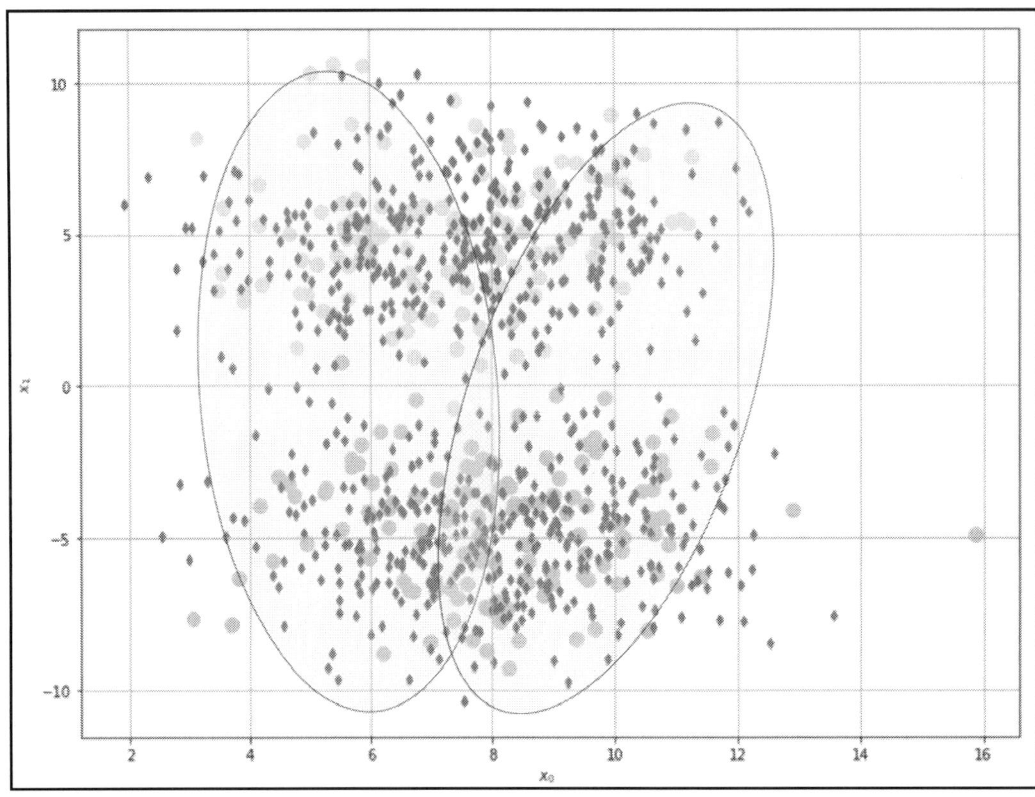

Biased final Gaussian mixture configuration

In this case, the means and covariance matrices of both Gaussian distributions have been biased by the unlabeled points and the resulting density estimation is clearly wrong. When this phenomenon happens, the best thing to do is to consider a double weighted log-likelihood. If the first *N* samples are labeled and the following *M* are unlabeled, the log-likelihood can be expressed as follows:

$$L(\bar{\theta}; \bar{w}) = \sum_{j=1}^{N} log \sum_{i} p(y_i|\bar{\theta})p(y_i|\bar{x}_j, \bar{\theta}) + \lambda \sum_{j=N+1}^{N+M} log \sum_{i} w_i p(\bar{x}_j|y_i, \bar{\theta})$$

In the previous formula, the term λ, if less than 1, can underweight the unlabeled terms, giving more importance to the labeled dataset. The modifications to the algorithm are trivial because each unlabeled weight has to be scaled according to λ, reducing its estimated probability. In *Semi-Supervised Learning, Chapelle O., Schölkopf B., Zien A., (edited by), The MIT Press,* the reader can find a very detailed discussion about the choice of λ. There are no golden rules; however, a possible strategy could be based on the cross-validation performed on the labeled dataset. Another (more complex) approach is to consider different increasing values of λ and pick the first one where the log-likelihood is maximum. I recommend the aforementioned book for further details and strategies.

Contrastive pessimistic likelihood estimation

As explained at the beginning of this chapter, in many real life problems, it's cheaper to retrieve unlabeled samples, rather than correctly labeled ones. For this reason, many researchers worked to find out the best strategies to carry out a semi-supervised classification that could outperform the supervised counterpart. The idea is to train a classifier with a few labeled samples and then improve its accuracy after adding weighted unlabeled samples. One of the best results is the **Contrastive Pessimistic Likelihood Estimation** (**CPLE**) algorithm, proposed by M. Loog (in *Loog M., Contrastive Pessimistic Likelihood Estimation for Semi-Supervised Classification, arXiv:1503.00269*).

Before explaining this algorithm, an introduction is necessary. If we have a labeled dataset (X, Y) containing N samples, it's possible to define the log-likelihood cost function of a generic estimator, as follows:

$$L(\bar{\theta}; \bar{x}, \bar{y}) = \sum_i log\, p(x_i, y_i | \bar{\theta})$$

After training the model, it should be possible to determine $p(y_i|x_i, \theta)$, which is the probability of a label given a sample x_i. However, some classifiers are not based on this approach (like SVM) and evaluate the right class, for example, by checking the sign of a parametrized function $f(x_i, \theta)$. As CPLE is a generic framework that can be used with any classification algorithm when the probabilities are not available, it's useful to implement a technique called Platt scaling, which allows transforming the decision function into a probability through a parametrized sigmoid. For a binary classifier, it can be expressed as follows:

$$p(y_i = +1|x_i, \bar{\theta}) = \frac{1}{1 + e^{\alpha f(x_i;\bar{\theta})+\beta}}$$

α and β are parameters that must be learned in order to maximize the likelihood. Luckily Scikit-Learn provides the method `predict_proba()`, which returns the probabilities for all classes. Platt scaling is performed automatically or on demand; for example, the SCV classifier needs to have the parameter `probability=True` in order to compute the probability mapping. I always recommend checking the documentation before implementing a custom solution.

We can consider a full dataset, made up of labeled and unlabeled samples. For simplicity, we can reorganize the original dataset, so that the first N samples are labeled, while the next M are unlabeled:

$$X_t = \{(\bar{x}_1, \bar{y}_1), (\bar{x}_2, \bar{y}_2), \ldots, (\bar{x}_N, \bar{y}_N), \bar{x}^u_{N+1}, \ldots, \bar{x}^u_{N+M})\}$$

As we don't know the labels for all x^u samples, we can decide to use M k-dimensional (k is the number of classes) soft-labels q_i that can be optimized during the training process:

$$Q = \{\bar{q}_1, \bar{q}_2, \ldots, \bar{q}_M\} \;\; where \;\; \bar{q}_i \in \mathbb{R}^k \;\; and \;\; \sum_k q_i^{(k)} = 1$$

The second condition in the previous formula is necessary to guarantee that each q_i represents a discrete probability (all the elements must sum up to 1.0). The complete log-likelihood cost function can, therefore, be expressed as follows:

$$L(\bar{\theta}; X_t, Q) = L(\bar{\theta}; \bar{x}, \bar{y}) + \sum_{i=N+1}^{N+M} \sum_k q_i^{(k)} \log p(\bar{x}^u_i, y^u_i = k|\bar{\theta})$$

The first term represents the log-likelihood for the supervised part, while the second one is responsible for the unlabeled points. If we train a classifier with only the labeled samples, excluding the second addend, we get a parameter set θ_{sup}. CPLE defines a contrastive condition (as a log-likelihood too), by defining the improvement in the total cost function given by the semi-supervised approach, compared to the supervised solution:

$$CL(\bar{\theta}, \bar{\theta}_{sup}, X_t, Q) = L(\bar{\theta}; X_t, Q) - L(\bar{\theta}_{sup}; X_t, Q)$$

This condition allows imposing that the semi-supervised solution must outperform the supervised one, in fact, maximizing it; we both increase the first term and reduce the second one, obtaining a proportional increase of CL (the term *contrastive* is very common in machine learning and it normally indicates a condition which is achieved as the difference between two opposite constraints). If CL doesn't increase, it probably means that the unlabeled samples have not been drawn from the marginal distribution $p(x)$ extracted from p_{data}.

Moreover, in the previous expression, we have implicitly used soft-labels, but as they are initially randomly chosen and there's no ground truth to support their values, it's a good idea not to trust them by imposing a pessimistic condition (as another log-likelihood):

$$CPL(\bar{\theta}, \bar{\theta}_{sup}, X_t, Q) = min_q \; CL(\bar{\theta}, \bar{\theta}_{sup}, X_t, Q)$$

By imposing this constraint, we try to find the soft-labels that minimize the contrastive log-likelihood; that's why this is defined as a pessimistic approach. It can seem a contradiction; however, trusting soft-labels can be dangerous, because the semi-supervised log-likelihood could be increased even with a large percentage of misclassification. Our goal is to find the best parameter set that is able to guarantee the highest accuracy starting from the supervised baseline (which has been obtained using the labeled samples) and improving it, without forgetting the structural features provided by the labeled samples.

Therefore, our final goal can be expressed as follows:

$$\bar{\theta}_{semi} = max_{\bar{\theta}} \; CPL(\bar{\theta}, \bar{\theta}_{sup}, X_t, Q)$$

Example of contrastive pessimistic likelihood estimation

We are going to implement the CPLE algorithm in Python using a subset extracted from the MNIST dataset. For simplicity, we are going to use only the samples representing the digits 0 and 1:

```
from sklearn.datasets import load_digits

import numpy as np

X_a, Y_a = load_digits(return_X_y=True)

X = np.vstack((X_a[Y_a == 0], X_a[Y_a == 1]))
Y = np.vstack((np.expand_dims(Y_a, axis=1)[Y_a==0],
np.expand_dims(Y_a, axis=1)[Y_a==1]))

nb_samples = X.shape[0]
nb_dimensions = X.shape[1]
nb_unlabeled = 150
Y_true = np.zeros((nb_unlabeled,))

unlabeled_idx = np.random.choice(np.arange(0, nb_samples, 1),
replace=False, size=nb_unlabeled)
Y_true = Y[unlabeled_idx].copy()
Y[unlabeled_idx] = -1
```

After creating the restricted dataset (*X*, *Y*) which contain 360 samples, we randomly select 150 samples (about 42%) to become unlabeled (the corresponding y is -1). At this point, we can measure the performance of logistic regression trained only on the labeled dataset:

```
from sklearn.linear_model import LogisticRegression

lr_test = LogisticRegression()
lr_test.fit(X[Y.squeeze() != -1], Y[Y.squeeze() != -1].squeeze())
unlabeled_score = lr_test.score(X[Y.squeeze() == -1], Y_true)

print(unlabeled_score)
0.573333333333
```

So, the logistic regression shows 57% accuracy for the classification of the unlabeled samples. We can also evaluate the cross-validation score on the whole dataset (before removing some random labels):

```
from sklearn.model_selection import cross_val_score
```

```
total_cv_scores = cross_val_score(LogisticRegression(), X,
Y.squeeze(), cv=10)

print(total_cv_scores)
[ 0.48648649  0.51351351  0.5         0.38888889  0.52777778
0.36111111
  0.58333333  0.47222222  0.54285714  0.45714286]
```

Thus, the classifier achieves an average 48% accuracy when using 10 folds (each test set contains 36 samples) if all the labels are known.

We can now implement a CPLE algorithm. The first thing is to initialize a `LogisticRegression` instance and the soft-labels:

```
lr = LogisticRegression()
q0 = np.random.uniform(0, 1, size=nb_unlabeled)
```

q0 is a random array of values bounded in the half-open interval [0, 1]; therefore, we also need a converter to transform q_i into an actual binary label:

$$y(q) = \begin{cases} 0 \ if \ q < 0.5 \\ 1 \ otherwise \end{cases}$$

We can achieve this using the NumPy function `np.vectorize()`, which allows us to apply a transformation to all the elements of a vector:

```
trh = np.vectorize(lambda x: 0.0 if x < 0.5 else 1.0)
```

In order to compute the log-likelihood, we need also a weighted log-loss (similar to the Scikit-Learn function `log_loss()`, which, however, computes the negative log-likelihood but doesn't support weights):

```
def weighted_log_loss(yt, p, w=None, eps=1e-15):
    if w is None:
        w_t = np.ones((yt.shape[0], 2))
    else:
        w_t = np.vstack((w, 1.0 - w)).T
    Y_t = np.vstack((1.0 - yt.squeeze(), yt.squeeze())).T
    L_t = np.sum(w_t * Y_t * np.log(np.clip(p, eps, 1.0 - eps)),
axis=1)
    return np.mean(L_t)
```

This function computes the following expression:

$$L(\bar{y}_i, \bar{p}, \bar{w}) = \frac{1}{N} \sum_i (y_{t_i} \, log(p_i) + (1 - y_{t_i}) log(1 - p_i))$$

We need also a function to build the dataset with variable soft-labels q_i:

```
def build_dataset(q):
    Y_unlabeled = trh(q)
    X_n = np.zeros((nb_samples, nb_dimensions))
    X_n[0:nb_samples - nb_unlabeled] = X[Y.squeeze()!=-1]
    X_n[nb_samples - nb_unlabeled:] = X[Y.squeeze()==-1]
    Y_n = np.zeros((nb_samples, 1))
    Y_n[0:nb_samples - nb_unlabeled] = Y[Y.squeeze()!=-1]
    Y_n[nb_samples - nb_unlabeled:] = np.expand_dims(Y_unlabeled,
axis=1)
    return X_n, Y_n
```

At this point, we can define our contrastive log-likelihood:

```
def log_likelihood(q):
    X_n, Y_n = build_dataset(q)
    Y_soft = trh(q)
    lr.fit(X_n, Y_n.squeeze())
    p_sup = lr.predict_proba(X[Y.squeeze() != -1])
    p_semi = lr.predict_proba(X[Y.squeeze() == -1])
    l_sup = weighted_log_loss(Y[Y.squeeze() != -1], p_sup)
    l_semi = weighted_log_loss(Y_soft, p_semi, q)
    return l_semi - l_sup
```

This method will be called by the optimizer, passing a different q vector each time. The first step is building the new dataset and computing `Y_soft`, which are the labels corresponding to q. Then the logistic regression classifier is trained with with the dataset (as `Y_n` is a (k, 1) array, it's necessary to squeeze it to avoid a warning. The same thing is done when using Y as a boolean indicator). At this point, it's possible to compute both p_{sup} and p_{semi} using the method `predict_proba()` and, finally, we can compute the semi-supervised and supervised log-loss, which is the term, a function of q_i, that we want to minimize, while the maximization of θ is done implicitly when training the logistic regression.

The optimization is carried out using the BFGS algorithm implemented in SciPy:

```
from scipy.optimize import fmin_bfgs

q_end = fmin_bfgs(f=log_likelihood, x0=q0, maxiter=5000, disp=False)
```

This is a very fast algorithm, but the user is encouraged to experiment with methods or libraries. The two parameters we need in this case are `f`, which is the function to minimize, and `x0`, which is the initial condition for the independent variables. `maxiter` is useful for avoiding an excessive number of iterations when no improvements are achieved. Once the optimization is complete, `q_end` contains the optimal soft-labels. We can, therefore, rebuild our dataset:

```
X_n, Y_n = build_dataset(q_end)
```

With this final configuration, we can retrain the logistic regression and check the cross-validation accuracy:

```
final_semi_cv_scores = cross_val_score(LogisticRegression(), X_n,
Y_n.squeeze(), cv=10)

print(final_semi_cv_scores)
[ 1.          1.          0.89189189  0.77777778  0.97222222
0.88888889
  0.61111111  0.88571429  0.94285714  0.48571429]
```

The semi-supervised solution based on the CPLE algorithms achieves an average 84% accuracy, outperforming, as expected, the supervised approach. The reader can try other examples using different classifiers, such SVM or Decision Trees, and verify when CPLE allows obtaining higher accuracy than other supervised algorithms.

Semi-supervised Support Vector Machines (S^3VM)

When we discussed the cluster assumption, we also defined the low-density regions as boundaries and the corresponding problem as low-density separation. A common supervised classifier which is based on this concept is a **Support Vector Machine** (**SVM**), the objective of which is to maximize the distance between the dense regions where the samples must be. For a complete description of linear and kernel-based SVMs, please refer to *Bonaccorso G., Machine Learning Algorithms, Packt Publishing;* however, it's useful to remind yourself of the basic model for a linear SVM with slack variables ξ_i:

$$\begin{cases} min_{\bar{w},b,\xi}\ \frac{1}{2}\bar{w}^T\bar{w} + C\sum_i \xi_i \\ y_i(\bar{w}^T\bar{x}_i + b) \geqslant 1 - \xi_i \ \ and \ \ \xi_i \geqslant 0 \ \ \forall \ i = 1..N \end{cases}$$

This model is based on the assumptions that y_i can be either -1 or 1. The slack variables ξ_i or soft-margins are variables, one for each sample, introduced to reduce the *strength* imposed by the original condition ($min \,||w||$), which is based on a hard margin that misclassifies all the samples that are on the wrong side. They are defined by the Hinge loss, as follows:

$$\xi_i = max\left(0, 1 - y_i(\bar{w}^T \cdot \bar{x}_i + b)\right)$$

With those variables, we allow some points to overcome the limit without being misclassified if they remain within a distance controlled by the corresponding slack variable (which is also minimized during the training phase, so as to avoid uncontrollable growth). In the following diagram, there's a schematic representation of this process:

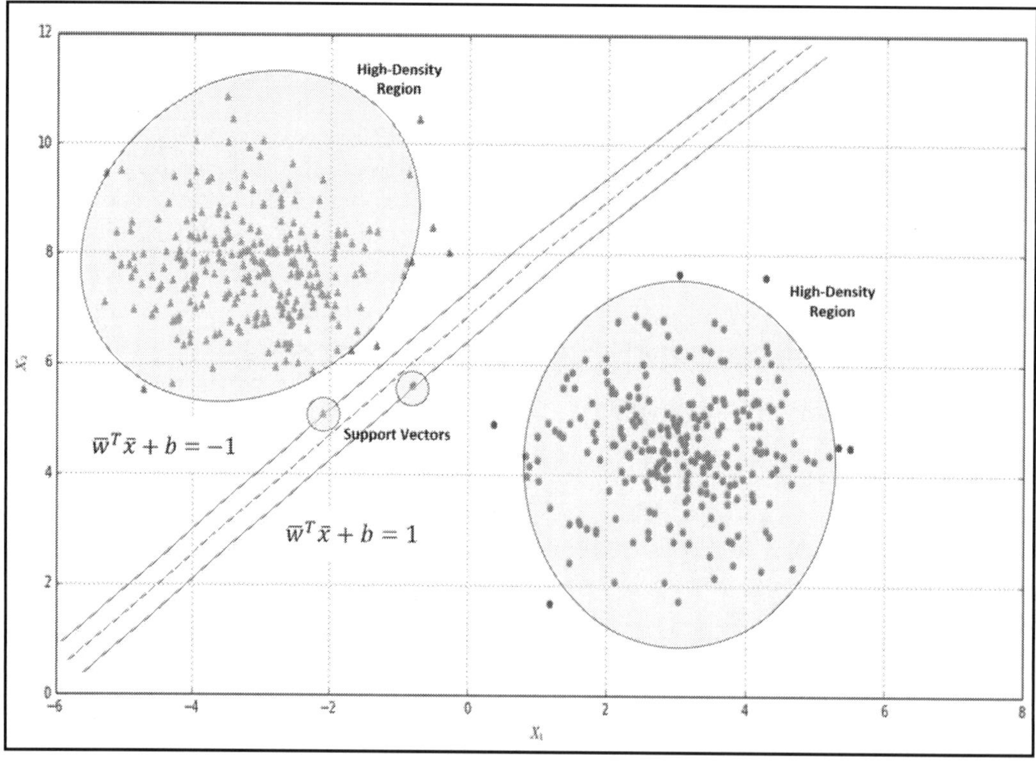

SVM generic scenario

The last elements of each high-density regions are the support vectors. Between them, there's a low-density region (it can also be zero-density in some cases) where our separating hyperplane lies. In `Chapter 1`, *Machine Learning Model Fundamentals*, we defined the concept of *empirical risk* as a proxy for expected risk; therefore, we can turn the SVM problem into the minimization of empirical risk under the Hinge cost function (with or without Ridge Regularization on w):

$$L(X,Y;\bar{w},b) = \frac{1}{N}\sum_{i} max\left(0, 1 - y_i(\bar{w}^T \cdot \bar{x}_i + b)\right)$$

Theoretically, every function which is always bounded by two hyperplanes containing the support vectors is a good classifier, but we need to minimize the empirical risk (and, so, the expected risk); therefore we look for the maximum margin between high-density regions. This model is able to separate two dense regions with irregular boundaries and, by adopting a kernel function, also in non-linear scenarios. The natural question, at this point, is about the best strategy to integrate labeled and unlabeled samples when we need to solve this kind of problem in a semi-supervised scenario.

The first element to consider is the ratio: if we have a low percentage of unlabeled points, the problem is mainly supervised and the generalization ability learned using the training set should be enough to correctly classify all the unlabeled points. On the other hand, if the number of unlabeled samples is much larger, we return to an almost pure clustering scenario (like the one discussed in the paragraph about the Generative Gaussian mixtures). In order to exploit the strength of semi-supervised methods in low-density separation problems, therefore, we should consider situations where the ratio labeled/unlabeled is about 1.0. However, even if we have the predominance of a class (for example, if we have a huge unlabeled dataset and only a few labeled samples), it's always possible to use the algorithms we're going to discuss, even if, sometimes, their performance could be equal to or lower than a pure supervised/clustering solution. Transductive SMVs, for example, showed better accuracies when the labeled/unlabeled ratio is very small, while other methods can behave in a completely different way. However, when working with semi-supervised learning (and its assumptions), it is always important to bear in mind that each problem is supervised and unsupervised at the same time and the best solution must be evaluated in every different context.

A solution for this problem is offered by the *Semi-Supervised SVM* (also known as S^3VM) algorithm. If we have N labeled samples and M unlabeled samples, the objective function becomes as follows:

$$min_{\bar{w},b,\bar{\eta},\bar{\xi},\bar{z}} \left[\|\bar{w}\| + C\left(\sum_{i=1}^{N} \eta_i + \sum_{j=N+1}^{N+M} min(\xi_j, z_j) \right) \right]$$

The first term imposes the standard SVM condition about the maximum separation distance, while the second block is divided into two parts:

- We need to add N slack variables η_i to guarantee a soft-margin for the labeled samples.
- At the same time, we have to consider the unlabeled points, which could be classified as +1 or -1. Therefore, we have two corresponding slack-variable sets ξ_i and z_i. However, we want to find the smallest variable for each possible pair, so as to be sure that the unlabeled sample is placed on the sub-space where the maximum accuracy is achieved.

The constraints necessary to solve the problems become as follows:

$$\begin{cases} y_i(\bar{w}^T \cdot x_i + b) \geqslant 1 - \eta_i \ \ and \ \ \eta_i \geqslant 0 \ \forall \ i = 1..N \\ (\bar{w}^T \cdot \bar{x}_j - b) \geqslant 1 - \xi_j \ \ and \ \ \xi_j \geqslant 0 \ \forall \ j = N+1 \ldots N+M \\ -(\bar{w}^T \cdot \bar{x}_j - b) \geqslant 1 - z_j \ \ and \ \ z_j \geqslant 0 \ \forall \ j = N+1 \ldots N+M \end{cases}$$

The first constraint is limited to the labeled points and it's the same as a supervised SVM. The following two, instead, take into account the possibility that an unlabeled sample could be classified as +1 or -1. Let's suppose, for example, that the label y_j for the sample x_j should be +1 and the first member of the second inequality is a positive number K (so the corresponding term of the third equation is $-K$). It's easy to verify that the first slack variable is $\xi_i \geq 1 - K$, while the second one is $z_j \geq 1 + K$.

Therefore, in the objective, ξ_i is chosen to be minimized. This method is inductive and yields good (if not excellent) performances; however, it has a very high computational cost and should be solved using optimized (native) libraries. Unfortunately, it is a non-convex problem and there are no standard methods to solve it so it always reaches the optimal configuration.

Example of S^3VM

We now implement an S^3VM in Python using the SciPy optimization methods, which are mainly based on C and FORTRAN implementations. The reader can try it with other libraries such as NLOpt and LIBSVM and compare the results. A possibility suggested by Bennet and Demiriz is to use the L1-norm for w, so as to linearize the objective function; however, this choice seems to produce good results only for small datasets. We are going to keep the original formulation based on the L2-norm, using an **Sequential Least Squares Programming** (**SLSQP**) algorithm to optimize the objective.

Let's start by creating a bidimensional dataset with both labeled and unlabeled samples:

```
from sklearn.datasets import make_classification

nb_samples = 500
nb_unlabeled = 200

X, Y = make_classification(n_samples=nb_samples, n_features=2,
n_redundant=0, random_state=1000)
Y[Y==0] = -1
Y[nb_samples - nb_unlabeled:nb_samples] = 0
```

For simplicity (and without any impact, because the samples are shuffled), we set last 200 samples as unlabeled ($y = 0$). The corresponding plot is shown in the following graph:

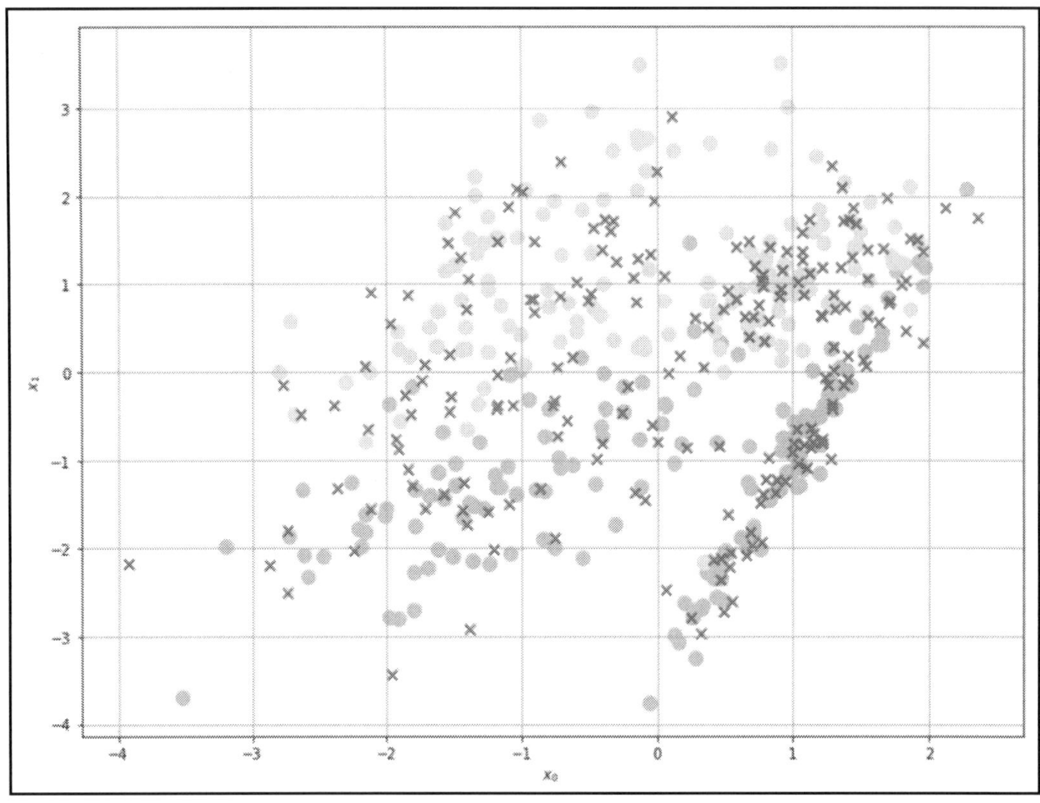

Original labeled and unlabeled dataset

The crosses represent unlabeled points, which are spread throughout the entire dataset. At this point we need to initialize all variables required for the optimization problem:

```
import numpy as np

w = np.random.uniform(-0.1, 0.1, size=X.shape[1])
eta = np.random.uniform(0.0, 0.1, size=nb_samples - nb_unlabeled)
xi = np.random.uniform(0.0, 0.1, size=nb_unlabeled)
zi = np.random.uniform(0.0, 0.1, size=nb_unlabeled)
b = np.random.uniform(-0.1, 0.1, size=1)
C = 1.0

theta0 = np.hstack((w, eta, xi, zi, b))
```

As the optimization algorithm requires a single array, we have stacked all vectors into a horizontal array `theta0` using the `np.hstack()` function. We also need to vectorize the `min()` function in order to apply it to arrays:

```
vmin = np.vectorize(lambda x1, x2: x1 if x1 <= x2 else x2)
```

Now, we can define the objective function:

```
def svm_target(theta, Xd, Yd):
    wt = theta[0:2].reshape((Xd.shape[1], 1))
    s_eta = np.sum(theta[2:2 + nb_samples - nb_unlabeled])
    s_min_xi_zi = np.sum(vmin(theta[2 + nb_samples - nb_unlabeled:2 +
nb_samples],
                              theta[2 + nb_samples:2 + nb_samples +
nb_unlabeled]))
    return C * (s_eta + s_min_xi_zi) + 0.5 * np.dot(wt.T, wt)
```

The arguments are the current `theta` vector and the complete datasets `Xd` and `Yd`. The dot product of w has been multiplied by 0.5 to keep the conventional notation used for supervised SVMs. The constant can be omitted without any impact. At this point, we need to define all the constraints, as they are based on the slack variables; each function (which shares the same parameters of the objectives) is parametrized with an index, `idx`. The labeled constraint is as follows:

```
def labeled_constraint(theta, Xd, Yd, idx):
    wt = theta[0:2].reshape((Xd.shape[1], 1))
    c = Yd[idx] * (np.dot(Xd[idx], wt) + theta[-1]) + \
    theta[2:2 + nb_samples - nb_unlabeled][idx] - 1.0
    return (c >= 0)[0]
```

The unlabeled constraints, instead, are as follows:

```
def unlabeled_constraint_1(theta, Xd, idx):
    wt = theta[0:2].reshape((Xd.shape[1], 1))
    c = np.dot(Xd[idx], wt) - theta[-1] + \
        theta[2 + nb_samples - nb_unlabeled:2 + nb_samples][idx -
nb_samples + nb_unlabeled] - 1.0
    return (c >= 0)[0]

def unlabeled_constraint_2(theta, Xd, idx):
    wt = theta[0:2].reshape((Xd.shape[1], 1))
    c = -(np.dot(Xd[idx], wt) - theta[-1]) + \
        theta[2 + nb_samples:2 + nb_samples + nb_unlabeled ][idx -
nb_samples + nb_unlabeled] - 1.0
    return (c >= 0)[0]
```

They are parametrized with the current `theta` vector, the `Xd` dataset, and an `idx` index. We need also to include the constraints for each slack variable (≥ 0):

```
def eta_constraint(theta, idx):
    return theta[2:2 + nb_samples - nb_unlabeled][idx] >= 0

def xi_constraint(theta, idx):
    return theta[2 + nb_samples - nb_unlabeled:2 + nb_samples][idx -
nb_samples + nb_unlabeled] >= 0

def zi_constraint(theta, idx):
    return theta[2 + nb_samples:2 + nb_samples+nb_unlabeled ][idx -
nb_samples + nb_unlabeled] >= 0
```

We can now set up the problem using the SciPy convention:

```
svm_constraints = []

for i in range(nb_samples - nb_unlabeled):
    svm_constraints.append({
            'type': 'ineq',
            'fun': labeled_constraint,
            'args': (X, Y, i)
        })
    svm_constraints.append({
            'type': 'ineq',
            'fun': eta_constraint,
            'args': (i,)
        })
for i in range(nb_samples - nb_unlabeled, nb_samples):
    svm_constraints.append({
            'type': 'ineq',
            'fun': unlabeled_constraint_1,
            'args': (X, i)
        })
    svm_constraints.append({
            'type': 'ineq',
            'fun': unlabeled_constraint_2,
            'args': (X, i)
        })
    svm_constraints.append({
            'type': 'ineq',
            'fun': xi_constraint,
            'args': (i,)
        })
    svm_constraints.append({
            'type': 'ineq',
            'fun': zi_constraint,
            'args': (i,)
        })
```

Each constraint is represented with a dictionary, where `type` is set to `ineq` to indicate that it is an inequality, `fun` points to the callable object and `args` contains all extra arguments (`theta` is the main x variable and it's automatically added). Using SciPy, it's possible to minimize the objective using the **Sequential Least Squares Programming (SLSQP)** or **Constraint Optimization by Linear Approximation (COBYLA)** algorithms. We preferred the former, because it works more rapidly and is more stable:

```
from scipy.optimize import minimize
```

```
result = minimize(fun=svm_target,
                  x0=theta0,
                  constraints=svm_constraints,
                  args=(X, Y),
                  method='SLSQP',
                  tol=0.0001,
                  options={'maxiter': 1000})
```

After the training process is complete, we can compute the labels for the unlabeled points:

```
theta_end = result['x']
w = theta_end[0:2]
b = theta_end[-1]

Xu= X[nb_samples - nb_unlabeled:nb_samples]
yu = -np.sign(np.dot(Xu, w) + b)
```

In the next graph, it's possible to compare the initial plot (left) with the final one where all points have been assigned a label (right):

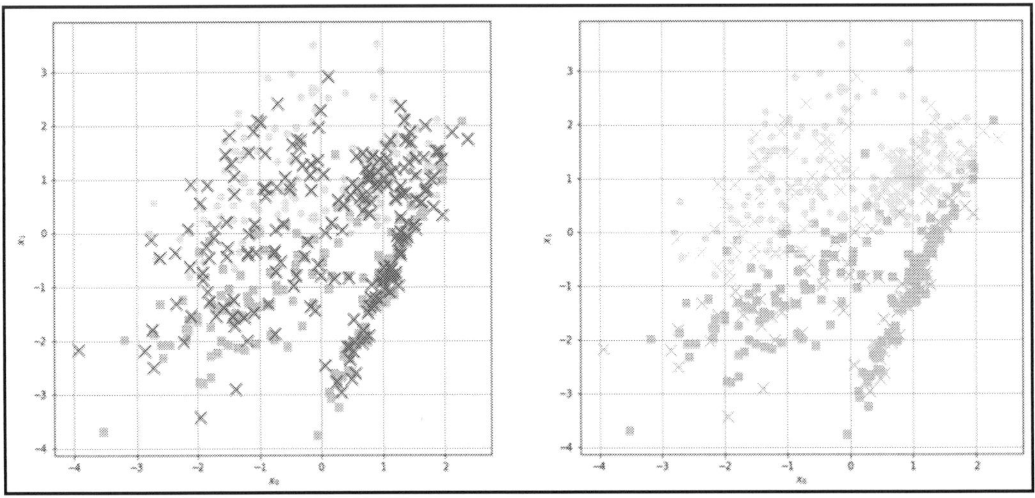

As you can see, S^3VM succeeded in finding the right label for all unlabeled points, confirming the existence of two very dense regions for x between *[0, 2]* (square dots) and y between *[0, 2]* (circular dots).

NLOpt is a complete optimization library developed at MIT. It is available for different operating systems and programming languages. The website is `https://nlopt.readthedocs.io`. LIBSVM is an optimized library for solving SVM problems and it is adopted by Scikit-Learn together with LIBLINEAR. It's also available for different environments. The homepage is `https://www.csie.ntu.edu.tw/~cjlin/libsvm/`.

Transductive Support Vector Machines (TSVM)

Another approach to the same problem is offered by the TSVM, proposed by T. Joachims (in *Transductive Inference for Text Classification using Support Vector Machines, Joachims T., ICML Vol. 99/1999*). The idea is to keep the original objective with two sets of slack variables: the first for the labeled samples and the other for the unlabeled ones:

$$min_{\bar{w},b,\bar{\eta},\bar{\xi}} \left[\|\bar{w}\| + C_L \sum_{i=1}^{N} \eta_i + C_U \sum_{j=N+1}^{N+M} \xi_j \right]$$

As this is a transductive approach, we need to consider the unlabeled samples as variable-labeled ones (subject to the learning process), imposing a constraint similar to the supervised points. As for the previous algorithm, we assume we have N labeled samples and M unlabeled ones; therefore, the conditions become as follows:

$$\begin{cases} y_i(\bar{w}^T \cdot x_i + b) \geqslant 1 - \eta_i \;\; and \;\; \eta_i \geqslant 0 \;\; \forall \;\; i = 1..N \\ y_j^{(u)}(\bar{w}^T \cdot x_j + b) \geqslant 1 - \xi_j \;\; and \;\; \xi_j \geqslant 0 \;\; \forall j = N+1, \ldots, N+M \\ y_j^{(u)} \in \{-1, 1\} \end{cases}$$

The first constraint is the classical SVM one and it works only on labeled samples. The second one uses the variable $y^{(u)}_j$ with the corresponding slack variables ξ_j to impose a similar condition on the unlabeled samples, while the third one is necessary to constrain the labels to being equal to -1 and 1.

Just like the semi-supervised SVMs, this algorithm is non-convex and it's useful to try different methods to optimize it. Moreover, the author, in the aforementioned paper, showed how TSVM works better when the test set (unlabeled) is large and the training set (labeled) is relatively small (when a standard supervised SVM is outperformed). On the other hand, with large training sets and small test sets, a supervised SVM (or other algorithms) are always preferable because they are faster and yield better accuracy.

Example of TSVM

In our Python implementation, we are going to use a bidimensional dataset similar to one employed in the previous method; however, in this case, we impose 400 unlabeled samples out of a total of 500 points:

```
from sklearn.datasets import make_classification

nb_samples = 500
nb_unlabeled = 400

X, Y = make_classification(n_samples=nb_samples, n_features=2,
n_redundant=0, random_state=1000)
Y[Y==0] = -1
Y[nb_samples - nb_unlabeled:nb_samples] = 0
```

The corresponding plot is shown in the following graph:

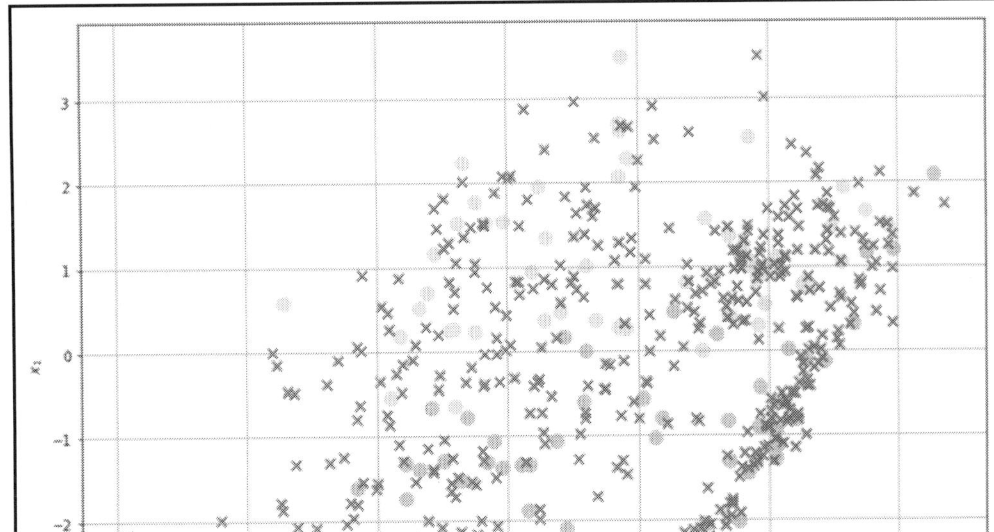

Original labeled and unlabeled dataset

The procedure is similar to the one we used before. First of all, we need to initialize our variables:

```
import numpy as np

w = np.random.uniform(-0.1, 0.1, size=X.shape[1])
eta_labeled = np.random.uniform(0.0, 0.1, size=nb_samples -
nb_unlabeled)
eta_unlabeled = np.random.uniform(0.0, 0.1, size=nb_unlabeled)
y_unlabeled = np.random.uniform(-1.0, 1.0, size=nb_unlabeled)
b = np.random.uniform(-0.1, 0.1, size=1)

C_labeled = 1.0
C_unlabeled = 10.0

theta0 = np.hstack((w, eta_labeled, eta_unlabeled, y_unlabeled, b))
```

In this case, we also need to define the `y_unlabeled` vector for variable-labels. The author also suggests using two C constants (`C_labeled` and `C_unlabeled`) in order to be able to weight the misclassification of labeled and unlabeled samples differently. We used a value of 1.0 for `C_labeled` and 10.0 for `C_unlabled`, because we want to penalize more the misclassification of unlabeled samples.

The objective function to optimize is as follows:

```
def svm_target(theta, Xd, Yd):
    wt = theta[0:2].reshape((Xd.shape[1], 1))
    s_eta_labeled = np.sum(theta[2:2 + nb_samples - nb_unlabeled])
    s_eta_unlabeled = np.sum(theta[2 + nb_samples - nb_unlabeled:2 +
nb_samples])
    return (C_labeled * s_eta_labeled) + (C_unlabeled *
s_eta_unlabeled) + (0.5 * np.dot(wt.T, wt))
```

While the labeled and unlabeled constraints are as follows:

```
def labeled_constraint(theta, Xd, Yd, idx):
    wt = theta[0:2].reshape((Xd.shape[1], 1))
    c = Yd[idx] * (np.dot(Xd[idx], wt) + theta[-1]) + \
    theta[2:2 + nb_samples - nb_unlabeled][idx] - 1.0
    return (c >= 0)[0]

def unlabeled_constraint(theta, Xd, idx):
    wt = theta[0:2].reshape((Xd.shape[1], 1))
    c = theta[2 + nb_samples:2 + nb_samples + nb_unlabeled][idx -
nb_samples + nb_unlabeled] * \
        (np.dot(Xd[idx], wt) + theta[-1]) + \
        theta[2 + nb_samples - nb_unlabeled:2 + nb_samples][idx -
nb_samples + nb_unlabeled] - 1.0
    return (c >= 0)[0]
```

We need also to impose the constraints on the slack variables and on the $y^{(u)}$:

```
def eta_labeled_constraint(theta, idx):
    return theta[2:2 + nb_samples - nb_unlabeled][idx] >= 0

def eta_unlabeled_constraint(theta, idx):
    return theta[2 + nb_samples - nb_unlabeled:2 + nb_samples][idx -
nb_samples + nb_unlabeled] >= 0

def y_constraint(theta, idx):
    return np.power(theta[2 + nb_samples:2 + nb_samples +
nb_unlabeled][idx], 2) == 1.0
```

As in the previous example, we can create the constraint dictionary needed by SciPy:

```
svm_constraints = []

for i in range(nb_samples - nb_unlabeled):
    svm_constraints.append({
            'type': 'ineq',
            'fun': labeled_constraint,
            'args': (X, Y, i)
        })
    svm_constraints.append({
            'type': 'ineq',
            'fun': eta_labeled_constraint,
            'args': (i,)
        })
for i in range(nb_samples - nb_unlabeled, nb_samples):
    svm_constraints.append({
            'type': 'ineq',
            'fun': unlabeled_constraint,
            'args': (X, i)
        })
    svm_constraints.append({
            'type': 'ineq',
            'fun': eta_unlabeled_constraint,
            'args': (i,)
        })

for i in range(nb_unlabeled):
    svm_constraints.append({
            'type': 'eq',
            'fun': y_constraint,
            'args': (i,)
        })
```

In this case, the last constraint is an equality, because we want to force $y^{(u)}$ to be equal either to -1 or 1. At this point, we minimize the objective function:

```
from scipy.optimize import minimize

result = minimize(fun=svm_target,
                  x0=theta0,
                  constraints=svm_constraints,
                  args=(X, Y),
                  method='SLSQP',
                  tol=0.0001,
                  options={'maxiter': 1000})
```

When the process is complete, we can compute the labels for the unlabeled samples and compare the plots:

```
theta_end = result['x']
w = theta_end[0:2]
b = theta_end[-1]

Xu= X[nb_samples - nb_unlabeled:nb_samples]
yu = -np.sign(np.dot(Xu, w) + b)
```

The plot comparison is shown in the following graph:

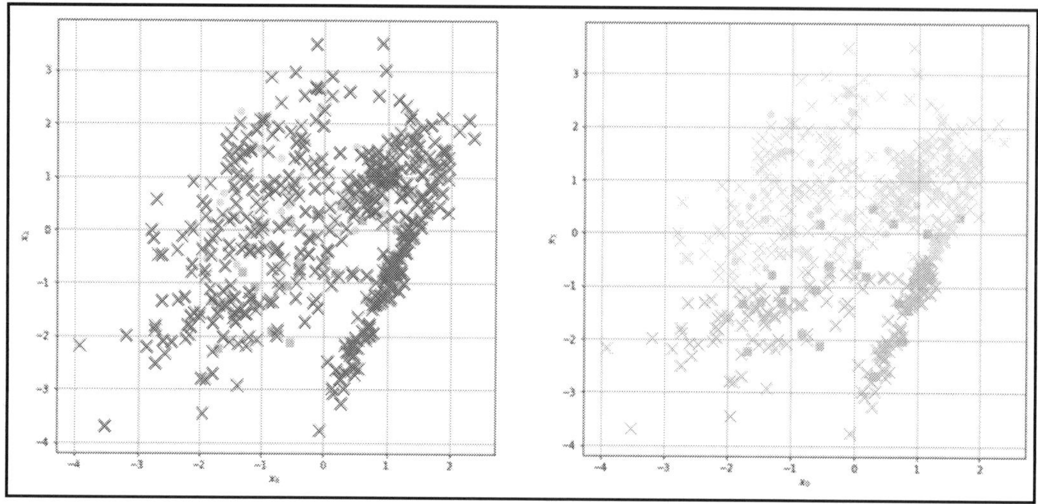

Original dataset (left). Final labeled dataset (right)

The misclassification (based on the density distribution) is slightly higher than S³VM, but it's possible to change the C values and the optimization method until the expected result has been reached. A good benchmark is provided by a supervised SVM, which can have better performances when the training set is huge enough (and when it represents the whole p_{data} correctly).

It's interesting to evaluate different combinations of the C parameters, starting from a standard supervised SVM. The dataset is smaller, with a high number of unlabeled samples:

```
nb_samples = 100
nb_unlabeled = 90

X, Y = make_classification(n_samples=nb_samples, n_features=2,
```

```
n_redundant=0, random_state=100)
Y[Y==0] = -1
Y[nb_samples - nb_unlabeled:nb_samples] = 0
```

We use the standard SVM implementation provided by Scikit-Learn (the `SVC()` class) with a linear kernel and `C=1.0`:

```
from sklearn.svm import SVC

svc = SVC(kernel='linear', C=1.0)
svc.fit(X[Y!=0], Y[Y!=0])

Xu_svc= X[nb_samples - nb_unlabeled:nb_samples]
yu_svc = svc.predict(Xu_svc)
```

The SVM is trained with the labeled samples and the vector `yu_svc` contains the prediction for the unlabeled samples. The resulting plot (in comparison with the original dataset) is shown in the following graph:

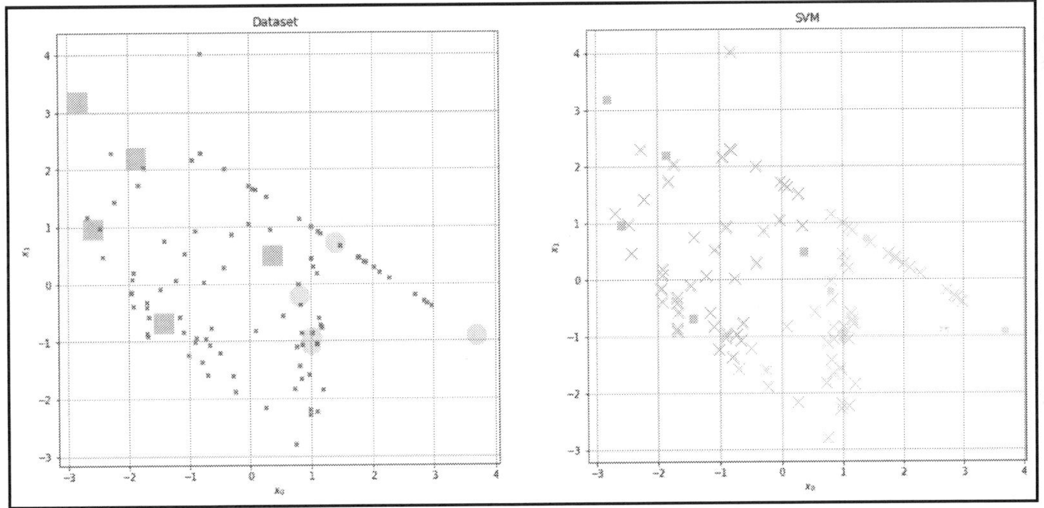

Original dataset (left). Final labeled dataset (right) with C = 1.0

All the labeled samples are represented with bigger squares and circles. The result meets our expectations, but there's an area *(X [-1, 0] - Y [-2, -1])*, where the SVM decided to impose the *circle* class even if the unlabeled points are close to a square. This hypothesis can't be acceptable considering the clustering assumption; in fact, in a high-density region there are samples belonging to two classes. A similar (or even worse) result is obtained using an S^3VM with **CL=10** and **CU=5**:

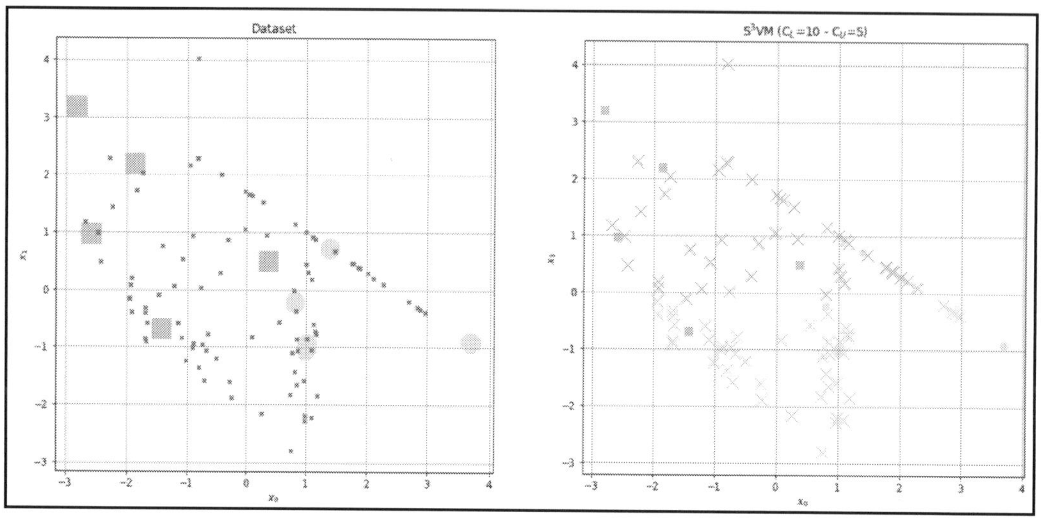

Original dataset (left). Final labeled dataset (right) with $C_L = 10$ and $C_U = 5$

In this case, the classification accuracy is lower because the penalty for the unlabeled samples is lower than the one imposed on the labeled points. A supervised SVM has obviously better performances. Let's try with **C_L=10** and **C_U=50**:

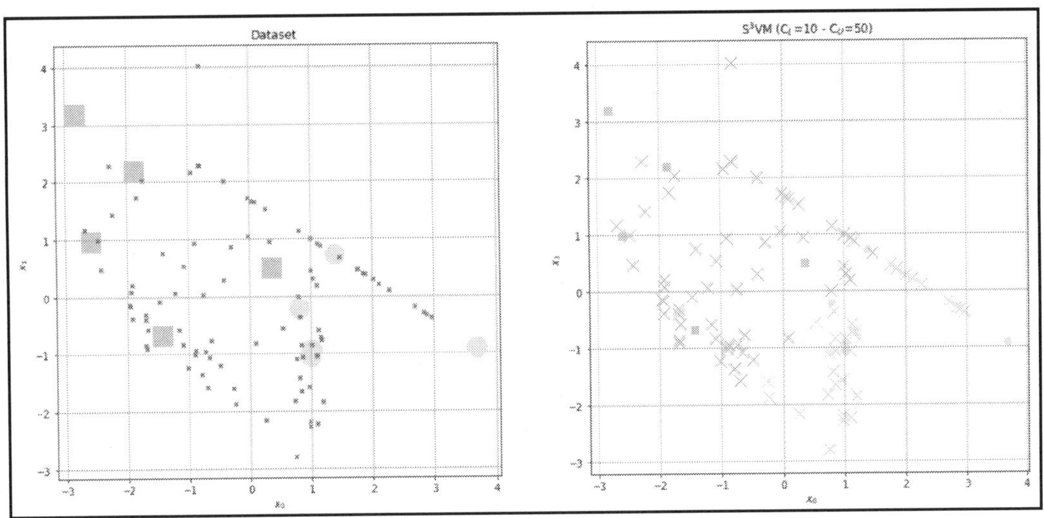

Original dataset (left). Final labeled dataset (right) with $C_L = 10$ and $C_U = 50$

Now, the penalty is quite a lot higher for the unlabeled samples and the result appears much more reasonable considering the clustering assumption. All the high-density regions are coherent and separated by low-density ones. These examples show how the value chosen for the parameters and the optimization method can dramatically change the result. My suggestion is to test several configurations (on sub-sampled datasets), before picking the final one. In *Semi-Supervised Learning, Chapelle O., Schölkopf B., Zien A., (edited by), The MIT Press,* there are further details about possible optimization strategies, with strengths and weaknesses.

Summary

In this chapter, we introduced semi-supervised learning, starting from the scenario and the assumptions needed to justify the approaches. We discussed the importance of the smoothness assumption when working with both supervised and semi-supervised classifiers in order to guarantee a reasonable generalization ability. Then we introduced the clustering assumption, which is strictly related to the geometry of the datasets and allows coping with density estimation problems with a strong structural condition. Finally, we discussed the manifold assumption and its importance in order to avoid the curse of dimensionality.

The chapter continued by introducing a generative and inductive model: Generative Gaussian mixtures, which allow clustering labeled and unlabeled samples starting from the assumption that the prior probabilities are modeled by multivariate Gaussian distributions.

The next topic was about a very important algorithm: contrastive pessimistic likelihood estimation, which is an inductive, semi-supervised classification framework that can be adopted together with any supervised classifier. The main concept is to define a contrastive log-likelihood based on soft-labels (representing the probabilities for the unlabeled samples) and impose a pessimistic condition in order to minimize the trust in the soft-labels. The algorithm can find the best configuration that maximizes the log-likelihood, taking into account both labeled and unlabeled samples.

Another inductive classification approach is provided by the S^3VM algorithm, which is an extension of the classical SVM approach, based on two extra optimization constraints to address the unlabeled samples. This method is relatively powerful, but it's non-convex and, therefore, very sensitive to the algorithms employed to minimize the objective function.

An alternative to S^3VM is provided by the TSVM, which tries to minimize the objective with a condition based on variable labels. The problem is, hence, divided into two parts: the supervised one, which is exactly the same as standard SVM, and the semi-supervised one, which has a similar structure but without fixed *y* labels. This problem is non-convex too and it's necessary to evaluate different optimization strategies to find the best trade-off between accuracy and computational complexity. In the reference section, there are some useful resources so you can examine all these problems in depth and find a suitable solution for each particular scenario.

In the next chapter, `Chapter 3`, *Graph-Based Semi-Supervised Learning* we're continuing this exploration by discussing some important algorithms based on the structure underlying the dataset. In particular, we're going to employ graph theory to perform the propagation of labels to unlabeled samples and to reduce the dimensionality of datasets in non-linear contexts.

3 Graph-Based Semi-Supervised Learning

In this chapter, we continue our discussion about semi-supervised learning, considering a family of algorithms that is based on the graph obtained from the dataset and the existing relationships among samples. The problems that we are going to discuss belong to two main categories: the propagation of class labels to unlabeled samples and the use of non-linear techniques based on the manifold assumption to reduce the dimensionality of the original dataset. In particular, this chapter covers the following propagation algorithms:

- Label propagation based on the weight matrix
- Label propagation in Scikit-Learn (based on transition probabilities)
- Label spreading
- Propagation based on Markov random walks

For the manifold learning section, we're discussing:

- Isomap algorithm and multidimensional scaling approach
- Locally linear embedding
- Laplacian Spectral Embedding
- t-SNE

Label propagation

Label propagation is a family of semi-supervised algorithms based on a graph representation of the dataset. In particular, if we have *N* labeled points (with bipolar labels +1 and -1) and *M* unlabeled points (denoted by *y=0*), it's possible to build an undirected graph based on a measure of geometric affinity among samples. If *G = {V, E}* is the formal definition of the graph, the set of vertices is made up of sample labels *V = { -1, +1, 0 }*, while the edge set is based on an **affinity matrix** *W* (often called **adjacency matrix** when the graph is unweighted), which depends only on the *X* values, not on the labels.

In the following graph, there's an example of such a structure:

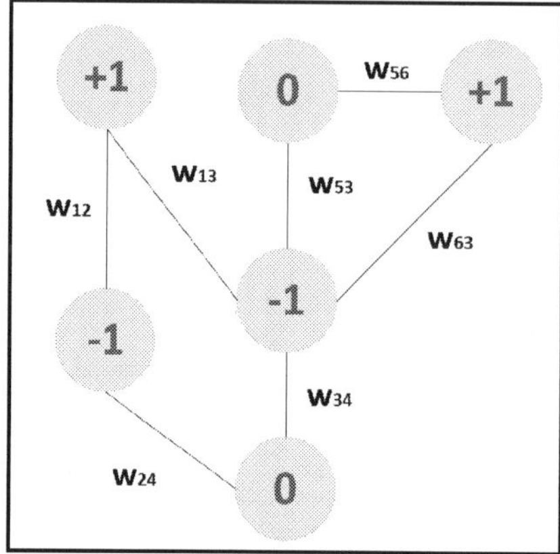

Example of binary graph

In the preceding example graph, there are four labeled points (two with *y=+1* and two with *y=-1*), and two unlabeled points (*y=0*). The affinity matrix is normally symmetric and square with dimensions equal to *(N+M) x (N+M)*. It can be obtained with different approaches. The most common ones, also adopted by Scikit-Learn, are:

- ***k*-Nearest Neighbors**:

$$W_{ij} = \begin{cases} 1 \; if \; \bar{x}_i \in kNN(\bar{x}_j) \\ 0 \; otherwise \end{cases}$$

- **Radial basis function kernel**:

$$W_{ij} = e^{-\gamma \|\bar{x}_i - \bar{x}_j\|^2}$$

Sometimes, in the radial basis function kernel, the parameter γ is represented as the reciprocal of $2\sigma^2$; however, small γ values corresponding to a large variance increase the radius, including farther points and *smoothing* the class over a number of samples, while large γ values restrict the boundaries to a subset that tends to a single sample. Instead, in the k-nearest neighbors kernel, the parameter k controls the number of samples to consider as neighbors.

To describe the basic algorithm, we also need to introduce the **degree matrix** (D):

$$D = diag\left(\left|\sum_j W_{ij}\right| \; \forall \; i = 1..N+M\right) = \begin{pmatrix} deg(v_1) & \cdots & 0 \\ \vdots & \ddots & \vdots \\ 0 & \cdots & deg(v_{N+M}) \end{pmatrix}$$

It is a diagonal matrix where each non-null element represents the *degree* of the corresponding vertex. This can be the number of incoming edges, or a measure proportional to it (as in the case of W based on the radial basis function). The general idea of label propagation is to let each node propagate its label to its neighbors and iterate the procedure until convergence.

Formally, if we have a dataset containing both labeled and unlabeled samples:

$$\begin{cases} X = \{\bar{x}_0, \bar{x}_1, \ldots, \bar{x}_N, \bar{x}_{N+1}, \ldots, \bar{x}_{N+M}\} \; where \; \bar{x}_i \in \mathbb{R}^k \\ Y = \{y_0, y_1, \ldots, y_N, 0, 0, \ldots, 0\} \; where \; y_i \in \{0, +1, -1\} \end{cases}$$

The complete steps of the **label propagation** algorithm (as proposed by Zhu and Ghahramani in *Learning from Labeled and Unlabeled Data with Label Propagation, Zhu X., Ghahramani Z., CMU-CALD-02-107*) are:

1. Select an affinity matrix type (KNN or RBF) and compute W
2. Compute the degree matrix D
3. Define $Y^{(0)} = Y$
4. Define $Y_L = \{y_0, y_1, ..., y_N\}$
5. Iterate until convergence of the following steps:

$$\begin{cases} \tilde{Y}^{(t+1)} = D^{-1}W\tilde{Y}^{(t)} \\ \tilde{Y}_L^{(t+1)} = Y_L \end{cases}$$

The first update performs a propagation step with both labeled and unlabeled points. Each label is spread from a node through its outgoing edges, and the corresponding weight, normalized with the degree, increases or decreases the *effect* of each contribution. The second command instead resets all y values for the labeled samples. The final labels can be obtained as:

$$Y_{Final} = sign(\tilde{Y}^{(t_{end})})$$

The proof of convergence is very easy. If we partition the matrix $D^{-1}W$ according to the relationship among labeled and unlabeled samples, we get:

$$D^{-1}W = \begin{pmatrix} A_{LL} & A_{LU} \\ A_{UL} & A_{UU} \end{pmatrix}$$

If we consider that only the first N components of Y are non-null and they are clamped at the end of each iteration, the matrix can be rewritten as:

$$D^{-1}W = \begin{pmatrix} A_{LL} & A_{LU} \\ A_{UL} & A_{UU} \end{pmatrix} = \begin{pmatrix} I & 0 \\ A_{UL} & A_{UU} \end{pmatrix}$$

We are interested in proving the convergence for the part regarding the unlabeled samples (the labeled ones are fixed), so we can write the update rule as:

$$\tilde{Y}_U^{(t+1)} = A_{UL}Y_L + A_{UU}\tilde{Y}_U^{(t)}$$

Transforming the recursion into an iterative process, the previous formula becomes:

$$\tilde{Y}_U^{(t+1)} = \sum_{k=1}^{t+1} \left((A_{UU})^{k-1}A_{UL}Y_L\right) + (A_{UU})^{t+1}Y_U$$

In the previous expression, the second term is null, so we need to prove that the first term converges; however, it's easy to recognize a truncated matrix geometrical series (Neumann series), and A_{uu} is constructed to have all eigenvalues $|\lambda_i| < 1$, therefore the series converges to:

$$\tilde{Y}_Y^{(\infty)} = \lim_{t \to \infty} \sum_{k=1}^{t+1} (A_{UU})^{k-1}A_{UL}Y_L = (I - A_{UU})^{-1}A_{UL}Y_L$$

Example of label propagation

We can implement the algorithm in Python, using a test bidimensional dataset:

```
from sklearn.datasets import make_classification

nb_samples = 100
nb_unlabeled = 75

X, Y = make_classification(n_samples=nb_samples, n_features=2,
n_informative=2, n_redundant=0, random_state=1000)
Y[Y==0] = -1
Y[nb_samples - nb_unlabeled:nb_samples] = 0
```

As in the other examples, we set *y = 0* for all unlabeled samples (75 out of 100). The corresponding plot is shown in the following graph:

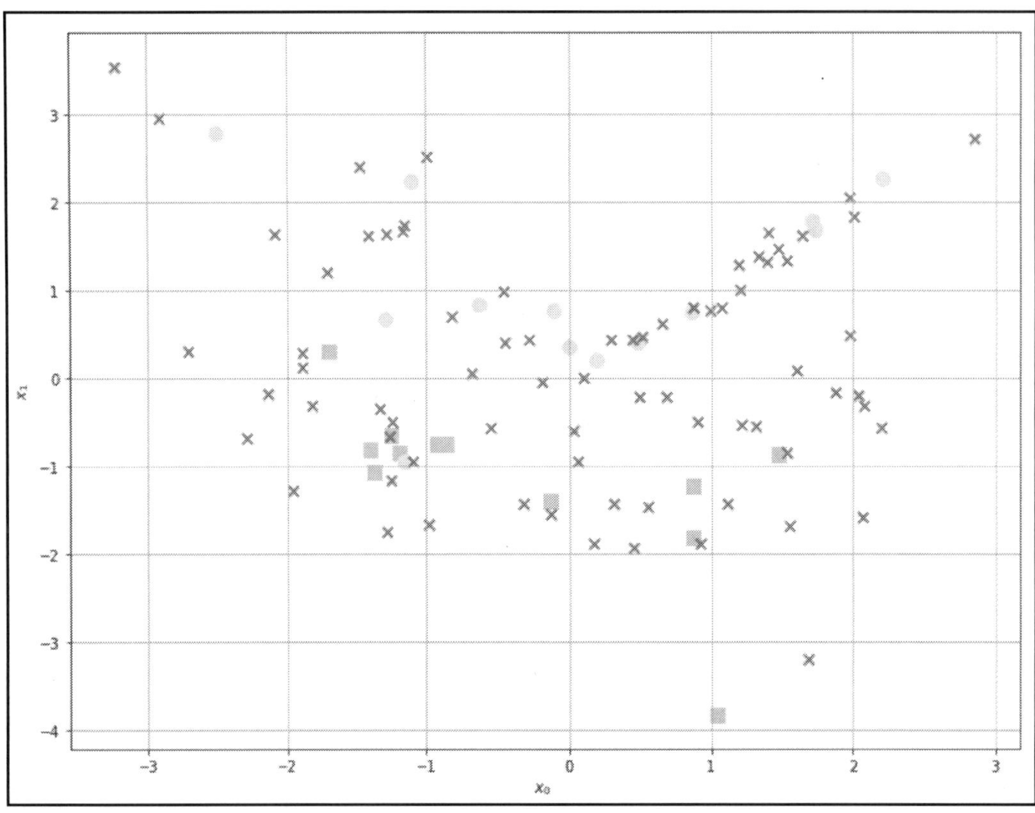

Partially labeled dataset

The dots marked with a cross are unlabeled. At this point, we can define the affinity matrix. In this case, we compute it using both methods:

```
from sklearn.neighbors import kneighbors_graph

nb_neighbors = 2

W_knn_sparse = kneighbors_graph(X, n_neighbors=nb_neighbors,
mode='connectivity', include_self=True)
W_knn = W_knn_sparse.toarray()
```

The KNN matrix is obtained using the Scikit-Learn function `kneighbors_graph()` with the parameters `n_neighbors=2` and `mode='connectivity'`; the alternative is `'distance'`, which returns the distances instead of 0 and 1 to indicate the absence/presence of an edge. The `include_self=True` parameter is useful, as we want to have $W_{ii} = 1$.

For the RBF matrix, we need to define it manually:

```
import numpy as np

def rbf(x1, x2, gamma=10.0):
    n = np.linalg.norm(x1 - x2, ord=1)
    return np.exp(-gamma * np.power(n, 2))

W_rbf = np.zeros((nb_samples, nb_samples))

for i in range(nb_samples):
    for j in range(nb_samples):
        W_rbf[i, j] = rbf(X[i], X[j])
```

The default value for γ is 10, corresponding to a standard deviation σ equal to 0.22. When using this method, it's important to set a correct value for γ; otherwise, the propagation can degenerate in the predominance of a class (γ too small). Now, we can compute the degree matrices and its inverse. As the procedure is identical, from this point on we continue using the RBF affinity matrix:

```
D_rbf = np.diag(np.sum(W_rbf, axis=1))
D_rbf_inv = np.linalg.inv(D_rbf)
```

The algorithm is implemented using a variable threshold. The value adopted here is `0.01`:

```
tolerance = 0.01

Yt = Y.copy()
Y_prev = np.zeros((nb_samples,))
iterations = 0

while np.linalg.norm(Yt - Y_prev, ord=1) > tolerance:
    P = np.dot(D_rbf_inv, W_rbf)
    Yt = np.dot(P, Yt)
    Yt[0:nb_samples - nb_unlabeled] = Y[0:nb_samples - nb_unlabeled]
    Y_prev = Yt.copy()

Y_final = np.sign(Yt)
```

The final result is shown in the following double plot:

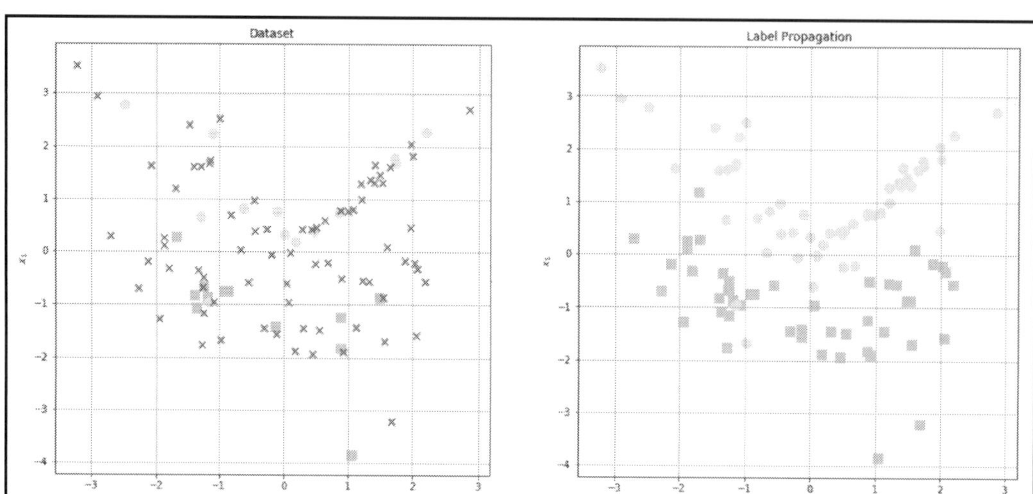

Original dataset (left): dataset after a complete label propagation (right)

As it's possible to see, in the original dataset there's a round dot surrounded by square ones (-0.9, -1). As this algorithm keeps the original labels, we find the same situation after the propagation of labels. This condition could be acceptable, even if both the smoothness and clustering assumptions are contradicted. Assuming that it's reasonable, it's possible to force a *correction* by relaxing the algorithm:

```
tolerance = 0.01

Yt = Y.copy()
Y_prev = np.zeros((nb_samples,))
iterations = 0

while np.linalg.norm(Yt - Y_prev, ord=1) > tolerance:
    P = np.dot(D_rbf_inv, W_rbf)
    Yt = np.dot(P, Yt)
    Y_prev = Yt.copy()

Y_final = np.sign(Yt)
```

In this way, we don't reset the original labels, letting the propagation change all those values that disagree with the neighborhood. The result is shown in the following plot:

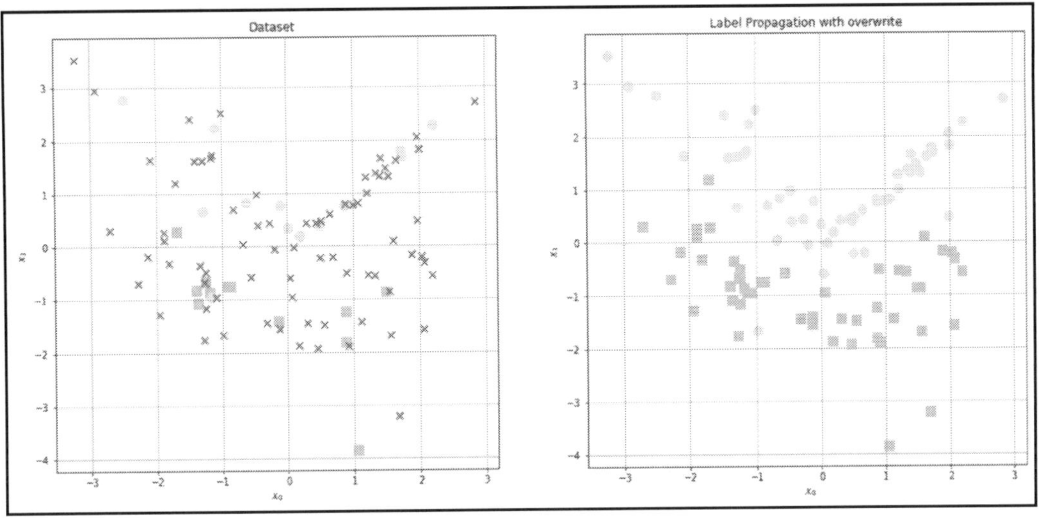

Original dataset (left): dataset after a complete label propagation with overwrite (right)

Label propagation in Scikit-Learn

Scikit-Learn implements a slightly different algorithm proposed by Zhu and Ghahramani (in the aforementioned paper) where the affinity matrix *W* can be computed using both methods (KNN and RBF), but it is normalized to become a probability transition matrix:

$$P_{ij}(i \rightarrow j) = \frac{w_{ij}}{\sum_k w_{kj}}$$

The algorithm operates like a Markov random walk, with the following sequence (assuming that there are *Q* different labels):

1. Define a matrix $Y^M_i = [P(label=y_0), P(label=y_1), ..., and\ P(label=y_Q)]$, where $P(label=yi)$ is the probability of the label *yi*, and each row is normalized so that all the elements sum up to *1*
2. Define $Y^{(0)} = Y^M$

3. Iterate until convergence of the following steps:

$$\begin{cases} \tilde{Y}_M^{(t+1)} = P\tilde{Y}_M^{(t)} \\ \tilde{Y}_M^{(t+1)}(i,j) = \frac{\tilde{Y}_M^{(t+1)}(i,j)}{\sum_k \tilde{Y}_M^{(t+1)}(k,j)} \\ \tilde{Y}_{ML}^{(t+1)} = Y_L \end{cases}$$

The first update performs a label propagation step. As we're working with probabilities, it's necessary (second step) to renormalize the rows so that their element sums up to *1*. The last update resets the original labels for all labeled samples. In this case, it means imposing a $P(label=y_i) = 1$ to the corresponding label, and setting all the others to zero. The proof of convergence is very similar to the one for label propagation algorithms, and can be found in *Learning from Labeled and Unlabeled Data with Label Propagation, Zhu X., Ghahramani Z., CMU-CALD-02-107*. The most important result is that the solution can be obtained in closed form (without any iteration) through this formula:

$$Y_U = (I - P_{uu})^{-1} P_{ul} Y_L$$

The first term is the sum of a generalized geometric series, where P_{uu} is the unlabeled-unlabeled part of the transition matrix *P*. P_{ul}, instead, is the unlabeled-labeled part of the same matrix.

For our Python example, we need to build the dataset differently, because Scikit-Learn considers a sample unlabeled if *y=-1*:

```
from sklearn.datasets import make_classification

nb_samples = 1000
nb_unlabeled = 750

X, Y = make_classification(n_samples=nb_samples, n_features=2,
n_informative=2, n_redundant=0, random_state=100)
Y[nb_samples - nb_unlabeled:nb_samples] = -1
```

We can now train a `LabelPropagation` instance with an RBF kernel and `gamma=10.0`:

```
from sklearn.semi_supervised import LabelPropagation

lp = LabelPropagation(kernel='rbf', gamma=10.0)
lp.fit(X, Y)

Y_final = lp.predict(X)
```

The result is shown in the following double plot:

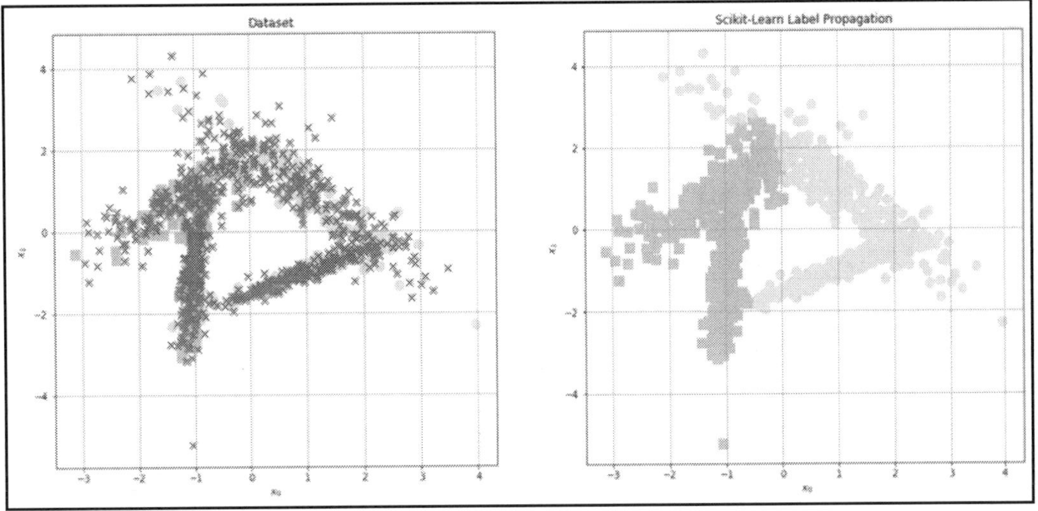

Original dataset (left). Dataset after a Scikit-Learn label propagation (right)

As expected, the propagation converged to a solution that respects both the smoothness and the clustering assumption.

Label spreading

The last algorithm (proposed by Zhou et al.) that we need to analyze is called **label spreading**, and it's based on the normalized graph Laplacian:

$$\mathcal{L} = D^{-\frac{1}{2}} W D^{-\frac{1}{2}}$$

This matrix has each a diagonal element l_{ii} equal to *1*, if the degree $deg(l_{ii}) > 0$ (0 otherwise) and all the other elements equal to:

$$l_{ij} = -\frac{1}{\sqrt{deg(v_i)}\sqrt{deg(v_j)}} \quad if\ v_i \in NN(v_j)$$

The behavior of this matrix is analogous to a discrete Laplacian operator, whose real-value version is the fundamental element of all diffusion equations. To better understand this concept, let's consider the generic heat equation:

$$\frac{\partial Q}{\partial t} = \rho \nabla^2 Q$$

This equation describes the behavior of the temperature of a room when a point is suddenly heated. From basic physics concepts, we know that heat will spread until the temperature reaches an equilibrium point and the speed of variation is proportional to the Laplacian of the distribution. If we consider a bidimensional grid at the equilibrium (the derivative with respect to when time becomes null) and we discretize the Laplacian operator ($\nabla^2 = \nabla \cdot \nabla$) considering the incremental ratios, we obtain:

$$\rho\left(Q(x+1,y) + Q(x-1,y) + Q(x,y+1) + Q(x,y-1) - 4Q(x,y)\right) = 0 \Rightarrow$$
$$Q(x,y) = \frac{Q(x+1,y) + Q(x-1,y) + Q(x,y+1) + Q(x,y-1)}{4}$$

Therefore, at the equilibrium, each point has a value that is the mean of the direct neighbors. It's possible to prove the finite-difference equation has a single fixed point that can be found iteratively, starting from every initial condition. In addition to this idea, label spreading adopts a clamping factor α for the labeled samples. If $\alpha=0$, the algorithm will always reset the labels to the original values (like for label propagation), while with a value in the interval *(0, 1]*, the percentage of clamped labels decreases progressively until $\alpha=1$, when all the labels are overwritten.

The complete steps of the **label spreading** algorithm are:

1. Select an affinity matrix type (KNN or RBF) and compute W
2. Compute the degree matrix D
3. Compute the normalized graph Laplacian L
4. Define $Y^{(0)} = Y$

5. Define α in the interval *[0, 1]*
6. Iterate until convergence of the following step:

$$\tilde{Y}^{(t+1)} = \alpha \mathcal{L} \tilde{Y}^{(t)} + (1 - \alpha) Y^{(0)}$$

It's possible to show (as demonstrated in *Semi-Supervised Learning, Chapelle O., Schölkopf B., Zien A.*, (edited by), *The MIT Press*) that this algorithm is equivalent to the minimization of a quadratic cost function with the following structure:

$$L(\tilde{Y}) = \left\|\tilde{Y}_L - Y_L\right\|^2 + \left\|\tilde{Y}_U\right\|^2 + \mu\left(D^{-\frac{1}{2}}\right)^T (D - W)(D^{-\frac{1}{2}}\tilde{Y})$$

The first term imposes consistency between original labels and estimated ones (for the labeled samples). The second term acts as a normalization factor, forcing the unlabeled terms to become zero, while the third term, which is probably the least intuitive, is needed to guarantee geometrical coherence in terms of smoothness. As we have seen in the previous paragraph, when a hard-clamping is adopted, the smoothness assumption could be violated. By minimizing this term (μ is proportional to α), it's possible to penalize the rapid changes inside the high-density regions. Also in this case, the proof of convergence is very similar to the one for label propagation algorithms, and will be omitted. The interested reader can find it in *Semi-Supervised Learning, Chapelle O., Schölkopf B., Zien A.*, (edited by), *The MIT Press*.

Example of label spreading

We can test this algorithm using the Scikit-Learn implementation. Let's start by creating a very dense dataset:

```
from sklearn.datasets import make_classification

nb_samples = 5000
nb_unlabeled = 1000

X, Y = make_classification(n_samples=nb_samples, n_features=2,
n_informative=2, n_redundant=0, random_state=100)
Y[nb_samples - nb_unlabeled:nb_samples] = -1
```

We can train a `LabelSpreading` instance with a clamping factor `alpha=0.2`. We want to preserve 80% of the original labels but, at the same time, we need a smooth solution:

```
from sklearn.semi_supervised import LabelSpreading

ls = LabelSpreading(kernel='rbf', gamma=10.0, alpha=0.2)
ls.fit(X, Y)

Y_final = ls.predict(X)
```

The result is shown, as usual, together with the original dataset:

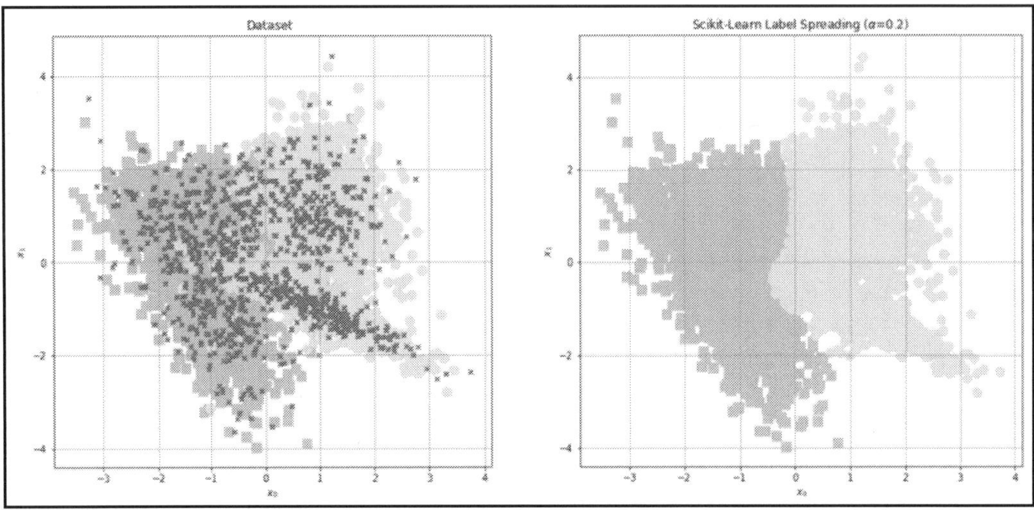

Original dataset (left). Dataset after a complete label spreading (right)

As it's possible to see in the first figure (left), in the central part of the cluster *(x [-1, 0])*, there's an area of circle dots. Using a hard-clamping, this *aisle* would remain unchanged, violating both the smoothness and clustering assumptions. Setting $\alpha > 0$, it's possible to avoid this problem. Of course, the choice of α is strictly correlated with each single problem. If we know that the original labels are absolutely correct, allowing the algorithm to change them can be counterproductive. In this case, for example, it would be better to preprocess the dataset, filtering out all those samples that violate the semi-supervised assumptions. If, instead, we are not sure that all samples are drawn from the same p_{data}, and it's possible to be in the presence of spurious elements, using a higher α value can smooth the dataset without any other operation.

Label propagation based on Markov random walks

The goal of this algorithm proposed by Zhu and Ghahramani is to find the probability distribution of target labels for unlabeled samples given a mixed dataset. This objective is achieved through the simulation of a stochastic process, where each unlabeled sample walks through the graph until it reaches a stationary absorbing state, a labeled sample where it stops acquiring the corresponding label. The main difference with other similar approaches is that in this case, we consider the probability of reaching a labeled sample. In this way, the problem acquires a closed form and can be easily solved.

The first step is to always build a k-nearest neighbors graph with all N samples, and define a weight matrix W based on an RBF kernel:

$$W_{ij} = e^{-\gamma \|\bar{x}_i - \bar{x}_j\|^2}$$

$W_{ij} = 0$ is x_i, and x_j are not neighbors and $W_{ii} = 1$. The transition probability matrix, similarly to the Scikit-Learn label propagation algorithm, is built as:

$$P_{ij}(i \rightarrow j) = \frac{w_{ij}}{\sum_k w_{kj}}$$

In a more compact way, it can be rewritten as $P = D^{-1}W$. If we now consider a *test sample*, starting from the state x_i and randomly walking until an absorbing labeled state is found (we call this label y^{∞}), the probability (referred to as **binary classification**) can be expressed as:

$$P(y^{\infty} = 1|\bar{x}_i) = \begin{cases} I_{y_i=1} \quad if\ x_i\ is\ labeled \\ \sum_{k=1}^{N} p(y^{\infty} = 1|x_k)p(x_i|x_k) \quad if\ x_i\ is\ unlabeled \end{cases}$$

When x_i is labeled, the state is final, and it is represented by the indicator function based on the condition $y_i=1$. When the sample is unlabeled, we need to consider the sum of all possible transitions starting from x_i and ending in the closest absorbing state, with label $y=1$ weighted by the relative transition probabilities.

We can rewrite this expression in matrix form. If we create a vector $P^\infty = [\ P_L(y^\infty=1 \mid X_L),\ P_U(y^\infty=1 \mid X_U)\ ]$, where the first component is based on labeled samples and the second on the unlabeled ones, we can write:

$$P^{\infty} = D^{-1}WP^{\infty}$$

If we now expand the matrices, we get:

$$P^{\infty} = \begin{pmatrix} D_U^{-1} & 0 \\ 0 & D_{uu}^{-1} \end{pmatrix} \begin{pmatrix} W_U & W_{LU} \\ W_{UL} & W_{UU} \end{pmatrix} P^{\infty} = \begin{pmatrix} D_U^{-1}W_U & D_U^{-1}W \\ D_{UU}^{-1}W_{UL} & D_{UU}^{-1}W_{UU} \end{pmatrix} P^{\infty}$$

As we are interested only in the unlabeled samples, we can consider only the second equation:

$$P_U(y^{\infty} = 1|X_U) = D_{UU}^{-1}W_{UL}P_L(y^{\infty} = 1|X_L) + D_{UU}^{-1}W_{UU}P_U(y^{\infty} = 1|X_U)$$

Simplifying the expression, we get the following linear system:

$$(D_{UU} - W_{UU})P_U(y^{\infty} = 1|X_U) = W_{UL}P_L(y^{\infty} = 1|X_L)$$

The term $(D_{uu} - W_{uu})$ is the unlabeled-unlabeled part of the unnormalized graph Laplacian $L = D - W$. By solving this system, we can get the probabilities for the class $y=1$ for all unlabeled samples.

Example of label propagation based on Markov random walks

For this Python example of label propagation based on Markov random walks, we are going to use a bidimensional dataset containing 50 labeled samples belonging to two different classes, and 1,950 unlabeled samples:

```
from sklearn.datasets import make_blobs

nb_samples = 2000
nb_unlabeled = 1950
nb_classes = 2

X, Y = make_blobs(n_samples=nb_samples,
                  n_features=2,
                  centers=nb_classes,
```

```
                    cluster_std=2.5,
                    random_state=500)

Y[nb_samples - nb_unlabeled:] = -1
```

The plot of the dataset is shown in the following diagram (the crosses represent the unlabeled samples):

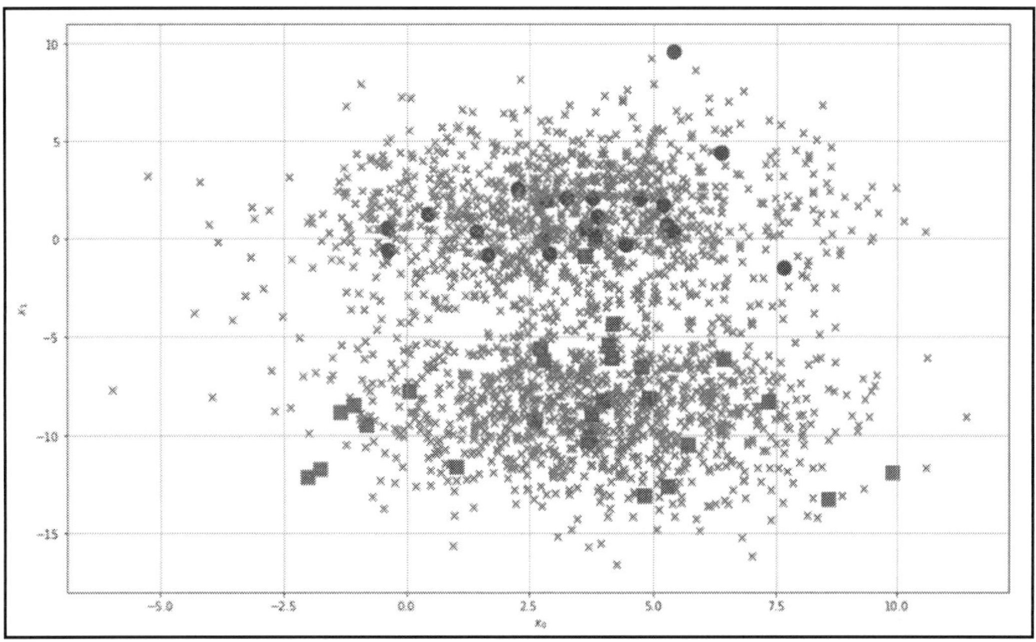

Partially labeled dataset

We can now create the graph (using `n_neighbors=15`) and the weight matrix:

```
import numpy as np

from sklearn.neighbors import kneighbors_graph

def rbf(x1, x2, sigma=1.0):
    d = np.linalg.norm(x1 - x2, ord=1)
    return np.exp(-np.power(d, 2.0) / (2 * np.power(sigma, 2)))

W = kneighbors_graph(X, n_neighbors=15, mode='connectivity',
include_self=True).toarray()

for i in range(nb_samples):
    for j in range(nb_samples):
        if W[i, j] != 0.0:
            W[i, j] = rbf(X[i], X[j])
```

Now, we need to compute the unlabeled part of the unnormalized graph Laplacian and the unlabeled-labeled part of the matrix *W*:

```
D = np.diag(np.sum(W, axis=1))
L = D - W
Luu = L[nb_samples - nb_unlabeled:, nb_samples - nb_unlabeled:]
Wul = W[nb_samples - nb_unlabeled:, 0:nb_samples - nb_unlabeled,]
Yl = Y[0:nb_samples - nb_unlabeled]
```

At this point, it's possible to solve the linear system using the NumPy function `np.linalg.solve()`, which accepts as parameters the matrix *A* and the vector *b* of a generic system in the form $Ax=b$. Once we have the solution, we can merge the new labels with the original ones (where the unlabeled samples have been marked with *-1*). In this case, we don't need to convert the probabilities, because we are using *0* and *1* as labels. In general, it's necessary to use a threshold (0.5) to select the right label:

```
Yu = np.round(np.linalg.solve(Luu, np.dot(Wul, Yl)))
Y[nb_samples - nb_unlabeled:] = Yu.copy()
```

Replotting the dataset, we get:

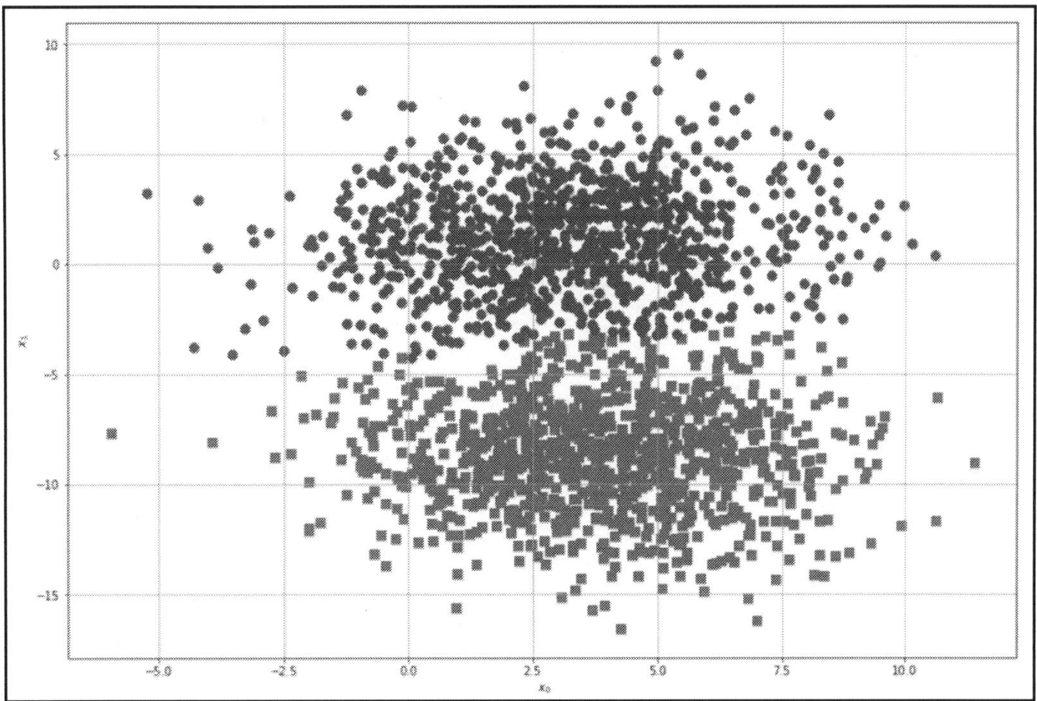

Dataset after a complete Markov random walk label propagation

As expected, without any iteration, the labels have been successfully propagated to all samples in perfect compliance with the clustering assumption. Both this algorithm and label propagation can work using a closed-form solution, so they are very fast even when the number of samples is high; however, there's a fundamental problem regarding the choice of σ/γ for the RBF kernel. As the same authors Zhu and Ghahramani remark, there is no standard solution, but it's possible to consider when $\sigma \to 0$ and when $\sigma \to \infty$. In the first case, only the nearest point has an influence, while in the second case, the influence is extended to the whole sample space, and the unlabeled points tend to acquire the same label. The authors suggest considering the entropy of all samples, trying to find the best σ value that minimizes it. This solution can be very effective, but sometimes the minimum entropy corresponds to a label configuration that isn't impossible to achieve using these algorithms. The best approach is to try different values (at different scales) and select the one corresponding to a valid configuration with the lowest entropy. In our case, it's possible to compute the entropy of the unlabeled samples as:

$$H(X_u) = -\sum_{i=N+1}^{N+M} p(x_i)\, log\, p(x_i)$$

The Python code to perform this computation is:

```
Pu = np.linalg.solve(Luu, np.dot(Wul, Yl))
H = -np.sum(Pu * np.log(Pu + 1e-6))
```

The term `1e-6` has been added to avoid numerical problems when the probability is null. Repeating this process for different values allows us to find a set of candidates that can be restricted to a single value with a direct evaluation of the labeling accuracy (for example, when there is no precise information about the real distribution, it's possible to consider the coherence of each cluster and the separation between them). Another approach is called **class rebalancing**, and it's based on the idea of reweighting the probabilities of unlabeled samples to rebalance the number of points belonging to each class when the new unlabeled samples are added to the set. If we have N labeled points and M unlabeled ones, with K classes, the weight factor w_j for the class j can be obtained as:

$$w_j = \frac{\frac{1}{N}\sum_{t=1}^{N} y_t^{(j)}}{\frac{1}{M}\sum_{t=N+1}^{N+M} \tilde{y}_t^{(j)}}$$

The numerator is the average computed over the labeled samples belonging to class *k*, while the denominator is the average over the unlabeled ones whose estimated class is *k*. The final decision about a class is no longer based only on the highest probability, but on:

$$\tilde{y}_t^{(j)} = argmax_j \left(w_j \cdot p(y_t = j) \right)$$

Manifold learning

In `Chapter 02`, *Introduction to Semi-Supervised Learning*, we discussed the manifold assumption, saying that high-dimensional data normally lies on low-dimensional manifolds. Of course, this is not a theorem, but in many real cases, the assumption is proven to be correct, and it allows us to work with non-linear dimensionality reduction algorithms that would be otherwise unacceptable. In this section, we're going to analyze some of these algorithms. They are all implemented in Scikit-Learn, therefore it's easy to try them with complex datasets.

Isomap

Isomap is one of the simplest algorithms, and it's based on the idea of reducing the dimensionality while trying to preserve the geodesic distances measured on the original manifold where the input data lies. The algorithm works in three steps. The first operation is a k-nearest neighbors clustering and the construction of the following graph. The vertices will be the samples, while the edges represent the connections among nearest neighbors, and their weight is proportional to the distance to the corresponding neighbor.

The second step adopts the **Dijkstra algorithm** to compute the shortest pairwise distances on the graph of all couples of samples. In the following graph, there's a portion of a graph, where some shortest distances are marked:

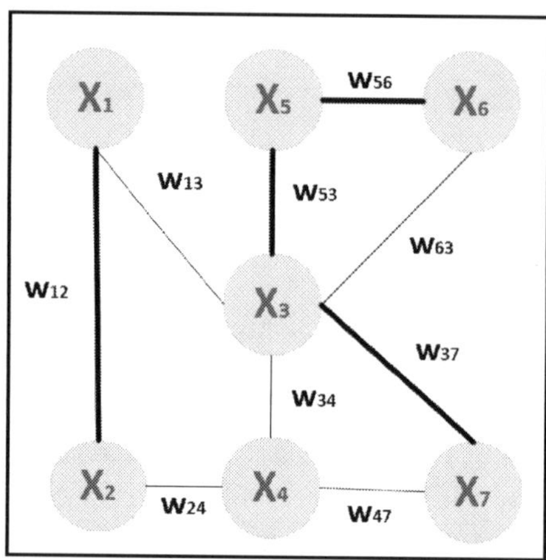

Example of a graph with marked shortest distances

For example, as x_3 is a neighbor of x_5 and x_7, applying the Dijkstra algorithm, we could get the shortest paths $d(x_3, x_5) = w_{53}$ and $d(x_3, x_7) = w_{73}$. The computational complexity of this step is about $O(n^2 log\ n + n^2 k)$, which is lower than $O(n^3)$ when $k << n$ (a condition normally met); however, for large graphs (with $n >> 1$), this is often the most expensive part of the whole algorithm.

The third step is called **metric multidimensional scaling**, which is a technique for finding a low-dimensional representation while trying to preserve the inner product among samples. If we have a *P*-dimensional dataset *X*, the algorithm must find a *Q*-dimensional set Φ with $Q < P$ minimizing the function:

$$L_{MDS} = \sum_{i,j}(\bar{x}_i \cdot \bar{x}_j - \bar{\phi}_i \cdot \bar{\phi}_j)^2$$

As proven in *Semi-Supervised Learning Chapelle O., Schölkopf B., Zien A.*, (edited by), *The MIT Press*, the optimization is achieved by taking the top Q eigenvectors of the Gram matrix $G_{ij} = x_i \cdot x_j$ (or in matrix form, $G=XX^T$ if $X \in \Re^{n \times M}$); however, as the **Isomap** algorithm works with pairwise distances, we need to compute the matrix D of squared distances:

$$D_{ij} = \|\bar{x}_i - \bar{x}_j\|^2$$

If the X dataset is zero-centered, it's possible to derive a simplified Gram matrix from D, as described by M. A. A. Cox and T. F. Cox:

$$G_D = -\frac{1}{2}(I - \bar{v}\bar{v}^T)D(I - \bar{v}\bar{v}^T) \;\; \bar{v} \in \mathbb{R}^P \; and \; \bar{v} = \left(\frac{1}{\sqrt{P}}, \frac{1}{\sqrt{P}}, \ldots, \frac{1}{\sqrt{P}}\right)$$

Isomap computes the top Q eigenvalues λ_1, $\lambda 2$, ..., λ_Q of G_D and the corresponding eigenvectors v_1, v_2, ..., v_Q and determines the Q-dimensional vectors as:

$$\bar{\phi}_i = \left(\lambda_1^{\frac{1}{2}} \bar{v}_1, \lambda_2^{\frac{1}{2}} \bar{v}_2, \ldots, \lambda_Q^{\frac{1}{2}} \bar{v}_Q\right)$$

As we're going to discuss in `Chapter 5`, *EM Algorithm and Applications* (and also as pointed out by Saul, Weinberger, Sha, Ham, and Lee in *Spectral Methods for Dimensionality Reduction, Saul L. K., Weinberger K. Q., Sha F., Ham J., and Lee D. D.*), this kind of projection is also exploited by **Principal Component Analysis** (**PCA**), which finds out the direction with the highest variance, corresponding to the top k eigenvectors of the covariance matrix. In fact, when applying the SVD to the dataset X, we get:

$$X = U\Lambda V^T \;\; where \;\; U \in \mathbb{R}^{M \times M}, \;\; \Lambda \; is \; diag(n \times n) \;\; and \;\; V \in \mathbb{R}^{n \times n}$$

The diagonal matrix Λ contains the eigenvalues of both XX^T and X^TX; therefore, the eigenvalues λ_{Gi} of G are equal to $M\lambda_{\Sigma i}$ where $\lambda_{\Sigma i}$ are the eigenvalues of the covariance matrix $\Sigma = M^{-1}X^TX$. Hence, Isomap achieves the dimensionality reduction, trying to preserve the pairwise distances, while projecting the dataset in the subspace determined by a group of eigenvectors, where the maximum explained variance is achieved. In terms of information theory, this condition guarantees the minimum loss with an effective reduction of dimensionality.

Scikit-Learn also implements the Floyd-Warshall algorithm, which is slightly slower. For further information, please refer to *Introduction to Algorithms, Cormen T. H., Leiserson C. E., Rivest R. L., The MIT Press*.

Example of Isomap

We can now test the Scikit-Learn **Isomap** implementation using the Olivetti faces dataset (provided by AT&T Laboratories, Cambridge), which is made up of 400 64 × 64 grayscale portraits belonging to 40 different people. Examples of these images are shown here:

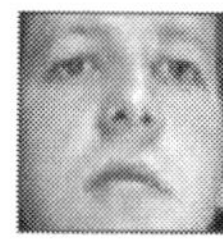

Subset of the Olivetti faces dataset

The original dimensionality is 4096, but we want to visualize the dataset in two dimensions. It's important to understand that using the Euclidean distance for measuring the similarity of images might not the best choice, and it's surprising to see how well the samples are clustered by such a simple algorithm.

The first step is loading the dataset:

```
from sklearn.datasets import fetch_olivetti_faces

faces = fetch_olivetti_faces()
```

The `faces` dictionary contains three main elements:

- `images`: Image array with shape 400 × 64 × 64
- `data`: Flattened array with shape 400 × 4096
- `target`: Array with shape 400 × 1 containing the labels (0, 39)

At this point, we can instantiate the `Isomap` class provided by Scikit-Learn, setting `n_components=2` and `n_neighbors=5` (the reader can try different configurations), and then fitting the model:

```
from sklearn.manifold import Isomap

isomap = Isomap(n_neighbors=5, n_components=2)
X_isomap = isomap.fit_transform(faces['data'])
```

As the resulting plot with 400 elements is very dense, I preferred to show in the following plot only the first 100 samples:

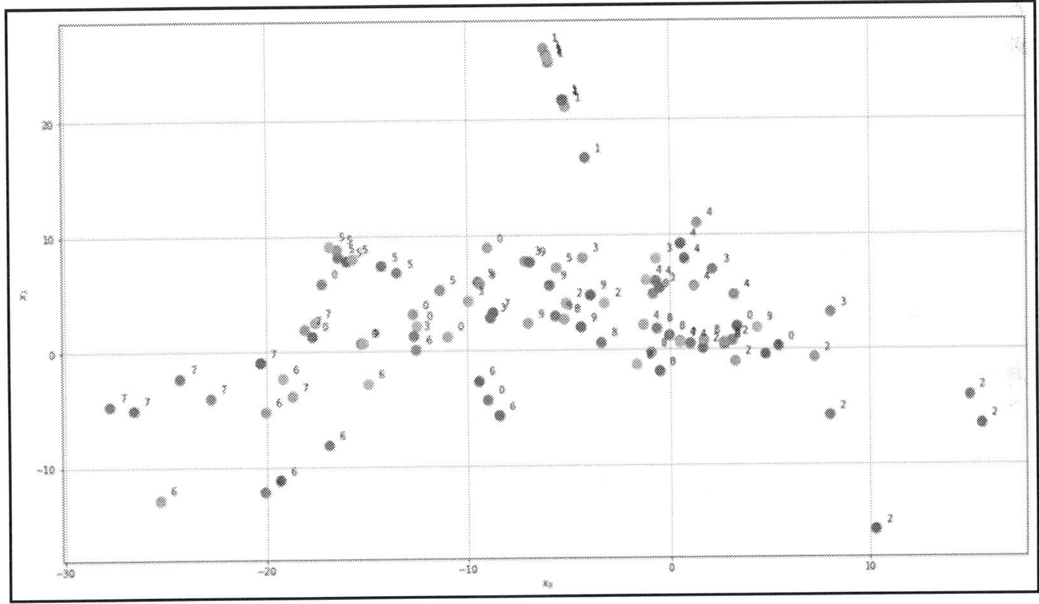

Isomap applied to 100 samples drawn from the Olivetti faces dataset

As it's possible to see, samples belonging to the same class are grouped in rather dense agglomerates. The classes that seem better separated are 7 and 1. Checking the corresponding faces, for class 7, we get:

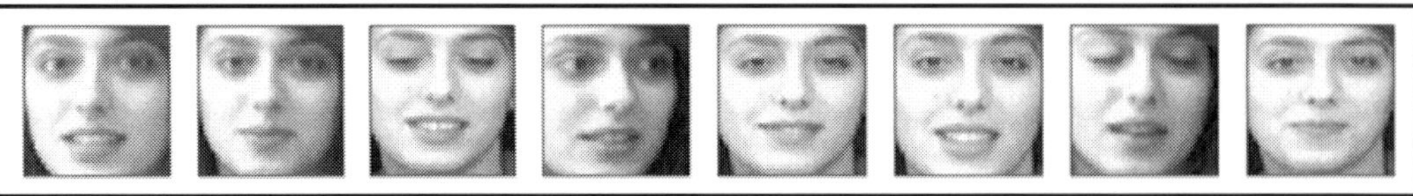

Samples belonging to class 7

The set contains portraits of a young woman with a fair complexion, quite different from the majority of other people. Instead, for class 1, we get:

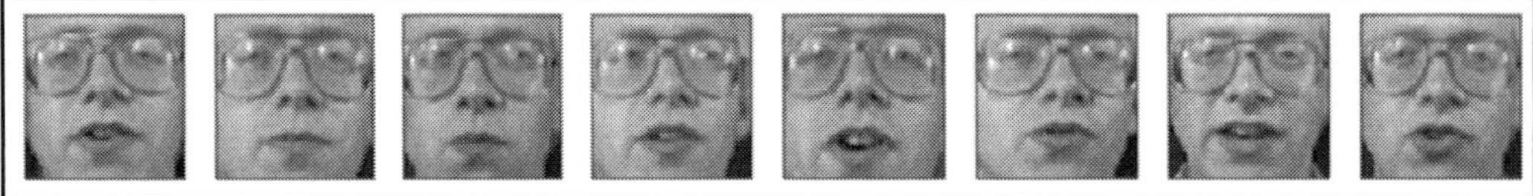

Samples belonging to class 1

In this case, it's a man with big glasses and a particular mouth expression. In the dataset, there are only a few people with glasses, and one of them has a dark beard. We can conclude that **Isomap** created a low-dimensional representation that is really coherent with the original geodesic distances. In some cases, there's a partial clustering overlap that can be mitigated by increasing the dimensionality or adopting a more complex strategy.

Locally linear embedding

Contrary to Isomap, which works with the pairwise distances, this algorithm is based on the assumption that a high-dimensional dataset lying on a smooth manifold can have local linear structures that it tries to preserve during the dimensionality reduction process. **Locally Linear Embedding** (**LLE**), like Isomap, is based on three steps. The first one is applying the *k*-nearest neighbor algorithm to create a directed graph (in Isomap, it was undirected), where the vertices are the input samples and the edges represent a neighborhood relationship. As the graph is direct, a point x_i can be a neighbor of x_j, but the opposite could be false. It means that the weight matrix can be asymmetric.

The second step is based on the main assumption of local linearity. For example, consider the following graph:

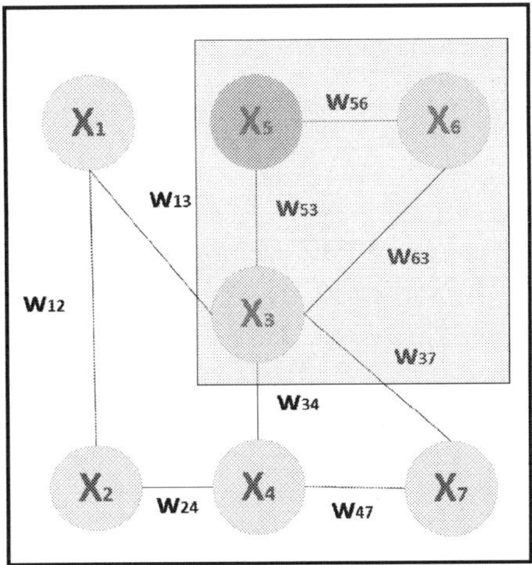

Graph where a neighborhood is marked with a shaded rectangle

The rectangle delimits a small neighboorhood. If we consider the point x_5, the local linearity assumption allows us to think that $x_5 = w_{56}x_6 + w_{53}x_3$, without considering the cyclic relationship. This concept can be formalized for all *N* *P*-dimensional points through the minimization of the following function:

$$L_W = \sum_{i=1}^{N} \left\| \bar{x}_i - \sum_{k \in NN(\bar{x}_i)} W_{ik}\bar{x}_k \right\|^2 \quad subject\ to \sum_{k \in NN(\bar{x}_i)} W_{ik} = 1$$

In order to address the problem of low-rank neighborhood matrices (think about the previous example, with a number of neighbors equal to 20), Scikit-Learn also implements a regularizer that is based on a small arbitrary additive constant that is added to the local weights (according to a variant called **Modified LLE** or **MLLE**). At the end of this step, the matrix W that better matches the linear relationships among neighbors will be selected for the next phase.

In the third step, locally linear embedding tries to determine the low-dimensional ($Q < P$) representation that best reproduces the original relationship among nearest neighbors. This is achieved by minimizing the following function:

$$L_{\Phi} = \sum_{i=1}^{N} \left\| \bar{\phi}_i - \sum_{k \in NN(\bar{\phi}_i)} W_{ik} \bar{\phi}_k \right\|^2 \quad subject\ to \sum_i \bar{\phi}_i = 0\ and\ Cov(\bar{\phi}_i, \bar{\phi}_j) = 1\ \forall\, i, j$$

The solution for this problem is obtained through the adoption of the **Rayleigh-Ritz method**, an algorithm to extract a subset of eigenvectors and eigenvalues from a very large sparse matrix. For further details, read *A spectrum slicing method for the Kohn–Sham problem, Schofield G. Chelikowsky J. R.; Saad Y., Computer Physics Communications. 183*. The initial part of the final procedure consists of determining the matrix D:

$$D = (I - W)^T (I - W)$$

It's possible to prove the last eigenvector (if the eigenvalues are sorted in descending order, it's the bottom one) has all components $v_1^{(N)}, v_2^{(N)}, \ldots, v_N^{(N)} = v$, and the corresponding eigenvalue is null. As Saul and Roweis (*An introduction to locally linear embedding, Saul L. K., Roweis S. T.*) pointed out, all the other Q eigenvectors (from the bottom) are orthogonal, and this allows them to have zero-centered embedding. Hence, the last eigenvector is discarded, while the remaining Q eigenvectors determine the embedding vectors φ_i.

For further details about MLLE, please refer to *MLLE: Modified Locally Linear Embedding Using Multiple Weights, Zhang Z., Wang J.*, `http://citeseerx.ist.psu.edu/viewdoc/summary?doi=10.1.1.70.382`.

Example of locally linear embedding

We can now apply this algorithm to the Olivetti faces dataset, instantiating the Scikit-Learn class `LocallyLinearEmbedding` with `n_components=2` and `n_neighbors=15`:

```
from sklearn.manifold import LocallyLinearEmbedding

lle = LocallyLinearEmbedding(n_neighbors=15, n_components=2)
X_lle = lle.fit_transform(faces['data'])
```

The result (limited to the first 100 samples) is shown in the following plot:

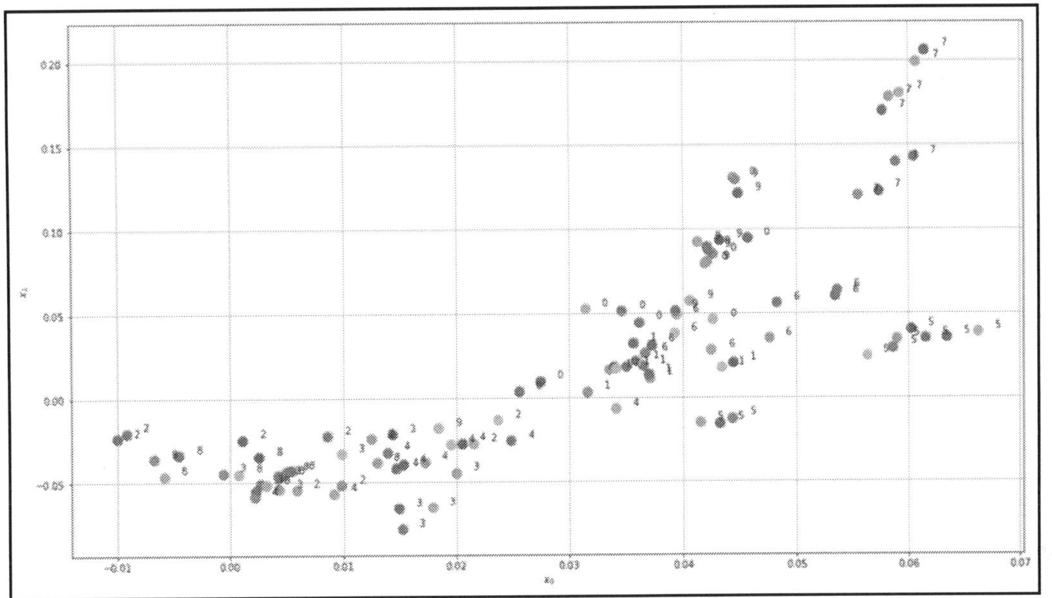

Locally linear embedding applied to 100 samples drawn from the Olivetti faces dataset

Even if the strategy is different from Isomap, we can determine some coherent clusters. In this case, the similarity is obtained through the conjunction of small linear blocks; for the faces, they can represent particular micro-features, like the shape of the nose or the presence of glasses, that remain invariant in the different portraits of the same person. LLE is, in general, preferable when the original dataset is intrinsically locally linear, possibly lying on a smooth manifold. In other words, LLE is a reasonable choice when small parts of a sample are structured in a way that allows the reconstruction of a point given the neighbors and the weights. This is often true for images, but it can be difficult to determine for a generic dataset. When the result doesn't reproduce the original clustering, it's possible to employ the next algorithm or **t-SNE**, which is one the most advanced.

Laplacian Spectral Embedding

This algorithm, based on the spectral decomposition of a graph Laplacian, has been proposed in order to perform a non-linear dimensionality reduction to try to preserve the nearness of points in the *P*-dimensional manifold when remapping on a *Q*-dimensional (with *Q* < *P*) subspace.

The procedure is very similar to the other algorithms. The first step is a *k*-nearest neighbor clustering to generate a graph where the vertices (we can assume to have *N* elements) are the samples, and the edges are weighted using an RBF kernel:

$$W_{ij} = e^{-\gamma\|\bar{x}_i - \bar{x}_j\|^2}$$

The resulting graph is undirected and symmetric. We can now define a pseudo-degree matrix *D*:

$$D = diag\left(\sum_j W_{1j}, \sum_j W_{2j}, \ldots, \sum_j W_{Nj}\right)$$

The low-dimensional representation *Φ* is obtained by minimizing the function:

$$L_\Phi = \sum_{i,j} \frac{W_{ij}\|\bar{\phi}_i - \bar{\phi}_j\|^2}{\sqrt{D_{ii}D_{jj}}} \quad subject\ to \sum_i \bar{\phi}_i = 0 \ \ and \ \ Cov(\bar{\phi}_i, \bar{\phi}_j) = 1\ \forall\, i, j$$

If the two points x_i and x_j are near, the corresponding W_{ij} is close to *1*, while it tends to 0 when the distance tends to ∞. D_{ii} is the sum of all weights originating from x_i (and the same for D_{jj}). Now, let's suppose that x_i is very close only to x_j so, to approximate $D_{ii} = D_{jj} \approx W_{ij}$. The resulting formula is a square loss based on the difference between the vectors φ_i and φ_j. When instead there are multiple *closeness* relationships to consider, the factor W_{ij} divided by the square root of $D_{ii}D_{jj}$ allows reweighting the new distances to find the best trade-off for the whole dataset. In practice, L_Φ is not minimized directly. In fact, it's possible to prove that the minimum can be obtained through the spectral decomposition of the symmetric normalized graph Laplacian (the name derives from this procedure):

$$\mathcal{L} = I - D^{-\frac{1}{2}} W D^{-\frac{1}{2}}$$

Just like for the LLE algorithm, Laplacian Spectral Embedding also works with the bottom $Q + 1$ eigenvectors. The mathematical theory behind the last step is always based on the application of the Rayleigh-Ritz method. The last one is discarded, and the remaining Q determines the low-dimensional representation φ_i.

Example of Laplacian Spectral Embedding

Let's apply this algorithm to the same dataset using the Scikit-Learn class `SpectralEmbedding`, with `n_components=2` and `n_neighbors=15`:

```
from sklearn.manifold import SpectralEmbedding

se = SpectralEmbedding(n_components=2, n_neighbors=15)
X_se = se.fit_transform(faces['data'])
```

The resulting plot (zoomed in due to the presence of a high-density region) is shown in the following graph:

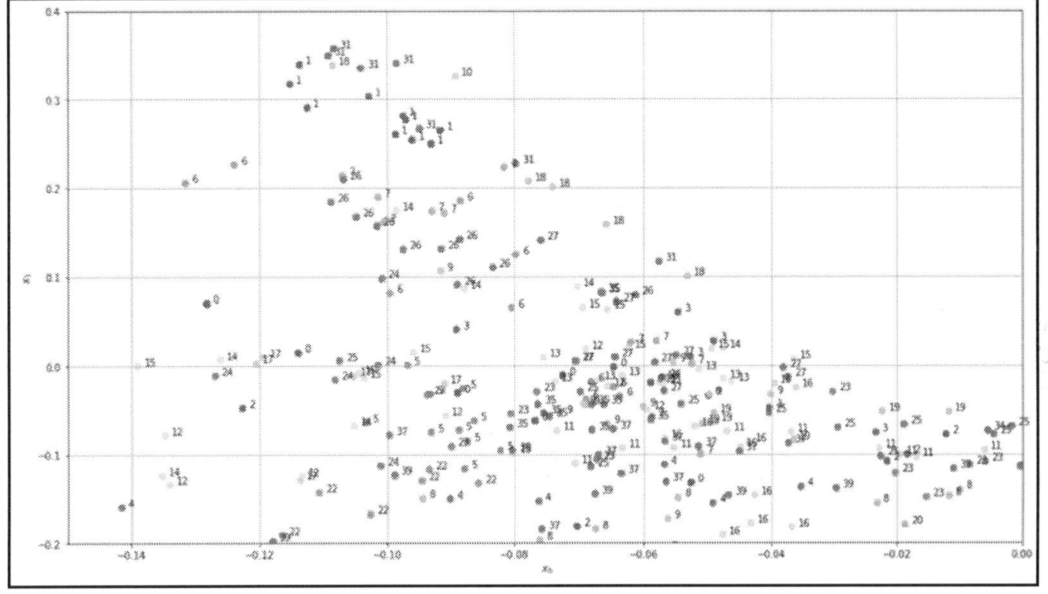

Laplacian Spectral Embedding applied to the Olivetti faces dataset

Even in this case, we can see that some classes are grouped into small clusters, but at the same time, we observe many agglomerates where there are mixed samples. Both this and the previous method work with local pieces of information, trying to find low-dimensional representations that could preserve the geometrical structure of micro-features. This condition drives to a mapping where close points *share* local features (this is almost always true for images, but it's very difficult to prove for generic samples). Therefore, we can observe small clusters containing elements belonging to the same class, but also some *apparent* outliers, which, on the original manifold, can be globally different even if they share local *patches*. Instead, methods like Isomap or t-SNE work with the whole distribution, and try to determine a representation that is almost isometric with the original dataset considering its global properties.

t-SNE

This algorithm, proposed by Van der Mateen and Hinton and formally known as **t-Distributed Stochastic Neighbor Embedding (t-SNE)**, is one of the most powerful manifold dimensionality reduction techniques. Contrary to the other methods, this algorithm starts with a fundamental assumption: the similarity between two *N*-dimensional points x_i and x_j can be represented as the conditional probability $p(x_j|x_i)$ where each point is represented by a Gaussian distribution centered in x_i and with variance σ_i. The variances are selected starting from the desired perplexity, defined as:

$$Perplexity(P) = 2^{H(P)}$$

Low-perplexity values indicate a low uncertainty, and are normally preferable. In common t-SNE tasks, values in the range *10÷50* are normally acceptable.

The assumption on the conditional probabilities can be interpreted thinking that if two samples are very similar, the probability associated with the first sample conditioned to the second one is high, while dissimilar points yield low conditional probabilities. For example, thinking about images, a point centered in the pupil can have as neighbors some points belonging to an eyelash. In terms of probabilities, we can think that *p(eyelash|pupil)* is quite high, while *p(nose|pupil)* is obviously lower. t-SNE models these conditional probabilities as:

$$p(\bar{x}_j|\bar{x}_i) = \frac{e^{-\frac{\|\bar{x}_i - \bar{x}_j\|^2}{2\sigma_i^2}}}{\sum_{k \neq i} e^{-\frac{\|\bar{x}_i - \bar{x}_k\|^2}{2\sigma_i^2}}}$$

The probabilities $p(x_i|x_i)$ are set to zero, so the previous formula can be extended to the whole graph. In order to solve the problem in an easier way, the conditional probabilities are also symmetrized:

$$p(\bar{x}_j|\bar{x}_i) = \frac{p(\bar{x}_i|\bar{x}_j) + p(\bar{x}_j|\bar{x}_i)}{2N}$$

The probability distribution so obtained represents the high-dimensional input relationship. As our goal is to reduce the dimensionality to a value $M < N$, we can think about a similar probabilistic representation for the target points φ_i, using a student-t distribution with one degree of freedom:

$$q(\bar{\phi}_i|\bar{\phi}_j) = \frac{\left(1 + \|\bar{\phi}_i - \bar{\phi}_j\|^2\right)^{-1}}{\sum_{k \neq j} \left(1 + \|\bar{\phi}_k - \bar{\phi}_j\|^2\right)^{-1}}$$

We want the low-dimensional distribution *Q* to be as close as possible to the high-dimensional distribution *P*; therefore, the aim of the **t-SNE** algorithm is to minimize the Kullback-Leibler divergence between *P* and *Q*:

$$D_{KL}(P\|Q) = \sum_{i,j} p(\bar{x}_j|\bar{x}_i)\, log \frac{p(\bar{x}_j|\bar{x}_i)}{q(\bar{\phi}_j|\bar{\phi}_i)} = H(P) - \sum_{i,j} p(\bar{x}_j|\bar{x}_i) log\, q(\bar{\phi}_j|\bar{\phi}_i)$$

The first term is the entropy of the original distribution *P*, while the second one is the cross-entropy *H(P, Q)*, which has to be minimized to solve the problem. The best approach is based on a gradient-descent algorithm, but there are also some useful variations that can improve the performance discussed in *Visualizing High-Dimensional Data Using t-SNE, Van der Maaten L.J.P., Hinton G.E., Journal of Machine Learning Research 9 (Nov), 2008.*

Example of t-distributed stochastic neighbor embedding

We can apply this powerful algorithm to the same Olivetti faces dataset, using the Scikit-Learn class `TSNE` with `n_components=2` and `perplexity=20`:

```
from sklearn.manifold import TSNE

tsne = TSNE(n_components=2, perplexity=20)
X_tsne = tsne.fit_transform(faces['data'])
```

The result for all 400 samples is shown in the following graph:

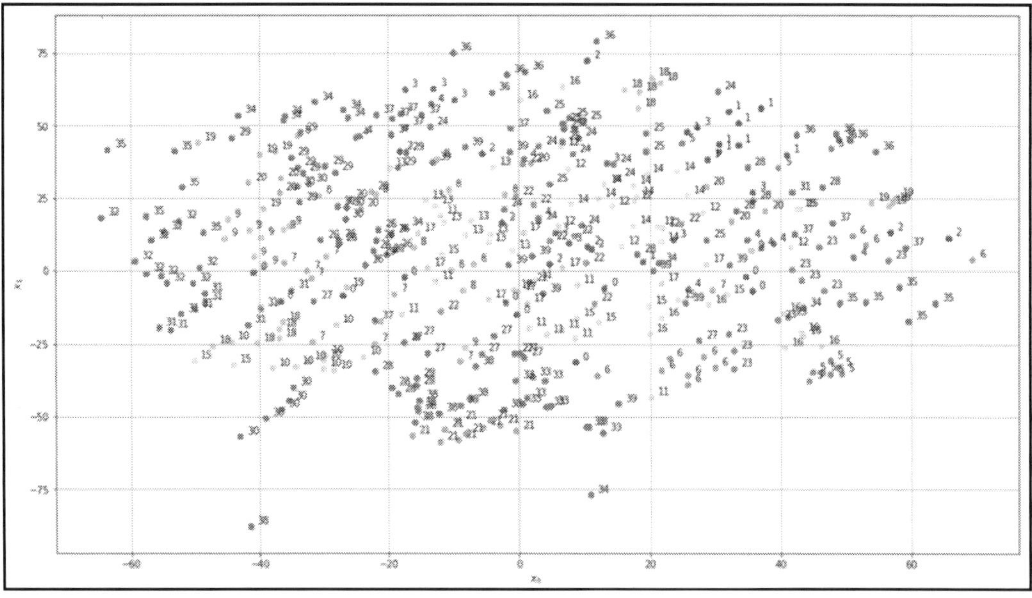

t-SNE applied to the Olivetti faces dataset

A visual inspection of the label distribution can confirm that t-SNE recreated the optimal clustering starting from the original high-dimensional distribution. This algorithm can be employed in several non-linear dimensionality reduction tasks, such as images, word embeddings, or complex feature vectors. Its main strength is hidden in the assumption to consider the similarities as probabilities, without the need to impose any constraint on the pairwise distances, either global or local. Under a certain viewpoint, it's possible to consider t-SNE as a reverse multiclass classification problem based on a cross-entropy cost function. Our goal is to find the labels (low-dimensional representation) given the original distribution and an assumption about the output distribution.

At this point, we could try to answer a natural question: which algorithm must be employed? The obvious answer is it depends on the single problem. When it's useful to reduce the dimensionality, preserving the global similarity among vectors (this is the case when the samples are long feature vectors without local properties, such as word embeddings or data encodings), t-SNE or Isomap are good choices. When instead it's necessary to keep the local distances (for example, the structure of a visual patch that can be shared by different samples also belonging to different classes) as close as possible to the original representation, locally linear embedding or spectral embedding algorithms are preferable.

Summary

In this chapter, we have introduced the most important label propagation techniques. In particular, we have seen how to build a dataset graph based on a weighting kernel, and how to use the geometric information provided by unlabeled samples to determine the most likely class. The basic approach works by iterating the multiplication of the label vector times the weight matrix until a stable point is reached and we have proven that, under simple assumptions, it is always possible.

Another approach, implemented by Scikit-Learn, is based on the transition probability from a state (represented by a sample) to another one, until the convergence to a labeled point. The probability matrix is obtained using a normalized weight matrix to encourage transitions associated to close points and discourage all the *long jumps*. The main drawback of these two methods is the hard-clamping of labeled samples; this constraint can be useful if we *trust* our dataset, but it can be a limitation in the presence of outliers whose label has been wrongly assigned.

Label spreading solves this problem by introducing a clamping factor that determines the percentage of clamped labels. The algorithm is very similar to label propagation, but it's based on graph Laplacian and can be employed in all those problems where the data-generating distribution is not well-determined and the probability of noise is high.

The propagation based on Markov random walks is a very simple algorithm that can estimate the class distribution of unlabeled samples through a stochastic process. It's possible to imagine it as a *test sample* that walks through the graph until it reaches a final labeled state (acquiring the corresponding label). The algorithm is very fast and it has a closed-form solution that can be found by solving a linear system.

The next topic was the introduction of manifold learning with the Isomap algorithm, which is a simple but powerful solution based on a graph built using a *k*-nearest neighbors algorithm (this is a common step in most of these algorithms). The original pairwise distances are processed using the multidimensional scaling technique, which allows obtaining a low-dimensional representation where the distances between samples are preserved.

Two different approaches, based on local pieces of information, are locally linear embedding and Laplacian Spectral Embedding. The former tries to preserve the local linearity present in the original manifold, while the latter, which is based on the spectral decomposition of the normalized graph Laplacian, tries to preserve the nearness of original samples. Both methods are suitable for all those tasks where it's important not to consider the whole original distribution, but the similarity induced by small data *patches*.

We closed this chapter by discussing t-SNE, which is a very powerful algorithm that tries to model a low-dimensional distribution that is as similar as possible to the original high-dimensional one. This task is achieved by minimizing the Kullback-Leibler divergence between the two distributions. t-SNE is a state-of-the-art algorithm, useful whenever it's important to consider the whole original distribution and the similarity between entire samples.

In the next chapter, `Chapter 4`, *Bayesian Networks and Hidden Markov Models* we're going to introduce Bayesian networks in both a static and dynamic context, and hidden Markov models, with practical prediction examples. These algorithms allow modeling complex probabilistic scenarios made up of observed and latent variables, and infer future states using optimized sampling methods based only on the observations.

4
Bayesian Networks and Hidden Markov Models

In this chapter, we're going to introduce the basic concepts of Bayesian models, which allow working with several scenarios where it's necessary to consider uncertainty as a structural part of the system. The discussion will focus on static (time-invariant) and dynamic methods that can be employed where necessary to model time sequences.

In particular, the chapter covers the following topics:

- Bayes' theorem and its applications
- Bayesian networks
- Sampling from a Bayesian network using direct methods and **Markov chain Monte Carlo** (**MCMC**) ones (Gibbs and Metropolis-Hastings samplers)
- Modeling a Bayesian network with PyMC3
- **Hidden Markov Models** (**HMMs**)
- Examples with hmmlearn

Conditional probabilities and Bayes' theorem

If we have a probability space S and two events A and B, the probability of A given B is called **conditional probability**, and it's defined as:

$$P(A|B) = \frac{P(A, B)}{P(B)}$$

As $P(A, B) = P(B, A)$, it's possible to derive **Bayes' theorem**:

$$\begin{cases} P(A,B) = P(A|B)P(B) \\ P(B,A) = P(B|A)P(A) \end{cases} \Rightarrow P(A|B) = \frac{P(B|A)P(A)}{P(B)}$$

This theorem allows expressing a conditional probability as a function of the opposite one and the two marginal probabilities $P(A)$ and $P(B)$. This result is fundamental to many machine learning problems, because, as we're going to see in this and in the next chapters, normally it's easier to work with a conditional probability in order to get the opposite, but it's hard to work directly from the latter. A common form of this theorem can be expressed as:

$$P(A|B) \propto P(B|A)P(A)$$

Let's suppose that we need to estimate the probability of an event A given some observations B, or using the standard notation, **the posterior probability of A**; the previous formula expresses this value as proportional to the term $P(A)$, which is the marginal probability of A, called **prior probability**, and the conditional probability of the observations B given the event A. $P(B|A)$ is called **likelihood**, and defines how event A is likely to determine B. Therefore, we can summarize the relation as *posterior probability* $\propto$ *likelihood* $\cdot$ *prior probability*. The proportion is not a limitation, because the term $P(B)$ is always a normalizing constant that can be omitted. Of course, the reader must remember to normalize $P(A|B)$ so that its terms always sum up to one.

This is a key concept of Bayesian statistics, where we don't directly trust the prior probability, but we reweight it using the likelihood of some observations. As an example, we can think to toss a coin 10 times (event A). We know that $P(A) = 0.5$ if the coin is fair. If we'd like to know what the probability is to get 10 heads, we could employ the Binomial distribution obtaining $P(10\ heads) = 0.5^k$; however, let's suppose that we don't know whether the coin is fair or not, but we suspect it's loaded with a prior probability $P(Loaded) = 0.7$ in favor of tails. We can define a complete prior probability $P(Coin\ status)$ using the indicator functions:

$$P(Coin\ status) = P(Fair)I_{Coin=Fair} + P(Loaded)I_{Coin=Loaded}$$

Where $P(Fair) = 0.5$ and $P(Loaded) = 0.7$, the indicator $I_{Coin=Fair}$ is equal to 1 only if the coin is fair, and 0 otherwise. The same happens with $I_{Coin=Loaded}$ when the coin is loaded. Our goal now is to determine the posterior probability $P(Coin\ status|B_1, B_2, ..., B_n)$ to be able to confirm or to reject our hypothesis.

Let's imagine to observe $n = 10$ events with $B_1 = Head$ and $B_2, ..., B_n = Tail$. We can express the probability using the binomial distribution:

$$P(Coin\ status|B_1, B_2, \ldots, B_n) \propto \left[\binom{10}{1}0.5(1-0.5)^9 \cdot 0.3I_{Fair} + \binom{10}{1}0.7(1-0.7)^9 \cdot 0.7I_{Loaded}\right]$$

After simplifying the expression, we get:

$$P(Coin\ status|B_1, B_2, \ldots, B_n) \propto (0.003I_{Fair} + 0.08I_{Loaded})$$

We still need to normalize by dividing both terms by 0.083 (the sum of the two terms), so we get the final posterior probability $P(Coin\ status \mid B_1, B_2, ..., Bn) = 0.04I_{Fair} + 0.96I_{Loaded}$. This result confirms and strengthens our hypothesis. The probability of a loaded coin is now about 96%, thanks to the sequence of nine tail observations after one head.

This example was presented to show how the data (observations) is plugged into the Bayesian framework. If the reader is interested in studying these concepts in more detail, in *Introduction to Statistical Decision Theory, Pratt J., Raiffa H., Schlaifer R., The MIT Press*, it's possible to find many interesting examples and explanations; however, before introducing Bayesian networks, it's useful to define two other essential concepts.

The first concept is called **conditional independence**, and it can be formalized considering two variables *A* and *B*, which are conditioned to a third one, *C*. We say that *A* and *B* are conditionally independent given *C* if:

$$P(A, B|C) = P(A|C)P(B|C)$$

Now, let's suppose we have an event *A* that is conditioned to a series of causes $C_1, C_2, ..., C_n$; the conditional probability is, therefore, $P(A \mid C_1, C_2, ..., C_n)$. Applying Bayes' theorem, we get:

$$P(A|C_1, C_2, \ldots, C_n) \propto P(C_1, C_2, \ldots, C_n|A)P(A)$$

If there is conditional independence, the previous expression can be simplified and rewritten as:

$$P(A|C_1, C_2, \ldots, C_n) \propto P(C_1|A)P(C_2|A)\ldots P(C_n|A)P(A) = P(A)\prod_{i=1}^{n} P(C_i|A)$$

This property is fundamental in Naive Bayes classifiers, where we assume that the effect produced by a cause does not influence the other causes. For example, in a spam detector, we could say that the length of the mail and the presence of some particular keywords are independent events, and we only need to compute *P(Length | Spam)* and *P(Keywords | Spam)* without considering the joint probability *P(Length, Keywords | Spam)*.

Another important element is the **chain rule** of probabilities. Let's suppose we have the joint probability $P(X_1, X_2, ..., X_n)$. It can be expressed as:

$$P(X_1, X_2, \ldots, X_n) = P(X_1|X_2, \ldots, X_n)P(X_2, \ldots, X_n)$$

Repeating the procedure with the joint probability on the right side, we get:

$$P(X_1, X_2, \ldots, X_n) = P(X_1|X_2, \ldots, X_n)P(X_2|X_3, \ldots, X_n)\ldots P(X_n) = \prod_{i=1}^{n} P(X_i|X_{i+1}, \ldots, X_n)$$

In this way, it's possible to express a full joint probability as the product of hierarchical conditional probabilities, until the last term, which is a marginal distribution. We are going to use this concept extensively in the next paragraph when exploring Bayesian networks.

Bayesian networks

A **Bayesian network** is a probabilistic model represented by a direct acyclic graph *G = {V, E}*, where the vertices are random variables X_i, and the edges determine a conditional dependence among them. In the following diagram, there's an example of simple Bayesian networks with four variables:

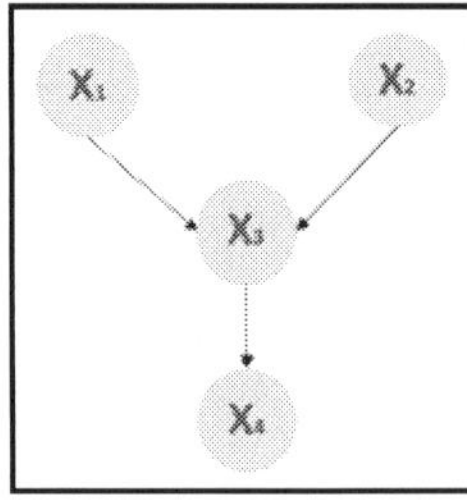

Example of Bayesian network

The variable x_4 is dependent on x_3, which is dependent on x_1 and x_2. To describe the network, we need the marginal probabilities $P(x_1)$ and $P(x_2)$ and the conditional probabilities $P(x_3|x_1,x_2)$ and $P(x_4|x_3)$. In fact, using the chain rule, we can derive the full joint probability as:

$$P(x_1, x_2, x_3, x_4) = P(x_4|x_3)P(x_3|x_1, x_2)P(x_2)P(x_1)$$

The previous expression shows an important concept: as the graph is direct and acyclic, each variable is conditionally independent of all other variables that are not successors given its predecessors. To formalize this concept, we can define the function $Predecessors(x_i)$, which returns the set of nodes that influence x_i directly, for example, $Predecessors(x_3) = \{x_1,x_2\}$ (we are using lowercase letters, but we are considering the random variable, not a sample). Using this function, it's possible to write a general expression for the full joint probability of a Bayesian network with N nodes:

$$P(x_1, x_2, \ldots, x_N) = \prod_{i=1}^{N} P\left(x_i|Predecessors(x_i)\right)$$

The general procedure to build a Bayesian network should always start with the first causes, adding their effects one by one, until the last nodes are inserted into the graph. If this rule is not respected, the resulting graph can contain useless relations that can increase the complexity of the model. For example, if x_4 is caused indirectly by both x_1 and x_2, therefore adding the edges $x_1 \rightarrow x_4$ and $x_2 \rightarrow x_4$ could seem a good modeling choice; however, we know that the final influence on x_4 is determined only by the values of x_3, whose probability must be conditioned on x_1 and x_2, hence we can remove the spurious edges. I suggest reading *Introduction to Statistical Decision Theory, Pratt J., Raiffa H., Schlaifer R., The MIT Press* to learn many best practices that should be employed in this procedure.

Sampling from a Bayesian network

Performing a direct inference on a Bayesian network can be a very complex operation when the number of variables and edges is high. For this reason, several sampling methods have been proposed. In this paragraph, we are going to show how to determine the full joint probability sampling from a network using a direct approach, and two MCMC algorithms.

Let's start considering the previous network and, for simplicity, let's assume to have only *Bernoulli* distributions. X_1 and X_2 are modeled as:

$$\begin{cases} X_1 \sim Bernoulli(0.35) \\ X_2 \sim Bernoulli(0.65) \end{cases}$$

The conditional distribution X_3 is defined as:

$$X_3 \sim Bernoulli(p) \;\; with\; p = \begin{cases} 0.75 & if\; x_1 = True\; and\; x_2 = True \\ 0.4 & otherwise \end{cases}$$

While the conditional distribution X_4 is defined as:

$$X_4 \sim Bernoulli(p) \;\; with\; p = \begin{cases} 0.65 & if\; x_3 = True \\ 0.5 & otherwise \end{cases}$$

We can now use a direct sampling to estimate the full joint probability $P(x_1, x_2, x_3, x_4)$ using the chain rule previously introduced.

Direct sampling

With **direct sampling**, our goal is to approximate the full joint probability through a sequence of samples drawn from each conditional distribution. If we assume that the graph is well-structured (without unnecessary edges) and we have *N* variables, the algorithm is made up of the following steps:

1. Initialize the variable $N_{Samples}$.
2. Initialize a vector *S* with shape $(N, N_{Samples})$.
3. Initialize a frequency vector $F_{Samples}$ with shape $(N, N_{Samples})$. In Python, it's better to employ a dictionary where the key is a combination $(x_1, x_2, x_3, ..., x_N)$.
4. For $t=1$ to $N_{Samples}$:
    1. For $i=1$ to N:
        1. Sample from $P(X_i \mid Predecessors(X_i))$
        2. Store the sample in $S[i, t]$
    2. If $F_{Samples}$ contains the sampled tuple $S[:, t]$:
        1. $F_{Samples}[S[:, t]] += 1$

2. Else:
    1. $F_{Samples}[S[:, t]] = 1$ (both these operations are immediate with Python dictionaries)

5. Create a vector $P_{Sampled}$ with shape $(N, 1)$.
6. Set $P_{Sampled}[i, 0] = F_{Samples}[i]/N$.

From a mathematical viewpoint, we are first creating a frequency vector $F_{Samples}(x_1, x_2, x_3, \ldots, x_N; N_{Samples})$ and then we approximate the full joint probability considering $N_{Samples} \rightarrow \infty$:

$$P(x_1, x_2, \ldots, x_N) = \lim_{N_{samples} \to \infty} F_{samples}(x_1, x_2, \ldots, x_N; N_{samples})$$

Example of direct sampling

We can now implement this algorithm in Python. Let's start by defining the sample methods using the NumPy function `np.random.binomial(1, p)`, which draws a sample from a *Bernoulli* distribution with probability `p`:

```
import numpy as np

def X1_sample(p=0.35):
    return np.random.binomial(1, p)

def X2_sample(p=0.65):
    return np.random.binomial(1, p)

def X3_sample(x1, x2, p1=0.75, p2=0.4):
    if x1 == 1 and x2 == 1:
        return np.random.binomial(1, p1)
    else:
        return np.random.binomial(1, p2)
def X4_sample(x3, p1=0.65, p2=0.5):
    if x3 == 1:
        return np.random.binomial(1, p1)
    else:
        return np.random.binomial(1, p2)
```

At this point, we can implement the main cycle. As the variables are Boolean, the total number of probabilities is 16, so we set `Nsamples` to `5000` (smaller values are also acceptable):

```
N = 4
```

```
Nsamples = 5000

S = np.zeros((N, Nsamples))
Fsamples = {}

for t in range(Nsamples):
    x1 = X1_sample()
    x2 = X2_sample()
    x3 = X3_sample(x1, x2)
    x4 = X4_sample(x3)
    sample = (x1, x2, x3, x4)
    if sample in Fsamples:
        Fsamples[sample] += 1
    else:
        Fsamples[sample] = 1
```

When the sampling is complete, it's possible to extract the full joint probability:

```
samples = np.array(list(Fsamples.keys()), dtype=np.bool_)
probabilities = np.array(list(Fsamples.values()), dtype=np.float64) /
Nsamples

for i in range(len(samples)):
    print('P{} = {}'.format(samples[i], probabilities[i]))

P[ True False  True  True] = 0.0286
P[ True  True False  True] = 0.024
P[ True  True  True False] = 0.06
P[False False False False] = 0.0708
P[ True False  True False] = 0.0166
P[False  True  True  True] = 0.1006
P[False False  True  True] = 0.054
...
```

We can also query the model. For example, we could be interested in $P(X_4=True)$. We can do this by looking for all the elements where $X_4=True$, and summing up the relative probabilities:

```
p4t = np.argwhere(samples[:, 3]==True)
print(np.sum(probabilities[p4t]))

0.5622
```

This value is coherent with the definition of X_4, which is always $p >= 0.5$. The reader can try to change the values and repeat the simulation.

A gentle introduction to Markov chains

In order to discuss the MCMC algorithms, it's necessary to introduce the concept of Markov chains. In fact, while the direct sample method draws samples without any particular order, the MCMC strategies draw a sequence of samples according to a precise transition probability from a sample to the following one.

Let's consider a time-dependent random variable *X(t)*, and let's assume a discrete time sequence $\mathbf{X}_1, \mathbf{X}_2, \ldots, \mathbf{X}_t, \mathbf{X}_{t+1}, \ldots$ where $\mathbf{X}_t$ represents the value assumed at time *t*. In the following diagram, there's a schematic representation of this sequence:

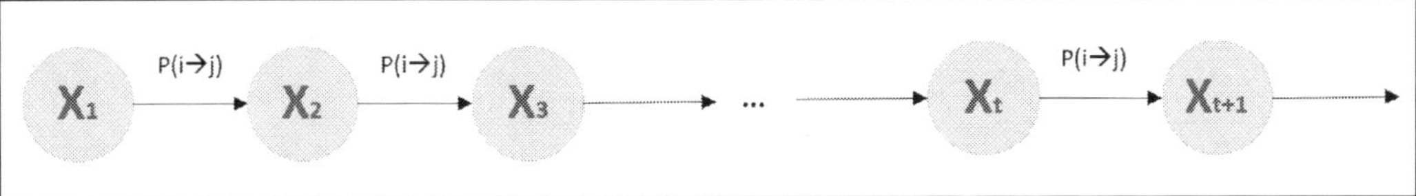

Structure of a generic Markov chain

We can suppose to have *N* different states s_i for *i=1..N*, therefore it's possible to consider the probability $P(X_t=s_i \mid X_{t-1}=s_j, \ldots, X_1=s_p)$. *X(t)* is defined as a **first-order Markov process** if:

$$P(X_t = s_i | X_{t-1} = s_j, \ldots, X_1 = s_p) = P(X_t = s_i | X_{t-1} = s_j)$$

In other words, in a Markov process (from now on, we omit *first-order*, even if there are cases when it's useful to consider more previous states), the probability that *X(t)* is in a certain state depends only on the state assumed in the previous time instant. Therefore, we can define a **transition probability** for every couple *i, j*:

$$P(j \to i) = P(X_t = s_i | X_{t-1} = s_j)$$

Considering all the couples *(i, j)*, it's also possible to build a transition probability matrix $T(i, j) = P(i \to j)$. The marginal probability that $X_t=s_i$ using a standard notation is defined as:

$$\pi_i(t) = P(X_t = s_i)$$

At this point, it's easy to prove (**Chapman-Kolmogorov** equation) that:

$$\pi_i(t+1) = \sum_k p(k \to i)\pi_k(t) \Rightarrow \bar{\pi}(t+1) = T^T \bar{\pi}(t)$$

In the previous expression, in order to compute $\pi_i(t+1)$, we need to sum over all possible previous states, considering the relative transition probability. This operation can be rewritten in matrix form, using a vector $\pi(t)$ containing all states and the transition probability matrix T (the uppercase superscript T means that the matrix is transposed). The evolution of the chain can be computed recursively:

$$\bar{\pi}(t+1) = T^T \bar{\pi}(t) = T^T \left(T^T \bar{\pi}(t-1)\right) = \ldots = (T^T)^t \bar{\pi}(1)$$

For our purposes, it's important to consider Markov chains that are able to reach a *stationary distribution* π_s:

$$\bar{\pi}_s = T^T \bar{\pi}_s$$

In other words, the state does not depend on the initial condition $\pi(1)$, and it's no longer able to change. The stationary distribution is unique if the underlying Markov process is *ergodic*. This concept means that the process has the same properties if averaged over time (which is often impossible), or averaged vertically (freezing the time) over the states (which is simpler in the majority of cases).

The process of ergodicity for Markov chains is assured by two conditions. The first is aperiodicity for all states, which means that it is impossible to find a positive number p so that the chain returns in the same state sequence after a number of instants equal to a multiple of p. The second condition is that all states must be positive recurrent: this means that, given a random variable $N_{instants}(i)$, describing the number of time instants needed to return to the state s_i, $E[N_{instants}(i)] < \infty$; therefore, potentially, all the states can be revisited in a finite time.

The reason why we need the ergodicity condition, and hence the existence of a unique stationary distribution, is that we are considering the sampling processes modeled as Markov chains, where the next value is sampled according to the current state. The transition from one state to another is done in order to find better samples, as we're going to see in the Metropolis-Hastings sampler, where we can also decide to reject a sample and keep the chain in the same state. For this reason, we need to be sure that the algorithms converge to the unique stable distribution (that approximates the real full joint distribution of our Bayesian network). It's possible to prove that a chain always reaches a stationary distribution if:

$$\forall\, i, j \Rightarrow P(i \rightarrow j)\pi_{s_i} = P(j \rightarrow i)\pi_{s_j}$$

The previous equation is called detailed balance, and implies the reversibility of the chain. Intuitively, it means that the probability of finding the chain in the state *A* times the probability of a transition to the state *B* is equal to the probability of finding the chain in the state *B* times the probability of a transition to *A*.

For both methods that we are going to discuss, it's possible to prove that they satisfy the previous condition, and therefore their convergence is assured.

Gibbs sampling

Let's suppose that we want to obtain the full joint probability for a Bayesian network $P(x_1, x_2, x_3, ..., x_N)$; however, the number of variables is large and there's no way to solve this problem easily in a closed form. Moreover, imagine that we would like to get some marginal distribution, such as $P(x_2)$, but to do so we should integrate the full joint probability, and this task is even harder. Gibbs sampling allows approximating of all marginal distributions with an iterative process. If we have *N* variables, the algorithm proceeds with the following steps:

1. Initialize the variable $N_{Iterations}$
2. Initialize a vector *S* with shape $(N, N_{Iterations})$
3. Randomly initialize $x_1^{(0)}, x_2^{(0)}, ..., x_N^{(0)}$ (the superscript index is referred to the iteration)
4. For $t=1$ to $N_{Iterations}$:
    1. Sample $x_1^{(t)}$ from $p(x_1|x_2^{(t-1)}, x_3^{(t-1)}, ..., x_N^{(t-1)})$ and store it in $S[0, t]$
    2. Sample $x_2^{(t)}$ from $p(x_2|x_1^{(t)}, x_3^{(t-1)}, ..., x_N^{(t-1)})$ and store it in $S[1, t]$
    3. Sample $x_3^{(t)}$ from $p(x_3|x_1^{(t)}, x_2^{(t)}, ..., x_N^{(t-1)})$ and store it in $S[2, t]$
    4. ...
    5. Sample $x_N^{(t)}$ from $p(x_N|x_1^{(t)}, x_2^{(t)}, ..., x_{N-1}^{(t)})$ and store it in $S[N-1, t]$

At the end of the iterations, vector *S* will contain $N_{Iterations}$ samples for each distribution. As we need to determine the probabilities, it's necessary to proceed like in the direct sampling algorithm, counting the number of single occurrences and normalizing dividing by $N_{Iterations}$. If the variables are continuous, it's possible to consider intervals, counting how many samples are contained in each of them.

For small networks, this procedure is very similar to direct sampling, except that when working with very large networks, the sampling process could become slow; however, the algorithm can be simplified after introducing the concept of the Markov blanket of X_i, which is the set of random variables that are predecessors, successors, and successors' predecessors of X_i (in some books, they use the terms *parents* and *children*). In a Bayesian network, a variable X_i is a conditional independent of all other variables given its Markov blanket. Therefore, if we define the function $MB(X_i)$, which returns the set of variables in the blanket, the generic sampling step can be rewritten as $p(x_i|MB(X_i))$, and there's no more need to consider all the other variables.

To understand this concept, let's consider the network shown in the following diagram:

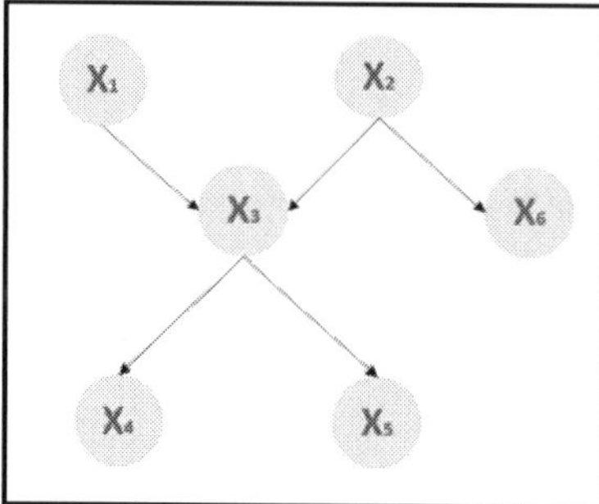

Bayesian network for the Gibbs sampling example

The Markov blankets are:

- $MB(X_1) = \{ X_2, X_3 \}$
- $MB(X_2) = \{ X_1, X_3, X_4 \}$
- $MB(X_3) = \{ X_1, X_2, X_4, X_5 \}$
- $MB(X_4) = \{ X_3 \}$
- $MB(X_5) = \{ X_3 \}$
- $MB(X_6) = \{ X_2 \}$

In general, if N is very large, the cardinality of $|MB(X_i)| << N$, thus simplifying the process (the *vanilla* Gibbs sampling needs $N-1$ conditions for each variable). We can prove that the Gibbs sampling generates samples from a Markov chain that is in detailed balance:

$$\begin{aligned} P(i \to j)\pi_{s_i} &= P(x_j | x_1, x_2, \dots, x_{j-1}, x_{j+1}, \dots, x_N)P(x_i) = \\ &= P(x_j, x_i | x_1, x_2, \dots, x_{j-1}, x_{j+1}, \dots, x_{i-1}, x_{i+1}, \dots, x_N) = \\ &= P(x_i | x_1, x_2, \dots, x_{i-1}, x_{i+1}, \dots, x_N)P(x_j) = P(j \to i)\pi_{s_j} \end{aligned}$$

Therefore, the procedure converges to the unique stationary distribution. This algorithm is quite simple; however, its performance is not excellent, because the random walks are not tuned up in order to explore the right regions of the state-space, where the probability to find good samples is high. Moreover, the trajectory can also return to bad states, slowing down the whole process. An alternative (also implemented by PyMC3 for continuous random variables) is the **No-U-Turn** algorithm, which we don't discuss in this book. The reader interested in this topic can find a full description in *The No-U-Turn Sampler: Adaptively Setting Path Lengths in Hamiltonian Monte Carlo, Hoffmann M. D., Gelman A., arXiv:1111.4246*.

Metropolis-Hastings sampling

We have seen that the full joint probability distribution of a Bayesian network $P(x_1, x_2, x_3, \dots, x_N)$ can become intractable when the number of variables is large. The problem can become even harder when it's needed to marginalize it in order to obtain, for example, $P(x_i)$, because it's necessary to integrate a very complex function. The same problem happens when applying the Bayes' theorem in simple cases. Let's suppose we have the expression $p(A|B) = K \cdot P(B|A)P(A)$. I've expressly inserted the normalizing constant K, because if we know it, we can immediately obtain the posterior probability; however, finding it normally requires integrating $P(B|A)P(A)$, and this operation can be impossible in closed form.

The Metropolis-Hastings algorithm can help us in solving this problem. Let's imagine that we need to sample from $P(x_1, x_2, x_3, \dots, x_N)$, but we know this distribution up to a normalizing constant, so $P(x_1, x_2, x_3, \dots, x_N) \propto g(x_1, x_2, x_3, \dots, x_N)$. For simplicity, from now on we collapse all variables into a single vector, so $P(x) \propto g(x)$.

Let's take another distribution $q(x'|x^{(i-1)})$, which is called **candidate-generating distribution**. There are no particular restrictions on this choice, only that q is easy to sample. In some situations, q can be chosen as a function very similar to the distribution $p(x)$, which is our target, while in other cases, it's possible to use a normal distribution with mean equal to $x^{(i-1)}$. As we're going to see, this function acts as a proposal-generator, but we're not obliged to accept all the samples drawn from it therefore, potentially any distribution with the same domain of $P(X)$ can be employed. When a sample is accepted, the Markov chain transitions to the next state, otherwise it remains in the current one. This decisional process is based on the idea that the sampler must explore the most important state-space regions and discard the ones where the probability to find good samples is low.

The algorithm proceeds with the following steps:

1. Initialize the variable $N_{Iterations}$
2. Initialize $x^{(0)}$ randomly
3. For $t=1$ to $N_{Iterations}$:
    1. Draw a candidate sample x' from $q(x'|x^{(i-1)})$
    2. Compute the following value:

       $$\alpha = \frac{g(x')q(x^{(t-1)}|x')}{g(x^{(t-1)})q(x'|x^{(t-1)})}$$

    3. If $\alpha \geq 1$:
        1. Accept the sample $x^{(t)} = x'$
    4. Else if $0 < \alpha < 1$:
        1. Accept the sample $x^{(t)} = x'$ with probability α; or
        2. Reject the sample x' setting $x^{(t)} = x^{(t-1)}$ with probability $1 - \alpha$

It's possible to prove (the proof will be omitted, but it's available in *Markov Chain Monte Carlo and Gibbs Sampling, Walsh B., Lecture Notes for EEB 596z*) that the transition probability of the Metropolis-Hastings algorithm satisfies the detailed balance equation, and therefore the algorithm converges to the true posterior distribution.

Example of Metropolis-Hastings sampling

We can implement this algorithm to find the posterior distribution $P(A|B)$ given the product of $P(B|A)$ and $P(A)$, without considering the normalizing constant that requires a complex integration.

Let's suppose that:

$$\begin{cases} p(A) \sim Exponential(\lambda = 0.1) \\ p(B|A) \sim Wald(\mu = 1.0, \lambda = 0.2) \end{cases}$$

Therefore, the resulting $g(x)$ is:

$$g(x) = 0.1e^{-0.1x}\sqrt{\frac{0.2}{2\pi x^3}}e^{-\frac{0.2(x-1)^2}{2x}}$$

To solve this problem, we adopt the random walk Metropolis-Hastings, which consists of choosing $q \sim Normal(\mu=x^{(t-1)})$. This choice allows simplifying the value α, because the two terms $q(x^{(t-1)}|x')$ and $q(x'|x^{(t-1)})$ are equal (thanks to the symmetry around the vertical axis passing through x_{mean}) and can be canceled out, so α becomes the ratio between $g(x')$ and $g(x^{(t-1)})$.

The first thing is defining the functions:

```
import numpy as np

def prior(x):
    return 0.1 * np.exp(-0.1 * x)

def likelihood(x):
    a = np.sqrt(0.2 / (2.0 * np.pi * np.power(x, 3)))
    b = - (0.2 * np.power(x - 1.0, 2)) / (2.0 * x)
    return a * np.exp(b)

def g(x):
    return likelihood(x) * prior(x)

def q(xp):
    return np.random.normal(xp)
```

Now, we can start our sampling process with 100,000 iterations and $x^{(0)} = 1.0$:

```
nb_iterations = 100000
x = 1.0
samples = []

for i in range(nb_iterations):
    xc = q(x)
    alpha = g(xc) / g(x)
    if np.isnan(alpha):
        continue
    if alpha >= 1:
        samples.append(xc)
        x = xc
    else:
        if np.random.uniform(0.0, 1.0) < alpha:
            samples.append(xc)
            x = xc
```

To get a representation of the posterior distribution, we need to create a histogram through the NumPy function `np.histogram()`, which accepts an array of values and the number of desired intervals (`bins`); in our case, we set `100` intervals:

```
hist, _ = np.histogram(samples, bins=100)
hist_p = hist / len(samples)
```

The resulting plot of *p(x)* is shown in the following graph:

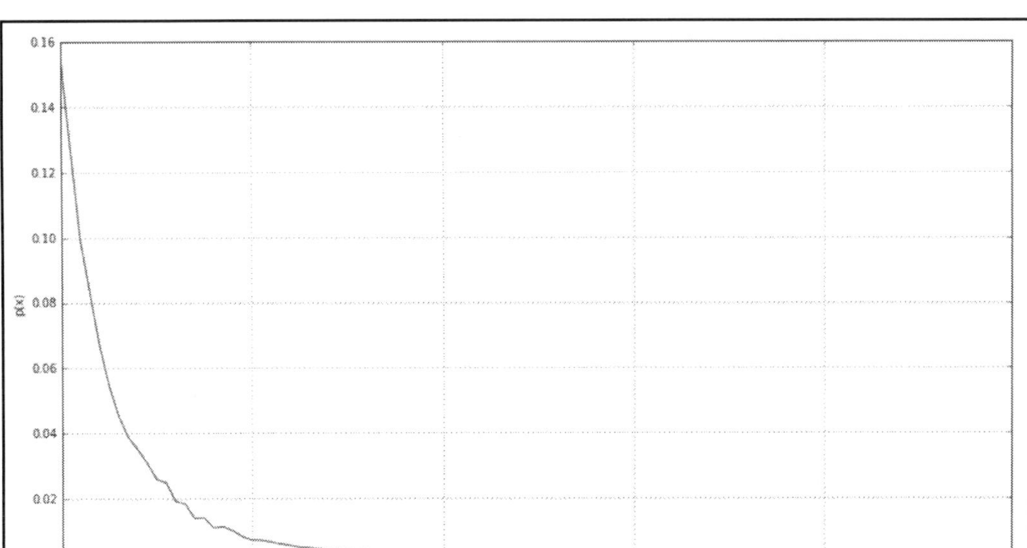

Sampled probability density function

Sampling example using PyMC3

PyMC3 is a powerful Python Bayesian framework that relies on Theano to perform high-speed computations (see the information box at the end of this paragraph for the installation instructions). It implements all the most important continuous and discrete distributions, and performs the sampling process mainly using the No-U-Turn and Metropolis-Hastings algorithms. For all the details about the API (distributions, functions, and plotting utilities), I suggest visiting the documentation home page `http://docs.pymc.io/index.html`, where it's also possible to find some very intuitive tutorials.

The example we want to model and simulate is based on this scenario: a daily flight from London to Rome has a scheduled departure time at 12:00 am, and a standard flight time of two hours. We need to organize the operations at the destination airport, but we don't want to allocate resources when the plane hasn't landed yet. Therefore, we want to model the process using a Bayesian network and considering some common factors that can influence the arrival time. In particular, we know that the onboarding process can be longer than expected, as well as the refueling one, even if they are carried out in parallel. London air traffic control can also impose a delay, and the same can happen when the plane is approaching Rome. We also know that the presence of rough weather can cause another delay due to a change of route. We can summarize this analysis with the following plot:

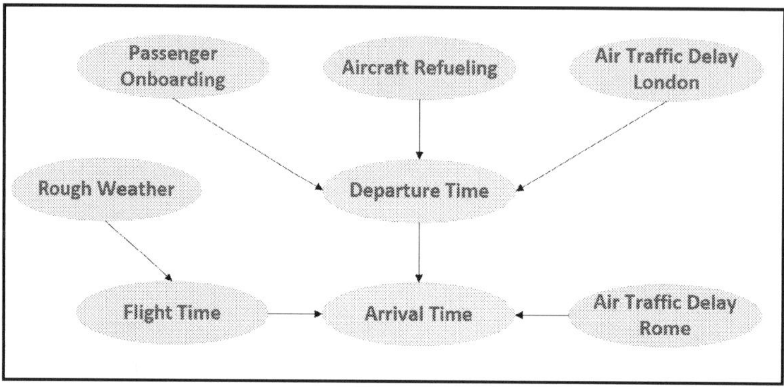

Bayesian network representing the air traffic control problem

Considering our experience, we decide to model the random variables using the following distributions:

- *Passenger onboarding ~ Wald(μ=0.5, λ=0.2)*
- *Refueling ~ Wald(μ=0.25, λ=0.5)*
- *Departure traffic delay ~ Wald(μ=0.1, λ=0.2)*
- *Arrival traffic delay ~ Wald(μ=0.1, λ=0.2)*
- *Departure time = 12 + Departure traffic delay + max(Passenger onboarding, Refueling)*
- *Rough weather ~ Bernoulli(p=0.35)*
- *Flight time ~ Exponential(λ=0.5 - (0.1 · Rough weather))* (The output of a Bernoulli distribution is *0* or *1* corresponding to False and True)
- *Arrival time = Departure time + Flight time + Arrival traffic delay*

The probability density functions are:

$$\begin{cases} f_{Wald}(x;\mu;\lambda) = \sqrt{\frac{\lambda}{2\pi x^3}} e^{-\frac{\lambda(x-\mu)^2}{2\mu^2 x}} \\ f_{Exponential}(x;\lambda) = \begin{cases} \lambda e^{-\lambda x} \ if \ x \geqslant 0 \\ 0 \ otherwise \end{cases} \\ f_{Bernoulli}(x;p) = \begin{cases} p \ if \ x = 1 \\ 1-p \ if \ x = 0 \end{cases} \end{cases}$$

`Departure Time` and `Arrival Time` are functions of random variables, and the parameter λ of `Flight Time` is also a function of `Rough Weather`.

Even if the model is not very complex, the direct inference is rather inefficient, and therefore we want to simulate the process using PyMC3.

The first step is to create a `model` instance:

```
import pymc3 as pm

model = pm.Model()
```

From now on, all operations must be performed using the context manager provided by the `model` variable. We can now set up all the random variables of our Bayesian network:

```
import pymc3.distributions.continuous as pmc
import pymc3.distributions.discrete as pmd
import pymc3.math as pmm

with model:
    passenger_onboarding = pmc.Wald('Passenger Onboarding', mu=0.5,
lam=0.2)
    refueling = pmc.Wald('Refueling', mu=0.25, lam=0.5)
    departure_traffic_delay = pmc.Wald('Departure Traffic Delay',
mu=0.1, lam=0.2)
    departure_time = pm.Deterministic('Departure Time',
                                      12.0 + departure_traffic_delay +
                                      pmm.switch(passenger_onboarding
>= refueling,
                                                 passenger_onboarding,
                                                 refueling))
    rough_weather = pmd.Bernoulli('Rough Weather', p=0.35)
```

```
    flight_time = pmc.Exponential('Flight Time', lam=0.5 - (0.1 *
rough_weather))
    arrival_traffic_delay = pmc.Wald('Arrival Traffic Delay', mu=0.1,
lam=0.2)
    arrival_time = pm.Deterministic('Arrival time',
                                    departure_time +
                                    flight_time +
                                    arrival_traffic_delay)
```

We have imported two namespaces, `pymc3.distributions.continuous` and `pymc3.distributions.discrete`, because we are using both kinds of variable. Wald and exponential are continuous distributions, while `Bernoulli` is discrete. In the first three rows, we declare the variables `passenger_onboarding`, `refueling`, and `departure_traffic_delay`. The structure is always the same: we need to specify the class corresponding to the desired distribution, passing the name of the variable and all the required parameters.

The `departure_time` variable is declared as `pm.Deterministic`. In PyMC3, this means that, once all the random elements have been set, its value becomes completely determined. Indeed, if we sample from `departure_traffic_delay`, `passenger_onboarding`, and `refueling`, we get a determined value for `departure_time`. In this declaration, we've also used the utility function `pmm.switch`, which operates a binary choice based on its first parameter (for example, if $A > B$, return A, else return B).

The other variables are very similar, except for `flight_time`, which is an exponential variable with a parameter λ, which is a function of another variable (`rough_weather`). As a Bernoulli variable outputs 1 with probability p and 0 with probability $1 - p$, $\lambda = 0.4$ if there's rough weather, and 0.5 otherwise.

Once the model has been set up, it's possible to simulate it through a sampling process. PyMC3 picks the best sampler automatically, according to the type of variables. As the model is not very complex, we can limit the process to `500` samples:

```
nb_samples = 500

with model:
    samples = pm.sample(draws=nb_samples, random_seed=1000)
```

The output can be analyzed using the built-in `pm.traceplot()` function, which generates the plots for each of the sample's variables. The following graph shows the detail of one of them:

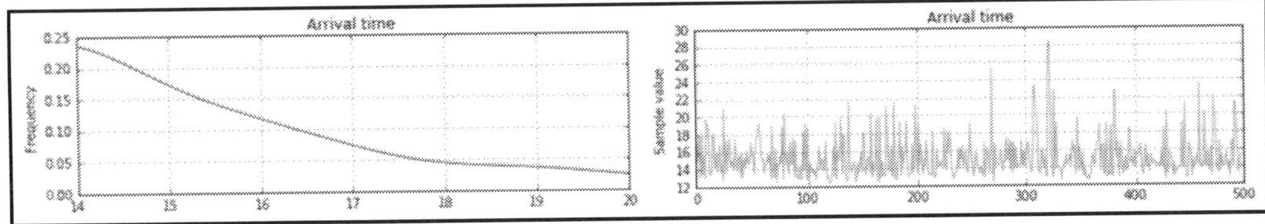

Distribution and samples for the arrival time random variable

The right column shown the samples generated for the random variable (in this case, the arrival time), while the left column shows the relative frequencies. This plot can be useful to have a visual confirmation of our initial ideas; in fact, the arrival time has the majority of its mass concentrated in the interval 14:00 to 16:00 (the numbers are always decimal, so it's necessary to convert the times); however, we should integrate to get the probabilities. Instead, through the `pm.summary()` function, PyMC3 provides a statistical summary that can help us in making the right decisions. In the following snippet, the output containing the summary of a single variable is shown:

```
pm.summary(samples)

...

Arrival time:

  Mean             SD               MC Error         95% HPD interval
  -------------------------------------------------------------------
  15.174           2.670            0.102            [12.174, 20.484]

  Posterior quantiles:
  2.5            25             50             75             97.5
  |--------------|==============|==============|--------------|
  12.492         13.459         14.419         16.073         22.557
```

For each variable, it contains mean, standard deviation, Monte Carlo error, 95% highest posterior density interval, and the posterior quantiles. In our case, we know that the plane will land at about 15:10 (`15.174`).

This is only a very simple example to show the power of Bayesian networks. For deep insight, I suggest the book *Introduction to Statistical Decision Theory, Pratt J., Raiffa H., Schlaifer R., The MIT Press*, where it's possible to study different Bayesian applications that are out of the scope of this book.

PyMC3 (`http://docs.pymc.io/index.html`) can be installed using the `pip install -U pymc3` command. As it requires Theano (which is installed automatically), it's also necessary to provide it with a C/C++ compiler. I suggest using distributions such as Anaconda (`https://www.anaconda.com/download/`), which allows installing MinGW through the `conda install -c anaconda mingw` command. For any problems, on the website you can find detailed installation instructions. For further information on how to configure Theano to work with GPU support (the default installation is based on CPU NumPy algorithms), please visit this page: `http://deeplearning.net/software/theano/`.

Hidden Markov Models (HMMs)

Let's consider a stochastic process *X(t)* that can assume *N* different states: $s_1, s_2, ..., s_N$ with first-order Markov chain dynamics. Let's also suppose that we cannot observe the state of *X(t)*, but we have access to another process *O(t)*, connected to *X(t)*, which produces observable outputs (often known as **emissions**). The resulting process is called a **Hidden Markov Model** (**HMM**), and a generic schema is shown in the following diagram:

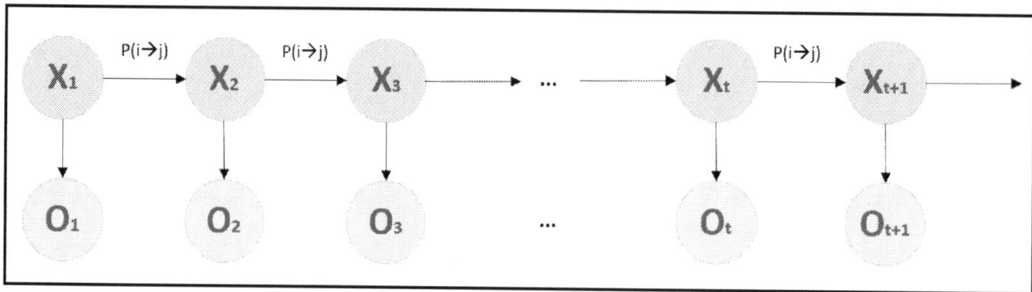

Structure of a generic Hidden Markov Model

For each hidden state s_i, we need to define a transition probability $P(i \rightarrow j)$, normally represented as a matrix if the variable is discrete. For the Markov assumption, we have:

$$P(j \rightarrow i) = P(X_t = s_i | X_{t-1} = s_j)$$

Moreover, given a sequence of observations $o_1, o_2, ..., o_M$, we also assume the following assumption about the independence of the **emission probability**:

$$P(o_i|o_1, o_2, \ldots, o_k, x_1, x_2, \ldots, x_k) = P(o_i|x_i)$$

In other words, the probability of the observation o_i (in this case, we mean the value at time *i*) is conditioned only by the state of the hidden variable at time *i* (x_i). Conventionally, the first state x_0 and the last one x_{Ending} are never emittied, and therefore all the sequences start with the index *1* and end with an extra timestep corresponding to the final state.

HMMs can be employed in all those contexts where it's impossible to measure the state of a system (we can only model it as a stochastic variable with a known transition probability), but it's possible to access some data connected to it. An example can be a complex engine that is made up of a large number of parts. We can define some internal states and learn a transition probability matrix (we're going to learn how to do that), but we can only receive measures provided by specific sensors.

Sometimes, even if not extremely realistic, but it's useful to include the Markov assumption and the emission probability independence into our model. The latter can be justified considering that we can sample all the *peak* emissions corresponding to precise states and, as the random process *O(t)* is implicitly dependent on *X(t)*, it's not unreasonable to think of it like a *pursuer* of *X(t)*.

The Markov assumption holds for many real-life processes if either they are naturally first-order Markov ones, or if the states contain all the history needed to justify a transition. In other words, in many cases, if the state is *A*, then there's a transit to *B* and finally to *C*. We assume that when in *C*, the system moved from a state *(B)* that carries a part of the information provided by *A*.

For example, if we are filling a tank, we can measure the level (the state of our system) at time *t*, *t+1*, ... If the water flow is modeled by a random variable because we don't have a stabilizer, we can find the probability that the water has reached a certain level at time *t*, $p(L_t=x|L_{t-1})$. Of course, it doesn't make sense to condition over all the previous states, because if the level is, for example, 80 m at time t-1, all the information needed to determine the probability of a new level (state) at time *t* is already contained in this state (80 m).

At this point, we can start analyzing how to train a hidden Markov model, and how to determine the most likely hidden states given a sequence of observations. For simplicity, we call A the transition probability matrix, and B the matrix containing all $P(o_i|x_t)$. The resulting model can be determined by the knowledge of those elements: $HMM = \{ A, B \}$.

Forward-backward algorithm

The **forward-backward algorithm** is a simple but effective method to find the transition probability matrix T given a sequence of observations $o_1, o_2, ..., o_t$. The first step is called the *forward phase*, and consists of determining the probability of a sequence of observations $P(o_1, o_2, ..., o_{Sequence\ Length} | A, B)$. This piece of information can be directly useful if we need to know the likelihood of a sequence and it's necessary, together with the *backward phase*, to estimate the structure (A and B) of the underlying HMM.

Both algorithms are based on the concept of dynamic programming, which consists of splitting a complex problem into sub-problems that can be easily solved, and reusing the solutions to solve more complex steps in a recursive/iterative fashion. For further information on this, please refer to *Dynamic Programming and Markov Process, Ronald A. Howard, The MIT Press.*

Forward phase

If we call p_{ij} the transition probability $P(i \rightarrow j)$, we define a recursive procedure considering the following probability:

$$f_t^i = P(o_1, o_2, \ldots, o_t, x_t = i | A, B)$$

The variable f_t^i represents the probability that the HMM is in the state i (at time t) after t observations (from 1 to t). Considering the HMM assumptions, we can state that f_t^i depends on all possible f_{t-1}^j. More precisely, we have:

$$f_t^i = \sum_j f_{t-1}^j p_{ji} P(o_t | x_j)$$

With this process, we are considering that the HMM can reach any of the states at time *t-1* (with the first *t-1* observations), and transition to the state *i* at time *t* with probability p_{ji}. We need also to consider the emission probability for the final state o_t conditioned to each of the possible previous states.

For definition, the initial and ending states are not emitting. It means that we can write any sequence of observations as $0, o_1, o_2, ..., o_{Sequence\ Length}, 0$, where the first and the final values are null. The procedure starts with computing the forward message at time *1*:

$$f_1^i = p_{0i} P(o_1|x_0)$$

The non-emitting ending state must be also considered:

$$f_{SequenceLength}^{Ending} = \sum_i f_{SequenceLength-1}^i p_{iEnding}$$

The expression for the last state x_{Ending} is interpreted here as the index of the ending state in both *A* and *B* matrices. For example, we indicate p_{ij} as *A[i, j]*, meaning the transition probability at a generic time instant from the state $x_t = i$ to the state $x_{t+1} = j$. In the same way, $p_{iEnding}$ is represented as $A[i, x_{Ending}]$, meaning the transition probability from the penultimate state $x_{Sequence\ Length-1} = i$ to the ending one $x_{Sequence\ Length} = Ending\ State$.

The Forward algorithm can, therefore, be summarized in the following steps (we assume to have *N* states, hence we need to allocate *N*+2 positions, considering the initial and the ending states):

1. Initialization of a *Forward* vector with shape (*N* + 2, *Sequence Length*).
2. Initialization of *A* (transition probability matrix) with shape (*N*, *N*). Each element is $P(x_i|x_j)$.
3. Initialization of *B* with shape (*Sequence Length*, *N*). Each element is $P(o_i|x_j)$.
4. For *i=1* to *N*:
    1. Set $Forward[i, 1] = A[0, i] \cdot B[1, i]$
5. For *t=2* to *Sequence Length-1*:
    1. For *i=1* to *N*:
        1. Set $S = 0$
    2. For *j=1* to *N*:
        1. Set $S = S + Forward[j, t-1] \cdot A[j, i] \cdot B[t, i]$
    3. Set $Forward[i, t] = S$

6. Set $S = 0$.
7. For i=1 to N:
    1. Set $S = S + Forward[i, Sequence\ Length] \cdot A[i, x_{Ending}]$
8. Set $Forward[x_{Ending}, Sequence\ Length] = S$.

Now it should be clear that the name **forward** derives from the procedure to propagate the information from the previous step to the next one, until the ending state, which is not emittied.

Backward phase

During the **backward phase**, we need to compute the probability of a sequence starting at time $t+1$: $o_{t+1}, o_{t+2}, \ldots, o_{Sequence\ Length}$, given that the state at time t is i. Just like we have done before, we define the following probability:

$$b_t^i = P(o_{t+1}, o_{t+2}, \ldots, o_{SequenceLength} | x_t = i, A, B)$$

The backward algorithm is very similar to the forward one, but in this case, we need to move in the opposite direction, assuming we know that the state at time t is i. The first state to consider is the last one x_{Ending}, which is not emitting, like the initial state; therefore we have:

$$b^i_{SequenceLenght} = p_{iEnding}$$

We terminate the recursion with the initial state:

$$b_1^0 = \sum_i b_1^i p_{0i} P(o_1 | x_i)$$

The steps are the following ones:

1. Initialization of a vector *Backward* with shape $(N + 2, Sequence\ Length)$.
2. Initialization of A (transition probability matrix) with shape (N, N). Each element is $P(x_i | x_j)$.
3. Initialization of B with shape $(Sequence\ Length, N)$. Each element is $P(o_i | x_j)$.

4. For *i=1* to *N*:
    1. Set $Backward[x_{Endind}, Sequence\ Length] = A[i, x_{Endind}]$
5. For *t=Sequence Length-1* to *1*:
    1. For *i=1* to *N*:
        1. Set $S = 0$
        2. For *j=1* to *N*
            1. Set $S = S + Backward[j, t+1] \cdot A[j, i] \cdot B[t+1, i]$
        3. Set $Backward[i, t] = S$
6. Set $S = 0$.
7. For *i=1* to *N*:
    1. Set $S = S + Backward[i, 1] \cdot A[0, i] \cdot B[1, i]$
8. Set $Backward[0, 1] = S$.

HMM parameter estimation

Now that we have defined both the forward and the backward algorithms, we can use them to estimate the structure of the underlying HMM. The procedure is an application of the Expectation-Maximization algorithm, which will be discussed in the next chapter, `Chapter 5`, *EM Algorithm and Applications*, and its goal can be summarized as defining how we want to estimate the values of *A* and *B*. If we define $N(i, j)$ as the number of transitions from the state *i* to the state *j*, and $N(i)$ the total number of transitions from the state *i*, we can approximate the transition probability $P(i \rightarrow j)$ with:

$$\tilde{a}_{ij} = \widetilde{P}(i \rightarrow j) = \frac{E[N(i,j)]}{E[N(i)]}$$

In the same way, if we define $M(i, p)$ the number of times we have observed the emission o_p in the state *i*, we can approximate the emission probability $P(o_p|x_i)$ with:

$$\tilde{b}_{ip} = \widetilde{P}(o_p|x_i) = \frac{E[M(i,p)]}{E[N(i)]}$$

Let's start with the estimation of the transition probability matrix *A*. If we consider the probability that the HMM is in the state *i* at time *t*, and in the state *j* at time *t+1* given the observations, we have:

$$\tilde{\alpha}_{ij}^{t} = P(x_t = i, x_{t+1} = j | o_1, o_2, \ldots, o_{SequenceLength}, A, B)$$

We can compute this probability using the forward and backward algorithms, given a sequence of observations $o_1, o_2, \ldots, o_{Sequence\ Length}$. In fact, we can use both the forward message f_t^i, which is the probability that the HMM is in the state *i* after *t* observations, and the backward message b_{t+1}^j, which is the probability of a sequence $o_{t+1}, o_{t+1}, \ldots, o_{Sequence\ Length}$ starting at time *t+1*, given that the HMM is in state *j* at time *t+1*. Of course, we need also to include the emission probability and the transition probability p_{ij}, which is what we are estimating. The algorithm, in fact, starts with a random hypothesis and iterates until the values of *A* become stable. The estimation α_{ij} at time *t* is equal to:

$$\tilde{\alpha}_{ij}^{t} = \frac{f_t^i p_{ij} b_{t+1}^j P(o_{t+1} | x_j)}{f_{SequenceLength}^{Ending}}$$

In this context, we are omitting the full proof due to its complexity; however, the reader can find it in *A tutorial on hidden Markov models and selected applications in speech recognition, Rabiner L. R., Proceedings of the IEEE 77.2*.

To compute the emission probabilities, it's easier to start with the probability of being in the state *i* at time *t* given the sequence of observations:

$$\tilde{\beta}_{i}^{t} = P(x_t = i | o_1, o_2, \ldots, o_{SequenceLength}, A, B)$$

In this case, the computation is immediate, because we can multiply the forward and backward messages computed at the same time *t* and state *i* (remember that considering the observations, the backward message is conditioned to $x_t = i$, while the forward message computes the probability of the observations joined with $x_t = i$. Hence, the multiplication is the unnormalized probability of being in the state *i* at time *t*). Therefore, we have:

$$\tilde{\beta}_{i}^{t} = \frac{f_t^i b_t^i}{f_{SequenceLength}^{Ending}}$$

The proof of how the normalizing constant is obtained can be found in the aforementioned paper. We can now plug these expressions to the estimation of a_{ij} and b_{ip}:

$$\begin{cases} \tilde{a}_{ij} = \dfrac{\sum_{t=1}^{SequenceLength-1} \tilde{\alpha}_{ij}^t}{\sum_{t=1}^{SequenceLength-1} \sum_{j=1}^{N} \tilde{\alpha}_{ij}^t} \\ \tilde{b}_{ip} = \dfrac{\sum_{t=1}^{SequenceLength} \tilde{\beta}_i^t \cdot I_{o_t=p}}{\sum_{t=1}^{SequenceLength} \tilde{\beta}_i^t} \end{cases}$$

In the numerator of the second formula, we adopted the indicator function (it's *1* only if the condition is true, *0* otherwise) to limit the sum only where those elements are $o_t = p$. During an iteration k, p_{ij} is the estimated value a_{ij} found in the previous iteration k-1.

The algorithm is based on the following steps:

1. Randomly initialize the matrices A and B
2. Initialize a tolerance variable Tol (for example, $Tol = 0.001$)
3. While $Norm(A^k - A^{k-1}) > Tol$ and $Norm(B^k - B^{k-1}) > Tol$ (k is the iteration index):
    1. For t=1 to *Sequence Length-1*:
        1. For i=1 to N:
            1. For j=1 to N:
                1. Compute α^t_{ij}
            2. Compute β^t_i
    2. Compute the estimations of a_{ij} and b_{ip} and store them in A^k

Alternatively, it's possible to fix the number of iterations, even if the best solution is using both a tolerance and a maximum number of iterations, to terminate the process when the first condition is met.

Example of HMM training with hmmlearn

For this example, we are going to use hmmlearn, which is a package for HMM computations (see the information box at the end of this section for further details). For simplicity, let's consider the airport example discussed in the paragraph about the Bayesian networks, and let's suppose we have a single hidden variable that represents the weather (of course, this is not a real hidden variable!), modeled as a multinomial distribution with two components (good and rough).

We observe the arrival time of our flight London-Rome (which partially depends on the weather conditions), and we want to train an HMM to infer future states and compute the posterior probability of hidden states corresponding to a given sequence.

The schema for our example is shown in the following diagram:

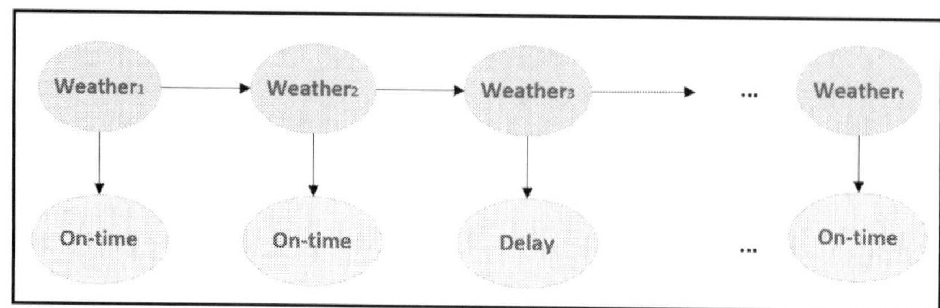

HMM for the weather-arrival delay problem

Let's start by defining our observation vector. As we have two states, its values will be `0` and `1`. Let's assume that `0` means **On-time** and `1` means **Delay**:

```
import numpy as np

observations = np.array([[0], [1], [1], [0], [1], [1], [1], [0], [1],
                         [0], [0], [0], [1], [0], [1], [1], [0], [1],
                         [0], [0], [1], [0], [1], [0], [0], [0], [1],
                         [0], [1], [0], [1], [0], [0], [0], [0], [0]],
dtype=np.int32)
```

We have 35 consecutive observations whose values are either `0` or `1`.

To build the HMM, we are going to use the `MultinomialHMM` class, with `n_components=2`, `n_iter=100`, and `random_state=1000` (it's important to always use the same seed to avoid differences in the results). The number of iterations is sometimes hard to determine; for this reason, hmmlearn provides a utility `ConvergenceMonitor` class which can be checked to be sure that the algorithm has successfully converged.

Now we can train our model using the `fit()` method, passing as argument the list of observations (the array must be always bidimensional with shape *Sequence Length* × $N_{Components}$):

```
from hmmlearn import hmm

hmm_model = hmm.MultinomialHMM(n_components=2, n_iter=100,
```

```
random_state=1000)
hmm_model.fit(observations)

print(hmm_model.monitor_.converged)
True
```

The process is very fast, and the monitor (available as instance variable `monitor`) has confirmed the convergence. If the model is very big and needs to be retrained, it's also possible to check smaller values of `n_iter`). Once the model is trained, we can immediately visualize the transition probability matrix, which is available as an instance variable `transmat_`:

```
print(hmm_model.transmat_)

[[ 0.0025384   0.9974616 ]
 [ 0.69191905  0.30808095]]
```

We can interpret these values as saying that the probability to transition from `0` (good weather) to `1` (rough weather) is higher (p_{01} is close to *1*) than the opposite, and it's more likely to remain in state `1` than in state `0` (p_{00} is almost null). We could deduce that the observations have been collected during the winter period! After explaining the Viterbi algorithm in the next paragraph, we can also check, given some observations, what the most likely hidden state sequence is.

hmmlearn (`http://hmmlearn.readthedocs.io/en/latest/index.html`) is a framework originally built to be a part of Scikit-Learn. It supports multinomial and Gaussian HMM, and allows training and inferring using the most common algorithms. It can be installed using the `pip install hmmlearn` command.

Viterbi algorithm

The **Viterbi algorithm** is one of most common decoding algorithms for HMM. Its goal is to find the most likely hidden state sequence corresponding to a series of observations. The structure is very similar to the forward algorithm, but instead of computing the probability of a sequence of observations joined with the state at the last time instant, this algorithm looks for:

$$v_t^i = max_{x_j} P(o_1, o_2, \ldots, o_t, x_1, x_2, \ldots, x_{t-1}, x_t = i|A, B)$$

The variable v_t^i represents that maximum probability of the given observation sequence joint with $x_t = i$, considering all possible hidden state paths (from time instant *1* to *t-1*). We can compute v_t^i recursively by evaluating all the v_{t-1}^j multiplied by the corresponding transition probabilities p_{ji} and emission probability $P(o_t|x_i)$, and always picking the maximum overall possible values of *j*:

$$v_t^i = max_j v_{t-1}^j p_{ji} P(o_t|x_i)$$

The algorithm is based on a backtracking approach, using a backpointer bp_t^i whose recursive expression is the same as v_t^i, but with the *argmax* function instead of *max*:

$$bp_t^i = argmax_j v_{t-1}^j p_{ji} P(o_t|x_i)$$

Therefore, bp_t^i represents the partial sequence of hidden states $x_1, x_2, ..., x_{t-1}$ that maximizes v_t^i. During the recursion, we add the timesteps one by one, so the previous path could be invalidated by the last observation. That's why we need to backtrack the partial result and replace the sequence built at time *t* that doesn't maximize v_{t+1}^i anymore.

The algorithm is based on the following steps (like in the other cases, the initial and ending states are not emitting):

1. Initialization of a vector *V* with shape *(N + 2, Sequence Length)*.
2. Initialization of a vector *BP* with shape *(N + 2, Sequence Length)*.
3. Initialization of *A* (transition probability matrix) with shape *(N, N)*. Each element is $P(x_i|x_j)$.
4. Initialization of *B* with shape *(Sequence Length, N)*. Each element is $P(o_i|x_j)$.
5. For *i=1* to *N*:
    1. Set $V[i, 1] = A[i, 0] \cdot B[1, i]$
    2. $BP[i, 1]$ = Null (or any other value that cannot be interpreted as a state)
6. For *t=1* to *Sequence Length*:
    1. For *i=1* to *N*:
        1. Set $V[i, t] = max_j\ V[j, t\text{-}1] \cdot A[j, i] \cdot B[t, i]$
        2. Set $BP[i, t] = argmax_j\ V[j, t\text{-}1] \cdot A[j, i] \cdot B[t, i]$
7. Set $V[x_{Endind}, Sequence\ Length] = max_j\ V[j, Sequence\ Length] \cdot A[j, x_{Endind}]$.

8. Set $BP[x_{Endind}, Sequence\ Length] = argmax_j\ V[j, Sequence\ Length] \cdot A[j, x_{Endind}]$.
9. Reverse *BP*.

The output of the Viterbi algorithm is a tuple with the most likely sequence *BP*, and the corresponding probabilities *V*.

Finding the most likely hidden state sequence with hmmlearn

At this point, we can continue with the previous example, using our model to find the most likely hidden state sequence given a set of possible observations. We can use either the `decode()` method or the `predict()` method. The first one returns the log probability of the whole sequence and the sequence itself; however, they all use the Viterbi algorithm as a default decoder:

```
sequence = np.array([[1], [1], [1], [0], [1], [1], [1], [0], [1],
                     [0], [1], [0], [1], [0], [1], [1], [0], [1],
                     [1], [0], [1], [0], [1], [0], [1], [0], [1],
                     [1], [1], [0], [0], [1], [1], [0], [1], [1]],
dtype=np.int32)

lp, hs = hmm_model.decode(sequence)

print(hs)
[0 1 1 0 1 1 1 0 1 0 1 0 1 0 1 1 0 1 1 0 1 0 1 0 1 0 1 1 1 1 0 1 1 0 1
1]

print(lp)
-30.489992468878615
```

The sequence is coherent with the transition probability matrix; in fact, it's more likely the persistence of rough weather (`1`) than the opposite. As a consequence, the transition from `1` to X is less likely than the one from `0` to `1`. The choice of state is made by selecting the highest probability; however, in some cases, the differences are minimal (in our example, it can happen to have $p = [0.49, 0.51]$, meaning that there's a high error chance), so it's useful to check the posterior probabilities for all the states in the sequence:

```
pp = hmm_model.predict_proba(sequence)
print(pp)

[[  1.00000000e+00   5.05351938e-19]
 [  3.76687160e-05   9.99962331e-01]
 [  1.31242036e-03   9.98687580e-01]
```

```
[  9.60384736e-01   3.96152641e-02]
[  1.27156616e-03   9.98728434e-01]
[  3.21353749e-02   9.67864625e-01]
[  1.23481962e-03   9.98765180e-01]

...
```

In our case, there are a couple of states that have $p \sim [0.495, 0.505]$, so even if the output state is *1* (rough weather), it's also useful to consider a moderate probability to observe good weather. In general, if a sequence is coherent with the transition probability previously learned (or manually input), those cases are not very common. I suggest trying different configurations and observations sequences, and to also assess the probabilities for the *strangest* situations (like a sequence of zero second). At that point, it's possible to retrain the model and recheck the new evidence has been correctly processed.

Summary

In this chapter, we have introduced Bayesian networks, describing their structure and relations. We have seen how it's possible to build a network to model a probabilistic scenario where some elements can influence the probability of others. We have also described how to obtain the full joint probability using the most common sampling methods, which allow reducing the computational complexity through an approximation.

The most common sampling methods belong to the family of MCMC algorithms, which model the transition probability from a sample to another one as a first-order Markov chain. In particular, the Gibbs sampler is based on the assumption that it's easier to sample from conditional distribution than work directly with the full joint probability. The method is very easy to implement, but it has some performance drawbacks that can be avoided by adopting more complex strategies. The Metropolis-Hastings sampler, instead, works with a candidate-generating distribution and a criterion to accept or reject the samples. Both methods satisfy the detailed balance equation, which guarantees the convergence (the underlying Markov chain will reach the unique stationary distribution).

In the last part of the chapter, we introduced HMMs, which allow modeling time sequences based on observations corresponding to a series of hidden states. The main concept of such models, in fact, is the presence of unobservable states that condition the emission of a particular observation (which is observable). We have discussed the main assumptions and how to build, train, and infer from a model. In particular, the Forward-Backward algorithm can be employed when it's necessary to learn the transition probability matrix and the emission probabilities, while the Viterbi algorithm is adopted to find the most likely hidden state sequence given a set of consecutive observations.

In the next chapter, `Chapter 5`, *EM Algorithm and Applications*, we're going to briefly discuss the Expectation-Maximization algorithm, focusing on some important applications based on the **Maximum Likelihood Estimation** (MLE) approach.

5 EM Algorithm and Applications

In this chapter, we are going to introduce a very important algorithmic framework for many statistical learning tasks: the EM algorithm. Contrary to its name, this is not a method to solve a single problem, but a methodology that can be applied in several contexts. Our goal is to explain the rationale and show the mathematical derivation, together with some practical examples. In particular, we are going to discuss the following topics:

- **Maximum Likelihood Estimation** (MLE) and **Maximum A Posteriori** (MAP) learning approaches
- The EM algorithm with a simple application for the estimation of unknown parameters
- The Gaussian mixture algorithm, which is one the most famous EM applications
- Factor analysis
- **Principal Component Analysis (PCA)**
- **Independent Component Analysis (ICA)**
- A brief explanation of the **Hidden Markov Models** (HMMs) forward-backward algorithm considering the EM steps

MLE and MAP learning

Let's suppose we have a data generating process p_{data}, used to draw a dataset X:

$$X = \{\bar{x}_1, \bar{x}_2, \dots, \bar{x}_N\} \ where \ \bar{x}_i \in \mathbb{R}^k$$

In many statistical learning tasks, our goal is to find the optimal parameter set θ according to a maximization criterion. The most common approach is based on the likelihood and is called MLE. In this case, the optimal set θ is found as follows:

$$\theta_{opt} = argmax_\theta \; L(\theta; X) = argmax_\theta \; p(X|\theta)$$

This approach has the advantage of being unbiased by wrong preconditions, but, at the same time, it excludes any possibility of incorporating prior knowledge into the model. It simply looks for the best θ in a wider subspace, so that $p(X|\theta)$ is maximized. Even if this approach is almost unbiased, there's a higher probability of finding a sub-optimal solution that can also be quite different from a reasonable (even if not sure) prior. After all, several models are too complex to allow us to define a suitable prior probability (think, for example, of reinforcement learning strategies where there's a huge number of complex states). Therefore, MLE offers the most reliable solution. Moreover, it's possible to prove that the MLE of a parameter θ converges in probability to the real value:

$$\forall \epsilon > 0 \;\; P\left(\left|\tilde{\theta}_k - \theta\right| < \epsilon\right) \rightarrow 1 \;\; when \;\; k \rightarrow \infty$$

On the other hand, if we consider Bayes' theorem, we can derive the following relation:

$$p(\theta|X) = \alpha p(X|\theta)p(\theta)$$

The posterior probability, $p(\theta|X)$, is obtained using both the likelihood and a prior probability, $p(\theta)$, and hence takes into account existing knowledge encoded in $p(\theta)$. The choice to maximize $p(\theta|X)$ is called the MAP approach and it's often a good alternative to MLE when it's possible to formulate trustworthy priors or, as in the case of **Latent Dirichlet Allocation (LDA)**, where the model is on purpose based on some specific prior assumptions.

Unfortunately, a wrong or incomplete prior distribution can bias the model leading to unacceptable results. For this reason, MLE is often the default choice even when it's possible to formulate reasonable assumptions on the structure of $p(\theta)$. To understand the impact of a prior on an estimation, let's consider to have observed n=1000 binomial distributed (θ corresponds to the parameter p) experiments and k=800 had a successful outcome. The likelihood is as follows:

$$p(X|\theta) = \binom{n}{k} \theta^k (1-\theta)^{n-k}$$

For simplicity, let's compute the log-likelihood:

$$log\, p(X|\theta) = log \binom{n}{k} + k\, log\theta + (n-k)\, log(1-\theta)$$

If we compute the derivative with respect to θ and set it equal to zero, we get the following:

$$\frac{\partial}{\partial \theta} log\, p(X|\theta) = \frac{k}{\theta} - \frac{n-k}{1-\theta} = 0 \Rightarrow \theta = \frac{\frac{1}{n-k}}{\frac{1}{k} + \frac{1}{n-k}} = \frac{k}{n}$$

So the MLE for θ is 0.8, which is coherent with the observations (we can say that after observing 1000 experiments with 800 successful outcomes, $p(X|Success)=0.8$). If we have only the data X, we could say that a success is more likely than a failure because 800 out of 1000 experiments are positive.

However, after this simple exercise, an expert can tell us that, considering the largest possible population, the marginal probability $p(Success)=0.001$ (Bernoulli distributed with $p(Failure) = 1 - P(success)$) and our sample is not representative. If we trust the expert, we need to compute the posterior probability using Bayes' theorem:

$$p(Success|X) = \frac{p(X|Success)p(Success)}{p(X|Success)p(Success) + p(X|Failure)(1-p(Success))} =$$
$$= \frac{0.8 \cdot 0.001}{(0.8 \cdot 0.001) + (0.2 \cdot 0.999)} = \frac{0.0008}{0.0008 + 0.1998} \approx 0.004$$

Surprisingly, the posterior probability is very close to zero and we should reject our initial hypothesis! At this point, there are two options: if we want to build a model based only on our data, the MLE is the only reasonable choice, because, considering the posterior, we need to accept we have a very poor dataset (this is probably a bias when drawing the samples from the data generating process p_{data}).

On the other hand, if we really trust the expert, we have a few options for managing the problem:

- Checking the sampling process in order to assess its quality (we can discover that a better sampling leads to a very lower k value)
- Increasing the number of samples
- Computing the MAP estimation of θ

I suggest that the reader tries both approaches with simple models, to be able to compare the relative accuracies. In this book, we're always going to adopt the MLE when it's necessary to estimate the parameters of a model with a statistical approach. This choice is based on the assumption that our datasets are correctly sampled from p_{data}. If this is not possible (think about an image classifier that must distinguish between horses, dogs, and cats, built with a dataset where there are pictures of 500 horses, 500 dogs, and 5 cats), we should expand our dataset or use data augmentation techniques to create artificial samples.

EM algorithm

The EM algorithm is a generic framework that can be employed in the optimization of many generative models. It was originally proposed in *Maximum likelihood from incomplete data via the em algorithm, Dempster A. P., Laird N. M., Rubin D. B., Journal of the Royal Statistical Society, B, 39(1):1–38, 11/1977*, where the authors also proved its convergence at different levels of genericity.

For our purposes, we are going to consider a dataset, *X*, and a set of latent variables, *Z*, that we cannot observe. They can be part of the original model or introduced artificially as a trick to simplify the problem. A generative model parameterized with the vector θ has a log-likelihood equal to the following:

$$L(\bar{\theta}|X, Z) = log\, P(X, Z|\bar{\theta})$$

Of course, a large log-likelihood implies that the model is able to generate the original distribution with a small error. Therefore, our goal is to find the optimal set of parameters θ that maximizes the marginalized log-likelihood (we need to sum—or integrate out for continuous variables—the latent variables out because we cannot observe them):

$$\bar{\theta}_{opt} = argmax_{\bar{\theta}} \; log \sum_z L(\bar{\theta}|X, z) = argmax_{\bar{\theta}} \; log \sum_z P(X, z|\bar{\theta})$$

Theoretically, this operation is correct, but, unfortunately, it's almost always impracticable because of its complexity (in particular, the logarithm of a sum is often very problematic to manage). However, the presence of the latent variables can help us in finding a good proxy that is easy to compute and whose maximization corresponds to the maximization of the original log-likelihood. Let's start by rewriting the expression of the likelihood using the chain rule:

$$log \sum_z P(X, z|\bar{\theta}) = log \sum_z P(X|z, \bar{\theta})P(z|\bar{\theta})$$

If we consider an iterative process, our goal is to find a procedure that satisfies the following condition:

$$L(\bar{\theta}_{opt}|X, Z) > L(\bar{\theta}_t|X, Z) > L(\bar{\theta}_{t-1}|X, Z) > \ldots > L(\bar{\theta}_0|X, Z)$$

We can start by considering a generic step:

$$L(\bar{\theta}|X) - L(\bar{\theta}_t|X) = log \sum_z P(X|z, \bar{\theta})P(z|\bar{\theta}) - log \, P(X|\bar{\theta}_t)$$

The first problem to solve is the logarithm of the sum. Fortunately, we can employ the *Jensen's inequality*, which allows us to move the logarithm inside the summation. Let's first define the concept of a *convex function*: a function, *f(x)*, defined on a convex set, *D*, is said to be convex if the following applies:

$$f(\lambda x_1 + (1-\lambda)x_2) \leqslant \lambda f(x_1) + (1-\lambda)f(x_2) \quad \forall \, x_1, x_2 \in D \; and \; \lambda \in [0,1]$$

If the inequality is strict, the function is said to be *strictly convex*. Intuitively, and considering a function of a single variable $f(x)$, the previous definition states that the function is never above the segment that connects two points $(x_1, f(x_1))$ and $(x_2, f(x_2))$. In the case of strict convexity, $f(x)$ is always below the segment. Inverting these definitions, we obtain the conditions for a function to be *concave* or *strictly concave*.

If a function $f(x)$ is concave in D, the function $-f(x)$ is convex in D; therefore, as $log(x)$ is concave in $[0, \infty)$ (or with an equivalent notation in $[0, \infty[)$, $-log(x)$ is convex in $[0, \infty)$, as shown in the following diagram:

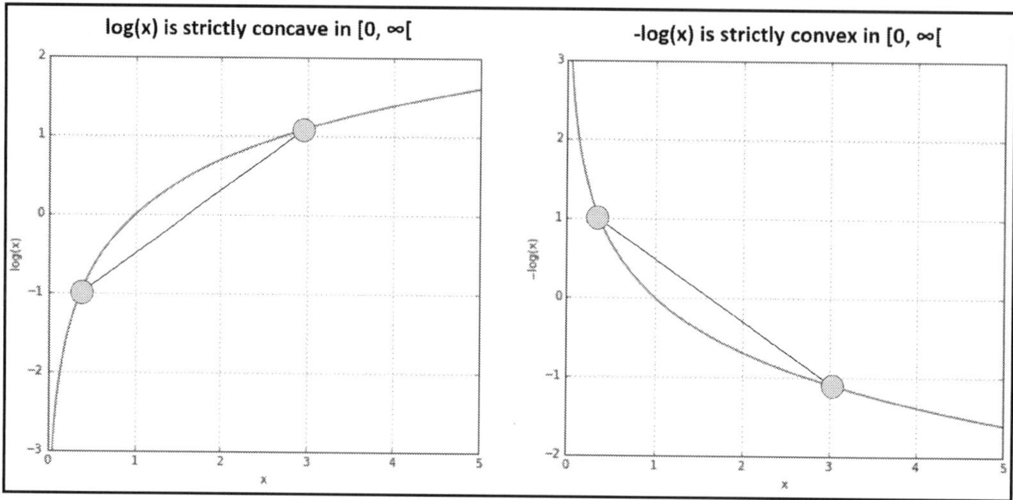

The *Jensen's inequality* (the proof is omitted but further details can be found in *Jensen's Operator Inequality, Hansen F., Pedersen G. K.*, arXiv:math/0204049 [math.OA] states that if $f(x)$ is a convex function defined on a convex set D, if we select n points $x_1, x_2, ..., x_n \in D$ and n constants $\lambda_1, \lambda_2, ..., \lambda_n \geq 0$ satisfying the condition $\lambda_1 + \lambda_2 + ... + \lambda_n = 1$, then the following applies:

$$f\left(\sum_i \lambda_i x_i\right) \leqslant \sum_i \lambda_i f(x_i)$$

Therefore, considering that *-log(x)* is convex, the *Jensen's inequality* for *log(x)* becomes as follows:

$$log\left(\sum_i \lambda_i x_i\right) \geqslant \sum_i \lambda_i log(x_i)$$

Hence, the generic iterative step can be rewritten, as follows:

$$\Delta L = L(\bar{\theta}|X) - L(\bar{\theta}_t|X) = log\sum_z P(X|z,\bar{\theta})P(z|\bar{\theta}) - log\,P(X|\bar{\theta}_t) =$$
$$= log\sum_z P(z|X,\bar{\theta}_t)\frac{P(X|z,\bar{\theta})P(z|\bar{\theta})}{P(z|X,\bar{\theta}_t)} - log\,P(X|\bar{\theta}_t)$$

Applying the Jensen's inequality, we obtain the following:

$$\Delta L \geqslant \sum_z P(z|X,\bar{\theta}_t)\,log\frac{P(X|z,\bar{\theta})P(z|\bar{\theta})}{P(z|X,\bar{\theta}_t)} - log\,P(X|\bar{\theta}_t) =$$
$$= \sum_z P(z|X,\bar{\theta}_t)\,log\frac{P(X|z,\bar{\theta})P(z|\bar{\theta})}{P(z|X,\bar{\theta}_t)P(X|\bar{\theta}_t)}$$

All the conditions are met, because the terms $P(z_i|X, \theta_t)$ are, by definition, bounded between [0, 1] and the sum over all *z* must always be equal to 1 (laws of probability). The previous expression implies that the following is true:

$$L(\bar{\theta}|X) \geqslant L(\bar{\theta}_t|X) + \sum_z P(z|X,\bar{\theta}_t)\,log\frac{P(X|z,\bar{\theta})P(z|\bar{\theta})}{P(z|X,\bar{\theta}_t)P(X|\bar{\theta}_t)}$$

Therefore, if we maximize the right side of the inequality, we also maximize the log-likelihood. However, the problem can be further simplified, considering that we are optimizing only the parameter vector θ and we can remove all the terms that don't depend on it. Hence, we can define a *Q function* whose expression is as follows:

$$Q(\bar{\theta}|\bar{\theta}_t) = \sum_z P(z|X,\bar{\theta}_t)\,log\,P(X|z,\bar{\theta})P(z|\bar{\theta}) = \sum_z P(z|X,\bar{\theta}_t)\,log\,P(X,z|\bar{\theta}) = E_{Z|X,\bar{\theta}_t}[log\,P(X,z|\bar{\theta})]$$

Q is the expected value of the log-likelihood considering the complete data $Y = (X, Z)$ and the current iteration parameter *set* θ_t. At each iteration, Q is computed considering the current estimation θ_t and it's maximized considering the variable θ. It's now clearer why the latent variables can be often artificially introduced: they allow us to apply the *Jensen's inequality* and transform the original expression into an expected value that is easy to evaluate and optimize.

At this point, we can formalize the EM algorithm:

1. Set a threshold Thr (for example, $Thr = 0.01$)
2. Set a random parameter vector θ_0.
3. While $|L(\theta_t|X, Z) - L(\theta_{t-1}|X, Z)| > Thr$:
    - **E-Step**: Compute the $Q(\theta|\theta_t)$. In general, this step consists in computing the conditional probability $p(z|X, \theta_t)$ or some of its moments (sometimes, the sufficient statistics are limited to mean and covariance) using the current parameter estimation θ_t.
    - **M-Step**: Find $\theta_{t+1} = argmax_\theta\, Q(\theta|\theta_t)$. The new parameter estimation is computed to maximize the Q function.

The procedure ends when the log-likelihood stops increasing or after a fixed number of iterations.

An example of parameter estimation

In this example, we see how it's possible to apply the EM algorithm for the estimation of unknown parameters (inspired by an example discussed in the original paper *Maximum likelihood from incomplete data via the em algorithm, Dempster A. P., Laird N. M., Rubin D. B., Journal of the Royal Statistical Society, B, 39(1):1–38, 11/1977*).

Let's consider a sequence of n independent experiments modeled with a multinomial distribution with three possible outcomes x_1, x_2, x_3 and corresponding probabilities p_1, p_2 and p_3. The probability mass function is as follows:

$$f(x_1, x_2, x_3; p_1, p_2, p_3) = \frac{n!}{\prod_{i=1}^{3} x_i!} \prod_{i=1}^{3} p_i^{x_i}$$

Let's suppose that we can observe $z_1 = x_1 + x_2$ and x_3, but we don't have any direct access to the single values x_1 and x_2. Therefore, x_1 and x_2 are latent variables, while z_1 and x_3 are observed ones. The probability vector p is parameterized in the following way:

$$\bar{p} = \begin{pmatrix} p_1 & p_2 & p_3 \end{pmatrix} = \begin{pmatrix} \frac{\theta}{6} & 1-\frac{\theta}{4} & \frac{\theta}{12} \end{pmatrix}$$

Our goal is to find the MLE for θ given n, z_1, and x_3. Let's start computing the log-likelihood:

$$L(\theta|x_1, x_2, x_3, z_1) = log\frac{n!}{\prod_{i=1}^{3} x_i!}\prod_{i=1}^{3} p_i^{x_i} = c + \sum_{i=1}^{3} x_i \; log \, p_i =$$
$$= c + x_1 \; log\frac{\theta}{6} + x_2 \; log\left(1 - \frac{\theta}{4}\right) + x_3 \; log \, \frac{\theta}{12}$$

We can derive the expression for the corresponding Q function, exploiting the linearity of the expected value operator $E[\bullet]$:

$$Q(\theta|\theta_t) = E\left[x_1|z_1, \bar{p}^{(t)}\right] log \, \frac{\theta}{6} + E\left[x_2|z_1, \bar{p}^{(t)}\right] log\left(1 - \frac{\theta}{4}\right) + x_3 \; log \, \frac{\theta}{12}$$

The variables x_1 and x_2, given z_1, are binomially distributed and can be expressed as a function of θ_t (we need to recompute them at each iteration). Hence, the expected value of $x_1^{(t+1)}$ becomes as follows:

$$E\left[x_1|z_1, \bar{p}^{(t)}\right] = z_1 \frac{p_1^{(t)}}{p_1^{(t)} + p_2^{(t)}} = z_1 \frac{\frac{\theta_t}{6}}{\frac{\theta}{6} + 1 - \frac{\theta_t}{4}} = z_1 \frac{2\theta_t}{12 - \theta_t}$$

While the expected value of $x_2^{(t+1)}$ is as follows:

$$E\left[x_2|z_1, \bar{p}^{(t)}\right] = z_1 \frac{p_2^{(t)}}{p_1^{(t)} + p_2^{(t)}} = z_1 \frac{1 - \frac{\theta_t}{4}}{\frac{\theta}{6} + 1 - \frac{\theta_t}{4}} = z_1 \frac{3(4 - \theta_t)}{12 - \theta_t}$$

If we apply these expressions in $Q(\theta|\theta_t)$ and compute the derivative with respect to θ, we get the following:

$$\frac{\partial Q}{\partial \theta} = 0 \Rightarrow \frac{E\left[x_1|z_1, \bar{p}^{(t)}\right] + x_3}{\theta} + \frac{E\left[x_2|z_1, \bar{p}^{(t)}\right]}{\theta - 4} = 0$$

Therefore, solving for θ, we get the following:

$$\theta = \frac{4\left(E\left[x_1^{(t+1)}|z_1, \bar{p}^{(t)}\right] + x_3\right)\Big)}{z_1 + x_3}$$

At this point, we can derive the iterative expression for θ:

$$\theta = \frac{4\left(z_1\frac{2\theta_t}{12-\theta_t} + x_3\right)\Big)}{z_1 + x_3} = \frac{8z_1\theta_t + 4x_3(12 - \theta_t)}{(z_1 + x_3)(12 - \theta_t)}$$

Let's compute the value of θ for $z_1 = 50$ and $x_3 = 10$:

```
def theta(theta_prev, z1=50.0, x3=10.0):
    num = (8.0 * z1 * theta_prev) + (4.0 * x3 * (12.0 - theta_prev))
    den = (z1 + x3) * (12.0 - theta_prev)
    return num / den

theta_v = 0.01

for i in range(1000):
    theta_v = theta(theta_v)

print(theta_v)
1.9999999999999999

p = [theta_v/6.0, (1-(theta_v/4.0)), theta_v/12.0]

print(p)
[0.33333333333333315, 0.5000000000000002, 0.16666666666666657]
```

In this example, we have parameterized all probabilities and, considering that $z_1 = x_1 + x_2$, we have one degree of freedom for the choice of θ. The reader can repeat the example by setting the value of one of p_1 or p_2 and leaving the other probabilities as functions of θ. The computation is almost identical but in this case, there are no degrees of freedom.

Gaussian mixture

In Chapter 2, *Introduction to Semi-Supervised Learning*, we discussed the generative Gaussian mixture model in the context of semi-supervised learning. In this paragraph, we're going to apply the EM algorithm to derive the formulas for the parameter updates.

Let's start considering a dataset, X, drawn from a data generating process, p_{data}:

$$X = \{\bar{x}_1, \bar{x}_2, \ldots, \bar{x}_N\} \; where \; \bar{x}_i \in \mathbb{R}^m$$

We assume that the whole distribution is generated by the sum of k Gaussian distributions so that the probability of each sample can be expressed as follows:

$$p(\bar{x}_i) = \sum_{j=1}^{k} P(N=j)\, N(\bar{x}_i|\bar{\mu}_j, \Sigma_j) = \sum_{j=1}^{k} w_j N(\bar{x}_i|\bar{\mu}_j, \Sigma_j)$$

In the previous expression, the term $w_j = P(N{=}j)$ is the relative weight of the jth Gaussian, while μ_j and Σ_j are the mean and the covariance matrix. For consistency with the laws of probability, we also need to impose the following:

$$\sum_j w_j = 1$$

Unfortunately, if we try to solve the problem directly, we need to manage the logarithm of a sum and the procedure becomes very complex. However, we have learned that it's possible to use latent variables as helpers, whenever this trick can simplify the solution.

Let's consider a single parameter set $\theta=(w_j, \mu_j, \Sigma_j)$ and a latent indicator matrix Z where each element z_{ij} is equal to 1 if the point x_i has been generated by the jth Gaussian, and 0 otherwise. Therefore, each z_{ij} is Bernoulli distributed with parameters equal to $p(j|x_i, \theta_t)$.

The joint log-likelihood can hence be expressed using the exponential-indicator notation, as follows:

$$L(\theta; X, Z) = log \prod_i \prod_j p(\bar{x}_i, j|\theta)^{z_{ij}} = \sum_i \sum_j z_{ij} log\, p(\bar{x}_i, j|\theta)$$

The index, *i*, is referred to the samples, while *j* refers to the Gaussian distributions. If we apply the chain rule and the properties of a logarithm, the expression becomes as follows:

$$L(\theta; X, Z) = \sum_i \sum_j z_{ij} log\, p(\bar{x}_i, j|\theta) = \sum_i \sum_j z_{ij} log\, p(\bar{x}_i|j, \theta) + z_{ij} log\, p(j|\theta)$$

The first term represents the probability of x_i under the jth Gaussian, while the second one is the relative weight of the jth Gaussian. We can now compute the $Q(\theta;\theta_t)$ function using the joint log-likelihood:

$$Q(\theta|\theta_t) = E_{Z|X,\theta_t}[L(\theta; X, Z)] = E_{Z|X,\theta_t}\left[\sum_i \sum_j z_{ij} log\, p(\bar{x}_i|j, \theta) + z_{ij} log\, p(j|\theta)\right]$$

Exploiting the linearity of *E[•]*, the previous expression becomes as follows:

$$\begin{aligned} Q(\theta|\theta_t) &= \sum_i \sum_j E_{Z|X,\theta_t}[z_{ij}]\, log\, p(\bar{x}_i|j, \theta) + E_{Z|X,\theta_t}[z_{ij}]\, log\, p(j|\theta) = \\ &= \sum_i \sum_j p(j|\bar{x}_i, \theta_t)\, log\, p(\bar{x}_i|j, \theta) + p(j|\bar{x}_i, \theta_t)\, log\, p(j|\theta) \end{aligned}$$

The term $p(j|x_i, \theta_t)$ corresponds to the expected value of z_{ij} considering the complete data, and expresses the probability of the jth Gaussian given the sample x_i. It can be simplified considering Bayes' theorem:

$$p(j|\bar{x}_i, \theta_t) = \alpha\, p(\bar{x}_i|j, \theta_t)\, p(j, \theta_t)$$

The first term is the probability of x_i under the jth Gaussian with parameters θ_t, while the second one is the weight of the jth Gaussian considering the same parameter set θ_t. In order to derive the iterative expressions for the parameters, it's useful to write the complete formula for the logarithm of a multivariate Gaussian distribution:

$$\begin{aligned} log\, p(\bar{x}_i|j, \theta) &= log \frac{1}{\sqrt{2\pi \det \Sigma_j}} e^{-\frac{1}{2}(\bar{x}_i - \bar{\mu}_j)^T \Sigma^{-1} (\bar{x}_i - \bar{\mu}_j)} = \\ &= -\frac{m}{2} log\, 2\pi - \frac{1}{2} log\, det\, \Sigma_j - \frac{1}{2}(\bar{x}_i - \bar{\mu}_j)^T \Sigma^{-1} (\bar{x}_i - \bar{\mu}_j) \end{aligned}$$

To simplify this expression, we use the trace trick. In fact, as $(x_i - \mu_j)^T \Sigma^{-1} (x_i - \mu_j)$ is a scalar, we can exploit the properties $tr(AB) = tr(BA)$ and $tr(c) = c$ where A and B are matrices and $c \in \Re$:

$$log\, p(\bar{x}_i | j, \theta) = -\frac{m}{2} log\, 2\pi - \frac{1}{2} log\, det\, \Sigma_j - \frac{1}{2} tr\left(\Sigma_j^{-1} (\bar{x}_i - \bar{\mu}_j)(\bar{x}_i - \bar{\mu}_j)^T\right)$$

Let's start considering the estimation of the mean (only the first term of $Q(\theta;\theta_t)$ depends on mean and covariance):

$$\frac{\partial Q}{\partial \mu_j} = -\frac{1}{2} \sum_i p(j|\bar{x}_i, \theta_t) \frac{\partial}{\partial \mu_j} tr\left(\Sigma_j^{-1} (\bar{x}_i - \bar{\mu}_j)(\bar{x}_i - \bar{\mu}_j)^T\right) = \\ = \sum_i p(j|\bar{x}_i, \theta_t)\, tr\left(\Sigma_j^{-1} (\bar{x}_i - \bar{\mu}_j)\right)$$

Setting the derivative equal to zero, we get the following:

$$\mu_j = \frac{\sum_i p(j|\bar{x}_i, \theta_t)\, \bar{x}_i}{\sum_i p(j|\bar{x}_i, \theta_t)}$$

In the same way, we obtain the expression of the covariance matrix:

$$\Sigma_j = \frac{\sum_i p(j|\bar{x}_i, \theta_t) \left[(\bar{x}_i - \bar{\mu}_j)(\bar{x}_i - \bar{\mu}_j)^T\right]}{\sum_i p(j|\bar{x}_i, \theta_t)}$$

To obtain the iterative expressions for the weights, the procedure is a little bit more complex, because we need to use the Lagrange multipliers (further information can be found in `http://www.slimy.com/~steuard/teaching/tutorials/Lagrange.html`). Considering that the sum of the weights must always be equal to 1, it's possible to write the following equation:

$$P = Q - \lambda\left(\sum_j w_j - 1\right) \Rightarrow \frac{\partial P}{\partial w_j} = \frac{\partial Q}{\partial w_j} - \lambda \text{ and } \frac{\partial P}{\partial \lambda} = \sum_j w_j - 1$$

Setting both derivatives equal to zero, from the first one, considering that $wj = p(j|\theta)$, we get the following:

$$\frac{\partial P}{\partial w_j} = \frac{\partial Q}{\partial w_j} - \lambda = 0 \Rightarrow \frac{\partial}{\partial w_j}\sum_i p(j|\bar{x}_i, \theta_t)\log p(j|\theta) = \lambda \Rightarrow \frac{\sum_i p(j|\bar{x}_i, \theta_t)}{w_j} = \lambda$$

$$w_j = \frac{\sum_i p(j|\bar{x}_i, \theta_t)}{\lambda}$$

While from the second derivative, we obtain the following:

$$\frac{\partial P}{\partial \lambda} = \sum_j w_j - 1 \Rightarrow \frac{\partial P}{\partial \lambda} = \frac{\sum_i \sum_j p(j|\bar{x}_i, \theta_t)}{\lambda} - 1 \Rightarrow \lambda = N$$

The last step derives from the fundamental condition:

$$\sum_j p(j|\bar{x}_i, \theta_t) = 1$$

Therefore, the final expression of the weights is as follows:

$$w_j = \frac{\sum_i p(j|\bar{x}_i, \theta_t)}{N}$$

At this point, we can formalize the Gaussian mixture algorithm:

- Set random initial values for $w_j^{(0)}$, $\theta^{(0)}_j$ and $\Sigma^{(0)}_j$
- **E-Step**: Compute $p(j|x_i, \theta_t)$ using Bayes' theorem: $p(j|x_i, \theta_t) = \alpha\, w^{(t)}_j\, p(x_i|j, \theta_t)$
- **M-Step**: Compute $w_j^{(t+1)}$, $\theta^{(t+1)}_j$ and $\Sigma^{(t+1)}_j$ using the formulas provided previously

The process must be iterated until the parameters become stable. In general, the best practice is using both a threshold and a maximum number of iterations.

An example of Gaussian Mixtures using Scikit-Learn

We can now implement the Gaussian mixture algorithm using the Scikit-Learn implementation. The direct approach has already been shown in `Chapter 2`, *Introduction to Semi-Supervised Learning*. The dataset is generated to have three cluster centers and a moderate overlap due to a standard deviation equal to 1.5:

```
from sklearn.datasets import make_blobs

nb_samples = 1000
X, Y = make_blobs(n_samples=nb_samples, n_features=2, centers=3,
cluster_std=1.5, random_state=1000)
```

The corresponding plot is shown in the following diagram:

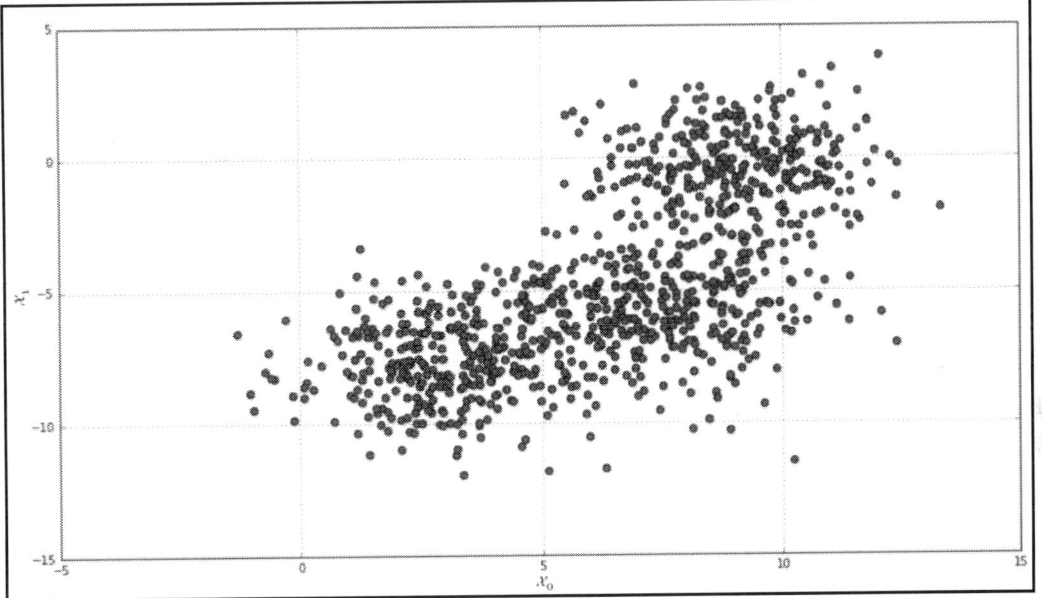

The Scikit-Learn implementation is based on the `GaussianMixture` class , which accepts as parameters the number of Gaussians (`n_components`), the type of covariance (`covariance_type`), which can be `full` (the default value), if all components have their own matrix, `tied` if the matrix is shared, `diag` if all components have their own diagonal matrix (this condition imposes an uncorrelation among the features), and `spherical` when each Gaussian is symmetric in every direction.

The other parameters allow setting regularization and initialization factors (for further information, the reader can directly check the documentation). Our implementation is based on full covariance:

```
from sklearn.mixture import GaussianMixture

gm = GaussianMixture(n_components=3)
gm.fit(X)
```

After fitting the model, it's possible to access to the learned parameters through the instance variables `weights_`, `means_`, and `covariances_`:

```
print(gm.weights_)

[ 0.32904743  0.33027731  0.34067526]

print(gm.means_)

[[ 3.03902183 -7.69186648]
 [ 9.04414279 -0.37455175]
 [ 7.37103878 -5.77496152]]

print(gm.covariances_)

[[[ 2.34943036  0.08492009]
  [ 0.08492009  2.36467211]]

 [[ 2.10999633  0.02602279]
  [ 0.02602279  2.21533635]]

 [[ 2.71755196 -0.0100434 ]
  [-0.0100434   2.39941067]]]
```

Considering the covariance matrices, we can already understand that the features are very uncorrelated and the Gaussians are almost spherical. The final plot can be obtained by assigning each point to the corresponding cluster (Gaussian distribution) through the `Yp = gm.transform(X)` command:

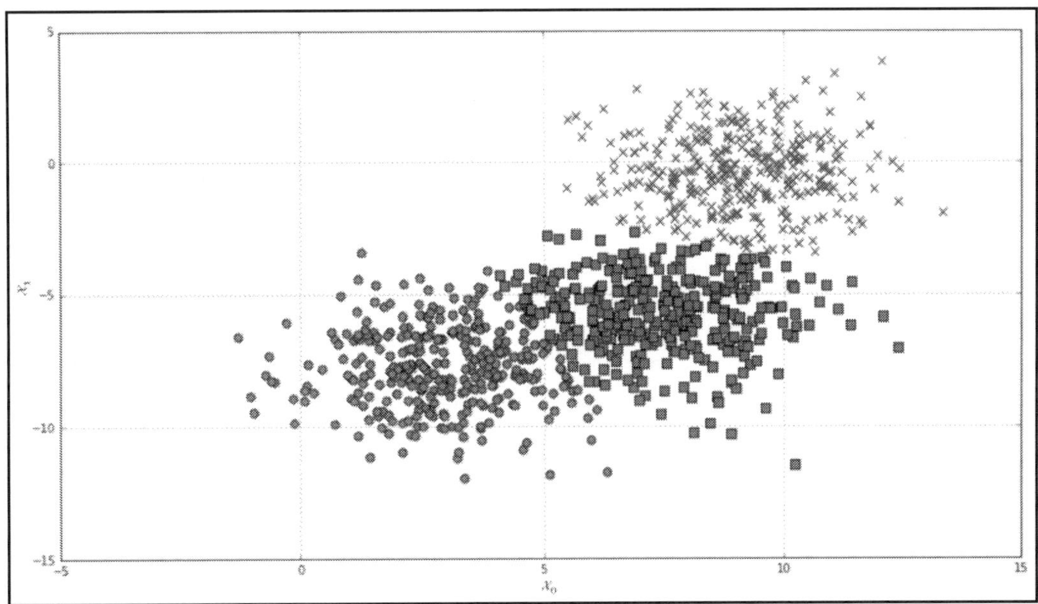

Labeled dataset obtained through the application of a Gaussian mixture with three components

The reader should have noticed a strong analogy between Gaussian mixture and k-means (which we're going to discuss in `Chapter 7`, *Clustering Algorithms*). In particular, we can state that K-means is a particular case of spherical Gaussian mixture with a covariance $\Sigma \to 0$. This condition transforms the approach from a soft clustering, where each sample belongs to all clusters with a precise probability distribution, into a hard clustering, where the assignment is done by considering the shortest distance between sample and centroid (or mean). For this reason, in some books, the Gaussian mixture algorithm is also called soft K-means. A conceptually similar approach that we are going to present is Fuzzy K-means, which is based on assignments characterized by membership functions, which are analogous to probability distributions.

Factor analysis

Let's suppose we have a Gaussian data generating process, $p_{data} \sim N(0, \Sigma)$, and M n-dimensional zero-centered samples drawn from it:

$$X = \{\bar{x}_1, \bar{x}_2, \ldots, \bar{x}_M\} \ \ where \ \ \bar{x}_i \in \mathbb{R}^n$$

If p_{data} has a mean $\mu \neq 0$, it's also possible to use this model, but it's necessary to account for this non-null value with slight changes in some formulas. As the zero-centering normally has no drawbacks, it's easier to remove the mean to simplify the model.

One of the most common problems in unsupervised learning is finding a lower dimensional distribution p_{lower} such that the Kullback-Leibler divergence with p_{data} is minimized. When performing a **factor analysis** (**FA**), following the original proposal published in *EM algorithms for ML factor analysis, Rubin D., Thayer D., Psychometrika,* 47/1982, Issue 1, and *The EM algorithm for Mixtures of Factor Analyzers, Ghahramani Z., Hinton G. E.,* CRC-TG-96-1, 05/1996, we start from the assumption to model the generic sample x as a linear combination of Gaussian latent variables, z, (whose dimension p is normally $p < n$) plus an additive and decorrelated Gaussian noise term, ν:

$$\bar{x} = A\bar{z} + \bar{\nu} \ \ where \ \ \bar{z} \sim N(0, I) \ \ and \ \ \bar{\nu} \sim N(0, \Omega) \ \ with \ \ \Omega = diag(\omega_0^2, \omega_1^2, \ldots, \omega_n^2)$$

The matrix, A, is called a *factor loading matrix* because it determines the contribution of each latent variable (factor) to the reconstruction of x. Factors and input data are assumed to be statistically independent. Instead, considering the last term, if $\omega_0^2 \neq \omega_1^2 \neq \ldots \neq \omega_n^2$ the noise is called *heteroscedastic*, while it's defined *homoscedastic* if the variances are equal $\omega_0^2 = \omega_1^2 = \ldots = \omega_n^2 = \omega^2$. To understand the difference between these two kinds of noise, think about a signal x which is the sum of two identical voices, recorded in different places (for example, an airport and a wood). In this case, we can suppose to also have different noise variances (the first one should be higher than the second considering the number of different noise sources). If instead both voices are recorded in a soundproofed room or even in the same airport, homoscedastic noise is surely more likely (we're not considering the power, but the difference between the variances).

One of the most important strengths of FA in respect to other methods (such as PCA) is its intrinsic robustness to heteroscedastic noise. In fact, including the noise term in the model (with only the constraint to be decorrelated) allows partial denoising filtering based on the single components, while one of the preconditions for the PCA is to impose only homoscedastic noise (which, in many cases, is very similar to the total absence of noise). Considering the previous example, we could make the assumption to have the first variance be $\omega_0^2 = k\,\omega_1^2$ with $k > 1$. In this way, the model will be able to understand that a high variance in the first component should be considered (with a higher probability) as the product of the noise and not an intrinsic property of the component.

Let's now analyze the linear relation:

$$\bar{x} = A\bar{z} + \bar{\nu}$$

Considering the properties of Gaussian distributions, we know that $x \sim N(\mu, \Sigma)$ and it's easy to determine either the mean or the covariance matrix:

$$\mu = E[X] = AE[Z] + E[\epsilon] = 0$$
$$\Sigma = E[X^T X] = AE[Z^T Z]A^T + E[\nu^T \nu] = AA^T + \Omega$$

Therefore, in order to solve the problem, we need to find the best $\theta=(A, \Omega)$ so that $AA^T + \Omega \approx \Sigma$ (with a zero-centered dataset, the estimation is limited to the input covariance matrix Σ).The ability to cope with noisy variables should be clearer now. If $AA^T + \Omega$ is exactly equal to Σ and the estimation of Ω is correct, the algorithm will optimize the factor loading matrix A, excluding the interference produced by the noise term; therefore, the components will be approximately denoised.

In order to adopt the EM algorithm, we need to determine the joint probability $p(X, z; \theta) = p(X|z; \theta)p(z|\theta)$. The first term on the right side can be easily determined, considering that $x - Az \sim N(0, \Omega)$; therefore, we get the following:

$$p(X, \bar{z}; \theta) = \prod_{i=1}^{M} \left(\frac{1}{\sqrt{(2\pi)^n det(\Omega)}} e^{-\frac{1}{2}(\bar{x}_i - A\bar{z})^T \Omega^{-1} (\bar{x}_i - A\bar{z})} \right) \left(\frac{1}{\sqrt{(2\pi)^p}} e^{-\frac{1}{2}\bar{z}^T \bar{z}} \right) =$$
$$= (2\pi)^{-\frac{Mn+p}{2}} det(\Omega)^{-\frac{M}{2}} \prod_{i=1}^{M} e^{-\frac{1}{2}\left[(\bar{x}_i - A\bar{z})^T \Omega^{-1} (\bar{x}_i - A\bar{z}) + \bar{z}^T \bar{z}\right]}$$

We can now determine the $Q(\theta;\theta_t)$ function, discarding the constant term $(2\pi)^k$ and term z^Tz, which don't depend on θ (in this particular case, as we're going to see, we don't need to compute the probability $p(z|X;\theta)$ because it's enough to obtain sufficient statistics for expected value and second moment). Moreover, it's useful to expand the multiplication in the exponential:

$$Q(\theta;\theta_t) = E_{Z|X;\theta}\left[log\, p(X|\bar{z};\theta)\right] =$$

$$E_{Z|X;\theta}\left[-\frac{M}{2}log\, det(\Omega) - \frac{1}{2}\sum_{i=1}^{M}\left(\bar{x}_i^T\Omega^{-1}\bar{x}_i - 2\bar{x}_i^T\Omega^{-1}A\bar{z} + \bar{z}^TA^T\Omega^{-1}A\bar{z}\right)\right]$$

Using the trace trick with the last term (which is a scalar), we can rewrite it as follows:

$$\bar{z}^TA^T\Omega^{-1}A\bar{z} = tr(\bar{z}^TA^T\Omega^{-1}A\bar{z}) = tr(A^T\Omega^{-1}A\bar{z}\bar{z}^T)$$

Exploiting the linearity of $E[\bullet]$, we obtain the following:

$$Q(\theta;\theta_t) = -\frac{M}{2}log\, det(\Omega) - \frac{1}{2}\sum_{i=1}^{M}\left(\bar{x}_i^T\Omega^{-1}\bar{x}_i - 2\bar{x}_i^T\Omega^{-1}AE_{\bar{z}|\bar{x}_i;\theta}[\bar{z}|\bar{x}_i] + A^T\Omega^{-1}AE_{\bar{z}|\bar{x}_i;\theta}[\bar{z}\bar{z}^T|\bar{x}_i]\right)$$

This expression is similar to what we have seen in the Gaussian mixture model, but in this case, we need to compute the conditional expectation and the conditional second moment of z. Unfortunately, we cannot do this directly, but it's possible to compute them exploiting the joint normality of x and z. In particular, using a classic theorem, we can partition the full joint probability $p(z, x)$, considering the following relations:

$$\bar{v} = \begin{pmatrix}\bar{z}\\ \bar{x}\end{pmatrix} \quad \bar{\mu}^* = \begin{pmatrix}E[\bar{z}]\\ E[\bar{x}]\end{pmatrix} = \begin{pmatrix}0\\ 0\end{pmatrix} \quad \Sigma^* = \begin{pmatrix}E[\bar{z}\bar{z}^T] & E[\bar{z}\bar{x}^T]\\ E[\bar{x}\bar{z}^T] & E[\bar{x}\bar{x}^T]\end{pmatrix} = \begin{pmatrix}I & A^T\\ A & AA^T+\Omega\end{pmatrix}$$

The conditional distribution $p(z|x=x_i)$ has a mean equal to the following:

$$E[\bar{z}|\bar{x}=\bar{x}_i] = E[\bar{z}] + E[\bar{z}\bar{x}^T]E[\bar{x}\bar{x}^T]^{-1}(\bar{x}_i - E[\bar{x}]) = A^T(AA^T+\Omega)^{-1}\bar{x}_i$$

The conditional variance is as follows:

$$E\left[(\bar{z} - E[\bar{z}|\bar{x}=\bar{x}_i])^2\right] = E[\bar{z}\bar{z}^T|\bar{x}=\bar{x}_i] - E[\bar{z}|\bar{x}=\bar{x}_i]E[\bar{z}|\bar{x}=\bar{x}_i]^T$$

Therefore, the conditional second moment is equal to the following:

$$E[\bar{z}\bar{z}^T|\bar{x}=\bar{x}_i] = E[\bar{z}\bar{z}^T|\bar{x}=\bar{x}_i] - E[\bar{z}\bar{x}^T|\bar{x}=\bar{x}_i]E[\bar{x}\bar{x}^T|\bar{x}=\bar{x}_i]^{-1}E[\bar{x}\bar{z}^T|\bar{x}=\bar{x}_i] + E[\bar{z}|\bar{x}=\bar{x}_i]E[\bar{z}|\bar{x}=\bar{x}_i]^T =$$
$$= I - A^T(AA^T+\Omega)^{-1}A + E[\bar{z}|\bar{x}=\bar{x}_i]E[\bar{z}|\bar{x}=\bar{x}_i]^T$$

If we define the auxiliary matrix $K = (AA^T + \Omega)^{-1}$, the previous expressions become as follows:

$$E[\bar{z}|\bar{x}=\bar{x}_i] = A^T K\bar{x}_i$$
$$E[\bar{z}\bar{z}^T|\bar{x}=\bar{x}_i] = I - A^T KA + A^T K\bar{x}_i\bar{x}_i^T K^T A$$

The reader in search of further details about this technique can read *Preview Introduction to Statistical Decision Theory, Pratt J., Raiffa H., Schlaifer R., The MIT Press.*

Using the previous expression, it's possible to build the inverse model (sometimes called a *recognition model* because it starts with the effects and rebuilds the causes), which is still Gaussian distributed:

$$\bar{z} = B\bar{x} + \bar{\lambda} \ where \ p(\bar{z}|\bar{x};\theta) \sim N(E[\bar{z}|\bar{x}], E\left[(\bar{z} - E[\bar{z}|\bar{x}=\bar{x}_i])^2\right]) = N(A^T K\bar{x}, I - A^T KA)$$

We are now able to maximize $Q(\theta;\theta_t)$ with respect to A and Ω, considering $\theta_t=(A_t, \Omega_t)$ and both the conditional expectation and the second moment computed according to the previous estimation $\theta_{t-1}=(A_{t-1}, \Omega_{t-1})$. For this reason, they are not involved in the derivation process. We are adopting the convention that the term subject to maximization is computed at time t, while all the others are obtained through the previous estimations (t - 1):

$$\frac{\partial Q}{\partial A} = -\sum_{i=1}^{M}\Omega_{t-1}^{-1}\bar{x}_i E_{Z|\bar{x}_i;\theta}[\bar{z}|\bar{x}=\bar{x}_i]^T + \sum_{j=1}^{M}\Omega_{t-1}^{-1}A_t E_{Z|\bar{x}_j;\theta}[\bar{z}\bar{z}^T|\bar{x}=\bar{x}_j] = 0$$

The expression for A_t is therefore as follows (Q is the biased input covariance matrix $E[X^TX]$ for a zero-centered dataset):

$$A_t = \left(\sum_{i=1}^{M}\bar{x}_i E_{Z|\bar{x}_i;\theta}[\bar{z}|\bar{x}=\bar{x}_i]^T\right)\left(\sum_{j=1}^{M}E_{Z|\bar{x}_j;\theta}[\bar{z}\bar{z}^T|\bar{x}=\bar{x}_j]\right)^{-1} =$$
$$= (QK_{t-1}^T A_{t-1})(I - A_{t-1}^T K_{t-1}A_{t-1} + A_{t-1}^T K_{t-1}QK_{t-1}^T A_{t-1})^{-1}$$

In the same way, we can obtain an expression for Ω_t by computing the derivative with respect to Ω^{-1} (this choice simplifies the calculation and doesn't affect the result, because we must set the derivative equal to zero):

$$\frac{\partial Q}{\partial \Omega^{-1}} = \frac{M}{2}\Omega_t - \frac{1}{2}\sum_{i=1}^{M}\left(\bar{x}_i\bar{x}_i^T - 2A_{t-1}E_{Z|\bar{x}_i;\theta}[\bar{z}|\bar{x} = \bar{x}_i] + A_{t-1}E[\bar{z}\bar{z}^T|\bar{x} = \bar{x}_i]A_{t-1}^T\right) =$$
$$\frac{M}{2}\Omega_t - \frac{1}{2}\sum_{i=1}^{M}\left(\bar{x}_i\bar{x}_i^T - A_{t-1}E_{Z|\bar{x}_i;\theta}[\bar{z}|\bar{x} = \bar{x}_i]\bar{x}_i^T\right) = 0$$

The derivative of the first term, which is the determinant of a real diagonal matrix, is obtained using the adjugate matrix $Adj(\Omega)$ and exploiting the properties of the inverse matrix $T^{-1} = det(T)^{-1}Adj(T)$ and the properties $det(T)^{-1} = det(T^{-1})$ and $det(T^T) = det(T)$:

$$\frac{\partial}{\partial \Omega^{-1}} log\ det(\Omega) = -\frac{\partial}{\partial \Omega^{-1}} log\ det(\Omega^{-1}) = det(\Omega)\frac{\partial}{\partial \Omega^{-1}} det(\Omega^{-1}) =$$
$$= det(\Omega)\frac{\partial}{\partial \Omega^{-1}}\Omega^{-1}\left(Adj(\Omega)^{-1}\right)^T = det(\Omega)\left(Adj(\Omega)^T\right)^{-1} = \Omega^T = \Omega$$

The expression for Ω_t (imposing the diagonality constraint) is as follows:

$$\Omega_t = \frac{1}{M} diag\left[\sum_{i=1}^{M}\left(\bar{x}_i\bar{x}_i^T - A_{t-1}E_{Z|\bar{x}_i;\theta}[\bar{z}|\bar{x} = \bar{x}_i]\bar{x}_i^T\right)\right] =$$
$$= diag\left(Q - A_{t-1}A_{t-1}^T K_{t-1}Q\right)$$

Summarizing the steps, we can define the complete FA algorithm:

1. Set random initial values for $A^{(0)}$ and $\Omega^{(0)}$
2. Compute the biased input covariance matrix $Q = E[X^TX]$
3. E-Step: Compute $A^{(t)}$, $\Omega^{(t)}$, and $K^{(t)}$
4. M-Step: Compute $A^{(t+1)}$, $\Omega^{(t+1)}$, and $K^{(t+1)}$ using the previous estimations and the formulas provided previously
5. Compute the matrices B and Ψ for the inverse model

The process must be repeated until $A^{(t)}$, $\Omega^{(t)}$, and $K^{(t)}$ stop modifying their values (using a threshold) together with a constraint on the maximum number of iterations. The factors can be easily obtained using the inverse model $z = Bx + \lambda$.

An example of factor analysis with Scikit-Learn

We can now make an example of FA with Scikit-Learn using the MNIST handwritten digits dataset (70,000 28 × 28 grayscale images) in the original version and with added heteroscedastic noise (ω_i randomly selected from [0, 0.75]).

The first step is to load and zero-center the original dataset (I'm using the functions defined in the first chapter, `Chapter 1`, *Machine Learning Model Fundamentals*):

```
import numpy as np

from sklearn.datasets import fetch_mldata

digits = fetch_mldata('MNIST original')
X = zero_center(digits['data'].astype(np.float64))
np.random.shuffle(X)

Omega = np.random.uniform(0.0, 0.75, size=X.shape[1])
Xh = X + np.random.normal(0.0, Omega, size=X.shape)
```

After this step, the `X` variable will contain the zero-center original dataset, while `Xh` is the noisy version. The following screenshot shows a random selection of samples from both versions:

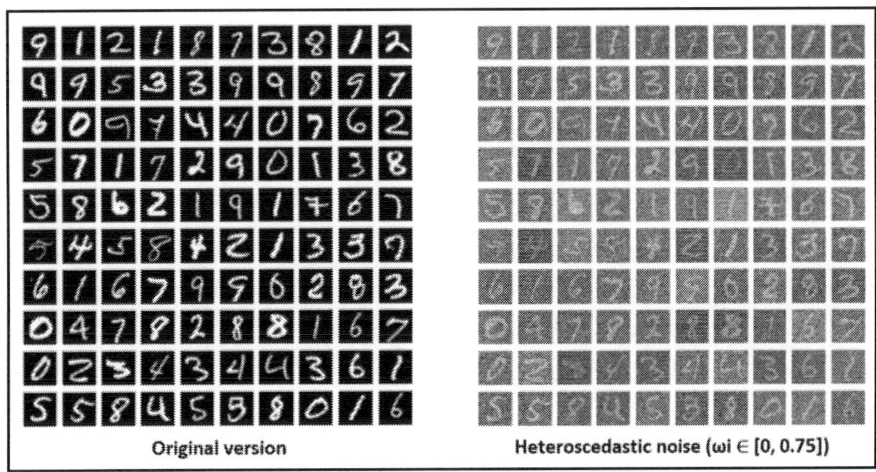

We can perform FA on both datasets using the Scikit-Learn `FactorAnalysis` class with the `n_components=64` parameter and check the score (the average log-likelihood over all samples). If the noise variance is known (or there's a good estimation), it's possible to include the starting point through the `noise_variance_init` parameter; otherwise, it will be initialized with the identity matrix:

```
from sklearn.decomposition import FactorAnalysis

fa = FactorAnalysis(n_components=64, random_state=1000)
fah = FactorAnalysis(n_components=64, random_state=1000)

Xfa = fa.fit_transform(X)
Xfah = fah.fit_transform(Xh)

print(fa.score(X))
-2162.70193446

print(fah.score(Xh))
-3046.19385694
```

As expected, the presence of noise has reduced the final accuracy (MLE). Following an example provided by *A. Gramfort* and *D. A. Engemann* in the original Scikit-Learn documentation, we can create a benchmark for the MLE using the *Lodoit-Wolf* algorithm (a shrinking method for improving the condition of the covariance that is beyond the scope of this book.

For further information, read *A Well-Conditioned Estimator for Large-Dimensional Covariance Matrices, Ledoit O., Wolf M., Journal of Multivariate Analysis*, 88, 2/2004":

```
from sklearn.covariance import LedoitWolf

ldw = LedoitWolf()
ldwh = LedoitWolf()

ldw.fit(X)
ldwh.fit(Xh)

print(ldw.score(X))
-2977.12971009

print(ldwh.score(Xh))
-2989.27874799
```

With the original dataset, FA performs much better than the benchmark, while it's slightly worse in the presence of heteroscedastic noise. The reader can try other combinations using the grid search with different numbers of components and noise variances, and experiment with the effect of removing the zero-centering step. It's possible to plot the extracted components using the `components_` instance variable:

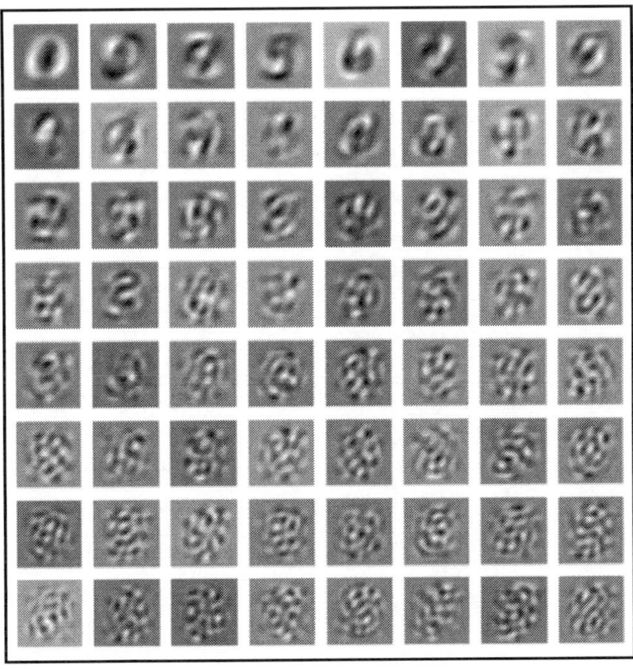

A plot of the 64 components extracted with the factor analysis on the original dataset

A careful analysis shows that the components are a superimposition of many low-level visual features. This is a consequence of the assumption to have a Gaussian prior distribution over the components ($z \sim N(0, I)$). In fact, one of the disadvantages of this distribution is its intrinsic denseness (the probability of sampling values far from the mean is often too high, while in some case, it would be desirable to have a peaked distribution that discourages values not close to its mean, to be able to observe more selective components).

Moreover, considering the distribution $p[Z|X; \theta]$, the covariance matrix ψ could not be diagonal (trying to impose this constraint can lead to an unsolvable problem), leading to a resulting multivariate Gaussian distribution, which isn't normally made up of independent components. In general, the single variables $z_{i,}$ (conditioned to an input sample, x_i) are statistically dependent and the reconstruction $x_{i,}$ is obtained with the participation of almost all extracted features. In all these cases, we say that the *coding is dense* and the dictionary of features in *under-complete* (the dimensionality of the components is lower than $dim(x_i)$).

The lack of independence can be also an issue considering that any orthogonal transformation Q applied to A (the factor loading matrix) don't affect the distribution $p[X|Z, \theta]$. In fact, as $QQ^T=I$, the following applies:

$$AA^T + \Omega = AQQ^T A^T + \Omega$$

In other words, any feature rotation $(x = AQz + v)$ is always a solution to the original problem and it's impossible to decide which is the real loading matrix. All these conditions lead to the further conclusion that the mutual information among components is not equal to zero and neither close to a minimum (in this case, each of them carries a specific portion of information). On the other side, our main goal was to reduce the dimensionality. Therefore, it's not surprising to have dependent components because we aim to preserve the maximum amount of original information contained in $p(X)$ (remember that the amount of information is related to the entropy and the latter is proportional to the variance).

The same phenomenon can be observed in the PCA (which is still based on the Gaussian assumption), but in the last paragraph, we're going to discuss a technique, called ICA, whose goal is to create a representation of each sample (without the constraint of the dimensionality reduction) after starting from a set of statistically independent features. This approach, even if it has its peculiarities, belongs to a large family of algorithms called *sparse coding*. In this scenario, if the corresponding dictionary has $dim(z_i) > dim(x_i)$,it is called *over-complete* (of course, the main goal is no longer the dimensionality reduction).

However, we're going to consider only the case when the dictionary is at most complete $dim(z_i) = dim(x_i)$, because ICA with over-complete dictionaries requires a more complex approach. The level of sparsity, of course, is proportional to $dim(z_i)$ and with ICA, it's always achieved as a secondary goal (the primary one is always the independence between components).

Principal Component Analysis

Another common approach to the problem of reducing the dimensionality of a high-dimensional dataset is based on the assumption that, normally, the total variance is not explained equally by all components. If p_{data} is a multivariate Gaussian distribution with covariance matrix Σ, then the entropy (which is a measure of the amount of information contained in the distribution) is as follows:

$$H(p) = \frac{1}{2} log\left(det(2\pi e\Sigma)\right)$$

Therefore, if some components have a very low variance, they also have a limited contribution to the entropy, providing little additional information. Hence, they can be removed without a high loss of accuracy.

Just as we've done with FA, let's consider a dataset drawn from $p_{data} \sim N(0, \Sigma)$ (for simplicity, we assume that it's zero-centered, even if it's not necessary):

$$X = \{\bar{x}_1, \bar{x}_2, \ldots, \bar{x}_M\} \quad where \quad \bar{x}_i \in \mathbb{R}^n$$

Our goal is to define a linear transformation, $z = A^T x$ (a vector is normally considered a column, therefore x has a shape $(n \times 1)$), such as the following:

$$\begin{cases} dim(\bar{z}_i) \ll n \\ H(p(z)) \approx H(p(x)) \end{cases}$$

As we want to find out the directions where the variance is higher, we can build our transformation matrix, A, starting from the eigen decomposition of the input covariance matrix, Σ (which is real, symmetric, and positive definite):

$$\Sigma = V\Omega V^T$$

V is an $(n \times n)$ matrix containing the eigenvectors (as columns), while Ω is a diagonal matrix containing the eigenvalues. Moreover, V is also orthogonal, hence the eigenvectors constitute a basis. An alternative approach is based on the **singular value decomposition** (**SVD**), which has an incremental variant and there are algorithms that can perform a decomposition truncated at an arbitrary number of components, speeding up the convergence process (such as the Scikit-Learn implementation `TruncatedSVD`).

In this case, it's immediately noticeable that the sample covariance is as follows:

$$\Sigma_s = \frac{1}{M} X^T X \ \ where \ \ X \in \mathbb{R}^{M \times n} \ \ and \ \ \Sigma_s \in \mathbb{R}^{n \times n}$$

If we apply the SVD to the matrix *X* (each row represents a single sample with a shape *(1, n)*), we obtain the following:

$$X = U \Lambda V^T \ \ where \ \ U \in \mathbb{R}^{M \times M}, \ \ \Lambda \ is \ diag(n \times n) \ \ and \ \ V \in \mathbb{R}^{n \times n}$$

U is a unitary matrix containing (as rows) the left singular vectors (the eigenvectors of XX^T), *V* (also unitary) contains (as rows) the right singular vectors (corresponding to the eigenvectors of X^TX), while Λ is a diagonal matrix containing the singular values of Σ_s (which are the square roots of the eigenvalues of both XX^T and X^TX). Conventionally, the eigenvalues are sorted by descending order and the eigenvectors are rearranged to match the corresponding position.

Hence, we can directly use the matrix Λ to select the most relevant eigenvalues (the square root is an increasing function and doesn't change the order) and the matrix *V* to retrieve the corresponding eigenvectors (the factor *1/M* is a proportionality constant). In this way, we don't need to compute and eigen decompose the covariance matrix Σ (contains $n \times n$ elements) and we can exploit some very fast approximate algorithms that work only with the dataset (without computing X^TX). Using the SVD, the transformation of *X* can be done directly, considering that *U* and *V* are unitary matrices (this means that $UU^T = U^TU = I$; therefore, the conjugate transpose is also the inverse):

$$Z = XA = U \Lambda V^T V = U \Lambda$$

Right now, *X* has only been projected in the eigenvector space (it has been simply rotated) and its dimensionality hasn't changed. However, from the definition of the eigenvector, we know that the following is true:

$$\Sigma \bar{v} = \lambda \bar{v}$$

If λ is large, the projection of v will be amplified proportionally to the variance explained by the direction of the corresponding eigenvector. Therefore, if it has not been already done, we can sort (and rename) the eigenvalues and the corresponding eigenvectors to have the following:

$$\lambda_1 > \lambda_2 > \ldots > \lambda_n$$

If we select the first top k eigenvalues, we can build a transformation matrix based on the corresponding eigenvectors (principal components) that projects X onto a subspace of the original eigenvector space:

$$A_k = \{\bar{v}_1, \bar{v}_2, \ldots, \bar{v}_k\} \quad where \quad A_k \in \mathbb{R}^{n \times k}$$

Using the SVD, instead of A_k, we can directly truncate U and Λ, creating the matrices U_k (which contains only the top k eigenvectors) and Λ_k, a diagonal matrix with the top k eigenvalues.

When choosing the value for k, we are assuming that the following is true:

$$ExplainedVariance[A_k] \approx ExplainedVariance[V]$$

To achieve this goal, it is normally necessary to compare the performances with a different number of components. In the following graph, there's a plot where the variance ratio (variance explained by component n/total variance) and the cumulative variance are plotted as functions of the components:

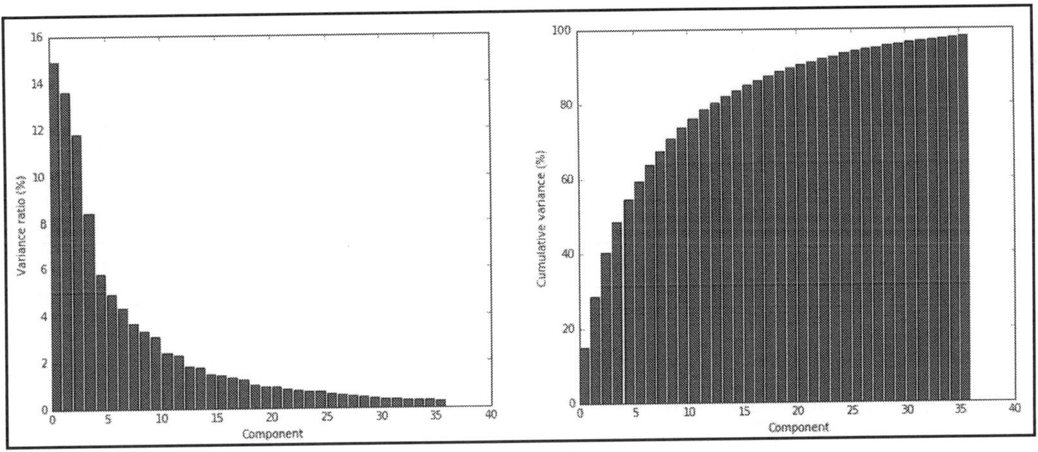

Explained variance per component (left) and cumulative variance per component (right)

In this case, the first 10 components are able to explain 80% of the total variance. The remaining 25 components have a slighter and slighter impact and could be removed. However, the choice must be always based on the specific context, considering the loss of value induced by the loss of information.

A trick for determining the right number of components is based on the analysis of the eigenvalues of X. After sorting them, it's possible to consider the differences between subsequent values d = $\{\lambda_1 - \lambda_2, \lambda_2 - \lambda_3, ..., \lambda_{n-1} - \lambda_n\}$. The highest difference $\lambda_k - \lambda_{k+1}$ determines the index k of a potential optimal reduction (obviously, it's necessary to consider a constraint on the minimum value, because normally $\lambda_1 - \lambda_2$ is the highest difference). For example, if d = {4, 4, 3, 0.2, 0.18, 0.05} the original dimensionality is n=6; however, $\lambda_4 - \lambda_5$ is the smallest difference, so, it's reasonable to reduce the dimensionality to $(n + 1) - k = 3$. The reason is straightforward, the eigenvalues determine the magnitude of each component, but we need a relative measure because the scale changes. In the example, the last three eigenvectors point to directions where the explained variance is negligible when compared to the first three components.

Once we've defined the transformation matrix A_k, it's possible to perform the actual projection of the original vectors in the new subspace, through the relation:

$$\bar{z} = A_k^T \bar{x} \;\; where \;\; \bar{z} \in \mathbb{R}^{k \times 1}, A_k^T \in \mathbb{R}^{n \times k} \;\; and \; \bar{x} \in \mathbb{R}^{n \times 1}$$

The complete transformation of the whole dataset is simply obtained as follows:

$$Z = XA_k = U_k \Lambda_k$$

Now, let's analyze the new covariance matrix $E[Z^T Z]$. If the original distribution $p_{data}\, x \sim N(0, \Sigma)$, $p(z)$ will also be Gaussian with mean and covariance:

$$\mu_z = E[Z] = A^T E[X] = 0$$
$$\Sigma_z = E[Z^T Z] = A^T E[X^T X] A = A^T \Sigma A = A^T V \Omega V^T A$$

We know that Σ is orthogonal; therefore, $v_i \bullet v_j = 0$ if $i \neq j$. If we analyze the term $A^T V$, we get the following:

$$A^T V = \begin{pmatrix} \bar{v}_1 \\ \bar{v}_2 \\ \vdots \\ \bar{v}_k \end{pmatrix} \begin{pmatrix} \bar{v}_1 & \bar{v}_2 & \cdots & \bar{v}_n \end{pmatrix} =$$

$$= \begin{pmatrix} \bar{v}_1 \cdot \bar{v}_1 & \bar{v}_1 \cdot \bar{v}_2 & \cdots & \bar{v}_1 \cdot \bar{v}_n \\ \bar{v}_2 \cdot \bar{v}_1 & \bar{v}_2 \cdot \bar{v}_2 & \cdots & \bar{v}_2 \cdot \bar{v}_n \\ \vdots & \vdots & \ddots & \vdots \\ \bar{v}_k \cdot \bar{v}_1 & \bar{v}_k \cdot \bar{v}_2 & \cdots & \bar{v}_k \cdot \bar{v}_n \end{pmatrix} = \begin{pmatrix} \bar{v}_1 \cdot \bar{v}_1 & 0 & 0 & 0 & \cdots & 0 \\ \vdots & \vdots & \vdots & \vdots & \cdots & 0 \\ 0 & 0 & \bar{v}_k \cdot \bar{v}_k & 0 & \cdots & 0 \end{pmatrix}$$

Considering that Ω is diagonal, the resulting matrix Σ_z will be diagonal as well. This means that the PCA decorrelates the transformed covariance matrix. At the same time, we can state that every algorithm that decorrelates the input covariance matrix performs a PCA (with or without dimensionality reduction). For example, the *whitening process* is a particular PCA without dimensionality reduction, while Isomap (see `Chapter 3`, *Graph-Based Semi-Supervised Learning*) performs the same operation working with the Gram matrix with a more geometric approach. This result will be used in `Chapter 6`, *Hebbian Learning*, to show how some particular neural networks can perform a PCA without eigen decomposing Σ.

Let's now consider a FA with homoscedastic noise. We have seen that the covariance matrix of the conditional distribution, $p(X|Z; \theta)$, is equal to $AA^T + \Omega$. In the case of homoscedastic noise, it becomes $AA^T + \omega I$. For a generic covariance matrix, Σ, it's possible to prove that adding a constant diagonal matrix $(\Sigma + aI)$ doesn't modify the original eigenvectors and shifts the eigenvalues by the same quantity:

$$\Sigma + aI = V\Psi V^T + aI = V\Psi V^T + aVIV^T = V(\Psi + aI)V^T$$

Therefore, we can consider the generic case of absence of noise without loss of generality. We know that the goal of FA (with $\Omega = (0)$) is finding the matrix, A, so that $AA^T \approx Q$ (the input covariance). Hence, thanks to the symmetry and imposing the asymptotic equality, we can write the following:

$$A_\infty A_\infty^T = Q \Rightarrow A_\infty A_\infty^T = V\Omega V^T = \left(V\left(\Omega^{\frac{1}{2}}\right)\left(\Omega^{\frac{1}{2}}\right)^T V^T \right) \Rightarrow A_\infty = V\Omega^{\frac{1}{2}}$$

This result implies that the FA is a more generic (and robust) way to manage the dimensionality reduction in the presence of heteroscedastic noise, and the PCA is a restriction to homoscedastic noise. When a PCA is performed on datasets affected by heteroscedastic noise, the MLE worsens because the different noise components, altering the magnitude of the eigenvalues at different levels, can drive to the selection of eigenvectors that, in the original dataset, explain only a low percentage of the variance (and in a noiseless scenario, it would be normally discarded in favor of more important directions). If you think of the example discussed at the beginning of the previous paragraph, we know that the noise is strongly heteroscedastic, but we don't have any tools to inform the PCA to cope with it and the variance of the first component will be much higher than expected, considering that the two sources are identical. Unfortunately, in a real- life scenario, the noise is correlated and neither a factor nor a PCA can efficiently solve the problem when the noise power is very high. In all those cases, more sophisticated denoising techniques must be employed. Whenever, instead, it's possible to define an approximate diagonal noise covariance matrix, FA is surely more robust and efficient than PCA. The latter should be considered only in noiseless or *quasi*-noiseless scenarios. In both cases, the results can never lead to well-separated features. For this reason, the ICA has been studied and many different strategies have been engineered.

The complete algorithm for the PCA is as follows:

1. Create a matrix $X^{(M \times n)}$ containing all the samples x_i as rows
    1. Eigen decomposition version:
        1. Compute the covariance matrix $\Sigma = [X^T X]$
        2. Eigen decompose $\Sigma = V \Omega V^T$
    2. SVD version:
        1. Compute the SVD on the matrix $X = U \Lambda V^T$
    3. Select the top k eigenvalues (from Ω or Λ) and the corresponding eigenvectors (from V)
    4. Create the matrix A with shape $(n \times k)$, whose columns are the top k eigenvectors (each of them has a shape $(n \times 1)$)
    5. Project the dataset into the low-dimensional space $Z = XA$ (eigen decomposition) or $Z = U\Lambda$ (SVD)

Some packages (such as Scipy, which is the backend for many NumPy function, such as`np.linalg.svd()`) return the matrix V (right singular vectors) already transposed. In this case, it's necessary to use V^T instead of V in step 3 of the algorithm. I suggest always checking the documentation when implementing these kinds of algorithms.

An example of PCA with Scikit-Learn

We can repeat the same experiment made with the FA and heteroscedastic noise to assess the MLE score of the PCA. We are going to use the `PCA` class with the same number of components (`n_components=64`). To achieve the maximum accuracy, we also set the `svd_solver='full'` parameter, to force Scikit-Learn to apply a full SVD instead of the truncated version. In this way, the top eigenvalues are selected only after the decomposition, avoiding the risk of imprecise estimations:

```
from sklearn.decomposition import PCA

pca = PCA(n_components=64, svd_solver='full', random_state=1000)
Xpca = pca.fit_transform(Xh)

print(pca.score(Xh))
-3772.7483580391995
```

The result is not surprising: the MLE is much lower than FA, because of the wrong estimations made due to the heteroscedastic noise. I invite the reader to compare the results with different datasets and noise levels, considering that the training performance of PCA is normally higher than FA. Therefore, when working with large datasets, a good trade-off is surely desirable. As with FA, it's possible to retrieve the components through the `components_` instance variable.

It's interesting to check the total explained variance (as a fraction of the total input variance) through the component-wise instance array `explained_variance_ratio_`:

```
print(np.sum(pca.explained_variance_ratio_))
0.862522337381
```

With 64 components, we are explaining 86% of the total input variance. Of course, it's also useful to compare the explained variance using a plot:

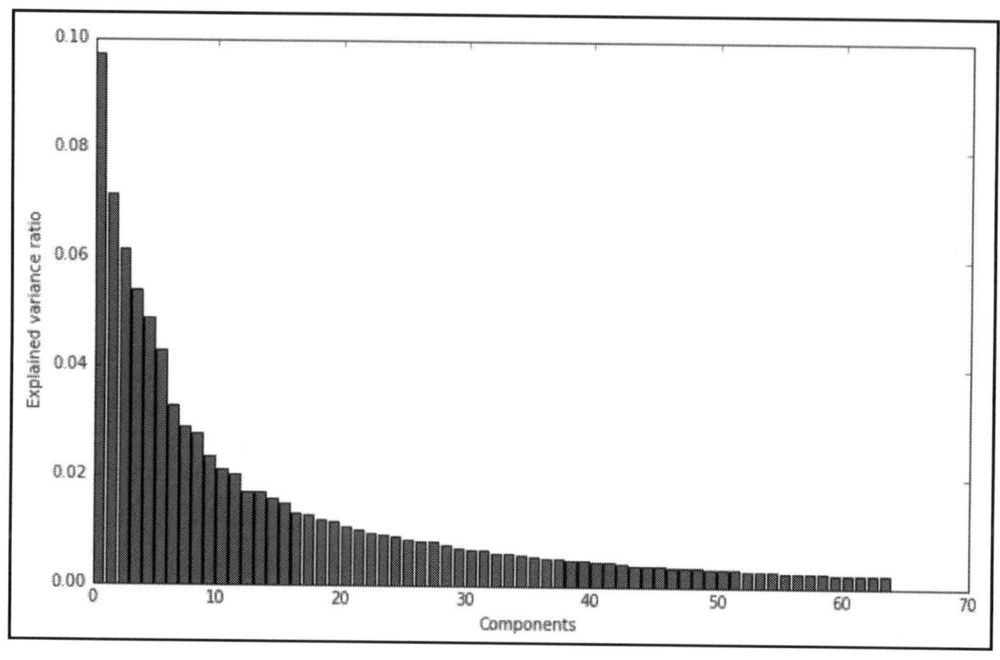

As usual, the first components explain the largest part of the variance; however, after about the twentieth component, each contribution becomes lower than 1% (decreasing till about 0%). This analysis suggests two observations: it's possible to further reduce the number of components with an acceptable loss (using the previous snippet, it's easy to extend the sum only the first *n* components and compare the results) and, at the same time, the PCA will be able to overcome a higher threshold (such as 95%) only by adding a large number of new components. In this particular case, we know that the dataset is made up of handwritten digits; therefore, we can suppose that the tail is due to secondary differences (a line slightly longer than average, a marked stroke, and so on); hence, we can drop all the components with n > 64 (or less) without problems (it's also easy to verify visually a rebuilt image using the `inverse_transform()` method). However, it is always best practice to perform a complete analysis before moving on to further processing steps, particularly when the dimensionality of X is high.

Another interesting approach to determine the optimal number of components has been proposed by Minka (*Automatic Choice of Dimensionality for PCA, Minka T.P., NIPS* 2000") and it's based on the Bayesian model selection. The idea is to use the MLE to optimize the likelihood *p(X|k)* where k is a parameter indicating the number of components. In other words, it doesn't start analyzing the explained variance, but determines a value of $k < n$ so that the likelihood keeps being the highest possible (implicitly, k will explain the maximum possible variance under the constraint of $max(k) = k_{max}$). The theoretical foundation (with tedious mathematical derivations) of the method is presented in the previously mentioned paper however, it's possible to use this method with Scikit-Learn by setting the `n_components='mle'` and `svd_solver='full'` parameters.

Independent component analysis

We have seen that the factors extracted by a PCA are decorrelated, but not independent. A classic example is the *cocktail party:* we have a recording of many overlapped voices and we would like to separate them. Every single voice can be modeled as a random process and it's possible to assume that they are statistically independent (this means that the joint probability can be factorized using the marginal probabilities of each source). Using FA or PCA, we are able to find uncorrelated factors, but there's no way to assess whether they are also independent (normally, they aren't). In this section, we are going to study a model that is able to produce sparse representations (when the dictionary isn't under-complete) with a set of statistically independent components.

Let's assume we have a zero-centered and whitened dataset X sampled from *N(0, I)* and noiseless linear transformation:

$$\bar{x} = A\bar{z} \;\; where \;\; x \sim N(0, I) \;\; and \;\; p(\bar{z};\theta) = \alpha \prod_k e^{f_k(\bar{z})}$$

In this case, the prior over, z, is modeled as a product of independent variables (α is the normalization factor), each of them represented as a generic exponential where the function $f_k(z)$ must be non-quadratic, that is, $p(z; \theta)$ cannot be Gaussian. Furthermore, we assume that the variance of z_i is equal to 1, therefore, $p(x|z; \theta) \sim N(Az, AA^T)$. The joint probability $p(X, z; \theta) = p(X|z; \theta)p(z|\theta)$ is equal to the following:

$$p(X, z; \theta) = \left(\prod_{i=1}^{M} \frac{1}{\sqrt{(2\pi)^n det(AA^T)}} e^{-\frac{1}{2}(\bar{x}_i - A\bar{z})^T (AA^T)^{-1} (\bar{x}_i - A\bar{z})}\right) \left(\alpha \prod_k e^{f_k(\bar{z})}\right)$$

If X has been whitened, A is orthogonal (the proof is straightforward); hence, the previous expression can be simplified. However, applying the EM algorithm requires determining $p(z|X; \theta)$ and this is quite difficult. The process could be easier after choosing a suitable prior distribution for z, that is, $f_k(z)$, but as we discussed at the beginning of the chapter, this assumption can have dramatic consequences if the real factors are distributed differently. For these reasons, other strategies have been studied.

The main concept that we need to enforce is having a non-Gaussian distribution of the factors. In particular, we'd like to have a peaked distribution (inducing sparseness) with heavy tails. From the theory, we know that the standardized fourth moment (also called *Kurtosis*) is a perfect measure:

$$Kurt(X) = E_{x \sim X}\left[\left(\frac{x - \mu_x}{\sigma_x}\right)^4\right]$$

For a Gaussian distribution, $Kurt[X]$ is equal to three (which is often considered as the reference point, determining the so called *Excess Kurtosis = Kurtosis - 3*), while it's larger for a family of distributions, called *Leptokurtotic* or super-Gaussian, which are peaked and heavy-tailed (also, the distributions with $Kurt[X] < 3$, called *Platykurtotic* or sub-Gaussian, can be good candidates, but they are less peaked and normally only the super-Gaussian distributions are taken into account). However, even if accurate, this measure is very sensitive to outliers because of the fourth power. For example, if $x \sim N(0, 1)$ and $z = x + v$, where v is a noise term that alters a few samples, increasing their value to two, the result can be a super-Gaussian ($Kurt[x] > 3$) even if, after filtering the outliers out, the distribution has $Kurt[x] = 3$ *(Gaussian)*.

To overcome this problem, Hyvärinen and Oja (*Independent Component Analysis: Algorithms and Applications, Hyvarinen A., Oja E.,* Neural Networks 13/2000) proposed a solution based on another measure, the *negentropy*. We know that the entropy is proportional to the variance and, given the variance, the Gaussian distribution has the maximum entropy (for further information, read *Mathematical Foundations of Information Theory, Khinchin A. I., Dover Publications*); therefore, we can define the measure:

$$H_N(X) = H\left(X_{\bar{x} \sim N(0,\Sigma)}\right) - H(X)$$

Formally, the negentropy of X is the difference between the entropy of a Gaussian distribution with the same covariance and the entropy of X (we are assuming both zero-centered). It's immediately possible to understand that $H_N(X) \geq 0$, hence the only way to maximize it is by reducing $H(X)$. In this way, X becomes less random, concentrating the probability around the mean (in other words, it becomes super-Gaussian). However, the previous expression cannot be easily adapted to closed-form solutions, because $H(X)$ needs to be computed over all the distribution of X, which must be estimated. For this reason, the same authors proposed an approximation based on non-quadratic functions (remember that in the context of ICA, a quadratic function can be never be employed because it would lead to a Gaussian distribution) that is useful to derive a fixed-point iterative algorithm called *FastICA* (indeed, it's really faster than EM).

Using k functions $f_k(x)$, the approximation becomes as follows:

$$H_N(X) \approx \sum_{i=1}^{k} \alpha_i \left(E[f_i(\bar{x})] - E[f_i(\bar{n})]\right)^2 \quad where \ \bar{n} \sim N(0, I) \ and \ \alpha_i > 0$$

In many real-life scenarios, a single function is enough to achieve a reasonable accuracy and one of the most common choices for f(x) is as follows:

$$f(x) = \frac{1}{a} log(cosh(ax)) = \frac{1}{a} log \frac{e^{ax} + e^{-ax}}{2}$$

In the aforementioned paper, the reader can find some alternatives that can be employed when this function fails in forcing statistical independence between components.

If we invert the model, we get $z = Wx$ with $W = A^{-1}$; therefore, considering a single sample, the approximation becomes as follows:

$$H_N(X) \approx \left(E[f(\bar{w}^T\bar{x})] - E[f(\bar{n})]\right)^2 \ where \ \bar{n} \sim N(0, I)$$

Clearly, the second term doesn't depend on w (in fact, it's only a reference) and can be excluded from the optimization. Moreover, considering the initial assumptions, $E[Z^TZ]=W\,E[X^TX]\,W^T = I$, therefore $WW^T = I$, *i.e.* $||w||^2 = 1$. Hence, our goal is to find the following:

$$\bar{w}_{opt} = argmax_{\bar{w}}\ E[f(\bar{w}^T\bar{x})]^2 \ \ subject\ to\ \ \|\bar{w}\|^2 = 1$$

In this way, we are forcing the matrix W to transform the input vector x, so that z has the lowest possible entropy; therefore, it's super-Gaussian. The maximization process is based on convex optimization techniques that are beyond the scope of this book (the reader can find all the details of Lagrange theorems in *Luenberger D. G., Optimization by Vector Space Methods, Wiley*); therefore, we directly provide the iterative step that must be performed:

$$w_{t+1} = E\left[\bar{x}f'(\bar{w}_t^T\bar{x})\right] - E\left[f''(\bar{w}_t^T\bar{x})\right]\bar{w}_t$$

Of course, to ensure $||w||^2 = 1$, after each step, the weight vector w must be normalized $(w_{t+1} = w_{t+1} / ||w_{t+1}||)$.

In a more general context, the matrix W contains more than one weight vector and, if we apply the previous rule to find out the independent factors, it can happen that some elements, w_i^Tx, are correlated. A strategy to avoid this problem is based on the gram-schmidt orthonormalization process, which decorrelates the components one by one, subtracting the projections of the current component (w_n) onto all the previous ones $(w_1, w_2, \ldots, w_{n-1})$ to w_n. In this way, w_n is forced to be orthogonal to all the other components.

Even if this method is simple and doesn't require much effort, it's preferable a global approach that can work directly with the matrix W at the end of an iteration (so that the order of the weights is not fixed). As explained in *Fast and robust fixedpoint algorithms for independent component analysis, Hyvarinen A., IEEE Transactions on Neural Networks* this result can be achieved with a simple sub-algorithm that we are including in the final *FastICA* algorithm:

1. Set random initial values for W_0
2. Set a threshold Thr (for example 0.001)
    1. Independent component extraction
    2. For each w in W:
        1. While $||w_{t+1} - w_t|| > Thr$:
            1. Compute $w_{t+1} = E[x \cdot f(w_t^T x)] - E[f'(w_t^T x)] w_t$
            2. $w_{t+1} = w_{t+1} / ||w_{t+1}||$
    3. Orthonormalization
    4. While $||W_{t+1} - W_t||_F > Thr$:
        1. $W_t = W_t / sqrt(||W_t W_t^T||)$
        2. $W_{t+1} = (3/2)W_t - (1/2)WW^T W$

This process can be also iterated for a fixed number of times, but the best approach is based on using both a threshold and a maximum number of iterations.

An example of FastICA with Scikit-Learn

Using the same dataset, we can now test the performance of the ICA. However, in this case, as explained, we need to zero-center and whiten the dataset, but fortunately these preprocessing steps are done by the Scikit-Learn implementation (if the parameter `whiten=True` is omitted).

To perform the ICA on the MNIST dataset, we're going to instantiate the `FastICA` class, passing the arguments `n_components=64` and the maximum number of iterations `max_iter=5000`. It's also possible to specify which function will be used to approximate the negentropy; however, the default is *log cosh(x)*, which is normally a good choice:

```
from sklearn.decomposition import FastICA

fastica = FastICA(n_components=64, max_iter=5000, random_state=1000)
fastica.fit(X)
```

At this point, we can visualize the components (which are always available through the `components_` instance variance):

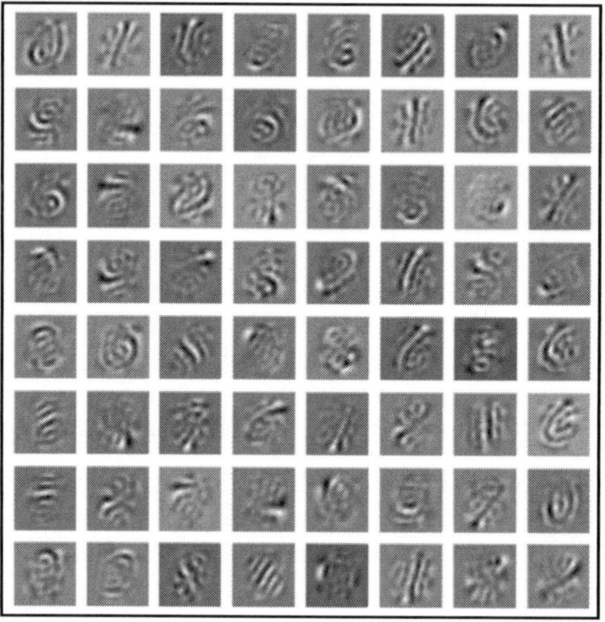

Independent components of the MNIST dataset extracted by the FastICA algorithm (64 components)

There are still some redundancies (the reader can try to increase the number of components) and background noise; however, it's now possible to distinguish some low-level features (such as oriented stripes) that are common to many digits. This representation isn't very sparse yet. In fact, we're always using 64 components (like for FA and PCA); therefore, the dictionary is under-complete (the input dimensionality is 28 × 28 = 784). To see the difference, we can repeat the experiment with a dictionary ten times larger, setting `n_components=640`:

```
fastica = FastICA(n_components=640, max_iter=5000, random_state=1000)
fastica.fit(Xs)
```

A subset of the new components (100) is shown in the following screenshot:

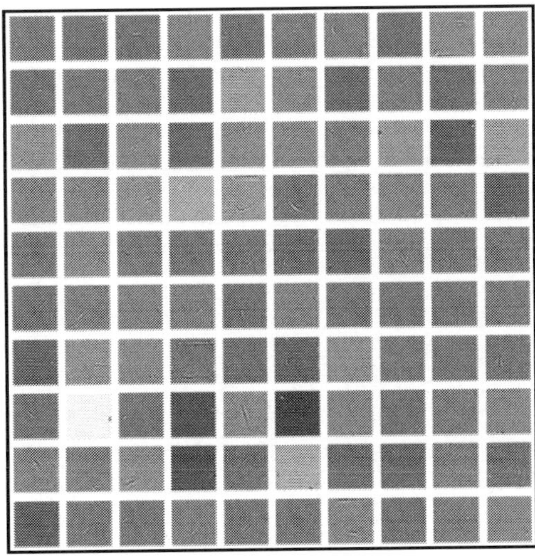

Independent components of the MNIST dataset extracted by the FastICA algorithm (640 components)

The structure of these components is almost elementary. They represent oriented stripes and positional dots. To check how an input is rebuilt, we can consider the mixing matrix *A* (which is available as the `mixing_` instance variable). Considering the first input sample, we can check how many factors have a weight less than half of the average:

```
M = fastica.mixing_
M0 = M[0] / np.max(M[0])

print(len(M0[np.abs(M0) < (np.mean(np.abs(M0)) / 2.0)]))
233
```

The sample is rebuilt using approximately 410 components. The level of sparsity is higher, but considering the granularity of the factors, it's easy to understand that many of them are needed to rebuild even a single structure (like the image of a 1) where long lines are present. However, this is not a drawback because, as already mentioned, the main goal of the ICA is to extract independent components. Considering an analogy with the *cocktail party* example, we could deduce that each component represents a phoneme, not the complete sound of a word or a sentence.

The reader can test a different number of components and compare the results with the ones achieved by other sparse coding algorithms (such as Dictionary Learning or Sparse PCA).

Addendum to HMMs

In the previous chapter, we discussed how it's possible to train a HMM using the forward-backward algorithm and we have seen that it is a particular application of the EM algorithm. The reader can now understand the internal dynamic in terms of E and M steps. In fact, the procedure starts with randomly initialized A and B matrices and proceeds in an alternating manner:

- **E-Step**:
    - The estimation of the probability α^t_{ij} that the HMM is in the state *i* at time *t* and in the state *j* at time *t+1* given the observations and the current parameter estimations (A and B)
    - The estimation of the probability β^t_i that the HMM is in the state *i* at time *t* given the observations and the current parameter estimations (A and B)
- **M-Step**:
    - Computing the new estimation for the transition probabilities a_{ij} *(A)* and for the emission probabilities b_{ip} *(B)*

The procedure is repeated until the convergence is reached. Even if there's no explicit definition of a Q function, the E-step determines a split expression for the expected complete data likelihood of the model given the observations (using both the Forward and Backward algorithms), while the M-Step corrects parameters A and B to maximize this likelihood.

Summary

In this chapter, we presented the EM algorithm, explaining the reasons that justify its application in many statistical learning contexts. We also discussed the fundamental role of hidden (latent) variables, in order to derive an expression that is easier to maximize (the Q function).

We applied the EM algorithm to solve a simple parameter estimation problem and afterward to prove the Gaussian Mixture estimation formulas. We showed how it's possible to employ the Scikit-Learn implementation instead of writing the whole procedure from scratch (like in `Chapter 2`, *Introduction to Semi-Supervised Learning*).

Afterward, we analyzed three different approaches to component extraction. FA assumes that we have a small number of Gaussian latent variables and a Gaussian decorrelated noise term. The only restriction on the noise is to have a diagonal covariance matrix, so two different scenarios are possible. When we are in the presence of heteroscedastic noise, the process is an actual FA. When, instead, the noise is homoscedastic, the algorithm becomes the equivalent of a PCA. In this case, the process is equivalent to check the sample space in order to find the directions where the variance is higher. Selecting only the most important directions, we can project the original dataset onto a low-dimensional subspace, where the covariance matrix becomes decorrelated.

One of the problems of both FA and PCA is their assumption to model the latent variables with Gaussian distributions. This choice simplifies the model, but at the same time, yields dense representations where the single components are statistically dependent. For this reason, we have investigated how it's possible to force the factor distribution to become sparse. The resulting algorithm, which is generally faster and more accurate than the MLE, is called FastICA and its goal is to extract a set of statistically independent components with the maximization of an approximation of the negentropy.

In the end, we provided a brief explanation of the HMM forward-backward algorithm (discussed in the previous chapter) considering the subdivision into E and M steps. Other EM-specific applications will be discussed in the next chapters.

In the next chapter, we are going to introduce the fundamental concepts of Hebbian learning and self-organizing maps, which are still very useful to solve many specific problems, such as principal component extraction, and have a strong neurophysiological foundation.

6
Hebbian Learning and Self-Organizing Maps

In this chapter, we're going to introduce the concept of Hebbian learning, based on the methods defined by the psychologist Donald Hebb. These theories immediately showed how a very simple biological law is able to describe the behavior of multiple neurons in achieving complex goals and was a pioneering strategy that linked the research activities in the fields of artificial intelligence and computational neurosciences.

In particular, we are going to discuss the following topics:

- The Hebb rule for a single neuron, which is a simple but biologically plausible behavioral law
- Some variants that have been introduced to overcome a few stability problems
- The final result achieved by a Hebbian neuron, which consists of computing the first principal component of the input dataset
- Two neural network models (Sanger's network and Rubner-Tavan's network) that can extract a generic number of principal components
- The concept of **Self-Organizing Maps (SOMs)** with a focus on the Kohonen Networks

Hebb's rule

Hebb's rule has been proposed as a conjecture in 1949 by the Canadian psychologist Donald Hebb to describe the synaptic plasticity of natural neurons. A few years after its publication, this rule was confirmed by neurophysiological studies, and many research studies have shown its validity in many application, of Artificial Intelligence. Before introducing the rule, it's useful to describe the generic Hebbian neuron, as shown in the following diagram:

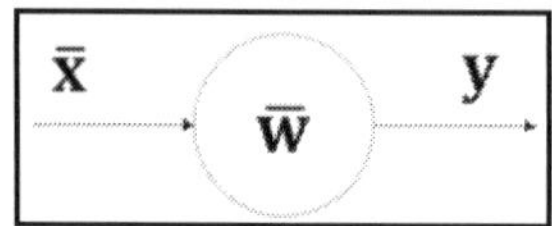

Generic Hebbian neuron with a vectorial input

The neuron is a simple computational unit that receives an input vector *x*, from the pre-synaptic units (other neurons or perceptive systems) and outputs a single scalar value, *y*. The internal structure of the neuron is represented by a weight vector, *w*, that models the strength of each synapse. For a single multi-dimensional input, the output is obtained as follows:

$$y = \bar{w} \cdot \bar{x}$$

In this model, we are assuming that each input signal is encoded in the corresponding component of the vector, *x*; therefore, x_i is processed by the synaptic weight $w_{i,}$ and so on. In the original version of Hebb's theory, the input vectors represent neural firing rates, which are always non-negative. This means that the synaptic weights can only be strengthened (the neuroscientific term for this phenomenon is **long-term potentiation** (LTP)). However, for our purposes, we assume that *x* is a real-valued vector, as is *w*. This condition allows modeling more artificial scenarios without a loss of generality.

The same operation performed on a single vector holds when it's necessary to process many input samples organized in a matrix. If we have *N* m-dimensional input vectors, the formula becomes as follows:

$$\bar{y} = X\bar{w} \;\; where \; X \in \mathbb{R}^{N \times m}, \; \bar{w} \in \mathbb{R}^m \; and \; \bar{y} \in \mathbb{R}^N$$

The basic form of Hebb's rule in a discrete form can be expressed (for a single input) as follows:

$$\Delta\bar{w} = \eta y\bar{x} = \eta(\bar{x} \cdot \bar{w})\bar{x}$$

The weight correction is hence a vector that has the same orientation of x and magnitude equal to $|x|$ multiplied by a positive parameter, η, which is called the learning rate and the corresponding output, y (which can have either a positive or a negative sign). The sense of Δw is determined by the sign of y; therefore, under the assumption that x and y are real values, two different scenarios arise from this rule:

- If $x_i > 0$ (< 0) and $y > 0$ (< 0), w_i is strengthened
- If $x_i > 0$ (< 0) and $y < 0$ (> 0), w_i is weakened

It's easy to understand this behavior considering two-dimensional vectors:

$$sign(y) = sign(\bar{w} \cdot \bar{x}) = sign(|w|\,|x|\,cos(\alpha))$$

Therefore, if the initial angle α between w and x is less than 90°, w will have the same orientation of x and viceversa if α is greater than 90°. In the following diagram, there's a schematic representation of this process:

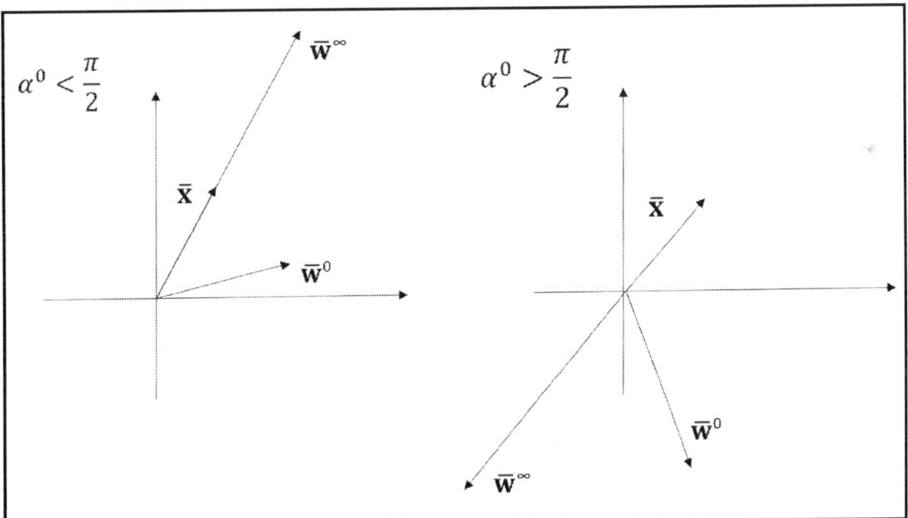

Vectorial analysis of Hebb's rule

It's possible to simulate this behavior using a very simple Python snippet. Let's start with a scenario where α is less than 90° and 50 iterations:

```
import numpy as np

w = np.array([1.0, 0.2])
x = np.array([0.1, 0.5])
alpha = 0.0

for i in range(50):
    y = np.dot(w, x.T)
    w += x*y
    alpha = np.arccos(np.dot(w, x.T) / (np.linalg.norm(w) *
np.linalg.norm(x)))

print(w)
[  8028.48942243  40137.64711215]

print(alpha * 180.0 / np.pi)
0.00131766983584
```

As expected, the final angle, α, is close to zero and w has the same orientation and sense of x. We can now repeat the experiment with α greater than 90° (we change only the value of w because the procedure is the same):

```
w = np.array([1.0, -1.0])

...

print(w)
[-16053.97884486 -80275.89422431]

print(alpha * 180.0 / np.pi)
179.999176456
```

In this case, the final angle, α, is about 180° and, of course, w has the opposite sense with respect to x.

The scientist S. Löwel expressed this concept with the famous sentence:

> *"Neurons that fire together wire together"*

We can re-express this concept (adapting it to a machine learning scenario) by saying that the main assumption of this approach is based on the idea that when pre- and post-synaptic units are coherent (their signals have the same sign), the connection between neurons becomes stronger and stronger. On the other side, if they are discordant, the corresponding synaptic weight is decreased. For the sake of precision, if x is a spiking rate, it should be represented as a real function $x(t)$ as well as $y(t)$. According to the original Hebbian theory, the discrete equation must be replaced by a differential equation:

$$\frac{d\bar{w}}{dt} = \eta y \bar{x}$$

If $x(t)$ and $y(t)$ have the same fire rate, the synaptic weight is strengthened proportionally to the product of both rates. If instead there's a relatively long delay between the pre-synaptic activity $x(t)$ and the post-synaptic one $y(t)$, the corresponding weight is weakened. This is a more biologically plausible explanation of the relation *fire together → wire together*.

However, even if the theory has a strong neurophysiological basis, some modifications are necessary. In fact, it's easy to understand that the resulting system is always unstable. If two inputs are repeatedly applied (both real values and firing rates), the norm of the vector, w, grows indefinitely and this isn't a plausible assumption for a biological system. In fact, if we consider a discrete iteration step, we have the following equation:

$$\bar{w}_{k+1} = \bar{w}_k + \eta(\bar{w}_k \cdot \bar{x})\bar{x} \Rightarrow \bar{w}_{k+1} \cdot \bar{x} = \bar{w}_k \cdot \bar{x} + \eta(\bar{w}_k \cdot \bar{x})\bar{x} \cdot \bar{x} \Rightarrow y_{k+1} = y_k(1 + \eta|\bar{x}|^2)$$

The previous output, $y_{k,}$ is always multiplied by a factor greater than 1 (except in the case of null input), therefore it grows without a bound. As $y = w \cdot x$, this condition implies that the magnitude of w increases (or remains constant if the magnitude of x is null) at each iteration (a more rigorous proof can be easily obtained considering the original differential equation).

Such a situation is not only biologically unacceptable, but it's also necessary to properly manage it in machine learning problems in order to avoid a numerical overflow after a few iterations. In the next paragraph, we're going to discuss some common methods to overcome this issue. For now, we can continue our analysis without introducing a correction factor.

Let's now consider a dataset, X:

$$X = \{\bar{x}_1, \bar{x}_2, \ldots, \bar{x}_N\} \; where \; \bar{x}_i \in \mathbb{R}^m$$

We can apply the rule iteratively to all elements, but it's easier (and more useful) to average the weight modifications over the input samples (the index now refers to the whole specific vector, not to the single components):

$$\Delta\bar{w} = \frac{\eta}{N}\sum_{i=1}^{N} y_i \bar{x}_i = \frac{\eta}{N}\sum_{i=1}^{N}(\bar{w}\cdot\bar{x}_i)\bar{x}_i = \frac{\eta}{N}\sum_{i=1}^{N}(\bar{x}_i^T\cdot\bar{x}_i)\bar{w} = \eta C\bar{w}$$

In the previous formula, C is the input correlation matrix:

$$C = \begin{pmatrix} \frac{1}{N}\sum_i x_1^i x_1^i & \cdots & \frac{1}{N}\sum_i x_1^i x_m^i \\ \vdots & \ddots & \vdots \\ \frac{1}{N}\sum_i x_m^i x_1^i & \cdots & \frac{1}{N}\sum_i x_m^i x_m^i \end{pmatrix} = \frac{1}{N}X^T X$$

For our purposes, however, it's useful to consider a slightly different Hebbian rule based on a threshold θ for the input vector (there's also a biological reason that justifies this choice, but it's beyond the scope of this book; the reader who is interested can find it in *Theoretical Neuroscience, Dayan P., Abbott F. L., The MIT Press*).

It's easy to understand that in the original theory where $x(t)$ and $y(t)$ are firing rates, this modification allows a phenomenon opposite to LTP and called **long-term depression** (**LTD**). In fact, when $x(t) < \theta$ and $y(t)$ is positive, the product $(x(t) - \theta)y(t)$ is negative and the synaptic weight is weakened.

If we set $\theta = \langle x \rangle \approx E[X]$, we can derive an expression very similar to the previous one, but based on the input covariance matrix (unbiased through the Bessel's correction):

$$\Delta\bar{w} = \frac{\eta}{N-1}\sum_{i=1}^{N} y_i(\bar{x}_i - \langle\bar{x}\rangle) = \frac{\eta}{N-1}\sum_{i=1}^{N}(\bar{w}\cdot(\bar{x}_i - \langle\bar{x}\rangle))(\bar{x}_i - \langle\bar{x}\rangle) =$$

$$= \frac{\eta}{N-1}\sum_{i=1}^{N}(\bar{x}_i - \langle\bar{x}\rangle)^T(\bar{x}_i - \langle\bar{x}\rangle)\bar{w} = \eta\Sigma\bar{w}$$

For obvious reasons, this variant of the original Hebb's rule is called the **covariance rule**.

It's also possible to use the **Maximum Likelihood Estimation** (**MLE**) (or biased) covariance matrix (dividing by *N*), but it's important to check which version is adopted by the mathematical package that is employed. When using NumPy, it's possible to decide the version using the `np.cov()` function and setting the `bias=True/False` parameter (the default value is `False`). However, when $N >> 1$, the difference between versions decreases and can often be discarded. In this book, we'll use the unbiased version. The reader who wants to see further details about the Bessel's correction can read *Applied Statistics, Warner R., SAGE Publications*.

Analysis of the covariance rule

The covariance matrix Σ is real and symmetric. If we apply the eigendecomposition, we get (for our purposes it's more useful to keep V^{-1} instead of the simplified version V^T):

$$\Sigma = V\Omega V^{-1}$$

V is an orthogonal matrix (thanks to the fact that Σ is symmetric) containing the eigenvectors of Σ (as columns), while Ω is a diagonal matrix containing the eigenvalues. Let's suppose we sort both eigenvalues ($\lambda_1, \lambda_2, ..., \lambda_m$) and the corresponding eigenvectors ($v_1, v_2, ..., v_m$) so that:

$$\lambda_1 > \lambda_2 > \ldots > \lambda_m$$

Moreover, let's suppose that λ_1 is dominant over all the other eigenvalues (it's enough that $\lambda_1 > \lambda_i$ with $i \neq 1$). As the eigenvectors are orthogonal, they constitute a basis and it's possible to express the vector w, with a linear combination of the eigenvectors:

$$\bar{w} = u_1\bar{v}_1 + u_2\bar{v}_2 + \ldots + u_m\bar{v}_m = V\bar{u}$$

The vector u contains the coordinates in the new basis. Let's now consider the modification to the covariance rule:

$$\Delta\bar{w} = \eta\Sigma\bar{w} = \eta V\Omega V^{-1}V\bar{u} = \eta\Sigma\bar{w} = \eta V\Omega\bar{u}$$

If we apply the rule iteratively, we get a matrix polynomial:

$$
\begin{gathered}
\bar{w}^{(0)} \\
\bar{w}^{(1)} = \bar{w}^{(0)} + \eta\Sigma\bar{w}^{(0)} \\
\bar{w}^{(2)} = \bar{w}^{(1)} + \eta\Sigma\bar{w}^{(1)} = \bar{w}^{(0)} + 2\eta\Sigma\bar{w}^{(0)} + \eta^2\Sigma^2\bar{w}^{(0)} \\
\bar{w}^{(3)} = \bar{w}^{(2)} + \eta\Sigma\bar{w}^{(2)} = \bar{w}^{(0)} + 3\eta\Sigma\bar{w}^{(0)} + 3\eta^2\Sigma^2\bar{w}^{(0)} + \eta^3\Sigma^3\bar{w}^{(0)} \\
\cdots
\end{gathered}
$$

Exploiting the Binomial theorem and considering that $\Sigma^0=I$, we can get a general expression for $w^{(k)}$ as a function of $w^{(0)}$:

$$\bar{w}^{(k)} = \sum_{i=0}^{k} \binom{k}{i} \eta^i \Sigma^i \bar{w}^{(0)}$$

Let's now rewrite the previous formula using the change of basis:

$$\bar{w}^{(k)} = \sum_{i=0}^{k} \binom{k}{i} \eta^i \Sigma^i \bar{w}^{(0)} = \sum_{i=0}^{k} \binom{k}{i} \eta^i V\Omega^i V^{-1} \bar{w}^{(0)} = \sum_{i=0}^{k} \binom{k}{i} \eta^i V\Omega^i \bar{u}^{(0)}$$

The vector $u^{(0)}$ contains the coordinates of $w^{(0)}$ in the new basis; hence, $w^{(k)}$ is expressed as a polynomial where the generic term is proportional to $V\Omega^i u^{(0)}$.

Let's now consider the diagonal matrix Ω^k:

$$\Omega^k = \begin{pmatrix} \lambda_1^k & 0 & 0 \\ \vdots & \ddots & \vdots \\ 0 & 0 & \lambda_m^k \end{pmatrix} \approx \begin{pmatrix} \lambda_1^k & 0 & 0 \\ \vdots & \ddots & \vdots \\ 0 & 0 & 0 \end{pmatrix}$$

The last step derives from the hypothesis that λ_1 is greater than any other eigenvalue and when $k \to \infty$, all $\lambda_{i\neq 1}^k \ll \lambda_1^k$. Of course, if $\lambda_{i\neq 1} > 1$, $\lambda_{i\neq 1}^k$ will grow as well as λ_1^k however, the contribution of the *secondary* eigenvalues to $w^{(k)}$ becomes significantly weaker when $k \to \infty$. Just to understand the validity of this approximation, let's consider the following situation where λ_1 is slightly larger that λ_2:

$$\Omega = \begin{pmatrix} 1.1 & 0 \\ 0 & 1.05 \end{pmatrix} \Rightarrow \Omega^{1000} \approx \begin{pmatrix} 2.5 \cdot 10^{41} & 0 \\ 0 & 1.5 \cdot 10^{21} \end{pmatrix}$$

The result shows a very important property: not only is the approximation correct, but as we're going to show, if an eigenvalue λ_i is larger than all the other ones, the covariance rule will always converge to the corresponding eigenvector v_i. No other stable fixed points exist!

This hypothesis is no more valid if $\lambda_1 = \lambda_2 = ... = \lambda_n$. In this case, the total variance is explained equally by the direction of each eigenvector (a condition that implies a symmetry which isn't very common in real-life scenarios). This situation can also happen when working with finite-precision arithmetic, but in general, if the difference between the largest eigenvalue and the second one is less than the maximum achievable precision (for example, 32-bit floating point), it's plausible to accept the equality.

Of course, we assume that the dataset is not whitened, because our goal (also in the next paragraphs) is to reduce the original dimensionality considering only a subset of components with the highest total variability (the decorrelation, like in **Principal Component Analysis** (**PCA**), must be an outcome of the algorithm, not a precondition). On the other side, zero-centering the dataset could be useful, even if not really necessary for this kind of algorithm.

If we rewrite the expression for w_k considering this approximation, we obtain the following:

$$\bar{w}^{(k)} = \sum_{i=0}^{k} \binom{k}{i} \eta^i V \Omega^i \bar{u}^{(0)} \approx \sum_{i=0}^{k} \binom{k}{i} \eta^i \left((\bar{v}_1\ \bar{v}_2\ \dots\ \bar{v}_m) \begin{pmatrix} \lambda_1^k & 0 & 0 \\ \vdots & \ddots & \vdots \\ 0 & 0 & 0 \end{pmatrix} \begin{pmatrix} u_1^{(0)} \\ \vdots \\ u_m^{(0)} \end{pmatrix} \right) =$$

$$= \left(\sum_{i=0}^{k} \binom{k}{i} \eta^i \lambda_1^i u_1^{(0)} \right) \bar{v}_1$$

As $a_1 v + a_2 v + ... + a_k v \propto v$, this result shows that, when $k \to \infty$, w_k will become proportional to the first eigenvector of the covariance matrix Σ (if $u_1^{(0)}$ is not null) and its magnitude, without normalization, will grow indefinitely. The spurious effect due to the other eigenvalues becomes negligible (above all, if w is divided by its norm, so that the length is always $||w|| = 1$) after a limited number of iterations.

However, before drawing our conclusions, an important condition must be added:

$$\bar{w}^{(0)} \cdot \bar{v}_1 \neq 0$$

In fact, if *w(0)* were orthogonal to *v1*, we would get (the eigenvectors are orthogonal to each other):

$$\begin{aligned}\bar{w}^{(0)} \cdot \bar{v}_1 = u_1^{(0)} \bar{v}_1 \cdot \bar{v}_1 + u_2^{(0)} \bar{v}_2 \cdot \bar{v}_1 + \ldots + u_m^{(0)} \bar{v}_m \cdot \bar{v}_1 = \\ = u_1^{(0)} \bar{v}_1 \cdot \bar{v}_1 = \\ = u_1^{(0)} |\bar{v}_1|^2 = 0 \Rightarrow u_1^{(0)} = 0\end{aligned}$$

This important result shows how a Hebbian neuron working with the covariance rule is able to perform a PCA limited to the first component without the need for eigendecomposing Σ. In fact, the vector *w* (we're not considering the problem of the increasing magnitude, which can be easily managed) will rapidly converge to the orientation where the input dataset *X* has the highest variance. In `Chapter 5`, *EM Algorithm and Applications,* we discussed the details of PCA; in the next paragraph, we're going to discuss a couple of methods to find the first N principal components using a variant of the Hebb's rule.

Example of covariance rule application

Before moving on, let's simulate this behavior with a simple Python example. We first generate `1000` values sampled from a bivariate Gaussian distribution (the variance is voluntarily asymmetric) and then we apply the covariance rule to find the first principal component ($w^{(0)}$ has been chosen so not to be orthogonal to v_1):

```
import numpy as np

rs = np.random.RandomState(1000)
X = rs.normal(loc=1.0, scale=(20.0, 1.0), size=(1000, 2))

w = np.array([30.0, 3.0])

S = np.cov(X.T)

for i in range(10):
    w += np.dot(S, w)
    w /= np.linalg.norm(w)
w *= 50.0
```

```
print(np.round(w, 1))
[ 50.  -0.]
```

The algorithm is straightforward, but there are a couple of elements that we need to comment on. The first one is the normalization of vector w at the end of each iteration. This is one of the techniques needed to avoid the uncontrolled growth of w. The second *tricky* element is the final multiplication, $w \cdot 50$. As we are multiplying by a positive scalar, the direction of w is not impacted, but it's easier to show the vector in the complete plot.

The result is shown in the following diagram:

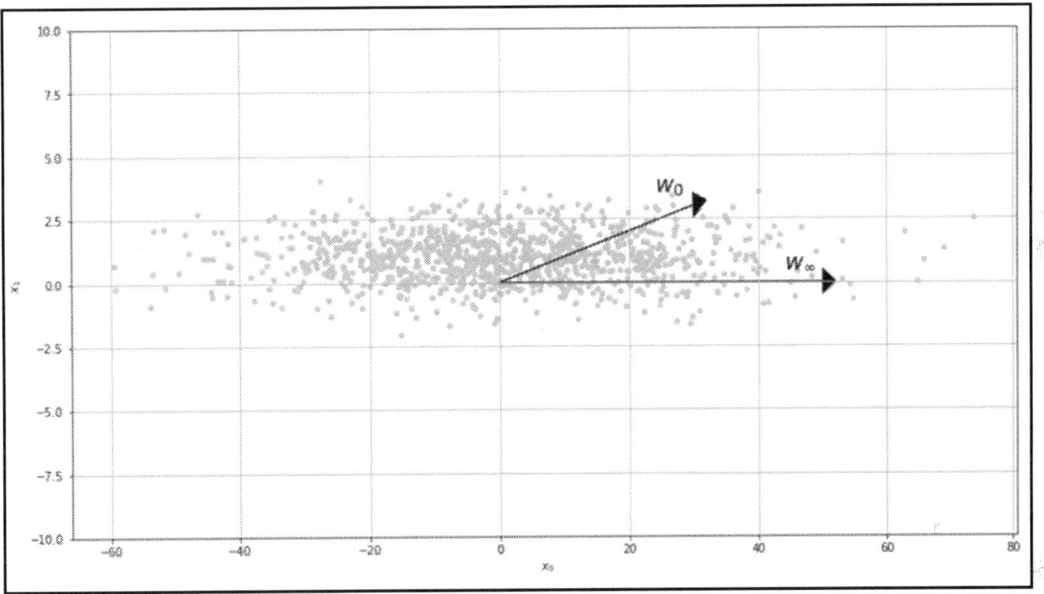

Application of the covariance rule. w_∞ becomes proportional to the first principal component

After a limited number of iterations, w_∞ has the same orientation of the principal eigenvector which is, in this case, parallel to the x axes. The sense depends on the initial value w_0; however, in a PCA, this isn't an important element.

Weight vector stabilization and Oja's rule

The easiest way to stabilize the weight vector is normalizing it after each update. In this way, its length will be always kept equal to one. In fact, in this kind of neural networks we are not interested in the magnitude, but only in the direction (that remains unchanged after the normalization). However, there are two main reasons that discourage this approach:

- It's non-local. To normalize vector w, we need to know all its values and this isn't biologically plausible. A real synaptic weight model should be self-limiting, without the need to have access to external pieces of information that cannot be available.
- The normalization must be performed after having applied the correction and hence needs a double iterative step.

In many machine learning contexts, these conditions are not limiting and they can be freely adopted, but when it's necessary to work with neuroscientific models, it's better to look for other solutions. In a discrete form, we need to determine a correction term for the standard Hebb's rule:

$$\bar{w}_{k+1} - \bar{w}_k = \eta y \bar{x} - f(\bar{w}_k, y_k, \bar{x})$$

The f function can work both as a local and non-local normalizer. An example of the first type is **Oja's rule**:

$$\Delta \bar{w} = \eta y_k \bar{x}_k - \alpha y_k^2 \bar{w}_k$$

The α parameter is a positive number that controls the strength of the normalization. A non-rigorous proof of the stability of this rule can be obtained considering the condition:

$$\Delta \bar{w} \cdot \bar{w} \to 0 \;\;\Rightarrow\;\; y_k(\bar{x} \cdot \bar{w}) - \alpha y_k^2 (\bar{w} \cdot \bar{w}) \to 0$$

The second expression implies that:

$$y_k^2 (1 - \alpha |\bar{w}|^2) \to 0 \;\;\Rightarrow\;\; |\bar{w}|^2 \to \frac{1}{\alpha}$$

Therefore, when $t \to \infty$, the magnitude of the weight correction becomes close to zero and the length of the weight vector w will approach a finite limit value:

$$\lim_{k \to \infty} |\bar{w}_k| = \frac{1}{\sqrt{\alpha}}$$

Sanger's network

A **Sanger's network** is a neural network model for online *Principal Component* extraction proposed by T. D. Sanger in *Optimal Unsupervised Learning in a Single-Layer Linear Feedforward Neural Network, Sanger T. D., Neural Networks, 1989/2*. The author started with the standard version of Hebb's rule and modified it to be able to extract a variable number of principal components ($v_1, v_2, ..., v_m$) in descending order ($\lambda_1 > \lambda_2 > ... > \lambda_m$). The resulting approach, which is a natural extension of Oja's rule, has been called the **Generalized Hebbian Rule** (**GHA**) (or Learning). The structure of the network is represented in the following diagram:

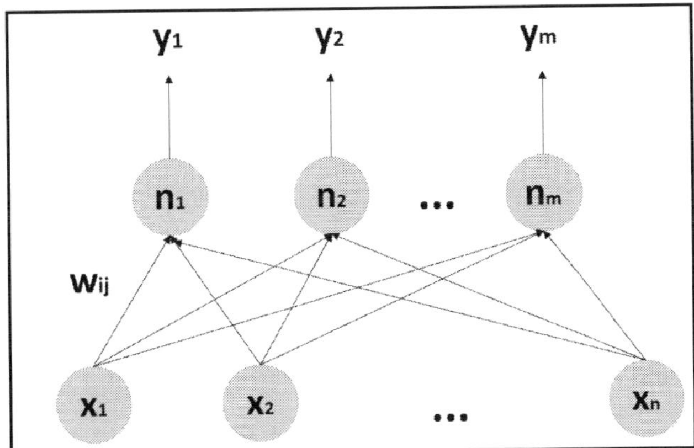

The network is fed with samples extracted from an n-dimensional dataset:

$$X = \{\bar{x}_1, \bar{x}_2, \ldots \bar{x}_N\} \;\; where \;\; \bar{x}_i \in \mathbb{R}^n$$

The m output neurons are connected to the input through a weight matrix, $W = \{w_{ij}\}$, where the first index refers to the input components (pre-synaptic units) and the second one to the neuron. The output of the network can be easily computed with a scalar product; however, in this case, we are not interested in it, because just like for the covariance (and Oja's) rules, the principal components are extracted through the weight updates.

The problem that arose after the formulation of Oja's rule was about the extraction of multiple components. In fact, if we applied the original rule to the previous network, all weight vectors (the rows of w) would converge to the first principal component. The main idea (based on the **Gram-Schmidt** orthonormalization method) to overcome this limitation is based on the observation that once we have extracted the first component w_1, the second one w_2 can be forced to be orthogonal to w_1, the third one w_3 can be forced to be orthogonal to w_1 and w_2, and so on. Consider the following representation:

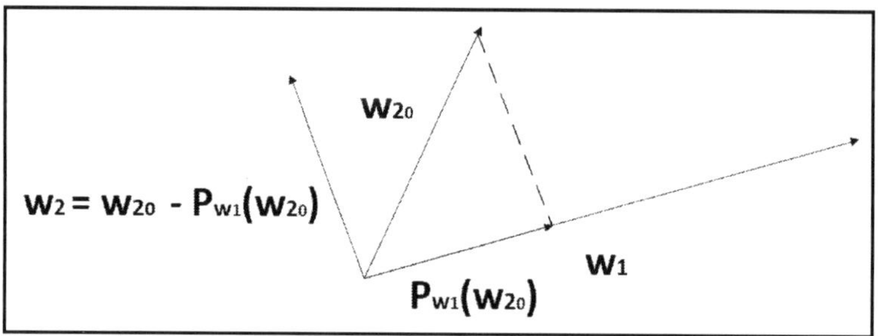

Orthogonalization of two weight vectors

In this case, we are assuming that w_1 is stable and w_{20} is another weight vector that is converging to w_1. The projection of w_{20} onto w_1 is as follows:

$$P_{\bar{w}_1}(\bar{w}_{2_0}) = (\bar{w}_1^T \bar{w}_{2_0}) \frac{\bar{w}_1}{\|\bar{w}_1\|}$$

In the previous formula, we can omit the norm if we don't need to normalize (in the network, this process is done after a complete weight update). The orthogonal component of w_{20} is simply obtained with a difference:

$$\bar{w}_2 = \bar{w}_{2_0} - P_{\bar{w}_1}(\bar{w}_{2_0})$$

Applying this method to the original Oja's rule, we obtain a new expression for the weight update (called Sanger's rule):

$$\Delta w_{ij} = \eta \left(y_i x_j - y_i \sum_{k=1}^{i} w_{kj} y_k \right)$$

The rule is referred to a single input vector x, hence x_j is the jth component of x. The first term is the classic Hebb's rule, which forces weight w to become parallel to the first principal component, while the second one acts in a way similar to the Gram-Schmidt orthogonalization, by subtracting a term proportional to the projection of w onto all the weights connected to the previous post-synaptic units and considering, at the same time, the normalization constraint provided by Oja's rule (which is proportional to the square of the output).

In fact, expanding the last term, we get the following:

$$y_i \sum_{k=1}^{i} w_{kj} y_k = y_i \sum_{k=1}^{i} w_{kj} (\bar{w}_k^T \bar{x}) = (\bar{w}_i^T \bar{x}) \left[w_{1j} (\bar{w}_1^T \bar{x}) + w_{2j} (\bar{w}_2^T \bar{x}) + \ldots + w_{ij} (\bar{w}_i^T \bar{x}) \right]$$

The term subtracted to each component w_{ij} is proportional to all the components where the index j is fixed and the first index is equal to $1, 2, \ldots, i$. This procedure doesn't produce an immediate orthogonalization but requires several iterations to converge. The proof is non-trivial, involving convex optimization and dynamic systems methods, but, it can be found in the aforementioned paper. Sanger showed that the algorithm converges always to the sorted first n principal components (from the largest eigenvalue to the smallest one) if the `learning_rate` $\eta(t)$ decreases monotonically and converges to zero when $t \rightarrow \infty$. Even if necessary for the formal proof, this condition can be relaxed (a stable $\eta < 1$ is normally sufficient). In our implementation, matrix W is normalized after each iteration, so that, at the end of the process, W^T (the weights are in the rows) is orthonormal and constitutes a basis for the eigenvector subspace.

In matrix form, the rule becomes as follows:

$$\Delta W = \eta \left(\bar{y} \bar{x}^T - Tril(\bar{y} \bar{y}^T) W \right)$$

Tril(•) is a matrix function that transforms its argument into a lower-triangular matrix and the term yy^T is equal to $Wxx^T W$.

The algorithm for a Sanger's network is as follows:

1. Initialize $W^{(0)}$ with random values. If the input dimensionality is n and m principal components must be extracted, the shape will be $(m \times n)$.
2. Set a `learning_rate` η (for example, `0.01`).
3. Set a `threshold` Thr (for example, `0.001`).
4. Set a counter $T = 0$.
5. While $||W^{(t)} - W^{(t-1)}||_F > Thr$:
    1. Set $\Delta W = 0$ (same shape of W)
    2. For each x in X:
        1. Set $T = T + 1$
        2. Compute $y = W^{(t)}x$
        3. Compute and accumulate ΔW += $\eta(yx^T - Tril(yy^T)W^{(t)}$
    3. Update $W^{(t+1)} = W^{(t)} + (\eta / T)\Delta W$
    4. Set $W^{(t+1)} = W^{(t+1)} / ||W^{(t+1)}||^{(rows)}$ (the norm must be computed row-wise)

The algorithm can also be iterated a fixed number of times (like in our example), or the two stopping approaches can be used together.

Example of Sanger's network

For this Python example, we consider a bidimensional zero-centered dataset `X` with 500 samples (we are using the function defined in the first chapter). After the initialization of `X`, we also compute the eigendecomposition, to be able to double-check the result:

```
import numpy as np

from sklearn.datasets import make_blobs

X, _ = make_blobs(n_samples=500, centers=2, cluster_std=5.0,
random_state=1000)
Xs = zero_center(X)

Q = np.cov(Xs.T)
eigu, eigv = np.linalg.eig(Q)

print(eigu)
[ 24.5106037   48.99234467]
```

```
print(eigv)
[[-0.75750566 -0.6528286 ]
 [ 0.6528286  -0.75750566]]

n_components = 2

W_sanger = np.random.normal(scale=0.5, size=(n_components,
Xs.shape[1]))
W_sanger /= np.linalg.norm(W_sanger, axis=1).reshape((n_components,
1))
```

The eigenvalues are in reverse order; therefore, we expect to have a final *W* with the rows swapped. The initial condition (with the weights multiplied by 15) is shown in the following diagram:

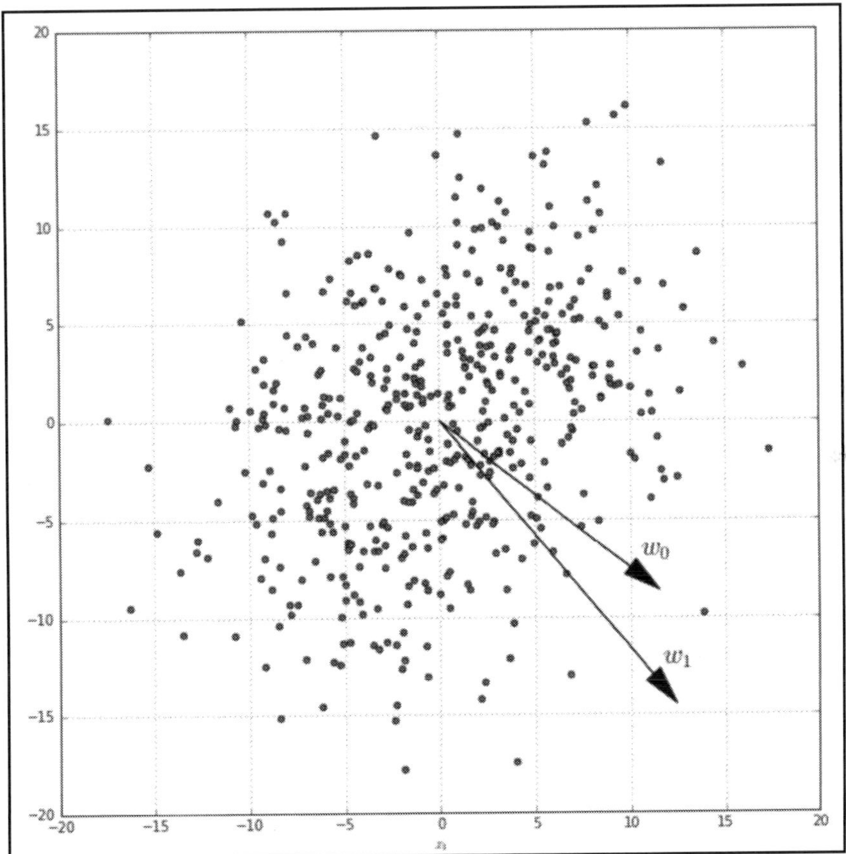

Dataset with *W* initial condition, we can implement the algorithm. For simplicity, we preferred a fixed number of iterations (`5000`) with a `learning_rate` of η=*0.01*. The reader can modify the snippet to stop when the weight matrix becomes stable:

```
learning_rate = 0.01
nb_iterations = 5000
t = 0.0

for i in range(nb_iterations):
    dw = np.zeros((n_components, Xs.shape[1]))
    t += 1.0
    for j in range(Xs.shape[0]):
        Ysj = np.dot(W_sanger, Xs[j]).reshape((n_components, 1))
        QYd = np.tril(np.dot(Ysj, Ysj.T))
        dw += np.dot(Ysj, Xs[j].reshape((1, X.shape[1]))) -
np.dot(QYd, W_sanger)
    W_sanger += (learning_rate / t) * dw
    W_sanger /= np.linalg.norm(W_sanger,
axis=1).reshape((n_components, 1))
```

The first thing to check is the final state of *W* (we transposed the matrix to be able to compare the columns):

```
print(W_sanger.T)
[[-0.6528286  -0.75750566]
 [-0.75750566  0.6528286 ]]
```

As expected, *W* has converged to the eigenvectors of the input correlation matrix (the sign – which is associated with the sense of w—is not important because we care only about the orientation). The second eigenvalue is the highest, so the columns are swapped. Replotting the diagram, we get the following:

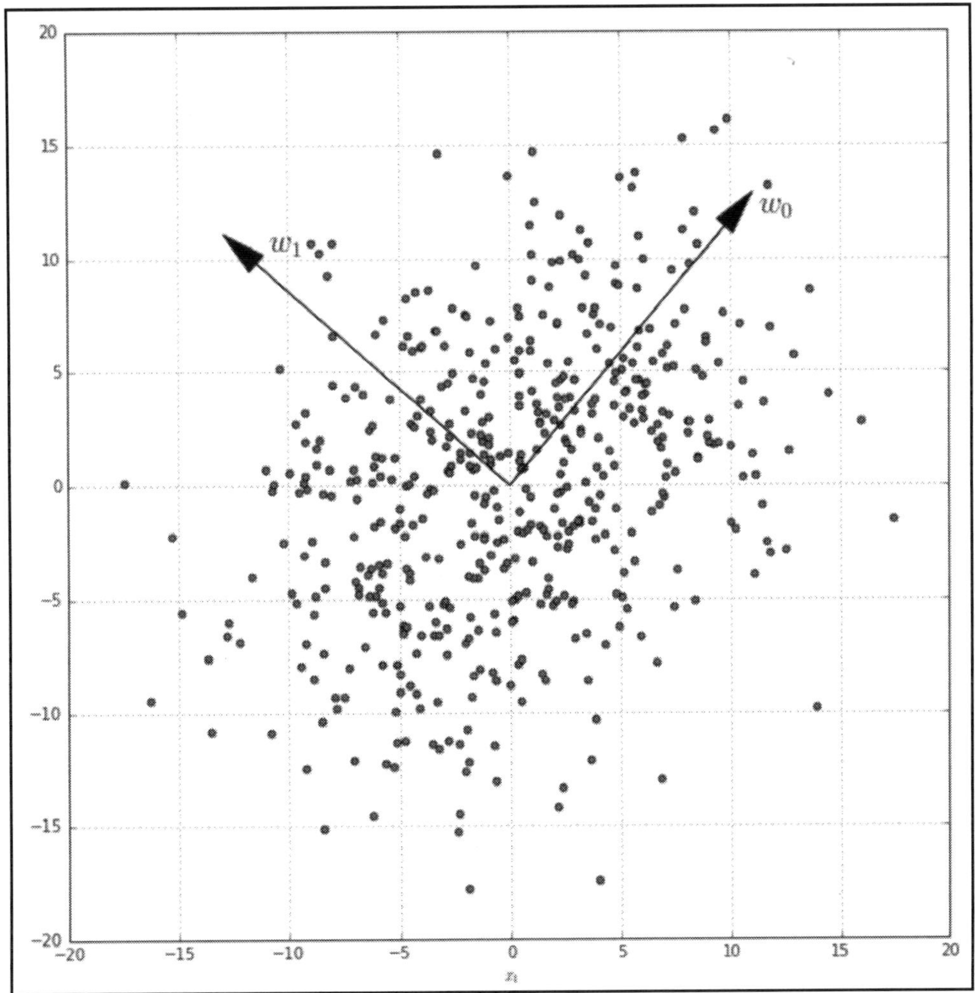

Final condition. w has converged to the two principal components

The two components are perfectly orthogonal (the final orientations can change according to the initial conditions or the random state) and w_0 points in the direction of the first principal component, while w_1 points in the direction of the second component. Considering this nice property, it's not necessary to check the magnitude of the eigenvalues; therefore, this algorithm can operate without eigendecomposing the input covariance matrix. Even if a formal proof is needed to explain this behavior, it's possible to understand it intuitively. Every single neuron converges to the first principal component given a full eigenvector subspace. This property is always maintained, but after the orthogonalization, the subspace is implicitly reduced by a dimension. The second neuron will always converge to the first component, which now corresponds to the global second component, and so on.

One of the advantages of this algorithm (and also of the next one) is that a standard PCA is normally a bulk process (even if there are batch algorithms), while a Sanger's network is an online algorithm that is trained incrementally. In general, the time performance of a Sanger's network is worse than the direct approach because of the iterations (some optimizations can be achieved using more vectorization or GPU support). On the other side, a Sanger's network is memory-saving when the number of components is less than the input dimensionality (for example, the covariance matrix for $n=1000$ has 10^6 elements, if $m = 100$, the weight matrix has 10^4 elements).

Rubner-Tavan's network

In `Chapter 5`, *EM Algorithm and Applications,* we said that any algorithm that decorrelates the input covariance matrix is performing a PCA without dimensionality reduction. Starting from this approach, Rubner, and Tavan (in the paper *A Self-Organizing Network for Principal-Components Analysis, Rubner J., Tavan P., Europhysics. Letters, 10(7), 1989*) proposed a neural model whose goal is decorrelating the output components to force the consequent decorrelation of the output covariance matrix (in lower-dimensional subspace). Assuming a zero-centered dataset and $E[y] = 0$, the output covariance matrix for m principal components is as follows:

$$Q = \begin{pmatrix} \frac{1}{N}\sum_i y_1^i y_1^i & \cdots & \frac{1}{N}\sum_i y_1^i y_m^i \\ \vdots & \ddots & \vdots \\ \frac{1}{N}\sum_i y_m^i y_1^i & \cdots & \frac{1}{N}\sum_i y_m^i y_m^i \end{pmatrix}$$

Hence, it's possible to achieve an approximate decorrelation, forcing the terms y_iy_j with $i \neq j$ to become close to zero. The main difference with a standard approach (such as whitening or vanilla PCA) is that this procedure is local, while all the standard methods operate globally, directly with the covariance matrix. The neural model proposed by the authors is shown in the following diagram (the original model was proposed for binary units, but it works quite well also for linear ones):

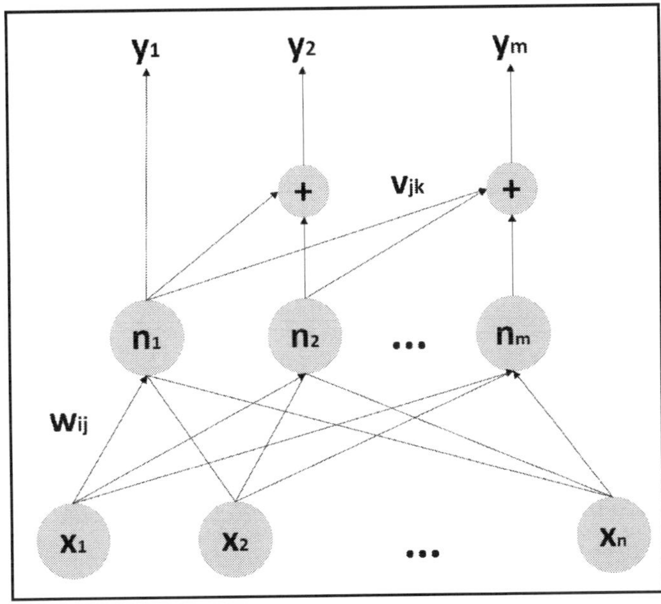

Rubner-Tavan network. The connections v_{jk} are based on the anti-Hebbian rule

The network has *m* output units and the last *m-1* neurons have a summing node that receives the weighted output of the previous units (hierarchical lateral connections). The dynamic is simple: the first output isn't modified. The second one is forced to become decorrelated with the first one. The third one is forced to become decorrelated with both the first and the second one and so on. This procedure must be iterated a number of times because the inputs are presented one by one and the cumulative term that appears in the correlation/covariance matrix (it's always easier to zero-center the dataset and work with the correlation matrix) must be implicitly split into its addends. It's not difficult to understand that the convergence to the only stable fixed point (which has been proven to exist by the authors) needs some iterations to correct the wrong output estimations.

The output of the network is made up of two contributions:

$$\bar{y}^{(i)} = \sum_{j=1}^{m} w_{ij}\bar{x}^{(j)} + \sum_{k=1}^{i-1} v_{jk}\bar{y}^{(k)}$$

The notation $y/x^{(i)}$ indicates the ith element of y/x. The first term produces a partial output based only on the input, while the second one uses hierarchical lateral connections to correct the values and enforce the decorrelation. The internal weights w_{ij} are updated using the standard version of Oja's rule (this is mainly responsible for the convergence of each weight vector to the first principal component):

$$\Delta w_{ij} = \eta y_i (x_j - w_{ij} y_i)$$

Instead, the external weights v_{jk} are updated using an anti-Hebbian rule:

$$\Delta v_{jk} = -\eta y_j (y_k + v_{jk} y_j) \ \ valid \ only \ for \ i \neq k$$

The previous formula can be split into two parts: the first term $-\eta y_j y_k$ acts in the opposite direction of a standard version of Hebb's rule (that's why it's called anti-Hebbian) and forces the decorrelation. The second one $-\eta y_j y_k v_{jk}$ acts as a regularizer and it's analogous to Oja's rule. The term $-\eta y_j y_k$ works as a feedback signal for the Oja's rule that readapts the updates according to the new magnitude of the actual output. In fact, after modifying the lateral connections, the outputs are also forced to change and this modification impacts on the update of w_{ij}. When all the outputs are decorrelated, the vectors w_i are implicitly obliged to be orthogonal. It's possible to imagine an analogy with the Gram-Schmidt orthogonalization, even if in this case the relation between the extraction of different components and the decorrelation is more complex. Like for Sanger's network, this model extracts the first m principal components in descending order (the reason is the same that has been intuitively explained), but for a complete (non-trivial) mathematical proof, please refer to the aforementioned paper.

If input dimensionality is n and the number of components is equal to m, it's possible to use a lower-triangular matrix $V (m \times m)$ with all diagonal elements set to 0 and a standard matrix for $W (n \times m)$.

The structure of W is as follows:

$$W = (\bar{w}_1 \;\; \bar{w}_2 \; \ldots \; \bar{w}_m)$$

Therefore, w_i is a column-vector that must converge to the corresponding eigenvector. The structure of V is instead:

$$V = Tril_{(if\ i=j\ V[i,j]=0)} \begin{pmatrix} \bar{v}_1 \\ \vdots \\ \bar{v}_m \end{pmatrix} = \begin{pmatrix} 0 & 0 & 0 & 0 \\ v_{21} & 0 & 0 & 0 \\ v_{31} & v_{32} & 0 & 0 \\ v_{41} & v_{42} & v_{43} & 0 \end{pmatrix}$$

Using this notation, the output becomes as follows:

$$y^{(t+1)} = W^T \bar{x} + V \bar{y}^{(t)}$$

As the output is based on recurrent lateral connections, its value must be stabilized by iterating the previous formula for a fixed number times or until the norm between two consecutive values becomes smaller than a predefined threshold. In our example, we use a fixed number of iterations equal to five. The update rules cannot be written directly in matrix notation, but it's possible to use the vectors w_i (columns) and v_j (rows):

$$\begin{cases} \Delta \bar{w}_i = \eta \bar{y}^{(i)} (\bar{x} - \bar{y}^{(i)} \bar{w}_i) \\ \Delta \bar{v}_i = -\eta \bar{y}^{(i)} (\bar{y} + \bar{y}^{(i)} \bar{v}_i) \end{cases}$$

In this case, $y^{(i)}$ means the ith component of y. The two matrices must be populated with a loop.

The complete Rubner-Tavan's network algorithm is (the dimensionality of x is n, the number of components is denoted with m):

1. Initialize $W^{(0)}$ randomly. The shape is $(n \times m)$.
2. Initialize $V^{(0)}$ randomly. The shape is $(m \times m)$.

3. Set $V^{(0)} = Tril(V^{(0)})$. $Tril(\bullet)$ transforms the input argument in a lower-triangular matrix.
4. Set all diagonal components of $V^{(0)}$ equal to 0.
5. Set the `learning_rate` η (for example, `0.001`).
6. Set a `threshold` Thr (for example, `0.0001`).
7. Set a cycle counter $T=0$.
8. Set a maximum number of iterations `max_iterations` (for example, 1000).
9. Set a number of `stabilization_cycles` (for example, `5`):
    1. While $||W^{(t)} - W^{(t-1)}||_F > Thr$ and T < `max_iterations`:
        1. Set $T = T + 1$.
        2. For each x in X:
            1. Set y_{prev} to zero. The shape is $(m, 1)$.
            2. For $i=1$ to `stabilization_cycles`:
                1. $y = W^T x + V y_{prev}$.
                2. $y_{prev} = y$.
            3. Compute the updates for W and V:
                1. Create two empty matrices ΔW $(n \times m)$ and ΔV $(m \times m)$
                2. for $t=1$ to m:
                    1. $\Delta w_t = \eta y^{(t)}(x - y^{(t)} w_t)$
                    2. $\Delta v_t = -\eta y^{(t)}(y + y^{(t)} v_t)$
                3. Update W and V:
                    1. $W^{(t+1)} = W^{(t)} + \Delta W$
                    2. $V^{(t+1)} = V^{(t)} + \Delta V$
                4. Set $V = Tril(V)$ and set all the diagonal elements to 0
                5. Set $W^{(t+1)} = W^{(t+1)} / ||W^{(t+1)}||^{(columns)}$ (The norm must be computed column-wise)

In this case, we have adopted both a threshold and a maximum number of iterations because this algorithms normally converges very quickly. Moreover, I suggest the reader always checks the shapes of vectors and matrices when performing dot products.

In this example, as well as in all the other ones, the NumPy random seed is set equal to `1000` (`np.random.seed(1000)`). Using different values (or repeating more times the experiments without resetting the seed) can lead to slightly different results (which are always coherent).

Example of Rubner-Tavan's network

For our Python example, we are going to use the same dataset already created for the Sanger's network (which is expected to be available in the variable `Xs`). Therefore, we can start setting up all the constants and variables:

```
import numpy as np

n_components = 2
learning_rate = 0.0001
max_iterations = 1000
stabilization_cycles = 5
threshold = 0.00001

W = np.random.normal(0.0, 0.5, size=(Xs.shape[1], n_components))
V = np.tril(np.random.normal(0.0, 0.01, size=(n_components,
n_components)))
np.fill_diagonal(V, 0.0)

prev_W = np.zeros((Xs.shape[1], n_components))
t = 0
```

At this point, it's possible to implement the training loop:

```
while(np.linalg.norm(W - prev_W, ord='fro') > threshold and t <
max_iterations):
    prev_W = W.copy()
    t += 1
    for i in range(Xs.shape[0]):
        y_p = np.zeros((n_components, 1))
        xi = np.expand_dims(Xs[i], 1)
        y = None

        for _ in range(stabilization_cycles):
            y = np.dot(W.T, xi) + np.dot(V, y_p)
            y_p = y.copy()
        dW = np.zeros((Xs.shape[1], n_components))
        dV = np.zeros((n_components, n_components))
        for t in range(n_components):
```

```
            y2 = np.power(y[t], 2)
            dW[:, t] = np.squeeze((y[t] * xi) + (y2 *
np.expand_dims(W[:, t], 1)))
            dV[t, :] = -np.squeeze((y[t] * y) + (y2 *
np.expand_dims(V[t, :], 1)))

        W += (learning_rate * dW)
        V += (learning_rate * dV)
        V = np.tril(V)
        np.fill_diagonal(V, 0.0)
        W /= np.linalg.norm(W, axis=0).reshape((1, n_components))
```

The final `W` and the output covariance matrix are as follows:

```
print(W)
[[-0.65992841  0.75897537]
 [-0.75132849 -0.65111933]]

Y_comp = np.zeros((Xs.shape[0], n_components))

for i in range(Xs.shape[0]):
        y_p = np.zeros((n_components, 1))
        xi = np.expand_dims(Xs[i], 1)

        for _ in range(stabilization_cycles):
            Y_comp[i] = np.squeeze(np.dot(W.T, xi) + np.dot(V.T, y_p))
            y_p = y.copy()

print(np.cov(Y_comp.T))
[[ 48.9901765   -0.34109965]
 [ -0.34109965  24.51072811]]
```

As expected, the algorithm has successfully converged to the eigenvectors (in descending order) and the output covariance matrix is almost completely decorrelated (the sign of the non-diagonal elements can be either positive or negative). Rubner-Tavan's networks are generally faster than Sanger's network, thanks to the feedback signal created by the anti-Hebbian rule; however, it's important to choose the right value for the learning rate. A possible strategy is to implement a temporal decay (as done in Sanger's network) starting with a value not greater than `0.0001`. However, it's important to reduce η when n increases (for example, $\eta = 0.0001 / n$), because the normalization strength of Oja's rule on the lateral connections v_{jk} is often not enough to avoid over and underflows when $n >> 1$. I don't suggest any extra normalization on V (which must be carefully analyzed considering that V is singular) because it can slow down the process and reduce the final accuracy.

Self-organizing maps

Self-organizing maps (SOMs) have been proposed by Willshaw and Von Der Malsburg (*Willshaw D. J., Von Der Malsburg C., How patterned neural connections can be set up by self-organization, Proceedings of the Royal Society of London, B/194, N. 1117*) to model different neurobiological phenomena observed in animals. In particular, they discovered that some areas of the brain develop structures with different areas, each of them with a high sensitivity for a specific input pattern. The process behind such a behavior is quite different from what we have discussed up until now, because it's based on competition among neural units based on a principle called **winner-takes-all**. During the training period, all the units are excited with the same signal, but only one will produce the highest response. This unit is automatically candidate to become the receptive basin for that specific pattern. The particular model we are going to present has been introduced by **Kohonen** (in the paper *Kohonen T., Self-organized formation of topologically correct feature maps, Biological Cybernetics, 43/1*) and it's named after him.

The main idea is to implement a gradual winner-takes-all paradigm, to avoid the premature convergence of a neuron (as a definitive winner) and increment the level of plasticity of the network. This concept is expressed graphically in the following graph (where we are considering a linear sequence of neurons):

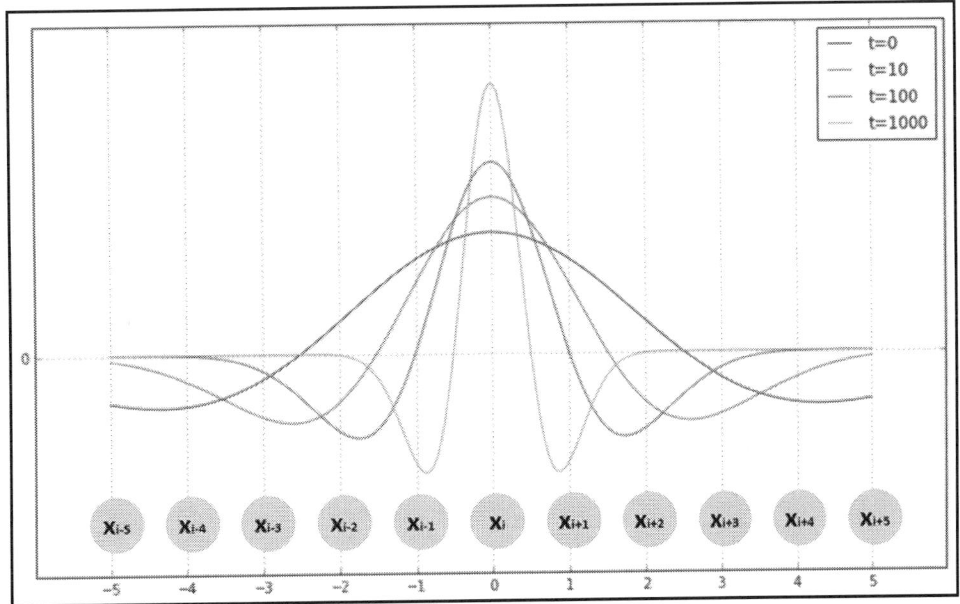

Mexican-hat dynamic implemented by a Kohonen network

In this case, the same pattern is presented to all the neurons. At the beginning of the training process (**t=0**), a positive response is observed in $\mathbf{x}_{i-2}$ to $\mathbf{x}_{i+2}$ with a peak in $\mathbf{x}_i$. The potential winner is obviously $\mathbf{x}_i$, but all these units are potentiated according to their distance from $\mathbf{x}_i$. In other words, the network (which is trained sequentially) is still receptive to change if other patterns produce a stronger activation. If instead $\mathbf{x}_i$ keeps on being the winner, the radius is slightly reduced, until the only potentiated unit will be $\mathbf{x}_i$. Considering the shape of this function, this dynamic is often called *Mexican Hat*. With this approach, the network remains plastic until all the patterns have been repeatedly presented. If, for example, another pattern elicits a stronger response in $\mathbf{x}_i$, it's important that its activation is still not too high, to allow a fast reconfiguration of the network. At the same time, the new winner will probably be a neighbor of $\mathbf{x}_i$, which has received a partial potentiation and can easily take the place of $\mathbf{x}_i$.

A **Kohonen SOM** (also known as Kohonen network or simply Kohonen map) is normally represented as a bidimensional map (for example, a square matrix $m \times m$, or any other rectangular shape), but 3D surfaces, such as spheres or toruses are also possible (the only necessary condition is the existence of a suitable metric). In our case, we always refer to a square matrix where each cell is a receptive neuron characterized by a synaptic weight w with the dimensionality of the input patterns:

$$X = \{\bar{x}_1, \bar{x}_2, \ldots, \bar{x}_N\} \quad where \ \bar{x}_i \in \mathbb{R}^n$$

During both training and working phases, the winning unit is determined according to a similarity measure between a sample and each weight vector. The most common metric is the Euclidean; hence, if we consider a bidimensional map W with a shape $(k \times p)$ so that $W \in \Re^{k \times p \times n}$, the winning unit (in terms of its coordinates) is computed as follows:

$$u^* = argmin_{k,p} \|W[k,p] - \bar{x}\|_2$$

As explained before, it's important to avoid the premature convergence because the complete final configuration could be quite different from the initial one. Therefore, the training process is normally subdivided into two different stages. During the first one, whose duration is normally about 10-20% of the total number of iterations (let's call this value t_{max}), the correction is applied to the winning unit and its neighbors (computed by adopting a decaying radius). Instead, during the second one, the radius is set to 1.0 and the correction is applied only to the winning unit. In this way, it's possible to analyze a larger number of possible configurations, automatically selecting the one associated with the least error. The neighborhood can have different shapes; it can be square (in closed 3D maps, the boundaries don't exist anymore), or, more easily, it's possible to employ a radial basis function based on an exponentially decaying distance-weight:

$$n(i,j) = e^{-\frac{\|u^* - (i,j)\|^2}{2\sigma(t)^2}} \quad where \quad \sigma(t) = \sigma_0 e^{-\frac{t}{\tau}}$$

The relative weight of each neuron is determined by the $\sigma(t)$. σ_0 function is the initial radius and τ is a time-constant that must be considered as a hyperparameter which determines the slope of the decaying weight. Suitable values are 5-10% of the total number of iterations. Adopting a radial basis function, it's not necessary to compute an actual neighborhood because the multiplication factor $n(i, j)$ becomes close to zero outside of the boundaries. A drawback is related to the computational cost, which is higher than a square neighborhood (as the function must be computed for the whole map); however, it's possible to speed up the process by precomputing all the squared distances (the numerator) and exploiting the vectorization features offered by packages such as NumPy (a single exponential is computed every time).

The update rule is very simple and it's based on the idea to move the winning unit synaptic weights closer to the pattern, x_i, (repeated for the whole dataset, X):

$$\Delta \bar{w}_{ij} = \eta(t) n(i,j)(\bar{x}_i - \bar{w}_{ij})$$

The $\eta(t)$ function is the learning rate, which can be fixed, but it's preferable to start with a higher value, η_0 and let it decay to a target final value, η_∞:

$$\eta(t) = \begin{cases} \eta_0 e^{-\frac{t}{\tau}} & if \ t < t_{max} \\ \eta_\infty & if \ t \geqslant t_{max} \end{cases}$$

In this way, the initial changes force the weights to align with the input patterns, while all the subsequent updates allow slight modifications to improve the overall accuracy. Therefore, each update is proportional to the learning rate, the neighborhood weighted distance, and the difference between each pattern and the synaptic vector. Theoretically, if Δw_{ij} is equal to 0.0 for the winning unit, it means that a neuron has become the attractor of a specific input pattern, and its neighbors will be receptive to noisy/altered versions. The most interesting aspect is that the complete final map will contain the attractors for all patterns which are organized to maximize the similarity between adjacent units. In this way, when a new pattern is presented, the area of neurons that maps the most similar shapes will show a higher response. For example, if the patterns are made up of handwritten digits, attractors for the digit 1 and for digit 7 will be closer than the attractor, for example, for digit 8. A malformed 1 (which could be interpreted as 7) will elicit a response that is between the first two attractors, allowing us to assign a relative probability based on the distance. As we're going to see in the example, this feature yields to a smooth transition between different variants of the same pattern class avoiding rigid boundaries that oblige a binary decision (like in a K-means clustering or in a hard classifier).

The complete Kohonen SOM algorithm is as follows:

1. Randomly initialize $W^{(0)}$. The shape is $(k \times p \times n)$.
2. Initialize `nb_iterations`, the total number of iterations, and t_{max} (for example, `nb_iterations` = 1000 and $t_{max} = 150$).
3. Initialize τ (for example, $\tau = 100$).
4. Initialize η_0 and η_∞ (for example, $\eta_0 = 1.0$ and $\eta_\infty = 0.05$).

5. For `t = 0` to `nb_iterations`:
    1. If $t < t_{max}$:
        1. Compute $\eta(t)$
        2. Compute $\sigma(t)$
    2. Otherwise:
        1. Set $\eta(t) = \eta_x$
        2. Set $\sigma(t) = \sigma_x$
    3. For each x_i in X:
        1. Compute the winning unit u^* (let's assume that the coordinates are i, j)
        2. Compute $n(i, j)$
        3. Apply the weight correction $\Delta w_{ij}^{(t)}$ to all synaptic weights $W^{(t)}$
    4. Renormalize $W^{(t)} = W^{(t)} / ||W^{(t)}||^{(columns)}$ (the norm must be computed column-wise)

Example of SOM

We can now implement an SOM using the Olivetti faces dataset. As the process can be very long, in this example we limit the number of input patterns to 100 (with a 5 × 5 matrix). The reader can try with the whole dataset and a larger map.

The first step is loading the data, normalizing it so that all values are bounded between 0.0 and 1.0, and setting the constants:

```
import numpy as np

from sklearn.datasets import fetch_olivetti_faces

faces = fetch_olivetti_faces(shuffle=True)

Xcomplete = faces['data'].astype(np.float64) / np.max(faces['data'])
np.random.shuffle(Xcomplete)

nb_iterations = 5000
nb_startup_iterations = 500
pattern_length = 64 * 64
pattern_width = pattern_height = 64
eta0 = 1.0
sigma0 = 3.0
```

```
tau = 100.0

X = Xcomplete[0:100]
matrix_side = 5
```

At this point, we can initialize the weight matrix using a normal distribution with a small standard deviation:

```
W = np.random.normal(0, 0.1, size=(matrix_side, matrix_side,
pattern_length))
```

Now, we need to define the functions to determine the winning unit based on the least distance:

```
def winning_unit(xt):
    distances = np.linalg.norm(W - xt, ord=2, axis=2)
    max_activation_unit = np.argmax(distances)
    return int(np.floor(max_activation_unit / matrix_side)),
max_activation_unit % matrix_side
```

It's also useful to define the functions $\eta(t)$ and $\sigma(t)$:

```
def eta(t):
    return eta0 * np.exp(-float(t) / tau)

def sigma(t):
    return float(sigma0) * np.exp(-float(t) / tau)
```

As explained before, instead of computing the radial basis function for each unit, it's preferable to use a precomputed distance matrix (in this case, 5 × 5 × 5 × 5) containing all the possible distances between couples of units. In this way, NumPy allows a faster calculation thanks to its vectorization features:

```
precomputed_distances = np.zeros((matrix_side, matrix_side,
matrix_side, matrix_side))

for i in range(matrix_side):
    for j in range(matrix_side):
        for k in range(matrix_side):
            for t in range(matrix_side):
                precomputed_distances[i, j, k, t] = \
                    np.power(float(i) - float(k), 2) +
np.power(float(j) - float(t), 2)

def distance_matrix(xt, yt, sigmat):
    dm = precomputed_distances[xt, yt, :, :]
    de = 2.0 * np.power(sigmat, 2)
    return np.exp(-dm / de)
```

The `distance_matrix` function returns the value of the radial basis function for the whole map given the center point (the winning unit) `xt, yt` and the current value of σ `sigmat`. Now, it's possible to start the training process (in order to avoid correlations, it's preferable to shuffle the input sequence at the beginning of each iteration):

```
sequence = np.arange(0, X.shape[0])
t = 0

for e in range(nb_iterations):
    np.random.shuffle(sequence)
    t += 1
    if e < nb_startup_iterations:
        etat = eta(t)
        sigmat = sigma(t)
    else:
        etat = 0.2
        sigmat = 1.0
    for n in sequence:
        x_sample = X[n]
        xw, yw = winning_unit(x_sample)
        dm = distance_matrix(xw, yw, sigmat)
        dW = etat * np.expand_dims(dm, axis=2) * (x_sample - W)
        W += dW
    W /= np.linalg.norm(W, axis=2).reshape((matrix_side, matrix_side,
1))
```

In this case, we have set η_∞ = `0.2` but I invite the reader to try different values and evaluate the final result. After training for `5000` epochs, we got the following weight matrix (each weight is plotted as a bidimensional array):

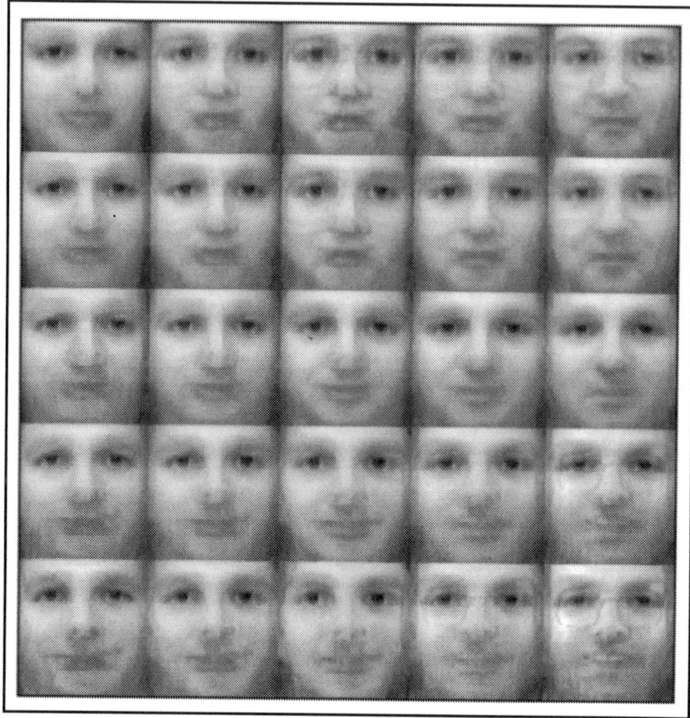

As it's possible to see, the weights have converged to faces with slightly different features. In particular, looking at the shapes of the faces and the expressions, it's easy to notice the transition between different attractors (some faces are smiling, while others are more serious; some have glasses, mustaches, and beards, and so on). It's also important to consider that the matrix is larger than the minimum capacity (there are ten different individuals in the dataset). This allows mapping more patterns that cannot be easily attracted by the right neuron. For example, an individual can have pictures with and without a beard and this can lead to confusion. If the matrix is too small, it's possible to observe an instability in the convergence process, while if it's too large, it's easy to see redundancies. The right choice depends on each different dataset and on the internal variance and there's no way to define a standard criterion. A good starting point is picking a matrix whose capacity is between 2.0 and 3.0 times larger than the number of desired attractors and then increasing or reducing its size until the accuracy reaches a maximum. The last element to consider is the labeling phase. At the end of the training process, we have no knowledge about the weight distribution in terms of winning neurons, so it's necessary to process the dataset and annotate the winning unit for each pattern. In this way, it's possible to submit new patterns to get the most likely label. This process has not been shown, but it's straightforward and the reader can easily implement it for every different scenario.

Summary

In this chapter, we have discussed Hebb's rule, showing how it can drive the computation of the first principal component of the input dataset. We have also seen that this rule is unstable because it leads to the infinite growth of the synaptic weights and how it's possible to solve this problem using normalization or Oja's rule.

We have introduced two different neural networks based on Hebbian learning (Sanger's and Rubner-Tavan's networks), whose internal dynamics are slightly different, which are able to extract the first n principal components in the right order (starting from the largest eigenvalue) without eigendecomposing the input covariance matrix.

Finally, we have introduced the concept of SOM and presented a model called a Kohonen network, which is able to map the input patterns onto a surface where some attractors (one per class) are placed through a competitive learning process. Such a model is able to recognize new patterns (belonging to the same distribution) by eliciting a strong response in the attractor, that is most similar to the pattern. In this way, after a labeling process, the model can be employed as a soft classifier that can easily manage noisy or altered patterns.

In the next chapter, we're going to discuss some important clustering algorithms, focusing on the difference (already discussed in the previous chapters) between hard and soft clustering and discussing the main techniques employed to evaluate the performance of an algorithm.

7
Clustering Algorithms

In this chapter, we are going to introduce some fundamental clustering algorithms, discussing both their strengths and weaknesses. The field of unsupervised learning, as well as any other machine learning approach, must be always based on the concept of Occam's razor. Simplicity must always be preferred when performance meets the requirements. However, in this case, the ground truth can be unknown. When a clustering algorithm is adopted as an exploratory tool, we can only assume that the dataset represents a precise data generating process. If this assumption is correct, the best strategy is to determine the number of clusters to maximize the internal cohesion (denseness) and the external separation. This means that we expect to find blobs (or isles) whose samples share some common and partially unique features.

In particular, the algorithms we are going to present are:

- **k-Nearest Neighbors** (**KNN**) based on KD Trees and Ball Trees
- K-means and K-means++
- Fuzzy C-means
- Spectral clustering based on the Shi-Malik algorithm

k-Nearest Neighbors

This algorithm belongs to a particular family called **instance-based** (the methodology is called **instance-based learning**). It differs from other approaches because it doesn't work with an actual mathematical model. On the contrary, the inference is performed by direct comparison of new samples with existing ones (which are defined as instances). KNN is an approach that can be easily employed to solve clustering, classification, and regression problems (even if, in this case, we are going to consider only the first technique). The main idea behind the clustering algorithm is very simple. Let's consider a data generating process p_{data} and a finite a dataset drawn from this distribution:

$$X = \{\bar{x}_1, \bar{x}_2, \ldots, \bar{x}_n\} \ \ where \ \ \bar{x}_i \in \mathbb{R}^N$$

Each sample has a dimensionality equal to N. We can now introduce a distance function $d(x_1, x_2)$, which in the majority of cases can be generalized with the Minkowski distance:

$$d_p(\bar{x}_1, \bar{x}_2) = \left(\sum_{j=1}^{N} \left| x_1^{(j)} - x_2^{(j)} \right|^p \right)^{\frac{1}{p}}$$

When $p = 2$, d_p represents the classical Euclidean distance, that is normally the default choice. In particular cases, it can be useful to employ other variants, such as $p = 1$ (which is the Manhattan distance) or $p > 2$. Even if all the properties of a metric function remain unchanged, different values of p yield results that can be *semantically* diverse. As an example, we can consider the distance between points $x_1 = (0, 0)$ and $x_2 = (15, 10)$ as a function of p:

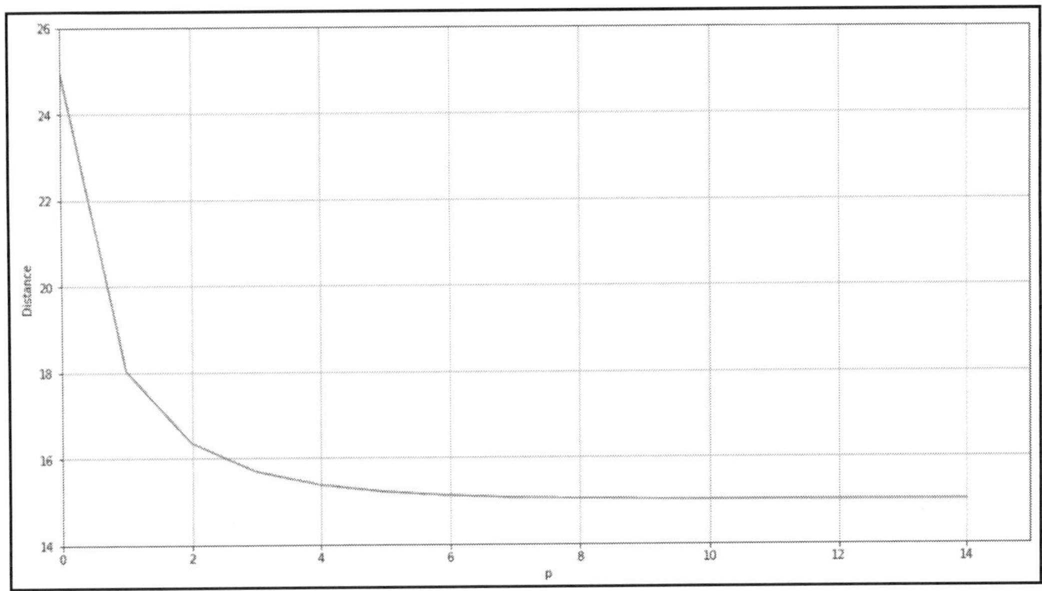

Minkowski distance between (0, 0) and (15, 10) as a function of parameter p

The distance decreases monotonically with p and converges to the largest component absolute difference, $|x_1^{(j)} - x_2^{(j)}|$, when $p \rightarrow \infty$. Therefore, whenever it's important to weight all the components in the same way in order to have a consistent metric, small values of p are preferable (for example, $p=1$ or 2). This result has also been studied and formalized by Aggarwal, Hinneburg, and Keim (in *On the Surprising Behavior of Distance Metrics in High Dimensional Space, Aggarwal C. C., Hinneburg A., Keim D. A., ICDT 2001*), who proved a fundamental inequality. If we consider a generic distribution G of M points $x_i \in (0, 1)^d$, a distance function based on the L_p norm, and the maximum D_{max}^p and minimum D_{min}^p distances (computed using the L_p norm) between two points, x_j and x_k drawn from G and $(0, 0)$, the following inequality holds:

$$C_p \leq \lim_{d\to\infty} E\left[\frac{D_{max}^p - D_{min}^p}{d^{\frac{1}{p}-\frac{1}{2}}}\right] \leqslant (M-1)C_p \quad where\ C_p \geqslant 0$$

It's clear that when the input dimensionality is very high and $p >> 2$, the expected value, $E[D_{max}^p - D_{min}^p]$, becomes bounded between two constants, $k_1 (C_p d^{1/p-1/2})$ and $k_2 ((M-1)C_p d^{1/p-1/2}) \rightarrow 0$, reducing the actual effect of almost any distance. In fact, given two generic couples of points (x_1, x_2) and (x_3, x_4) drawn from G, the natural consequence of the following inequality is that $d_p(x_1, x_2) \approx d_p(x_3, x_4)$ when $p \rightarrow \infty$, independently of their relative positions. This important result confirms the importance of choosing the right metric according to the dimensionality of the dataset and that $p = 1$ is the best choice when $d >> 1$, while $p >> 1$ can produce inconsistent results due the ineffectiveness of the metric. To see direct confirmation of this phenomenon, it's possible to run the following snippet, which computes the average difference between maximum and minimum distances considering `100` sets containing `100` samples drawn from a uniform distribution, $G \sim U(0, 1)$. In the snippet, the case of `d=2, 100, 1000` is analyzed with Minkowski metrics with `P= 1, 2, 10, 100` (the final values depend on the random seed and how many times the experiment is repeated):

```
import numpy as np

from scipy.spatial.distance import pdist

nb_samples = 100
nb_bins = 100

def max_min_mean(p=1.0, d=2):
    Xs = np.random.uniform(0.0, 1.0, size=(nb_bins, nb_samples, d))
    pd_max = np.zeros(shape=(nb_bins, ))
    pd_min = np.zeros(shape=(nb_bins, ))

    for i in range(nb_bins):
        pd = pdist(Xs[i], metric='minkowski', p=p)
        pd_max[i] = np.max(pd)
        pd_min[i] = np.min(pd)
    return np.mean(pd_max - pd_min)

print('P=1 -> {}'.format(max_min_mean(p=1.0)))
print('P=2 -> {}'.format(max_min_mean(p=2.0)))
print('P=10 -> {}'.format(max_min_mean(p=10.0)))
print('P=100 -> {}'.format(max_min_mean(p=100.0)))

P=1 -> 1.79302317381
P=2 -> 1.27290283592
P=10 -> 0.989257369005
P=100 -> 0.983016242436

print('P=1 -> {}'.format(max_min_mean(p=1.0, d=100)))
```

```
print('P=2 -> {}'.format(max_min_mean(p=2.0, d=100)))
print('P=10 -> {}'.format(max_min_mean(p=10.0, d=100)))
print('P=100 -> {}'.format(max_min_mean(p=100.0, d=100)))

P=1 -> 17.1916057948
P=2 -> 1.76155714836
P=10 -> 0.340453945928
P=100 -> 0.288625281313

print('P=1 -> {}'.format(max_min_mean(p=1.0, d=1000)))
print('P=2 -> {}'.format(max_min_mean(p=2.0, d=1000)))
print('P=10 -> {}'.format(max_min_mean(p=10.0, d=1000)))
print('P=100 -> {}'.format(max_min_mean(p=100.0, d=1000)))

P=1 -> 55.2865105705
P=2 -> 1.77098913218
P=10 -> 0.130444336657
P=100 -> 0.0925427145923
```

A particular case, that is a direct consequence of the previous inequality is when the largest absolute difference between components determines the most important factor of a distance, large values of p can be employed. For example, if we consider three points, $x_1 = (0, 0)$, $x_2 = (15, 10)$, and $x_3 = (15, 0)$, $d_2(x_1, x_2) \approx 18$ and $d_2(x_1, x_3) = 15$. So, if we set a threshold at $d = 16$ centered at x_1, x_2 is outside the boundaries. If instead $p = 15$, both distances become close to 15 and the two points (x_2 and x_3) are inside the boundaries. A particular use of large values of p is when it's important to take into account the inhomogeneity among components. For example, some feature vectors can represent the age and height of a set of people. Considering a test person $x = (30, 175)$, with large p values, the distances between x and two samples $(35, 150)$ and $(25, 151)$ are almost identical (about 25.0), and the only dominant factor becomes the height difference (independent from the age).

The KNN algorithm determines the k closest samples of each training point. When a new sample is presented, the procedure is repeated with two possible variants:

- With a predefined value of k, the KNN are computed
- With a predefined radius/threshold r, all the neighbors whose distance is less than or equal to the radius are computed

The philosophy of KNN is that similar samples can share their features. For example, a recommendation system can cluster users using this algorithm and, given a new user, find the most similar ones (based, for example, on the products they bought) to recommend the same category of items. In general, a similarity function is defined as the reciprocal of a distance (there are some exceptions, such as the cosine similarity):

$$s(\bar{x}_1, \bar{x}_2) = f(d_p(\bar{x}_1, \bar{x}_2)) = \frac{1}{d_p(\bar{x}_1, \bar{x}_2)} \quad for \ d_p(\bar{x}_1, \bar{x}_2) \neq 0$$

Two different users, *A* and *B*, who are classified as neighbors, will differ under some viewpoints, but, at the same time, they will share some peculiar features. This statement authorizes us to increase the homogeneity by *suggesting the differences*. For example, if *A* liked book b_1 and *B* liked b_2, we can recommend b_1 to *B* and b_2 to *A*. If our hypothesis was correct, the similarity between *A* and *B* will be increased; otherwise, the two users will move towards other clusters that better represent their behavior.

Unfortunately, the *vanilla* algorithm (in Scikit-Learn it is called the **brute-force** algorithm) can become extremely slow with a large number of samples because it's necessary to compute all the pairwise distances in order to answer any query. With *M* points, this number is equal to M^2, which is often unacceptable (if $M = 1,000$, each query needs to compute a million distances). More precisely, as the computation of a distance in an N-dimensional space requires *N* operations, the total complexity becomes $O(M^2N)$, which can be reasonable only for small values of both *M* and *N*. That's why some important strategies have been implemented to reduce the computational complexity.

KD Trees

As all KNN queries can be considered search problems, one of the most efficient way to reduce the overall complexity is to reorganize the dataset into a tree structure. In a binary tree (one-dimensional data), the average computational complexity of a query is $O(\log M)$, because we assume we have almost the same number of elements in each branch (if the tree is completely unbalanced, all the elements are inserted sequentially and the resulting structure has a single branch, so the complexity becomes $O(M)$). In general, the real complexity is slightly higher than $O(\log M)$, but the operation is always much more efficient than a vanilla search, which is $O(M^2)$.

However, we normally work with N-dimensional data and the previous structure cannot be immediately employed. KD Trees extend the concept of a binary for $N > 1$. In this case, a split cannot be immediately performed and a different strategy must be chosen. The easiest way to solve this problem is to select a feature at each level *(1, 2, ..., N)* and repeat the process until the desired depth is reached. In the following diagram, there's an example of KD Trees with three-dimensional points:

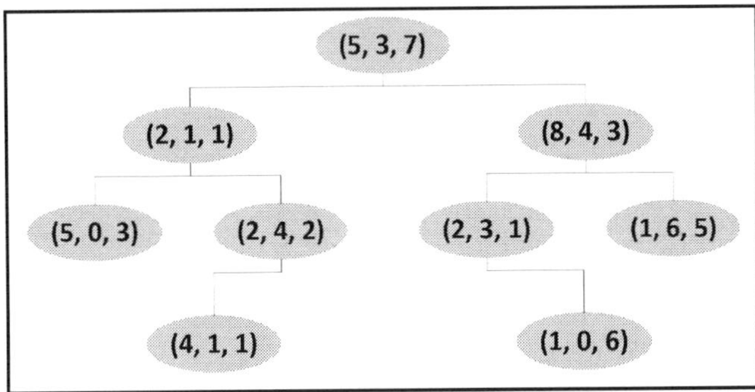

Example of three-dimensional KD Tree

The root is point **(5, 3, 7)**. The first split is performed considering the first feature, so two children are **(2, 1, 1)** and **(8, 4, 3)**. The second one operates on the second feature and so on. The average computational complexity is $O(N \log M)$, but if the distribution is very asymmetric, the probability that the tree becomes unbalanced is very high. To mitigate this issue, it's possible to select the feature corresponding to the median of the (sub-)dataset and to continue splitting with this criterion. In this way, the tree is guaranteed to be balanced. However, the average complexity is always proportional to the dimensionality and this can dramatically affect the performance.

For example, if $M = 10{,}000$ and $N = 10$, using the $\log_{10}$, $O(N \log M) = O(40)$, while, with $N = 1{,}000$, the complexity becomes $O(40{,}000)$. Generally, KD Trees suffers the *curse of dimensionality* and when N becomes large, the average complexity is about $O(MN)$, which is always better than the *vanilla* algorithm, but often too expensive for real-life applications. Therefore, KD Trees is really effective only when the dimensionality is not too high. In all other cases, the probability of having an unbalanced tree and the resulting computational complexity suggest employing a different method.

Ball Trees

An alternative to KD Trees is provided by **Ball Trees**. The idea is to rearrange the dataset in a way that is almost insensitive to high-dimensional samples. A ball is defined as a set of points whose distance from a center sample is less than or equal to a fixed radius:

$$B_R(\bar{x}_c) = \{\bar{x}_i : d_p(\bar{x}_i, \bar{x}_c) \leqslant R\}$$

Starting from the first main ball, it's possible to build smaller ones nested into the parent ball and stop the process when the desired depth has been reached. A fundamental condition is that a point can always belong to a single ball. In this way, considering the cost of the N-dimensional distance, the computational complexity is *O(N log M)* and doesn't suffer the curse of dimensionality like KD Trees. The structure is based on hyperspheres, whose boundaries are defined by the equations (given a center point x and a radius R_i):

$$x_1^2 + x_2^2 + \ldots + x_N^2 = R_i^2$$

Therefore, the only operation needed to find the right ball is measuring the distance between a sample and the centers starting from the smallest balls. If a point is outside the ball, it's necessary to move upwards and check the parents, until the ball containing the sample is found. In the following diagram, there's an example of Ball Trees with two levels:

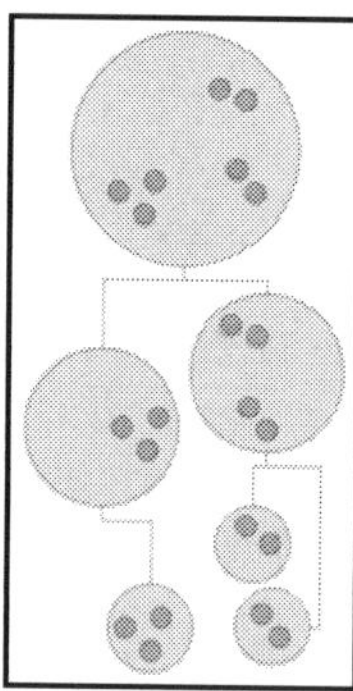

Example of Ball Trees with seven bidimensional points and two levels

In this example, the seven bidimensional points are split first into two balls containing respectively three and four points. At the second level, the second ball is split again into two smaller balls containing two points each. This procedure can be repeated until a fixed depth is reached or by imposing the maximum number of elements that a leaf must contain (in this case, it can be equal to *3*).

Both KD Trees and Ball Trees can be efficient structures to reduce the complexity of KNN queries. However, when fitting a model, it's important to consider both the *k parameter* (which normally represents the average or the standard number of neighbors computed in a query) and the maximum tree depth. These particular structures are not employed for common tasks (such as sorting) and their efficiency is maximized when all the requested neighbors can be found in the same sub-structure (with a size $K \ll M$, to avoid an implicit fallback to the *vanilla* algorithm). In other words, the tree has the role of reducing the dimensionality of the search space by partitioning it into reasonably small regions.

At the same time, if the number of samples contained in a leaf is small, the number of tree nodes grows and the complexity is subsequently increased. The negative impact is doubled because on average it's necessary to explore more nodes and if k is much greater than the number of elements contained in a node, it's necessary to merge the samples belonging to different nodes. On the other side, a very large number of samples per node leads to a condition that is close to the *vanilla* algorithm. For example, if $M = 1{,}000$ and each node contains 250 elements, once the right node is computed, the number of distances to compute is comparable with the initial dataset size and no real advantage is achieved by employing a tree structure. An acceptable practice is to set the size of a life equal to $5 \div 10$ times the average value of k, to maximize the probability to find all the neighbors inside the same leaf. However, every specific problem must be analyzed (while also benchmarking the performances) in order to find the most appropriate value. If different values for k are necessary, it's important to consider the relative frequencies of the queries. For example, if a program needs 10 *5-NN* queries and 1 *50-NN* query, it's probably better to set a leaf size equal to 25, even if the *50-NN* query will be more expensive. In fact, setting a good value for a second query (for example, 200) will dramatically increase the complexity of the first 10 queries, driving to a performance loss.

Example of KNN with Scikit-Learn

In order to test the KNN algorithm, we are going to use the MNIST handwritten digit dataset provided directly by Scikit-Learn. It is made up of 1,797 8 × 8 grayscale images representing the digits from 0 to 9. The first step is loading it and normalizing all the values to be bounded between 0 and 1:

```
import numpy as np

from sklearn.datasets import load_digits

digits = load_digits()
X_train = digits['data'] / np.max(digits['data'])
```

The dictionary `digits` contains both the images, `digits['images']`, and the flattened 64-dimensional arrays, `digits['data']`. Scikit-Learn implements different classes (for example, it's possible to work directly with KD Trees and Ball Trees using the KDTree and BallTree classes) that can be used in the context of KNN (as clustering, classification, and regression algorithms). However, we're going to employ the main class, `NearestNeighbors`, which allows performing clustering and queries based either on the number of neighbors or on the radius of a ball centered on a sample:

```
from sklearn.neighbors import NearestNeighbors

knn = NearestNeighbors(n_neighbors=50, algorithm='ball_tree')
knn.fit(X_train)
```

We have chosen to have a default number of neighbors equal to `50` and an algorithm based on a `ball_tree`. The leaf size (`leaf_size`) parameter has been kept to its default value equal to `30`. We have also employed the default metric (Euclidean), but it's possible to change it using the `metric` and `p` parameters (which is the order of the Minkowski metric). Scikit-Learn supports all the metrics implemented by SciPy in the `scipy.spatial.distance` package. However, in the majority of cases, it's sufficient to use a Minkowski metric and adjust the value of `p` if the results are not acceptable with any number of neighbors. Other metrics, such as the cosine distance, can be employed when the similarity must not be affected by the Euclidean distance, but only by the angle between two vectors pointing at the samples. Applications that use this metric include, for example, deep learning models for natural language processing, where the words are embedded into feature vectors whose semantic similarity is proportional to their Cosine distance.

We can now query the model in order to find 50 neighbors of a sample. For our purposes, we have selected the sample with index 100, which represents a 4 (the images have a very low resolution, but it's always possible to distinguish the digit):

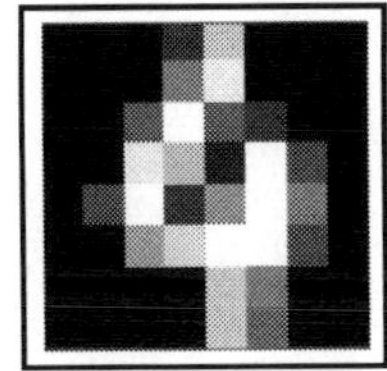

Sample digit used to query the KNN model

The query can be performed using the instance method `kneighbors`, which allows specifying the number of neighbors (`n_neighbors` parameter the default is the value selected during the instantiation of the class) and whether we want to also get the distances of each neighbor (the `return_distance` parameter). In this example, we are also interested in evaluating *how far* the neighbors are from the center, so we set `return_distance=True`:

```
distances, neighbors = knn.kneighbors(X_train[100].reshape(1, -1),
return_distance=True)

print(distances[0])

[ 0.          0.91215747  1.16926793  1.22633855  1.24058958
1.32139841
  1.3564084   1.36645069  1.41972709  1.43341812  1.45236875
1.50130152
  1.52709897  1.5499496   1.62379763  1.62620148  1.6345871
1.64292993
  1.66770801  1.70934929  1.71619128  1.71619128  1.72187216
1.73317808
  1.74888357  1.75445861  1.75668367  1.75779514  1.76555586
1.77878118
  1.788636    1.79408751  1.79626348  1.80169191  1.80277564
1.80385871
  1.80494113  1.8125      1.81572988  1.83498978  1.84771819
1.87291551
  1.87916205  1.88020112  1.88538789  1.88745861  1.88952706
1.90906554
  1.91213232  1.92333532]
```

The first neighbor is always the center, so its distance is `0`. The other ones range from 0.9 to 1.9. Considering that, in this case, the maximum possible distance is 8 (between a 64-dimensional vector $a = (1, 1, ..., 1)$ and the null vector), the result could be acceptable. In order to get confirmation, we can plot the neighbors as bidimensional 8 × 8 arrays (the returned array, `neighbors`, contains the indexes of the samples). The result is shown in the following screenshot:

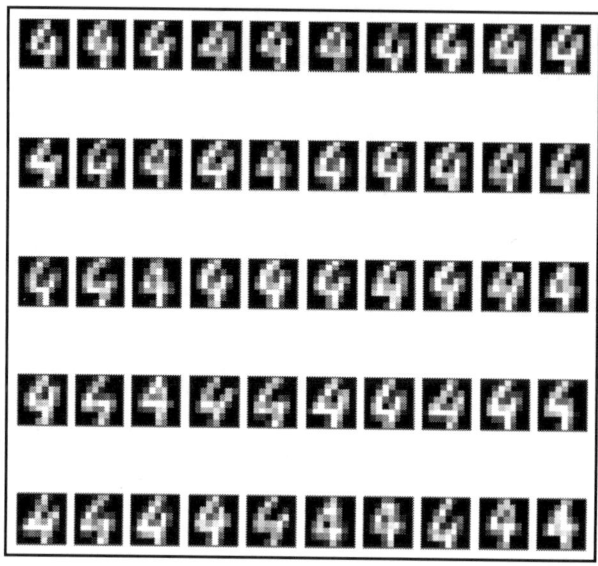

50 neighbors selected by the KNN model

As it's possible to see, there are no errors, but all the shapes are slightly different. In particular, the last one, which is also the farthest, has a lot of white pixels (corresponding to the value 1.0), explaining the reason of a distance equal to about 2.0. I invite the reader to test the `radius_neighbors` method until spurious values appear among the results. It's also interesting to try this algorithm with the Olivetti faces dataset, whose complexity is higher and many more geometrical parameters can influence the similarity.

K-means

When we discussed the Gaussian mixture algorithm, we defined it as *Soft K-means*. The reason is that each cluster was represented by three elements: mean, variance, and weight. Each sample always belongs to all clusters with a probability provided by the Gaussian distributions. This approach can be very useful when it's possible to manage the probabilities as weights, but in many other situations, it's preferable to determine a single cluster per sample. Such an approach is called hard clustering and K-means can be considered the hard version of a Gaussian mixture. In fact, when all variances $\Sigma_i \rightarrow 0$, the distributions degenerate to Dirac's Deltas, which represent perfect spikes centered at a specific point. In this scenario, the only possibility to determine the most appropriate cluster is to find the shortest distance between a sample point and all the centers (from now on, we are going to call them *centroids*). This approach is also based on an important double principle that should be taken into account in every clustering algorithm. The clusters must be set up to maximize:

- The intra-cluster cohesion
- The inter-cluster separation

This means that we expect to label high-density regions that are well separated from each other. When this is not possible, the criterion must try to minimize the intra-cluster average distance between samples and centroid. This quantity is also called *inertia* and it's defined as:

$$S = \sum_{j=1}^{k} \sum_{\bar{x}_j \in C_j} \left\| \bar{x}_i - \bar{\mu}_j \right\|^2$$

High levels of inertia imply low cohesion because there are probably too many points belongings to clusters whose centroids are too far away. The problem can be solved by minimizing the previous quantity. However, the computational complexity needed to find the global minimum is exponential (K-means belongs to the class of NP-Hard problems). The alternative approach employed by the K-means algorithm, also known as **Lloyd's algorithm**, is iterative and starts from selecting k random centroids (in the next section, we're going to analyze a more efficient method) and adjusting them until their configuration becomes stable.

The dataset to cluster (with M samples) is represented as:

$$X = \{\bar{x}_1, \bar{x}_2, \ldots, \bar{x}_M\} \ \ where \ \ \bar{x}_i \in \mathbb{R}^N$$

An initial guess for the centroids is:

$$M^{(0)} = \left\{\bar{\mu}_0^{(0)}, \bar{\mu}_1^{(0)}, \ldots, \bar{\mu}_k^{(0)}\right\} \ \ where \ \ \bar{\mu}_i^{(0)} \in \mathbb{R}^N$$

There are no particular restrictions on the initial values. However, the choice can influence both the convergence speed and the minimum that is found. The iterative procedure will loop over the dataset, computing the Euclidean distance between x_i and each μ_j and assigning a cluster based on the criterion:

$$C^{(t)}(\bar{x}_i) = argmin_j \ d(\bar{x}_i, \bar{\mu}_j^{(t)})$$

Once all the samples have been clustered, the new centroids are computed:

$$\bar{\mu}_j^{(t)} = \frac{1}{N_{C_j}} \sum_{i \in C_j} \bar{x}_i \ \ \forall j \in [1, k]$$

The quantity N_{Cj} represents the number of points belonging to cluster j. At this point, the inertia is recomputed and the new value is compared with the previous one. The procedure will stop either after a fixed number of iterations or when the variations in the inertia become smaller than a predefined threshold. Lloyd's algorithm is very similar to a particular case of the EM algorithm. In fact, the first step of each iteration is the computation of an *expectation* (the centroid configuration), while the second step maximizes the intra-cluster cohesion by minimizing the inertia.

The complete vanilla K-means algorithm is:

1. Set a maximum number of iterations N_{max}.
2. Set a tolerance *Thr*.
3. Set the value of k (number of expected clusters).
4. Initialize vector $C^{(0)}$ with random values. They can be points belonging to the dataset or sampled from a suitable distribution.
5. Compute the initial inertia $S^{(0)}$

6. Set $N = 0$.
7. While $N < N_{max}$ or $||S^{(t)} - S^{(t-1)}|| > Thr$:
    1. $N = N + 1$
    2. For x_i in X:
        1. Assign x_i to a cluster using the shortest distance between x_i and μ_j
    3. Recompute the centroid vector $C^{(t)}$
    4. Recompute the inertia $S^{(t)}$

The algorithm is quite simple and intuitive, and there are many real-life applications based on it. However, there are two important elements to consider. The first one is the convergence speed. It's easy to show that every initial guess drives to a convergence point, but the number of iterations is dramatically influenced by this choice and there's no guarantee to find the global minimum. If the initial centroids are close to the final ones, the algorithm needs only a few steps to correct the values, but when the choice is totally random, it's not uncommon to need a very high number of iterations. If there are N samples and k centroids, Nk distances must be computed at each iteration, leading to an inefficient result. In the next paragraph, we'll show how it's possible to initialize the centroids to minimize the convergence time.

Another important aspect is that, contrary to KNN, K-means needs to predefine the number of expected clusters. In some cases, this is a secondary problem because we already know the most appropriate value for k. However, when the dataset is high-dimensional and our knowledge is limited, this choice could be hazardous. A good approach to solve the issue is to analyze the final inertia for a different number of clusters. As we expect to maximize the intra-cluster cohesion, a small number of clusters will lead to an increased inertia. We try to pick the highest point below a maximum tolerable value. Theoretically, we can also pick $k = N$. In this case, the inertia becomes zero because each point represents the centroid of its cluster, but a large value for k transforms the clustering scenario into a fine-grained partitioning that might not be the best strategy to capture the feature of a consistent group. It's impossible to define a rule for the upper bound k_{max}, but we assume that this value is always much less than N. The best choice is achieved by selecting k to minimize the inertia, selecting the values from a set bounded, for example, between 2 and k_{max}.

K-means++

We have said that a good choice for the initial centroids can improve the convergence speed and leads to a minimum that is closer to the global optimum of the inertia S. Arthur and Vassilvitskii (in *The Advantages of Careful Seeding, Arthur, D., Vassilvitskii S., k-means++: Proceedings of the Eighteenth Annual ACM-SIAM Symposium on Discrete Algorithms*) proposed a method called K-means++, which allows increasing the accuracy of the initial centroid guess considering the most likely final configuration.

In order to expose the algorithm, it's useful to introduce a function, *D(x, i)*, which is defined as:

$$D(\bar{x}, i) = min_i \; d(\bar{x}, \bar{\mu}_i) \; for \; i = 1 \; to \, p \leqslant k$$

D(x, i) defines the shortest distance between each sample and one of the centroids already selected. As the process is incremental, this function must be recomputed after all steps. For our purposes, let's also define an auxiliary probability distribution (we omit the index variable for simplicity):

$$G(\bar{x}) = \frac{D(\bar{x})^2}{\sum_{j=1}^{M} D(\bar{x}_j)^2}$$

The first centroid μ_0 is sampled from *X* using a uniform distribution. The next steps are:

1. Compute *D(x, i)* for all $x \in X$ considering the centroids already selected
2. Compute *G(x)*
3. Select the next centroid μ_i from *X* with a probability *G(x)*

In the aforementioned paper, the authors showed a very important property. If we define S^* as the global optimum of *S*, a K-means++ initialization determines an upperbound for the expected value of the actual inertia:

$$E[S] \leqslant 8S^* (log \, k + 2)$$

This condition is often expressed by saying that K-means++ is *O(log k)*-competitive. When *k* is sufficiently small, the probability of finding a local minimum close to the global one increases. However, K-means++ is still a probabilistic approach and different initializations on the same dataset lead to different initial configurations. A good practice is to run a limited number of initializations (for example, ten) and pick the one associated with the smallest inertia. When training complexity is not a primary issue, this number can be increased, but different experiments showed that the improvement achievable with a very large number of trials is negligible when compared to the actual computational cost. The default value in Scikit-Learn is ten and the author suggests to keep this value in the majority of cases. If the result continues to be poor, it's preferable to pick another method. Moreover, there are problems that cannot be solved using K-means (even with the best possible initialization), because one of the assumptions of the algorithm is that each cluster is a hypersphere and the distances are measured using a Euclidean function. In the following sections, we're going to analyze other algorithms that are not constrained to work with such limitations and can easily solve clustering problems using asymmetric cluster geometries.

Example of K-means with Scikit-Learn

In this example, we continue using the MNIST dataset (the `X_train` array is the same defined in the paragraph dedicated to KNN), but we want also to analyze different clustering evaluation methods. The first step is visualizing the inertia corresponding to different numbers of clusters. We are going to use the `KMeans` class, which accepts the `n_clusters` parameter and employs the K-means++ initialization as the default method (as explained in the previous section, in order to find the best initial configuration, Scikit-Learn performs several attempts and selects the configuration with the lowest inertia; it's possible to change the number of attempts through the `n_iter` parameter):

```
import numpy as np

from sklearn.cluster import KMeans

min_nb_clusters = 2
max_nb_clusters = 20

inertias = np.zeros(shape=(max_nb_clusters - min_nb_clusters + 1,))
```

```
for i in range(min_nb_clusters, max_nb_clusters + 1):
    km = KMeans(n_clusters=i, random_state=1000)
    km.fit(X_train)
    inertias[i - min_nb_clusters] = km.inertia_
```

We are supposing to analyze the range [2, 20]. After each training session, the final inertia can be retrieved using the `inertia_` instance variable. The following graph shows the plot of the values as a function of the number of clusters:

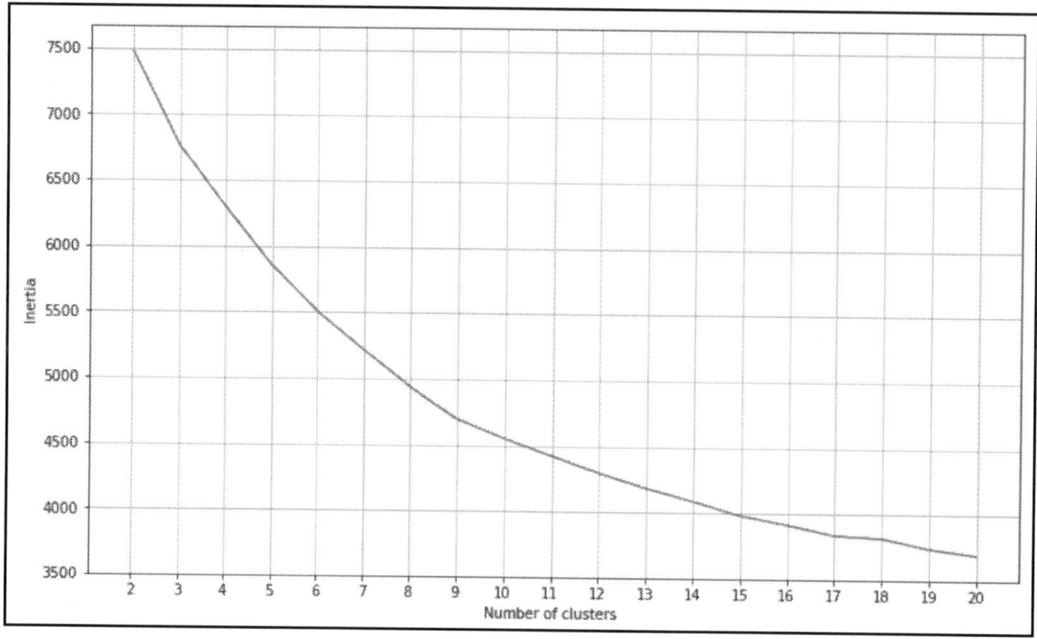

Inertia as a function of the number of clusters

As expected, the function is decreasing, starting from a value of about 7,500 and reaching about 3,700 with **20** clusters. In this case, we know that the real number is **10**, but it's possible to discover it by observing the trend. The slope is quite high before **10**, but it starts decreasing more and more slowly after this threshold. This is a signal that informs us that some clusters are not well separated, even if their internal cohesion is high. In order to confirm this hypothesis, we can set `n_clusters=10` and, first of all, check the centroids at the end of the training process:

```
km = KMeans(n_clusters=10, random_state=1000)
Y = km.fit_predict(X_train)
```

The centroids are available through the `cluster_centers_` instance variable. In the following screenshot, there's a plot of the corresponding bidimensional arrays:

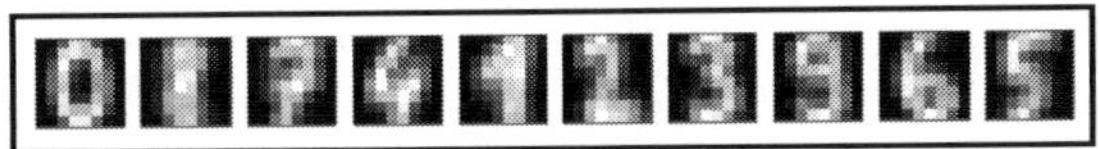

K-means centroid at the end of the training process

All the digits are present and there are no duplicates. This confirms that the algorithm has successfully separated the sets, but the final inertia (which is about 4,500) informs us that there are probably wrong assignments. To obtain confirmation, we can plot the dataset using a dimensionality-reduction method, such as t-SNE (see `Chapter 3`, *Graph-Based Semi-Supervised Learning* for further details):

```
from sklearn.manifold import TSNE

tsne = TSNE(n_components=2, perplexity=20.0, random_state=1000)
X_tsne = tsne.fit_transform(X_train)
```

At this point, we can plot the bidimensional dataset with the corresponding cluster labels:

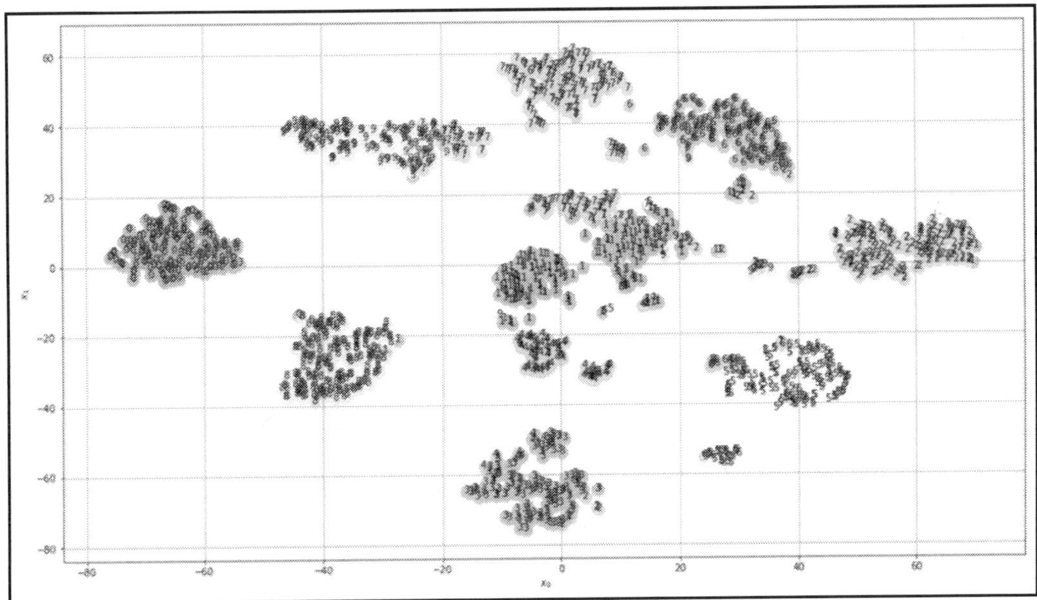

t-SNE representation of the MNIST dataset: the labels correspond to the clusters

The plot confirms that the dataset is made up of well-separated blobs, but a few samples are assigned to the wrong cluster (this is not surprising considering the similarity between some pairs of digits). An important observation can further explain the trend of the inertia. In fact, the point where the slope changes almost abruptly corresponds to 9 clusters. Observing the t-SNE plot, we can immediately discover the reason: the cluster corresponding to the digit 7 is indeed split into 3 blocks. The main one contains the majority of samples, but there are another 2 smaller blobs that are wrongly *attached* to clusters **1** and **9**. This is not surprising, considering that the digit **7** can be very similar to a distorted **1** or **9**. However, these two spurious blobs are always at the boundaries of the wrong clusters (remember that the geometric structures are hyperspheres), confirming that the metric has successfully detected a low similarity. If a group of wrongly assigned samples were in the middle of a cluster, it would have meant that the separation failed dramatically and another method should be employed.

Evaluation metrics

In many cases, it's impossible to evaluate the performance of a clustering algorithm using only a visual inspection. Moreover, it's important to use standard objective metrics that allow for comparing different approaches. We are now going to introduce some methods based on the knowledge of the ground truth (the correct assignment for each sample) and one common strategy employed when the true labels are unknown.

Before discussing the scoring functions, we need to introduce a standard notation. If there are *k* clusters, we define the true labels as:

$$Y_{true} = \left\{ y_1^{true}, y_2^{true}, \ldots, y_M^{true} \right\} \;\; where \;\; y_i^{true} \in \{1, 2, \ldots, k\}$$

In the same way, we can define the predicted labels:

$$Y_{pred} = \left\{ y_1^{pred}, y_2^{pred}, \ldots, y_M^{pred} \right\} \;\; where \;\; y_i^{pred} \in \{1, 2, \ldots, k\}$$

Both sets can be considered as sampled from two discrete random variables (for simplicity, we denote them with the same names), whose probability mass functions are $P_{true}(y)$ and $P_{pred}(y)$ with a generic $y \in \{y_1, y_2, ..., y_k\}$ (y_i represents the index of the ith cluster). These two probabilities can be approximated with a frequency count; so, for example, the probability $P_{true}(1)$ is computed as the number of samples whose true label is 1 $n_{true}(1)$ over the total number of samples M. In this way, we can define the entropies:

$$\begin{cases} H(Y_{true}) = -\sum_{i=1}^{k} p(y_i^{true}) \; log \; p(y_i^{true}) \\ H(Y_{pred}) = -\sum_{i=1}^{k} p(y_i^{pred}) \; log \; p(y_i^{pred}) \end{cases}$$

These quantities describe the intrinsic uncertainty of the random variables. They are maximized when all the classes have the same probability, while, for example, they are null if all the samples belong to a single class (minimum uncertainty). We also need to know the uncertainty of a random variable Y given another one X. This can be achieved using the conditional entropy $H(Y|X)$. In this case, we need to compute the joint probability $p(x, y)$ because the definition of $H(Y|X)$ is:

$$H(Y|X) = -\sum_{x}\sum_{y} p(x, y) \; log \; \frac{p(x, y)}{p(x)}$$

In order to approximate the previous expression, we can define the function $n(i_{true}, j_{pred})$, which counts the number of samples with the true label i assigned to cluster j. In this way, if there are M samples, the approximated conditional entropies become:

$$\begin{cases} H(Y_{true}|Y_{pred}) = -\sum_{i_{true}=1}^{M} \sum_{j_{pred}=1}^{M} \frac{n(i_{true}, j_{pred})}{M} \; log \; \frac{n(i_{true}, j_{pred})}{n_{pred}(j_{pred})} \\ H(Y_{pred}|Y_{true}) = -\sum_{i_{pred}=1}^{M} \sum_{j_{true}=1}^{M} \frac{n(i_{true}, j_{pred})}{M} \; log \; \frac{n(i_{true}, j_{pred})}{n_{true}(i_{true})} \end{cases}$$

Homogeneity score

This score is useful to check whether the clustering algorithm meets an important requirement: a cluster should contain only samples belonging to a single class. It's defined as:

$$h = 1 - \frac{H(Y_{true}|Y_{pred})}{H(Y_{true})}$$

It's bounded between *0* and *1*, with low values indicating a low homogeneity. In fact, when the knowledge of Y_{pred} reduces the uncertainty of Y_{true}, $H(Y_{true} | Y_{pred})$ becomes smaller ($h \rightarrow 1$) and viceversa. For our example, the homogeneity score can be computed as:

```
from sklearn.metrics import homogeneity_score

print(homogeneity_score(digits['target'], Y))
0.739148799605
```

The `digits['target']` array contains the true labels while `Y` contains the predictions (all the functions we are going to use accept the true labels as the first parameter and the predictions as the second one). The homogeneity score confirms that the clusters are rather homogeneous, but there's still a moderate level of uncertainty because some clusters contain wrong assignments. This method, together with the other ones, can be used to search for the right number of clusters and tune up all supplementary hyperparameters (such as the number of iterations or the metric function).

Completeness score

This score is complementary to the previous one. Its purpose is to provide a piece of information about the assignment of samples belonging to the same class. More precisely, a good clustering algorithm should assign all samples with the same true label to the same cluster. From our previous analysis, we know that, for example, the digit 7 has been wrongly assigned to both clusters 9 and 1; therefore, we expect a non-perfect completeness score. The definition is symmetric to the homogeneity score:

$$c = 1 - \frac{H(Y_{pred}|Y_{true})}{H(Y_{pred})}$$

The rationale is very intuitive. When $H(Y_{pred} | Y_{true})$ is low $(c \rightarrow 1)$, it means that the knowledge of the ground truth reduces the uncertainty about the predictions. Therefore, if we know that all the sample of subset A have the same label y_i, we are quite sure that all the corresponding predictions have been assigned to the same cluster. The completeness score for our example is:

```
from sklearn.metrics import completeness_score

print(completeness_score(digits['target'], Y))
0.747718831945
```

Again, the value confirms our hypothesis. The residual uncertainty is due to a lack of completeness because a few samples with the same label have been split into blocks that are assigned to wrong clusters. It's obvious that a perfect scenario is characterized by having both homogeneity and completeness scores equal to 1.

Adjusted Rand Index

This score is useful to compare the original label distribution with the clustering prediction. Ideally, we'd like to reproduce the exact ground truth distribution, but in general, this is very difficult in real-life scenarios. A way to measure the discrepancy is provided by the Adjusted Rand Index. In order to compute this score, we need to define the auxiliary variables:

- a: Number of sample pairs (y_i, y_j) that have the same true label and that are assigned to the same cluster
- b: Number of sample pairs (y_i, y_j) that have a different true label and that are assigned to different clusters

The Rand Index is defined as:

$$R = \frac{a + b}{\binom{M}{2}}$$

The Adjusted Rand Index is the Rand Index corrected for chance and it's defined as:

$$R_A = \frac{R - E[R]}{max(R) - E[R]}$$

The R_A measure is bounded between *-1* and *1*. A value close to *-1* indicates a prevalence of wrong assignments, while a value close to *1* indicates that the clustering algorithm is correctly reproducing the ground truth distribution. The Adjusted Rand Score for our example is:

```
from sklearn.metrics import adjusted_rand_score

print(adjusted_rand_score(digits['target'], Y))
0.666766395716
```

This value confirms that the algorithm is working well (because it's positive), but it can be further optimized by trying to reduce the number of wrong assignments. The Adjusted Rand Score is a very powerful tool when the ground truth is known and can be employed as a single method to optimize all the hyperparameters.

Silhouette score

This measure doesn't need to know the ground truth and can be used to check, at the same time, the intra-cluster cohesion and the inter-cluster separation. In order to define the Silhouette score, we need to introduce two auxiliary functions. The first one is the average intra-cluster distance of a sample x_i belonging to a cluster C_j:

$$a(\bar{x}_i) = \frac{1}{n(j)} \sum_p d(\bar{x}_i, \bar{x}_p) \ \forall \ \bar{x}_p \in C_j$$

In the previous expression, *n(k)* is the number of samples assigned to the cluster C_j and *d(a, b)* is a standard distance function (in the majority of cases, the Euclidean distance is chosen). We need also to define the lowest inter-cluster distance which can be interpreted as the average nearest-cluster distance. In the sample $x_i \in C_j$, let's call C_t the nearest cluster; therefore, the function is defined as:

$$b(\bar{x}_i) = \frac{1}{n(t)} \sum_t d(\bar{x}_i, \bar{x}_t) \ \forall \ \bar{x}_t \in C_t$$

The Silhouette score for sample x_i is:

$$s(\bar{x}_i) = \frac{b(\bar{x}_i) - a(\bar{x}_i)}{max\left(a(\bar{x}_i), b(\bar{x}_i)\right)}$$

The value of $s(x_i)$, like for the Adjusted Rand Index, is bounded between *-1* and *1*. A value close to *-1* indicates that $b(x_i) \ll a(x_i)$, so the average intra-cluster distance is greater than the average nearest-cluster index and sample x_i is wrongly assigned. Viceversa, a value close to *1* indicates that the algorithm achieved a very good level of internal cohesion and inter-cluster separation (because $a(x_i) \ll b(x_i)$). Contrary to the other measure, the Silhouette score isn't a cumulative function and must be computed for each sample. A feasible strategy is to analyze the average value, but in this way, it's not possible to determine which clusters have the highest impact on the result. Another approach (the most common), is based on Silhouette plots, which display the score for each cluster in descending order. In the following snippet, we create plots for four different values of `n_clusters` (`3`, `5`, `10`, `12`):

```
import matplotlib.pyplot as plt
import matplotlib.cm as cm

import numpy as np

from sklearn.cluster import KMeans
from sklearn.metrics import silhouette_samples

fig, ax = plt.subplots(2, 2, figsize=(15, 10))

nb_clusters = [3, 5, 10, 12]
mapping = [(0, 0), (0, 1), (1, 0), (1, 1)]

for i, n in enumerate(nb_clusters):
    km = KMeans(n_clusters=n, random_state=1000)
    Y = km.fit_predict(X_train)

    silhouette_values = silhouette_samples(X_train, Y)

    ax[mapping[i]].set_xticks([-0.15, 0.0, 0.25, 0.5, 0.75, 1.0])
    ax[mapping[i]].set_yticks([])
    ax[mapping[i]].set_title('%d clusters' % n)
    ax[mapping[i]].set_xlim([-0.15, 1])
    ax[mapping[i]].grid()
    y_lower = 20

    for t in range(n):
```

```
        ct_values = silhouette_values[Y == t]
        ct_values.sort()

        y_upper = y_lower + ct_values.shape[0]

        color = cm.Accent(float(t) / n)
        ax[mapping[i]].fill_betweenx(np.arange(y_lower, y_upper), 0,
ct_values, facecolor=color, edgecolor=color)

        y_lower = y_upper + 20
```

The result is shown in the following graph:

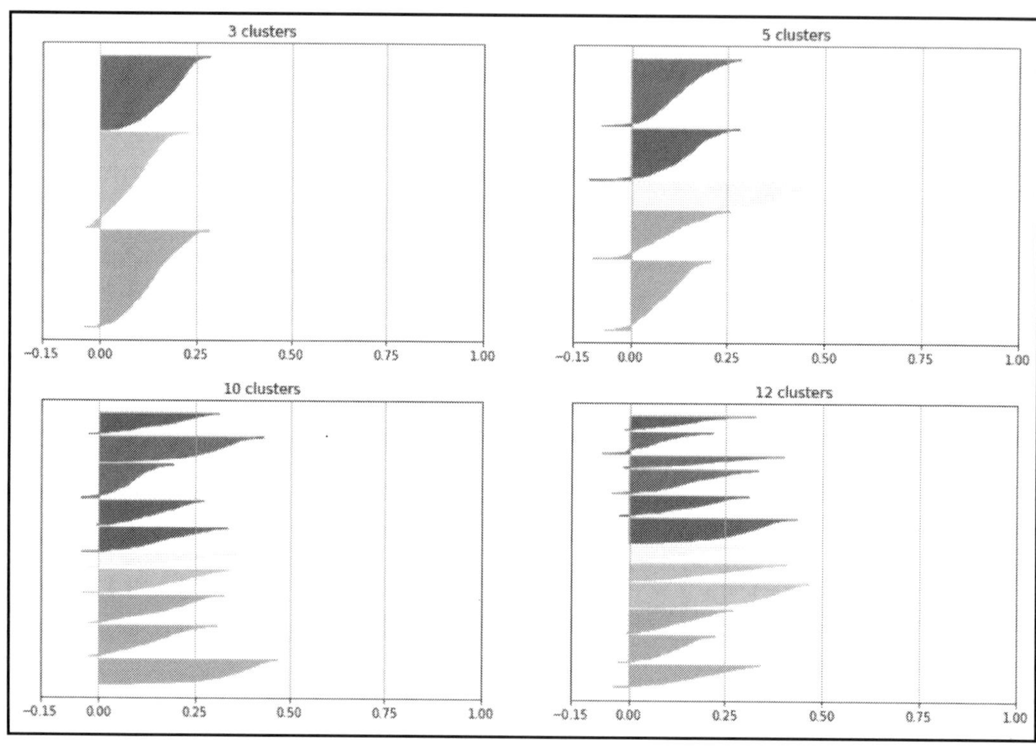

Silhouette plots for different number of clusters

The analysis of a Silhouette plot should follow some common guidelines:

- The width of each block must be proportional to the number of samples that are expected to belong to the corresponding cluster. If the label distribution is uniform, all the blocks must have a similar width. Any asymmetry indicates wrong assignments. For example, in our case, we know that the right number of clusters is ten, but a couple of blocks are thinner than the other ones. This means that a cluster contains fewer samples than expected and the remaining ones have been assigned to wrong partitions.
- The shape of a block shouldn't be sharp and peaked (like a knife) because it means that many samples have a low Silhouette score. The ideal (realistic) scenario is made up of shapes similar to cigars with a minimum difference between the highest and lowest values. Unfortunately, this is not always possible to achieve, but it's always preferable to tune up the algorithm if the shapes are like the ones plotted in the first diagram (three clusters).
- The maximum Silhouette score should be close to *1*. Lower values (like in our example) indicate the presence of partial overlaps and wrong assignments. Negative values must be absolutely avoided (or limited to a very small number of samples) because they show a failure in the clustering process. Moreover, it's possible to prove that convex clusters (like K-means hyperspheres) lead to higher values. This is due to the properties of the commons distance functions (like the Euclidean distance) that can suggest a low internal cohesion whenever the shape of a cluster is concave (think about a circle and a half-moon). In this case, the process of embedding the shape into a convex geometry leads to a lower density and this negatively affects the Silhouette score.

In our particular case, we cannot accept having a number of clusters different from ten. However, the corresponding Silhouette plot is not perfect. We know the reasons for such imperfections (the structure of the samples and the high similarity of different digits) and it's quite difficult to avoid them using an algorithm like K-means. The reader can try to improve the performances by increasing the number of iterations, but in these cases, if the result doesn't meet the requirements, it's preferable to adopt another method (like the spectral clustering method, which can manage asymmetric clusters and more complex geometries).

Fuzzy C-means

We have already talked about the difference between hard and soft clustering, comparing K-means with Gaussian mixtures. Another way to address this problem is based on the concept of **fuzzy logic**, which was proposed for the first time by Lotfi Zadeh in 1965 (for further details, a very good reference is *An Introduction to Fuzzy Sets, Pedrycz W., Gomide F., The MIT Press*). Classic logic sets are based on the law of excluded middle that, in a clustering scenario, can be expressed by saying that a sample x_i can belong only to a single cluster c_j. Speaking more generally, if we split our universe into labeled partitions, a hard clustering approach will assign a label to each sample, while a fuzzy (or soft) approach allows managing a membership degree (in Gaussian mixtures, this is an actual probability), w_{ij} which expresses how strong the relationship is between sample x_i and cluster c_j. Contrary to other methods, by employing fuzzy logic it's possible to define asymmetric sets that are not representable with continuous functions (such as trapezoids). This allows for achieving further flexibility and an increased ability to adapt to more complex geometries. In the following graph, there's an example of fuzzy sets:

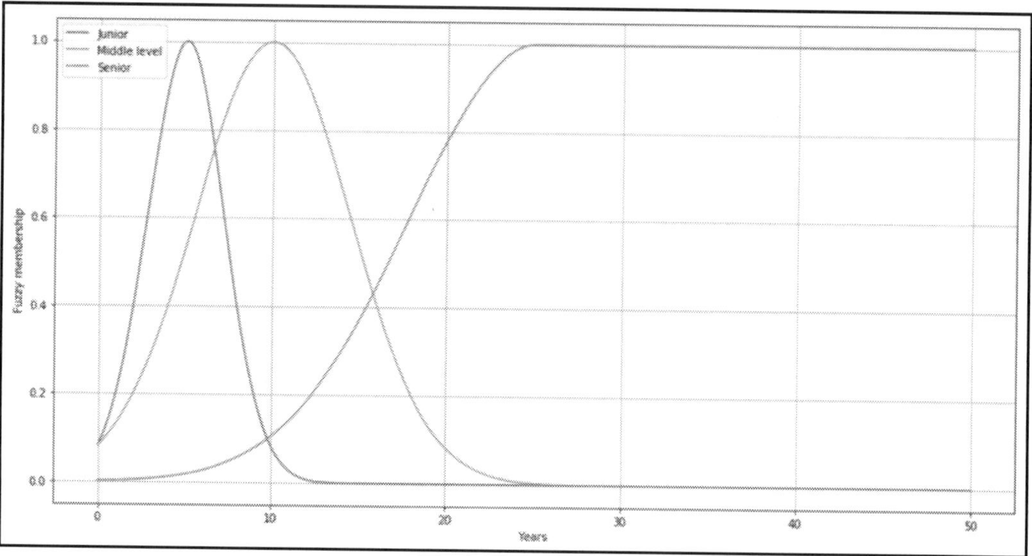

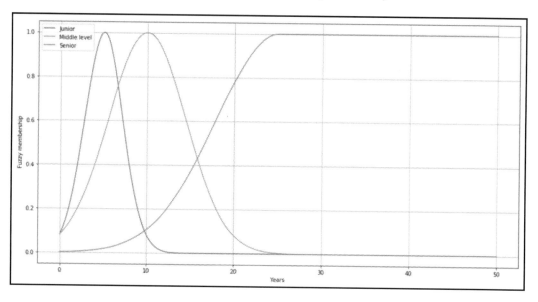

Example of fuzzy sets representing the seniority level of an employee according to years of experience

The graph represents the seniority level of an employee given his/her years of experience. As we want to cluster the entire population into three groups (**Junior**, **Middle level**, and **Senior**), three fuzzy sets have been designed. We have assumed that a young employee is keen and can quickly reach a **Junior** level after an initial apprenticeship period. The possibility to work with complex problems allows him/her to develop skills that are fundamental to allowing the transition between the **Junior** and **Middle** levels. After about **10** years, the employee can begin to consider himself/herself as a *senior apprentice* and, after about 25 years, the experience is enough to qualify him/her as a full **Senior** until the end of his/her career. As this is an imaginary example, we haven't tuned all the values up, but it's easy to compare, for example, employee A with 9 years of experience with another employee B with 18 years of experience. The former is about 50% **Junior** (decreasing), 90% **Middle level** (reaching its climax), and 10% **Senior** (increasing). The latter, instead, is 0% **Junior** (ending plateau), 30% **Middle level** (decreasing), and 60% **Senior** (increasing). In both cases, the values are not normalized so always sum up to 1 because we are more interested in showing the process and the proportions. The fuzziness level is lower in extreme cases, while it becomes higher when two sets intersect. For example, at about 15%, the **Middle level** and **Senior** are about 50%. As we're going to discuss, it's useful to avoid a very high fuzziness when clustering a dataset because it can lead to a lack of precision as the boundaries *fade out*, becoming completely fuzzy.

Fuzzy C-means is a generalization of a standard K-means, with a soft assignment and more *flexible* clusters. The dataset to cluster (containing M samples) is represented by:

$$X = \{\bar{x}_1, \bar{x}_2, \ldots, \bar{x}_M\} \;\; where \;\; \bar{x}_i \in \mathbb{R}^N$$

If we assume we have k clusters, it's necessary to define a matrix $W \in \Re^{M \times k}$ containing the membership degrees for each sample:

$$W = \begin{pmatrix} w_{11} & \cdots & w_{1k} \\ \vdots & \ddots & \vdots \\ w_{M1} & \cdots & w_{Mk} \end{pmatrix}$$

Each degree $w_{ij} \in [0, 1]$ and all rows must be normalized so that they always sum up to *1*. In this way, the membership degrees can be considered as probabilities (with the same semantics) and it's easier to make decisions with a prediction result. If a hard assignment is needed, it's possible to employ the same approach normally used with Gaussian mixtures: the winning cluster is selected by applying the *argmax* function. However, it's a good practice to employ soft clustering only when it's possible to manage the vectorial output. For example, the probabilities/membership degrees can be fed into a classifier in order to yield more complex predictions.

As with K-means, the problem can be expressed as the minimization of a *generalized inertia*:

$$S_f = \sum_{j=1}^{k} \sum_{\bar{x}_i \in C_j} w_{ij}^m \left\| \bar{x}_i - \bar{\mu}_j \right\|^2$$

The constant m $(m > 1)$ is an exponent employed to re-weight the membership degrees. A value very close to *1* doesn't affect the actual values. Greater m values reduce their magnitude. The same parameter is also used when recomputing the centroids and the new membership degrees and can drive to a different clustering result. It's rather difficult to define a global acceptable value; therefore, a good practice is to start with an average m (for example, 1.5) and perform a grid search (it's possible to sample from a Gaussian or uniform distribution) until the desired accuracy has been achieved.

Minimizing the previous expression is even more difficult than with a standard inertia; therefore, a *pseudo-Lloyd's algorithm* is employed. After a random initialization, the algorithm proceeds, alternating two steps (like an EM procedure) in order to determine the centroids, and recomputing the membership degrees to maximize the internal cohesion. The centroids are determined by a weighted average:

$$\bar{\mu}_j = \frac{\sum_{i=1}^{M} w_{ij}^m \, \bar{x}_i}{\sum_{i=1}^{M} w_{ij}^m}$$

Contrary to K-means, the sum is not limited to the points belonging to a specific cluster because the weight factor will force the farthest points ($w_{ij} \approx 0.0$) to produce a contribution close to 0. At the same time, as this is a soft-clustering algorithm, no exclusions are imposed, to allow a sample to belong to any number of clusters with different membership degrees. Once the centroids have been recomputed, the membership degrees must be updated using this formula:

$$w_{ij} = \frac{1}{\sum_{p=1}^{k}\left(\frac{\|\bar{x}_i-\bar{\mu}_j\|}{\|\bar{x}_i-\bar{\mu}_p\|}\right)^{\frac{2}{m-1}}}$$

This function behaves like a similarity. In fact, when sample x_i is very close to centroid μ_j (and relatively far from μ_p with $p \neq j$), the denominator becomes small and w_{ij} increases. The exponent m directly influences the fuzzy partitioning, because when $m \approx 1$ $(m > 1)$, the denominator is a sum of *quasi*-squared terms and the closest centroid can dominate the sum, yielding to a higher preference for a specific cluster. When $m >> 1$, all the terms in the sum tend to 1, producing a more flat weight distribution with no well-defined preference. It's important to understand that, even when working with soft clustering, a fuzziness excess leads to inaccurate decisions because there are no factors that push a sample to clearly belong to a specific cluster. This means that problem is either ill-posed or, for example, the number of expected clusters is too high and doesn't represent the real underlying data structure. A good way to measure how much this algorithm is similar to a hard-clustering approach (such as K-means) is provided by the normalized **Dunn's partitioning coefficient**:

$$P_C = \frac{w_c - \frac{1}{k}}{1 - \frac{1}{k}} \quad where \quad w_c = \frac{1}{M}\sum_{i=1}^{M}\sum_{j=1}^{k} w_{ij}^2$$

When P_c is bounded between *0* and *1*, when it's close to *0*, it means that the membership degrees have a flat distribution and the level of fuzziness is the highest possible. On the other side, if it's close to *1*, each row of *W* has a single dominant value, while all the others are negligible. This scenario resembles a hard-clustering approach. Higher P_c values are normally preferable because, even without renouncing to a degree of fuzziness, it allows making more precise decisions. Considering the previous example, P_c tends to *1* when the sets don't intersect, while it becomes 0 (complete fuzziness) if, for example, the three seniority levels are chosen to be identical and overlapping. Of course, we are interested in avoiding such extreme scenarios by limiting the number of borderline cases. A grid search can be performed by analyzing different numbers of clusters and *m* values (in the example, we're going to do it with the MNIST handwritten digit dataset). A reasonable rule of thumb is to accept P_c values higher than *0.8*, but in some cases, that can be impossible. If we are sure that the problem is well-posed, the best approach is to choose the configuration that maximizes P_c, considering, however, that a final value less than *0.3-0.5* will lead to a very high level of uncertainty because the clusters are extremely overlapping.

The complete **Fuzzy C-means** algorithm is:

1. Set a maximum number of iteration N_{max}
2. Set a tolerance *Thr*
3. Set the value of *k* (number of expected clusters)
4. Initialize the matrix $W^{(0)}$ with random values and normalize each row, dividing it by its sum
5. Set $N = 0$
6. While $N < N_{max}$ or $||W^{(t)} - W^{(t-1)}|| > Thr$:
    1. $N = N + 1$
    2. For $j = 1$ to k:
        1. Compute the centroid vectors μ_j
    3. Recompute the weight matrix $W^{(t)}$
    4. Normalize the rows of $W^{(t)}$

Example of fuzzy C-means with Scikit-Fuzzy

Scikit-Fuzzy (`http://pythonhosted.org/scikit-fuzzy/`) is a Python package based on SciPy that allows implementing all the most important fuzzy logic algorithms (including fuzzy C-means). In this example, we continue using the MNIST dataset, but with a major focus on fuzzy partitioning. To perform the clustering, Scikit-Fuzzy implements the `cmeans` method (in the `skfuzzy.cluster` package) which requires a few mandatory parameters: `data`, which must be an array $D \in \Re^{N \times M}$ (N is the number of features; therefore, the array used with Scikit-Learn must be transposed); `c`, the number of clusters; the coefficient `m`, `error`, which is the maximum tolerance; and `maxiter`, which is the maximum number of iterations. Another useful parameter (not mandatory) is the `seed` parameter which allows specifying the random seed to be able to easily reproduce the experiments. I invite the reader to check the official documentation for further information.

The first step of this example is performing the clustering:

```
from skfuzzy.cluster import cmeans

fc, W, _, _, _, _, pc = cmeans(X_train.T, c=10, m=1.25, error=1e-6,
maxiter=10000, seed=1000)
```

The `cmeans` function returns many values, but for our purposes, the most important are: the first one, which is the array containing the cluster centroids; the second one, which is the final membership degree matrix; and the last one, the partition coefficient. In order to analyze the result, we can start with the partition coefficient:

```
print(pc)
0.632070870735
```

This value informs us that the clustering is not very far from a hard assignment, but there's still a residual fuzziness. In this particular case, such a situation may be reasonable because we know that many digits are partially distorted and may appear very similar to other ones (such as 1, 7, and 9). However, I invite the reader to try different values for `m` and check how the partition coefficient changes. We can now display the centroids:

Centroids obtained by fuzzy C-means

All the different digit classes have been successfully found, but now, contrary to K-means, we can check the fuzziness of a *problematic* digit (representing a 7, with index 7), as shown in the following diagram:

Sample digit (a 7) selected to test the fuzziness

The membership degrees associated with the previous sample are:

```
print(W[:, 7])
[ 0.00373221  0.01850326  0.00361638  0.01032591  0.86078292
0.02926149
  0.03983662  0.00779066  0.01432076  0.0118298 ]
```

The corresponding plot is:

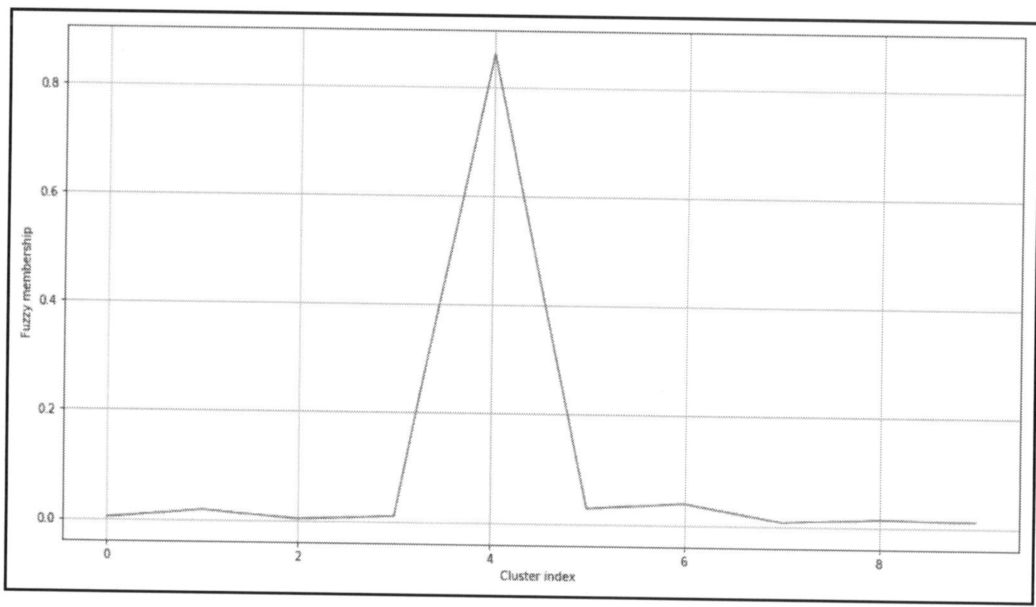

Fuzzy membership plot corresponding to a digit representing a 7

In this case, the choice of *m* has forced the algorithm to reduce the fuzziness. However, it's still possible to see three smaller peaks corresponding to the clusters centered respectively on 1, 8, and 5 (remember that the cluster indexes correspond to digits shown previously in the centroid plot). I invite the reader to analyze the fuzzy partitioning of different digits and replot it with different values of the `m` parameter. It will be possible to observe an increased fuzziness (corresponding also to smaller partitioning coefficients) with larger *m* values. This effect is due to a stronger overlap among clusters (observable also by plotting the centroids) and could be useful when it's necessary to detect the distortion of a sample. In fact, even if the main peak indicates the right cluster, the secondary ones, in descending order, inform us how much the sample is similar to other centroids and, therefore, if it contains features that are characteristics of other subsets.

Contrary to Scikit-Learn, in order to perform predictions, Scikit-Fuzzy implements the `cmeans_predict` method (in the same package), which requires the same parameters of `cmeans`, but instead of the number of clusters, `c` needs the final centroid array (the name of the parameter is `cntr_trained`). The function returns as a first value the corresponding membership degree matrix (the other ones are the same as `cmeans`). In the following snippet, we repeat the prediction for the same sample digit (representing a `7`):

```
import numpy as np

from skfuzzy.cluster import cmeans_predict

new_sample = np.expand_dims(X_train[7], axis=1)
Wn, _, _, _, _, _ = cmeans_predict(new_sample, cntr_trained=fc,
m=1.25, error=1e-6, maxiter=10000, seed=1000)

print(Wn.T)
[[ 0.00373221  0.01850326  0.00361638  0.01032591  0.86078292
0.02926149
   0.03983662  0.00779066  0.01432076  0.0118298 ]]
```

Scikit-Fuzzy can be installed using the `pip install -U scikit-fuzzy` command. For further instructions, please visit `http://pythonhosted.org/scikit-fuzzy/install.html`

Spectral clustering

One of the most common problems of K-means and other similar algorithms is the assumption we have only hyperspherical clusters. This condition can be acceptable when the dataset is split into blobs that can be easily embedded into a regular geometric structure. However, it fails whenever the sets are not separable using regular shapes. Let's consider, for example, the following bidimensional dataset:

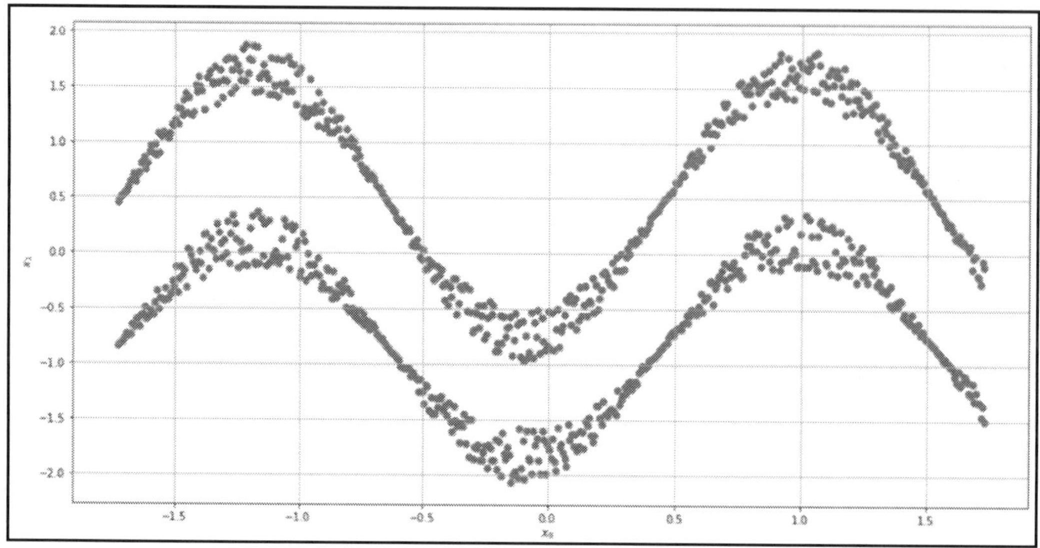

Sinusoidal dataset

As we are going to see in the example, any attempt to separate the upper sinusoid from the lower one using K-means will fail. The reason is quite obvious: a circle that contains the upper set will also contain part of the (or the whole) lower set. Considering the criterion adopted by K-means and imposing two clusters, the inertia will be minimized by a vertical separation corresponding to about $x_0 = 0$. Therefore, the resulting clusters are completely mixed and only a dimension is contributing to the final configuration. However, the two sinusoidal sets are well-separated and it's not difficult to check that, selecting a point x_i from the lower set, it's always possible to find a ball containing only samples belonging to the same set. We have already discussed this kind of problem when Label Propagation algorithms were discussed and the logic behind **spectral clustering** is essentially the same.

Let's suppose we have a dataset X sampled from a data generating process p_{data}:

$$X = \{\bar{x}_1, \bar{x}_2, \ldots, \bar{x}_M\} \;\; where \;\; \bar{x}_i \in \mathbb{R}^N$$

We can build a graph $G = \{V, E\}$, where the vertices are the points and the edges are determined using an *affinity matrix* W. Each element w_{ij} must express the affinity between sample x_i and sample x_j. W is normally built using two different approaches:

- KNN: In this case, we can build the number of neighbors to take into account for each point x_i. W can be built as a *connectivity matrix* (expressing only the existence of a connection between two samples) if we adopt the criterion:

  $$w_{ij} = \begin{cases} 1 \;\; if \;\; \bar{x}_j \in kNN(\bar{x}_i) \\ 0 \;\; otherwise \end{cases}$$

  Alternatively, it's possible to build a *distance matrix*:

  $$w_{ij} = \begin{cases} d(\bar{x}_i, \bar{x}_j) \;\; if \;\; \bar{x}_j \in kNN(\bar{x}_i) \\ 0 \;\; otherwise \end{cases}$$

- **Radial basis function** (**RBF**): The previous methods can lead to graphs which are not fully connected because samples can exist that have no neighbors. In order to obtain a fully connected graph, it's possible to employ an RBF (this approach has also been used in the Kohonen map algorithm):

  $$w_{ij} = e^{-\gamma \|\bar{x}_i - \bar{x}_j\|^2}$$

  The γ parameter allows controlling the amplitude of the Gaussian function, reducing or increasing the number of samples with a high weight (so *actual neighbors*). However, a weight is assigned to all points and the resulting graph will always be connected (even if many elements are close to zero).

In both cases, the elements of W will represent a measure of affinity (or *closeness*) between points and no restrictions are imposed on the global geometry (contrary to K-means). In particular, using a KNN connectivity matrix, we are implicitly segmenting the original dataset into smaller regions with a high level of internal cohesion. The problem that we need to solve now is to find out a way to merge all the regions belonging to the same cluster. The approach we are going to present here has been proposed by *Normalized Cuts and Image Segmentation, J. Shi* and *J. Malik, IEEE Transactions on Pattern Analysis and Machine Intelligence, Vol. 22, 08/2000,* and it's based on the normalized graph Laplacian:

$$L_n = I - D^{-1}W$$

The matrix D, called the degree matrix, is the same as discussed in `Chapter 3`, *Graph-Based Semi-Supervised Learning* and it's defined as:

$$D = diag\left(\left[\sum_j w_{ij}\right] \forall\, i \in [1, M]\right)$$

It's possible to prove the following properties (the formal proofs are omitted but they can be found in texts such as *Functions and Graphs Vol. 2, Gelfand I. M., Glagoleva E. G., Shnol E. E., The MIT Press*:

- The eigenvalues λ_i and the eigenvectors v_i of L_n can be found by solving the problem $Lv = \lambda Dv$, where L is the unnormalized graph Laplacian $L = D - W$
- L_n always has an eigenvalue equal to 0 (with a multiplicity k) with a corresponding eigenvector $v_o = (1, 1, ..., 1)$
- As G is undirected and all $w_{ij} \geq 0$, the number of connected components k of G is equal to the multiplicity of the null eigenvalue

In other words, the normalized graph Laplacian encodes the information about the number of connected components and provides us with a new reference system where the clusters can be separated using regular geometric shapes (normally hyperspheres). To better understand how this approach works without a non-trivial mathematical approach, it's important to expose another property of L_n.

From linear algebra, we know that each eigenvalue λ of a matrix $M \in \Re^{n \times n}$ spans a corresponding eigenspace, which is a subset of $\Re^n$ containing all eigenvectors associated with λ plus the null vector.

Moreover, given a set $S \subseteq \Re n$ and a countable subset C (it's possible to extend the definition to generic subsets but in our context the datasets are always countable), we can define a vector $v \in \Re^n$ as an *indicator vector*, if $v^{(i)} = 1$ if the vector $c_i \in S$ and $v^{(i)} = 0$ otherwise. If we consider the null eigenvalues of L_n and we assume that their number is k (corresponding to the multiplicity of the eigenvalue 0), it's possible to prove that the corresponding eigenvectors are indicator vectors for eigenspaces spanned by each of them. From the previous statements, we know that these eigenspaces correspond to the connected components of the graph G; therefore, performing a standard clustering (like K-means or K-means++) with the points projected into these subspaces allows for an easy separation with symmetric shapes.

As $L_n \in \Re^{M \times M}$, its eigenvectors $v_i \in \Re^M$. Selecting the first k eigenvectors, it's possible to build a matrix $A \in \Re^{M \times k}$:

$$A = \begin{pmatrix} v_1^{(1)} & v_2^{(1)} & \cdots & v_k^{(1)} \\ v_1^{(2)} & v_2^{(2)} & \cdots & v_1^{(k)} \\ \vdots & \vdots & \ddots & \vdots \\ v_1^{(M)} & v_2^{(M)} & \cdots & v_k^{(M)} \end{pmatrix}$$

Each row of A, $a_j \in \Re^k$ can be considered as the projection of an original sample x_j in the low-dimensional subspace spanned by each of the null eigenvalues of L_n. At this point, the separability of the new dataset $A = \{a_j\}$ depends only on the structure of the graph G and, in particular, on the number of neighbors or the γ parameter for RBFs. As in many other similar cases, it's impossible to define a standard value suitable for all problems, above all when the dimensionality doesn't allow a visual inspection. A reasonable approach should start with a small number of neighbors (for example, five) or $\gamma = 1.0$ and increase the values until a performance metric (such as the Adjusted Rand Index) reaches its maximum. Considering the nature of the problems, it can also be useful to measure the homogeneity and the completeness because these two measures are more sensitive to irregular geometric structures and can easily show when the clustering is not separating the sets correctly. If the ground truth is unknown, the Silhouette score can be employed to assess the intra-cluster cohesion and the inter-cluster separation as functions of all hyperparameters (number of clusters, number of neighbors, or γ).

The complete **Shi-Malik spectral clustering** algorithm is:

1. Select a graph construction a method between KNN (1) and RBF (2):
    1. Select parameter k
    2. Select parameter γ
2. Select the expected number of clusters N_k.
3. Compute the matrices W and D.
4. Compute the normalized graph Laplacian L_n.
5. Compute the first k eigenvectors of L_n.
6. Build the matrix A.
7. Cluster the rows of A using K-means++ (or any other symmetric algorithm). The output of this process is this set of clusters: $C_{km}^{(1)}, C_{km}^{(2)}, ..., C_{km}^{(Nk)}$.

Example of spectral clustering with Scikit-Learn

In this example, we are going to use the sinusoidal dataset previously shown. The first step is creating it (with 1,000 samples):

```
import numpy as np

from sklearn.preprocessing import StandardScaler

nb_samples = 1000

X = np.zeros(shape=(nb_samples, 2))

for i in range(nb_samples):
    X[i, 0] = float(i)
    if i % 2 == 0:
        X[i, 1] = 1.0 + (np.random.uniform(0.65, 1.0) *
np.sin(float(i) / 100.0))
    else:
        X[i, 1] = 0.1 + (np.random.uniform(0.5, 0.85) *
np.sin(float(i) / 100.0))
ss = StandardScaler()
Xs = ss.fit_transform(X)
```

At this point, we can try to cluster it using K-means (with `n_clusters=2`):

```
from sklearn.cluster import KMeans

km = KMeans(n_clusters=2, random_state=1000)
Y_km = km.fit_predict(Xs)
```

The result is shown in the following graph:

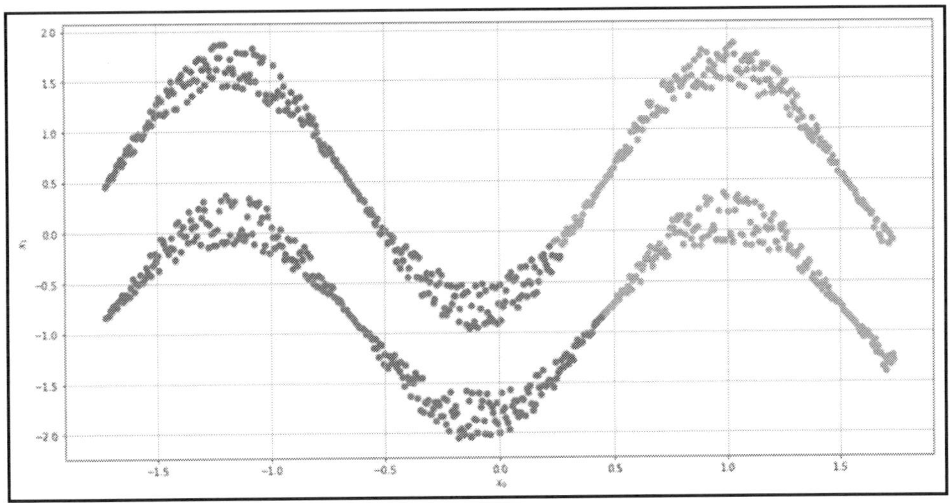

K-means clustering result using the sinusoidal dataset

As expected, K-means isn't able to separate the two sinusoids. The reader is free to try with different parameters, but the result will always be unacceptable because K-means bidimensional clusters are circles and no valid configurations exist. We can now employ spectral clustering using an affinity matrix based on the KNN algorithm (in this case, Scikit-Learn can produce a warning because the graph is not fully connected, but this normally doesn't affect the results). Scikit-Learn implements the `SpectralClustering` class, whose most important parameters are `n_clusters`, the number of expected clusters; `affinity`, which can be either `'rbf'` or `'nearest_neighbors'`; `gamma` (only for RBF); and `n_neighbors` (only for KNN). For our test, we have chosen to have `20` neighbors:

```
from sklearn.cluster import SpectralClustering

sc = SpectralClustering(n_clusters=2, affinity='nearest_neighbors',
n_neighbors=20, random_state=1000)
Y_sc = sc.fit_predict(Xs)
```

The result of the spectral clustering is shown in the following graph:

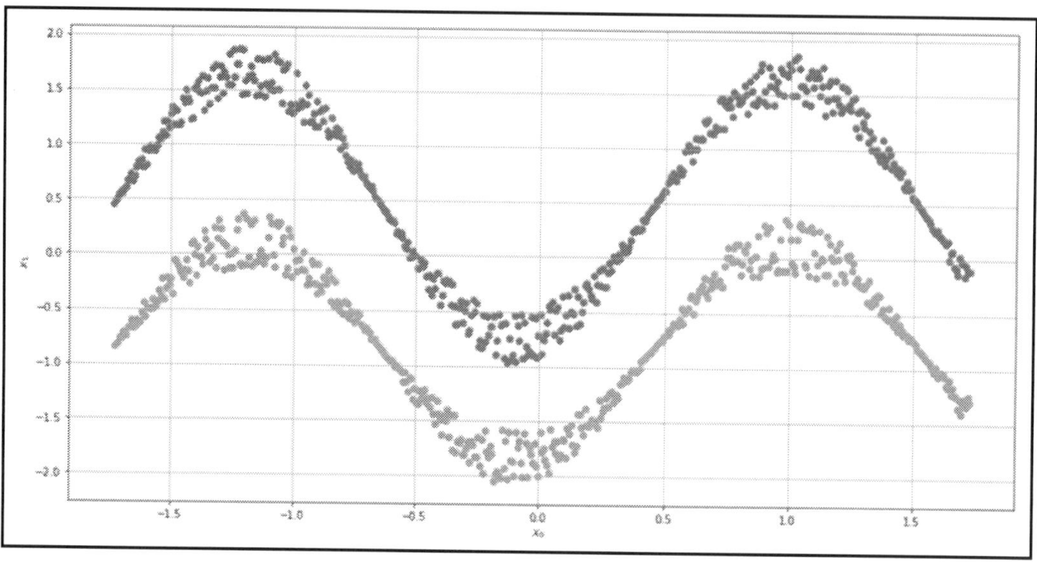

Spectral clustering result using the sinusoidal dataset

As expected, the algorithm was able to separate the two sinusoids perfectly. As an exercise, I invite the reader to apply this method to the MNIST dataset, using both an RBF (with different gamma values) and KNN (with different numbers of neighbors). I also suggest to replot the t-SNE diagram and compare all the assignment errors. As the clusters are strictly non-convex, we don't expect a high Silhouette score. Other useful exercises can be: drawing the Silhouette plot and checking the result, assigning ground truth labels, and measuring the homogeneity and the completeness.

Summary

In this chapter, we presented some fundamental clustering algorithms. We started with KNN, which is an instance-based method that restructures the dataset to find the most similar samples given a query point. We discussed three approaches: a naive one, which is also the most expensive in terms of computational complexity, and two strategies based respectively on the construction of a KD Tree and a Ball Tree. These two data structures can dramatically improve performance even when the number of samples is very large.

The next topic was a classic algorithm: K-means, which is a symmetric partitioning strategy, comparable to a Gaussian mixture with variances close to zero, that can solve many real-life problems. We discussed both a vanilla algorithm, which wasn't able to find a valid sub-optimal solution, and an optimized initialization method, called K-means++, which was able to speed up the convergence towards solutions quite close to the global minimum. In the same section, we also presented some evaluation methods that can be employed to assess the performance of a generic clustering algorithm.

We also presented a soft-clustering method called fuzzy C-means, which resembles the structure of a standard K-means, but allows managing membership degrees (analogous to probabilities) that encode the similarity of a sample with all cluster centroids. This kind of approach allows processing the membership vectors in a more complex pipeline, where the output of a clustering process, for example, is fed into a classifier.

One of the most important limitations of K-means and similar algorithms is the symmetric structure of the clusters. This problem can be solved with methods such as spectral clustering, which is a very powerful approach based on the dataset graph and is quite similar to non-linear dimensionality reduction methods. We analyzed an algorithm proposed by Shi and Malik, showing how it can easily separate a non-convex dataset.

8
Advanced Neural Models

In this chapter, we will explore pragmatic world of deep learning, analyzing two very important elements: deep convolutional networks and **recurrent neural networks (RNN)**. The former represents the most accurate and best performing visual processing technique for almost any purpose. Results like the ones obtained in fields such as real-time image recognition, self-driving cars, and Deep Reinforcement Learning have been possible thanks to the expressivity of this kind of network. On the other hand, in order to fully manage the temporal dimension, it is necessary to introduce advanced recurrent layers, whose performance must be greater than any other regression method. Employing these two techniques together with all the elements already discussed in the previous chapter makes it possible to achieve extraordinary results in the field of video processing, decoding, segmentation, and generation.

In particular, in this chapter, we are going to discuss the following topics:

- Deep convolutional networks
- Convolutions, atrous convolutions, separable convolutions, and transpose convolutions
- Pooling and other support layers
- Recurrent neural networks
- LSTM and GRU cells
- Transfer learning

Deep convolutional networks

As the fully-connected layers are *horizontal*, the images, which in general are three-dimensional structures (*width* × *height* × *channels*), must be flattened and transformed into one-dimensional arrays where the geometric properties are definitively lost. With more complex datasets, where the distinction between classes depends on more details and on their relationships, this approach can yield moderate accuracies, but it can never reach the precision required by production-ready applications.

The conjunction of neuroscientific studies and image processing techniques suggested experimenting with neural networks where the first layers work with bidimensional structures (without the channels), trying to extract a hierarchy of features that are strictly dependent on the geometric properties of the image. In fact, as confirmed by neuroscientific research about the visual cortex, a human being doesn't decode an image directly. The process is sequential and starts by detecting low-level elements such as lines are orientations; progressively, it proceeds by focusing on sub-properties that define more and more complex shapes, different colors, structural features, and so on, until the amount of information is enough to resolve any possible ambiguity (for further scientific details, I recommend the book *Vision and Brain: How We Perceive the World, Stone J. V., MIT Press*).

For example, we can image the decoding process of an eye as a sequence made up of these filters (of course, this is only a didactic example): directions (dominant horizontal dimension), a central circle inside an ellipsoidal shape, a darker center (pupil) and a clear background (bulb), a smaller darker circle in the middle of the pupil, the presence of eyebrows, and so on. Even if the process is not biologically correct, it can be considered as a reasonable hierarchical process where a higher level sub-feature is obtained after a lower-level filtering.

This approach has been synthesized using the bidimensional convolutional operator, which was already known as a powerful image processing tool. However, in this case, there's a very important difference: the structure of the filters is not pre-imposed but learned by the network using the same back-propagation algorithm employed for MLPs. In this way, the model can adapt the weights considering a final goal (which is the classification output), without taking into account any pre-processing steps. In fact, a deep convolutional network, more than an MLP, is based on the concept of end-to-end learning, which is a different way to express what we have described before. The input is the source; in the middle, there's a flexible structure; and, at the end, we define a global cost function, measuring the accuracy of the classification. The learning process has to back-propagate the errors and correct the weights to reach a specific goal, but we don't know exactly how this process works. What we can easily do is analyze the structure of the filters at the end of the learning phase, discovering that the network has specialized the first layers on low-level details (such as orientations) and the last ones on high-level, sometimes recognizable, ones (such as the components of a face). It's not surprising that such models achieved state-of-the-art performance in tasks such as image recognition, segmentation (detecting the boundaries of different parts composing an image), and tracking (detecting the position of moving objects). Nevertheless, deep convolutional networks have become the first block of many different architectures (such as deep reinforcement learning or neural style transfer) and, even with a few known limitations, continue to be the first choice for solving several complex real-life problems. The main drawback of such models (which is also a common objection) is that they require very large datasets to reach high accuracies. All the most important models are trained with millions of images and their generalization ability (that is, the main goal) is proportional to the number of different samples. There were researchers who noticed that a human being learns to generalize without this huge amount of experience and, in the coming decades, we are likely to observe improvements under this viewpoint. However, deep convolutional networks have revolutionized many Artificial Intelligence fields, allowing results that were considered almost impossible just a few years ago.

In this section, we are going to discuss different kinds of convolutions and how they can be implemented using Keras; therefore, for specific technical details I continue suggesting to check the official documentation and the book *Deep Learning with Keras, Gulli A, Pal S., Packt*.

Convolutions

Even if we work only with finite and discrete convolutions, it's useful to start providing the standard definition based on integrable functions. For simplicity, let's suppose that $f(\tau)$ and $k(\tau)$ are two real functions of a single variable defined in $\Re$. The convolution of $f(\tau)$ and $k(\tau)$ (conventionally denoted as $f * k$), which we are going to call kernel, is defined as follows:

$$f * k = \int_{-\infty}^{\infty} f(\tau)k(t-\tau)d\tau$$

The expression may not be very easy to understand without a mathematical background, but it can become exceptionally simple with a few considerations. First of all, the integral sums over all values of τ; therefore, the convolution is a function of the remaining variable, t. The second fundamental element is a sort of dynamic property: the kernel is reversed ($-\tau$) and transformed into a function of a new variable $z = t - \tau$. Without deep mathematical knowledge, it's possible to understand that this operation shifts the function along the τ (independent variable) axis. In the following graphs, there's an example based on a parabola:

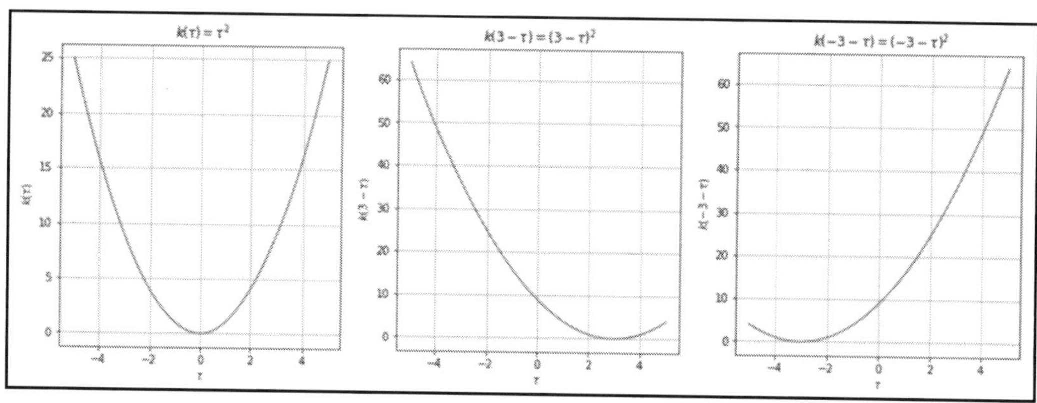

The first diagram is the original kernel (which is also symmetric). The other two plots show, respectively, a forward and a backward shift. It should be clearer now that a convolution multiplies the function $f(\tau)$ times the shifted kernel and computes the area under the resulting curve. As the variable t is not integrated, the area is a function of t and defines a new function, which is the convolution itself. In other words, the value of convolution of $f(\tau)$ and $k(\tau)$ computed for $t = 5$ is the area under the curve obtained by the multiplication $f(\tau)k(5 - \tau)$. By definition, a convolution is commutative $(f * k = k * f)$ and distributive $(f * (k + g) = (f * k) + (f * g))$. Moreover, it's also possible to prove that it's associative $(f * (k * g) = (f * k) * g)$.

However, in deep learning, we never work with continuous convolutions; therefore, I omit all the properties and mathematical details, focusing the attention on the discrete case. The reader who is interested in the theory can find further details in *Circuits, Signals, and Systems, Siebert W. M., MIT Press*. A common practice is, instead, to stack multiple convolutions with different kernels (often called filters), to transform an input containing n channels into an output with m channels, where m corresponds to the number of kernels. This approach allows the unleashing of the full power of convolutions, thanks to the synergic actions of different outputs. Conventionally, the output of a convolution layer with n filters is called a **feature map** $(w^{(t)} \times h^{(t)} \times n)$, because its structure is no longer related to a specific image but resembles the overlap of different feature detectors. In this chapter, we often talk about images (considering a hypothetical first layer), but all the considerations are implicitly extended to any feature map.

Bidimensional discrete convolutions

The most common type of convolution employed in deep learning is based on bidimensional arrays with any number of channels (such as grayscale or RGB images). For simplicity, let's analyze a single layer (channel) convolution because the extension to n layers is straightforward. If $X \in \Re^{w \times h}$ and $k \in \Re^{n \times m}$, the convolution $X * k$ is defined as (the indexes start from 0):

$$(X * k)(x, y) = \sum_{i \in [0, n-1],\ j \in [0, m-1]} k(i, j) X(x + i, y + j)$$

It's clear that the previous expression is a natural derivation of the continuous definition. In the following graph, there's an example with a 3 × 3 kernel:

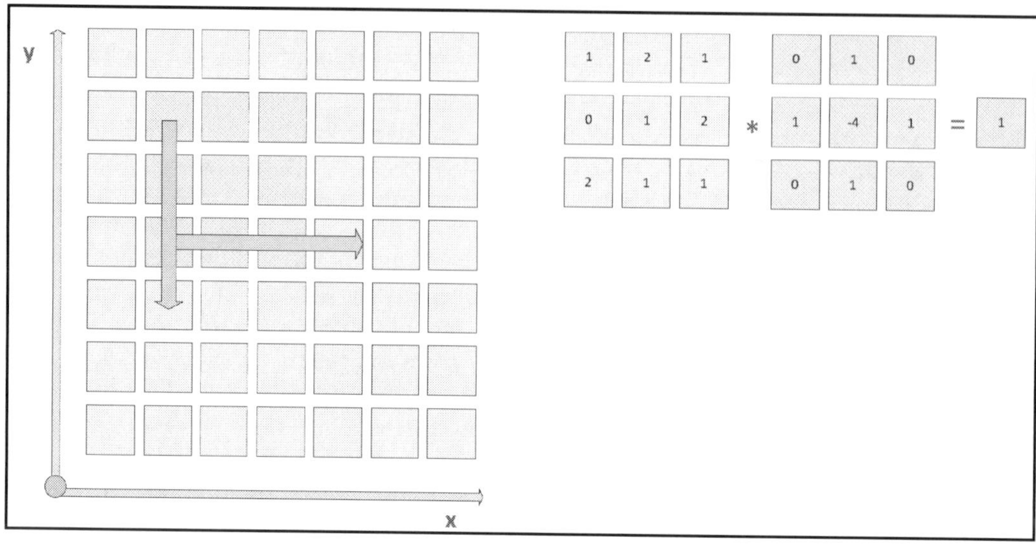

Example of bidimensional convolution with a 3x3 kernel

The kernel is shifted horizontally and vertically, yielding the sum of the element-wise multiplication of corresponding elements. Therefore, every operation leads to the output of a single pixel. The kernel employed in the example is called the **discrete Laplacian operator** (because it's obtained by discretizing the real Laplacian); let's observe the effect of this kernel on a complete greyscale diagram:

Example of convolution with a Discrete Laplacian Kernel

As it's possible to notice, the effect of the convolution is to emphasize the borders of the various shapes. The reader can now understand how variable kernels can be tuned up in order to fulfill precise requirements. However, instead of trying to do it manually, a deep convolutional network leaves this tasks to the learning process, which is subject to a precise goal expressed as the minimization of a cost function. A parallel application of different filters yields complex overlaps that can simplify the extraction of those features that are really important for a classification. The main difference between a fully-connected layer and a convolutional one is the ability of the latter to work with an existing geometry, which encodes all the elements needed to distinguish an object from another one. These elements cannot be immediately generalizable (think about the branches of a decision tree, where a split defines a precise path towards a final class), but require subsequent processing steps to perform a necessary disambiguation. Considering the previous photo, for example, eyes and nose are rather similar. How is it possible to segment the picture correctly? The answer is provided by a double analysis: there are subtle differences that can be discovered by fine-grained filters and, above all, the global geometry of real objects is based on internal relationships that are almost invariant. For example (only for didactic purposes), eyes and nose should make up an isosceles triangle, because the symmetry of a face implies the same distance between each eye and the nose. This consideration can be made *apriori*, like in many visual processing techniques, or, thanks to the power of deep learning, it can be left to the training process. As the cost function and the output classes implicitly control the differences, a deep convolutional network can learn what is important to reach a specific goal, discarding at the same time all those details that are useless.

In the previous section, we have said that the feature extraction process is mainly hierarchical. Now, it should be clear that different kernel sizes and subsequent convolutions achieve exactly this objective. Let's suppose that we have a 100×100 image and a (3×3) kernel. The resulting image will be 98×98 pixels (we will explain this concept later). However, each pixel encodes the information of a 3×3 block and, as these blocks are overlapping, two consecutive pixels will share some knowledge but, at the same time, they emphasize the difference between the corresponding blocks.

In the following diagram, the same Laplacian Kernel is applied to a simple white square on a black background:

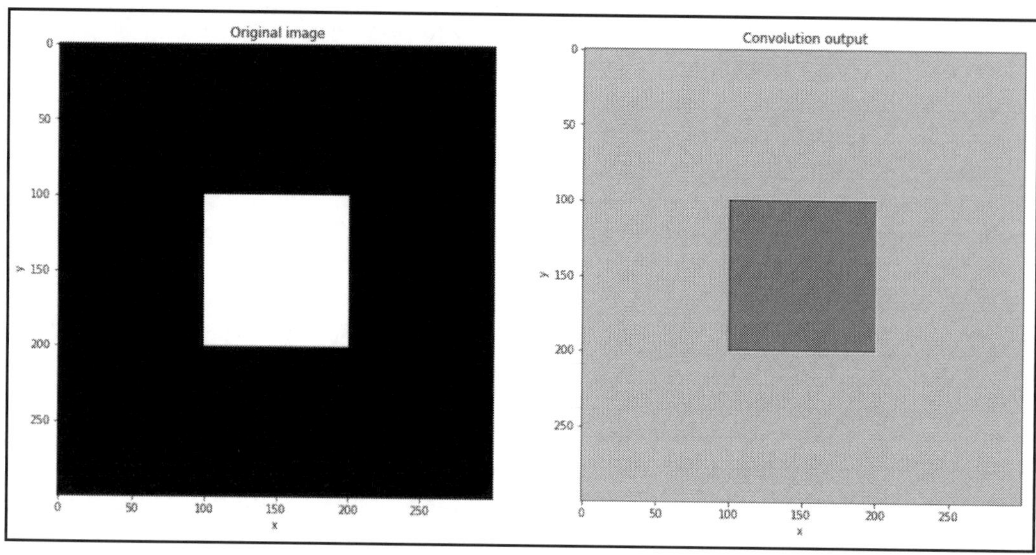

Orginal image (left): convolution with Laplacian kernel result (right)

Even if the image is very simple, it's possible to notice that the result of a convolution enriched the output image with some very important pieces of information: the borders of the square are now clearly visible (they are black and white) and they can be immediately detected by thresholding the image. The reason is straightforward: the effect of the kernel on the compact surfaces is compact too but, when the kernel is shifted upon the border, the effect of the difference becomes visible. Three adjacent pixels in the original image can be represented as *(0, 1, 1)*, indicating the horizontal transition between black and white. After the convolution, the result is approximately *(0.75, 0.0, 0.25)*. All the original black pixels have been transformed into a light gray, the white square became darker, and the border (which is not marked in the original picture) is now black (or white, depending on the shift direction). Reapplying the same filter to the output of the previous convolution, we obtain the following:

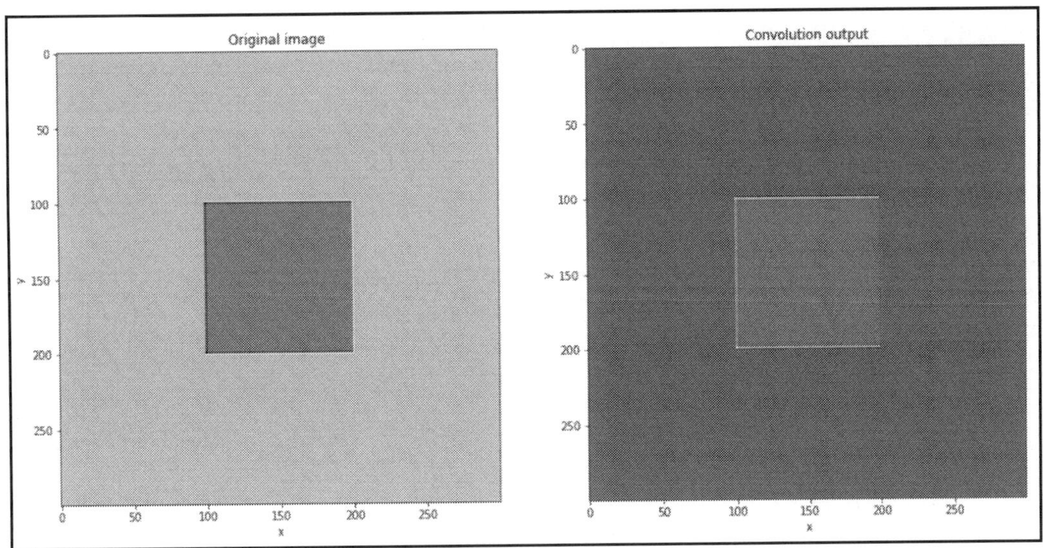

Second application of the Laplacian kernel

A sharp eye can immediately notice three results: the compact surfaces (black and white) are becoming more and more similar, the borders are still visible, and, above all, the top and lower left corners are now more clearly marked with white pixels. Therefore, the result of the second convolution added a finer-grained piece of information, which was much more difficult to detect in the original image. Indeed, the effect of the Laplacian operator is very straightforward and it's useful only for didactic purposes. In real deep convolutional networks, the filters are trained to perform more complex processing operations that can reveal details (together with their internal and external relationships) that are not immediately exploited to classify the image. Their isolation (obtained thanks to the effect of many parallel filters) allows the network to mark similar elements (like the corners of the square) in a different way and make more accurate decisions.

The purpose of this example is to show how a sequence of convolutions allows the generation of a hierarchical process that will extract coarse-grained features at the beginning and very high-level ones at the end, without losing the information already collected. Metaphorically, we could say that a deep convolutional network starts placing labels indicating lines, orientations, and borders and proceeds by enriching the existing ontology with further details (such as corners, particular shapes, and so on). Thanks to this ability, such models can easily outperform any MLP and reach almost to the Bayes level if the number of training samples is large enough. The main drawback of this models is their inability to easily recognize objects after the application of affine transformations (such as rotations or translations). In other words, if a network is trained with a dataset containing only faces in their natural position, it will achieve poor performance when a rotated (or upside-down) sample is presented. In the next sections, we are going to discuss a couple of methods that are helpful for mitigating this problem (in the case of translations); however, a new experimental architecture called a **capsule network** (which is beyond the scope of this book) has been proposed in order to solve this problem with a slightly different and much more robust approach (the reader can find further details in *Dynamic Routing Between Capsules, Sabour S., Frosst N., Hinton G. E., arXiv:1710.09829 [cs.CV]*).

Strides and padding

Two important parameters common to all convolutions are **padding** and **strides**. Let's consider the bidimensional case, but keep in mind that the concepts are always the same. When a kernel ($n \times m$ with $n, m > 1$) is shifted upon an image and it arrives at the end of a dimension, there are two possibilities. The first one, called **valid padding**, consists of not continuing even if the resulting image is smaller than the original. In particular, if X is a $w \times h$ matrix, the resulting convolution output will have dimensions equal to $(w - n + 1) \times (h - m + 1)$. However, there are many cases when it's useful to keep the original dimensions, for example, to be able to sum different outputs. This approach is called **same padding** and it's based on the simple idea to add $n - 1$ blank columns and $m - 1$ blank rows to allow the kernel to shift over the original image, yielding a number of pixels equal to the initial dimensions. In many implementations, the default value is set to valid padding.

The other parameter, called **strides**, defines the number of pixels to skip during each shift. For example, a value set to (*1, 1*) corresponds to a standard convolution, while strides set to (*2, 1*) are shown in the following diagram:

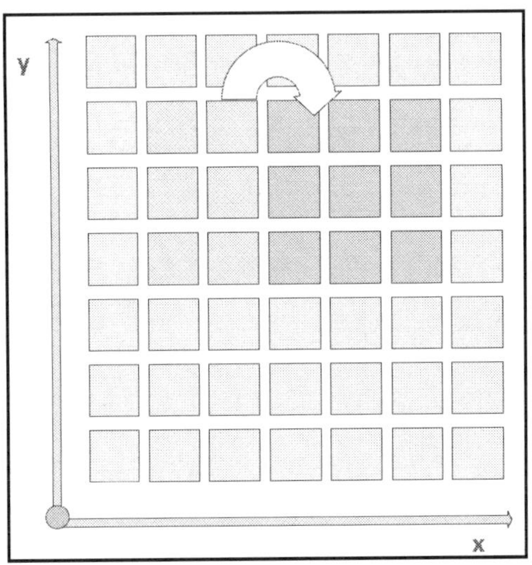

Example of bidimensional convolution with strides=2 on the x-axis

In this case, every horizontal shift skips a pixel. Larger strides force a dimensionality reduction when a high granularity is not necessary (for example, in the first layers), while strides set to (*1, 1*) are normally employed in the last layers to capture smaller details. There are no standard rules to find out the optimal value and testing different configurations is always the best approach. Like any other hyperparameter, too many elements should be taken into account when determining whether a choice is acceptable or not; however, some general pieces of information about the dataset (and therefore about the underlying data generating process) can help in making a reasonable initial decision. For example, if we are working with pictures of buildings whose dimension is vertical, it's possible to start picking a value of (*1, 2*), because we can assume that there's more informative redundancy in the *y*-axis than in the *x*-axis. This choice can dramatically speed up the training process, as the output has one dimension, which is half (with the same padding) of the original one. In this way, larger strides produce a partial denoising and can improve the training speed. At the same time, the information loss could have a negative impact on the accuracy. If that happens, it probably means that the scale isn't high enough to allow skipping some elements without compromising the *semantics*. For example, an image with very small faces could be irreversibly *damaged* with large strides, yielding an inability to detect the right feature and a consequent worsening of the classification accuracy.

Atrous convolution

In some cases, a stride larger than one could be a good solution because it reduces the dimensionality and speeds up the training process, but it can lead to distorted images where the main features are not detectable anymore. An alternative approach is provided by the **atrous convolution** (also known as **dilated convolution**). In this case, the kernel is applied to a larger image patch, but skips some pixels inside the area itself (that's why someone called it convolution with holes). In the following graph, there's an example with (3×3) and dilation rate set to 2:

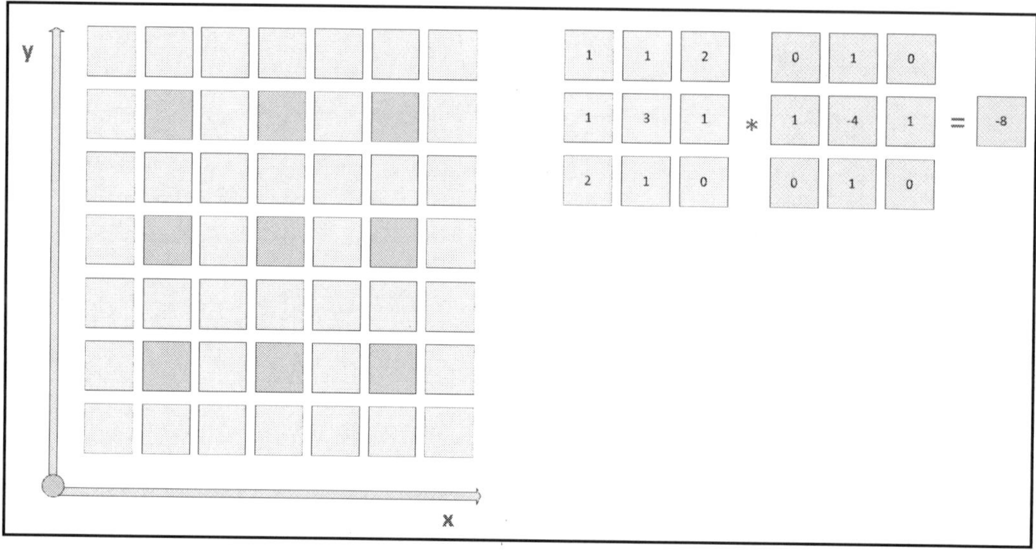

Example of atrous convolution with a Laplacian kernel

Every patch is now 9×9, but the kernel remains a 3×3 Laplacian operator. The effect of this approach is more robust than increasing the strides because the kernel *perimeter* will always contain a group of pixels with the same geometrical relationships. Of course, fine-grained features could be distorted, but as the strides are normally set to *(1, 1)*, the final result is normally more coherent. The main difference with a standard convolution is that in this case, we are assuming that farther elements can be taken into account to determine the nature of an output pixel. For example, if the main features don't contain very small details, an atrous convolution can consider larger areas, focusing directly on elements that a standard convolution can detect only after several operations. The choice of this technique must be made considering the final accuracy, but just like for the strides, it can be considered from the beginning whenever the geometric properties can be detected more efficiently, considering larger patches with a few representative elements. Even if this method can be very effective in particular contexts, it isn't normally the first choice for very deep models. In the most important image classification models, standard convolutions (with or without larger strides) are employed because they have been proven to yield the best performance with very generic datasets (such as ImageNet or Microsoft Coco). However, I suggest the reader experiment with this method and compare the results. In particular, it would be a good idea to analyze which classes are better classified and try to find a rational explanation for the observed behavior.

In some frameworks, such as Keras, there are no explicit layers to define an atrous convolution. Instead, a standard convolutional layer normally has a parameter to define the dilation rate (in Keras, it's called `dilation_rate`). Of course, the default value is 1, meaning that the kernel will be applied to patches matching its size.

Separable convolution

If we consider an image $X \in \Re^{w \times h}$ (single channel) and a kernel $k \in \Re^{n \times m}$, the number of operations is *nmwh*. When the kernel is not very small and the image is large, the cost of this computation can be quite high, even with GPU support. An improvement can be achieved by taking into account the associated property of convolutions. In particular, if the original kernel can be split into the dot product of two vectorial kernels, $k^{(1)}$ with dimensions $(n \times 1)$ and $k^{(2)}$ with dimensions $(1 \times m)$, the convolution is said to be **separable**. This means that we can perform a $(n \times m)$ convolution with two subsequent operations:

$$X * k \sim \left(X * \begin{pmatrix} k_1^{(1)} \\ \vdots \\ k_n^{(1)} \end{pmatrix} \right) * \begin{pmatrix} k_1^{(2)} & \cdots & k_m^{(2)} \end{pmatrix}$$

The advantage is clear, because now the number of operations is $(n + m)wh$. In particular, when $nm \gg n + m$, it's possible to avoid a large number of multiplications and speed up both the training and the prediction process.

A slightly different approach has been proposed in *Xception: Deep Learning with Depthwise Separable Convolutions, Chollet F., arXiv:1610.02357 [cs.CV]*. In this case, which is properly called **depthwise separable convolution**, the process is split into two steps. The first one operates along the channel axis, transforming it into a single dimensional map with a variable number of channels (for example, if the original diagram is $768 \times 1024 \times 3$, the output of the first stage will be $n \times 768 \times 1024 \times 1$). Then, a standard convolution is applied to the single layer (which can have indeed more than one channel). In the majority of implementations, the default number of output channels for the depthwise convolution is 1 (this is conventionally expressed by saying that the **depth multiplier** is 1). This approach allows a dramatic parameter reduction with respect to a standard convolution. In fact, if the input generic feature map is $X \in \Re^{w \times h \times p}$ and we want to perform a standard convolution with q kernels $k^{(i)} \in \Re^{n \times m}$, we need to learn *nmqp* parameters (each kernel $k^{(i)}$ is applied to all input channels). Employing the Depthwise Separable Convolution, the first step (working with only the channels) requires *nmp* parameters. As the output has still p feature maps and we need to output q channels, the process employs a *trick*: processing each feature map with q 1×1 kernels (in this way, the output will have q layers and the same dimensions).

The number of parameters required for the second step is *pq*, so the total number of parameters becomes *nmp* + *pq*. Comparing this value with the one required for a standard convolution, we obtain an interesting result:

$$nmp + pq < nmpq \quad \Rightarrow \quad nm + q < nmq \quad \Rightarrow \quad nm < q(nm-1) \quad \Rightarrow \quad q > \frac{nm}{nm-1}$$

As this condition is easily true, this approach is extremely effective in optimizing the training and prediction processes, as well as the memory consumption in any scenario. It's not surprising that the Xception model has been immediately implemented in mobile devices, allowing real-time image classification with very limited resources. Of course, depthwise separable convolutions don't always have the same accuracy as standard ones, because they are based on the assumption that the geometrical features observable inside a channel of a composite feature map are independent of each other. This is not always true, because we know that the effect of multiple layers is based also on their combinations (which increases the expressivity of a network). However, in many cases the final result has an accuracy comparable to some state-of-the-art models; therefore, this technique can very often be considered as a valid alternative to a standard convolution.

Since version 2.1.5, Keras has introduced a layer called `DepthwiseConv2D` that implements a depthwise separable convolution. This layer extends the existing `SeparableConv2D`.

Transpose convolution

A **transpose convolution** (sometimes wrongly called deconvolution, even if the mathematical definition is different) is not very different from a standard convolution, but its goal is to rebuild a structure with the same features as the input sample. Let's suppose that the output of a convolutional network is the feature map $X \in \Re^{w' \times h' \times p}$ and we need to build an output element $Y \in \Re^{w \times h \times 3}$ (assuming the w and h are the original dimensions). We can achieve this result by applying a transpose convolution with appropriate strides and padding to *X*. For example, let's suppose that $X \in \Re^{128 \times 128 \times 256}$ and our output must be $512 \times 512 \times 3$. The last transpose convolution must learn three filters with strides set to four and same padding. The main difference is the cost function, because when a transpose convolution is used as the last layer, the comparison must be done between a target image and a reconstructed one.

Pooling layers

In a deep convolutional network, **pooling layers** are extremely useful elements. There are mainly two kinds of these structures: **max pooling** and **average pooling**. They both work on patches $p \in \Re^{n \times m}$, shifting horizontally and vertically according to the predefined stride value and transforming the patches into single pixels according to the following rules:

$$\begin{cases} f_{MaxPooling}(X) = max_{i,j} X(i,j) \\ f_{AveragePooling}(X) = \frac{1}{n+m} \sum_{i=1}^{n} \sum_{j=1}^{m} X(i,j) \end{cases}$$

There are two main reasons that justify the use of these layers. The first one is a dimensionality reduction with limited information loss (for example, setting the strides to (2, 2), it's possible to halve the dimensions of an image/feature map). Clearly, all pooling techniques can be more or less lossy (in particular max pooling) and the specific result depends on the single image. In general, pooling layers try to summarize the information contained in a small chunk into a single pixel. This idea is supported by a perceptual-oriented approach; in fact, when the pools are not too large, it's rather unlikely to find high variances in subsequent shifts (natural images have very few isolated pixels). Therefore, all the pooling operations allow us to set up strides greater than one with a mitigated risk of compromising the information content. However, considering several experiments and architectures, I suggest that you set up larger strides in the convolutional layers (in particular, in the first layer of a convolutional sequence) instead of in pooling ones. In this way, it's possible to apply the transformation with a minimum loss and to fully exploit the next fundamental property.

The second (and probably the most important) reason is that they slightly increase the robustness to translations and limited distortions with an effect that is proportional to the pool size. Let's consider the following diagram, representing an original image of a cross and the version after a 10-pixel diagonal translation:

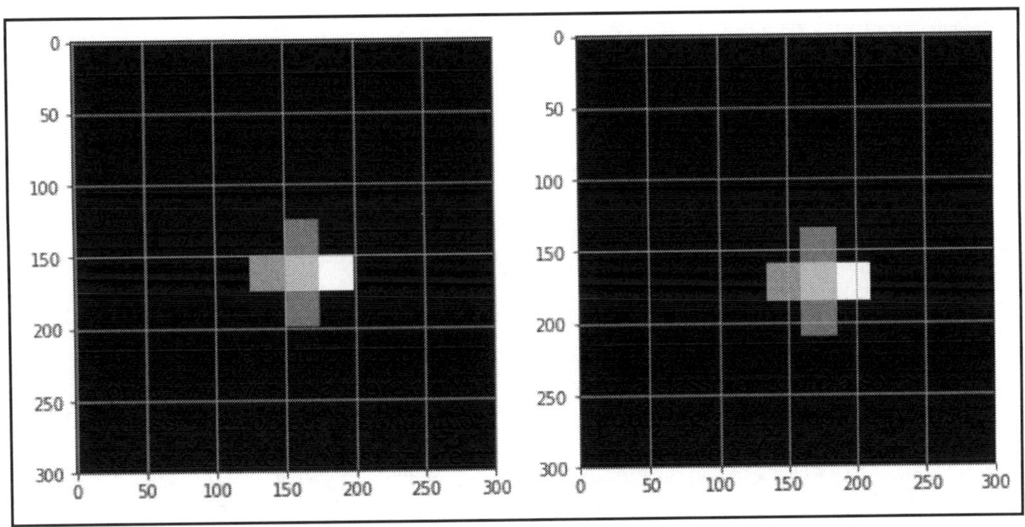

Original image (left): diagonally translated image (right)

This is a very simple example and the translated image is not very different from the original one. However, in a more complex scenario, a classifier could also fail to correctly classify an object in similar conditions. Applying a max pooling (with a (2 × 2) pool size and 2-pixel strides) on the translated image, we get the following:

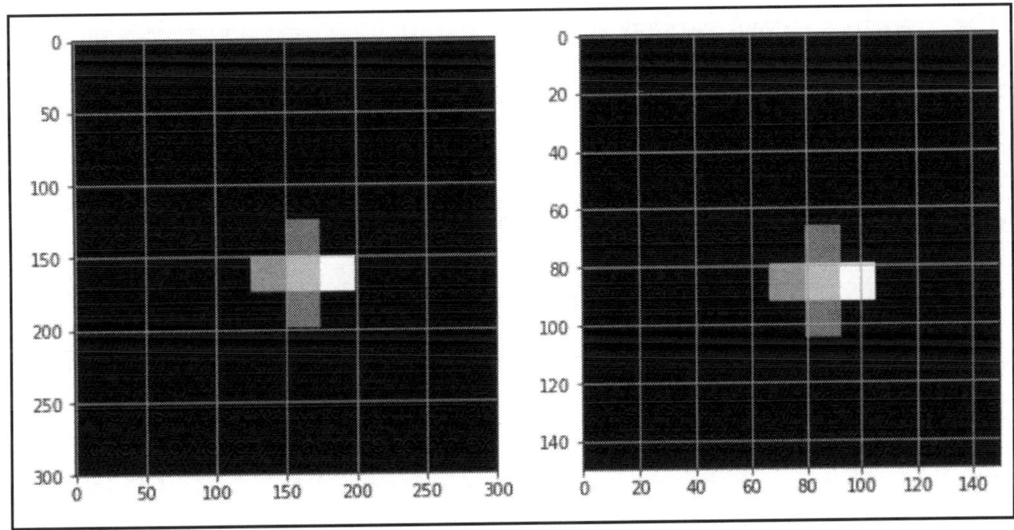

Original image (left): result of a max pooling on the translated image (right)

The result is a larger cross, whose arms are slightly more aligned to the axis. When compared with the original image, it's easier for a classifier with a good generalization ability to filter out the spurious elements and recognize the original shape (which can be considered a cross surrounded by a noisy frame). Repeating the same experiment with average pooling (same parameters), we obtain the following:

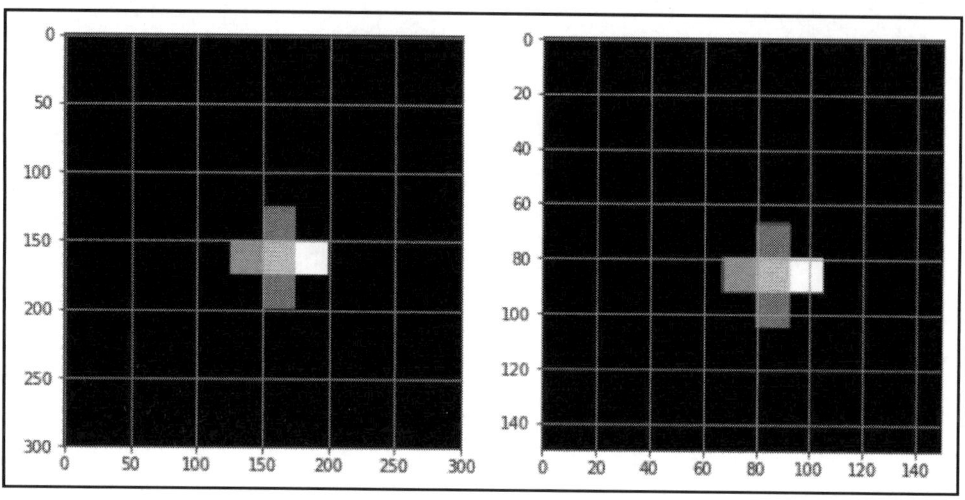

Original image (left): result of an average pooling on the translated image (right)

In this case, the picture is partially smoothed, but it's still possible to see a better alignment (thanks mainly to the fading effect). Also, if these methods are simple and somewhat effective, the robustness to invariant transformations is never dramatically improved and higher levels of invariance are possible only by increasing the pool size. This choice leads to coarser-grained feature maps whose amount of information is drastically reduced; therefore, whenever it's necessary to extend the classification to samples that can be distorted or rotated, it can be a good idea (which allows working with a dataset that better represents the real data generating process) to use a data augmentation technique to produce artificial images and to also train the classifier on them. However, as pointed out in *Deep Learning, Goodfellow I., Bengio Y., Courville A., MIT Press*, pooling layers can also provide a robust invariance to rotations when they are used together with the output of a multiple convolution layer or a rotated image stack. In fact, in these cases, a single pattern response is elicited and the effect of the pooling layer becomes similar to a collector that standardizes the output. In other words, it will produce the same result without an explicit selection of the best matching pattern. For this reason, if the dataset contains enough samples, pooling layers in intermediate positions of the network can provide a moderate robustness to small rotations, increasing the generalization ability of the whole deep architecture.

As it's easy to see in the previous example, the main difference between the two variants is the final result. Average pooling performs a sort of very simple interpolation, smoothing the borders and avoiding abrupt changes. On the other hand, max pooling is less noisy and can yield better results when the features need to be detected without any kind of smoothing (which could alter their geometry). I always suggest testing both techniques, because it's almost impossible to pick the best method with the right pool size according only to heuristic considerations (above all, when the datasets are not made up of very simple images).

Clearly, it's always preferable to use these layers after a group of convolutions, avoiding very large pool sizes that can irreversibly destroy the information content. In many important deep architectures, the pooling layers are always based on *(2, 2)* or *(3, 3)* pools, independently of their position, and the strides are always set to 1 or 2. In both cases, the information loss is proportional to the pool size/strides; therefore, large pools are normally avoided when small features must be detected together with larger ones (for example, foreground and background faces).

Other useful layers

Even if convolution and pooling layers are the backbone of almost all deep convolutional networks, other layers can be helpful to manage specific situations. They are as follows:

- **Padding layers**: These can be employed to increase the size of a feature map (for example, to align it with another one) by surrounding it with a blank frame (*n* black pixels are added before and after each side).
- **Upsampling layers**: These increase the size of a feature map by creating larger blocks out of a single pixel. To a certain extent, they can be considered as a transformation opposite to a pooling layer, even if, in this case, the upsampling is not based on any kind of interpolation. These kinds of layers can be used to prepare the feature maps for transformations similar to the ones obtained with a transpose convolution, even if many experiments confirmed that using larger strides can yield very accurate results without the need of an extra computational step.

- **Cropping layers**: These are helpful for selecting specific rectangular areas of an image/feature map. They are particularly useful in modular architectures, where the first part determines the cropping boundaries (for example, of a face), while the second part, after having removed the background, can perform high-level operations such as detail segmentation (marking the areas of eyes, nose, mouth, and so on). The possibility of inserting these layers directly into a deep neural model avoids multiple data transfers. Unfortunately, many frameworks (such as Keras) don't allow us to use variable boundaries, limiting *de facto* the number of possible use cases.
- **Flattening layers:** These are the conjunction link between feature maps and fully-connected layers. Normally, a single flattening layer is used before processing the output of the convolutional blocks, with a few dense layers terminating in a final Softmax layer (for classifications). The operation is computationally very cheap as it works only with the metadata and doesn't perform any calculations.

Examples of deep convolutional networks with Keras

In the first example, we want to consider again the complete MNIST handwritten digit dataset, but instead of using an MLP, we are going to employ a small deep convolutional network. The first step consists of loading and normalizing the dataset:

```
import numpy as np

from keras.datasets import mnist
from keras.utils import to_categorical

(X_train, Y_train), (X_test, Y_test) = mnist.load_data()

width = height = X_train.shape[1]

X_train = X_train.reshape((X_train.shape[0], width, height,
1)).astype(np.float32) / 255.0
 X_test = X_test.reshape((X_test.shape[0], width, height,
1)).astype(np.float32) / 255.0

Y_train = to_categorical(Y_train, num_classes=10)
Y_test = to_categorical(Y_test, num_classes=10)
```

We can now define the model architecture. The samples are rather small (*28 × 28*); therefore it can be helpful to use small kernels. This is not a general rule and it's useful to also evaluate larger kernels (in particular in the first layers); however, many state-of-the-art architectures confirmed large kernel sizes with small images can lead to a performance loss. In my personal experiments, I've always obtained the best results when the largest kernels were *8 ÷ 10* smaller than the image dimensions. Our model is made up of the following layers:

1. Input dropout 25%.
2. Convolution with 16 filters, (3 × 3) kernel, strides equal to 1, ReLU activation, and the same padding (the default weight initializer is Xavier). Keras implements the `Conv2D` class, whose main parameters are immediately understandable.
3. Dropout 50%.
4. Convolution with 32 filters, (3 × 3) kernel, strides equal to 1, ReLU activation, and the same padding.
5. Dropout 50%.
6. Average pooling with (2 × 2) pool size and strides equal to 1 (using the Keras class `AveragePooling2D`).
7. Convolution with 64 filters, (3 × 3) kernel, strides equal to 1, ReLU activation, and the same padding.
8. Average pooling with (2 × 2) pool size and strides equal to 1.
9. Convolution with 64 filters, (3 × 3) kernel, strides equal to 1, ReLU activation, and the same padding.
10. Dropout 50%.
11. Average pooling with (2 × 2) pool size and strides equal to 1.
12. Fully-connected layer with 1024 ReLU units.
13. Dropout 50%.
14. Fully-connected layer with 10 Softmax units.

The goal is to capture the low-level features (horizontal and vertical lines, intersections, and so on) in the first layers and use the pooling layers and all the subsequent convolutions to increase the accuracy when distorted samples are presented. At this point, we can create and compile the model (using the Adam optimizer with $\eta = 0.001$ and a decay rate equal to 10^{-5}):

```
from keras.models import Sequential
from keras.layers import Dense, Activation, Dropout, Conv2D,
AveragePooling2D, Flatten
```

```
from keras.optimizers import Adam

model = Sequential()

model.add(Dropout(0.25, input_shape=(width, height, 1), seed=1000))

model.add(Conv2D(16, kernel_size=(3, 3), padding='same'))
model.add(Activation('relu'))
model.add(Dropout(0.5, seed=1000))

model.add(Conv2D(32, kernel_size=(3, 3), padding='same'))
model.add(Activation('relu'))
model.add(Dropout(0.5, seed=1000))

model.add(AveragePooling2D(pool_size=(2, 2), padding='same'))

model.add(Conv2D(64, kernel_size=(3, 3), padding='same'))
model.add(Activation('relu'))

model.add(AveragePooling2D(pool_size=(2, 2), padding='same'))

model.add(Conv2D(64, kernel_size=(3, 3), padding='same'))
model.add(Activation('relu'))
model.add(Dropout(0.5, seed=1000))

model.add(AveragePooling2D(pool_size=(2, 2), padding='same'))

model.add(Flatten())

model.add(Dense(1024))
model.add(Activation('relu'))
model.add(Dropout(0.5, seed=1000))

model.add(Dense(10))
model.add(Activation('softmax'))

model.compile(optimizer=Adam(lr=0.001, decay=1e-5),
              loss='categorical_crossentropy',
              metrics=['accuracy'])
```

We can now proceed to train the model with 200 epochs and a batch size of 256 samples:

```
history = model.fit(X_train, Y_train,
                    epochs=200,
                    batch_size=256,
                    validation_data=(X_test, Y_test))
```

```
Train on 60000 samples, validate on 10000 samples
Epoch 1/200
60000/60000 [==============================] - 30s 496us/step - loss:
0.4474 - acc: 0.8531 - val_loss: 0.0993 - val_acc: 0.9693
Epoch 2/200
60000/60000 [==============================] - 20s 338us/step - loss:
0.1497 - acc: 0.9530 - val_loss: 0.0682 - val_acc: 0.9780
Epoch 3/200
60000/60000 [==============================] - 21s 346us/step - loss:
0.1131 - acc: 0.9647 - val_loss: 0.0598 - val_acc: 0.9839

...

Epoch 199/200
60000/60000 [==============================] - 21s 349us/step - loss:
0.0083 - acc: 0.9974 - val_loss: 0.0137 - val_acc: 0.9950
Epoch 200/200
60000/60000 [==============================] - 22s 373us/step - loss:
0.0083 - acc: 0.9972 - val_loss: 0.0143 - val_acc: 0.9950
```

The final validation accuracy is now `0.9950`, which means that only 50 samples (out of 10,000) have been misclassified. To better understand the behavior, we can plot the accuracy and loss diagrams:

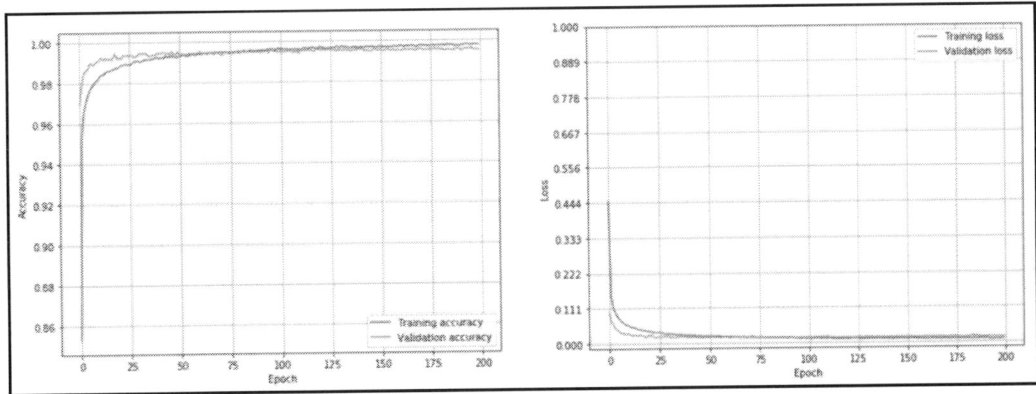

As it's possible to see, both validation accuracy and loss easily reach the optimal values. In particular, the initial validation accuracy is about 0.97 and the remaining epochs are necessary to improve the performance with all those samples, whose shapes can lead to confusion (for example, malformed 8s that resemble 0s, or 7s that are very similar to 1s). It's evident that the *geometric* approach employed by convolutions guarantees a much higher robustness than a standard fully-connected network, thanks also to the contribution of pooling layers, which reduce the variance due to noisy samples.

Example of a deep convolutional network with Keras and data augmentation

In this example, we are going to use the Fashion MNIST dataset, which was freely provided by Zalando as a more difficult replacement for the standard MNIST dataset. In this case, instead of handwritten digits, there are greyscale photos of different articles of clothing. An example of a few samples is shown in the following screenshot:

However, in this case, we want to employ a utility class provided by Keras (`ImageDataGenerator`) in order to create a data-augmented sample set to improve the generalization ability of the deep convolutional network. This class allows us to add random transformations (such as standardization, rotations, shifting, flipping, zooming, shearing, and so on) and output the samples using a Python generator (with an infinite loop). Let's start loading the dataset (we don't need to standardize it, as this transformation is performed by the generator):

```
from keras.datasets import fashion_mnist

(X_train, Y_train), (X_test, Y_test) = fashion_mnist.load_data()
```

At this point, we can create the generators, selecting the transformation that best suits our case. As the dataset is rather *standard* (all the samples are represented only in a few positions), we've decided to augment the dataset by applying a sample-wise standardization (which doesn't rely on the entire dataset), horizontal flip, zooming, small rotations, and small shears. This choice has been made according to an objective analysis, but I suggest the reader repeat the experiment with different parameters (for example, adding whitening, vertical flip, horizontal/vertical shifting, and extended rotations). Of course, increasing the augmentation variability needs larger processed sets. In our case, we are going to use 384,000 training samples (the original size is 60,000), but larger values can be employed to train deeper networks:

```
import numpy as np

from keras.preprocessing.image import ImageDataGenerator
from keras.utils import to_categorical

nb_classes = 10
train_batch_size = 256
test_batch_size = 100
```

```
train_idg = ImageDataGenerator(rescale=1.0 / 255.0,
                               samplewise_center=True,
                               samplewise_std_normalization=True,
                               horizontal_flip=True,
                               rotation_range=10.0,
                               shear_range=np.pi / 12.0,
                               zoom_range=0.25)

train_dg = train_idg.flow(x=np.expand_dims(X_train, axis=3),
                          y=to_categorical(Y_train,
num_classes=nb_classes),
                          batch_size=train_batch_size,
                          shuffle=True,
                          seed=1000)

test_idg = ImageDataGenerator(rescale=1.0 / 255.0,
                              samplewise_center=True,
                              samplewise_std_normalization=True)

test_dg = train_idg.flow(x=np.expand_dims(X_test, axis=3),
                         y=to_categorical(Y_test,
num_classes=nb_classes),
                         shuffle=False,
                         batch_size=test_batch_size,
                         seed=1000)
```

Once an image data generator has been initialized, it must be fitted, specifying the input dataset and the desired batch size (the output of this operation is the actual Python generator). The test image generator is voluntarily kept without transformations except for normalization and standardization, in order to avoid a validation on a dataset drawn from a different distribution. At this point, we can create and compile our network, using 2D convolutions based on Leaky ReLU activations (using the `LeakyReLU` class, which replaces the standard layer `Activation`), batch normalizations, and max poolings:

```
from keras.models import Sequential
from keras.layers import Activation, Dense, Flatten, LeakyReLU,
Conv2D, MaxPooling2D, BatchNormalization
from keras.optimizers import Adam

model = Sequential()

model.add(Conv2D(filters=32,
                 kernel_size=(3, 3),
                 padding='same',
                 input_shape=(X_train.shape[1], X_train.shape[2], 1)))
```

```
model.add(BatchNormalization())
model.add(LeakyReLU(alpha=0.1))

model.add(Conv2D(filters=64,
                 kernel_size=(3, 3),
                 padding='same'))

model.add(BatchNormalization())
model.add(LeakyReLU(alpha=0.1))

model.add(MaxPooling2D(pool_size=(2, 2)))

model.add(Conv2D(filters=64,
                 kernel_size=(3, 3),
                 padding='same'))

model.add(BatchNormalization())
model.add(LeakyReLU(alpha=0.1))

model.add(Conv2D(filters=128,
                 kernel_size=(3, 3),
                 padding='same'))

model.add(BatchNormalization())
model.add(LeakyReLU(alpha=0.1))

model.add(Conv2D(filters=128,
                 kernel_size=(3, 3),
                 padding='same'))

model.add(BatchNormalization())
model.add(LeakyReLU(alpha=0.1))

model.add(MaxPooling2D(pool_size=(2, 2)))

model.add(Flatten())

model.add(Dense(units=1024))
model.add(BatchNormalization())
model.add(LeakyReLU(alpha=0.1))

model.add(Dense(units=1024))
model.add(BatchNormalization())
model.add(LeakyReLU(alpha=0.1))

model.add(Dense(units=nb_classes))
model.add(Activation('softmax'))
```

```
model.compile(loss='categorical_crossentropy',
              optimizer=Adam(lr=0.0001, decay=1e-5),
              metrics=['accuracy'])
```

All the batch normalizations are always applied to the linear transformation before the activation function. Considering the additional complexity, we are also going to use a callback, which is a class that Keras uses in order to perform in-training operations. In our case, we want to reduce the learning rate when the validation loss stops improving. The specific callback is called `ReduceLROnPlateau` and it's tuned in order to reduce η multiplying it by `0.1` (after a number of epochs equal to the value of the `patience` parameter) with a cooldown period (the number of epochs to wait before restoring the original learning rate) of 1 epoch and a minimum $\eta = 10^{-6}$. The training method is now `fit_generator()`, which accepts Python generators instead of finite datasets and the number of iterations per epoch (all the other parameters are the same as implemented by `fit()`):

```
from keras.callbacks import ReduceLROnPlateau

nb_epochs = 100
steps_per_epoch = 1500

history = model.fit_generator(generator=train_dg,
                              epochs=nb_epochs,
                              steps_per_epoch=steps_per_epoch,
                              validation_data=test_dg,
                              validation_steps=int(X_test.shape[0] /
test_batch_size),
                              callbacks=[
                                  ReduceLROnPlateau(factor=0.1,
patience=1, cooldown=1, min_lr=1e-6)
                              ])

Epoch 1/100
1500/1500 [==============================] - 471s 314ms/step - loss:
0.3457 - acc: 0.8722 - val_loss: 0.2863 - val_acc: 0.8952
Epoch 2/100
1500/1500 [==============================] - 464s 309ms/step - loss:
0.2325 - acc: 0.9138 - val_loss: 0.2721 - val_acc: 0.8990
Epoch 3/100
1500/1500 [==============================] - 460s 307ms/step - loss:
0.1929 - acc: 0.9285 - val_loss: 0.2522 - val_acc: 0.9112

...

Epoch 99/100
1500/1500 [==============================] - 449s 299ms/step - loss:
```

```
0.0438 - acc: 0.9859 - val_loss: 0.2142 - val_acc: 0.9323
Epoch 100/100
1500/1500 [==============================] - 449s 299ms/step - loss:
0.0443 - acc: 0.9857 - val_loss: 0.2136 - val_acc: 0.9339
```

In this case, the complexity is higher and the result is not as accurate as the one obtained with the standard MNIST dataset. The validation and loss plots are shown in the following graph:

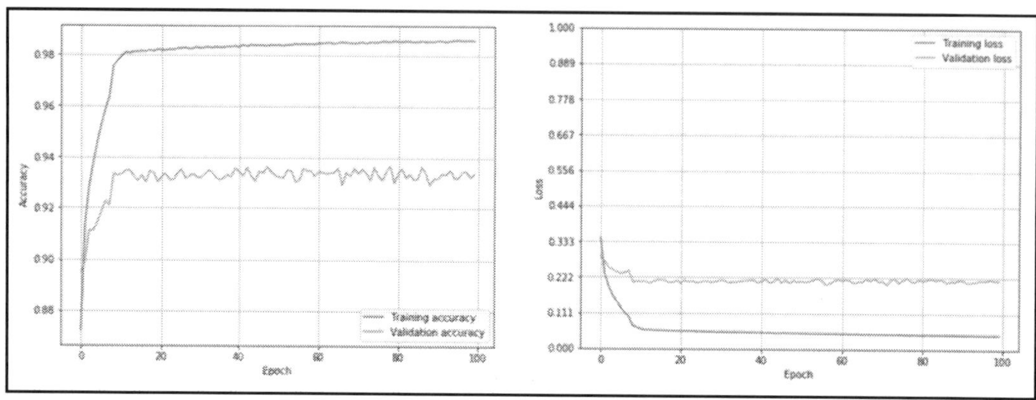

The loss plot doesn't show a U-curve, but it seems that there are no real improvements starting from the 20th epoch. This is also confirmed by the validation plot, which continues oscillating between 0.935 and about 0.94. On the other side, the training loss hasn't reached its minimum (nor has the training accuracy), mainly because of the batch normalizations. However, considering several benchmarks, the result is not bad (even if state-of-the-art models can reach a validation accuracy of about 0.96). I suggest that the reader try different configurations (with and without dropout and other activations) based on deeper architectures with larger training sets. This example offers many chances to practice with this kind of models, as the complexity is not as high as to require dedicated hardware, but at the same time, there are many ambiguities (for example, between shirts and t-shirts) that can reduce the generalization ability.

Recurrent networks

All the models that we have analyzed until now have a common feature. Once the training process is completed, the weights are frozen and the output depends only on the input sample. Clearly, this is the expected behavior of a classifier, but there are many scenarios where a prediction must take into account the history of the input values. A time series is a classic example. Let's suppose that we need to predict the temperature for the next week. If we try to use only the last known $x^{(t)}$ value and an MLP trained to predict $x^{(t+1)}$, it's impossible to take into account temporal conditions like the season, the history of the season over the years, the position in the season, and so on. The regressor will be able to associate the output that yields the minimum average error, but in real-life situations, this isn't enough. The only reasonable way to solve this problem is to define a new architecture for the artificial neuron, to provide it with a memory. This concept is shown in the following diagram:

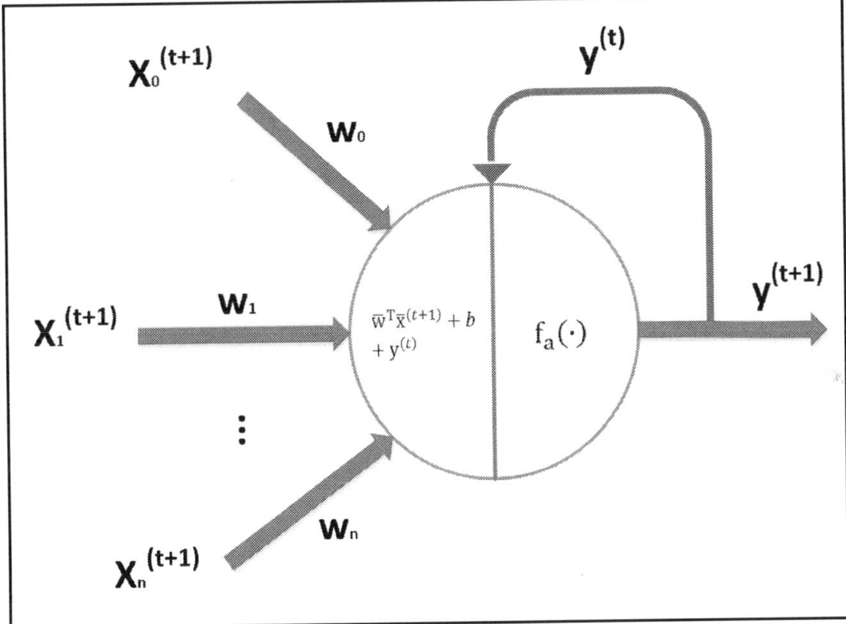

Now the neuron is no longer a pure feed-forward computational unit because the feedback connection forces it to remember its past and use it in order to predict new values. The new dynamic rule is now as follows:

$$\begin{cases} y^{(t+1)} = f_a\left(\bar{w}^T \bar{x}^{(t+1)} + b + y^{(t)}\right) \quad for \ t > 0 \\ y^{(0)} = 0 \end{cases}$$

The previous prediction is fed back and summed to new linear output. The resulting value is transformed by the activation function in order to produce the actual new output (conventionally the first output is null, but this is not a constraint). An immediate consideration concerns the activation function—this is a dynamic system that could easily become unstable. The only way to prevent this phenomenon is to employ saturating functions (such as the sigmoid or hyperbolic tangent). In fact, whatever the input is, the output can never *explode* by moving towards $+\infty$ or $-\infty$.

Suppose that, instead, we were to use a ReLU activation—under some conditions, the output will grow indefinitely, leading to an overflow. Clearly, the situation is even worse with a linear activation and could be very similar even when using a Leaky ReLU or ELU. Hence, it's obvious that we need to select saturating functions, but is this enough to ensure stability? Even if a hyperbolic tangent (as well as a sigmoid) has two stable points (*-1* and *+1*), this isn't enough to ensure stability. Let's imagine that the output is affected by noise and oscillates around 0.0. The unit cannot converge towards a value and remains trapped in a limit cycle.

Luckily, the possibility to learn the weights allows us to increase the robustness to noise, avoiding that limited changes in the input could invert the dynamic of the neuron. This is a very important (and easy to prove) result that guarantees stability under very simple conditions, but again, what is the price that we need to pay? Is it anything simple and straightforward? Unfortunately, the answer is negative and the price for stability is extremely high. However, before discussing this problem, let's show how a simple recurrent network can be trained.

Backpropagation through time (BPTT)

The simplest way to train an RNN is based on a representational trick. As the input sequences are limited and their length can be fixed, it's possible to restructure the simple neuron with a feedback connection as an unrolled feed-forward network. In the following diagram, there's an example with *k* timesteps:

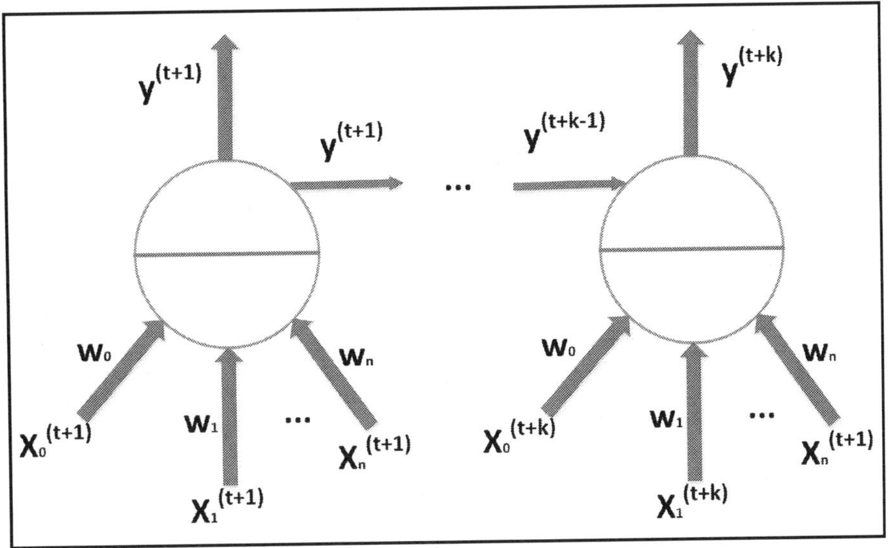

Example of unrolled recurrent network

This network (which can be easily extended to more complex architecture with several layers) is exactly like an MLP, but in this case, the weights of each *clone* are the same. The algorithm called **BPTT** is the natural extension of the standard learning technique to unrolled recurrent networks. The procedure is straightforward. Once all the outputs have been computed, it's possible to determine the value of the cost function for every single network. At this point, starting from the last step, the corrections (the gradients) are computed and stored, and the process is repeated until the initial step. Then, all of the gradients are summed and applied to the network. As every single contribution is based on a precise *temporal experience* (made up of a local sample and a previous memory element), the standard backpropagation will learn how to manage a dynamic condition as if it were a point-wise prediction. However, we know that the actual network is not unrolled and the past dependencies are theoretically propagated and remembered. I voluntarily used the word *theoretically,* because all practical experiments show a completely different behavior that we are going to discuss. This technique is very easy to implement, but it can be very expensive for deep networks that must be unrolled for a large number of timesteps. For this reason, a variant called **truncated backpropagation through time** (**TBPTT**) has been proposed (in *Subgrouping reduces complexity and speeds up learning in recurrent networks, Zipser D., Advances in Neural Information Processing Systems, II 1990*).

The idea is to use two sequence lengths t_1 and t_2 (with $t_1 >> t_2$)—the longer one (t_1) is employed for the feed-forward phase, while the shorter length (t_2) is used to train the network. At first sight, this version seems like a normal BPTT with a short sequence; however, the key idea is to force the network to update the hidden states with more pieces of information and then compute the corrections according to the result of the longer sequence (even if the updates are propagated to a limited number of previous timesteps). Clearly, this is an approximation that can speed up the training process, but the final result is normally comparable with the one obtained by processing long sequences, in particular when the dependencies can be split into shorter temporal chunks (and therefore the assumption is that there are no very long dependencies).

Even if the BPTT algorithm is mathematically correct and it's not difficult to learn short-term dependencies (corresponding to short unrolled networks), several experiments confirmed that it's extremely difficult (or almost impossible) learning long-term dependencies. In other words, it's easy to exploit past experiences whose contribution is limited to a short window (and therefore whose importance is limited because they cannot manage the most complex trends) but the network cannot easily learn all behaviors that, for example, have a periodicity of hundreds of timesteps. In 1994, Bengio, Simard, and Frasconi provided a theoretical explanation of the problem (in *Learning Long-Term Dependencies with Gradient Descent is Difficult, Bengio Y., Simard P., Frasconi P., IEEE Transactions on Neural Networks, 5/1994*). The mathematical details are rather complex, because they involve dynamic system theory; however, the final result is that a network whose neurons are forced to become robust to noise (the normal expected behavior) is affected by the vanishing gradients problem when $t \rightarrow \infty$. More generally, we can represent a vectorial recurrent neuron dynamic as follows:

$$\bar{y}^{(t+1)} = f_a\left(W^T \bar{x}^{(t+1)} + \bar{b} + \bar{y}^{(t)}\right)$$

The multiplicative effect of BPTT forces the gradients to be proportional to W^t. If the largest absolute eigenvalue (also known as spectral radius) of W is smaller than 1, then the following applies:

$$\lim_{t \to \infty} W^t = 0$$

More simply, we can re-express the result saying that the magnitude of the gradients is proportional to the length of the sequences and even if the condition is asymptotically valid, many experiments confirmed that the limited precision of numeric computations and the exponential decay due to subsequent multiplications can force the gradients to vanish even when the sequences are not extremely long. This seems to be the end of any RNN architecture, but luckily more recent approaches have been designed and proposed to resolve this problem, allowing RNNs to learn both short and long-term dependencies without particular complications. A new era of RNNs started and the results were immediately outstanding.

LSTM

This model (which represents the state-of-the-art recurrent cell in many fields) was proposed in 1997 by Hochreiter and Schmidhuber (in *Long Short-Term Memory, Hochreiter S., Schmidhuber J., Neural Computation, Vol. 9, 11/1997*) with the emblematic name **long-short-term memory** (**LSTM**). As the name suggests, the idea is to create a more complex artificial recurrent neuron that can be plugged into larger networks and trained without the risk of vanishing and, of course, exploding gradients. One of the key elements of classic recurrent networks is that they are focused on learning, but not on selectively forgetting. This ability is indeed necessary for optimizing the memory in order to remember what is really important and removing all those pieces of information that are not necessary to predict new values.

To achieve this goal, LSTM exploits two important features (it's helpful to expose them before discussing the model). The first one is an explicit state, which is a separate set of variables that store the elements necessary to build long and short-term dependencies, including the current state. These variables are the building blocks of a mechanism called **constant error carousel** (**CEC**), named in this way because it's responsible for the cyclical and internal management of the error provided by the backpropagation algorithm. This approach allows the correction of the weights without suffering the multiplicative effect anymore. The internal LSTM dynamics allow better understanding of how the error is safely fed back; however, the exact explanation of the training procedure (which is always based on the gradient descent) is beyond the scope of this book and can be found in the aforementioned paper.

The second feature is the presence of gates. We can simply define a gate as an element that can modulate the amount of information flowing through it. For example, if $y = ax$ and a is a variable bounded between 0 and 1, it can be considered as a gate, because when it's equal to 0, it blocks the input x; when it's equal to 1, it allows the input to flow in without restrictions; and when it has an intermediate value, it reduces the amount of information proportionally. In LSTMs, gates are managed by sigmoid functions, while the activations are based on hyperbolic tangents (whose symmetry guarantees better performances). At this point, we can show the structural diagram of an LSTM cell and discuss its internal dynamics:

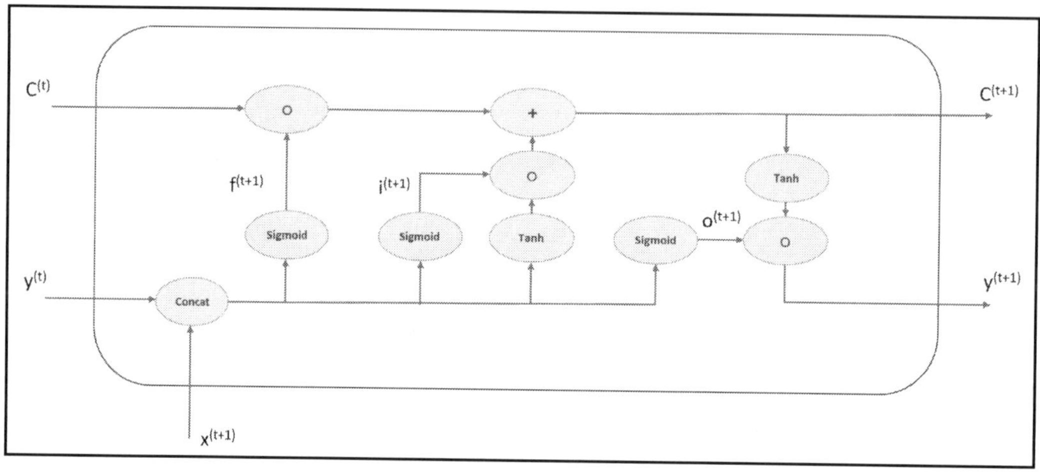

The first (and most important) element is the memory state, which is responsible for the dependencies and for the actual output. In the diagram, it is represented by the upper line and its dynamics are represented by the following general equation:

$$C^{(t+1)} = g_1(C^{(t)}) + g_2(\bar{x}^{(t+1)}, \bar{y}^{(t)})$$

So, the state depends on the previous value, on the current input, and on the previous output. Let's start with the first term, introducing the forget gate. As the name says, it's responsible for the persistence of the existing memory elements or for their deletion. In the diagram, it's represented by the first vertical block and its value is obtained by considering the concatenation of previous output and current input:

$$\bar{f}^{(t+1)} = \sigma\left(W_f \cdot \begin{pmatrix} \bar{y}^{(t)} \\ \bar{x}^{(t+1)} \end{pmatrix} + \bar{b}_f\right)$$

The operation is a classical neuron activation with a vectorial output. An alternative version can use two weight matrices and keep the input elements separated:

$$\bar{f}^{(t+1)} = \sigma\left(W_f \cdot \bar{x}^{(t+1)} + V_f \cdot \bar{y}^{(t)} + \bar{b}_f\right)$$

However, I prefer the previous version, because it can better express the homogeneity of input and output, and also their consequentiality. Using the forget gate, it's possible to determine the value of $g_1(C^{(t)})$ using the Hadamard (or element-wise) product:

$$g_1(C^{(t)}) = \bar{f}^{(t+1)} \circ C^{(t)}$$

The effect of this computation is filtering the content of $C^{(t)}$ that must be preserved and the validity degree (which is proportional to the value of $f^{(t+1)}$). If the forget gate outputs a value close to 1, the corresponding element is still considered valid, while lower values determine a sort of obsolescence that can even lead the cell to completely remove an element when the forget gate value is 0 or close to it. The next step is to consider the amount of the input sample that must be considered to update the state. This task is achieved by the input gate (second vertical block). The equation is perfectly analogous to the previous one:

$$\bar{i}^{(t+1)} = \sigma\left(W_i \cdot \begin{pmatrix} \bar{y}^{(t)} \\ \bar{x}^{(t+1)} \end{pmatrix} + \bar{b}_i\right)$$

However, in this case, we also need to compute the term that must be added to the current state. As already mentioned, LSTM cells employ hyperbolic tangents for the activations; therefore, the new contribution to the state is obtained as follows:

$$\hat{C}^{(t+1)} = tanh\left(W_c \cdot \begin{pmatrix} \bar{y}^{(t)} \\ \bar{x}^{(t+1)} \end{pmatrix} + \bar{b}_c\right)$$

Using the input gate and the state contribution, it's possible to determine the function $g_2(x^{(t+1)}, y^{(t)})$:

$$g_2(\bar{x}^{(t+1)}, \bar{y}^{(t)}) = \bar{i}^{(t+1)} \circ \hat{C}^{(t+1)}$$

Hence, the complete state equation becomes as follows:

$$C^{(t+1)} = \left(\bar{f}^{(t+1)} \circ C^{(t)}\right) + \left(\bar{i}^{(t+1)} \circ \hat{C}^{(t+1)}\right)$$

Now, the inner logic of an LSTM cell is more evident. The state is based on the following:

- A dynamic balance between previous experience and its re-evaluation according to new experience (modulated by the forget gate)
- The *semantic* effect of the current input (modulated by the input gate) and the potential additive activation

Realistic scenarios are many. It's possible that a new input forces the LSTM to reset the state and store the new incoming value. On the other hand, the input gate can also remain closed, giving a very low priority to the new input (together with the previous output). In this case, the LSTM, considering the long-term dependencies, can decide to discard a sample that is considered noisy and not necessarily able to contribute to an accurate prediction. In other situations, both the forget and input gates can be partially open, letting only some values influence the state. All these possibilities are managed by the learning process through the correction of the weight matrices and the biases. The difference with BPTT is that the long-term dependencies are no longer impeded by the vanishing gradients problem.

The last step is determining the output. The third vertical block is called the output gate and controls the information that must transit from the state to the output unit. Its equation is as follows:

$$\bar{o}^{(t+1)} = \sigma\left(W_o \cdot \begin{pmatrix} \bar{y}^{(t)} \\ \bar{x}^{(t+1)} \end{pmatrix} + \bar{b}_o\right)$$

The actual output is hence determined as follows:

$$\bar{y}^{(t+1)} = \bar{o}^{(t+1)} \circ tanh(C^{(t+1)})$$

An important consideration concerns the gates. They are all fed with the same vector, containing the previous output and the current input. As they are homogenous values, the concatenation yields a coherent entity that encodes a sort of *inverse* cause-effect relationship (this is an improper definition, as we work with previous effect and current cause). The gates work like logistic regressions without thresholding; therefore, they can be considered as pseudo-probability vectors (not distributions, as each element is independent). The forget gate expresses the probability that last sequence (effect, cause) is more important than the current state; however, only the input gate has the responsibility to grant it the right to influence the new state. Moreover, the output gate expresses the probability that the current sequence is able to let the current state flow out. The dynamic is indeed very complex and has some drawbacks. For example, when the output gate remains closed, the output is close to zero and this influences both forget and input gates. As they control the new state and the CEC, they could limit the amount of incoming information and consequent corrections, leading to poor performance.

A simple solution that can mitigate this problem is provided by a variant called **peephole LSTM**. The idea is to feed the previous state to every gate so that they can take decisions more independently. The generic gate equation becomes as follows:

$$\bar{g}^{(t+1)} = \sigma\left(W_g \cdot \begin{pmatrix} \bar{y}^{(t)} \\ \bar{x}^{(t+1)} \end{pmatrix} + U_g \cdot C^{(t)} + \bar{b}_g\right)$$

The new set of weights U_g (for all three gates) must be learned in the same way as the standard W_g and b_g. The main difference with a classic LSTM is that the sequential dynamic: forget gate | input gate | new state | output gate | actual output is now partially shortcutted. The presence of the state in every gate activation allows them to exploit multiple recurrent connections, yielding a better accuracy in many complex situations. Another important consideration is about the learning process: in this case, the peepholes are closed and the only feedback channel is the output gate. Unfortunately, not every LSTM implementation support peepholes; however, several studies confirmed that in most cases all the models yield similar performances.

Xingjian et al. (in *Convolutional LSTM Network: A Machine Learning Approach for Precipitation Nowcasting, Xingjian S., Zhourong C., Hao W., Dit-Yan Y., Wai-kin W., Wang-Chun W., arXiv:1506.04214 [cs.CV]*) proposed a variant called **convolutional LSTM**, which clearly mixes Convolutions and LSTM cells. The main internal difference concerns the gate computations, which now become (without peepholes, which however, can always be added):

$$\bar{g}^{(t+1)} = \sigma\left(W_g * \begin{pmatrix} \bar{y}^{(t)} \\ \bar{x}^{(t+1)} \end{pmatrix} + \bar{b}_g\right)$$

W_g is now a kernel that is convoluted with the input-output vector (which is usually the concatenation of two images). Of course, it's possible to train any number of kernels to increase the decoding power of the cell and the output will have a shape equal to (*batch size* × *width* × *height* × *kernels*). This kind of cell is particularly useful for joining spatial processing with a robust temporal approach. Given a sequence of images (for example, satellite images, game screenshots, and so on), a convolutional LSTM network can learn long-term relationships that are manifested through geometric feature evolutions (for example, cloud movements or specific sprite strategies that it's possible to anticipate considering a long history of events). This approach (even with a few modifications) is widely employed in Deep Reinforcement Learning in order to solve complex problems where the only input is provided by a sequence of images. Of course, the computational complexity is very high, in particular when many subsequent layers are used; however, the results outperformed any existing method and this approach became one of the first choices to manage this kind of problem.

Another important variant, which is common to many Recurrent Neural Networks, is provided by a bidirectional interface. This isn't an actual layer, but a strategy that is employed in order to join the forward analysis of a sequence with the backward one. Two cellblocks are fed with a sequence and its inverse and the output, for example, is concatenated and used for further processing steps. In fields such as NLP, this method allows us to dramatically improve the accuracy of classifications and real-time translations. The reason is strictly related to the rules underlying the structure of a sequence. In natural language, a sentence $w_1\ w_2\ ...\ w_n$ has forward relationships (for example, a singular noun can be followed by *is*), but the knowledge of backward relationships (for example, the sentence *this place is pretty awful*) permits avoiding common mistakes that, in the past, had to be corrected using post-processing steps (the initial translation of *pretty* could be similar to the translation of *nice*, but a subsequent analysis can reveal that the adjective mismatches and a special rule can be applied). Deep learning, on the other side, is not based on *special rules*, but on the ability to learn an internal representation that should be autonomous in making final decisions (without further external aids) and bidirectional LSTM networks help in reaching this goal in many important contexts.

Keras implements the classes `LSTM` since its origins. It also provides a `Bidirectional` class wrapper that can be used with every RNN layer in order to obtain a double output (computed with the forward and backward sequences). Moreover, in Keras 2 there are optimized versions of LSTM based on NVIDIA CUDA (`CuDNNLSTM`), which provide very high performance when a compatible GPU is available. In the same package, it's possible to also find the `ConvLSTM2D` class, which implements a convolutional LSTM layer. In this case, the reader can immediately identify many of the parameters, as they are the same as a standard convolutional layer.

GRU

This model, named **Gated recurrent unit** (**GRU**), proposed by Cho et al. (in *Learning Phrase Representations using RNN Encoder-Decoder for Statistical Machine Translation, Cho K., Van Merrienboer B., Gulcehre C., Bahdanau D., Bougares F., Schwenk H., Bengio Y., arXiv:1406.1078 [cs.CL]*) can be considered as a simplified LSTM with a few variations. The structure of a generic full-gated unit is represented in the following diagram:

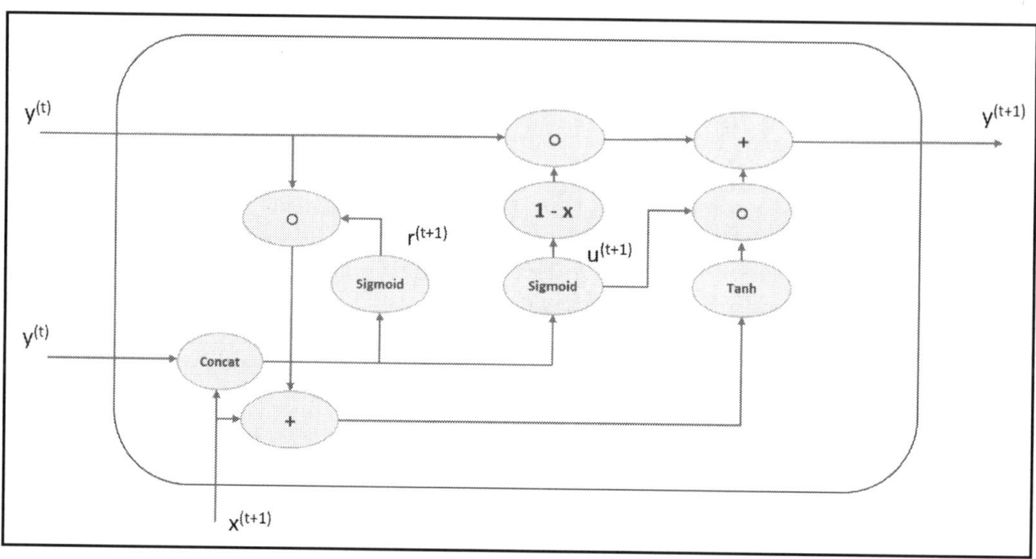

The main differences from LSTM are the presence of only two gates and the absence of an explicit state. These simplifications can speed both the training and the prediction phases while avoiding the vanishing gradient problem.

The first gate is called the **reset gate** (conventionally denoted with the letter *r*) and its function is analogous to the forget gate:

$$\bar{r}^{(t+1)} = \sigma\left(W_r \cdot \begin{pmatrix} \bar{y}^{(t)} \\ \bar{x}^{(t+1)} \end{pmatrix} + \bar{b}_r\right)$$

Similar to the forget gate, its role is to decide what content of the previous output must be preserved and the relative degree. In fact, the additive contribution to new output is obtained as follows:

$$\hat{y}^{(t+1)} = tanh\left(W_y \cdot \bar{x}^{(t+1)} + \bar{r}^{(t+1)} \circ \left(V_y \cdot \bar{y}^{(t)}\right) + \bar{b}_y\right)$$

In the previous expression, I've preferred to separate the weight matrices to better exposes the behavior. The argument of *tanh(•)* is the sum of a linear function of the new input and a weighted term that is a function of the previous state. Now, it's clear how the reset gate works: it modulates the amount of history (accumulated in the previous output value) that must be preserved and what instead can be discarded. However, the reset gate is not enough to determine the right output with enough accuracy, considering both short and long-term dependencies. In order to increase the expressivity of the unit, an update gate (with a role similar to the LSTM input gate) has been added:

$$\bar{u}^{(t+1)} = \sigma\left(W_u \cdot \begin{pmatrix} \bar{y}^{(t)} \\ \bar{x}^{(t+1)} \end{pmatrix} + \bar{b}_u\right)$$

The update gate controls the amount of information that must contribute to the new output (and hence to the state). As it's a value bounded between *0* and *1*, GRUs are trained to mix old output and new additive contribution with an operation similar to a weighted average:

$$\bar{y}^{(t+1)} = \bar{u}^{(t+1)} \circ \hat{y}^{(t+1)} + \left(I - \bar{u}^{(t+1)}\right) \circ \bar{y}^{(t)}$$

Therefore, the update gate becomes a modulator that can select which components of each flow must be output and stored for the next operation. This unit is structurally simpler than an LSTM, but several studies confirmed that its performance is on average, equivalent to LSTM, with some particular cases when GRU has even outperformed the more complex cell. My suggestion is that you test both models, starting with LSTM. The computational cost has been dramatically reduced by modern hardware and in many contexts the advantage of GRUs is negligible. In both cases, the philosophy is the same: the error is kept inside the cell and the weights of the gates are corrected in order to maximize the accuracy. This behavior prevents the multiplicative cascade of small gradients and increases the ability to learn very complex temporal behaviors.

However, a single cell/layer would not be able to successfully achieve the desired accuracy. In all these cases, it's possible to stack multiple layers made up of a variable number of cells. Every layer can normally output the last value or the entire sequence. The former is used when connecting the LSTM/GRU layer to a fully-connected one, while the whole sequence is necessary to feed another recurrent layer. We are going to see how to implement these techniques with Keras in the following example.

Just like for LSTMs, Keras implements the`GRU` class and its NVIDIA CUDA optimized version `CuDNNGRU`.

Example of an LSTM network with Keras

In this example, we want to test the ability of an LSTM network to learn long-term dependencies. For this reason, we employ a dataset called Zuerich Monthly Sunspots (freely provided by Andrews and Herzberg in 1985) containing the numbers observed in all the months starting from 1749 to 1983 (please read the information box for how to download the dataset). As we are not interested in the dates, we need to parse the file in order to extract only the values needed for the time series (which contains 2,820 steps):

```
import numpy as np

dataset_filename = '<YOUR_PATH>\dataset.csv'

n_samples = 2820
data = np.zeros(shape=(n_samples, ), dtype=np.float32)

with open(dataset_filename, 'r') as f:
    lines = f.readlines()
for i, line in enumerate(lines):
    if i == 0:
        continue
    if i == n_samples + 1:
        break
    _, value = line.split(',')
    data[i-1] = float(value)
```

Alternatively, it's possible to load the CSV dataset using pandas (`https://pandas.pydata.org`), which is a powerful data manipulation/analysis library (for further information, please refer to *Learning pandas Second Edition, Heydt M., Packt*):

```
import pandas as pd

dataset_filename = '<YOUR_PATH>\dataset.csv'

df = pd.read_csv(dataset_filename, index_col=0, header=0).dropna()
data = df.values.astype(np.float32).squeeze()
```

The values are unnormalized and as LSTMs work with hyperbolic tangents, it's helpful to normalize them in the interval `-1` and `1`. We can easily perform this step using the Scikit-Learn class `MinMaxScaler`:

```
from sklearn.preprocessing import MinMaxScaler

mmscaler = MinMaxScaler((-1.0, 1.0))
data = mmscaler.fit_transform(data.reshape(-1, 1))
```

The complete dataset is shown in the following diagram:

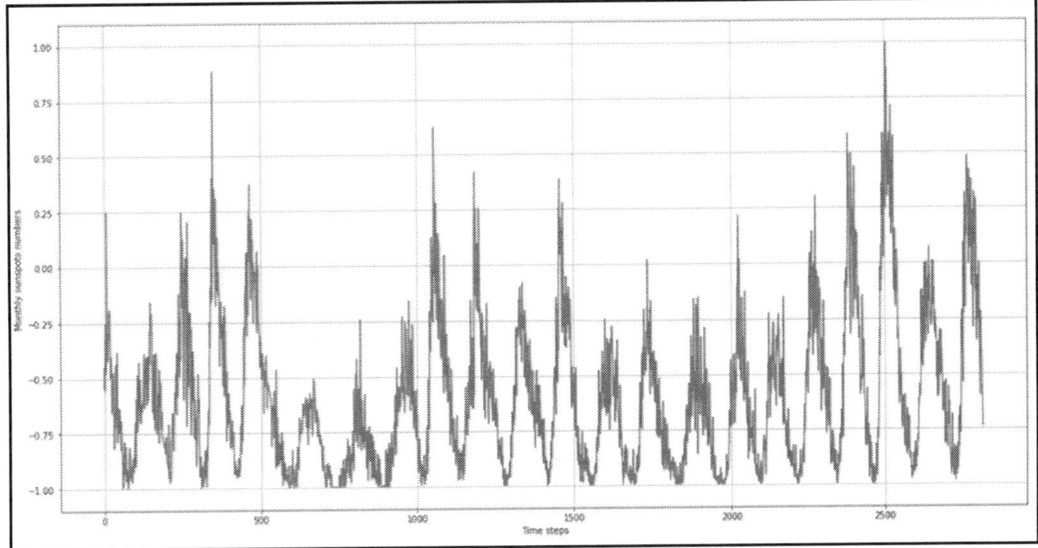

In order to train the model, we have decided to use 2,300 samples for training and the remaining 500 for validation (corresponding to about 42 years). The input of the model is a batch of sequences of 15 samples (shifted along the time axis) and the output is the subsequent month; therefore, before training, we need to prepare the dataset:

```
sequence_length = 15

X_ts = np.zeros(shape=(n_samples - sequence_length, sequence_length,
1), dtype=np.float32)
Y_ts = np.zeros(shape=(n_samples - sequence_length, 1),
dtype=np.float32)

for i in range(0, data.shape[0] - sequence_length):
    X_ts[i] = data[i:i + sequence_length]
    Y_ts[i] = data[i + sequence_length]

X_ts_train = X_ts[0:2300, :]
Y_ts_train = Y_ts[0:2300]

X_ts_test = X_ts[2300:2800, :]
Y_ts_test = Y_ts[2300:2800]
```

Now, we can create and compile a simple model with a single stateful LSTM layer containing four cells, followed by a hyperbolic tangent output neuron (I always suggest that the reader experiment with more complex architectures and different parameters):

```
from keras.models import Sequential
from keras.layers import LSTM, Dense, Activation
from keras.optimizers import Adam

model = Sequential()

model.add(LSTM(4, stateful=True, batch_input_shape=(20,
sequence_length, 1)))

model.add(Dense(1))
model.add(Activation('tanh'))

model.compile(optimizer=Adam(lr=0.001, decay=0.0001),
              loss='mse',
              metrics=['mse'])
```

Setting the `stateful=True` parameter in the `LSTM` class forces Keras not to reset the state after each batch. In fact, our goal is learning long-term dependencies and the internal LSTM state must reflect the overall trend. When an LSTM network is stateful, it's also necessary to specify the batch size in the input shape (through the `batch_input_shape` parameter). In our case, we have selected a batch size equal to 20 samples. The optimizer is `Adam` with a higher decay (to avoid instabilities) and a loss based on the mean squared error (which is the most common choice in this kind of scenario). At this point, we can train the model (for 100 epochs):

```
model.fit(X_ts_train, Y_ts_train,
          batch_size=20,
          epochs=100,
          shuffle=False,
          validation_data=(X_ts_test, Y_ts_test))

Train on 2300 samples, validate on 500 samples
Epoch 1/100
2300/2300 [==============================] - 11s 5ms/step - loss:
0.4905 - mean_squared_error: 0.4905 - val_loss: 0.1827 -
val_mean_squared_error: 0.1827
Epoch 2/100
2300/2300 [==============================] - 4s 2ms/step - loss:
0.1214 - mean_squared_error: 0.1214 - val_loss: 0.1522 -
val_mean_squared_error: 0.1522
Epoch 3/100
2300/2300 [==============================] - 4s 2ms/step - loss:
0.0796 - mean_squared_error: 0.0796 - val_loss: 0.1154 -
val_mean_squared_error: 0.1154

...

Epoch 99/100
2300/2300 [==============================] - 4s 2ms/step - loss:
0.0139 - mean_squared_error: 0.0139 - val_loss: 0.0247 -
val_mean_squared_error: 0.0247
Epoch 100/100
2300/2300 [==============================] - 4s 2ms/step - loss:
0.0139 - mean_squared_error: 0.0139 - val_loss: 0.0247 -
val_mean_squared_error: 0.0247
```

This is an example whose purpose is only didactic; therefore, the final validation mean squared error is not extremely low. However, as it's possible to see in the following diagram (representing the predictions on the validation set), the model has successfully learned the global trend:

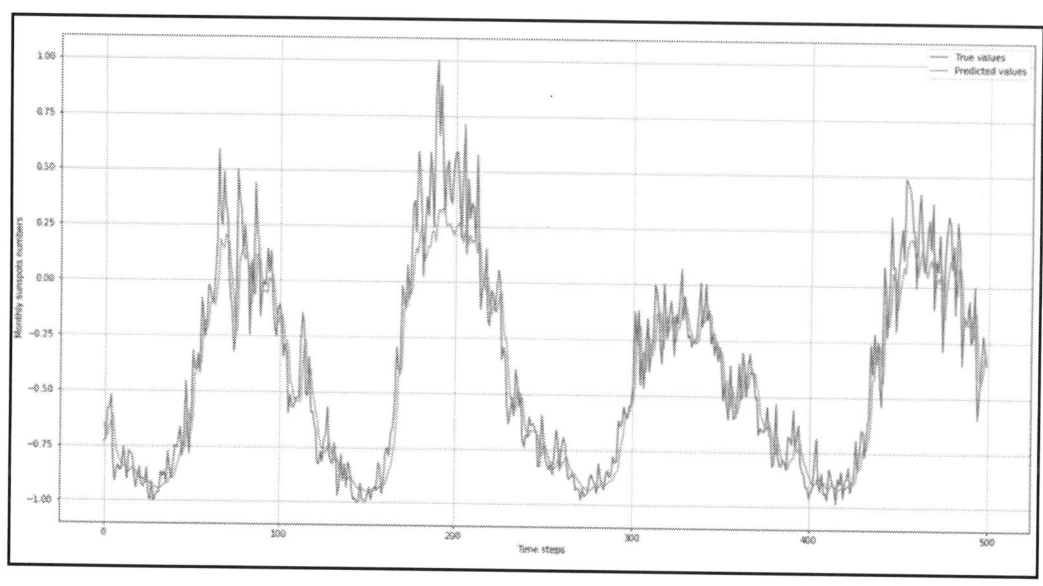

LSTM predictions on the Zuerich dataset

The model is still unable to achieve a very high accuracy in correspondence of all the very rapid spikes, but it's able to correctly model the amplitude of the oscillations and the length of the tails. For the sake of intellectual honesty, we must consider that this validation is performed on true data; however, when working with time series, it's normal to predict a new value using the ground truth. In this case, it's like a moving prediction where each value is obtained using the training history and a set of real observations. It's clear that the model is able to predict the long-term oscillations and also some local ones (for example, the sequence starting from step 300), but it can be improved in order to have better performance on the whole validation set. To achieve this goal, it is necessary to increase the network complexity and tune up the learning rate (it's a very interesting exercise on a real dataset).

Observing the previous diagram, it's possible to see that the model is relatively more accurate at some high frequencies (rapid changes), while it's more imprecise on others. This is not a strange behavior, because very oscillating functions *need more non-linearity* (think about the Taylor expansion and the relative error when it's truncated to a specific degree) to achieve high accuracies (this means employing more layers). My suggestion is that you repeat the experiment using more LSTM layers, considering that we need to pass the whole output sequence to the following recurrent layer (this can be achieved by setting the `return_sequences=True` parameter). The last layer, instead, must return only the final value (which is the default behavior). I also suggest testing the GRU layers, comparing the performance with the LSTM version and picking the simplest (benchmarking the training time) and most accurate solution.

The dataset can be freely downloaded in CSV format from `https://datamarket.com/data/set/22ti/zuerich-monthly-sunspot-numbers-1749-1983#!ds=22tidisplay=line`.

Transfer learning

We have discussed how deep learning is fundamentally based on gray-box models that learn how to associate input patterns to specific classification/regression outcomes. All the processing pipeline that is often employed to prepare the data for specific detections is absorbed by the complexity of the neural architecture. However, the price to pay for high accuracies is a proportionally large number of training samples. State-of-the-art visual networks are trained with millions of images and, obviously, each of them must be properly labeled. Even if there are many free datasets that can be employed to train several models, many specific scenarios need hard preparatory work that sometimes is very difficult to achieve.

Luckily, deep neural architectures are hierarchical models that learn in a structured way. As we have seen in the examples of deep convolutional networks, the first layers become more and more sensitive to detect low-level features, while the higher ones concentrate their work on extracting more detailed high-level features. In several tasks, it's reasonable to think that a network trained, for example, with a large visual dataset (such as ImageNet or Microsoft Coco) could be reused to achieve a specialization in a slightly different task.

This concept is known as **transfer learning** and it's one of the most useful techniques when it's necessary to create state-of-the-art models with brand new datasets and specific objectives. For example, a customer can ask for a system to monitor a few cameras with the goal to segment the images and highlight the boundaries of specific targets.

The input is made up of video frames with the same geometric properties as thousands of images employed in training very powerful models (for example, Inception, ResNet, or VGG); therefore, we can take a pre-trained model, remove the highest layers (normally dense ones ending in a softmax classification layer) and connect the flattening layer to an MLP that outputs the coordinates of the bounding boxes. The first part of the network can be *frozen* (the weights are not modified anymore), while the SGD is applied to tune up the weights of the newly specialized sub-network.

Clearly, such an approach can dramatically speed up the training process, because the most complex part of the model is already trained and can also guarantee an extremely high accuracy (with respect to a naive solution), thanks to the optimization already performed on the original model. Obviously, the most natural question is how does this method work? Is there any formal proof? Unfortunately, there are no mathematical proofs, but there's enough evidence to assure about us of this approach. Generally speaking, the goal of a neural training process is to specialize each layer in order to provide a more particular (detailed, filtered, and so on) representation to the following one. Convolutional networks are a clear example of this behavior, but the same is observable in MLPs as well. The analysis of very deep convolutional networks showed how the content is still *visual* until reaching the flattening layer, where it's sent to a series of dense layers that are responsible for feeding the final softmax layer. In other words, the output of the convolutional block is a higher-level, segmented representation of the input, which is seldom affected by the specific classification problem. For this reason, transfer learning is generally sound and doesn't normally require a retraining of the lower layers. However, it's difficult to understand which model can yield the best performances and it's very useful to know which dataset has been used to train the original network. General purpose datasets (for example, ImageNet) are very useful in many contexts, while specific ones (such as Cifar-10 or Fashion; MNIST can be too restrictive). Luckily, Keras offers (in the package `keras.applications`) many models (even quite complex ones) that are always trained with ImageNet datasets and that can be immediately employed in a production-ready application. Even if using them is extremely simple, it requires a deeper knowledge of this framework, which is beyond the scope of this book. I invite the reader interested in this topic to check the book *Deep Learning with Keras, Gulli A., Pal S., Packt.*

Summary

In this chapter, we have presented the concept of a deep convolutional network, which is a generic architecture that can be employed in any visual processing task. The idea is based on hierarchical information management, aimed at extracting the features starting from low-level elements and moving forward until the high-level details that can be helpful to achieve specific goals.

The first topic was the concept of convolution and how it's applied in discrete and finite samples. We discussed the properties of standard convolution, before analyzing some important variants such as atrous (or dilated convolution), separable (and depthwise separable) convolution and, eventually, transpose convolution. All these methods can work with 1D, 2D, and 3D samples, even if the most diffused applications are based on bidimensional (not considering the channels) matrices representing static images. In the same section, we also discussed how pooling layers can be employed to reduce the dimensionality and improve the robustness to small translations.

In the next section, we introduced the concept of RNN, emphasizing the issues that normally arise when classic models are trained using the backpropagation through time algorithm. In particular, we explained why these networks cannot easily learn long-term dependencies. For this reason, new models have been proposed, whose performance was immediately outstanding. We discussed the most famous recurrent cell, called **Long-short-term memory** (**LSTM**), which can be used in layers that can easily learn all the most important dependencies of a sequence, allowing us to minimize the prediction error even in contexts with a very high variance (such as stock market quotations). The last topic was a simplified version of the idea implemented in LSTMs, which led to a model called a **Gated recurrent unit** (**GRU**). This cell is simpler and more computationally efficient, and many benchmarks confirmed that its performance is approximately the same as LSTM.

9
Classical Machine Learning with TensorFlow

Machine learning is an area of computer science that involves research, development, and application of algorithms to make computing machines learn from data. The models learned by computing machines are used to make predictions and forecasts. Machine learning researchers and engineers achieve this goal by building models and then using these models for predictions. It's common knowledge now that machine learning has been used highly successfully in various areas such as natural language understanding, video processing, image recognition, speech, and vision.

Let's talk about models. All of the machine learning problems are abstracted to the following equation in one form or another:

$$y = f(x)$$

Here, y is the output or target and x is the input or features. If x is a collection of features, we also call it a feature vector and denote with X. When we say model, we mean to find the function f that maps features to targets. Thus once we find f, we can use the new value of x to predict values of y.

Machine learning is centered around finding the function f that can be used to predict y from values of x. As you might be able to recall from your high school mathematics days, the equation of the line is as follows:

$$y = mx + c$$

We can rewrite the preceding simple equation as follows:

$$y = Wx + b$$

Here, W is known as the weight and b is known as the bias. Don't worry about the terms weight and bias as of now, we will cover them later. For now, you can just think of W as the equivalent of m and b as the equivalent of c in the equation of the line. Thus, now the machine learning problem can be stated as a problem of finding W and b from current values of X, such that the equation can be used to predict the values of y.

Regression analysis or regression modeling refers to the methods and techniques used to estimate relationships among variables. The variables that are input to regression models are called independent variables or predictors or features and the output variable from regression models is called dependent variable or target. Regression models are defined as follows:

$$Y \approx f(X, \beta)$$

where Y is the target variable, X is a vector of features, and β is a vector of parameters

Often, we use a very simple form of regression known as simple linear regression to estimate the parameter β.

In machine learning problems, we have to learn the model parameters β_0 and β_1 from the given data so that we have an estimated model to predict the value of Y from future values of X. We use the term *weight* for β_1 and *bias* for β_0 and represent them with w and b in the code, respectively.

Thus the model becomes as follows:

$$y = X \times w + b$$

Classification is one of the classical problems in machine learning. Data under consideration could belong to one or other classes, for example, if the images provided are data, they could be pictures of cats or dogs. Thus the classes, in this case, are cats and dogs. Classification means to identify or recognize the label or class of the data or objects under consideration. Classification falls under the umbrella of supervised machine learning. In classification problems, the training dataset is provided that has features or inputs and their corresponding outputs or labels. Using this training dataset, a model is trained; in other words, parameters of the model are computed. The trained model is then used on new data to find its correct labels.

Classification problems can be of two types: **binary class** or **multiclass**. Binary class means the data is to be classified in two distinct and discrete labels, for example, the patient has cancer or the patient does not have cancer, the images are of cats or dogs. Multiclass means the data is to be classified among multiple classes, for example, an email classification problem will divide emails into social media emails, work-related emails, personal email, family-related emails, spam emails, shopping offer emails, and so on. Another example would be the example of pictures of digits; each picture could be labeled between 0 to 9, depending on what digit the picture represents. In this chapter, we will see an example of both kinds of classification.

In this chapter, we are going to further expand on the following topics:

- Regression
    - Simple linear regression
    - Multi regression
    - Regularized regression
    - Lasso regularization
    - Ridge regularization
    - ElasticNet regularization
- Classification
    - Classification using logistic regression
    - Binary classification
    - Multiclass classification

Simple linear regression

You might have used other machine learning libraries; now let's practice learning the simple linear regression model using TensorFlow. We will explain the concepts first using a generated dataset before moving on to domain-specific examples.

We will use generated datasets so that readers from all different domains can learn without getting overwhelmed with the details of the specific domain of the example.

You can follow along with the code in the Jupyter notebook `ch-04a_Regression`.

Data preparation

To generate the dataset, we use the `make_regression` function from the `datasets` module of the `sklearn` library:

```
from sklearn import datasets as skds
X, y = skds.make_regression(n_samples=200,
                            n_features=1,
                            n_informative=1,
                            n_targets=1,
                            noise = 20.0)
```

This generates a dataset for regression with 200 sample values for one feature and one target each, with some noise added. As we are generating only one target, the function generates y with a one-dimensional NumPy Array; thus, we reshape y to have two dimensions:

```
if (y.ndim == 1):
    y = y.reshape(len(y),1)
```

We plot the generated dataset to look at the data with the following code:

```
import matplotlib.pyplot as plt
plt.figure(figsize=(14,8))
plt.plot(X,y,'b.')
plt.title('Original Dataset')
plt.show()
```

We get the following plot. As the data generated is random, you might get a different plot:

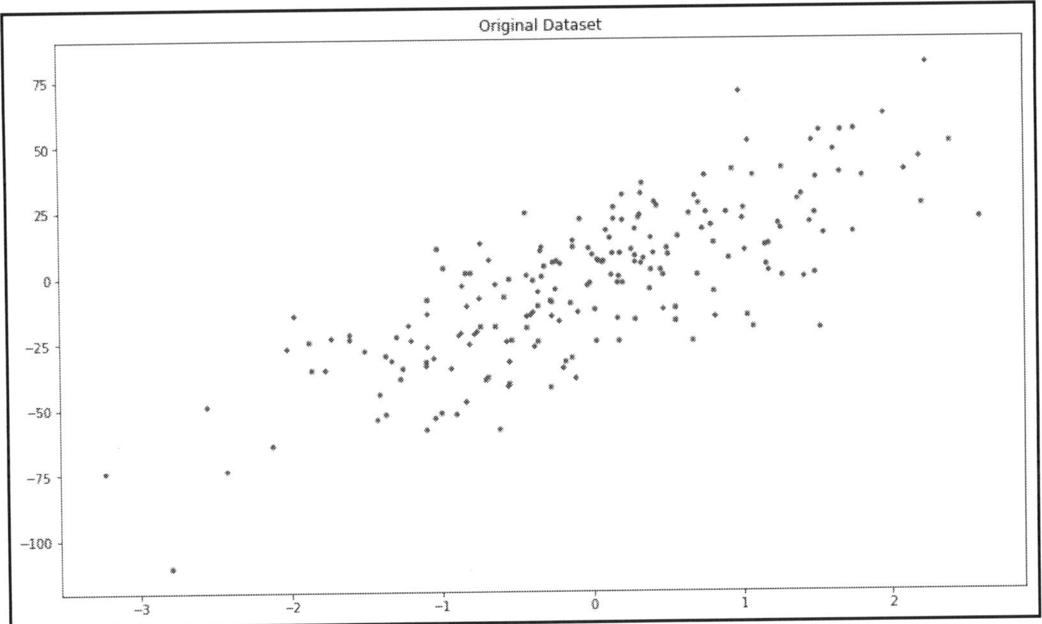

Now let's divide the data into train and test sets:

```
X_train, X_test, y_train, y_test = skms.train_test_split(X, y,
                                        test_size=.4,
                                        random_state=123)
```

Building a simple regression model

To build and train a regression model in TensorFlow, the following steps are taken in general:

1. Defining the inputs, parameters, and other variables.
2. Defining the model.
3. Defining the loss function.
4. Defining the optimizer function.
5. Training the model for a number of iterations known as epochs.

Defining the inputs, parameters, and other variables

Before we get into building and training the regression model using TensorFlow, let's define some important variables and operations. We find out the number of output and input variables from `X_train` and `y_train` and then use these numbers to define the *x*(`x_tensor`), *y* (`y_tensor`), *weights* (`w`), and *bias* (`b`):

```
num_outputs = y_train.shape[1]
num_inputs = X_train.shape[1]

x_tensor = tf.placeholder(dtype=tf.float32,
                         shape=[None, num_inputs],
                         name="x")
y_tensor = tf.placeholder(dtype=tf.float32,
                         shape=[None, num_outputs],
                         name="y")

w = tf.Variable(tf.zeros([num_inputs,num_outputs]),
                dtype=tf.float32,
                name="w")
b = tf.Variable(tf.zeros([num_outputs]),
                dtype=tf.float32,
                name="b")
```

- `x_tensor` is defined as having a shape of variable rows and `num_inputs` columns and the number of columns is only one in our example
- `y_tensor` is defined as having a shape of variable rows and `num_outputs` columns and the number of columns is only one in our example
- `w` is defined as a variable of dimensions `num_inputs` x `num_outputs`, which is **1 x 1** in our example
- `b` is defined as a variable of dimension `num_outputs`, which is one in our example

Defining the model

Next, we define the model as $(x\_tensor \times w) + b$:

```
model = tf.matmul(x_tensor, w) + b
```

Defining the loss function

Next, we define the loss function using the **mean squared error** (**MSE**). MSE is defined as follows:

$$\frac{1}{n}\sum(y_i - \hat{y}_i)^2$$

More details about MSE can be found from the following links:
https://en.wikipedia.org/wiki/Mean_squared_error
http://www.statisticshowto.com/mean-squared-error/

The difference in the actual and estimated value of y is known as **residual**. The loss function calculates the mean of squared residuals. We define it in TensorFlow in the following way:

```
loss = tf.reduce_mean(tf.square(model - y_tensor))
```

- `model - y_tensor` calculates the residuals
- `tf.square(model - y_tensor)` calculates the squares of each residual
- `tf.reduce_mean( ... )` finally calculates the mean of squares calculated in the preceding step

We also define the **mean squared error** (**mse**) and **r-squared** (**rs**) functions to evaluate the trained model. We use a separate `mse` function, because in the next chapters, the loss function will change but the `mse` function would remain the same.

```
# mse and R2 functions
mse = tf.reduce_mean(tf.square(model - y_tensor))
y_mean = tf.reduce_mean(y_tensor)
total_error = tf.reduce_sum(tf.square(y_tensor - y_mean))
unexplained_error = tf.reduce_sum(tf.square(y_tensor - model))
rs = 1 - tf.div(unexplained_error, total_error)
```

Defining the optimizer function

Next, we instantiate the `theGradientDescentOptimizer` function with a learning rate of 0.001 and set it to minimize the loss function:

```
learning_rate = 0.001
optimizer =
tf.train.GradientDescentOptimizer(learning_rate).minimize(loss)
```

More details about gradient descent can be found at the following links:
`https://en.wikipedia.org/wiki/Gradient_descent`
`https://www.analyticsvidhya.com/blog/2017/03/introduction-to-gradient-descent-algorithm-along-its-variants/`

TensorFlow offers many other optimizer functions such as Adadelta, Adagrad, and Adam. We will cover some of them in the following chapters.

Training the model

Now that we have the model, loss function, and optimizer function defined, train the model to learn the parameters, *w*, and *b*. To train the model, define the following global variables:

- `num_epochs`: The number of iterations to run the training for. With every iteration, the model learns better parameters, as we will see in the plots later.
- `w_hat` and `b_hat`: To collect the estimated *w* and *b* parameters.
- `loss_epochs`, `mse_epochs`, `rs_epochs`: To collect the total error value on the training dataset, along with the mse and r-squared values of the model on the test dataset in every iteration.
- `mse_score` and `rs_score`: To collect mse and r-squared values of the final trained model.

```
num_epochs = 1500
w_hat = 0
b_hat = 0
loss_epochs = np.empty(shape=[num_epochs],dtype=float)
mse_epochs = np.empty(shape=[num_epochs],dtype=float)
rs_epochs = np.empty(shape=[num_epochs],dtype=float)

mse_score = 0
rs_score = 0
```

After initializing the session and the global variables, run the training loop for `num_epoch` times:

```
with tf.Session() as tfs:
    tf.global_variables_initializer().run()
    for epoch in range(num_epochs):
```

Within each iteration of the loop, run the optimizer on the training data:

```
tfs.run(optimizer, feed_dict={x_tensor: X_train, y_tensor:
y_train})
```

Using the learned *w* and *b* values, calculate the error and save it in `loss_val` to plot it later:

```
loss_val = tfs.run(loss,feed_dict={x_tensor: X_train, y_tensor:
y_train})
loss_epochs[epoch] = loss_val
```

Calculate the mean squared error and r-squared value for the predicted values of the test data:

```
mse_score = tfs.run(mse,feed_dict={x_tensor: X_test, y_tensor:
y_test})
mse_epochs[epoch] = mse_score

rs_score = tfs.run(rs,feed_dict={x_tensor: X_test, y_tensor: y_test})
rs_epochs[epoch] = rs_score
```

Finally, once the loop is finished, save the values of `w` and `b` to plot them later:

```
w_hat,b_hat = tfs.run([w,b])
w_hat = w_hat.reshape(1)
```

Let's print the model and final mean squared error on the test data after 2,000 iterations:

```
print('model : Y = {0:.8f} X + {1:.8f}'.format(w_hat[0],b_hat[0]))
print('For test data : MSE = {0:.8f}, R2 = {1:.8f} '.format(
    mse_score,rs_score))
```

This gives us the following output:

```
model : Y = 20.37448120 X + -2.75295663
For test data : MSE = 297.57995605, R2 = 0.66098368
```

Thus, the model that we trained is not a very good model, but we will see how to improve it using neural networks in later chapters.

The goal of this chapter is to introduce how to build and train regression models using TensorFlow without using neural networks.

Let's plot the estimated model along with the original data:

```
plt.figure(figsize=(14,8))
plt.title('Original Data and Trained Model')
x_plot = [np.min(X)-1,np.max(X)+1]
y_plot = w_hat*x_plot+b_hat
plt.axis([x_plot[0],x_plot[1],y_plot[0],y_plot[1]])
plt.plot(X,y,'b.',label='Original Data')
plt.plot(x_plot,y_plot,'r-',label='Trained Model')
plt.legend()
plt.show()
```

We get the following plot of the original data vs. the data from the trained model:

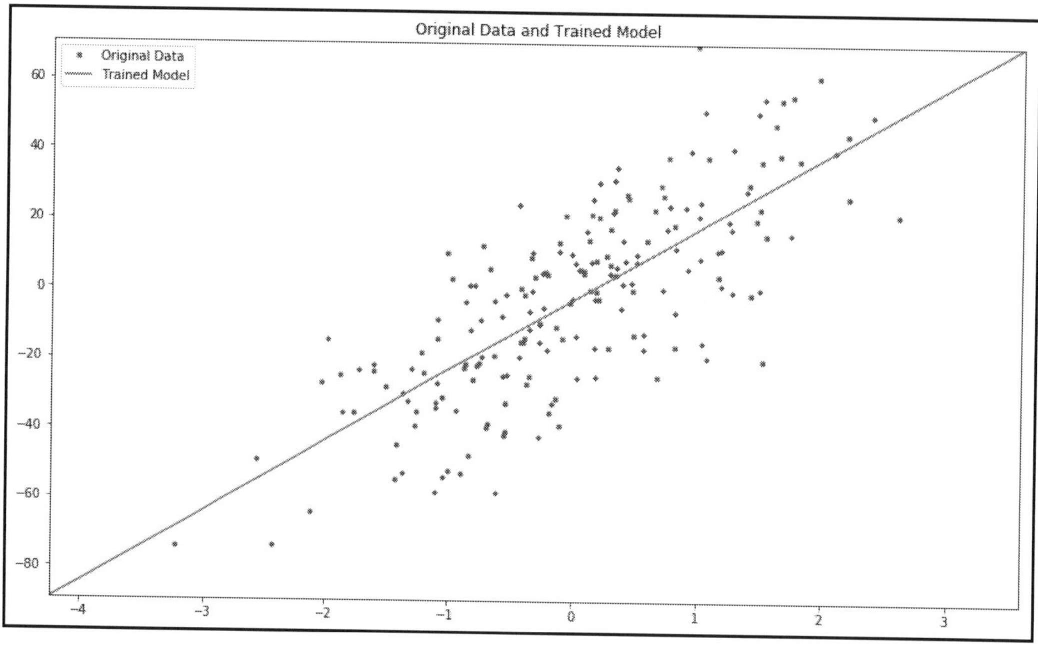

Let's plot the mean squared error for the training and test data in each iteration:

```
plt.figure(figsize=(14,8))

plt.axis([0,num_epochs,0,np.max(loss_epochs)])
plt.plot(loss_epochs, label='Loss on X_train')
plt.title('Loss in Iterations')
plt.xlabel('# Epoch')
plt.ylabel('MSE')

plt.axis([0,num_epochs,0,np.max(mse_epochs)])
plt.plot(mse_epochs, label='MSE on X_test')
plt.xlabel('# Epoch')
plt.ylabel('MSE')
plt.legend()

plt.show()
```

We get the following plot that shows that with each iteration, the mean squared error reduces and then remains at the same level near 500:

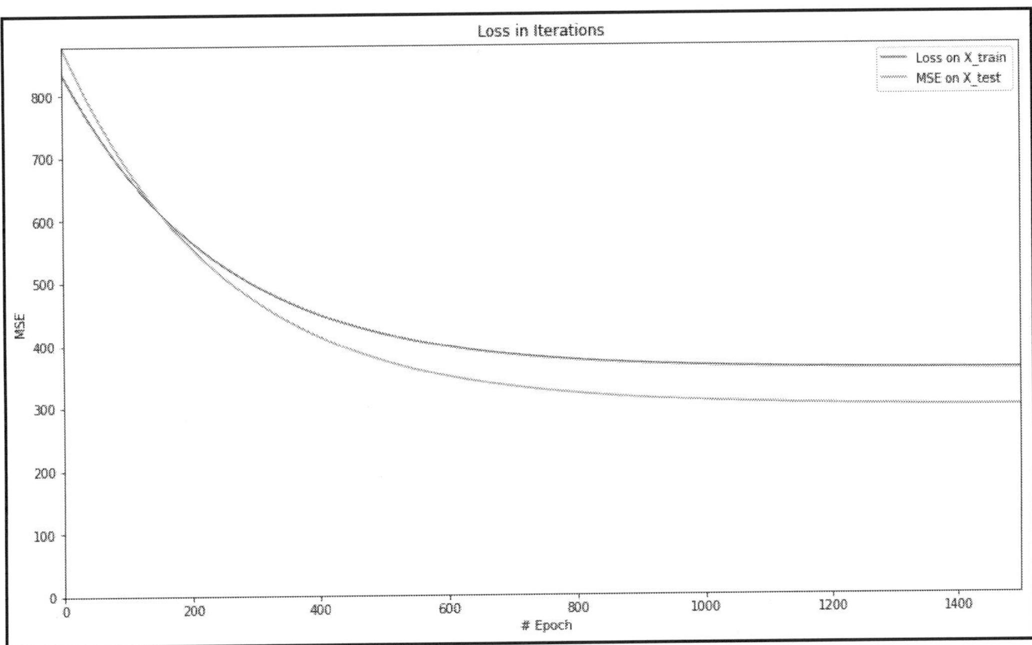

Let's plot the value of r-squared:

```
plt.figure(figsize=(14,8))
plt.axis([0,num_epochs,0,np.max(rs_epochs)])
plt.plot(rs_epochs, label='R2 on X_test')
plt.xlabel('# Epoch')
plt.ylabel('R2')
plt.legend()
plt.show()
```

We get the following plot when we plot the value of r-squared over epochs:

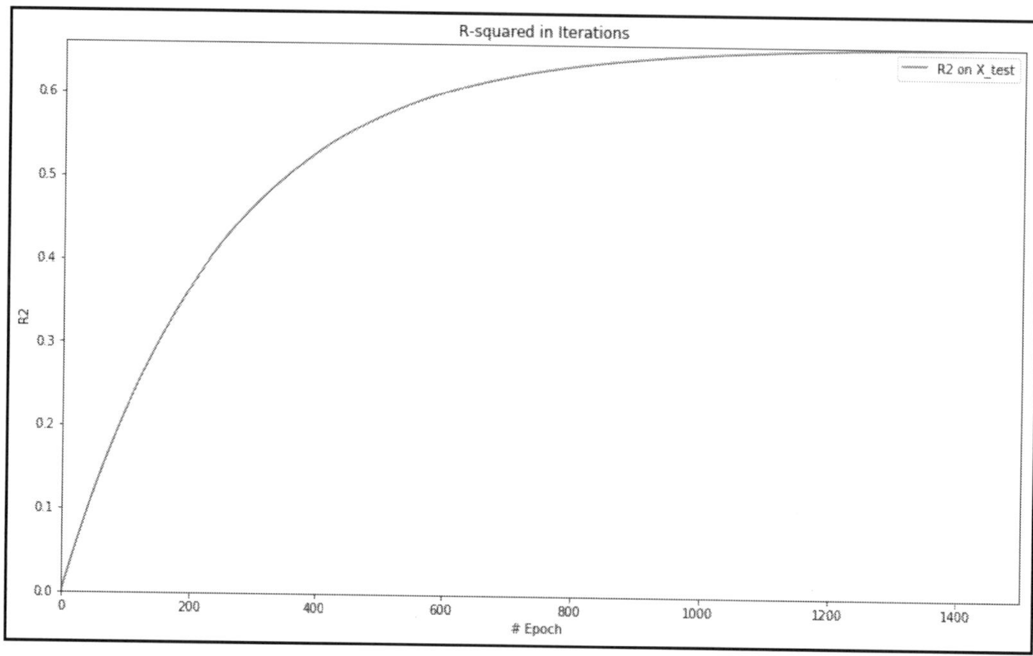

This basically shows that the model starts with a very low value of r-squared, but as the model gets trained and reduces the error, the value of r-squared starts getting higher and finally becomes stable at a point little higher than 0.6.

Plotting MSE and r-squared allows us to see how quickly our model is getting trained and where it starts becoming stable such that further training results in marginal or almost no benefits in reducing the error.

Using the trained model to predict

Now that you have the trained model, it can be used to make predictions about new data. The predictions from the linear model are made with the understanding of some minimum mean squared error that we saw in the previous plot because the straight line may not fit the data perfectly.

To get a better fitting model, we have to extend our model using different methods such as adding the linear combination of variables.

Multi-regression

Now that you have learned how to create a basic regression model with TensorFlow, let's try to run it on example datasets from different domains. The dataset that we generated as an example dataset is univariate, namely, the target was dependent only on one feature.

Most of the datasets, in reality, are multivariate. To emphasize a little more, the target depends on multiple variables or features, thus the regression model is called **multi-regression** or **multidimensional regression**.

We first start with the most popular Boston dataset. This dataset contains 13 attributes of 506 houses in Boston such as the average number of rooms per dwelling, nitric oxide concentration, weighted distances to five Boston employment centers, and so on. The target is the median value of owner-occupied homes. Let's dive into exploring a regression model for this dataset.

Load the dataset from the *sklearn* library and look at its description:

```
boston=skds.load_boston()
print(boston.DESCR)
X=boston.data.astype(np.float32)
y=boston.target.astype(np.float32)
if (y.ndim == 1):
    y = y.reshape(len(y),1)
X = skpp.StandardScaler().fit_transform(X)
```

We also extract `X`, a matrix of features, and `y`, a vector of targets in the preceding code. We reshape `y` to make it two-dimensional and scale the features in `x` to have a mean of zero and standard deviation of one. Now let's use this `X` and `y` to train the regression model, as we did in the previous example:

You may observe that the code for this example is similar to the code in the previous section on simple regression; however, we are using multiple features to train the model so it is called multi-regression.

```
X_train, X_test, y_train, y_test = skms.train_test_split(X, y,
    test_size=.4, random_state=123)
num_outputs = y_train.shape[1]
num_inputs = X_train.shape[1]

x_tensor = tf.placeholder(dtype=tf.float32,
    shape=[None, num_inputs], name="x")
y_tensor = tf.placeholder(dtype=tf.float32,
    shape=[None, num_outputs], name="y")

w = tf.Variable(tf.zeros([num_inputs,num_outputs]),
    dtype=tf.float32, name="w")
b = tf.Variable(tf.zeros([num_outputs]),
    dtype=tf.float32, name="b")

model = tf.matmul(x_tensor, w) + b
loss = tf.reduce_mean(tf.square(model - y_tensor))
# mse and R2 functions
mse = tf.reduce_mean(tf.square(model - y_tensor))
y_mean = tf.reduce_mean(y_tensor)
```

```
total_error = tf.reduce_sum(tf.square(y_tensor - y_mean))
unexplained_error = tf.reduce_sum(tf.square(y_tensor - model))
rs = 1 - tf.div(unexplained_error, total_error)

learning_rate = 0.001
optimizer =
tf.train.GradientDescentOptimizer(learning_rate).minimize(loss)

num_epochs = 1500
loss_epochs = np.empty(shape=[num_epochs],dtype=np.float32)
mse_epochs = np.empty(shape=[num_epochs],dtype=np.float32)
rs_epochs = np.empty(shape=[num_epochs],dtype=np.float32)

mse_score = 0
rs_score = 0

with tf.Session() as tfs:
    tfs.run(tf.global_variables_initializer())
    for epoch in range(num_epochs):
        feed_dict = {x_tensor: X_train, y_tensor: y_train}
        loss_val, _ = tfs.run([loss, optimizer], feed_dict)
        loss_epochs[epoch] = loss_val

        feed_dict = {x_tensor: X_test, y_tensor: y_test}
        mse_score, rs_score = tfs.run([mse, rs], feed_dict)
        mse_epochs[epoch] = mse_score
        rs_epochs[epoch] = rs_score

print('For test data : MSE = {0:.8f}, R2 = {1:.8f} '.format(
    mse_score, rs_score))
```

We get the following output from the model:

```
For test data : MSE = 30.48501778, R2 = 0.64172244
```

Let's plot the MSE and R-squared values.

The following image shows the plotting of MSE:

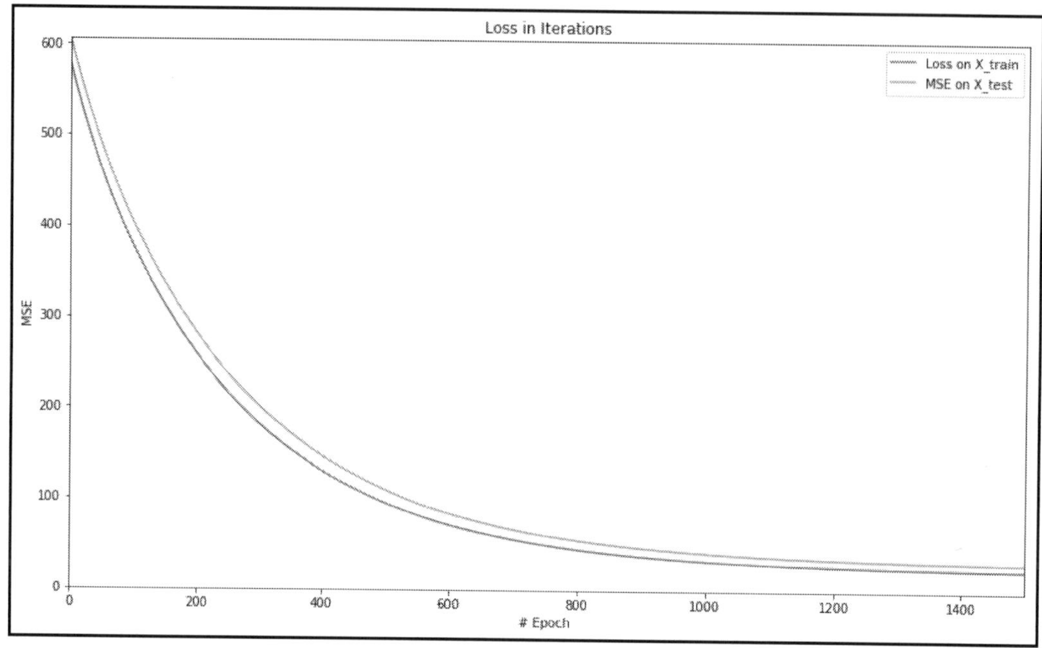

The following image shows the plotting of R-squared values:

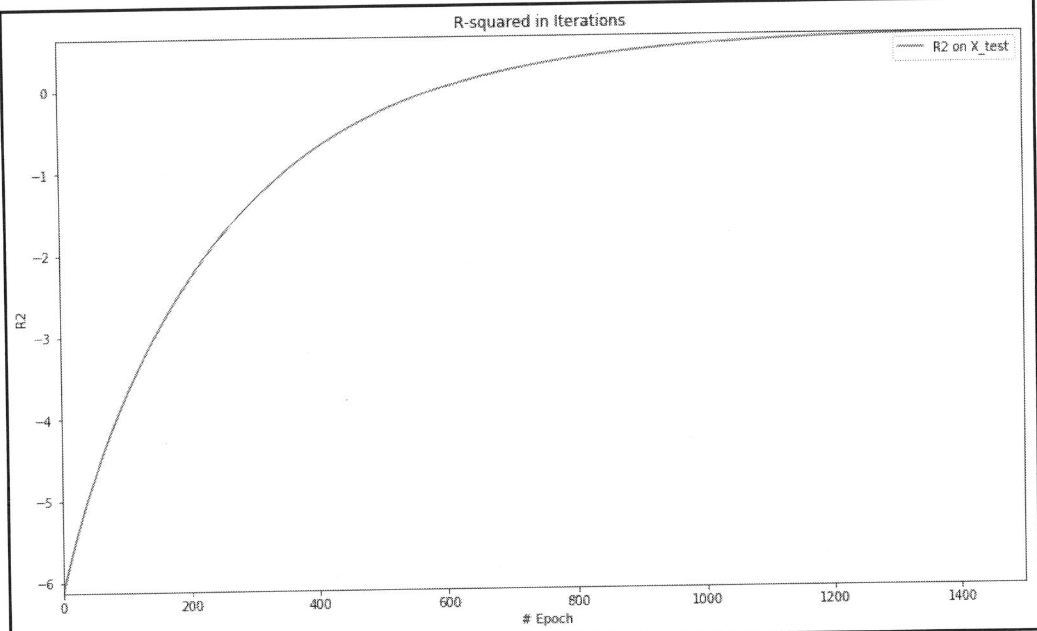

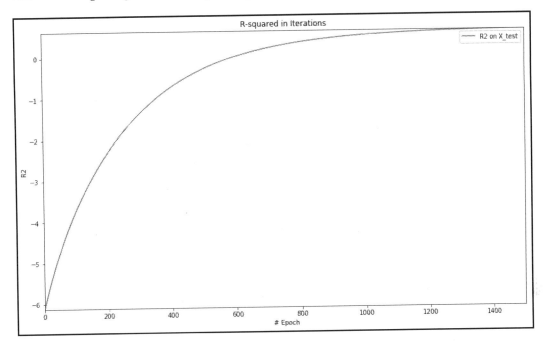

We see a similar pattern for MSE and r-squared, just as we saw for the univariate dataset.

Regularized regression

In linear regression, the model that we trained returns the best-fit parameters on the training data. However, finding the best-fit parameters on the training data may lead to overfitting.

Overfitting means that the model fits best to the training data but gives a greater error on the test data. Thus, we generally add a penalty term to the model to obtain a simpler model.

This penalty term is called a **regularization** term, and the regression model thus obtained is called a regularized regression model. There are three main types of regularization models:

- **Lasso regression**: In lasso regularization, also known as L1 regularization, the regularization term is the lasso parameter α multiplied with the sum of absolute values of the weights w. Thus, the loss function is as follows:

$$\frac{1}{n}\sum_{i=1}^{n}(y_i - \hat{y}_i)^2 + \alpha\frac{1}{n}\sum_{i=1}^{n}|w_i|$$

- **Ridge regression**: In ridge regularization, also known as L2 regularization, the regularization term is the ridge parameter α multiplied with the ith sum of the squares of the weights w. Thus, the loss function is as follows:

$$\frac{1}{n}\sum_{i=1}^{n}(y_i - \hat{y}_i)^2 + \alpha\frac{1}{n}\sum_{i=1}^{n}w_i^2$$

- **ElasticNet regression**: When we add both lasso and ridge regularization terms, the resulting regularization is known as the ElasticNet regularization. Thus, the loss function is as follows:

$$\frac{1}{n}\sum_{i=1}^{n}(y_i - \hat{y}_i)^2 + \alpha_1\frac{1}{n}\sum_{i=1}^{n}|w_i| + \alpha_2\frac{1}{n}\sum_{i=1}^{n}w_i^2$$

Refer to the following resources on the internet for further details on regularization:
`http://www.statisticshowto.com/regularization/`.

A simple rule of thumb is to use L1 or Lasso when we want to remove some features, thus reducing computation time, but at the cost of reduced accuracy.

Now let's see these regularization loss functions implemented in TensorFlow. We will continue with the Boston dataset that we used in the previous example.

Lasso regularization

We define the lasso parameter to have the value 0.8:

```
lasso_param = tf.Variable(0.8, dtype=tf.float32)
lasso_loss = tf.reduce_mean(tf.abs(w)) * lasso_param
```

Setting the lasso parameter as zero means no regularization as the term becomes zero. Higher the value of the regularization term, higher the penalty. The following is the complete code for lasso regularized regression to train the model in order to predict Boston house pricing:

The code below assumes that train and test datasets have been split as per the previous example.

```
num_outputs = y_train.shape[1]
num_inputs = X_train.shape[1]

x_tensor = tf.placeholder(dtype=tf.float32,
                          shape=[None, num_inputs], name='x')
y_tensor = tf.placeholder(dtype=tf.float32,
                          shape=[None, num_outputs], name='y')

w = tf.Variable(tf.zeros([num_inputs, num_outputs]),
                dtype=tf.float32, name='w')
b = tf.Variable(tf.zeros([num_outputs]),
                dtype=tf.float32, name='b')

model = tf.matmul(x_tensor, w) + b

lasso_param = tf.Variable(0.8, dtype=tf.float32)
lasso_loss = tf.reduce_mean(tf.abs(w)) * lasso_param

loss = tf.reduce_mean(tf.square(model - y_tensor)) + lasso_loss

learning_rate = 0.001
optimizer =
tf.train.GradientDescentOptimizer(learning_rate).minimize(loss)

mse = tf.reduce_mean(tf.square(model - y_tensor))
y_mean = tf.reduce_mean(y_tensor)
total_error = tf.reduce_sum(tf.square(y_tensor - y_mean))
unexplained_error = tf.reduce_sum(tf.square(y_tensor - model))
rs = 1 - tf.div(unexplained_error, total_error)
```

```
num_epochs = 1500
loss_epochs = np.empty(shape=[num_epochs],dtype=np.float32)
mse_epochs = np.empty(shape=[num_epochs],dtype=np.float32)
rs_epochs = np.empty(shape=[num_epochs],dtype=np.float32)

mse_score = 0.0
rs_score = 0.0

num_epochs = 1500
loss_epochs = np.empty(shape=[num_epochs], dtype=np.float32)
mse_epochs = np.empty(shape=[num_epochs], dtype=np.float32)
rs_epochs = np.empty(shape=[num_epochs], dtype=np.float32)

mse_score = 0.0
rs_score = 0.0

with tf.Session() as tfs:
    tfs.run(tf.global_variables_initializer())
    for epoch in range(num_epochs):
        feed_dict = {x_tensor: X_train, y_tensor: y_train}
        loss_val,_ = tfs.run([loss,optimizer], feed_dict)
        loss_epochs[epoch] = loss_val

        feed_dict = {x_tensor: X_test, y_tensor: y_test}
        mse_score,rs_score = tfs.run([mse,rs], feed_dict)
        mse_epochs[epoch] = mse_score
        rs_epochs[epoch] = rs_score

print('For test data : MSE = {0:.8f}, R2 = {1:.8f} '.format(
    mse_score, rs_score))
```

We get the following output:

```
For test data : MSE = 30.48978233, R2 = 0.64166653
```

Let's plot the values of MSE and r-squared using the following code:

```
plt.figure(figsize=(14,8))

plt.axis([0,num_epochs,0,np.max([loss_epochs,mse_epochs])])
plt.plot(loss_epochs, label='Loss on X_train')
plt.plot(mse_epochs, label='MSE on X_test')
plt.title('Loss in Iterations')
plt.xlabel('# Epoch')
plt.ylabel('Loss or MSE')
plt.legend()

plt.show()
```

```
plt.figure(figsize=(14,8))

plt.axis([0,num_epochs,np.min(rs_epochs),np.max(rs_epochs)])
plt.title('R-squared in Iterations')
plt.plot(rs_epochs, label='R2 on X_test')
plt.xlabel('# Epoch')
plt.ylabel('R2')
plt.legend()

plt.show()
```

We get the following plot for loss:

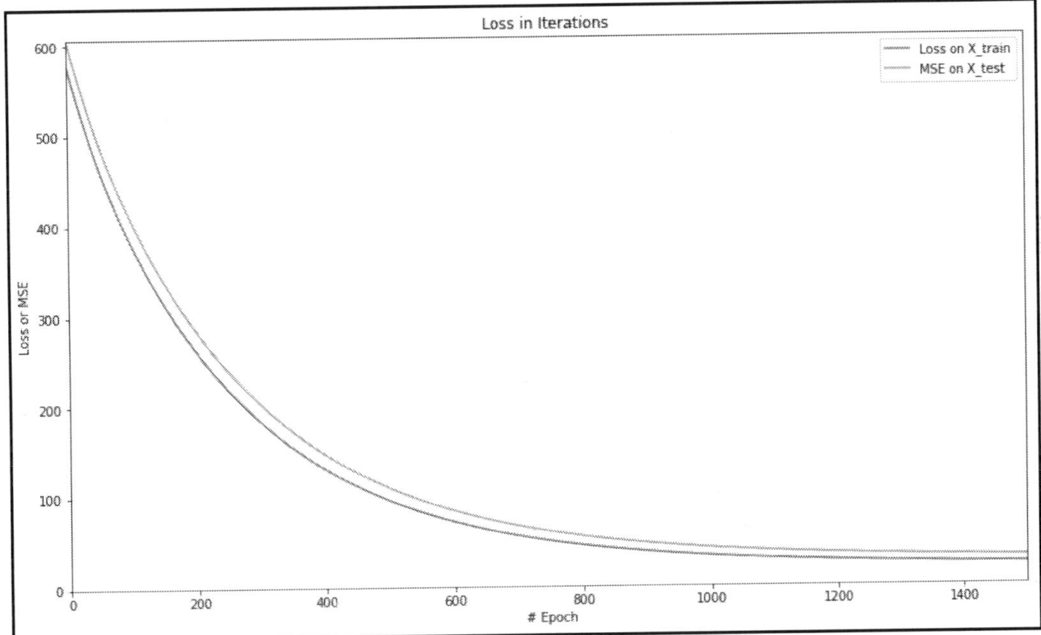

The plot for R-squared in iterations is as follows:

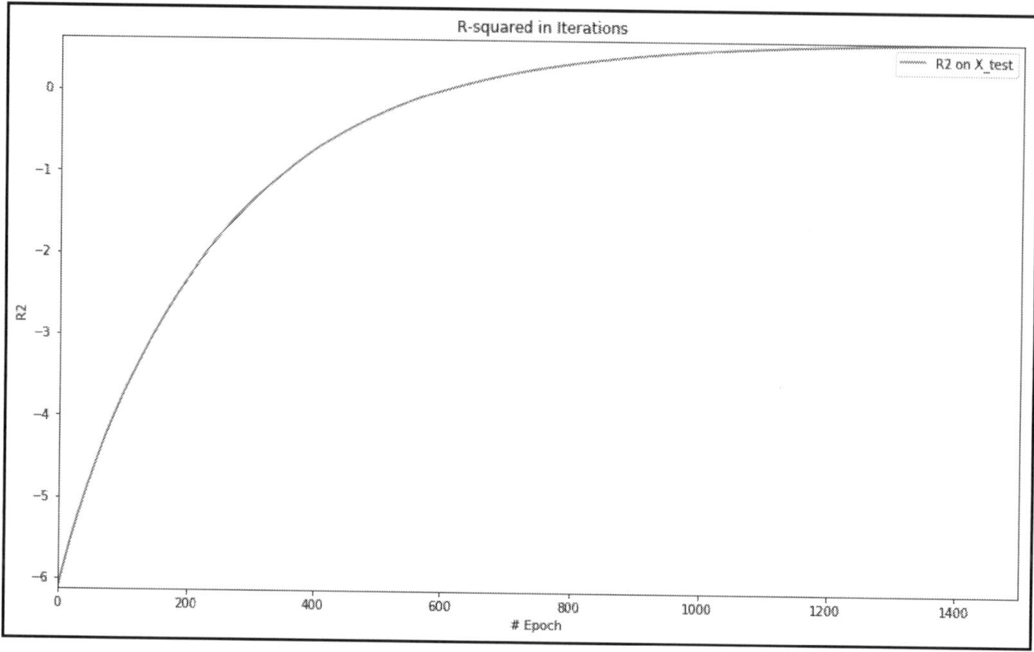

Let's repeat the same example with ridge regression.

Ridge regularization

The following is the complete code for ridge regularized regression to train the model in order to predict Boston house pricing:

```
num_outputs = y_train.shape[1]
num_inputs = X_train.shape[1]

x_tensor = tf.placeholder(dtype=tf.float32,
                          shape=[None, num_inputs], name='x')
y_tensor = tf.placeholder(dtype=tf.float32,
                          shape=[None, num_outputs], name='y')

w = tf.Variable(tf.zeros([num_inputs, num_outputs]),
                dtype=tf.float32, name='w')
b = tf.Variable(tf.zeros([num_outputs]),
                dtype=tf.float32, name='b')

model = tf.matmul(x_tensor, w) + b
```

```
ridge_param = tf.Variable(0.8, dtype=tf.float32)
ridge_loss = tf.reduce_mean(tf.square(w)) * ridge_param

loss = tf.reduce_mean(tf.square(model - y_tensor)) + ridge_loss

learning_rate = 0.001
optimizer =
tf.train.GradientDescentOptimizer(learning_rate).minimize(loss)

mse = tf.reduce_mean(tf.square(model - y_tensor))
y_mean = tf.reduce_mean(y_tensor)
total_error = tf.reduce_sum(tf.square(y_tensor - y_mean))
unexplained_error = tf.reduce_sum(tf.square(y_tensor - model))
rs = 1 - tf.div(unexplained_error, total_error)

num_epochs = 1500
loss_epochs = np.empty(shape=[num_epochs],dtype=np.float32)
mse_epochs = np.empty(shape=[num_epochs],dtype=np.float32)
rs_epochs = np.empty(shape=[num_epochs],dtype=np.float32)

mse_score = 0.0
rs_score = 0.0

with tf.Session() as tfs:
    tfs.run(tf.global_variables_initializer())
    for epoch in range(num_epochs):
        feed_dict = {x_tensor: X_train, y_tensor: y_train}
        loss_val, _ = tfs.run([loss, optimizer], feed_dict=feed_dict)
        loss_epochs[epoch] = loss_val

        feed_dict = {x_tensor: X_test, y_tensor: y_test}
        mse_score, rs_score = tfs.run([mse, rs], feed_dict=feed_dict)
        mse_epochs[epoch] = mse_score
        rs_epochs[epoch] = rs_score

print('For test data : MSE = {0:.8f}, R2 = {1:.8f} '.format(
    mse_score, rs_score))
```

We get the following result:

```
For test data : MSE = 30.64177132, R2 = 0.63988018
```

Plotting the values of loss and MSE, we get the following plot for loss:

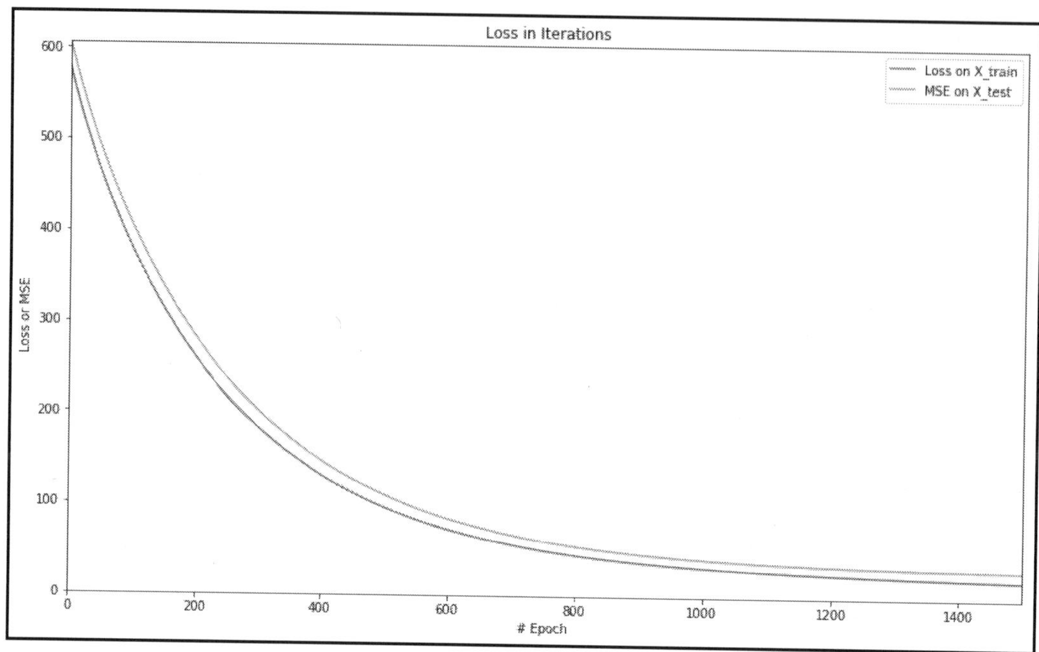

We get the following plot for R-squared:

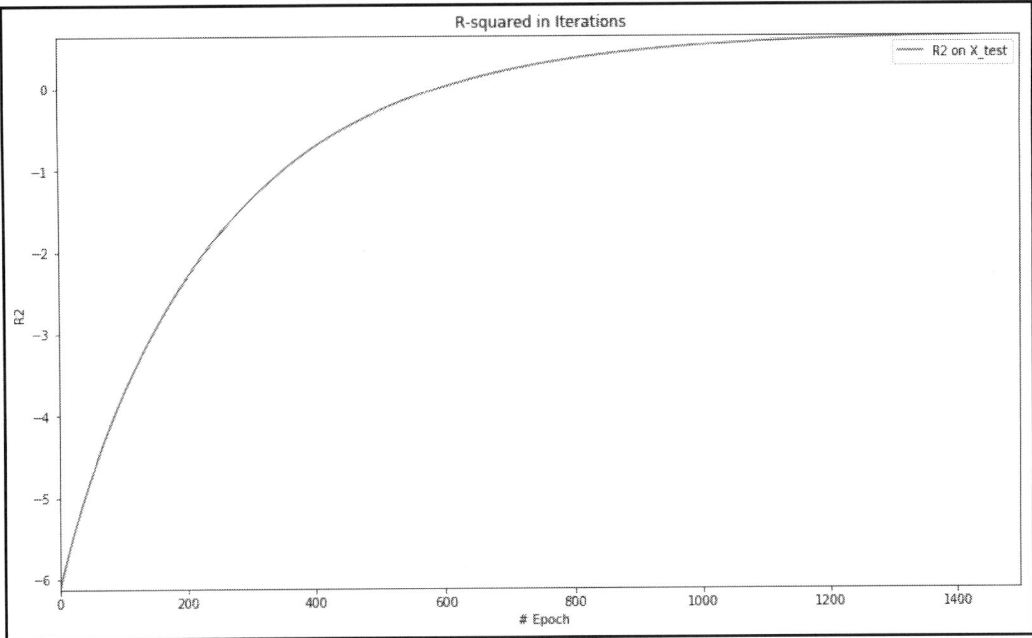

Let's look at the combination of lasso and ridge regularization methods.

ElasticNet regularization

The complete code for ElasticNet regularized regression to train the model to predict the Boston house pricing is provided in the notebook `ch-04a_Regression`. On running the model, we get the following result:

```
For test data : MSE = 30.64861488, R2 = 0.63979971
```

Plotting the values of loss and MSE, we get the following plots:

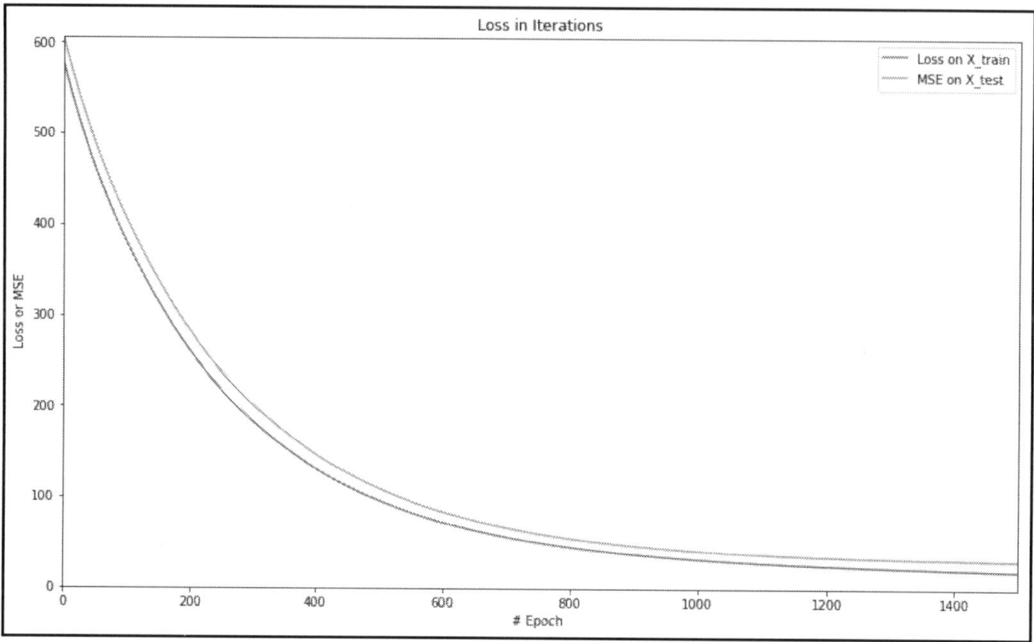

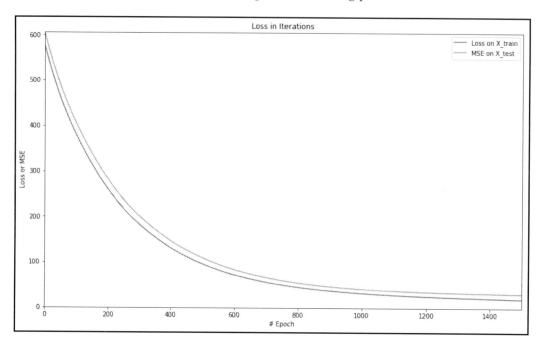

We get the following plot for R-squared:

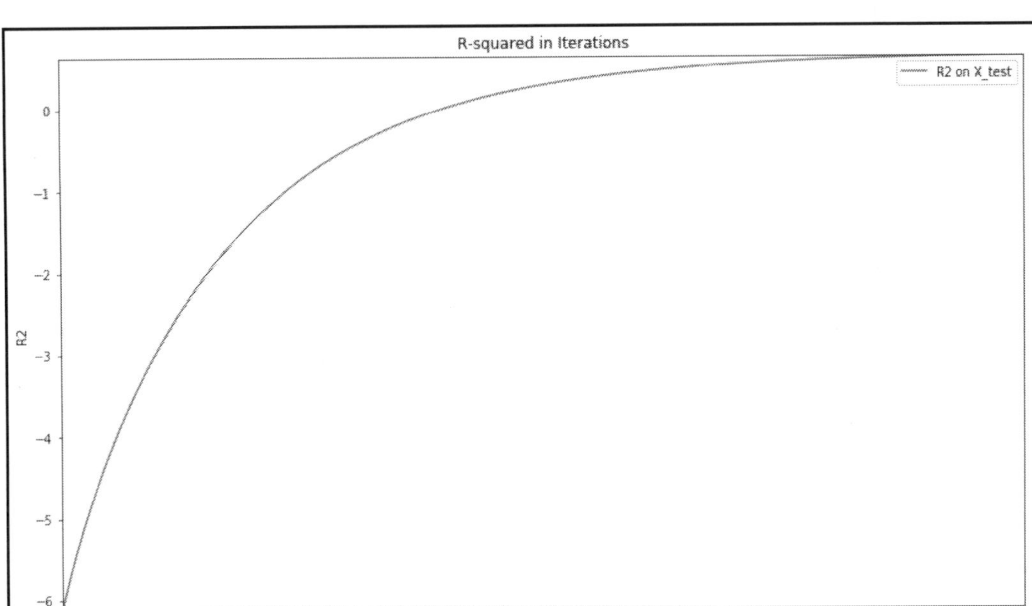

Classification using logistic regression

The most common method for classification is using logistic regression. Logistic regression is a probabilistic and linear classifier. The probability that vector of input features is a member of a specific class can be written formally as the following equation:

$$P(Y = i|x, w, b) = \phi(z)$$

In the above equation:

- Y represents the output,
- i represents one of the classes
- x represents the inputs

- w represents the weights
- b represents the biases
- z represents the regression equation $z = w \times x + b$
- ϕ represents the smoothing function or model in our case

The preceding equation represents that probability that x belongs to class i when w and b are given, is represented by function $\phi(z)$. Thus the model has to be trained to maximize the value of probability.

Logistic regression for binary classification

For binary classification, we define the model function $\phi(z)$ to be the sigmoid function, written as follows:

$$\phi(z) = \frac{1}{1+e^{-z}} = \frac{1}{1+e^{-(w \times x + b)}}$$

The sigmoid function produces the value of y to lie between the range [0,1]. Thus we can use the value of $y=\phi(z)$ to predict the class: if $y > 0.5$ then class is equal to 1, else class is equal to 0.

As we saw in the previous sections in this chapter that for linear regression, the model can be trained by finding parameters that minimize the loss function and loss function could be the sum of squared error or mean squared error. For logistic regression, we want to maximize the likelihood: $L(w) = P(y|x, w, b)$.

However, as it is easier to maximize the log-likelihood, thus we use the log-likelihood $l(w)$ as the cost function. The loss function ($J(w)$) is thus written as $-l(w)$ that can be minimized using the optimization algorithms such as gradient descent.

The loss function for binary logistic regression is written mathematically as follows:

$$J(w) = -\sum_{i=1}^{n}[(y_i \times log(\phi(z_i))) + ((1 - y_i) \times (1 - log(\phi(z_i))))]$$

where $\phi(z)$ is the sigmoid function.

We will implement this loss function in the next section.

Logistic regression for multiclass classification

When there are more than two classes involved, the logistic regression is known multinomial logistic regression. In multinomial logistic regression, instead of sigmoid, we use softmax function that is one of the most popular functions. Softmax can be represented mathematically as follows:

$$softmax\ \ \phi_i(z) = \frac{e_i^z}{\sum_j e_j^z} = \frac{e_i^{(w \times x + b)}}{\sum_j e_j^{(w \times x + b)}} =$$

Softmax function produces the probabilities for each class, and the probabilities vector adds to 1. While predicting, the class with highest softmax value becomes the output or predicted class. The loss function, as we discussed earlier, is the negative log-likelihood function $-l(w)$ that can be minimized by the optimizers such as gradient descent.

The loss function for multinomial logistic regression is written formally as follows:

$$J(w) = -\sum_{i=1}^{n}[y_i \times log(\phi(z_i))]$$

where $\phi(z)$ is the softmax function.

We will implement this loss function later in this chapter.

Let's dig into some examples in the next sections.

You can follow along with the code in the Jupyter notebook `ch-04b_Classification`.

Binary classification

Binary classification refers to problems with only two distinct classes. As we did in the previous chapter, we will generate a dataset using the convenience function, `make_classification()`, in the SciKit Learn library:

```
X, y = skds.make_classification(n_samples=200,
   n_features=2,
   n_informative=2,
   n_redundant=0,
   n_repeated=0,
   n_classes=2,
   n_clusters_per_class=1)
if (y.ndim == 1):
    y = y.reshape(-1,1)
```

The arguments to `make_classification()` are self-explanatory; `n_samples` is the number of data points to generate, `n_features` is the number of features to be generated, and `n_classes` is the number of classes, which is 2:

- `n_samples` is the number of data points to generate. We have kept it to 200 to keep the dataset small.
- `n_features` is the number of features to be generated; we are using only two features so that we can keep it a simple problem to understand the TensorFlow commands.
- `n_classes` is the number of classes, which is 2 as it is a binary classification problem.

Let's plot the data using the following code:

```
plt.scatter(X[:,0],X[:,1],marker='o',c=y)
plt.show()
```

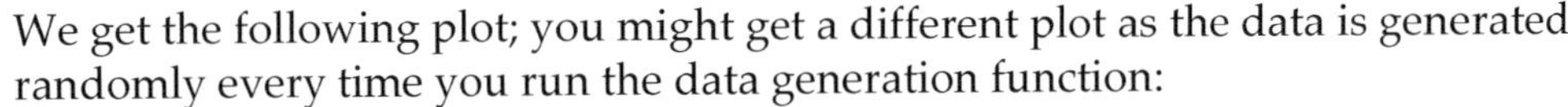

We get the following plot; you might get a different plot as the data is generated randomly every time you run the data generation function:

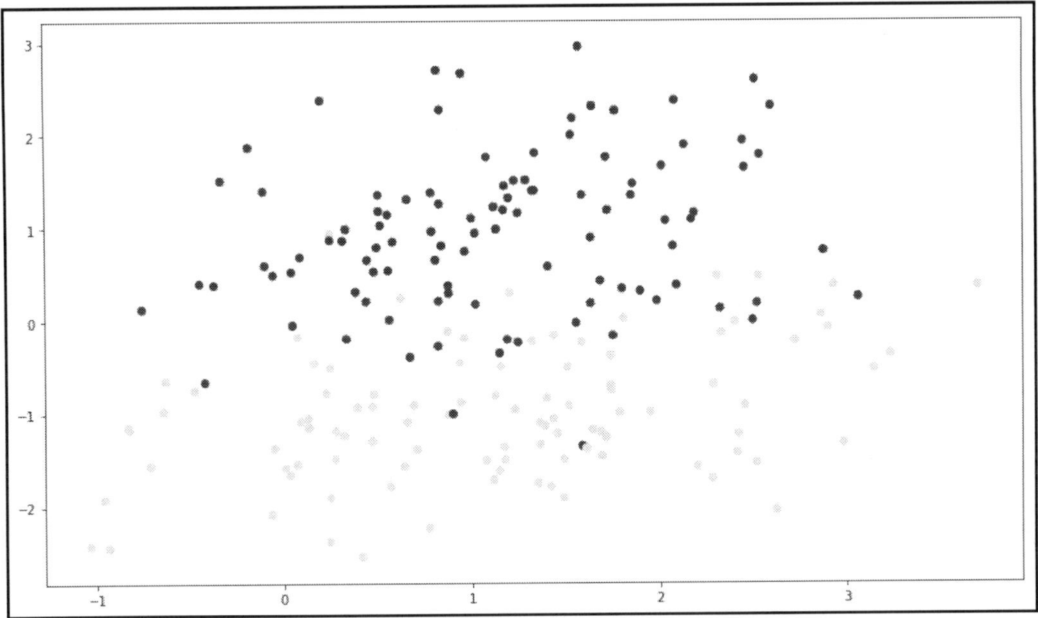

Then we use the NumPy `eye` function to convert *y* to one-hot encoded targets:

```
print(y[0:5])
y=np.eye(num_outputs)[y]
print(y[0:5])
```

The one-hot encoded targets appear as follows:

```
[1 0 0 1 0]
[[ 0.  1.]
 [ 1.  0.]
 [ 1.  0.]
 [ 0.  1.]
 [ 1.  0.]]
```

Divide the data into train and test categories:

```
X_train, X_test, y_train, y_test = skms.train_test_split(
    X, y, test_size=.4, random_state=42)
```

In classification, we use the sigmoid function to quantify the value of model such that the output value lies between the range [0,1]. The following equations denote the sigmoid function indicated by $\phi(z)$, where z is the equation $w \times x + b$. The loss function now changes to the one indicated by $J(\theta)$, where θ represents the parameters.

$$z_i = w_i \times x_i + b$$

$$\phi(z) = \frac{1}{1 + e^{-z}}$$

$$J(w) = -\sum_{i=1}^{n}[(y_i \times log(\phi(z_i))) + ((1 - y_i) \times (1 - log(\phi(z_i))))]$$

We implement the new model and loss function using the following code:

```
num_outputs = y_train.shape[1]
num_inputs = X_train.shape[1]

learning_rate = 0.001

# input images
x = tf.placeholder(dtype=tf.float32, shape=[None, num_inputs],
name="x")
# output labels
y = tf.placeholder(dtype=tf.float32, shape=[None, num_outputs],
name="y")

# model paramteres
w = tf.Variable(tf.zeros([num_inputs,num_outputs]), name="w")
b = tf.Variable(tf.zeros([num_outputs]), name="b")
model = tf.nn.sigmoid(tf.matmul(x, w) + b)

loss = tf.reduce_mean(-tf.reduce_sum(
    (y * tf.log(model)) + ((1 - y) * tf.log(1 - model)), axis=1))
optimizer = tf.train.GradientDescentOptimizer(
    learning_rate=learning_rate).minimize(loss)
```

Finally, we run our classification model:

```
num_epochs = 1
with tf.Session() as tfs:
    tf.global_variables_initializer().run()
    for epoch in range(num_epochs):
        tfs.run(optimizer, feed_dict={x: X_train, y: y_train})
        y_pred = tfs.run(tf.argmax(model, 1), feed_dict={x: X_test})
        y_orig = tfs.run(tf.argmax(y, 1), feed_dict={y: y_test})

        preds_check = tf.equal(y_pred, y_orig)
        accuracy_op = tf.reduce_mean(tf.cast(preds_check, tf.float32))
        accuracy_score = tfs.run(accuracy_op)
        print("epoch {0:04d} accuracy={1:.8f}".format(
            epoch, accuracy_score))

        plt.figure(figsize=(14, 4))
        plt.subplot(1, 2, 1)
        plt.scatter(X_test[:, 0], X_test[:, 1], marker='o', c=y_orig)
        plt.title('Original')
        plt.subplot(1, 2, 2)
        plt.scatter(X_test[:, 0], X_test[:, 1], marker='o', c=y_pred)
        plt.title('Predicted')
        plt.show()
```

We get a pretty good accuracy of about 96 percent and the original and predicted data graphs look like this:

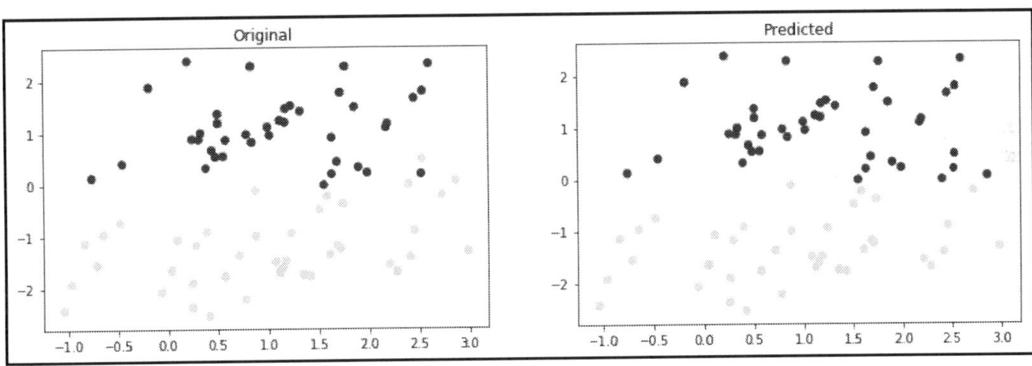

Pretty neat!! Now let's make our problem complicated and try to predict more than two classes.

Multiclass classification

One of the popular examples of multiclass classification is to label the images of handwritten digits. The classes or labels in this examples are {0,1,2,3,4,5,6,7,8,9}. In the following example, we will use MNIST. Let's load the MNIST images as we did in the earlier chapter with the following code:

```
from tensorflow.examples.tutorials.mnist import input_data
mnist = input_data.read_data_sets(os.path.join(
    datasetslib.datasets_root, 'mnist'), one_hot=True)
```

If the MNIST dataset is already downloaded as per instructions from an earlier chapter, then we would get the following output:

```
Extracting /Users/armando/datasets/mnist/train-images-idx3-ubyte.gz
Extracting /Users/armando/datasets/mnist/train-labels-idx1-ubyte.gz
Extracting /Users/armando/datasets/mnist/t10k-images-idx3-ubyte.gz
Extracting /Users/armando/datasets/mnist/t10k-labels-idx1-ubyte.gz
```

Now let's set some parameters, as shown in the following code:

```
num_outputs = 10 # 0-9 digits
num_inputs = 784 # total pixels

learning_rate = 0.001
num_epochs = 1
batch_size = 100
num_batches = int(mnist.train.num_examples/batch_size)
```

The parameters in the above code are as follows:

- `num_outputs`: As we have to predict that image represents which digit out of the ten digits, thus we set the number of outputs as 10. The digit is represented by the output that is turned on or set to one.
- `num_inputs`: We know that our input digits are 28 x 28 pixels, thus each pixel is an input to the model. Thus we have a total of 784 inputs.
- `learning_rate`: This parameter represents the learning rate for the gradient descent optimizer algorithm. We set the learning rate arbitrarily to 0.001.
- `num_epochs`: We will run our first example only for one iteration, hence we set the number of epochs to 1.

- `batch_size`: In the real world, we might have a huge dataset and loading the whole dataset in order to train the model may not be possible. Hence, we divide the input data into batches that are chosen randomly. We set the `batch_size` to 100 images that can be selected at a time using TensorFlow's inbuilt algorithm.
- `num_batches`: This parameter sets the number of times the batches should be selected from the total dataset; we set this to be equal to the number of items in the dataset divided by the number of items in a batch.

You are encouraged to experiment with different values of these parameters.

Now let's define the inputs, outputs, parameters, model, and loss function using the following code:

```
# input images
x = tf.placeholder(dtype=tf.float32, shape=[None, num_inputs],
name="x")
# output labels
y = tf.placeholder(dtype=tf.float32, shape=[None, num_outputs],
name="y")

# model paramteres
w = tf.Variable(tf.zeros([784, 10]), name="w")
b = tf.Variable(tf.zeros([10]), name="b")
model = tf.nn.softmax(tf.matmul(x, w) + b)

loss = tf.reduce_mean(-tf.reduce_sum(y * tf.log(model), axis=1))
optimizer = tf.train.GradientDescentOptimizer(
    learning_rate=learning_rate).minimize(loss)
```

The code is similar to the binary classification example with one significant difference: we use `softmax` instead of `sigmoid` function. Softmax is used for multiclass classification whereas sigmoid is used for binary class classification. Softmax function is a generalization of the sigmoid function that converts an n-dimensional vector z of arbitrary real values to an n-dimensional vector $\sigma(z)$ of real values in the range (0, 1] that add up to 1.

Now let's run the model and print the accuracy:

```
with tf.Session() as tfs:
    tf.global_variables_initializer().run()
    for epoch in range(num_epochs):
        for batch in range(num_batches):
            batch_x, batch_y = mnist.train.next_batch(batch_size)
            tfs.run(optimizer, feed_dict={x: batch_x, y: batch_y})
        predictions_check = tf.equal(tf.argmax(model, 1), tf.argmax(y,
1))
        accuracy_function = tf.reduce_mean(
            tf.cast(predictions_check, tf.float32))
        feed_dict = {x: mnist.test.images, y: mnist.test.labels}
        accuracy_score = tfs.run(accuracy_function, feed_dict)
        print("epoch {0:04d} accuracy={1:.8f}".format(
            epoch, accuracy_score))
```

We get the following accuracy:

```
epoch 0000  accuracy=0.76109999
```

Let's try training our model in multiple iterations, such that it learns with different batches in each iteration. We build two supporting functions to help us with this:

```
def mnist_batch_func(batch_size=100):
    batch_x, batch_y = mnist.train.next_batch(batch_size)
    return [batch_x, batch_y]
```

The preceding function takes the number of examples in a batch as input and uses the `mnist.train.next_batch()` function to return a batch of features (`batch_x`) and targets (`batch_y`):

```
def tensorflow_classification(num_epochs, num_batches, batch_size,
                              batch_func, optimizer, test_x, test_y):
    accuracy_epochs = np.empty(shape=[num_epochs], dtype=np.float32)
    with tf.Session() as tfs:
        tf.global_variables_initializer().run()
        for epoch in range(num_epochs):
            for batch in range(num_batches):
                batch_x, batch_y = batch_func(batch_size)
                feed_dict = {x: batch_x, y: batch_y}
                tfs.run(optimizer, feed_dict)
            predictions_check = tf.equal(
                tf.argmax(model, 1), tf.argmax(y, 1))
            accuracy_function = tf.reduce_mean(
                tf.cast(predictions_check, tf.float32))
            feed_dict = {x: test_x, y: test_y}
            accuracy_score = tfs.run(accuracy_function, feed_dict)
```

```
            accuracy_epochs[epoch] = accuracy_score
            print("epoch {0:04d} accuracy={1:.8f}".format(
                epoch, accuracy_score))

    plt.figure(figsize=(14, 8))
    plt.axis([0, num_epochs, np.min(
        accuracy_epochs), np.max(accuracy_epochs)])
    plt.plot(accuracy_epochs, label='Accuracy Score')
    plt.title('Accuracy over Iterations')
    plt.xlabel('# Epoch')
    plt.ylabel('Accuracy Score')
    plt.legend()
    plt.show()
```

The preceding function takes the parameters and performs the training iterations, printing the accuracy score for each iteration and prints the accuracy scores. It also saves the accuracy scores for each epoch in the `accuracy_epochs` array. Later, it plots the accuracy in each epoch. Let's run this function for 30 epochs using the parameters we set previously, using the following code:

```
num_epochs=30
tensorflow_classification(num_epochs=num_epochs,
    num_batches=num_batches,
    batch_size=batch_size,
    batch_func=mnist_batch_func,
    optimizer=optimizer,
    test_x=mnist.test.images,test_y=mnist.test.labels)
```

We get the following accuracy and graph:

```
epoch 0000  accuracy=0.76020002
epoch 0001  accuracy=0.79420000
epoch 0002  accuracy=0.81230003
epoch 0003  accuracy=0.82309997
epoch 0004  accuracy=0.83230001
epoch 0005  accuracy=0.83770001

--- epoch 6 to 24 removed for brevity ---

epoch 0025  accuracy=0.87930000
epoch 0026  accuracy=0.87970001
epoch 0027  accuracy=0.88059998
epoch 0028  accuracy=0.88120002
epoch 0029  accuracy=0.88180000
```

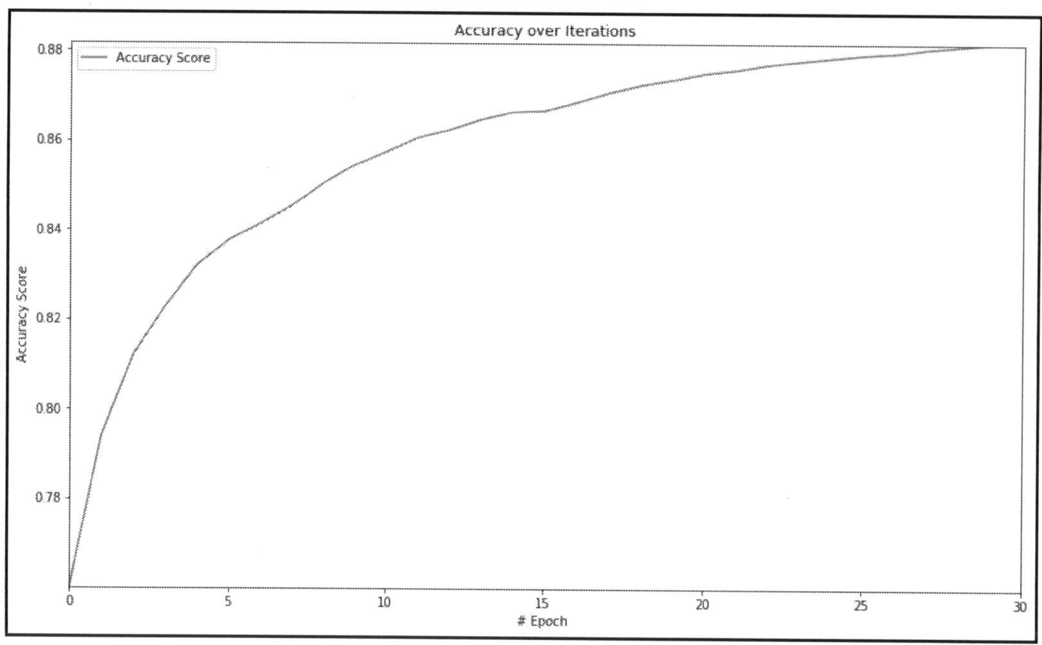

As we can see from the graph, accuracy improves very sharply in initial iterations and then the rate of improvement in accuracy slows down. Later, we will see how we can use the full power of neural networks in TensorFlow and bring this classification accuracy to a larger value.

Summary

In this chapter, we learned about applying classical machine learning algorithms in TensorFlow, without using neural networks. In the first section of the chapter, we learned about regression models. We explained how to train the models for linear regression with one or multiple features. We used TensorFlow to write the linear regression code. We also discussed that regularization is basically adding a penalty term so that the model does not overfit to the training data while learning the parameters in the training phase. We implemented Lasso, Ridge, and ElasticNet regularizations using TensorFlow. TensorFlow has some built-in regularization methods that we will study in the next chapters.

In the subsequent sections of this chapter, we learned about the classification problem in supervised machine learning. We discussed the model function, smoothing functions, and loss functions for binary class and multiclass classification. We used logistic regression in this chapter as that is the simplest method to implement classification. For binary classification, we used the sigmoid function and for multiclass classification, we used the softmax function to smooth the values of our linear model to produce the probabilities of output being in a specific class.

We implemented the logic for model and loss functions in TensorFlow and trained the model for binary classification and multiclass classification. Although we used the classical machine learning methods in this chapter and implemented them using TensorFlow, the full power of TensorFlow is unleashed when we implement neural networks and deep neural networks to solve machine learning problems. We will study such advanced methods in neural network-related chapters in this book.

You are encouraged to read the following books to learn more details on regression and classification:

Sebastian Raschka, *Python Machine Learning, 2nd Edition*. Packt Publishing, 2017

Trevor Hastie, Robert Tibshirani, Jerome Friedman, *The Elements of Statistical Learning*. Second Edition. Springer, 2013

10
Neural Networks and MLP with TensorFlow and Keras

The neural network is a modeling technique that was inspired by the structure and functioning of the brain. Just as the brain contains millions of tiny interconnected units known as neurons, the neural networks of today consist of millions of tiny interconnected computing units arranged in layers. Since the computing units of neural networks only exist in the digital world, as against the physical neurons of the brain, they are also called artificial neurons. Similarly, the **neural networks** (**NN**) are also known as the **artificial neural networks** (**ANN**).

In this chapter, we are going to further expand on the following topics:

- The perceptron (artificial neuron)
- Feed forward neural networks
- **MultiLayer Perceptron** (**MLP**) for image classification
    - TensorFlow-based MLP for MNIST image classification
    - Keras-based MLP for MNIST classification
    - TFLearn-based MLP for MNIST classification
- MLP for time series regression

The perceptron

Let's understand the most basic building block of a neural network, the **perceptron,** also known as the **artificial neuron**. The concept of the perceptron originated in the works of Frank Rosenblatt in 1962.

You may want to read the following work to explore the origins of neural networks:

Frank Rosenblatt, *Principles of Neurodynamics: Perceptrons and the Theory of Brain Mechanisms*. Spartan Books, 1962

In the most simplified view, a perceptron is modeled after the biological neurons such that it takes one or multiple inputs and combines them to generate output.

As shown in the following image, the perceptron takes three inputs and adds them to generate output *y*:

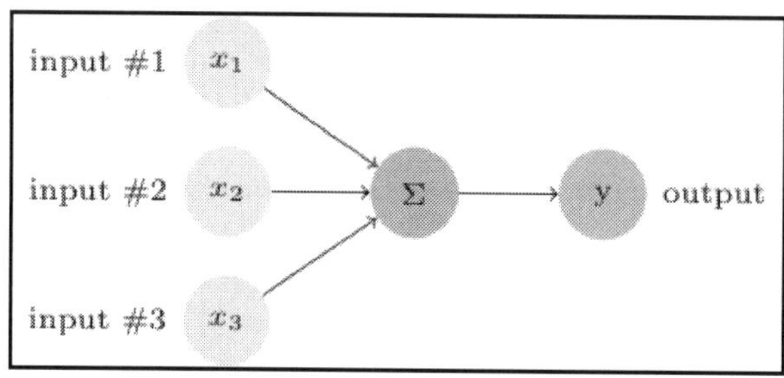

Simple perceptron

This perceptron is too simple to be of any practical use. Hence, it has been enhanced by adding the concept of weights, bias, and activation function. The weights are added to each input to get the weighted sum. If the weighted sum $\sum w_i x_i$ is less than the threshold value, then the output is 0, else output is 1:

$$y = \begin{cases} 0 & if \sum w_i x_i < threshold \\ 1 & if \sum w_i x_i \geq threshold \end{cases}$$

The threshold value is known as the **bias**. Let's move the bias to the left of the equation and denote it with b and represent $\Sigma w_i x_i$ with vector dot product of w and x. The equation for perceptron now becomes as follows:

$$y = \begin{cases} 0 & if \sum w \cdot x + b < 0 \\ 1 & if \sum w \cdot x + b \geq 0 \end{cases}$$

The perceptron now looks like the following image:

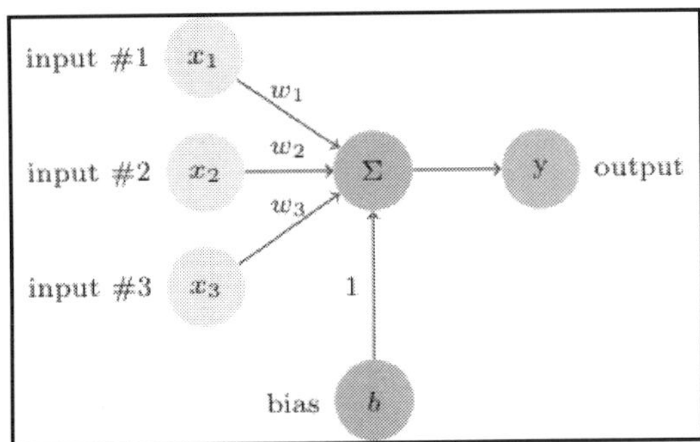

Simple perceptron with weights and bias

So far, the neuron is a linear function. In order to make this neuron produce a nonlinear decision boundary, run the output of summation through a nonlinear function known as the **activation** or transfer function. There are many popular activation functions available:

- `ReLU`: **Rectified Linear Unit**, smoothens the value to the range *(0,x)*, $ReLU(x) = max(0, x)$
- `sigmoid`: **Sigmoid** smoothens the value to the range *(0,1)*, $sigmoid(x) = \frac{1}{1+e^{-x}} = \frac{e^x}{1+e^x}$
- `tanh`: **Hyperbolic Tangent** smoothens the value to the range *(-1,1)*, $tanh(x) = \frac{e^x - e^{-x}}{e^x + e^{-x}}$

With the activation function, the equation for the perceptron becomes:

$$y = \varphi(w \cdot x + b)$$

where $\varphi(\cdot)$ is an activation function.

The neuron looks like the following image:

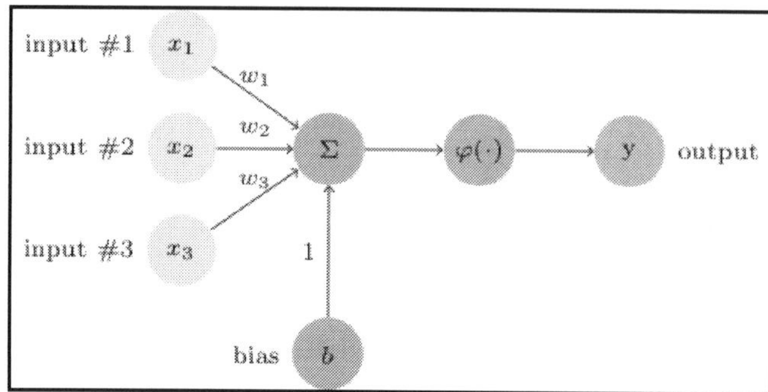

Simple perceptron with activation function, weights, and bias

MultiLayer Perceptron

When we connect the artificial neurons together, based on a well-defined structure, we call it a neural network. Here is the simplest neural network with one neuron:

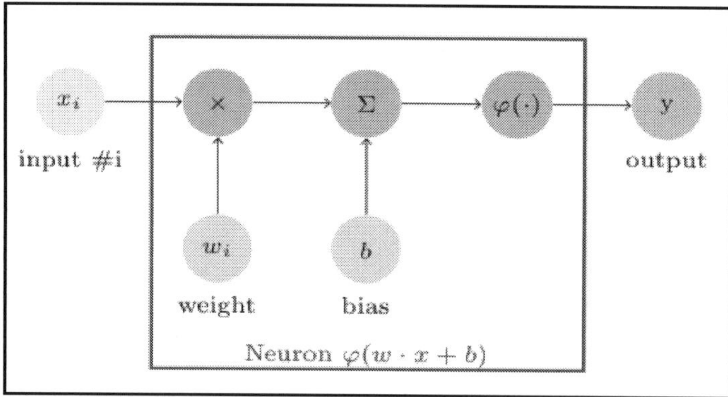

Neural network with one neuron

We connect the neurons such that the output of one layer becomes the input of the next layer, until the final layer's output becomes the final output. Such neural networks are called **feed forward neural networks (FFNN)**. As these FFNNs are made up of layers of neurons connected together, they are hence called **MultiLayer Perceptrons (MLP)** or **deep neural networks (DNN)**.

As an example, the MLP depicted in the following diagram has three features as inputs: two hidden layers of five neurons each and one output y. The neurons are fully connected to the neurons of the next layer. Such layers are also called dense layers or affine layers and such models are also known as sequential models.

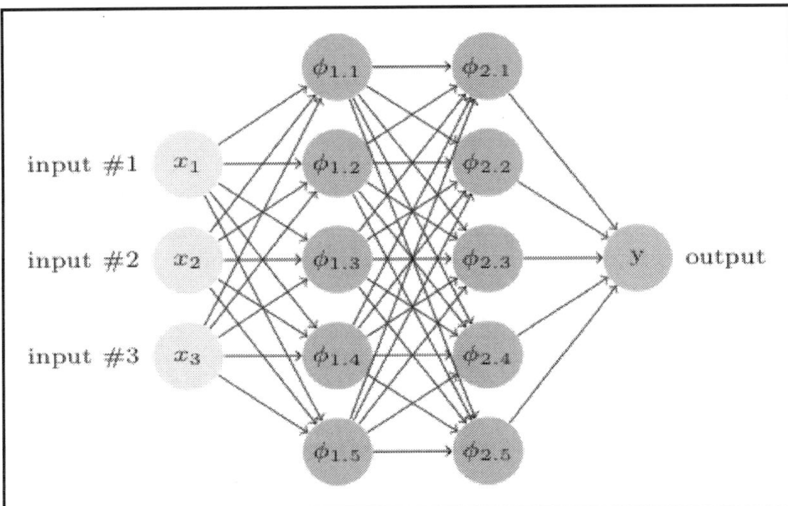

Let's revisit some of the example datasets that we explored earlier and build simple neural networks (MLP or DNN) in TensorFlow.

You can follow along with the code in the Jupyter notebook `ch-05_MLP`.

MLP for image classification

Let's build the MLP network for image classification using different libraries, such as TensorFlow, Keras, and TFLearn. We shall use the MNIST data set for the examples in this section.

The MNIST dataset contains the 28x28 pixel images of handwritten digits from 0 to 9, and their labels, 60K for the training set and 10K for the test set. The MNIST dataset is the most widely used data set, including in TensorFlow examples and tutorials.

The MNIST dataset and related documentation are available from the following link: `http://yann.lecun.com/exdb/mnist/`.

Let us start with the pure TensorFlow approach.

TensorFlow-based MLP for MNIST classification

First, load the MNIST dataset, and define the training and test features and the targets using the following code:

```
from tensorflow.examples.tutorials.mnist import input_data
mnist_home = os.path.join(datasetslib.datasets_root, 'mnist')
mnist = input_data.read_data_sets(mnist_home, one_hot=True)

X_train = mnist.train.images
X_test = mnist.test.images
Y_train = mnist.train.labels
Y_test = mnist.test.labels

num_outputs = 10 # 0-9 digits
num_inputs = 784 # total pixels
```

We create three helper functions that will help us create a simple MLP with only one hidden layer, followed by a larger MLP with multiple layers and multiple neurons in each layer.

The `mlp()` function builds the network layers with the following logic:

1. The `mlp()` function takes five inputs:
    - *x* is the input features tensor
    - `num_inputs` is the number of input features
    - `num_outputs` is the number of output targets
    - `num_layers` is the number of hidden layers required
    - `num_neurons` is the list containing the number of neurons for each layer
2. Set the weights and biases lists to empty:

```
w=[]
b=[]
```

3. Run a loop for the number of hidden layers to create weights and bias tensors and append them to their respective lists:
    - The tensors are given the names `w_<layer_num>` and `b_<layer_num>` respectively. Naming the tensors helps in the debugging and locating problems with the code.
    - The tensors are initialized with normal distribution using `tf.random_normal()`.
    - The first dimension of the weight tensor is the number of inputs from the previous layer. For the first hidden layer, the first dimension is `num_inputs`. The second dimension of the weights tensor is the number of neurons in the current layer.
    - The biases are all one-dimensional tensors, where the dimension equals the number of neurons in the current layer.

```
for i in range(num_layers):
    # weights
    w.append(tf.Variable(tf.random_normal(
          [num_inputs if i == 0 else num_neurons[i - 1],
           num_neurons[i]]),
          name="w_{0:04d}".format(i)
          ))
    # biases
    b.append(tf.Variable(tf.random_normal(
          [num_neurons[i]]),
          name="b_{0:04d}".format(i)
          ))
```

4. Create the weights and biases for the last hidden layer. In this case, the dimensions of the weights tensor are equal to the number of neurons in the last hidden layer and the number of output targets. The bias would be a tensor having a single dimension of the size of the number of output features:

```
    w.append(tf.Variable(tf.random_normal(
        [num_neurons[num_layers - 1] if num_layers > 0 else
num_inputs,
         num_outputs]), name="w_out"))
    b.append(tf.Variable(tf.random_normal([num_outputs]),
        name="b_out"))
```

5. Now start defining the layers. First, treat `x` as the first most visible input layer:

```
    # x is input layer
    layer = x
```

6. Add the hidden layers in a loop. Each hidden layer represents the linear function `tf.matmul(layer, w[i]) + b[i]` being made nonlinear by the activation function `tf.nn.relu()`:

```
    # add hidden layers
    for i in range(num_layers):
        layer = tf.nn.relu(tf.matmul(layer, w[i]) + b[i])
```

7. Add the output layer. The one difference between the output layer and the hidden layer is the absence of activation function in the output layer:

```
    layer = tf.matmul(layer, w[num_layers]) + b[num_layers]
```

8. Return the `layer` object that contains the MLP network:

```
    return layer
```

The complete code of the entire MLP function is as follows:

```
def mlp(x, num_inputs, num_outputs, num_layers, num_neurons):
    w = []
    b = []
    for i in range(num_layers):
        # weights
        w.append(tf.Variable(tf.random_normal(
            [num_inputs if i == 0 else num_neurons[i - 1],
             num_neurons[i]]),
            name="w_{0:04d}".format(i)
        ))
        # biases
        b.append(tf.Variable(tf.random_normal(
            [num_neurons[i]]),
            name="b_{0:04d}".format(i)
        ))
    w.append(tf.Variable(tf.random_normal(
        [num_neurons[num_layers - 1] if num_layers > 0 else
num_inputs,
         num_outputs]), name="w_out"))
    b.append(tf.Variable(tf.random_normal([num_outputs]),
name="b_out"))

    # x is input layer
    layer = x
    # add hidden layers
    for i in range(num_layers):
        layer = tf.nn.relu(tf.matmul(layer, w[i]) + b[i])
    # add output layer
    layer = tf.matmul(layer, w[num_layers]) + b[num_layers]

    return layer
```

The helper function `mnist_batch_func()` wraps the TensorFlow's batch function for the MNIST dataset to provide the next batch of images:

```
def mnist_batch_func(batch_size=100):
    X_batch, Y_batch = mnist.train.next_batch(batch_size)
    return [X_batch, Y_batch]
```

This function is self-explanatory. TensorFlow provides this function for the MNIST dataset; however, for other datasets, we may have to write our own batch function.

The helper function, `tensorflow_classification()`, trains and evaluates the model.

1. The `tensorflow_classification()` function takes several inputs:
   - `n_epochs` is the number of training loops to run
   - `n_batches` is the number of randomly sampled batches for which the training in each cycle should be run
   - `batch_size` is the number of samples in each batch
   - `batch_func` is the function that takes the `batch_size` and returns the sample batch of `X` and `Y`
   - `model` is the actual neural network or layers with neurons
   - `optimizer` is the optimization function defined using TensorFlow
   - `loss` is the loss of cost function that the optimizer would optimize the parameters for
   - `accuracy_function` is the function that calculates the accuracy score
   - `X_test` and `Y_test` are the datasets for the testing
2. Start the TensorFlow session to run the training loop:

```
with tf.Session() as tfs:
    tf.global_variables_initializer().run()
```

3. Run the training for `n_epoch` cycles:

```
for epoch in range(n_epochs):
```

4. In each cycle, take the `n_batches` number of sample sets and train the model, calculate the loss for each batch, calculate the average loss for each epoch:

```
epoch_loss = 0.0
            for batch in range(n_batches):
                X_batch, Y_batch = batch_func(batch_size)
                feed_dict = {x: X_batch, y: Y_batch}
                _, batch_loss = tfs.run([optimizer, loss],
feed_dict)
                epoch_loss += batch_loss
            average_loss = epoch_loss / n_batches
            print("epoch: {0:04d} loss = {1:0.6f}".format(
                epoch, average_loss))
```

5. When all the epoch cycles are finished, calculate and print the accuracy score calculated with the `accuracy_function`:

```
feed_dict = {x: X_test, y: Y_test}
accuracy_score = tfs.run(accuracy_function,
                         feed_dict=feed_dict)
print("accuracy={0:.8f}".format(accuracy_score))
```

The complete code of `tensorflow_classification()` function is given below:

```
def tensorflow_classification(n_epochs, n_batches,
                              batch_size, batch_func,
                              model, optimizer, loss,
accuracy_function,
                              X_test, Y_test):
    with tf.Session() as tfs:
        tfs.run(tf.global_variables_initializer())
        for epoch in range(n_epochs):
            epoch_loss = 0.0
            for batch in range(n_batches):
                X_batch, Y_batch = batch_func(batch_size)
                feed_dict = {x: X_batch, y: Y_batch}
                _, batch_loss = tfs.run([optimizer, loss], feed_dict)
                epoch_loss += batch_loss
            average_loss = epoch_loss / n_batches
            print("epoch: {0:04d} loss = {1:0.6f}".format(
                epoch, average_loss))
        feed_dict = {x: X_test, y: Y_test}
        accuracy_score = tfs.run(accuracy_function,
feed_dict=feed_dict)
        print("accuracy={0:.8f}".format(accuracy_score))
```

Now let's define the input and output placeholders, *x* and *y*, and other hyper-parameters:

```
# input images
x = tf.placeholder(dtype=tf.float32, name="x",
                   shape=[None, num_inputs])
# target output
y = tf.placeholder(dtype=tf.float32, name="y",
                   shape=[None, num_outputs])
num_layers = 0
num_neurons = []
learning_rate = 0.01
n_epochs = 50
batch_size = 100
n_batches = int(mnist.train.num_examples/batch_size)
```

The parameters are described below:

- `num_layers` is the number of hidden layers. We first practice with no hidden layer, only the input, and output layers.
- `num_neurons` is the empty list because there are no hidden layers.
- `learning_rate` is 0.01, a randomly selected small number.
- `num_epochs` represents the 50 iterations to learn the parameters for the only neuron that connects the inputs to the output.
- `batch_size` is kept at 100, again a matter of choice. Larger batch size does not necessarily offer higher benefits. You might have to explore different batch sizes to find the optimum batch size for your neural networks.
- `n_batches`: Number of batches is calculated approximately to be the number of examples divided by the number of samples in a batch.

Now let's put everything together and define the network, `loss` function, `optimizer` function, and `accuracy` function using the variables defined so far.

```
model = mlp(x=x,
            num_inputs=num_inputs,
            num_outputs=num_outputs,
            num_layers=num_layers,
            num_neurons=num_neurons)

loss = tf.reduce_mean(
    tf.nn.softmax_cross_entropy_with_logits(logits=model, labels=y))
optimizer = tf.train.GradientDescentOptimizer(
    learning_rate=learning_rate).minimize(loss)

predictions_check = tf.equal(tf.argmax(model, 1), tf.argmax(y, 1))
accuracy_function = tf.reduce_mean(tf.cast(predictions_check,
tf.float32))
```

In this code, we use a new tensorflow function to define the loss function:

```
tf.nn.softmax_cross_entropy_with_logits(logits=model, labels=y)
```

When the `softmax_cross_entropy_with_logits()` function is used, make sure that the output is unscaled and has not been passed through the `softmax` activation function. This function internally uses *softmax* to scale the output.

This function computes the softmax entropy between the model (the estimated value *y*) and the actual value of *y*. The entropy function is used when the output belongs to one class and not more than one class. As in our example, the image can only belong to one of the digits.

More information on this entropy function can be found at `https://www.tensorflow.org/api_docs/python/tf/nn/softmax_cross_entropy_with_logits`.

Once everything is defined, run the `tensorflow_classification` function to train and evaluate the model:

```
tensorflow_classification(n_epochs=n_epochs,
   n_batches=n_batches,
   batch_size=batch_size,
   batch_func=mnist_batch_func,
   model = model,
   optimizer = optimizer,
   loss = loss,
   accuracy_function = accuracy_function,
   X_test = mnist.test.images,
   Y_test = mnist.test.labels
   )
```

We get the following output from running the classification:

```
epoch: 0000   loss = 8.364567
epoch: 0001   loss = 4.347608
epoch: 0002   loss = 3.085622
epoch: 0003   loss = 2.468341
epoch: 0004   loss = 2.099220
epoch: 0005   loss = 1.853206

--- Epoch 06 to 45 output removed for brevity ---

epoch: 0046   loss = 0.684285
epoch: 0047   loss = 0.678972
epoch: 0048   loss = 0.673685
epoch: 0049   loss = 0.668717
accuracy=0.85720009
```

We see that the single neuron network slowly reduces the loss from 8.3 to 0.66 over 50 iterations, finally getting an accuracy of almost 85 percent. This is pretty bad accuracy for this specific example because this was only a demonstration of using TensorFlow for classification using MLP.

We ran the same code with more layers and neurons and got the following accuracy:

Number of Layers	Number of Neurons in Each Hidden Layer	Accuracy
0	0	0.857
1	8	0.616
2	256	0.936

Thus, by adding two rows and 256 neurons to each layer, we brought the accuracy up to 0.936. You are encouraged to try the code with different values of variables to observe how it affects the loss and accuracy.

Keras-based MLP for MNIST classification

Now let's build the same MLP network with Keras, a high-level library for TensorFlow. We keep all the parameters the same as we used for the TensorFlow example in this chapter, for example, the activation function for the hidden layers is kept as the ReLU function.

1. Import the required modules from the Keras:

```
import keras
from keras.models import Sequential
from keras.layers import Dense
from keras.optimizers import SGD
```

2. Define the hyper-parameters (we assume that the dataset has already been loaded into the `X_train`, `Y_train`, `X_test`, and `Y_test` variables):

```
num_layers = 2
num_neurons = []
for i in range(num_layers):
   num_neurons.append(256)
learning_rate = 0.01
n_epochs = 50
batch_size = 100
```

3. Create a sequential model:

```
model = Sequential()
```

4. Add the first hidden layer. Only in the first hidden layer, we have to specify the shape of the input tensor:

```
model.add(Dense(units=num_neurons[0], activation='relu',
    input_shape=(num_inputs,)))
```

5. Add the second layer:

```
model.add(Dense(units=num_neurons[1], activation='relu'))
```

6. Add the output layer with the activation function softmax:

```
model.add(Dense(units=num_outputs, activation='softmax'))
```

7. Print the model details:

```
model.summary()
```

We get the following output:

```
_________________________________________________________________
Layer (type)                 Output Shape              Param #
=================================================================
dense_1 (Dense)              (None, 256)               200960
_________________________________________________________________
dense_2 (Dense)              (None, 256)               65792
_________________________________________________________________
dense_3 (Dense)              (None, 10)                2570
=================================================================
Total params: 269,322
Trainable params: 269,322
Non-trainable params: 0
_________________________________________________________________
```

8. Compile the model with an SGD optimizer:

```
model.compile(loss='categorical_crossentropy',
   optimizer=SGD(lr=learning_rate),
   metrics=['accuracy'])
```

9. Train the model:

```
model.fit(X_train, Y_train,
   batch_size=batch_size,
   epochs=n_epochs)
```

As the model is being trained, we can observe the loss and accuracy of each training iteration:

```
Epoch 1/50
55000/55000 [========================] - 4s - loss: 1.1055 - acc:
0.7413
Epoch 2/50
55000/55000 [========================] - 3s - loss: 0.4396 - acc:
0.8833
Epoch 3/50
55000/55000 [========================] - 3s - loss: 0.3523 - acc:
0.9010
Epoch 4/50
55000/55000 [========================] - 3s - loss: 0.3129 - acc:
0.9112
Epoch 5/50
55000/55000 [========================] - 3s - loss: 0.2871 - acc:
0.9181

--- Epoch 6 to 45 output removed for brevity ---

Epoch 46/50
55000/55000 [========================] - 4s - loss: 0.0689 - acc:
0.9814
Epoch 47/50
55000/55000 [========================] - 4s - loss: 0.0672 - acc:
0.9819
Epoch 48/50
55000/55000 [========================] - 4s - loss: 0.0658 - acc:
0.9822
Epoch 49/50
55000/55000 [========================] - 4s - loss: 0.0643 - acc:
0.9829
Epoch 50/50
55000/55000 [========================] - 4s - loss: 0.0627 - acc:
0.9829
```

10. Evaluate the model and print the loss and accuracy:

```
score = model.evaluate(X_test, Y_test)
print('\n Test loss:', score[0])
print('Test accuracy:', score[1])
```

We get the following output:

```
Test loss: 0.089410082236
Test accuracy: 0.9727
```

The complete code for MLP for MNIST classification using Keras is provided in the notebook `ch-05_MLP`.

TFLearn-based MLP for MNIST classification

Now let's see how to implement the same MLP using TFLearn, another high-level library for TensorFlow:

1. Import the TFLearn library:

    ```
    import tflearn
    ```

2. Define the hyper-parameters (we assume that the dataset has already been loaded into the `X_train`, `Y_train`, `X_test`, and `Y_test` variables):

    ```
    num_layers = 2
    num_neurons = []
    for i in range(num_layers):
    num_neurons.append(256)

    learning_rate = 0.01
    n_epochs = 50
    batch_size = 100
    ```

3. Build the input layer, two hidden layers, and the output layer (the same architecture as examples in TensorFlow and Keras sections):

    ```
    # Build deep neural network
    input_layer = tflearn.input_data(shape=[None, num_inputs])
    dense1 = tflearn.fully_connected(input_layer, num_neurons[0],
        activation='relu')
    dense2 = tflearn.fully_connected(dense1, num_neurons[1],
        activation='relu')
    softmax = tflearn.fully_connected(dense2, num_outputs,
        activation='softmax')
    ```

4. Define the optimizer function, neural network, and MLP model (known as DNN in TFLearn) using the DNN built in the last step (in the variable `softmax`):

    ```
    optimizer = tflearn.SGD(learning_rate=learning_rate)
    net = tflearn.regression(softmax, optimizer=optimizer,
                             metric=tflearn.metrics.Accuracy(),
                             loss='categorical_crossentropy')
    model = tflearn.DNN(net)
    ```

5. Train the model:

```
model.fit(X_train, Y_train, n_epoch=n_epochs,
          batch_size=batch_size,
          show_metric=True, run_id="dense_model")
```

We get the following output once the training is finished:

```
Training Step: 27499  | total loss: 0.11236 | time: 5.853s
| SGD | epoch: 050 | loss: 0.11236 - acc: 0.9687 -- iter: 54900/55000
Training Step: 27500  | total loss: 0.11836 | time: 5.863s
| SGD | epoch: 050 | loss: 0.11836 - acc: 0.9658 -- iter: 55000/55000
--
```

6. Evaluate the model and print the accuracy score:

```
score = model.evaluate(X_test, Y_test)
print('Test accuracy:', score[0])
```

We get the following output:

```
Test accuracy: 0.9637
```

We get a pretty comparable accuracy from using TFLearn as well.

The complete code for MLP for MNIST classification using TFLearn is provided in the notebook `ch-05_MLP`.

Summary of MLP with TensorFlow, Keras, and TFLearn

In the previous sections, we learned how to build a simple MLP architecture using TensorFLow and its high-level libraries. We got an accuracy of about 0.93-0.94 with pure TensorFlow, 0.96-0.98 with Keras, and 0.96-0.97 with TFLearn. Even though all the examples of our code use TensorFlow underneath, the difference in accuracy for the same architecture and parameters can be attributed to the fact that although we initialized some important hyper-parameters, the high-level libraries and TensorFlow abstract away many other hyper-parameters that we did not modify from their default values.

We observe that the code in TensorFlow is very detailed and lengthy as compared to Keras and TFLearn. The high-level libraries make it easier for us to build and train neural network models.

MLP for time series regression

We have seen examples of classification for image data; now let's look at regression for time series data. We shall build and use MLP for a smaller univariate time series dataset known as the international airline passengers dataset. This dataset contains the total number of passengers over the years. The dataset is available at the following links:

- `https://www.kaggle.com/andreazzini/international-airline-passengers/data`
- `https://datamarket.com/data/set/22u3/international-airline-passengers-monthly-totals-in-thousands-jan-49-dec-60`

Let us start by preparing our dataset.

1. First, load the dataset using the following code:

```
filename = os.path.join(datasetslib.datasets_root,
                        'ts-data',
                        'international-airline-passengers-
cleaned.csv')
dataframe = pd.read_csv(filename,usecols=[1],header=0)
dataset = dataframe.values
dataset = dataset.astype('float32')
```

2. With a utility function from the `datasetslib`, we split the dataset into test and train sets. For time series datasets, we have a separate function that does not shuffle the observations because for time series regression we need to maintain the order of the observations. We use 67 percent data for training and 33 percent for testing. You may want to try the example with a different ratio.

```
train,test=dsu.train_test_split(dataset,train_size=0.67)
```

3. For time series regression, we convert the dataset to build a supervised data set. We use a lag of two time steps in this example. We set `n_x` to 2 and the `mvts_to_xy()` function returns the input and output (`X` and `Y`) train and test sets such that X has values for time {t-1,t} in two columns and Y has values for time {t+1} in one column. Our learning algorithm assumes that values at time t+1 can be learned by finding the relationship between values for time {t-1, t, t+1}.

```
# reshape into X=t-1,t and Y=t+1
n_x=2
```

```
n_y=1
X_train, Y_train, X_test, Y_test = tsd.mvts_to_xy(train,
                                        test,n_x=n_x,n_y=n_y)
```

More information on converting time series datasets as supervised learning problems can be found at the following link: `http://machinelearningmastery.com/convert-time-series-supervised-learning-problem-python/`.

Now we build and train the model on our train dataset:

1. Import the required Keras modules:

```
from keras.models import Sequential
from keras.layers import Dense
from keras.optimizers import SGD
```

2. Set the hyper-parameters required to build the model:

```
num_layers = 2
num_neurons = [8,8]
n_epochs = 50
batch_size = 2
```

Note that we use a batch size of two as the dataset is very small. We use a two-layer MLP with only eight neurons in each layer because of the small size of our example problem.

3. Build, compile, and train the model:

```
model = Sequential()
model.add(Dense(num_neurons[0], activation='relu',
    input_shape=(n_x,)))
model.add(Dense(num_neurons[1], activation='relu'))
model.add(Dense(units=1))
model.summary()

model.compile(loss='mse', optimizer='adam')

model.fit(X_train, Y_train,
   batch_size=batch_size,
   epochs=n_epochs)
```

Note that instead of SGD, we use the Adam optimizer. You may want to try out the different optimizers available in TensorFlow and Keras.

4. Evaluate the model and print the Mean Square Error (MSE) and the Root Mean Square Error (RMSE):

```
score = model.evaluate(X_test, Y_test)
print('\nTest mse:', score)
print('Test rmse:', math.sqrt(score))
```

We get the following output:

```
Test mse: 5619.24934188
Test rmse: 74.96165247566114
```

5. Predict the values using our model and plot them, both for test and train datasets:

```
# make predictions
Y_train_pred = model.predict(X_train)
Y_test_pred = model.predict(X_test)

# shift train predictions for plotting
Y_train_pred_plot = np.empty_like(dataset)
Y_train_pred_plot[:, :] = np.nan
Y_train_pred_plot[n_x-1:len(Y_train_pred)+n_x-1, :] =
Y_train_pred

# shift test predictions for plotting
Y_test_pred_plot = np.empty_like(dataset)
Y_test_pred_plot[:, :] = np.nan
Y_test_pred_plot[len(Y_train_pred)+(n_x*2)-1:len(dataset)-1,
:] = \
    Y_test_pred

# plot baseline and predictions
plt.plot(dataset,label='Original Data')
plt.plot(Y_train_pred_plot,label='Y_train_pred')
plt.plot(Y_test_pred_plot,label='Y_test_pred')
plt.legend()
plt.show()
```

We get the following plot for our original and predicted time series values:

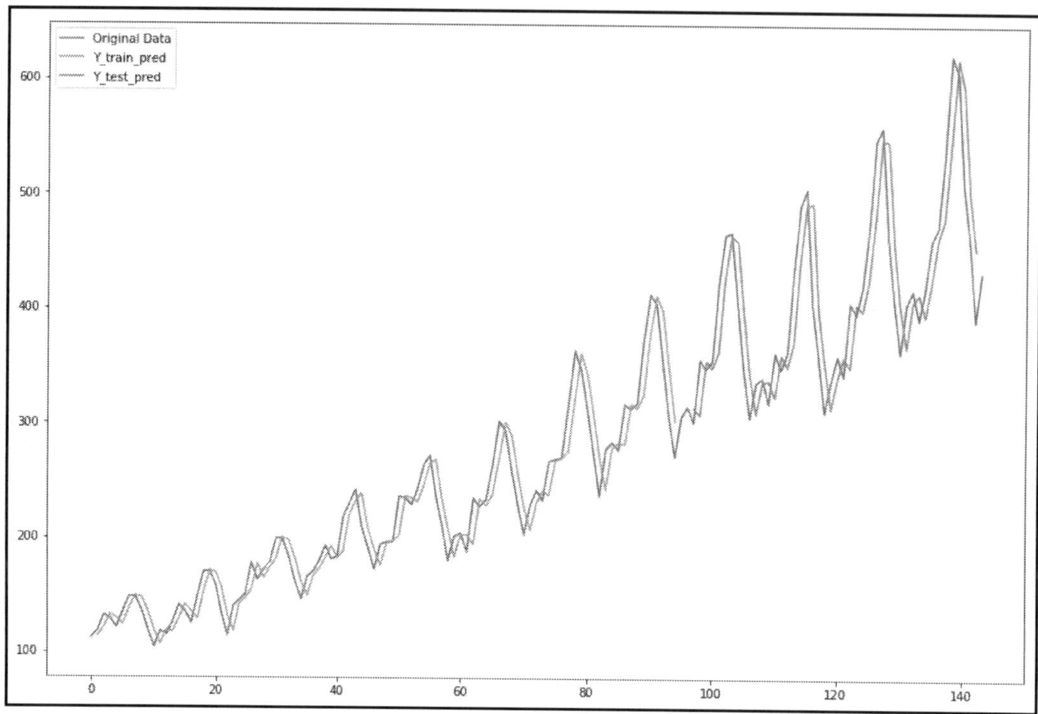

As you can see, it's a pretty good estimation. However, in real life, the data is multivariate and complex in nature. Hence, we shall see recurrent neural network architectures for timeseries data, in the following chapters.

Summary

In this chapter, we learned about multilayer perceptrons. We explained how to build and train MLP models for classification and regression problems. We built MLP models with pure TensorFlow, Keras, and TFLearn. For classification, we used image data, and for regression, we used the time series data.

The techniques to build and train MLP network models are the same for any other kind of data, such as numbers or text. However, for image datasets, the CNN architectures have proven to be the best architectures, and for sequence datasets, such as time series and text, the RNN models have proven to be the best architectures.

While we only used simple dataset examples to demonstrate the MLP architecture in this chapter, in the further chapters, we shall cover CNN and RNN architectures with some large and advanced datasets.

11
RNN with TensorFlow and Keras

In problems involving ordered sequences of data, such as **time series Forecasting** and **natural language processing**, the context is very valuable to predict the output. The context for such problems can be determined by ingesting the whole sequence, not just one last data point. Thus, the previous output becomes part of the current input, and when repeated, the last output turns out to be the results of all the previous inputs along with the last input. **Recurrent Neural Network** (**RNN**) architecture is a solution for handling machine learning problems that involve sequences.

Recurrent Neural Network (**RNN**) is a specialized neural network architecture for handling sequential data. The sequential data could be the sequence of observations over a period of time, as in time series data, or sequence of characters, words, and sentences, as in textual data.

One of the assumptions for the standard neural network is that the input data is arranged in a way that one input has no dependency on another. However, for time series data and textual data, this assumption does not hold true, since the values appearing later in the sequence are often influenced by the values that appeared before.

In order to achieve that, RNN extends the standard neural networks in the following ways:

- RNN adds the ability to use the output of one layer as an input to the same or previous layer, by adding loops or cycles in the computation graph.
- RNN adds the memory unit to store previous inputs and outputs that can be used in the current computation.

In this chapter, we cover the following topics to learn about RNN:

- Simple Recurrent Neural Networks
- RNN variants
- Long Short-Term Memory networks
- Gated Recurrent Unit networks
- TensorFlow for RNN
- Keras for RNN
- RNN in Keras for MNIST data

Simple Recurrent Neural Network

Here is what a simple neural network with loops looks like:

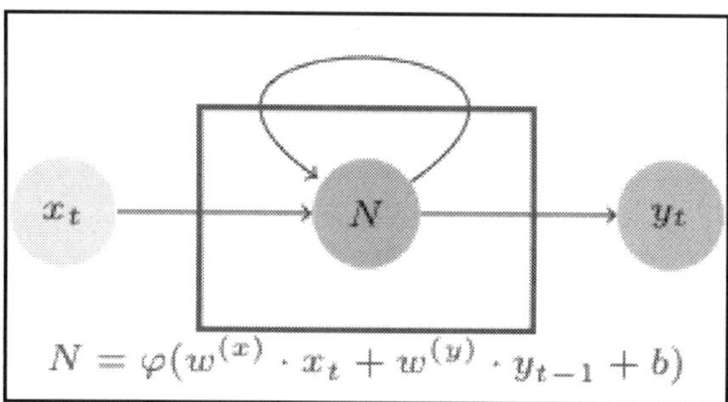

RNN Network

In this diagram, a Neural Network *N* takes input x_t to produce output y_t. Due to the loop, at the next time step $t+1$, it takes the input y_t along with input x_{t+1} to produce output y_{t+1}. Mathematically, we represent this as the following equation:

$$y_t = \varphi(w^{(x)} \cdot x_t + w^{(y)} \cdot y_{t-1} + b)$$

When we unroll the loop, the RNN architecture looks as follows at time step t_1:

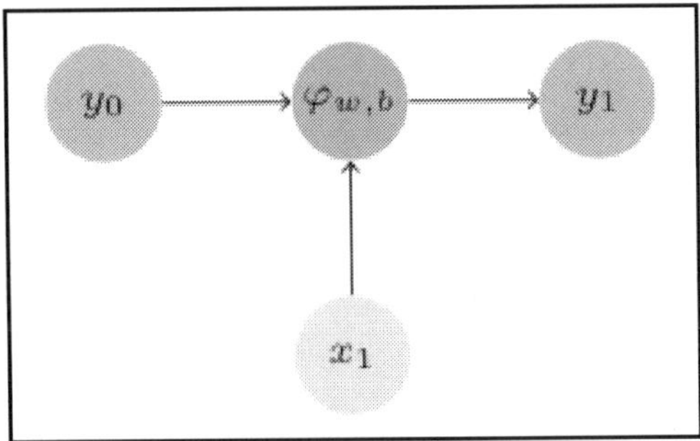

Unrolled RNN at timestep t_1

As the time steps evolve, this loop unrolls as follows at time step 5:

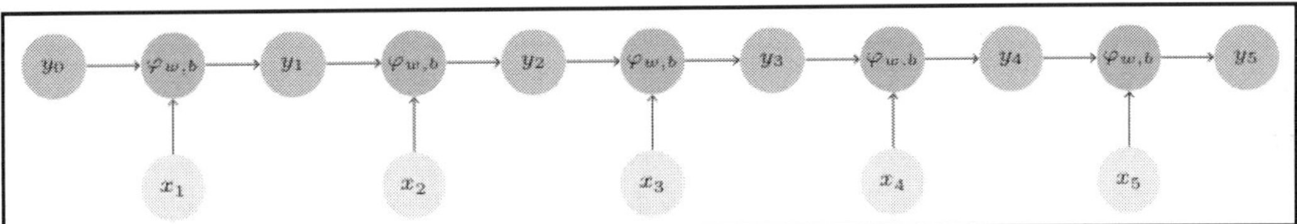

Unrolled RNN at timestep t_5

At every time step, the same learning function, $\varphi(\cdot)$, and the same parameters, *w* and *b*, are used.

The output *y* is not always produced at every time step. Instead, an output *h* is produced at every time step, and another activation function is applied to this output *h* to produce the output *y*. The equations for the RNN look like this now:

$$h_t = \varphi(w^{(hx)} \cdot x_t + w^{(hh)} \cdot h_{t-1} + b^{(h)})$$

$$y_t = \varphi(w^{(yh)} \cdot h_t + b^{(y)})$$

where,

- $w^{(hx)}$ is the weight vector for *x* inputs that are connected to the hidden layer

- $w^{(hh)}$ is the weight vector for the value of h from the previous time step
- $w^{(yh)}$ is the weight vector for layer connecting the hidden layer to the output layer
- The function used for h_t is usually a nonlinear function, such as tanh or ReLU

In RNN, same parameters ($w^{(hx)}, w^{(hh)}, w^{(yh)}, b^{(h)}, b^{(y)}$) are used at every time step. This fact greatly reduces the number of parameters we need to learn for sequence-based models.

With this, the RNN unrolls as follows at time step t_5, assuming that the output y is only produced at time step t_5:

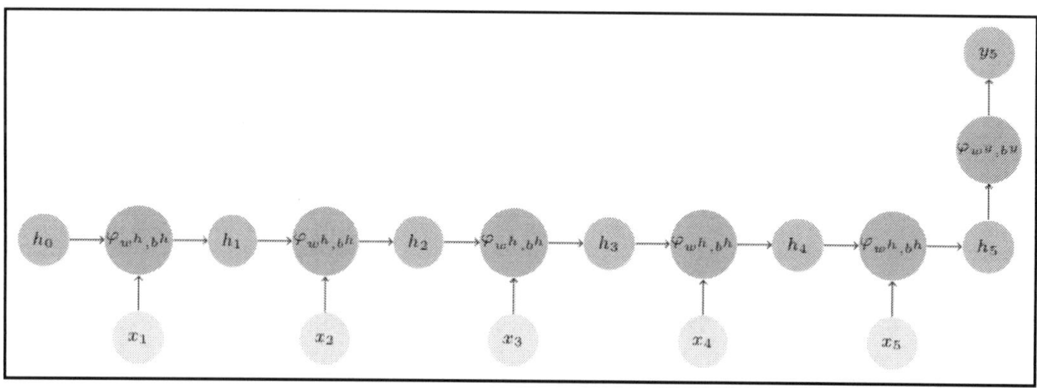

Unrolled RNN with one output at timestep t_5

Simple RNN was introduced by Elman in 1990, thus it is also known as Elman network. However, simple RNN falls short of our processing needs today, hence we will learn about the variants of the RNN in the next section.

Read the Elman's original research paper to learn about origins of RNN architecture:

J. L. Elman, Finding Structure in Time, Cogn. Sci., vol. 14, no. 2, pp. 179–211, 1990.

RNN variants

The RNN architecture has been extended in many ways to accommodate the extra needs in certain problems and to overcome the shortcomings of simple RNN models. We list some of the major extensions to the RNN architecture below.

- **Bidirectional RNN** (**BRNN**) is used when the output depends on both the previous and future elements of a sequence. BRNN is implemented by stacking two RNNs, known as forward and backward Layer, and the output is the result of the hidden state of both the RNNs. In the forward layer, the memory state h flows from time step *t* to time step *t+1* and in the backward layer the memory state flows from time step *t* to time step *t-1*. Both the layers take same input x_t at time step *t*, but they jointly produce the output at time step *t*.

- **Deep Bidirectional RNN** (**DBRNN**) extends the BRNN further by adding multiple layers. The BRNN has hidden layers or cells across the time dimensions. However, by stacking BRNN, we get the hierarchical presentation in DBRNN. One of the significant difference is that in BRNN we use the same parameters for each cell in the same layer, but in DBRNN we use different parameters for each stacked layer.
- **Long Short-Term Memory** (**LSTM**) network extends the RNN by using an architecture that involves multiple nonlinear functions instead of one simple nonlinear function to compute the hidden state. The LSTM is composed of black boxes called **cells** that take the three inputs: the working memory at time $t-1$ (h_{t-1}), current input (x_t) and long-term memory at time $t-1$ (c_{t-1}), and produce the two outputs: updated working memory (h_t) and long-term memory (c_t). The cells use the functions known as gates, to make decisions about saving and erasing the content selectively from the memory. We describe the LSTM in detail in the sections below.

Read the following research paper on LSTM to get more information about origins of LSTM:

S. Hochreiter and J. Schmidhuber, Long Short-Term Memory, Neural Comput., vol. 9, no. 8, pp. 1735–1780, 1997. `http://www.bioinf.jku.at/publications/older/2604.pdf`

- **Gated Recurrent Unit** (**GRU**) network is a simplified variation of LSTM. It combines the function of the *forget* and the *input* gates in a simpler *update* gate. It also combines the *hidden state* and *cell state* into one single state. Hence, GRU is computationally less expensive as compared to LSTM. We describe the GRU in detail in the sections below.

Read the following research papers to explore more details on GRU:

K. Cho, B. van Merrienboer, C. Gulcehre, D. Bahdanau, F. Bougares, H. Schwenk, and Y. Bengio, Learning Phrase Representations using RNN Encoder-Decoder for Statistical Machine Translation, 2014. `https://arxiv.org/abs/1406.1078`

J. Chung, C. Gulcehre, K. Cho, and Y. Bengio, Empirical Evaluation of Gated Recurrent Neural Networks on Sequence Modeling, pp. 1–9, 2014. `https://arxiv.org/abs/1412.3555`

- The **seq2seq** model combines the encoder-decoder architecture with RNN architectures. In seq2seq architecture, the model is trained on sequences of data, such as text data or time series data, and then the model is used to generate the output sequences. For example, train the model on English text and then generate Spanish text from the model. The seq2seq model consists of an encoder and a decoder model, both of them built with the RNN architecture. The seq2seq models can be stacked to build hierarchical multi-layer models.

LSTM network

When RNNs are trained over very long sequences of data, the gradients tend to become either very large or very small that they vanish to almost zero. **Long Short-Term Memory (LSTM)** networks address the vanishing/exploding gradient problem by adding gates for controlling the access to past information. LSTM concept was first introduced by Hochreiter and Schmidhuber in 1997.

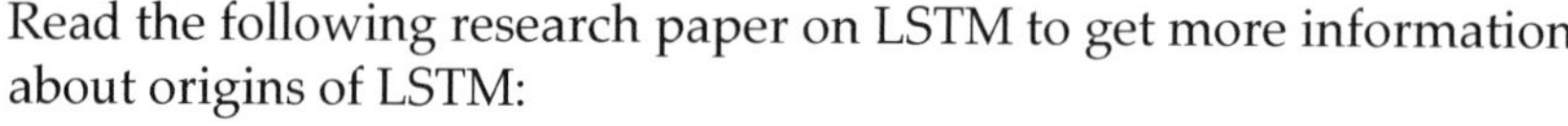

Read the following research paper on LSTM to get more information about origins of LSTM:

S. Hochreiter and J. Schmidhuber, Long Short-Term Memory, Neural Comput., vol. 9, no. 8, pp. 1735–1780, 1997. `http://www.bioinf.jku.at/publications/older/2604.pdf`

In RNN, a single neural network layer of repeatedly used learning function φ is used, whereas, in LSTM, a repeating module consisting of four main functions is used. The module that builds the LSTM network is called the **cell**. The LSTM cell helps train the model more effectively when long sequences are passed, by selectively learning or erasing information. The functions composing the cell are also known as gates as they act as gatekeeper for the information that is passed in and out of the cell.

The LSTM model has two kinds of memory:

- working memory denoted with $\boldsymbol{h}$ (hidden state) and
- long-term memory denoted with with $\boldsymbol{c}$ (cell state).

The cell state or long-term memory flows from cell to cell with only two linear interactions. The LSTM adds information to the long term memory, or removes information from the long-term memory, through gates.

Following diagram depicts the LSTM cell:

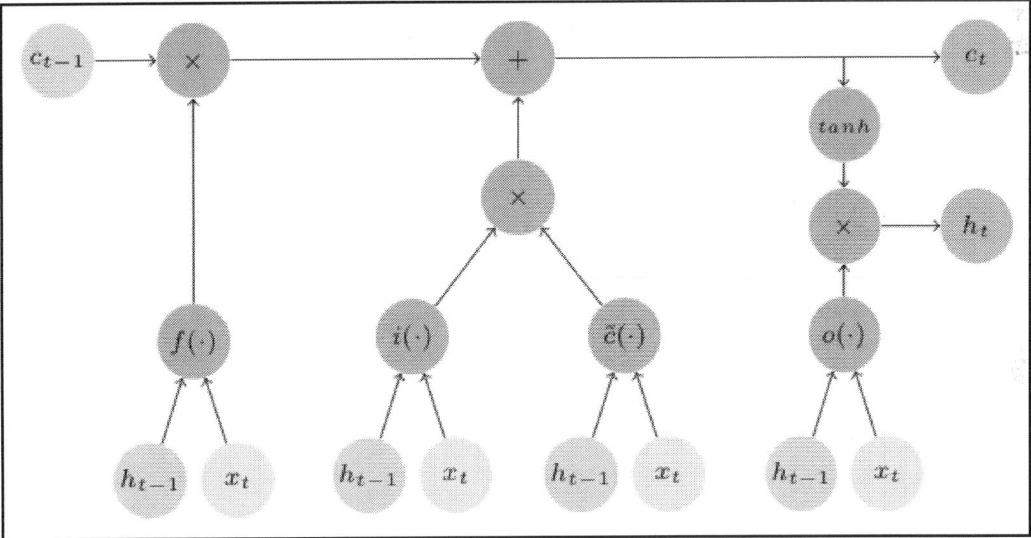

The LSTM Cell

The internal flow through the gates in the LSTM cell is as follows:

1. **Forget Gate f( ) (or remember gate)**: The h_{t-1} and x_t flows as input to *f( )* gate as per the following equation:
   $$f(\cdot) = \sigma(w^{(fx)} \cdot x_t + w^{(fh)} \cdot h_{t-1} + b^{(f)})$$
   The function of *forget gate* is to decide which information to forget and which information to remember. The *sigmoid* activation function is used here, so that an output of 1 represents that the information is carried over to the next step within the cell, and an output of 0 represents that the information is selectively discarded.

2. **Input Gate i( ) (or save gate)**: The h_{t-1} and x_t flows as input to *i( )* gate as per the following equation:
   $$i(\cdot) = \sigma(w^{(ix)} \cdot x_t + w^{(ih)} \cdot h_{t-1} + b^{(i)})$$
   The function of *input gate* is to decide whether to save or discard the input. The input function also allows the cell to learn which part of candidate memory to keep or discard.
3. **Candidate Long-Term Memory**: The candidate long-term memory is computed from h_{t-1} and x_t using an activation function, which is mostly *tanh*, as per the following equation:
   $$\tilde{c}(\cdot) = tanh(w^{(\tilde{c}x)} \cdot x_t + w^{(\tilde{c}h)} \cdot h_{t-1} + b^{(\tilde{c})})$$
4. Next, the preceding three calculations are combined to get the update long-term memory, denoted by c_t as per the following equation:
   $$c_t = c_{t-1} \times f(\cdot) + i(\cdot) \times \tilde{c}(\cdot)$$
5. **Output o( ) (or focus/attention gate)**: The h_{t-1} and x_t flows as input to the *o( )* gate as per the following equation:
   $$o(\cdot) = \sigma(w^{(ox)} \cdot x_t + w^{(oh)} \cdot h_{t-1} + b^{(o)})$$
   The function of *output gate* is to decide how much information can be used to update the working memory.
6. Next, working memory h_t is updated from the long-term memory c_t and the focus/attention vector as per the following equation:
   $$h_t = \varphi(c_t) \times o(\cdot)$$
   where $\varphi(\cdot)$ is an activation function, that is usually *tanh*.

GRU network

LSTM Network is computationally expensive, hence, researchers found an almost equally effective configuration of RNNs, known as **Gated Recurrent Unit** (**GRU**) architecture.

In GRU, instead of a working and a long-term memory, only one kind of memory is used, indicated with *h* (hidden state). The GRU cell adds information to this state memory or removes information from this state memory through **reset** and **update** gates.

Following diagram depicts the GRU cell (explanation follows the diagram):

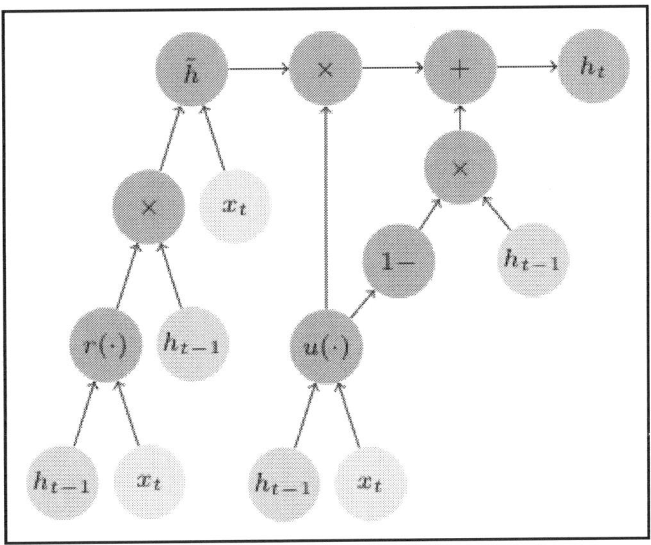

The GRU Cell

The internal flow through the gates in the GRU cell is as follows:

1. **Update gate u( )**: The input h_{t-1} and x_t flows to the *u( )* gate as per the following equation:
   $$u(\cdot) = \sigma(w^{(ux)} \cdot x_t + w^{(uh)} \cdot h_{t-1} + b^{(u)})$$
2. **Reset Gate r( )**: The input h_{t-1} and x_t flows to the *r( )* gate as per the following equation:
   $$r(\cdot) = \sigma(w^{(rx)} \cdot x_t + w^{(rh)} \cdot h_{t-1} + b^{(r)})$$

3. **Candidate State Memory**: The candidate long-term memory is computed from the output of the *r( )* gate, h_{t-1}, and x_t, as per the following equation:
$$\tilde{h}(\cdot) = tanh(w^{(\tilde{h}x)} \cdot x_t + w^{(\tilde{h}h)} \cdot (r_t \cdot h_{t-1}) + b^{(\tilde{h})})$$
4. Next, the preceding three calculations are combined to get the updated state memory, denoted by h_t, as per following equation:
$$h_t = (u_t \cdot \tilde{h}_t) + ((1 - u_t) \cdot h_{t-1})$$

Read the following research papers to explore more details on GRU:

K. Cho, B. van Merrienboer, C. Gulcehre, D. Bahdanau, F. Bougares, H. Schwenk, and Y. Bengio, Learning Phrase Representations using RNN Encoder-Decoder for Statistical Machine Translation, 2014. `https://arxiv.org/abs/1406.1078`

J. Chung, C. Gulcehre, K. Cho, and Y. Bengio, Empirical Evaluation of Gated Recurrent Neural Networks on Sequence Modeling, pp. 1–9, 2014. `https://arxiv.org/abs/1412.3555`

TensorFlow for RNN

The basic workflow for creating RNN models in low-level TensorFlow library is almost the same as MLP:

- First create the input and output placeholders of shape (None, # TimeSteps, # Features) or (Batch Size, # TimeSteps, # Features)
- From the input placeholder, create a list of length # TimeSteps, containing Tensors of Shape (None, #Features) or (Batch Size, # Features)
- Create a cell of the desired RNN type from the `tf.rnn.rnn_cell` module
- Use the cell and the input tensor list created previously to create a static or dynamic RNN
- Create the output weights and bias variables, and define the loss and optimizer functions
- For the required number of epochs, train the model using the loss and optimizer functions

Let us look at the various classes available to support the previous workflow.

TensorFlow RNN Cell Classes

The `tf.nn.rnn_cell` module contains the following classes for creating different kinds of cells in TensorFlow:

Class	Description
BasicRNNCell	Provides simple RNN cell
BasicLSTMCell	Provides simple LSTM RNN cell, based on `http://arxiv.org/abs/1409.2329`
LSTMCell	Provides LSTM RNN cell, based on `http://deeplearning.cs.cmu.edu/pdfs/Hochreiter97_lstm.pdf` and `https://research.google.com/pubs/archive/43905.pdf`
GRUCell	Provides GRU RNN cell, based on `http://arxiv.org/abs/1406.1078`
MultiRNNCell	Provides RNN cell made of multiple simple cells joined sequentially

The `tf.contrib.rnn` module provides the following additional classes for creating different kinds of cells in TensorFlow:

Class	Description
LSTMBlockCell	Provides the block LSTM RNN cell, based on `http://arxiv.org/abs/1409.2329`
LSTMBlockFusedCell	Provides the block fused LSTM RNN cell, based on `http://arxiv.org/abs/1409.2329`
GLSTMCell	Provides the group LSTM cell, based on `https://arxiv.org/abs/1703.10722`
GridLSTMCell	Provides the grid LSTM RNN cell, based on `http://arxiv.org/abs/1507.01526`
GRUBlockCell	Provides the block GRU RNN cell, based on `http://arxiv.org/abs/1406.1078`
BidirectionalGridLSTMCell	Provides bidirectional grid LSTM with bi-direction only in frequency and not in time
NASCell	Provides neural architecture search RNN cell, based on `https://arxiv.org/abs/1611.01578`
UGRNNCell	Provides update gate RNN cell, based on `https://arxiv.org/abs/1611.09913`

TensorFlow RNN Model Construction Classes

TensorFlow provides classes to create RNN models from the RNN cell objects. The static RNN classes add unrolled cells for time steps at the compile time, while dynamic RNN classes add unrolled cells for time steps at the run time.

- `tf.nn.static_rnn`
- `tf.nn.static_state_saving_rnn`
- `tf.nn.static_bidirectional_rnn`
- `tf.nn.dynamic_rnn`
- `tf.nn.bidirectional_dynamic_rnn`
- `tf.nn.raw_rnn`
- `tf.contrib.rnn.stack_bidirectional_dynamic_rnn`

TensorFlow RNN Cell Wrapper Classes

TensorFlow also provides classes that wrap other cell classes:

- `tf.contrib.rnn.LSTMBlockWrapper`
- `tf.contrib.rnn.DropoutWrapper`
- `tf.contrib.rnn.EmbeddingWrapper`
- `tf.contrib.rnn.InputProjectionWrapper`
- `tf.contrib.rnn.OutputProjectionWrapper`
- `tf.contrib.rnn.DeviceWrapper`
- `tf.contrib.rnn.ResidualWrapper`

Latest documentation on RNN in TensorFlow at the following link: `https://www.tensorflow.org/api_guides/python/contrib.rnn`.

Keras for RNN

Creating RNN in Keras is much easier as compared to the TensorFlow. To build the RNN model, you have to add layers from the `kera.layers.recurrent` module. Keras provides the following kinds of recurrent layers in the `keras.layers.recurrent` module:

- SimpleRNN
- LSTM
- GRU

Stateful Models

Keras recurrent layers also support RNN models that save state between the batches. You can create a stateful RNN, LSTM, or GRU model by passing `stateful` parameters as `True`. For stateful models, the batch size specified for the inputs has to be a fixed value. In stateful models, the hidden state learnt from training a batch is reused for the next batch. If you want to reset the memory at some point during training, it can be done with extra code by calling the `model.reset_states()` or `layer.reset_states()` functions.

The latest documentation on Recurrent Layers in Keras can be found at the following link: `https://keras.io/layers/recurrent/`.

Application areas of RNNs

Some of the application areas where RNNs are used more often are as follows:

- **Natural Language Modeling**: The RNN models have been used in natural language processing (NLP) for natural language understanding and natural language generation tasks. In NLP, an RNN model is given a sequence of words and it predicts another sequence of words. Thus, the trained models can be used for generating the sequence of words, a field known as Text Generation. For example, generating stories, and screenplays. Another area of NLP is language translation, where given a sequence of words in one language, the model predicts a sequence of words in another language.

- **Voice and Speech Recognition**: The RNN models have great use in building models for learning from the audio data. In speech recognition, an RNN model is given audio data and it predicts a sequence of phonetic segments. It can be used to train the models to recognize the voice commands, or even for conversation with speech based chatbots.
- **Image/Video Description or Caption Generation**: The RNN models can be used in combination with CNN to generate the descriptions of elements found in images and videos. Such descriptions can also be used to generate captions for images and videos.
- **TimeSeries Data**: Most importantly, RNNs are very useful for TimeSeries data. Most of the sensors and systems generate data where the temporal order is important. The RNN models fit very well to finding patterns and forecasting such data.

Explore more information about RNN at the following links:

`http://karpathy.github.io/2015/05/21/rnn-effectiveness/`
`http://colah.github.io/posts/2015-08-Understanding-LSTMs/`
`http://www.wildml.com/2015/09/recurrent-neural-networks-tutorial-part-1-introduction-to-rnns/`
`https://r2rt.com/written-memories-understanding-deriving-and-extending-the-lstm.html`

RNN in Keras for MNIST data

Although RNN is mostly used for sequence data, it can also be used for image data. We know that images have minimum two dimensions - height and width. Now think of one of the dimensions as time steps, and other as features. For MNIST, the image size is 28 x 28 pixels, thus we can think of an MNIST image as having 28 time steps with 28 features in each timestep.

Let us build and train an RNN for MNIST in Keras to quickly glance over the process of building and training the RNN models.

You can follow along with the code in the Jupyter notebook `ch-06_RNN_MNIST_Keras`.

Import the required modules:

```
import keras
from keras.models import Sequential
from keras.layers import Dense, Activation
from keras.layers.recurrent import SimpleRNN
from keras.optimizers import RMSprop
from keras.optimizers import SGD
```

Get the MNIST data and transform the data from 784 pixels in 1-D to 28 x 28 pixels in 2-D:

```
from tensorflow.examples.tutorials.mnist import input_data
mnist =
input_data.read_data_sets(os.path.join(datasetslib.datasets_root,
                                                       'mnist'),
                                  one_hot=True)
X_train = mnist.train.images
X_test = mnist.test.images
Y_train = mnist.train.labels
Y_test = mnist.test.labels
n_classes = 10
n_classes = 10
X_train = X_train.reshape(-1,28,28)
X_test = X_test.reshape(-1,28,28)
```

Build the SimpleRNN model in Keras:

```
# create and fit the SimpleRNN model
model = Sequential()
model.add(SimpleRNN(units=16, activation='relu', input_shape=(28,28)))
model.add(Dense(n_classes))
model.add(Activation('softmax'))

model.compile(loss='categorical_crossentropy',
              optimizer=RMSprop(lr=0.01),
              metrics=['accuracy'])
model.summary()
```

The model appears as follows:

```
Layer (type)                 Output Shape              Param #
=================================================================
simple_rnn_1 (SimpleRNN)     (None, 16)                720
_________________________________________________________________
dense_1 (Dense)              (None, 10)                170
_________________________________________________________________
activation_1 (Activation)    (None, 10)                0
=================================================================
Total params: 890
Trainable params: 890
Non-trainable params: 0
_________________________________________________________________
```

Train the model and print the accuracy of test data set:

```
model.fit(X_train, Y_train,
          batch_size=100, epochs=20)

score = model.evaluate(X_test, Y_test)
print('\nTest loss:', score[0])
print('Test accuracy:', score[1])
```

We get the following results:

```
Test loss: 0.520945608187
Test accuracy: 0.8379
```

Summary

In this chapter, we learned about Recurrent Neural Networks (RNNs). We learned about the various variants of RNN and described two of them in detail: Long Short-Term Memory (LSTM) networks and Gated Recurrent Unit (GRU) networks. We also described the classes available for constructing RNN cells, models, and layers in TensorFlow and Keras. We built a simple RNN network for classifying the digits of the MNIST dataset.

12
CNN with TensorFlow and Keras

Convolutional Neural Network (**CNN**) is a special kind of feed-forward neural network that includes convolutional and pooling layers in its architecture. Also known as ConvNets, the general pattern for the CNN architecture is to have these layers in the following sequence:

1. Fully connected input layer
2. Multiple combinations of convolutional, pooling, and fully connected layers
3. Fully connected output layer with softmax activation

CNN architectures have proven to be highly successful in solving problems that involve learning from images, such as image recognition and object identification.

In this chapter, we shall learn the following topics related to ConvNets:

- Understanding Convolution
- Understanding Pooling
- CNN architecture pattern-LeNet
- LeNet for MNIST dataset
    - LeNet for MNIST with TensorFlow
    - LeNet for MNIST with Keras
- LeNet for CIFAR dataset
    - LeNet CNN for CIFAR10 with TensorFlow
    - LeNet CNN for CIFAR10 with Keras

Let us start by learning the core concepts behind the ConvNets.

Understanding convolution

Convolution is the central concept behind the CNN architecture. In simple terms, convolution is a mathematical operation that combines information from two sources to produce a new set of information. Specifically, it applies a special matrix known as the *kernel* to the input tensor to produce a set of matrices known as the *feature maps*. The kernel can be applied to the input tensor using any of the popular algorithms.

The most commonly used algorithm to produce the convolved matrix is as follows:

```
N_STRIDES = [1,1]
1. Overlap the kernel with the top-left cells of the image matrix.
2. Repeat while the kernel overlaps the image matrix:
    2.1 c_col = 0
    2.2 Repeat while the kernel overlaps the image matrix:
        2.1.1 set c_row = 0
        2.1.2 convolved_scalar = scalar_prod(kernel, overlapped cells)
        2.1.3 convolved_matrix(c_row,c_col) = convolved_scalar
        2.1.4 Slide the kernel down by N_STRIDES[0] rows.
        2.1.5 c_row = c_row  + 1
    2.3 Slide the kernel to (topmost row, N_STRIDES[1] columns right)
    2.4 c_col = c_col + 1
```

For example, let us assume the kernel matrix is a 2 x 2 matrix, and the input image is a 3 x 3 matrix. The following diagrams show the above algorithm step by step:

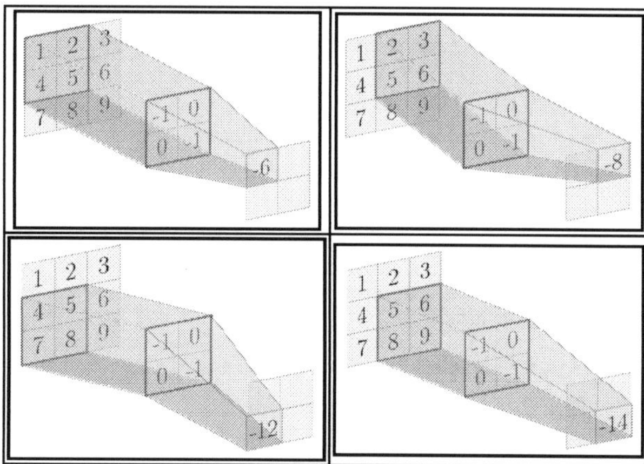

At the end of the convolution operation we get the following feature map:

-6	-8
-12	-14

In the example above the resulting feature map is smaller in size as compared to the original input to the convolution. Generally, the size of the feature maps gets reduced by (kernel size-1). Thus the size of feature map is :

$$size_{feature\_map} = size_{features} - size_{kernel} + 1$$

The 3-D Tensor

For 3-D tensors with an additional depth dimension, you can think of the preceding algorithm being applied to each layer in the depth dimension. The output of applying convolution to a 3D tensor is also a 2D tensor as convolution operation adds the three channels.

The Strides

The ***strides*** in array N_STRIDES is the number the rows or columns by which you want to slide the kernel across. In our example, we used a stride of 1. If we use a higher number of strides, then the size of the feature map gets reduced further as per the following equation:

$$size_{feature\_map} = \frac{size_{features} - size_{kernel}}{n_{strides}} + 1$$

The Padding

If we do not wish to reduce the size of the feature map, then we can use padding on all sides of the input such that the size of features is increased by double of the padding size. With padding, the size of the feature map can be calculated as follows:

$$size_{feature\_map} = \frac{size_{features} + 2 * size_{padding} - size_{kernel}}{n_{strides}} + 1$$

TensorFlow allows two kinds of padding: SAME or VALID. The SAME padding means to add a padding such that the output feature map has the same size as input features. VALID padding means no padding.

The result of applying the previously-mentioned convolution algorithm is the feature map which is the filtered version of the original tensor. For example, the feature map could have only the outlines filtered from the original image. Hence, the kernel is also known as the filter. For each kernel, you get a separate 2D feature map.

Depending on which features you want the network to learn, you have to apply the appropriate filters to emphasize the required features. However, with CNN, the model can automatically learn which kernels work best in the convolution layer.

Convolution Operation in TensorFlow

TensorFlow provides the convolutional layers that implement the convolution algorithm. For example, the `tf.nn.conv2d()` operation with the following signature:

```
tf.nn.conv2d(
  input,
  filter,
  strides,
  padding,
  use_cudnn_on_gpu=None,
  data_format=None,
  name=None
)
```

`input` and `filter` represent the data tensor of the shape `[batch_size, input_height, input_width, input_depth]` and kernel tensor of the shape `[filter_height, filter_width, input_depth, output_depth]`. The `output_depth` in he kernel tensor represents the number of kernels that should be applied to the input. The `strides` tensor represents the number of cells to slide in each dimension. The `padding` is VALID or SAME as described above.

You can find more information on convolution operations available in TensorFlow at the following link: `https://www.tensorflow.org/api_guides/python/nn#Convolution`

You can find more information on convolution layers available in Keras at the following link: `https://keras.io/layers/convolutional/`

The following links provide a detailed mathematical explanation of convolution:

http://colah.github.io/posts/2014-07-Understanding-Convolutions/
http://ufldl.stanford.edu/tutorial/supervised/FeatureExtractionUsingConvolution/

The convolution layer or operation connects the input values or neurons to the next hidden layer neurons. Each hidden layer neuron is connected to the same number of input neurons as the number of elements in the kernel. So in our previous example, the kernel has 4 elements, thus the hidden layer neuron is connected to 4 neurons (out of the 3 x 3 neurons) of the input layer. This area of 4 neurons of the input layer in our example is known as the **receptive field** in CNN theory.

The convolution layer has the separate weights and bias parameters for each kernel. The number of weight parameters is equal to the number of elements in the kernel, and only one bias parameter. All connections for the kernel share the same weights and bias parameters. Thus in our example, there would be 4 weight parameters and 1 bias parameter, but if we use 5 kernels in our convolution layer, then there would be total of 5 x 4 weight parameters and 5 x 1 bias parameters, a set of (4 weights, 1 bias) parameters for each feature map.

Understanding pooling

Generally, in the convolution operation several different kernels are applied that result in generation of several feature maps. Thus, the convolution operation results in generating a large sized dataset.

As an example, applying a kernel of shape 3 x 3 x 1 to an MNIST dataset that has images of shape 28 x 28 x 1 pixels, produces a feature map of shape 26 x 26 x 1. If we apply 32 such filters in a convolutional layer, then the output will be of shape 32 x 26 x 26 x 1, that is, 32 feature maps of shape 26 x 26 x 1.

This is a huge dataset as compared to the original dataset of shape 28 x 28 x 1. Thus, to simplify the learning for the next layer, we apply the concept of *pooling*.

Pooling refers to calculating the aggregate statistic over the regions of the convolved feature space. Two most popular aggregate statistics are the maximum and the average. The output of applying max-pooling is the maximum of the region selected, while the output of applying the average-pooling is the mean of the numbers in the region.

As an example, let us say the feature map is of shape 3 x 3 and the pooling region of shape 2 x 2. The following images show the max pool operation applied with a stride of [1,1]:

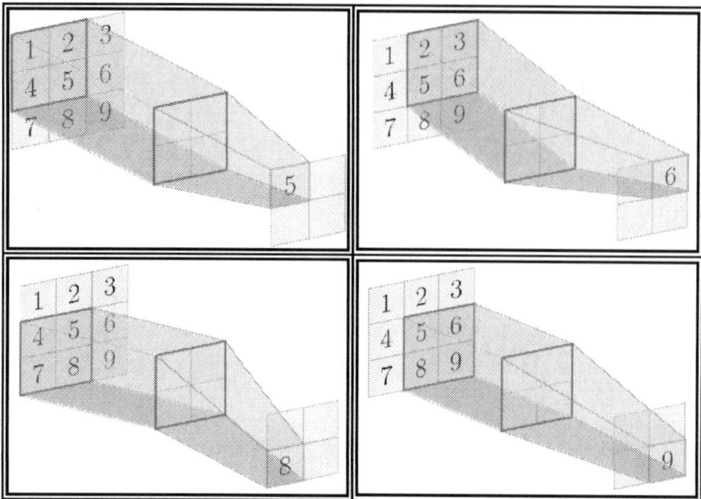

At the end of the max pool operation we get the following matrix:

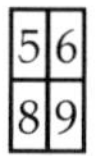

Generally, the pooling operation is applied with non-overlapping regions, thus the stride tensor and the region tensor are set to the same values.

As an example, TensorFlow has the `max_pooling` operation with the following signature:

```
max_pool(
  value,
  ksize,
  strides,
  padding,
  data_format='NHWC',
  name=None
)
```

`value` represents the input tensor of the shape `[batch_size, input_height, input_width, input_depth]`. The pooling operation is performed on rectangular regions of shape `ksize`. These regions are offset by the shape `strides`.

You can find more information on the pooling operations available in TensorFlow at the following link: `https://www.tensorflow.org/api_guides/python/nn#Pooling`

Find more information on the pooling layers available in Keras at the following link: `https://keras.io/layers/pooling/`

`The following link provides a detailed mathematical explanation of the pooling: http://ufldl.stanford.edu/tutorial/supervised/Pooling/`

CNN architecture pattern - LeNet

LeNet is a popular architectural pattern for implementing CNN. In this chapter, we shall learn to build CNN model based on LeNet pattern by creating the layers in the following sequence:

1. The input layer
2. The convolutional layer 1 that produces a set of feature maps, with ReLU activation
3. The pooling layer 1 that produces a set of statistically aggregated feature maps
4. The convolutional layer 2 that produces a set of feature maps, with ReLU activation
5. The pooling layer 2 that produces a set of statistically aggregated feature maps
6. The fully connected layer that flattens the feature maps, with ReLU activation
7. The output layer that produces the output by applying simple linear activation

LeNet family of models were introduced by Yann LeCun and his fellow researchers. More details on the LeNet family of models can be found at the following link: `http://yann.lecun.com/exdb/publis/pdf/lecun-01a.pdf`.

Yann LeCun maintains a list of the LeNet family of models at the following link: `http://yann.lecun.com/exdb/lenet/index.html`.

LeNet for MNIST data

You can follow along with the code in the Jupyter notebook `ch-09a_CNN_MNIST_TF_and_Keras`.

Prepare the MNIST data into test and train sets:

```
from tensorflow.examples.tutorials.mnist import input_data
mnist = input_data.read_data_sets(os.path.join('.','mnist'),
one_hot=True)
X_train = mnist.train.images
X_test = mnist.test.images
Y_train = mnist.train.labels
Y_test = mnist.test.labels
```

LeNet CNN for MNIST with TensorFlow

In TensorFlow, apply the following steps to build the LeNet based CNN models for MNIST data:

1. Define the hyper-parameters, and the placeholders for x and y (input images and output labels):

```
n_classes = 10 # 0-9 digits
n_width = 28
n_height = 28
n_depth = 1
n_inputs = n_height * n_width * n_depth # total pixels
learning_rate = 0.001
n_epochs = 10
batch_size = 100
```

```
n_batches = int(mnist.train.num_examples/batch_size)

# input images shape: (n_samples,n_pixels)
x = tf.placeholder(dtype=tf.float32, name="x", shape=[None,
n_inputs])
# output labels
y = tf.placeholder(dtype=tf.float32, name="y", shape=[None,
n_classes])
```

Reshape the input x to shape (`n_samples`, `n_width`, `n_height`, `n_depth`):

```
x_ = tf.reshape(x, shape=[-1, n_width, n_height, n_depth])
```

2. Define the first convolutional layer with 32 kernels of shape 4 x 4, thus producing 32 feature maps.

- First, define the weights and biases for the first convolutional layer. We populate the parameters with the normal distribution:

```
layer1_w =
tf.Variable(tf.random_normal(shape=[4,4,n_depth,32],
            stddev=0.1),name='l1_w')
layer1_b = tf.Variable(tf.random_normal([32]),name='l1_b')
```

- Next, define the convolutional layer with the `tf.nn.conv2d` function. The function argument `stride` defines the elements by which the kernel tensor should slide in each dimension. The dimension order is determined by `data_format`, which could be either `'NHWC'` or `'NCHW'` (by default, `'NHWC'`).
  Generally, the first and last element in `stride` is set to '1'. The function argument `padding` could be `SAME` or `VALID`. `SAME padding` means that the input would be padded with zeroes such that after convolution the output is of the same shape as the input. Add the `relu` activation using the `tf.nn.relu()` function:

```
layer1_conv = tf.nn.relu(tf.nn.conv2d(x_,layer1_w,
                                      strides=[1,1,1,1],
                                      padding='SAME'
                                     ) +
                         layer1_b
                        )
```

- Define the first pooling layer with the `tf.nn.max_pool()` function. The argument `ksize` represents the pooling operation using 2 x 2 x 1 regions, and the argument `stride` represents to slide the regions by 2 x 2 x 1 pixels. Thus the regions do not overlap with each other. Since we use `max_pool`, pooling operation selects the maximum in 2 x 2 x 1 regions:

```
layer1_pool = tf.nn.max_pool(layer1_conv,ksize=[1,2,2,1],
                  strides=[1,2,2,1],padding='SAME')
```

The first convolution layer produces 32 feature maps of size 28 x 28 x 1, which are then pooled into data of shape 32 x 14 x 14 x 1.

3. Define the second convolutional layer that takes this data as input and produces 64 feature maps.

- First, define the weights and biases for the second convolutional layer. We populate the parameters with a normal distribution:

```
layer2_w = tf.Variable(tf.random_normal(shape=[4,4,32,64],
           stddev=0.1),name='l2_w')
layer2_b = tf.Variable(tf.random_normal([64]),name='l2_b')
```

- Next, define the convolutional layer with the `tf.nn.conv2d` function:

```
layer2_conv = tf.nn.relu(tf.nn.conv2d(layer1_pool,
                                      layer2_w,
                                      strides=[1,1,1,1],
                                      padding='SAME'
                                     ) +
                         layer2_b
                        )
```

- Define the second pooling layer with the `tf.nn.max_pool` function:

```
layer2_pool = tf.nn.max_pool(layer2_conv,
                             ksize=[1,2,2,1],
                             strides=[1,2,2,1],
                             padding='SAME'
                            )
```

The output of the second convolution layer is of shape 64 x 14 x 14 x 1, which then gets pooled into an output of shape 64 x 7 x 7 x 1.

4. Reshape this output before feeding into the fully connected layer of 1024 neurons to produce a flattened output of size 1024:

```
layer3_w = tf.Variable(tf.random_normal(shape=[64*7*7*1,1024],
                       stddev=0.1),name='l3_w')
layer3_b = tf.Variable(tf.random_normal([1024]),name='l3_b')
layer3_fc = tf.nn.relu(tf.matmul(tf.reshape(layer2_pool,
            [-1, 64*7*7*1]),layer3_w) + layer3_b)
```

5. The output of the fully connected layer is fed into a linear output layer with 10 outputs. We did not use softmax in this layer because our loss function automatically applies the softmax to the output:

```
layer4_w = tf.Variable(tf.random_normal(shape=[1024,
n_classes],
                                        stddev=0.1),name='l)
layer4_b =
tf.Variable(tf.random_normal([n_classes]),name='l4_b')
layer4_out = tf.matmul(layer3_fc,layer4_w)+layer4_b
```

This creates our first CNN model that we save in the variable `model`:

```
model = layer4_out
```

The reader is encouraged to explore different convolutional and pooling operators available in TensorFlow with different hyper-parameter values.

For defining the loss, we use the `tf.nn.softmax_cross_entropy_with_logits` function, and for optimizer, we use the `AdamOptimizer` function. You should try to explore the different optimizer functions available in TensorFlow.

```
entropy = tf.nn.softmax_cross_entropy_with_logits(logits=model,
labels=y)
loss = tf.reduce_mean(entropy)
optimizer = tf.train.AdamOptimizer(learning_rate).minimize(loss)
```

Finally, we train the model by iterating over `n_epochs`, and within each epoch train over `n_batches`, each batch of the size of `batch_size`:

```
with tf.Session() as tfs:
    tf.global_variables_initializer().run()
    for epoch in range(n_epochs):
        total_loss = 0.0
        for batch in range(n_batches):
            batch_x,batch_y = mnist.train.next_batch(batch_size)
```

```
                feed_dict={x:batch_x, y: batch_y}
                batch_loss,_ = tfs.run([loss, optimizer],
                                        feed_dict=feed_dict)
                total_loss += batch_loss
            average_loss = total_loss / n_batches
            print("Epoch: {0:04d} loss =
{1:0.6f}".format(epoch,average_loss))
        print("Model Trained.")

        predictions_check = tf.equal(tf.argmax(model,1),tf.argmax(y,1))
        accuracy = tf.reduce_mean(tf.cast(predictions_check, tf.float32))
        feed_dict = {x:mnist.test.images, y:mnist.test.labels}
        print("Accuracy:", accuracy.eval(feed_dict=feed_dict))
```

We get the following output:

```
Epoch: 0000   loss = 1.418295
Epoch: 0001   loss = 0.088259
Epoch: 0002   loss = 0.055410
Epoch: 0003   loss = 0.042798
Epoch: 0004   loss = 0.030471
Epoch: 0005   loss = 0.023837
Epoch: 0006   loss = 0.019800
Epoch: 0007   loss = 0.015900
Epoch: 0008   loss = 0.012918
Epoch: 0009   loss = 0.010322
Model Trained.
Accuracy: 0.9884
```

Now that is some pretty good accuracy as compared to the approaches we have seen in the previous chapters so far. Aren't CNN models almost magical when it comes to learning from the image data?

LeNet CNN for MNIST with Keras

Let us revisit the same LeNet architecture with the same dataset to build and train the CNN model in Keras:

1. Import the required Keras modules:

    ```
    import keras
    from keras.models import Sequential
    from keras.layers import Conv2D,MaxPooling2D, Dense, Flatten,
    Reshape
    from keras.optimizers import SGD
    ```

2. Define the number of filters for each layer:

```
n_filters=[32,64]
```

3. Define other hyper-parameters:

```
learning_rate = 0.01
n_epochs = 10
batch_size = 100
```

4. Define the sequential model and add the layer to reshape the input data to shape `(n_width,n_height,n_depth)`:

```
model = Sequential()
model.add(Reshape(target_shape=(n_width,n_height,n_depth),
                  input_shape=(n_inputs,))
         )
```

5. Add the first convolutional layer with 4 x 4 kernel filter, `SAME` padding and `relu` activation:

```
model.add(Conv2D(filters=n_filters[0],kernel_size=4,
                 padding='SAME',activation='relu')
         )
```

6. Add the pooling layer with region size of 2 x 2 and stride of 2 x 2:

```
model.add(MaxPooling2D(pool_size=(2,2),strides=(2,2)))
```

7. Add the second convolutional and pooling layer in the same way as we added the first layer:

```
model.add(Conv2D(filters=n_filters[1],kernel_size=4,
                 padding='SAME',activation='relu')
         )
model.add(MaxPooling2D(pool_size=(2,2),strides=(2,2)))
```

8. Add a layer to flatten the output of the second pooling layer and a fully connected layer of 1024 neurons to handle the flattened output:

```
model.add(Flatten())
model.add(Dense(units=1024, activation='relu'))
```

9. Add the final output layer with the `softmax` activation:

```
model.add(Dense(units=n_outputs, activation='softmax'))
```

10. See the model summary with the following code:

```
model.summary()
```

The model is described as follows:

```
Layer (type)                 Output Shape              Param #
=================================================================
===
reshape_1 (Reshape)          (None, 28, 28, 1)         0
_________________________________________________________________
___
conv2d_1 (Conv2D)            (None, 28, 28, 32)        544
_________________________________________________________________
___
max_pooling2d_1 (MaxPooling2 (None, 14, 14, 32)        0
_________________________________________________________________
___
conv2d_2 (Conv2D)            (None, 14, 14, 64)        32832
_________________________________________________________________
___
max_pooling2d_2 (MaxPooling2 (None, 7, 7, 64)          0
_________________________________________________________________
___
flatten_1 (Flatten)          (None, 3136)              0
_________________________________________________________________
___
dense_1 (Dense)              (None, 1024)              3212288
_________________________________________________________________
___
dense_2 (Dense)              (None, 10)                10250
=================================================================
===
Total params: 3,255,914
Trainable params: 3,255,914
Non-trainable params: 0
_________________________________________________________________
___
```

11. Compile, train, and evaluate the model:

```
model.compile(loss='categorical_crossentropy',
              optimizer=SGD(lr=learning_rate),
              metrics=['accuracy'])
model.fit(X_train, Y_train,batch_size=batch_size,
          epochs=n_epochs)
score = model.evaluate(X_test, Y_test)
print('\nTest loss:', score[0])
```

```
        print('Test accuracy:', score[1])
```

We get the following output:

```
Epoch 1/10
55000/55000 [====================] - 267s - loss: 0.8854 - acc: 0.7631
Epoch 2/10
55000/55000 [====================] - 272s - loss: 0.2406 - acc: 0.9272
Epoch 3/10
55000/55000 [====================] - 267s - loss: 0.1712 - acc: 0.9488
Epoch 4/10
55000/55000 [====================] - 295s - loss: 0.1339 - acc: 0.9604
Epoch 5/10
55000/55000 [====================] - 278s - loss: 0.1112 - acc: 0.9667
Epoch 6/10
55000/55000 [====================] - 279s - loss: 0.0957 - acc: 0.9714
Epoch 7/10
55000/55000 [====================] - 316s - loss: 0.0842 - acc: 0.9744
Epoch 8/10
55000/55000 [====================] - 317s - loss: 0.0758 - acc: 0.9773
Epoch 9/10
55000/55000 [====================] - 285s - loss: 0.0693 - acc: 0.9790
Epoch 10/10
55000/55000 [====================] - 217s - loss: 0.0630 - acc: 0.9804
Test loss: 0.0628845927377
Test accuracy: 0.9785
```

The difference in accuracy could be attributed to the fact that we used SGD optimizer here, which does not implement some of the advanced features provided by AdamOptimizer we used for the TensorFlow model.

LeNet for CIFAR10 Data

Now that we have learned to build and train the CNN model using MNIST data set with TensorFlow and Keras, let us repeat the exercise with CIFAR10 dataset.

The CIFAR-10 dataset consists of 60,000 RGB color images of the shape 32x32 pixels. The images are equally divided into 10 different categories or classes: airplane, automobile, bird, cat, deer, dog, frog, horse, ship, and truck. CIFAR-10 and CIFAR-100 are subsets of a large image dataset comprising of 80 million images. The CIFAR data sets were collected and labelled by Alex Krizhevsky, Vinod Nair, and Geoffrey Hinton. The numbers 10 and 100 represent the number of classes of images.

More details about the CIFAR dataset are available at the following links: `http://www.cs.toronto.edu/~kriz/cifar.html` and `http://www.cs.toronto.edu/~kriz/learning-features-2009-TR.pdf`.

We picked CIFAR 10, since it has 3 channels, i.e. the depth of the images is 3, while the MNIST data set had only one channel. For the sake of brevity, we leave out the details to download and split the data into training and test set and provide the code in the datasetslib package in the code bundle for this book.

You can follow along with the code in the Jupyter notebook `ch-09b_CNN_CIFAR10_TF_and_Keras`.

We load and preprocess the CIFAR10 data using the following code:

```
from datasetslib.cifar import cifar10
from datasetslib import imutil
dataset = cifar10()
dataset.x_layout=imutil.LAYOUT_NHWC
dataset.load_data()
dataset.scaleX()
```

The data is loaded such that the images are in the `'NHWC'` format, that makes the data variable of shape (`number_of_samples, image_height, image_width, image_channels`). We refer to image channels as image depth. Each pixel in the images is a number from 0 to 255. The dataset is scaled using MinMax scaling to normalize the images by dividing all pixel values with 255.

The loaded and pre-processed data becomes available in the dataset object variables as `dataset.X_train`, `dataset.Y_train`, `dataset.X_test`, and `dataset.Y_test`.

ConvNets for CIFAR10 with TensorFlow

We keep the layers, filters, and their sizes the same as in the MNIST examples earlier, with one new addition of regularization layer. Since this data set is complex as compared to the MNIST, we add additional dropout layers for the purpose of regularization:

```
tf.nn.dropout(layer1_pool, keep_prob)
```

The placeholder `keep_prob` is set to 1 during prediction and evaluation. That way we can reuse the same model for training as well as prediction and evaluation.

The complete code for LeNet model for CIFAR10 data is provided in the notebook `ch-09b_CNN_CIFAR10_TF_and_Keras`.

On running the model we get the following output:

```
Epoch: 0000   loss = 2.115784
Epoch: 0001   loss = 1.620117
Epoch: 0002   loss = 1.417657
Epoch: 0003   loss = 1.284346
Epoch: 0004   loss = 1.164068
Epoch: 0005   loss = 1.058837
Epoch: 0006   loss = 0.953583
Epoch: 0007   loss = 0.853759
Epoch: 0008   loss = 0.758431
Epoch: 0009   loss = 0.663844
Epoch: 0010   loss = 0.574547
Epoch: 0011   loss = 0.489902
Epoch: 0012   loss = 0.410211
Epoch: 0013   loss = 0.342640
Epoch: 0014   loss = 0.280877
Epoch: 0015   loss = 0.234057
Epoch: 0016   loss = 0.195667
Epoch: 0017   loss = 0.161439
Epoch: 0018   loss = 0.140618
Epoch: 0019   loss = 0.126363
Model Trained.
Accuracy: 0.6361
```

We did not get good accuracy as compared to the accuracy we achieved on the MNIST data. It is possible to achieve much better accuracy by tuning the different hyper-parameters and varying the combinations of convolutional and pooling layers. We leave it as a challenge for the reader to explore and try different variations of the LeNet architecture and hyper-parameters to achieve better accuracy.

ConvNets for CIFAR10 with Keras

Let us repeat the LeNet CNN model building and training for CIFAR10 data in Keras. We keep the architecture same as previous examples in order to explain the concepts easily. In Keras, the dropout layer is added as follows:

```
model.add(Dropout(0.2))
```

The complete code in Keras for CIFAR10 CNN model is provided in the notebook `ch-09b_CNN_CIFAR10_TF_and_Keras`.

On running the model we get the following model description:

```
_________________________________________________________________
Layer (type)                 Output Shape              Param #
=================================================================
conv2d_1 (Conv2D)            (None, 32, 32, 32)        1568
_________________________________________________________________
max_pooling2d_1 (MaxPooling2 (None, 16, 16, 32)        0
_________________________________________________________________
dropout_1 (Dropout)          (None, 16, 16, 32)        0
_________________________________________________________________
conv2d_2 (Conv2D)            (None, 16, 16, 64)        32832
_________________________________________________________________
max_pooling2d_2 (MaxPooling2 (None, 8, 8, 64)          0
_________________________________________________________________
dropout_2 (Dropout)          (None, 8, 8, 64)          0
_________________________________________________________________
flatten_1 (Flatten)          (None, 4096)              0
_________________________________________________________________
dense_1 (Dense)              (None, 1024)              4195328
_________________________________________________________________
dropout_3 (Dropout)          (None, 1024)              0
_________________________________________________________________
dense_2 (Dense)              (None, 10)                10250
=================================================================
Total params: 4,239,978
Trainable params: 4,239,978
Non-trainable params: 0
_________________________________________________________________
```

We get the following training and evaluation output:

```
Epoch 1/10
50000/50000 [====================] - 191s - loss: 1.5847 - acc: 0.4364
Epoch 2/10
50000/50000 [====================] - 202s - loss: 1.1491 - acc: 0.5973
Epoch 3/10
50000/50000 [====================] - 223s - loss: 0.9838 - acc: 0.6582
Epoch 4/10
50000/50000 [====================] - 223s - loss: 0.8612 - acc: 0.7009
Epoch 5/10
50000/50000 [====================] - 224s - loss: 0.7564 - acc: 0.7394
Epoch 6/10
50000/50000 [====================] - 217s - loss: 0.6690 - acc: 0.7710
Epoch 7/10
50000/50000 [====================] - 222s - loss: 0.5925 - acc: 0.7945
Epoch 8/10
50000/50000 [====================] - 221s - loss: 0.5263 - acc: 0.8191
Epoch 9/10
50000/50000 [====================] - 237s - loss: 0.4692 - acc: 0.8387
Epoch 10/10
50000/50000 [====================] - 230s - loss: 0.4320 - acc: 0.8528
Test loss: 0.849927025414
Test accuracy: 0.7414
```

Once again, we leave it as a challenge for the reader to explore and try different variations of the LeNet architecture and hyper-parameters to achieve better accuracy.

Summary

In this chapter, we learned how to create convolutional neural networks with TensorFlow and Keras. We learned the core concepts of convolution and pooling, that lay the foundation of CNN. We learned the LeNet family of architectures and created, trained, and evaluated the LeNet family model for MNIST and CIFAR datasets. TensorFlow and Keras offer many convolutional and pooling layers and operations. The reader is encouraged to explore the layers and operations that were not covered in this chapter.

In the next chapter, we shall continue our journey to learn how to apply TensorFlow on image data with the AutoEncoder architecture.

13
Autoencoder with TensorFlow and Keras

Autoencoder is a neural network architecture that is often associated with unsupervised learning, dimensionality reduction, and data compression. Autoencoders learn to produce the same output as given to the input layer by using lesser number of neurons in the hidden layers. This allows hidden layers to learn the features of input with lesser number of parameters. This process of using lesser number of neurons to learn the features of the input data, in turn, reduces the dimensionality of the input dataset.

An autoencoder architecture has two stages: encoder and decoder. In the encoder stage, the model learns to represent the input to a compressed vector with lesser dimensions, and in the decoder stage, the model learns to represent the compressed vector to an output vector. The loss is calculated as entropy distance between the output and input, thus by minimizing the loss, we learn parameters that encode the input into a representation that is capable of producing the input back, with yet another set of learned parameters.

In this chapter, you will learn how to use TensorFlow and Keras to create autoencoder architectures in the following topics:

- Autoencoder types
- Stacked autoencoder in TensorFlow and Keras
- Denoising autoencoder in TensorFlow and Keras
- Variational autoencoder in TensorFlow and Keras

Autoencoder types

Autoencoder architectures can be found in a variety of configurations such as simple autoencoders, sparse autoencoders, denoising autoencoders, and convolutional autoencoders.

- **Simple autoencoder:** In simple autoencoder, the hidden layers have lesser number of nodes or neurons as compared to the input. For example, in the MNIST dataset, an input of 784 features can be connected to the hidden layer of 512 nodes or 256 nodes, which is connected to the 784-feature output layer. Thus, during training, the 784 features would be learned by only 256 nodes. Simple autoencoders are also known as *undercomplete* autoencoders.
  Simple autoencoder could be single-layer or multi-layer. Generally, single-layer autoencoder does not perform very good in production. Multi-layer autoencoder has more than one hidden layer, divided into encoder and decoder groupings. Encoder layers encode a large number of features into a smaller number of neurons, and decoder layers then decode the learned compressed features back into the original or a reduced number of features. Multi-layer autoencoder is known as the **stacked autoencoder**.

- **Sparse autoencoder**: In sparse autoencoder, a regularization term is added as the penalty and hence, the representation becomes more sparse as compared to simple autoencoders.
- **Denoising autoencoder** (DAE): In the DAE architecture, the input is introduced with stochastic noise. The DAE recreates the input and attempts to remove noise. The loss function in the DAE compares the denoised recreated output to the original uncorrupted input.
- **Convolutional autoencoder** (CAE): The autoencoders discussed previously use fully-connected layers, a pattern similar to the multilayer perceptron models. We can also use convolutional layers instead of fully connected or dense layers. When we use convolutional layers to create an autoencoder, it is known as a convolutional autoencoder. As an example, we could have the following layers for the CAE:
  input -> convolution -> pooling -> convolution -> pooling -> output

  The first set of convolution and pooling layers acts as the encoder, reducing the high-dimensional input feature space to low dimensional feature space. The second set of convolutional and pooling layers acts as the decoder, converting it back to high-dimensional feature space.

- **Variational autoencoder** (VAE): The variational autoencoder architecture is the latest development in the field of autoencoders. VAE is a kind of generative model, that is, it produces parameters of the probability distribution from which the original data or the data very similar to original data can be generated.
  In a VAE, the encoder turns the input samples into parameters in latent space using which the latent points are sampled. The decoder then uses the latent points to regenerate the original input data. Hence, the focus of learning in VAE shifts to maximizing the probability of the input data in place of trying to recreate the output from input.

Now let's build autoencoders in TensorFlow and Keras in the following sections. We will use the MNIST dataset to build the autoencoders. The autoencoder will learn to represent the handwritten digits of MNIST dataset with a lesser number of neurons or features.

You can follow along with the code in the Jupyter notebook `ch-10_AutoEncoders_TF_and_Keras`.

As usual, we first read the MNIST dataset with the following code:

```
from tensorflow.examples.tutorials.mnist.input_data import input_data
dataset_home = os.path.join(datasetslib.datasets_root,'mnist')
mnist = input_data.read_data_sets(dataset_home,one_hot=False)

X_train = mnist.train.images
X_test = mnist.test.images
Y_train = mnist.train.labels
Y_test = mnist.test.labels

pixel_size = 28
```

We extract four distinct images and their respective labels from training and test datasets:

```
while True:
     train_images,train_labels = mnist.train.next_batch(4)
     if len(set(train_labels))==4:
        break
while True:
     test_images,test_labels = mnist.test.next_batch(4)
     if len(set(test_labels))==4:
        break
```

Now let's look at the code to build an autoencoder using the MNIST dataset.

You can follow along with the code in the Jupyter notebook `ch-10_AutoEncoders_TF_and_Keras`.

Stacked autoencoder in TensorFlow

The steps to build a stacked autoencoder model in TensorFlow are as follows:

1. First, define the hyper-parameters as follows:

```
learning_rate = 0.001
n_epochs = 20
batch_size = 100
n_batches = int(mnist.train.num_examples/batch_size)
```

2. Define the number of inputs (that is, features) and outputs (that is, targets). The number of outputs will be the same as the number of inputs:

```
# number of pixels in the MNIST image as number of inputs
n_inputs = 784
n_outputs = n_inputs
```

3. Define the placeholders for input and output images:

```
x = tf.placeholder(dtype=tf.float32, name="x", shape=[None,
n_inputs])
y = tf.placeholder(dtype=tf.float32, name="y", shape=[None,
n_outputs])
```

4. Add the number of neurons for encoder and decoder layers as `[512,256,256,512]`:

```
# number of hidden layers
n_layers = 2
# neurons in each hidden layer
n_neurons = [512,256]
# add number of decoder layers:
n_neurons.extend(list(reversed(n_neurons)))
n_layers = n_layers * 2
```

5. Define the w and b parameters:

```
w=[]
b=[]

for i in range(n_layers):
    w.append(tf.Variable(tf.random_normal([n_inputs \
                 if i==0 else n_neurons[i-1],n_neurons[i]]),
                        name="w_{0:04d}".format(i)
                       )
            )
    b.append(tf.Variable(tf.zeros([n_neurons[i]]),
                        name="b_{0:04d}".format(i)
                       )
            )
w.append(tf.Variable(tf.random_normal([n_neurons[n_layers-1] \
                     if n_layers > 0 else n_inputs,n_outputs]),
                      name="w_out"
                     )
        )
b.append(tf.Variable(tf.zeros([n_outputs]),name="b_out"))
```

6. Build the network and use the sigmoid activation function for each layer:

```
# x is input layer
layer = x
# add hidden layers
for i in range(n_layers):
layer = tf.nn.sigmoid(tf.matmul(layer, w[i]) + b[i])
# add output layer
layer = tf.nn.sigmoid(tf.matmul(layer, w[n_layers]) +
b[n_layers])
model = layer
```

7. Define the `loss` function using `mean_squared_error` and the `optimizer` function using `AdamOptimizer`:

```
mse = tf.losses.mean_squared_error
loss = mse(predictions=model, labels=y)
optimizer =
tf.train.AdamOptimizer(learning_rate=learning_rate)
optimizer = optimizer.minimize(loss)
```

8. Train the model and predict the images for the `train` as well as `test` sets:

```
with tf.Session() as tfs:
    tf.global_variables_initializer().run()
    for epoch in range(n_epochs):
        epoch_loss = 0.0
        for batch in range(n_batches):
            X_batch, _ = mnist.train.next_batch(batch_size)
            feed_dict={x: X_batch,y: X_batch}
            _,batch_loss = tfs.run([optimizer,loss],
feed_dict)
            epoch_loss += batch_loss
        if (epoch%10==9) or (epoch==0):
            average_loss = epoch_loss / n_batches
            print('epoch: {0:04d} loss = {1:0.6f}'
                  .format(epoch,average_loss))
    # predict images using trained autoencoder model
    Y_train_pred = tfs.run(model, feed_dict={x: train_images})
    Y_test_pred = tfs.run(model, feed_dict={x: test_images})
```

9. We see the following output as the loss reduces significantly after 20 epochs:

```
epoch: 0000   loss = 0.156696
epoch: 0009   loss = 0.091367
epoch: 0019   loss = 0.078550
```

10. Now that the model is trained, let's display the predicted images from the trained model. We wrote a helper function `display_images` to help us display images:

```
import random

# Function to display the images and labels
# images should be in NHW or NHWC format
def display_images(images, labels, count=0, one_hot=False):
    # if number of images to display is not provided, then
display all the images
    if (count==0):
        count = images.shape[0]

    idx_list = random.sample(range(len(labels)),count)
    for i in range(count):
        plt.subplot(4, 4, i+1)
        plt.title(labels[i])
        plt.imshow(images[i])
        plt.axis('off')
    plt.tight_layout()
```

```
            plt.show()
```

Using this function, we first display the four images from the training set and the images predicted by the autoencoder.

The first row indicates the actual images and second row indicates the generated images:

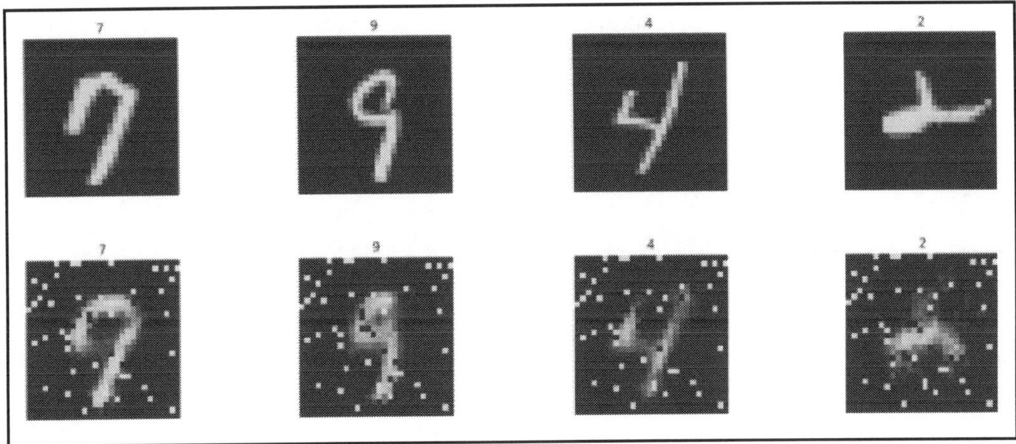

The images generated have a little bit of noise that can be removed with more training and hyper-parameter tuning. Now predicting the training set images is not magical as we trained the autoencoder on those images, hence it knows about them. Let's see the result of predicting the test set images. The first row indicates the actual images and second row indicates the generated images:

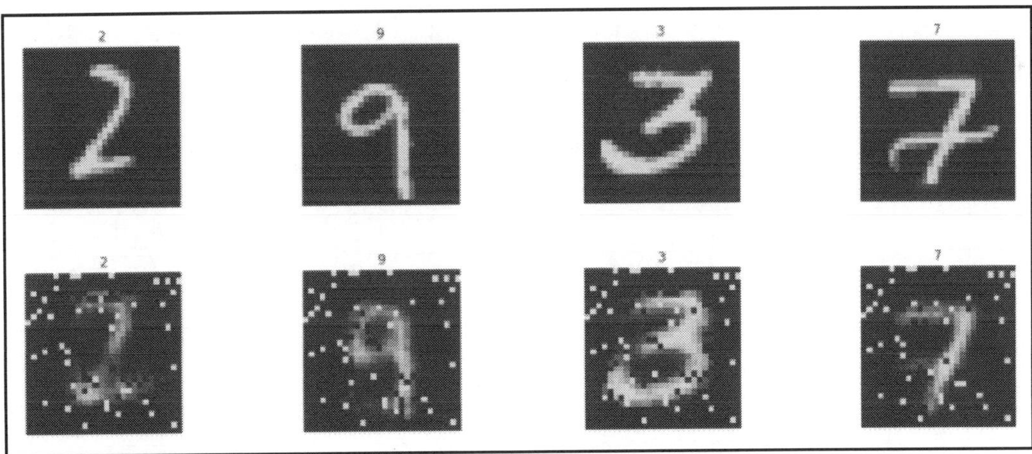

Wow! The trained autoencoder was able to generate the same digits with just 256 features that it learned out of 768. The noise in generated images can be improved by hyper-parameter tuning and more training.

Stacked autoencoder in Keras

Now let's build the same autoencoder in Keras.

We clear the graph in the notebook using the following commands so that we can build a fresh graph that does not carry over any of the memory from the previous session or graph:

```
tf.reset_default_graph()
keras.backend.clear_session()
```

1. First, we import the keras libraries and define hyperparameters and layers:

```
import keras
from keras.layers import Dense
from keras.models import Sequential

learning_rate = 0.001
n_epochs = 20
batch_size = 100
n_batches = int(mnist.train.num_examples/batch_sizee
# number of pixels in the MNIST image as number of inputs
n_inputs = 784
n_outputs = n_i
# number of hidden layers
n_layers = 2
# neurons in each hidden layer
n_neurons = [512,256]
# add decoder layers:
n_neurons.extend(list(reversed(n_neurons)))
n_layers = n_layers * 2
```

2. Next, we build a sequential model and add dense layers to it. For a change, we use `relu` activation for the hidden layers and `linear` activation for the final layer:

    ```
    model = Sequential()

    # add input to first layer
    model.add(Dense(units=n_neurons[0], activation='relu',
        input_shape=(n_inputs,)))

    for i in range(1,n_layers):
        model.add(Dense(units=n_neurons[i], activation='relu'))

    # add last layer as output layer
    model.add(Dense(units=n_outputs, activation='linear'))
    ```

3. Now let's display the model summary to see how the model looks:

    ```
    model.summary()
    ```

    The model has a total of 1,132,816 parameters in five dense layers:

```
_________________________________________________________________
Layer (type)                 Output Shape              Param #
=================================================================
dense_1 (Dense)              (None, 512)               401920
_________________________________________________________________
dense_2 (Dense)              (None, 256)               131328
_________________________________________________________________
dense_3 (Dense)              (None, 256)               65792
_________________________________________________________________
dense_4 (Dense)              (None, 512)               131584
_________________________________________________________________
dense_5 (Dense)              (None, 784)               402192
=================================================================
Total params: 1,132,816
Trainable params: 1,132,816
Non-trainable params: 0
_________________________________________________________________
```

4. Let's compile the model with the mean squared loss as in the previous example:

```
model.compile(loss='mse',
    optimizer=keras.optimizers.Adam(lr=learning_rate),
    metrics=['accuracy'])

model.fit(X_train, X_train,batch_size=batch_size,
    epochs=n_epochs)
```

Just in 20 epochs, we are able to get a loss of 0.0046 as compared to 0.078550 that we got before:

```
Epoch 1/20
55000/55000 [==========================] - 18s - loss: 0.0193 - acc:
0.0117
Epoch 2/20
55000/55000 [==========================] - 18s - loss: 0.0087 - acc:
0.0139
...
...
...
Epoch 20/20
55000/55000 [==========================] - 16s - loss: 0.0046 - acc:
0.0171
```

Now let's predict and display the train and test images generated by the model. The first row indicates the actual images and second row indicates the generated images. The following are the train set images:

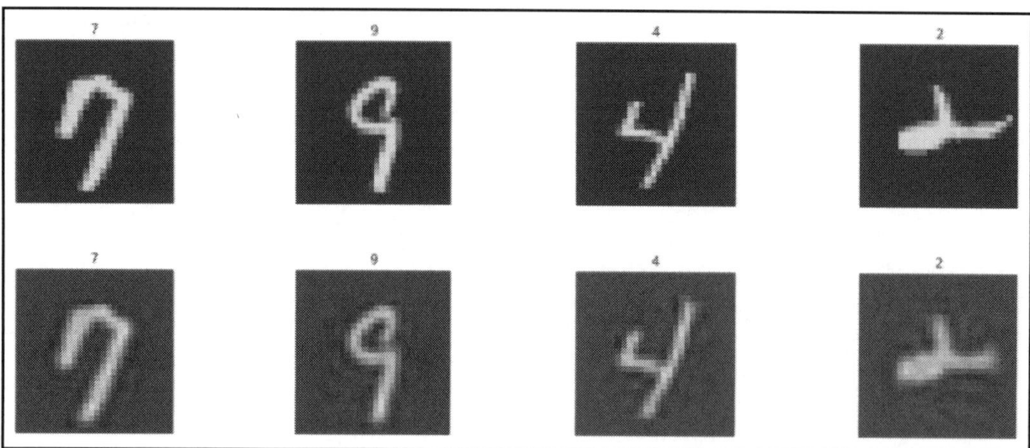

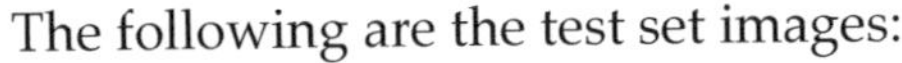

The following are the test set images:

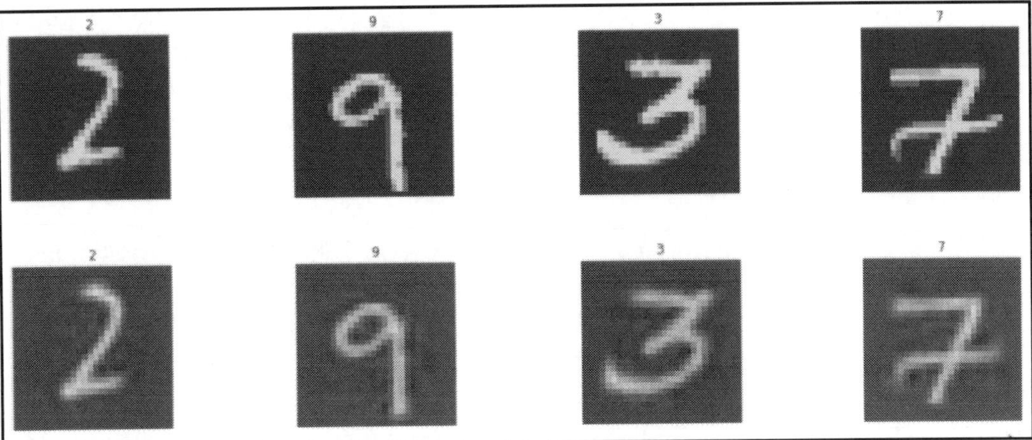

This is pretty good accuracy that we achieved in being able to generate the images from just 256 features.

Denoising autoencoder in TensorFlow

As you learned in the first section of this chapter, denoising autoencoders can be used to train the models such that they are able to remove the noise from the images input to the trained model:

1. For the purpose of this example, we write the following helper function to help us add noise to the images:

```
def add_noise(X):
    return X + 0.5 * np.random.randn(X.shape[0],X.shape[1])
```

2. Then we add noise to test images and store it in a separate list:

```
test_images_noisy = add_noise(test_images)
```

We will use these test images to test the output from our denoising model examples.

3. We build and train the denoising autoencoder as in the preceding example, with one difference: While training, we input the noisy images to the input layer and we check the reconstruction and denoising error with the non-noisy images, as the following code shows:

```
X_batch, _ = mnist.train.next_batch(batch_size)
X_batch_noisy = add_noise(X_batch)
feed_dict={x: X_batch_noisy, y: X_batch}
_,batch_loss = tfs.run([optimizer,loss], feed_dict=feed_dict)
```

The complete code for the denoising autoencoder is provided in the notebook `ch-10_AutoEncoders_TF_and_Keras`.

Now let's first display the test images generated from the DAE model; the first row indicates the original non-noisy test images and second row indicates the generated test images:

```
display_images(test_images.reshape(-1,pixel_size,pixel_size),test_labe
ls)
display_images(Y_test_pred1.reshape(-1,pixel_size,pixel_size),test_lab
els)
```

The result of the preceding code is as follows:

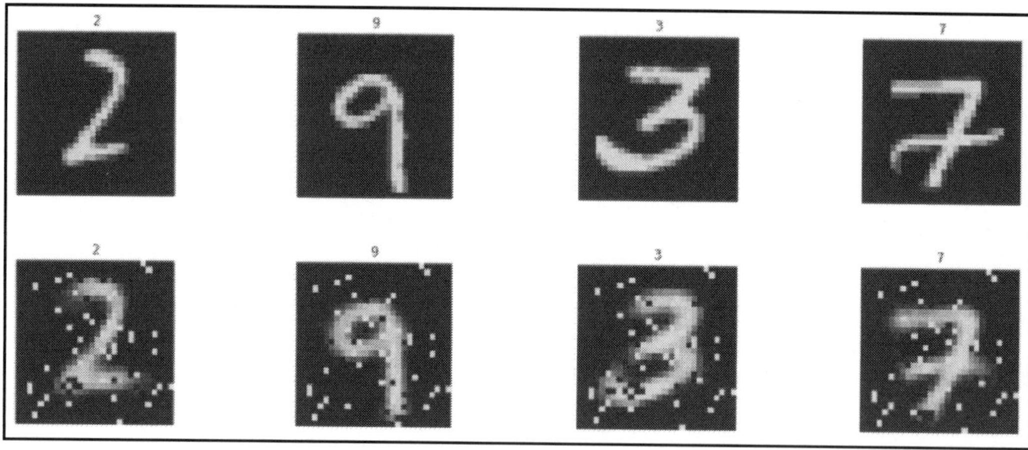

Next, we display the generated images when we input the noisy test images:

```
display_images(test_images_noisy.reshape(-1,pixel_size,pixel_size),
    test_labels)
display_images(Y_test_pred2.reshape(-1,pixel_size,pixel_size),test_lab
els)
```

The result of the preceding code is as follows:

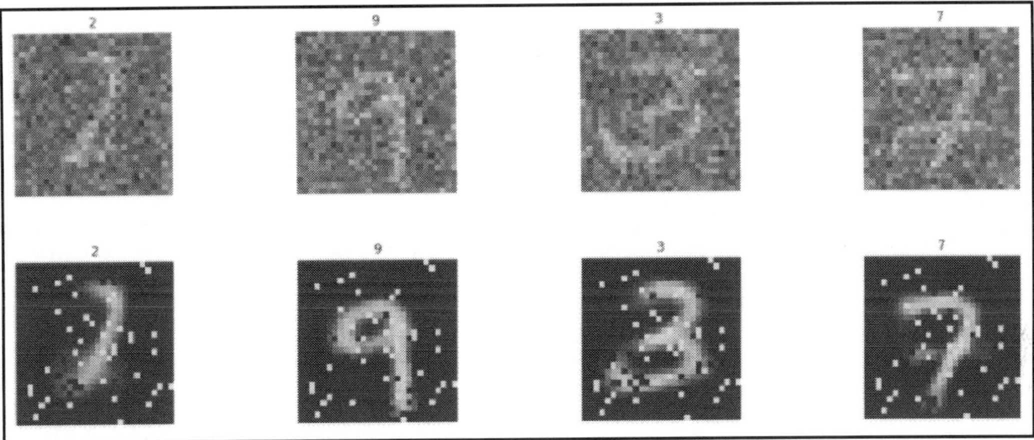

That is super cool!! The model learned the images and generated almost correct images even from a very noisy set. The quality of regeneration can be further improved with proper hyperparameter tuning.

Denoising autoencoder in Keras

Now let's build the same denoising autoencoder in Keras.

As Keras takes care of feeding the training set by batch size, we create a noisy training set to feed as input for our model:

```
X_train_noisy = add_noise(X_train)
```

The complete code for the DAE in Keras is provided in the notebook `ch-10_AutoEncoders_TF_and_Keras`.

The DAE Keras model looks like the following:

```
Layer (type)                 Output Shape              Param #
=================================================================
dense_1 (Dense)              (None, 512)               401920
_________________________________________________________________
dense_2 (Dense)              (None, 256)               131328
_________________________________________________________________
dense_3 (Dense)              (None, 256)               65792
_________________________________________________________________
dense_4 (Dense)              (None, 512)               131584
_________________________________________________________________
dense_5 (Dense)              (None, 784)               402192
=================================================================
Total params: 1,132,816
Trainable params: 1,132,816
Non-trainable params: 0
```

As DAE models are complex, for the purpose of demonstration, we had to increase the number of epochs to 100 to train the model:

```
n_epochs=100

model.fit(x=X_train_noisy, y=X_train,
      batch_size=batch_size,
      epochs=n_epochs,
      verbose=0)

Y_test_pred1 = model.predict(test_images)
Y_test_pred2 = model.predict(test_images_noisy)
```

Print the resulting images:

```
display_images(test_images.reshape(-1,pixel_size,pixel_size),test_labe
ls)
display_images(Y_test_pred1.reshape(-1,pixel_size,pixel_size),test_lab
els)
```

The first row is the original test images and the second row is the generated test images:

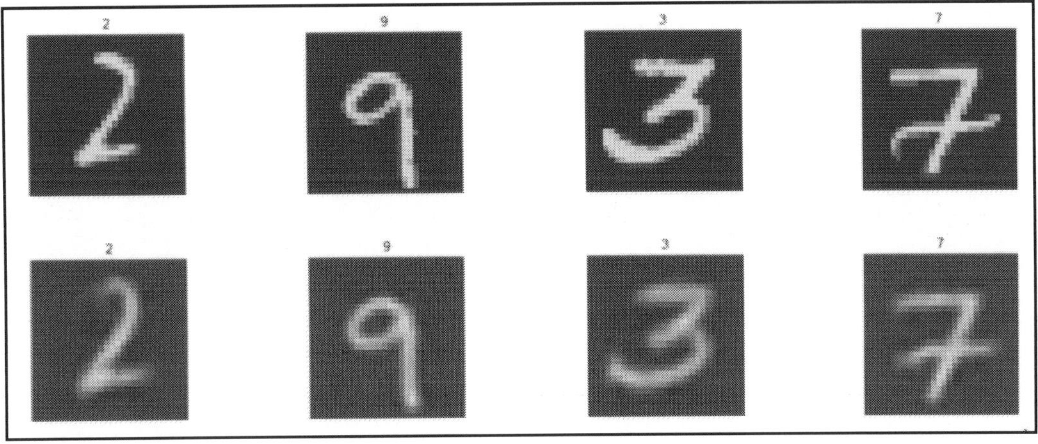


```
display_images(test_images_noisy.reshape(-1,pixel_size,pixel_size),
    test_labels)
display_images(Y_test_pred2.reshape(-1,pixel_size,pixel_size),test_lab
els)
```

The first row is the noisy test images and the second row is the generated test images:

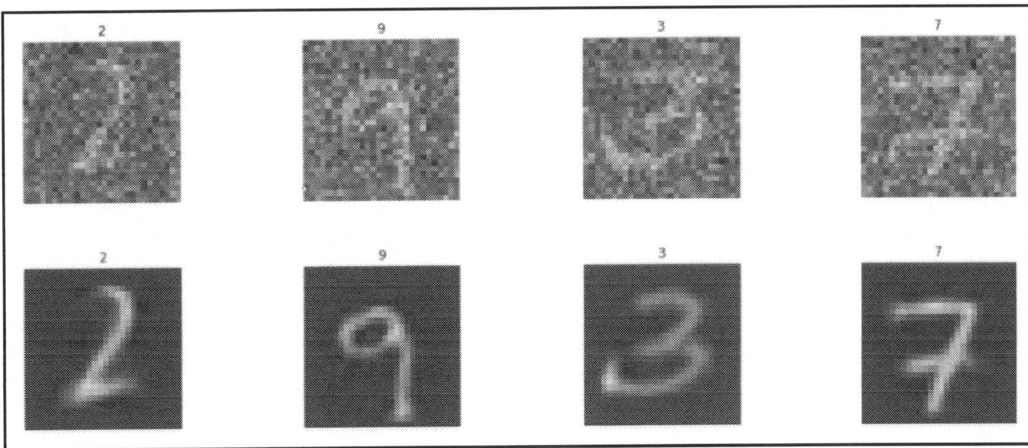

As we can see, the denoising autoencoder does a pretty good job of generating the images from the noisy version of the images.

Variational autoencoder in TensorFlow

Variational autoencoders are the modern generative version of autoencoders. Let's build a variational autoencoder for the same preceding problem. We will test the autoencoder by providing images from the original and noisy test set.

We will use a different coding style to build this autoencoder for the purpose of demonstrating the different styles of coding with TensorFlow:

1. Start by defining the hyper-parameters:

    ```
    learning_rate = 0.001
    n_epochs = 20
    batch_size = 100
    n_batches = int(mnist.train.num_examples/batch_size)
    # number of pixels in the MNIST image as number of inputs
    n_inputs = 784
    n_outputs = n_inputs
    ```

2. Next, define a parameter dictionary to hold the weight and bias parameters:

    ```
    params={}
    ```

3. Define the number of hidden layers in each of the encoder and decoder:

    ```
    n_layers = 2
    # neurons in each hidden layer
    n_neurons = [512,256]
    ```

4. The new addition in a variational encoder is that we define the dimensions of the latent variable `z`:

    ```
    n_neurons_z = 128 # the dimensions of latent variables
    ```

5. We use the activation `tanh`:

    ```
    activation = tf.nn.tanh
    ```

6. Define input and output placeholders:

    ```
    x = tf.placeholder(dtype=tf.float32, name="x",
                       shape=[None, n_inputs])
    y = tf.placeholder(dtype=tf.float32, name="y",
                       shape=[None, n_outputs])
    ```

7. Define the input layer:

```
# x is input layer
layer = x
```

8. Define the biases and weights for the encoder network and add layers. The encoder network for variational autoencoders is also known as recognition network or inference network or probabilistic encoder network:

```
for i in range(0,n_layers):
    name="w_e_{0:04d}".format(i)
    params[name] = tf.get_variable(name=name,
        shape=[n_inputs if i==0 else n_neurons[i-1],
        n_neurons[i]],
        initializer=tf.glorot_uniform_initializer()
        )
    name="b_e_{0:04d}".format(i)
    params[name] = tf.Variable(tf.zeros([n_neurons[i]]),
        name=name
        )
    layer = activation(tf.matmul(layer,
        params["w_e_{0:04d}".format(i)]
        ) + params["b_e_{0:04d}".format(i)]
        )
```

9. Next, add the layers for mean and variance of the latent variables:

```
name="w_e_z_mean"
params[name] = tf.get_variable(name=name,
    shape=[n_neurons[n_layers-1], n_neurons_z],
    initializer=tf.glorot_uniform_initializer()
    )
name="b_e_z_mean"
params[name] = tf.Variable(tf.zeros([n_neurons_z]),
    name=name
    )
z_mean = tf.matmul(layer, params["w_e_z_mean"]) +
            params["b_e_z_mean"]
name="w_e_z_log_var"
params[name] = tf.get_variable(name=name,
    shape=[n_neurons[n_layers-1], n_neurons_z],
    initializer=tf.glorot_uniform_initializer()
    )
name="b_e_z_log_var"
params[name] = tf.Variable(tf.zeros([n_neurons_z]),
    name="b_e_z_log_var"
    )
```

```
z_log_var = tf.matmul(layer, params["w_e_z_log_var"]) +
            params["b_e_z_log_var"]
```

10. Next, define the epsilon variable representing the noise distribution of the same shape as the variable holding the variance of *z*:

```
epsilon = tf.random_normal(tf.shape(z_log_var),
    mean=0,
    stddev=1.0,
    dtype=tf.float32,
    name='epsilon'
    )
```

11. Define a posterior distribution based on the mean, log variance, and noise:

```
z = z_mean + tf.exp(z_log_var * 0.5) * epsilon
```

12. Next, define the weights and biases for the decoder network and add the decoder layers. The decoder network in variational autoencoder is also known as probabilistic decoder or generator network.

```
# add generator / probablistic decoder network parameters and
layers
layer = z

for i in range(n_layers-1,-1,-1):
name="w_d_{0:04d}".format(i)
    params[name] = tf.get_variable(name=name,
    shape=[n_neurons_z if i==n_layers-1 else n_neurons[i+1],
    n_neurons[i]],
    initializer=tf.glorot_uniform_initializer()
    )
name="b_d_{0:04d}".format(i)
params[name] = tf.Variable(tf.zeros([n_neurons[i]]),
    name=name
    )
layer = activation(tf.matmul(layer,
params["w_d_{0:04d}".format(i)]) +
    params["b_d_{0:04d}".format(i)])
```

13. Finally, define the output layer:

```
name="w_d_z_mean"
params[name] = tf.get_variable(name=name,
    shape=[n_neurons[0],n_outputs],
    initializer=tf.glorot_uniform_initializer()
    )
name="b_d_z_mean"
    params[name] = tf.Variable(tf.zeros([n_outputs]),
    name=name
    )
name="w_d_z_log_var"
params[name] = tf.Variable(tf.random_normal([n_neurons[0],
    n_outputs]),
    name=name
    )
name="b_d_z_log_var"
params[name] = tf.Variable(tf.zeros([n_outputs]),
    name=name
    )
layer = tf.nn.sigmoid(tf.matmul(layer, params["w_d_z_mean"]) +
    params["b_d_z_mean"])

model = layer
```

14. In variation autoencoders, we have the reconstruction loss and the regularization loss. Define the loss function as the sum of reconstruction loss and regularization loss:

```
rec_loss = -tf.reduce_sum(y * tf.log(1e-10 + model) + (1-y)
                        * tf.log(1e-10 + 1 - model), 1)
reg_loss = -0.5*tf.reduce_sum(1 + z_log_var -
tf.square(z_mean)
                             - tf.exp(z_log_var), 1)
loss = tf.reduce_mean(rec_loss+reg_loss)
```

15. Define the optimizer function based on `AdapOptimizer`:

```
optimizer =
tf.train.AdamOptimizer(learning_rate=learning_rate)
        .minimize(loss)
```

16. Now let's train the model and generate the images from non-noisy and noisy test images:

```
with tf.Session() as tfs:
    tf.global_variables_initializer().run()
    for epoch in range(n_epochs):
        epoch_loss = 0.0
        for batch in range(n_batches):
            X_batch, _ = mnist.train.next_batch(batch_size)
            feed_dict={x: X_batch,y: X_batch}
            _,batch_loss = tfs.run([optimizer,loss],
                                    feed_dict=feed_dict)
            epoch_loss += batch_loss
        if (epoch%10==9) or (epoch==0):
            average_loss = epoch_loss / n_batches
            print("epoch: {0:04d} loss = {1:0.6f}"
                  .format(epoch,average_loss))

# predict images using autoencoder model trained
Y_test_pred1 = tfs.run(model, feed_dict={x: test_images})
Y_test_pred2 = tfs.run(model, feed_dict={x:
test_images_noisy})
```

We get the following output:

```
epoch: 0000   loss = 180.444682
epoch: 0009   loss = 106.817749
epoch: 0019   loss = 102.580904
```

Now let's display the images:

```
display_images(test_images.reshape(-1,pixel_size,pixel_size),test_labe
ls)
display_images(Y_test_pred1.reshape(-1,pixel_size,pixel_size),test_lab
els)
```

The result is as follows:

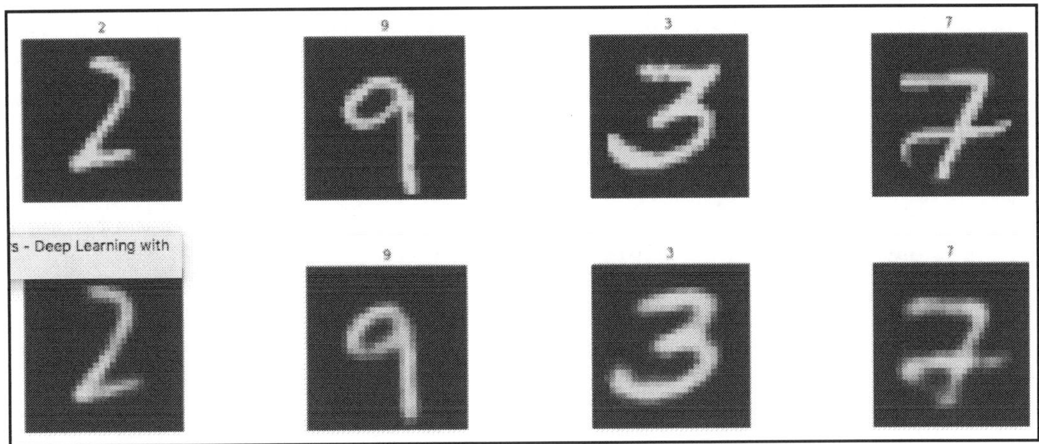


```
display_images(test_images_noisy.reshape(-1,pixel_size,pixel_size),
    test_labels)
display_images(Y_test_pred2.reshape(-1,pixel_size,pixel_size),test_labels)
```

The result is as follows:

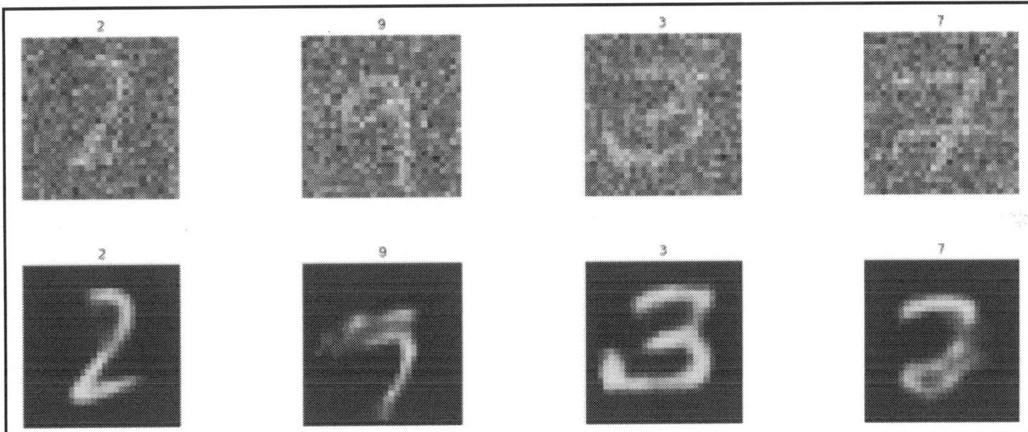

Again, the results can be improved with hyperparameter tuning and increasing the amount of learning.

Variational autoencoder in Keras

In Keras, building the variational autoencoder is much easier and with lesser lines of code. The Keras variational autoencoders are best built using the functional style. So far we have used the sequential style of building the models in Keras, and now in this example, we will see the functional style of building the VAE model in Keras. The steps to build a VAE in Keras are as follows:

1. Define the hyper-parameters and the number of neurons in the hidden layers and the latent variables layer:

```
import keras
from keras.layers import Lambda, Dense, Input, Layer
from keras.models import Model
from keras import backend as K

learning_rate = 0.001
batch_size = 100
n_batches = int(mnist.train.num_examples/batch_size)
# number of pixels in the MNIST image as number of inputs
n_inputs = 784
n_outputs = n_inputs
# number of hidden layers
n_layers = 2
# neurons in each hidden layer
n_neurons = [512,256]
# the dimensions of latent variables
n_neurons_z = 128
```

2. Build the input layer:

```
x = Input(shape=(n_inputs,), name='input')
```

3. Build the encoder layers, along with mean and variance layers for the latent variables:

```
# build encoder
layer = x
for i in range(n_layers):
    layer = Dense(units=n_neurons[i],
activation='relu',name='enc_{0}'.format(i))(layer)

z_mean = Dense(units=n_neurons_z,name='z_mean')(layer)
z_log_var = Dense(units=n_neurons_z,name='z_log_v')(layer)
```

4. Create the noise and posterior distributions:

```
# noise distribution
epsilon = K.random_normal(shape=K.shape(z_log_var),
              mean=0,stddev=1.0)

# posterior distribution
z = Lambda(lambda zargs: zargs[0] + K.exp(zargs[1] * 0.5) *
epsilon,
    name='z')([z_mean,z_log_var])
```

5. Add the decoder layers:

```
# add generator / probablistic decoder network layers
layer = z
for i in range(n_layers-1,-1,-1):
    layer = Dense(units=n_neurons[i], activation='relu',
              name='dec_{0}'.format(i))(layer)
```

6. Define the final output layer:

```
y_hat = Dense(units=n_outputs, activation='sigmoid',
          name='output')(layer)
```

7. Finally, define the model from the input layer and the output layer and display the model summary:

```
model = Model(x,y_hat)
model.summary()
```

We see the following summary:

```
______________________________________________________________________
____
Layer (type)            Output Shape          Param #     Connected to
======================================================================
===
input (InputLayer)      (None, 784)           0
______________________________________________________________________
____
enc_0 (Dense)           (None, 512)           401920      input[0][0]
______________________________________________________________________
____
enc_1 (Dense)           (None, 256)           131328      enc_0[0][0]
______________________________________________________________________
____
z_mean (Dense)          (None, 128)           32896       enc_1[0][0]
______________________________________________________________________
```

```
___
z_log_v (Dense)          (None, 128)          32896        enc_1[0][0]
________________________________________________________________________
___
z (Lambda)               (None, 128)          0            z_mean[0][0]
                                                           z_log_v[0][0]
________________________________________________________________________
___
dec_1 (Dense)            (None, 256)          33024        z[0][0]
________________________________________________________________________
___
dec_0 (Dense)            (None, 512)          131584       dec_1[0][0]
________________________________________________________________________
___
output (Dense)           (None, 784)          402192       dec_0[0][0]
========================================================================
===
Total params: 1,165,840
Trainable params: 1,165,840
Non-trainable params: 0
________________________________________________________________________
___
```

8. Define a function that calculates the sum of reconstruction and regularization loss:

```
def vae_loss(y, y_hat):
    rec_loss = -K.sum(y * K.log(1e-10 + y_hat) + (1-y) *
                K.log(1e-10 + 1 - y_hat), axis=-1)
    reg_loss = -0.5 * K.sum(1 + z_log_var - K.square(z_mean) -
                K.exp(z_log_var), axis=-1)
    loss = K.mean(rec_loss+reg_loss)
    return loss
```

9. Use this loss function to compile the model:

```
model.compile(loss=vae_loss,
    optimizer=keras.optimizers.Adam(lr=learning_rate))
```

10. Let's train the model for 50 epochs and predict the images, as we have done in previous sections:

```
n_epochs=50
model.fit(x=X_train_noisy,y=X_train,batch_size=batch_size,
    epochs=n_epochs,verbose=0)
Y_test_pred1 = model.predict(test_images)
Y_test_pred2 = model.predict(test_images_noisy)
```

Let's display the resulting images:

```
display_images(test_images.reshape(-1,pixel_size,pixel_size),test_labe
ls)
display_images(Y_test_pred1.reshape(-1,pixel_size,pixel_size),test_lab
els)
```

We get the result as follows:

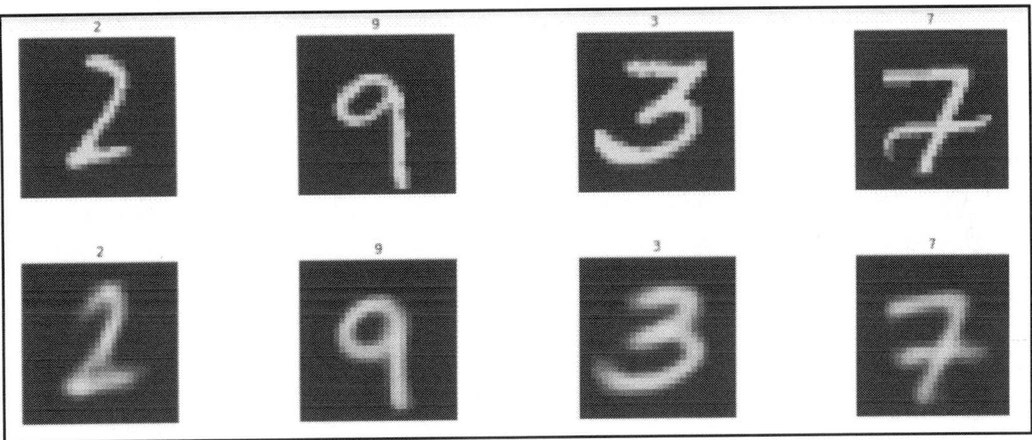

```
display_images(test_images_noisy.reshape(-1,pixel_size,pixel_size),
    test_labels)
display_images(Y_test_pred2.reshape(-1,pixel_size,pixel_size),test_lab
els)
```

We get the following results:

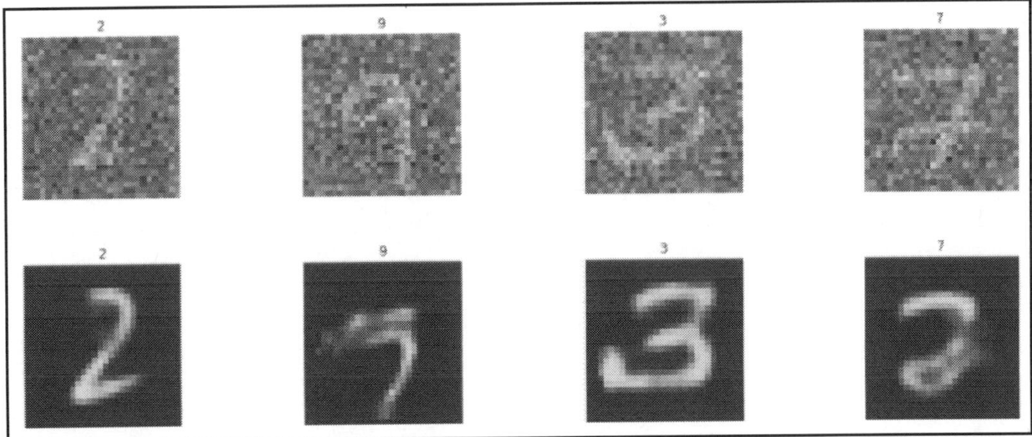

This is great!! The resulting generated images are much clearer and sharper.

Summary

Autoencoders are a great tool for unsupervised learning from data. They are often used for dimensionality reduction so that data can be represented by the lesser number of features. In this chapter, you learned about various types of autoencoders. We practiced building the three types of autoencoders using TensorFlow and Keras: stacked autoencoders, denoising autoencoders, and variational autoencoders. We used the MNIST dataset as an example.

In the last chapters, you have learned how to build various kinds of machine learning and deep learning models with TensorFlow and Keras, such as regression, classification, MLP, CNN, RNN, and autoencoders. In the next chapter, you will learn about advanced features of TensorFlow and Keras that allow us to take the models to production.

14
TensorFlow Models in Production with TF Serving

The TensorFlow models are trained and validated in the development environment. Once released, they need to be hosted somewhere to be made available to application engineers and software engineers to integrate into various applications. TensorFlow provides a high-performance server for this purpose, known as TensorFlow Serving.

For serving TensorFlow models in production, one would need to save them after training offline and then restore the trained models in the production environment. A TensorFlow model consists of the following files when saved:

- **meta-graph**: The meta-graph represents the protocol buffer definition of the graph. The meta-graph is saved in files with the `.meta` extension.
- **checkpoint**: The checkpoint represents the values of various variables. The checkpoint is saved in two files: one with the `.index` extension and one with the `.data-00000-of-00001` extension.

In this chapter, we shall learn various ways to save and restore models and how to serve them using the TF Serving. We will use the MNIST example to keep things simple and cover the following topics:

- Saving and restoring Models in TensorFlow with the `Saver` class
- Saving and restoring Keras models
- TensorFlow Serving
- Installing TF Serving
- Saving the model for TF Serving

- Serving the model with TF Serving
- TF Serving in the Docker container
- TF Serving on the Kubernetes

Saving and Restoring models in TensorFlow

You can save and restore the models and the variables in TensorFlow by one of the following two methods:

- A saver object created from the `tf.train.Saver` class
- A `SavedModel` format based object created from the `tf.saved_model_builder.SavedModelBuilder` class

Let us see both the methods in action.

You can follow along with the code in the Jupyter notebook `ch-11a_Saving_and_Restoring_TF_Models`.

Saving and restoring all graph variables with the saver class

We proceed as follows:

1. To use the `saver` class, first an object of this class is created:

```
saver = tf.train.Saver()
```

2. The simplest way to save all the variables in a graph is to call the `save()` method with the following two parameters: the session object and the path to the file on the disk where the variables will be saved:

```
with tf.Session() as tfs:
   ...
   saver.save(tfs,"saved-models/model.ckpt")
```

3. To restore the variables, the `restore()` method is called:

```
with tf.Session() as tfs:
    saver.restore(tfs,"saved-models/model.ckpt")
    ...
```

4. The code to save the variables in the graph in the simple example is as follows:

```
# Assume Linear Model y = w * x + b
# Define model parameters
w = tf.Variable([.3], tf.float32)
b = tf.Variable([-.3], tf.float32)
# Define model input and output
x = tf.placeholder(tf.float32)
y = w * x + b
output = 0

# create saver object
saver = tf.train.Saver()

with tf.Session() as tfs:
    # initialize and print the variable y
    tfs.run(tf.global_variables_initializer())
    output = tfs.run(y,{x:[1,2,3,4]})
    saved_model_file = saver.save(tfs,
        'saved-models/full-graph-save-example.ckpt')
    print('Model saved in {}'.format(saved_model_file))
    print('Values of variables w,b: {}{}'
        .format(w.eval(),b.eval()))
    print('output={}'.format(output))
```

We get the following output:

```
Model saved in saved-models/full-graph-save-example.ckpt
Values of variables w,b: [ 0.30000001][-0.30000001]
output=[ 0.          0.30000001  0.60000002  0.90000004]
```

5. Now let us restore the variables from the checkpoint file we just created:

```
# Assume Linear Model y = w * x + b
# Define model parameters
w = tf.Variable([0], dtype=tf.float32)
b = tf.Variable([0], dtype=tf.float32)
# Define model input and output
x = tf.placeholder(dtype=tf.float32)
y = w * x + b
output = 0
```

```
# create saver object
saver = tf.train.Saver()

with tf.Session() as tfs:
    saved_model_file = saver.restore(tfs,
        'saved-models/full-graph-save-example.ckpt')
    print('Values of variables w,b: {}{}'
        .format(w.eval(),b.eval()))
    output = tfs.run(y,{x:[1,2,3,4]})
    print('output={}'.format(output))
```

You will notice that in the restore code we did not call `tf.global_variables_initializer()`, because there is no need to initialize the variables since they will be restored from the file. We get the following output, which is calculated from the restored variables:

```
INFO:tensorflow:Restoring parameters from saved-models/full-graph-
save-example.ckpt
Values of variables w,b: [ 0.30000001][-0.30000001]
output=[ 0.          0.30000001  0.60000002  0.90000004]
```

Saving and restoring selected variables with the saver class

By default, the `Saver()` class saves all the variables in a graph, but you can select which variables to save by passing the list of variables to the constructor of the `Saver()` class:

```
# create saver object
saver = tf.train.Saver({'weights': w})
```

The variables names can be passed either as a list or as a dictionary. In case the variable names are passed as a list then each variable in the list will be saved with its own name. The variables can also be passed as a dictionary consisting of key-value pairs where the key is the name to be used for saving and the value is the name of the variable to be saved.

The following is the code for the example we just saw, but this time we are only saving weights from the `w` variable; name it `weights` when you save it:

```
# Saving selected variables in a graph in TensorFlow

# Assume Linear Model y = w * x + b
# Define model parameters
```

```
w = tf.Variable([.3], tf.float32)
b = tf.Variable([-.3], tf.float32)
# Define model input and output
x = tf.placeholder(tf.float32)
y = w * x + b
output = 0

# create saver object
saver = tf.train.Saver({'weights': w})

with tf.Session() as tfs:
    # initialize and print the variable y
    tfs.run(tf.global_variables_initializer())
    output = tfs.run(y,{x:[1,2,3,4]})
    saved_model_file = saver.save(tfs,
        'saved-models/weights-save-example.ckpt')
    print('Model saved in {}'.format(saved_model_file))
    print('Values of variables w,b: {}{}'
        .format(w.eval(),b.eval()))
    print('output={}'.format(output))
```

We get the following output:

```
Model saved in saved-models/weights-save-example.ckpt
Values of variables w,b: [ 0.30000001][-0.30000001]
output=[ 0.          0.30000001  0.60000002  0.90000004]
```

The checkpoint file has only saved weights and not the biases. Now let us initialize the biases and weights to zero, and restore the weights. The code is given here for this example:

```
# Restoring selected variables in a graph in TensorFlow
tf.reset_default_graph()
# Assume Linear Model y = w * x + b
# Define model parameters
w = tf.Variable([0], dtype=tf.float32)
b = tf.Variable([0], dtype=tf.float32)
# Define model input and output
x = tf.placeholder(dtype=tf.float32)
y = w * x + b
output = 0

# create saver object
saver = tf.train.Saver({'weights': w})

with tf.Session() as tfs:
    b.initializer.run()
    saved_model_file = saver.restore(tfs,
```

```
        'saved-models/weights-save-example.ckpt')
    print('Values of variables w,b: {}{}'
        .format(w.eval(),b.eval()))
    output = tfs.run(y,{x:[1,2,3,4]})
    print('output={}'.format(output))
```

As you can see, this time we had to initialize biases by using `b.initializer.run()`. We do not use `tfs.run(tf.global_variables_initializer())` since that would initialize all the variables, and there is no need to initialize the weights since they would be restored from the checkpoint file.

We get the following output, as the calculations use only the restored weights while the biases are set to zero:

```
INFO:tensorflow:Restoring parameters from saved-models/weights-save-example.ckpt
Values of variables w,b: [ 0.30000001][ 0.]
output=[ 0.30000001  0.60000002  0.90000004  1.20000005]
```

Saving and restoring Keras models

In Keras, saving and restoring models is very simple. Keras provides three options:

- Save the complete model with its network architecture, weights (parameters), training configuration, and optimizer state.
- Save only the architecture.
- Save only the weights.

For saving the complete model, use the `model.save(filepath)` function. This will save the complete model in an HDF5 file. The saved model can be loaded back using the `keras.models.load_model(filepath)` function. This function loads everything back, and then also compiles the model.

For saving the architecture of a model, use either the `model.to_json()` or `model.to_yaml()` function. These functions return a string that can be written to the disk file. While restoring the architecture, the string can be read back and the model architecture restored using the `keras.models.model_from_json(json_string)` or the `keras.models.model_from_yaml(yaml_string)` function. Both these functions return a model instance.

For saving the weights of a model, use the `model.save_weights(path_to_h5_file)` function. The weights can be restored using the `model.load_weights(path_to_h5_file)` function.

TensorFlow Serving

TensorFlow Serving (TFS) is a high-performance server architecture for serving the machine learning models in production. It offers out-of-the-box integration with the models built using TensorFlow.

In TFS, a **model** is composed of one or more **servables**. A servable is used to perform computation, for example:

- A lookup table for embedding lookups
- A single model returning predictions
- A tuple of models returning a tuple of predictions
- A shard of lookup tables or models

The ***manager*** component manages the full lifecycle for the *servables* including loading/unloading a *servable* and serving the *servable*.

The internal architecture and workflow of TensorFlow Serving is described at the following link: `https://www.tensorflow.org/serving/architecture_overview`.

Installing TF Serving

Follow the instructions in this section to install the TensorFlow ModelServer on Ubuntu using `aptitude`.

1. First, add TensorFlow Serving distribution URI as a package source (one-time setup) with the following command at shell prompt:

```
$ echo "deb [arch=amd64]
http://storage.googleapis.com/tensorflow-serving-apt stable
tensorflow-model-server tensorflow-model-server-universal" |
sudo tee /etc/apt/sources.list.d/tensorflow-serving.list

$ curl
https://storage.googleapis.com/tensorflow-serving-apt/tensorfl
```

```
ow-serving.release.pub.gpg | sudo apt-key add -
```

2. Install and update TensorFlow ModelServer with the following command at shell prompt:

```
$ sudo apt-get update && sudo apt-get install tensorflow-
model-server
```

This installs the version of ModelServer that uses platform-specific compiler optimizations, such as utilizing the SSE4 and AVX instructions. However, if the optimized version install does not work on older machines, then you can install the universal version:

```
$ sudo apt-get remove tensorflow-model-server
$ sudo apt-get update && sudo apt-get install tensorflow-
model-server-universal
```

For other operating systems and for installing from source, refer to the following link: `https://www.tensorflow.org/serving/setup`

When the new versions of ModelServer are released, you can upgrade to newer versions using the following command:

```
$ sudo apt-get update && sudo apt-get upgrade tensorflow-
model-server
```

3. Now that ModelServer is installed, run the server with the following command:

```
$ tensorflow-model-server
```

4. To connect to `tensorflow-model-server`, install the python client package with pip:

```
$ sudo pip2 install tensorflow-serving-api
```

The TF Serving API is only available for Python 2 and not yet available for Python 3.

Saving models for TF Serving

In order to serve the models, they need to be saved first. In this section, we demonstrate a slightly modified version of the MNIST example from the official TensorFlow documentation, available at the following link: `https://www.tensorflow.org/serving/serving_basic`.

The TensorFlow team recommends using SavedModel for saving and restoring models built and trained in TensorFlow. According to the TensorFlow documentation:

> *SavedModel is a language-neutral, recoverable, hermetic serialization format. SavedModel enables higher-level systems and tools to produce, consume, and transform TensorFlow models.*

You can follow along with the code in the Jupyter notebook `ch-11b_Saving_TF_Models_with_SavedModel_for_TF_Serving`.

We proceed with saving models as follows:

1. Define the model variables:

```
model_name = 'mnist'
model_version = '1'
model_dir = os.path.join(models_root,model_name,model_version)
```

2. Get the MNIST data as we did in chapter 9 - MLP models:

```
from tensorflow.examples.tutorials.mnist import input_data
dataset_home = os.path.join('.','mnist')
mnist = input_data.read_data_sets(dataset_home, one_hot=True)
x_train = mnist.train.images
x_test = mnist.test.images
y_train = mnist.train.labels
y_test = mnist.test.labels
pixel_size = 28
num_outputs = 10 # 0-9 digits
num_inputs = 784 # total pixels
```

3. Define an MLP function that would build and return the model:

```
def mlp(x, num_inputs, num_outputs,num_layers,num_neurons):
    w=[]
    b=[]
```

```
    for i in range(num_layers):
        w.append(tf.Variable(tf.random_normal(
            [num_inputs if i==0 else num_neurons[i-1],
            num_neurons[i]]),name="w_{0:04d}".format(i)
             )
            )
        b.append(tf.Variable(tf.random_normal(
                [num_neurons[i]]),
                name="b_{0:04d}".format(i)
             )
            )
    w.append(tf.Variable(tf.random_normal(
        [num_neurons[num_layers-1] if num_layers > 0 \
        else num_inputs, num_outputs]),name="w_out"))
    b.append(tf.Variable(tf.random_normal([num_outputs]),
            name="b_out"))

    # x is input layer
    layer = x
    # add hidden layers
    for i in range(num_layers):
        layer = tf.nn.relu(tf.matmul(layer, w[i]) + b[i])
    # add output layer
    layer = tf.matmul(layer, w[num_layers]) + b[num_layers]
    model = layer
    probs = tf.nn.softmax(model)

    return model,probs
```

The `mlp()` function described above returns model and probabilities. Probabilities are the softmax activation applied to the model.

4. Define the `x_p` and `y_p` placeholders for image input and target output:

```
# input images
serialized_tf_example = tf.placeholder(tf.string,
        name='tf_example')
feature_configs = {'x': tf.FixedLenFeature(shape=[784],
        dtype=tf.float32),}
tf_example = tf.parse_example(serialized_tf_example,
        feature_configs)
# use tf.identity() to assign name
x_p = tf.identity(tf_example['x'], name='x_p')
# target output
y_p = tf.placeholder(dtype=tf.float32, name="y_p",
        shape=[None, num_outputs])
```

5. Create the model, along with the loss, optimizer, accuracy, and training functions:

```
num_layers = 2
num_neurons = []
for i in range(num_layers):
   num_neurons.append(256)

learning_rate = 0.01
n_epochs = 50
batch_size = 100
n_batches = mnist.train.num_examples//batch_size

model,probs = mlp(x=x_p,
    num_inputs=num_inputs,
    num_outputs=num_outputs,
    num_layers=num_layers,
    num_neurons=num_neurons)

loss_op = tf.nn.softmax_cross_entropy_with_logits
loss = tf.reduce_mean(loss_op(logits=model, labels=y_p))
optimizer = tf.train.GradientDescentOptimizer(learning_rate)
train_op = optimizer.minimize(loss)

pred_check = tf.equal(tf.argmax(probs,1), tf.argmax(y_p,1))
accuracy_op = tf.reduce_mean(tf.cast(pred_check, tf.float32))

values, indices = tf.nn.top_k(probs, 10)
table = tf.contrib.lookup.index_to_string_table_from_tensor(
        tf.constant([str(i) for i in range(10)]))
prediction_classes = table.lookup(tf.to_int64(indices))
```

6. In a TensorFlow session, train the model as we did before, but use the builder object to save the model:

```
from tf.saved_model.signature_constants import \
        CLASSIFY_INPUTS
from tf.saved_model.signature_constants import \
        CLASSIFY_OUTPUT_CLASSES
from tf.saved_model.signature_constants import \
        CLASSIFY_OUTPUT_SCORES
from tf.saved_model.signature_constants import \
        CLASSIFY_METHOD_NAME
from tf.saved_model.signature_constants import \
        PREDICT_METHOD_NAME
from tf.saved_model.signature_constants import \
        DEFAULT_SERVING_SIGNATURE_DEF_KEY
```

```
with tf.Session() as tfs:
    tfs.run(tf.global_variables_initializer())
    for epoch in range(n_epochs):
        epoch_loss = 0.0
        for batch in range(n_batches):
            x_batch, y_batch =
mnist.train.next_batch(batch_size)
            feed_dict = {x_p: x_batch, y_p: y_batch}
            _,batch_loss = tfs.run([train_op,loss],
                                feed_dict=feed_dict)
            epoch_loss += batch_loss
        average_loss = epoch_loss / n_batches
        print("epoch: {0:04d}   loss = {1:0.6f}"
            .format(epoch,average_loss))
    feed_dict={x_p: x_test, y_p: y_test}
    accuracy_score = tfs.run(accuracy_op, feed_dict=feed_dict)
    print("accuracy={0:.8f}".format(accuracy_score))

    # save the model

    # definitions for saving the models
    builder =
tf.saved_model.builder.SavedModelBuilder(model_dir)
    # build signature_def_map
    bti_op = tf.saved_model.utils.build_tensor_info
    bsd_op = tf.saved_model.utils.build_signature_def

    classification_inputs = bti_op(serialized_tf_example)
    classification_outputs_classes =
bti_op(prediction_classes)
    classification_outputs_scores = bti_op(values)
    classification_signature = (bsd_op(
        inputs={CLASSIFY_INPUTS: classification_inputs},
        outputs={CLASSIFY_OUTPUT_CLASSES:
                    classification_outputs_classes,
                 CLASSIFY_OUTPUT_SCORES:
                    classification_outputs_scores
               },
        method_name=CLASSIFY_METHOD_NAME))

    tensor_info_x = bti_op(x_p)
    tensor_info_y = bti_op(probs)

    prediction_signature = (bsd_op(
            inputs={'inputs': tensor_info_x},
            outputs={'outputs': tensor_info_y},
            method_name=PREDICT_METHOD_NAME))
```

```
        legacy_init_op = tf.group(tf.tables_initializer(),
            name='legacy_init_op')
        builder.add_meta_graph_and_variables(
            tfs, [tf.saved_model.tag_constants.SERVING],
            signature_def_map={
                'predict_images':prediction_signature,
                DEFAULT_SERVING_SIGNATURE_DEF_KEY:
                    classification_signature,
            },
            legacy_init_op=legacy_init_op)

        builder.save()
```

The model is saved once we see the following output:

```
accuracy=0.92979997
INFO:tensorflow:No assets to save.
INFO:tensorflow:No assets to write.
INFO:tensorflow:SavedModel written to:
b'/home/armando/models/mnist/1/saved_model.pb'
```

Next, we run the ModelServer and serve the model we just saved.

Serving models with TF Serving

To run the ModelServer, execute the following command:

```
$ tensorflow_model_server --model_name=mnist --
model_base_path=/home/armando/models/mnist
```

The server starts serving the model on port 8500:

```
I tensorflow_serving/model_servers/main.cc:147] Building single
TensorFlow model file config: model_name: mnist model_base_path:
/home/armando/models/mnist
I tensorflow_serving/model_servers/server_core.cc:441] Adding/updating
models.
I tensorflow_serving/model_servers/server_core.cc:492] (Re-)adding
model: mnist
I tensorflow_serving/core/basic_manager.cc:705] Successfully reserved
resources to load servable {name: mnist version: 1}
I tensorflow_serving/core/loader_harness.cc:66] Approving load for
servable version {name: mnist version: 1}
I tensorflow_serving/core/loader_harness.cc:74] Loading servable
version {name: mnist version: 1}
I
external/org_tensorflow/tensorflow/contrib/session_bundle/bundle_shim.
```

```
cc:360] Attempting to load native SavedModelBundle in bundle-shim
from: /home/armando/models/mnist/1
I external/org_tensorflow/tensorflow/cc/saved_model/loader.cc:236]
Loading SavedModel from: /home/armando/models/mnist/1
I
external/org_tensorflow/tensorflow/core/platform/cpu_feature_guard.cc:
137] Your CPU supports instructions that this TensorFlow binary was
not compiled to use: AVX2 FMA
I external/org_tensorflow/tensorflow/cc/saved_model/loader.cc:155]
Restoring SavedModel bundle.
I external/org_tensorflow/tensorflow/cc/saved_model/loader.cc:190]
Running LegacyInitOp on SavedModel bundle.
I external/org_tensorflow/tensorflow/cc/saved_model/loader.cc:284]
Loading SavedModel: success. Took 29853 microseconds.
I tensorflow_serving/core/loader_harness.cc:86] Successfully loaded
servable version {name: mnist version: 1}
E1121 ev_epoll1_linux.c:1051] grpc epoll fd: 3
I tensorflow_serving/model_servers/main.cc:288] Running ModelServer at
0.0.0.0:8500 ...
```

To test the server by calling the model to classify images, follow along with notebook `ch-11c_TF_Serving_MNIST`.

The first two cells of the notebook provide the test client functions from TensorFlow official examples in the serving repository. We have modified the example to send the `'input'` and receive the `'output'` in the function signature for calling the ModelServer.

Call the test client functions in the third cell of the notebook with the following code:

```
error_rate = do_inference(hostport='0.0.0.0:8500',
                          work_dir='/home/armando/datasets/mnist',
                          concurrency=1,
                          num_tests=100)
print('\nInference error rate: %s%%' % (error_rate * 100))
```

We get an almost 7% error rate! (you might get a different value):

```
Extracting /home/armando/datasets/mnist/train-images-idx3-ubyte.gz
Extracting /home/armando/datasets/mnist/train-labels-idx1-ubyte.gz
Extracting /home/armando/datasets/mnist/t10k-images-idx3-ubyte.gz
Extracting /home/armando/datasets/mnist/t10k-labels-idx1-ubyte.gz

..................................................
..................................................
Inference error rate: 7.0%
```

TF Serving in the Docker containers

Docker is a platform for packaging and deploying the application in containers. If you do not already know about the Docker containers, then visit the tutorials and information at the following link: `https://www.docker.com/what-container`.

We can also install and run the TensorFlow Serving in the Docker containers. The instructions for Ubuntu 16.04 provided in this section are derived from the links on TensorFlow's official website:

- `https://www.tensorflow.org/serving/serving_inception`
- `https://www.tensorflow.org/serving/serving_basic`

Let us dive right in!

Installing Docker

We install Docker as follows:

1. First, remove the previous installations of Docker:

   ```
   $ sudo apt-get remove docker docker-engine docker.io
   ```

2. Install the pre-requisite software:

   ```
   $ sudo apt-get install \
       apt-transport-https \
       ca-certificates \
       curl \
       software-properties-common
   ```

3. Add the GPG key for Docker repositories:

   ```
   $ curl -fsSL https://download.docker.com/linux/ubuntu/gpg |
   sudo apt-key add -
   ```

4. Add the Docker repository:

   ```
   $ sudo add-apt-repository \
      "deb [arch=amd64] https://download.docker.com/linux/ubuntu
   \
      $(lsb_release -cs) \
      stable"
   ```

5. Install the Docker community edition:

```
$ sudo apt-get update && sudo apt-get install docker-ce
```

6. Once the installation is successfully completed, add the Docker as a system service:

```
$ sudo systemctl enable docker
```

7. To run Docker as a non-root user or without `sudo`, add the `docker` group:

```
$ sudo groupadd docker
```

8. Add your user to the `docker` group:

```
$ sudo usermod -aG docker $USER
```

9. Now log off and log in again so that group membership takes effect. Once logged in, run the following command to test Docker installation:

```
$ docker run --name hello-world-container hello-world
```

You should see output similar to the following:

```
Unable to find image 'hello-world:latest' locally
latest: Pulling from library/hello-world
ca4f61b1923c: Already exists
Digest:
sha256:be0cd392e45be79ffeffa6b05338b98ebb16c87b255f48e297ec7f98e123905
c
Status: Downloaded newer image for hello-world:latest

Hello from Docker!
This message shows that your installation appears to be working
correctly.

To generate this message, Docker took the following steps:
 1. The Docker client contacted the Docker daemon.
 2. The Docker daemon pulled the "hello-world" image from the Docker
Hub.
 (amd64)
 3. The Docker daemon created a new container from that image which
runs the
 executable that produces the output you are currently reading.
 4. The Docker daemon streamed that output to the Docker client, which
sent it
 to your terminal.
```

```
To try something more ambitious, you can run an Ubuntu container with:
 $ docker run -it ubuntu bash

Share images, automate workflows, and more with a free Docker ID:
 https://cloud.docker.com/

For more examples and ideas, visit:
 https://docs.docker.com/engine/userguide/
```

Docker is installed successfully. Now let us build a Docker image for TensorFlow Serving.

Building a Docker image for TF serving

We proceed with the Docker image for serving as follows:

1. Create the file named `dockerfile` with the following content:

```
FROM ubuntu:16.04
MAINTAINER Armando Fandango <armando@geekysalsero.com>

RUN apt-get update && apt-get install -y \
 build-essential \
 curl \
 git \
 libfreetype6-dev \
 libpng12-dev \
 libzmq3-dev \
 mlocate \
 pkg-config \
 python-dev \
 python-numpy \
 python-pip \
 software-properties-common \
 swig \
 zip \
 zlib1g-dev \
 libcurl3-dev \
 openjdk-8-jdk\
 openjdk-8-jre-headless \
 wget \
 && \
 apt-get clean && \
 rm -rf /var/lib/apt/lists/*

RUN echo "deb [arch=amd64]
```

```
http://storage.googleapis.com/tensorflow-serving-apt stable
tensorflow-model-server tensorflow-model-server-universal" \
 | tee /etc/apt/sources.list.d/tensorflow-serving.list

RUN curl
https://storage.googleapis.com/tensorflow-serving-apt/tensorfl
ow-serving.release.pub.gpg \
 | apt-key add -

RUN apt-get update && apt-get install -y \
 tensorflow-model-server

RUN pip install --upgrade pip
RUN pip install mock grpcio tensorflow tensorflow-serving-api

CMD ["/bin/bash"]
```

2. Run the following command to build the Docker image from this `dockerfile`:

```
$ docker build --pull -t $USER/tensorflow_serving -f
dockerfile .
```

3. It will take a while to create the image. When you see something similar to the following, then you know the image is built:

```
Removing intermediate container 1d8e757d96e0
Successfully built 0f95ddba4362
Successfully tagged armando/tensorflow_serving:latest
```

4. Run the following command to start the container:

```
$ docker run --name=mnist_container -it
$USER/tensorflow_serving
```

5. You will be logged into the container when you see the following prompt:

```
root@244ea14efb8f:/#
```

6. Give the `cd` command to go to the home folder.
7. In the home folder, give the following command to check that TensorFlow is serving code. We will be using examples from this code to demonstrate, but you can check out your own Git repository to run your own models:

```
$ git clone --recurse-submodules
https://github.com/tensorflow/serving
```

Once the repository is cloned, we are ready to build, train, and save the MNIST model.

8. Remove the temp folder, if you haven't already, with the following command:

```
$ rm -rf /tmp/mnist_model
```

9. Run the following command to build, train, and save the MNIST model.

```
$ python
serving/tensorflow_serving/example/mnist_saved_model.py
/tmp/mnist_model
```

You will see something similar to the following:

```
Training model...
Successfully downloaded train-images-idx3-ubyte.gz 9912422
bytes.
Extracting /tmp/train-images-idx3-ubyte.gz
Successfully downloaded train-labels-idx1-ubyte.gz 28881
bytes.
Extracting /tmp/train-labels-idx1-ubyte.gz
Successfully downloaded t10k-images-idx3-ubyte.gz 1648877
bytes.
Extracting /tmp/t10k-images-idx3-ubyte.gz
Successfully downloaded t10k-labels-idx1-ubyte.gz 4542 bytes.
Extracting /tmp/t10k-labels-idx1-ubyte.gz
2017-11-22 01:09:38.165391: I
tensorflow/core/platform/cpu_feature_guard.cc:137] Your CPU
supports instructions that this TensorFlow binary was not
compiled to use: SSE4.1 SSE4.2 AVX AVX2 FMA
training accuracy 0.9092
Done training!
Exporting trained model to /tmp/mnist_model/1
Done exporting!
```

10. Detach from the Docker image by pressing *Ctrl+P* and *Ctrl+Q*.
11. Commit the changes to the new image and stop the container with the following commands:

```
$ docker commit mnist_container $USER/mnist_serving
$ docker stop mnist_container
```

12. Now you can run this container at any time by giving the following command:

```
$ docker run --name=mnist_container -it $USER/mnist_serving
```

13. Remove the temporary MNIST container we built to save the image:

```
$ docker rm mnist_container
```

Serving the model in the Docker container

To serve the model in the container, the instructions are as follows:

1. Start the MNIST container built in the previous section:

```
$ docker run --name=mnist_container -it $USER/mnist_serving
```

2. Give the `cd` command to go to the home folder.
3. Run the ModelServer with the following command:

```
$ tensorflow_model_server  --model_name=mnist --
model_base_path=/tmp/mnist_model/ &> mnist_log &
```

4. Check the prediction from the model with the sample client:

```
$ python serving/tensorflow_serving/example/mnist_client.py --
num_tests=100 --server=localhost:8500
```

5. We see the error rate to be 7%, just like our previous notebook example execution:

```
Extracting /tmp/train-images-idx3-ubyte.gz
Extracting /tmp/train-labels-idx1-ubyte.gz
Extracting /tmp/t10k-images-idx3-ubyte.gz
Extracting /tmp/t10k-labels-idx1-ubyte.gz
...............................................................
......................................
Inference error rate: 7.0%
```

That's it! You have built a Docker image and served your model in the Docker image. Issue the `exit` command to get out of the container.

TensorFlow Serving on Kubernetes

According to `https://kubernets.io`:

> *Kubernetes is an open-source system for automating deployment, scaling, and management of containerized applications.*

TensorFlow models can be scaled to be served from hundreds or thousands of `TF Serving` services using Kubernetes clusters in the production environment. Kubernetes clusters can be run on all popular public clouds, such as GCP, AWS, Azure, as well as in your on-premises private cloud. So let us dive right in to learn to install Kubernetes and then deploy the MNIST model on Kubernetes Cluster.

Installing Kubernetes

We installed Kubernetes on Ubuntu 16.04 in a single-node local cluster mode as per the following steps:

1. Install LXD and Docker, which are prerequisites to install Kubernetes locally. LXD is the container manager that works with linux containers. We already learned how to install Docker in the previous section. To install LXD, run the following command:

```
$ sudo snap install lxd
lxd 2.19 from 'canonical' installed
```

2. Initialize `lxd` and create the virtual network:

```
$ sudo /snap/bin/lxd init --auto
LXD has been successfully configured.

$ sudo /snap/bin/lxc network create lxdbr0 ipv4.address=auto
ipv4.nat=true ipv6.address=none ipv6.nat=false
If this is your first time using LXD, you should also run: lxd
init
 To start your first container, try: lxc launch ubuntu:16.04

Network lxdbr0 created
```

3. Add your user to the `lxd` group:

```
$ sudo usermod -a -G lxd $(whoami)
```

4. Install `conjure-up` and restart the machine:

```
$ sudo snap install conjure-up --classic
conjure-up 2.3.1 from 'canonical' installed
```

5. Fire up `conjure-up` to install Kubernetes:

```
$ conjure-up kubernetes
```

6. From the list of spells select **Kubernetes Core**.
7. From the list of available clouds select **localhost.**
8. From the list of networks select **lxbr0 bridge.**
9. Provide the sudo password for the option: **Download the kubectl and kubefed client programs to your local host**.
10. In the next screen, it would ask to select the apps to install. Install all five of the remaining apps.

You know the Kubernetes cluster is ready to brew when the final screen during install looks like this:

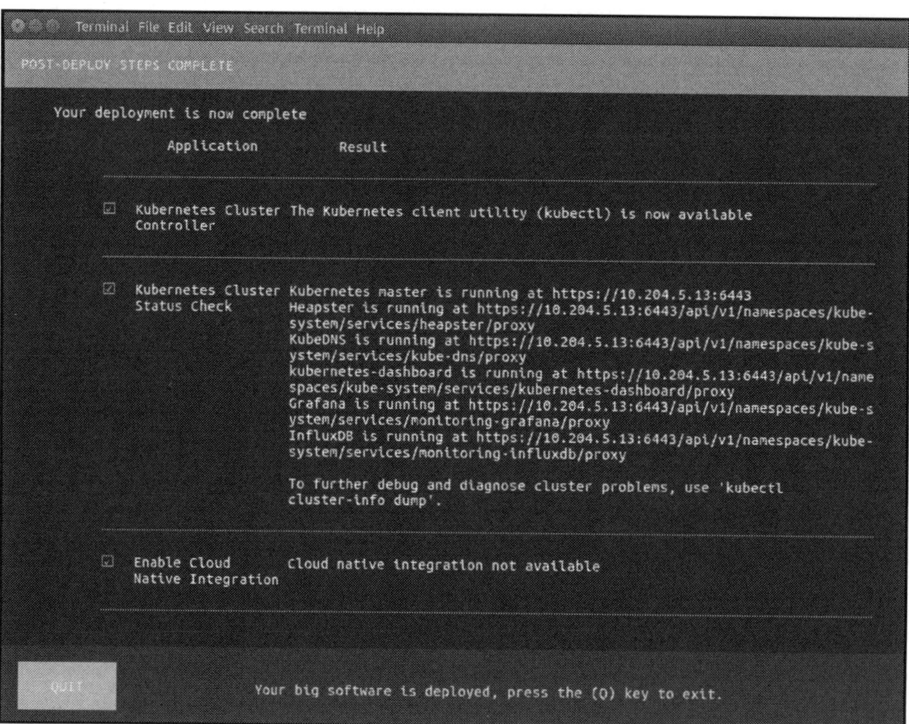

If you are having problems with the installation, please search for help on the internet, starting with the documentation at the following links:

`https://kubernetes.io/docs/getting-started-guides/ubuntu/local/`
`https://kubernetes.io/docs/getting-started-guides/ubuntu/`
`https://tutorials.ubuntu.com/tutorial/install-kubernetes-with-conjure-up`

Uploading the Docker image to the dockerhub

The steps to upload the Docker image to the dockerhub are as follows:

1. Create an account on the dockerhub if you haven't already.
2. Log in to the dockerhub account with the following command:

```
$ docker login --username=<username>
```

3. Tag the MNIST image with a repo that you have created on dockerhub. For example, we created `neurasights/mnist-serving`:

```
$ docker tag $USER/mnist_serving neurasights/mnist-serving
```

4. Push the tagged image to the dockerhub account.

```
$ docker push neurasights/mnist-serving
```

Deploying in Kubernetes

We proceed with deployment in Kubernotes as follows:

1. Create the `mnist.yaml` file with the following content:

```
apiVersion: extensions/v1beta1
kind: Deployment
metadata:
  name: mnist-deployment
spec:
  replicas: 3
  template:
    metadata:
      labels:
```

```
          app: mnist-server
      spec:
        containers:
        - name: mnist-container
          image: neurasights/mnist-serving
          command:
          - /bin/sh
          args:
          - -c
          - tensorflow_model_server --model_name=mnist --
model_base_path=/tmp/mnist_model
          ports:
          - containerPort: 8500
---
apiVersion: v1
kind: Service
metadata:
  labels:
    run: mnist-service
  name: mnist-service
spec:
  ports:
  - port: 8500
    targetPort: 8500
  selector:
    app: mnist-server
#  type: LoadBalancer
```

If you are running it in AWS or GCP clouds then uncomment the `LoadBalancer` line from the preceding file. Since we are running the whole cluster locally on a single node, we do not have external LoadBalancer.

2. Create the Kubernetes deployment and service:

```
$ kubectl create -f mnist.yaml
deployment "mnist-deployment" created
service "mnist-service" created
```

3. Check the deployments, pods, and services:

```
$ kubectl get deployments
NAME                DESIRED   CURRENT   UP-TO-DATE   AVAILABLE
AGE
mnist-deployment    3         3         3            0
1m

$ kubectl get pods
```

```
NAME                                   READY  STATUS
RESTARTS  AGE
default-http-backend-bbchw             1/1    Running
3         9d
mnist-deployment-554f4b674b-pwk8z      0/1    ContainerCreating
0         1m
mnist-deployment-554f4b674b-vn6sd      0/1    ContainerCreating
0         1m
mnist-deployment-554f4b674b-zt4xt      0/1    ContainerCreating
0         1m
nginx-ingress-controller-724n5         1/1    Running
2         9d

$ kubectl get services
NAME                   TYPE            CLUSTER-IP
EXTERNAL-IP   PORT(S)            AGE
default-http-backend   ClusterIP       10.152.183.223   <none>
80/TCP          9d
kubernetes             ClusterIP       10.152.183.1     <none>
443/TCP         9d
mnist-service          LoadBalancer    10.152.183.66
<pending>     8500:32414/TCP    1m

$ kubectl describe service mnist-service
Name:                     mnist-service
Namespace:                default
Labels:                   run=mnist-service
Annotations:              <none>
Selector:                 app=mnist-server
Type:                     LoadBalancer
IP:                       10.152.183.66
Port:                     <unset>  8500/TCP
TargetPort:               8500/TCP
NodePort:                 <unset>  32414/TCP
Endpoints:
10.1.43.122:8500,10.1.43.123:8500,10.1.43.124:8500
Session Affinity:         None
External Traffic Policy:  Cluster
Events:                   <none>
```

4. Wait until the status of all the pods is `Running`:

```
$ kubectl get pods
NAME                                  READY    STATUS
RESTARTS   AGE
default-http-backend-bbchw            1/1      Running   3
9d
mnist-deployment-554f4b674b-pwk8z     1/1      Running   0
```

```
3m
mnist-deployment-554f4b674b-vn6sd   1/1       Running   0
3m
mnist-deployment-554f4b674b-zt4xt   1/1       Running   0
3m
nginx-ingress-controller-724n5      1/1       Running   2
9d
```

5. Check the logs of one of the pods, and you should see something like this :

```
$ kubectl logs mnist-deployment-59dfc5df64-g7prf
I tensorflow_serving/model_servers/main.cc:147] Building
single TensorFlow model file config: model_name: mnist
model_base_path: /tmp/mnist_model
I tensorflow_serving/model_servers/server_core.cc:441]
Adding/updating models.
I tensorflow_serving/model_servers/server_core.cc:492] (Re-
)adding model: mnist
I tensorflow_serving/core/basic_manager.cc:705] Successfully
reserved resources to load servable {name: mnist version: 1}
I tensorflow_serving/core/loader_harness.cc:66] Approving load
for servable version {name: mnist version: 1}
I tensorflow_serving/core/loader_harness.cc:74] Loading
servable version {name: mnist version: 1}
I
external/org_tensorflow/tensorflow/contrib/session_bundle/bund
le_shim.cc:360] Attempting to load native SavedModelBundle in
bundle-shim from: /tmp/mnist_model/1
I
external/org_tensorflow/tensorflow/cc/saved_model/loader.cc:23
6] Loading SavedModel from: /tmp/mnist_model/1
I
external/org_tensorflow/tensorflow/core/platform/cpu_feature_g
uard.cc:137] Your CPU supports instructions that this
TensorFlow binary was not compiled to use: AVX2 FMA
I
external/org_tensorflow/tensorflow/cc/saved_model/loader.cc:15
5] Restoring SavedModel bundle.
I
external/org_tensorflow/tensorflow/cc/saved_model/loader.cc:19
0] Running LegacyInitOp on SavedModel bundle.
I
external/org_tensorflow/tensorflow/cc/saved_model/loader.cc:28
4] Loading SavedModel: success. Took 45319 microseconds.
I tensorflow_serving/core/loader_harness.cc:86] Successfully
loaded servable version {name: mnist version: 1}
E1122 12:18:04.566415410 6 ev_epoll1_linux.c:1051] grpc epoll
fd: 3
```

```
I tensorflow_serving/model_servers/main.cc:288] Running
ModelServer at 0.0.0.0:8500 ...
```

6. You can also look at the UI console with the following command:

```
$ kubectl proxy xdg-open http://localhost:8001/ui
```

The Kubernetes UI console looks like the following images:

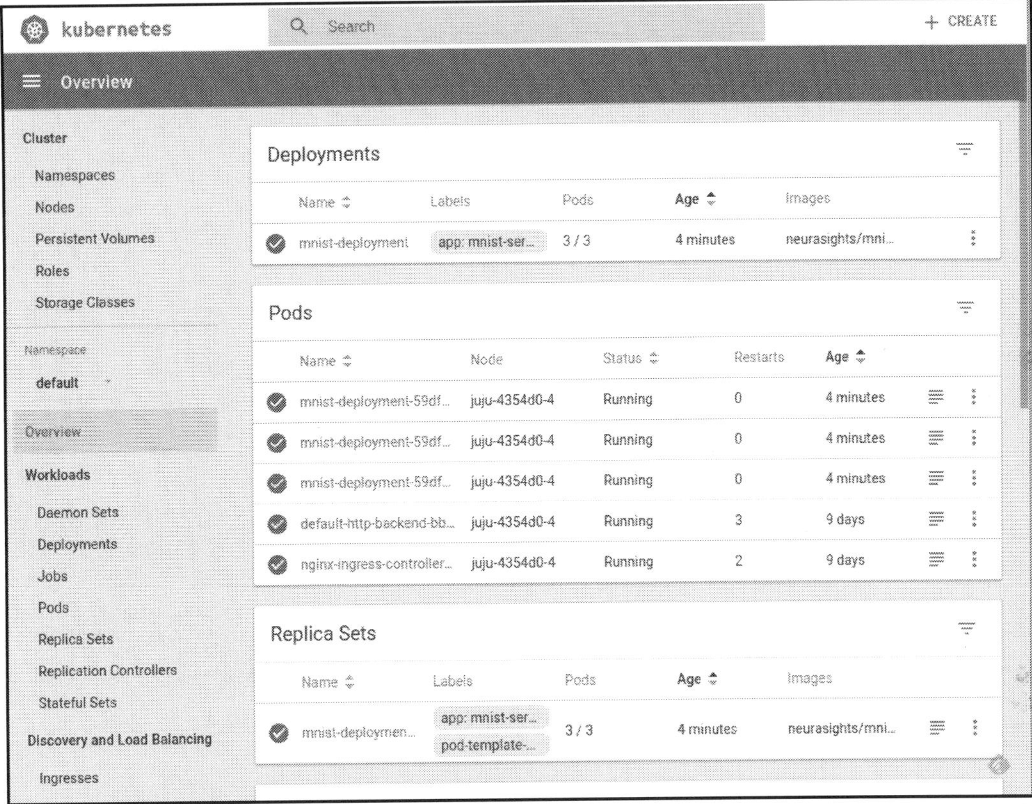

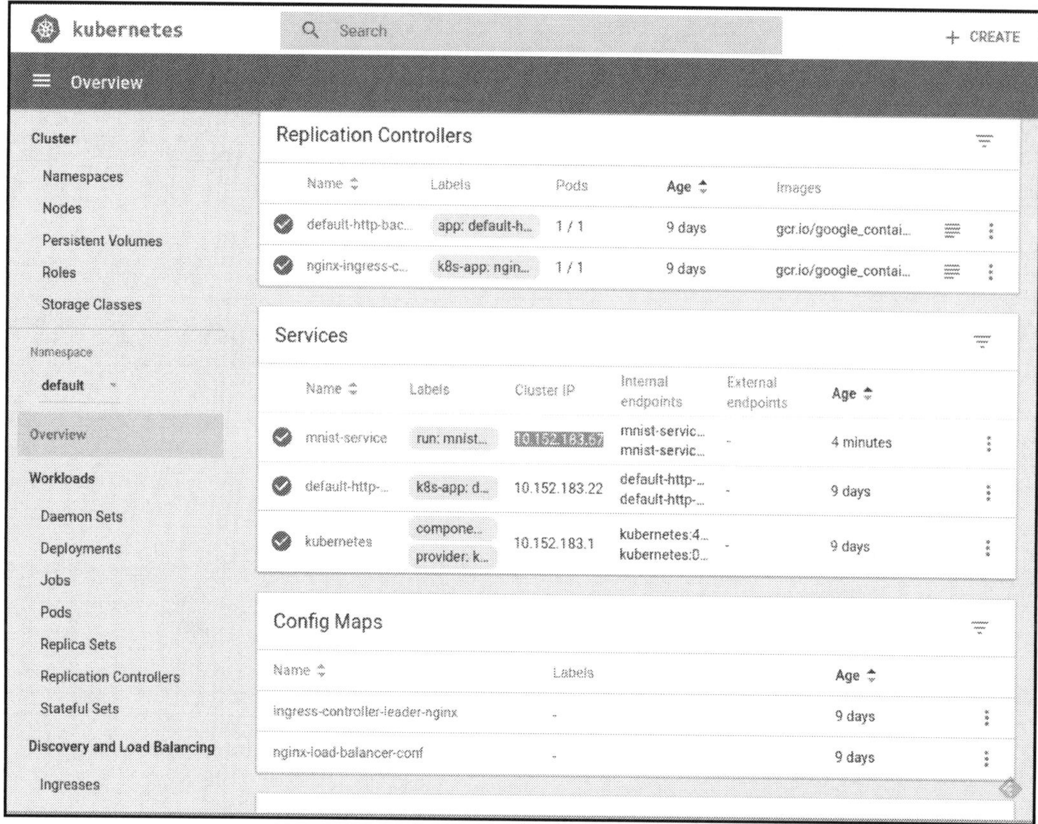

Since we are running the cluster locally on single Node, thus our service is only exposed within the cluster and cannot be accessed from outside. Log in to one of the three pods that we just instantiated:

```
$ kubectl exec -it mnist-deployment-59dfc5df64-bb24q -- /bin/bash
```

Change to the home directory and run the MNIST client to test the service:

```
$ kubectl exec -it mnist-deployment-59dfc5df64-bb24q -- /bin/bash
root@mnist-deployment-59dfc5df64-bb24q:/# cd
root@mnist-deployment-59dfc5df64-bb24q:~# python
serving/tensorflow_serving/example/mnist_client.py --num_tests=100 --
server=10.152.183.67:8500
Extracting /tmp/train-images-idx3-ubyte.gz
Extracting /tmp/train-labels-idx1-ubyte.gz
Extracting /tmp/t10k-images-idx3-ubyte.gz
Extracting /tmp/t10k-labels-idx1-ubyte.gz
....................................................................
```

```
..............................
Inference error rate: 7.0%
root@mnist-deployment-59dfc5df64-bb24q:~#
```

We learned how to deploy TensorFlow serving on the Kubernetes cluster running on single node locally. You can use the same conceptual knowledge to deploy the serving across the public clouds or private clouds on your premises.

Summary

In this chapter, we learned how to leverage the TensorFlow Serving to serve the models in production environments. We also learned how to save and restore full models or selective models using both TensorFlow and Keras. We built a Docker container and served the sample MNIST example code in the Docker container from the official TensorFlow Serving repository. We also installed a local Kubernetes cluster and deployed the MNIST model to serve from TensorFlow Serving running in Kubernetes pods. We encourage the reader to build upon these examples and try out serving different models. TF Serving documentation describes various options and provides additional information enabling you to explore this topic further.

15
Deep Reinforcement Learning

Reinforcement learning is a form of learning in which a software agent observes the environment and takes actions so as to maximize its rewards from the environment, as depicted in the following diagram:

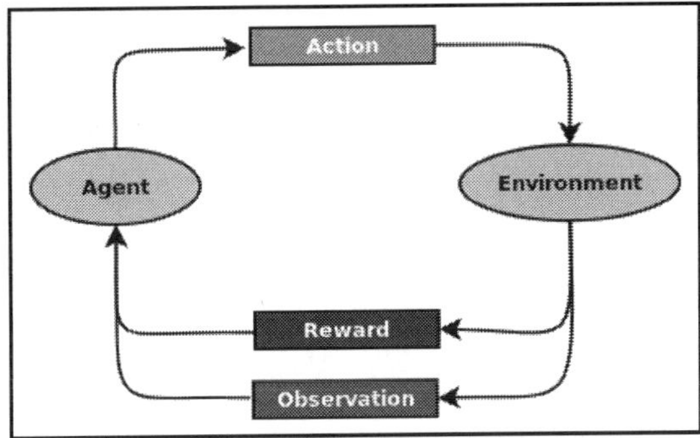

This metaphor can be used to represent real-life situations such as the following:

- A stock trading agent observes the trade information, news, analysis, and other form information, and takes actions to buy or sell trades so as to maximize the reward in the form of short-term profit or long-term profit.
- An insurance agent observes the information about the customer and then takes action to define the amount of insurance premium, so as to maximize the profit and minimize the risk.
- A humanoid robot observes the environment and then takes action, such as walking, running, or picking up objects, so as to maximize the reward in terms of the goal achieved.

Reinforcement learning has been successfully applied to many applications such as advertising optimization, stock market trading, self-driving vehicles, robotics, and games, to name a few.

Reinforcement learning is different from supervised learning in the sense that there are no labels in advance to tune the parameters of the model. The model learns from the rewards received from the runs. Although the short-term rewards are available instantly, long-term rewards are only available after a couple of steps. This phenomenon is also known as **delayed feedback**.

Reinforcement learning is also different from unsupervised learning because in unsupervised learning there are no labels available, whereas in reinforcement learning the feedback is available in terms of the rewards.

In this chapter, we shall learn about reinforcement learning and its implementation in TensorFlow and Keras by covering the following topics:

- OpenAI Gym 101
- Applying simple policies to a cartpole game
- Reinforcement Learning 101
    - Q function
    - Exploration and exploitation
    - V function
    - RL techniques
- Simple neural network policy for RL
- Implementing Q-Learning
    - Initializing and discretizing for Q-Learning
    - Q-Learning with Q-Table
    - Deep Q networks: Q-Learning with Q-Network

We shall demonstrate our examples in OpenAI Gym, so let us first learn about OpenAI Gym.

OpenAI Gym 101

OpenAI Gym is a Python-based toolkit for the research and development of reinforcement learning algorithms. OpenAI Gym provides more than 700 opensource contributed environments at the time of writing. With OpenAI, you can also create your own environments. The biggest advantage is that OpenAI provides a unified interface for working with these environments, and takes care of running the simulation while you focus on the reinforcement learning algorithms.

The research paper describing OpenAI Gym is available at this link: `http://arxiv.org/abs/1606.01540`.

You can install OpenAI Gym using the following command:

```
pip3 install gym
```

If the above command does not work, then you can find further help with installation at the following link: `https://github.com/openai/gym#installation`.

1. Let us print the number of available environments in OpenAI Gym:

You can follow along with the code in the Jupyter notebook `ch-13a_Reinforcement_Learning_NN` in the code bundle of this book.

```
all_env = list(gym.envs.registry.all())
print('Total Environments in Gym version {} : {}'
    .format(gym.__version__,len(all_env)))

Total Environments in Gym version 0.9.4 : 777
```

2. Let us print the list of all environments:

```
for e in list(all_env):
    print(e)
```

The partial list from the output is as follows:

```
EnvSpec(Carnival-ramNoFrameskip-v0)
EnvSpec(EnduroDeterministic-v0)
EnvSpec(FrostbiteNoFrameskip-v4)
EnvSpec(Taxi-v2)
EnvSpec(Pooyan-ram-v0)
EnvSpec(Solaris-ram-v4)
EnvSpec(Breakout-ramDeterministic-v0)
EnvSpec(Kangaroo-ram-v4)
EnvSpec(StarGunner-ram-v4)
EnvSpec(Enduro-ramNoFrameskip-v4)
EnvSpec(DemonAttack-ramDeterministic-v0)
EnvSpec(TimePilot-ramNoFrameskip-v0)
EnvSpec(Amidar-v4)
```

Each environment, represented by the `env` object, has a standardized interface, for example:

- An `env` object can be created with the `env.make(<game-id-string>)` function by passing the id string.
- Each `env` object contains the following main functions:
    - The `step()` function takes an action object as an argument and returns four objects:
        - *observation*: An object implemented by the environment, representing the observation of the environment.
        - *reward*: A signed float value indicating the gain (or loss) from the previous action.
        - *done*: A Boolean value representing if the scenario is finished.
        - *info*: A Python dictionary object representing the diagnostic information.
    - The `render()` function creates a visual representation of the environment.
    - The `reset()` function resets the environment to the original state.
- Each `env` object comes with well-defined actions and observations, represented by `action_space` and `observation_space`.

One of the most popular games in the gym to learn reinforcement learning is CartPole. In this game, a pole attached to a cart has to be balanced so that it doesn't fall. The game ends if either the pole tilts by more than 15 degrees or the cart moves by more than 2.4 units from the center. The home page of `OpenAI.com` emphasizes the game in these words:

> *The small size and simplicity of this environment make it possible to run very quick experiments, which is essential when learning the basics.*

The game has only four observations and two actions. The actions are to move a cart by applying a force of +1 or -1. The observations are the position of the cart, the velocity of the cart, the angle of the pole, and the rotation rate of the pole. However, knowledge of the semantics of observation is not necessary to learn to maximize the rewards of the game.

Now let us load a popular game environment, CartPole-v0, and play it with stochastic control:

1. Create the `env` object with the standard `make` function:

   ```
   env = gym.make('CartPole-v0')
   ```

2. The number of episodes is the number of game plays. We shall set it to one, for now, indicating that we just want to play the game once. Since every episode is stochastic, in actual production runs you will run over several episodes and calculate the average values of the rewards. Additionally, we can initialize an array to store the visualization of the environment at every timestep:

   ```
   n_episodes = 1
   env_vis = []
   ```

3. Run two nested loops—an external loop for the number of episodes and an internal loop for the number of timesteps you would like to simulate for. You can either keep running the internal loop until the scenario is done or set the number of steps to a higher value.
   - At the beginning of every episode, reset the environment using `env.reset()`.
   - At the beginning of every timestep, capture the visualization using `env.render()`.

   ```
   for i_episode in range(n_episodes):
       observation = env.reset()
       for t in range(100):
   ```

```
        env_vis.append(env.render(mode = 'rgb_array'))
        print(observation)
        action = env.action_space.sample()
        observation, reward, done, info = env.step(action)
        if done:
            print("Episode finished at t{}".format(t+1))
            break
```

4. Render the environment using the helper function:

```
env_render(env_vis)
```

5. The code for the helper function is as follows:

```
def env_render(env_vis):
    plt.figure()
    plot = plt.imshow(env_vis[0])
    plt.axis('off')
    def animate(i):
        plot.set_data(env_vis[i])

    anim = anm.FuncAnimation(plt.gcf(),
                             animate,
                             frames=len(env_vis),
                             interval=20,
                             repeat=True,
                             repeat_delay=20)
    display(display_animation(anim, default_mode='loop'))
```

We get the following output when we run this example:

```
[-0.00666995 -0.03699492 -0.00972623  0.00287713]
[-0.00740985  0.15826516 -0.00966868 -0.29285861]
[-0.00424454 -0.03671761 -0.01552586 -0.00324067]
[-0.0049789  -0.2316135  -0.01559067  0.28450351]
[-0.00961117 -0.42650966 -0.0099006   0.57222875]
[-0.01814136 -0.23125029  0.00154398  0.27644332]
[-0.02276636 -0.0361504   0.00707284 -0.01575223]
[-0.02348937  0.1588694   0.0067578  -0.30619523]
[-0.02031198 -0.03634819  0.00063389 -0.01138875]
[-0.02103895  0.15876466  0.00040612 -0.3038716 ]
[-0.01786366  0.35388083 -0.00567131 -0.59642642]
[-0.01078604  0.54908168 -0.01759984 -0.89089036]
[  1.95594914e-04   7.44437934e-01  -3.54176495e-02  -1.18905344e+00]
[ 0.01508435  0.54979251 -0.05919872 -0.90767902]
[ 0.0260802   0.35551978 -0.0773523  -0.63417465]
[ 0.0331906   0.55163065 -0.09003579 -0.95018025]
[ 0.04422321  0.74784161 -0.1090394  -1.26973934]
```

```
[ 0.05918004  0.55426764 -0.13443418 -1.01309691]
[ 0.0702654   0.36117014 -0.15469612 -0.76546874]
[ 0.0774888   0.16847818 -0.1700055  -0.52518186]
[ 0.08085836  0.3655333  -0.18050913 -0.86624457]
[ 0.08816903  0.56259197 -0.19783403 -1.20981195]
Episode finished at t22
```

It took 22 time-steps for the pole to become unbalanced. At every run, we get a different time-step value because we picked the action scholastically by using `env.action_space.sample()`.

Since the game results in a loss so quickly, randomly picking an action and applying it is probably not the best strategy. There are many algorithms for finding solutions to keeping the pole straight for a longer number of time-steps that you can use, such as Hill Climbing, Random Search, and Policy Gradient.

Some of the algorithms for solving the Cartpole game are available at the following links:
`https://openai.com/requests-for-research/#cartpole`
`http://kvfrans.com/simple-algoritms-for-solving-cartpole/`
`https://github.com/kvfrans/openai-cartpole`

Applying simple policies to a cartpole game

So far, we have randomly picked an action and applied it. Now let us apply some logic to picking the action instead of random chance. The third observation refers to the angle. If the angle is greater than zero, that means the pole is tilting right, thus we move the cart to the right (1). Otherwise, we move the cart to the left (0). Let us look at an example:

1. We define two policy functions as follows:

```
def policy_logic(env,obs):
    return 1 if obs[2] > 0 else 0
def policy_random(env,obs):
    return env.action_space.sample()
```

2. Next, we define an experiment function that will run for a specific number of episodes; each episode runs until the game is lost, namely when `done` is `True`. We use `rewards_max` to indicate when to break out of the loop as we do not wish to run the experiment forever:

    ```
    def experiment(policy, n_episodes, rewards_max):
        rewards=np.empty(shape=(n_episodes))
        env = gym.make('CartPole-v0')
        for i in range(n_episodes):
            obs = env.reset()
            done = False
            episode_reward = 0
            while not done:
                action = policy(env,obs)
                obs, reward, done, info = env.step(action)
                episode_reward += reward
                if episode_reward > rewards_max:
                    break
            rewards[i]=episode_reward
        print('Policy:{}, Min reward:{}, Max reward:{}'
              .format(policy.__name__,
                      min(rewards),
                      max(rewards)))
    ```

3. We run the experiment 100 times, or until the rewards are less than or equal to `rewards_max`, that is set to 10,000:

    ```
    n_episodes = 100
    rewards_max = 10000
    experiment(policy_random, n_episodes, rewards_max)
    experiment(policy_logic, n_episodes, rewards_max)
    ```

We can see that the logically selected actions do better than the randomly selected ones, but not that much better:

```
Policy:policy_random, Min reward:9.0, Max reward:63.0, Average
reward:20.26
Policy:policy_logic, Min reward:24.0, Max reward:66.0, Average
reward:42.81
```

Now let us modify the process of selecting the action further—to be based on parameters. The parameters will be multiplied by the observations and the action will be chosen based on whether the multiplication result is zero or one. Let us modify the random search method in which we initialize the parameters randomly. The code looks as follows:

```
def policy_logic(theta,obs):
```

```
    # just ignore theta
    return 1 if obs[2] > 0 else 0

def policy_random(theta,obs):
    return 0 if np.matmul(theta,obs) < 0 else 1

def episode(env, policy, rewards_max):
    obs = env.reset()
    done = False
    episode_reward = 0
    if policy.__name__ in ['policy_random']:
        theta = np.random.rand(4) * 2 - 1
    else:
        theta = None
    while not done:
        action = policy(theta,obs)
        obs, reward, done, info = env.step(action)
        episode_reward += reward
        if episode_reward > rewards_max:
            break
    return episode_reward
def experiment(policy, n_episodes, rewards_max):
    rewards=np.empty(shape=(n_episodes))
    env = gym.make('CartPole-v0')
    for i in range(n_episodes):
        rewards[i]=episode(env,policy,rewards_max)
        #print("Episode finished at t{}".format(reward))
    print('Policy:{}, Min reward:{}, Max reward:{}, Average reward:{}'
          .format(policy.__name__,
                  np.min(rewards),
                  np.max(rewards),
                  np.mean(rewards)))

n_episodes = 100
rewards_max = 10000
experiment(policy_random, n_episodes, rewards_max)
experiment(policy_logic, n_episodes, rewards_max)
```

We can see that random search does improve the results:

```
Policy:policy_random, Min reward:8.0, Max reward:200.0, Average
reward:40.04
Policy:policy_logic, Min reward:25.0, Max reward:62.0, Average
reward:43.03
```

With the random search, we have improved our results to get the max rewards of 200. On average, the rewards for random search are lower because random search tries various bad parameters that bring the overall results down. However, we can select the best parameters from all the runs and then, in production, use the best parameters. Let us modify the code to train the parameters first:

```
def policy_logic(theta,obs):
    # just ignore theta
    return 1 if obs[2] > 0 else 0

def policy_random(theta,obs):
    return 0 if np.matmul(theta,obs) < 0 else 1

def episode(env,policy, rewards_max,theta):
    obs = env.reset()
    done = False
    episode_reward = 0

    while not done:
        action = policy(theta,obs)
        obs, reward, done, info = env.step(action)
        episode_reward += reward
        if episode_reward > rewards_max:
            break
    return episode_reward

def train(policy, n_episodes, rewards_max):

    env = gym.make('CartPole-v0')
    theta_best = np.empty(shape=[4])
    reward_best = 0

    for i in range(n_episodes):
        if policy.__name__ in ['policy_random']:
            theta = np.random.rand(4) * 2 - 1
        else:
            theta = None
        reward_episode=episode(env,policy,rewards_max, theta)
        if reward_episode > reward_best:
            reward_best = reward_episode
            theta_best = theta.copy()
    return reward_best,theta_best
def experiment(policy, n_episodes, rewards_max, theta=None):
    rewards=np.empty(shape=[n_episodes])
    env = gym.make('CartPole-v0')
    for i in range(n_episodes):
        rewards[i]=episode(env,policy,rewards_max,theta)
```

```
        #print("Episode finished at t{}".format(reward))
    print('Policy:{}, Min reward:{}, Max reward:{}, Average reward:{}'
          .format(policy.__name__,
                  np.min(rewards),
                  np.max(rewards),
                  np.mean(rewards)))

n_episodes = 100
rewards_max = 10000

reward,theta = train(policy_random, n_episodes, rewards_max)
print('trained theta: {}, rewards: {}'.format(theta,reward))
experiment(policy_random, n_episodes, rewards_max, theta)
experiment(policy_logic, n_episodes, rewards_max)
```

We train for 100 episodes and then use the best parameters to run the experiment for the random search policy:

```
n_episodes = 100
rewards_max = 10000

reward,theta = train(policy_random, n_episodes, rewards_max)
print('trained theta: {}, rewards: {}'.format(theta,reward))
experiment(policy_random, n_episodes, rewards_max, theta)
experiment(policy_logic, n_episodes, rewards_max)
```

We find the that the training parameters gives us the best results of 200:

```
trained theta: [-0.14779543  0.93269603  0.70896423  0.84632461],
rewards: 200.0
Policy:policy_random, Min reward:200.0, Max reward:200.0, Average
reward:200.0
Policy:policy_logic, Min reward:24.0, Max reward:63.0, Average
reward:41.94
```

We may optimize the training code to continue training until we reach a maximum reward. The code for this optimization is provided in the notebook `ch-13a_Reinforcement_Learning_NN`.

Now that we have learned the basics of OpenAI Gym, let us learn about reinforcement learning.

Reinforcement learning 101

Reinforcement learning is described by an agent getting inputs of the *observation* and *reward* from the previous time-step and producing output as an *action* with the goal of maximizing cumulative rewards.

The agent has a policy, value function, and model:

- The algorithm used by the agent to pick the next action is known as the **policy**. In the previous section, we wrote a policy that would take a set of parameters theta and would return the next action based on the multiplication between the observation and the parameters. The policy is represented by the following equation:
  $\pi(s) : S \rightarrow A$,
  S is set of states and A is set of actions.
- A policy is deterministic or stochastic.
    - A deterministic policy returns the same action for the same state in each run:
      $\pi(s) = a$
    - A stochastic policy returns the different probabilities for the same action for the same state in each run:
      $\pi(a|s) = P(A = a|S = s)$
- The **value function** predicts the amount of long-term reward based on the selected action in the current state. Thus, the value function is specific to the policy used by the agent. The reward indicates the immediate gain from the action while the value function indicates the cumulative or long-term future gain from the action. The reward is returned by the environment and the value function is estimated by the agent at every time-step.
- The **model** is a representation of the environment kept internally by the agent. The model could be an imperfect representation of the environment. The agent uses the model to estimate the reward and the next state from the selected action.

The goal of an agent can also be to find the optimal policy for the Markovian Decision Process (MDP). MDP is a mathematical representation of the observations, actions, rewards, and transitions from one state to another. We will omit the discussion of MDP for the sake of brevity and advise the curious reader to search for resources on the internet for diving deeper into MDP.

Q function (learning to optimize when the model is not available)

If the model is not available then the agent learns the model and optimal policy by trial and error. When the model is not available, the agent uses a Q function, which is defined as follows:

$$Q : S \times A \to \mathbb{R}$$

The Q function basically maps the pairs of states and actions to a real number that denotes the expected total reward if the agent at state s selects an action a.

Exploration and exploitation in the RL algorithms

In the absence of a model, at every step the agent either explores or exploits. **Exploration** means that the agent selects an unknown action to find out the reward and the model. **Exploitation** means that the agent selects the best-known action to get the maximum reward. If the agent always decides to exploit then it might get stuck in a local optimal value. Hence, sometimes the agent takes a detour from learned policy to explore unknown actions. Similarly, if an agent always decides to explore then it may fail to find an optimal policy. Thus, it is important to have a balance of exploration and exploitation. In our code, we implement this by using a probability p to select a random action and probability $1-p$ to select the optimal action.

V function (learning to optimize when the model is available)

If the model is known beforehand then the agent can perform a **policy search** to find the optimal policy that maximizes the value function. When the model is available, the agent uses a value function that can be defined naively as a sum of the rewards of the future states:

$$V^{\pi}(s) = \sum_{i} R_i \quad \forall s \in S$$

Thus, the value at time-step t for selecting actions using the policy p would be:

$$V_t^{\pi} = R_t + R_{t+1} + \ldots + R_{t+n}$$

V is the value and R is the reward, and the value function is estimated only up to n time-steps in the future.

When the agent estimates the reward with this approach, it treats that reward as a result of all actions equally. In the pole cart example, if the poll falls at step 50, it will treat all the steps up to the 50th step as being equally responsible for the fall. Hence, instead of adding the future rewards, the weighted sum of future rewards is estimated. Usually, the weights are a discount rate raised to the power of the time-step. If the discount rate is zero then the value function becomes the naive function discussed above, and if the value of the discount rate is close to one, such as 0.9 or 0.92, then the future rewards have less effect when compared to the current rewards.

Thus, now the value at time-step t for action a would be:

$$V_t^{\pi} = R_t + r \times R_{t+1} = R_t + rR_{t+1} + r^2 R_{t+2} + \ldots + r^n R_{t+n}$$

V is the value, R is the rewards, and r is the discount rate.

The relationship between the V function and the Q function:

V*(s) is the optimal value function at state s that gives the maximum reward, and Q*(s,a) is the optimal Q function at state s that gives the maximum expected reward by selecting action a. Thus, V*(s) is the maximum of all optimal Q functions Q*(s,a) over all possible actions:

$$V^*(s) = \max_a Q^*(s,a) \quad \forall s \in S$$

Reinforcement learning techniques

Reinforcement learning techniques can be categorized on the basis of the availability of the model as follows:

- **Model is available**: If the model is available then the agent can plan offline by iterating over policies or the value function to find the optimal policy that gives the maximum reward.
    - **Value-iteration learning**: In the value-iteration learning approach, the agent starts by initializing the *V(s)* to a random value and then repeatedly updates the *V(s)* until a maximum reward is found.
    - **Policy-iterative learning**: In the policy-iteration learning approach, the agent starts by initializing a random policy *p*, and then repeatedly updates the policy until a maximum reward is found.
- **Model is not available**: If the model is not available, then an agent can only learn by observing the results of its actions. Thus, from the history of observations, actions, and rewards, an agent either tries to estimate the model or tries to directly derive the optimal policy:
    - **Model-based learning**: In model-based learning, the agent first estimates the model from the history, and then uses a policy or value-based approach to find the optimal policy.
    - **Model-free learning**: In model-free learning, the agent does not estimate the model, but rather estimates the optimal policy directly from the history. Q-Learning is an example of model-free learning.

As an example, the algorithm for the value-iteration learning is as follows:

```
initialize V(s) to random values for all states
Repeat
    for s in states
        for a in actions
            compute Q[s,a]
        V(s) = max(Q[s])    # maximum of Q for all actions for that
state
Until optimal value of V(s) is found for all states
```

The algorithm for the policy-iteration learning is as follows:

```
initialize a policy P_new to random sequence of actions for all states
Repeat
    P = P_new
    for s in states
        compute V(s) with P[s]
        P_new[s] = policy of optimal V(s)
Until P == P_new
```

Naive Neural Network policy for Reinforcement Learning

We proceed with the policy as follows:

1. Let us implement a naive neural network-based policy. Define a new policy to use the neural network based predictions to return the actions:

```
def policy_naive_nn(nn,obs):
    return np.argmax(nn.predict(np.array([obs])))
```

2. Define nn as a simple one layer MLP network that takes the observations having four dimensions as input, and produces the probabilities of the two actions:

```
from keras.models import Sequential
from keras.layers import Dense
model = Sequential()
model.add(Dense(8,input_dim=4, activation='relu'))
model.add(Dense(2, activation='softmax'))
model.compile(loss='categorical_crossentropy',optimizer='adam'
)
model.summary()
```

This is what the model looks like:

```
Layer (type)                 Output Shape              Param #
=================================================================
dense_16 (Dense)             (None, 8)                 40
_________________________________________________________________
dense_17 (Dense)             (None, 2)                 18
=================================================================
Total params: 58
Trainable params: 58
Non-trainable params: 0
```

3. This model needs to be trained. Run the simulation for 100 episodes and collect the training data only for those episodes where the score is more than 100. If the score is less then 100, then those states and actions are not worth recording since they are not examples of good play:

```
# create training data
env = gym.make('CartPole-v0')
n_obs = 4
n_actions = 2
theta = np.random.rand(4) * 2 - 1
n_episodes = 100
r_max = 0
t_max = 0

x_train, y_train = experiment(env,
                              policy_random,
                              n_episodes,
                              theta,r_max,t_max,
                              return_hist_reward=100 )
y_train = np.eye(n_actions)[y_train]
print(x_train.shape,y_train.shape)
```

We are able to collect 5732 samples for training:

```
(5732, 4) (5732, 2)
```

4. Next, train the model:

```
model.fit(x_train, y_train, epochs=50, batch_size=10)
```

5. The trained model can be used to play the game. However, the model will not learn from the further plays of the game until we incorporate a loop updating the training data:

```
n_episodes = 200
r_max = 0
```

```
t_max = 0

_ = experiment(env,
               policy_naive_nn,
               n_episodes,
               theta=model,
               r_max=r_max,
               t_max=t_max,
               return_hist_reward=0 )

_ = experiment(env,
               policy_random,
               n_episodes,
               theta,r_max,t_max,
               return_hist_reward=0 )
```

We can see that this naive policy performs almost in the same way, albeit a little better than the random policy:

```
Policy:policy_naive_nn, Min reward:37.0, Max reward:200.0, Average
reward:71.05
Policy:policy_random, Min reward:36.0, Max reward:200.0, Average
reward:68.755
```

We can improve the results further with network tuning and hyper-parameters tuning, or by learning from more gameplay. However, there are better algorithms, such as Q-Learning.

In the rest of this chapter, we shall focus on the Q-Learning algorithm since most real-life problems involve model-free learning.

Implementing Q-Learning

Q-Learning is a model-free method of finding the optimal policy that can maximize the reward of an agent. During initial gameplay, the agent learns a Q value for each pair of (state, action), also known as the exploration strategy, as explained in previous sections. Once the Q values are learned, then the optimal policy will be to select an action with the largest Q-value in every state, also known as the exploitation strategy. The learning algorithm may end in locally optimal solutions, hence we keep using the exploration policy by setting an `exploration_rate` parameter.

The Q-Learning algorithm is as follows:

```
initialize Q(shape=[#s,#a]) to random values or zeroes
Repeat (for each episode)
    observe current state s
    Repeat
        select an action a (apply explore or exploit strategy)
        observe state s_next as a result of action a
        update the Q-Table using bellman's equation
        set current state s = s_next
    until the episode ends or a max reward / max steps condition is
reached
Until a number of episodes or a condition is reached
        (such as max consecutive wins)
```

The *Q(s, a)* in the preceding algorithm represents the Q function that we described in the previous sections. The values of this functions are used for selecting the action instead of the rewards, thus this function represents the reward or discounted rewards. The values for the Q-function are updated using the values of the Q function in the future state. The well-known *bellman equation* captures this update:

$$Q(s_t, a_t) = r_t + \gamma \max_a Q(s_{t+1}, a)$$

This basically means that at time step t, in state s, for action a, the maximum future reward (Q) is equal to the reward from the current state plus the max future reward from the next state.

Q(s,a) can be implemented as a Q-Table or as a neural network known as a Q-Network. In both cases, the task of the Q-Table or the Q-Network is to provide the best possible action based on the Q value of the given input. The Q-Table-based approach generally becomes intractable as the Q-Table becomes large, thus making neural networks the best candidate for approximating the Q-function through Q-Network. Let us look at both of these approaches in action.

You can follow along with the code in the Jupyter notebook `ch-13b_Reinforcement_Learning_DQN` in the code bundle of this book.

Initializing and discretizing for Q-Learning

The observations returned by the pole-cart environment involves the state of the environment. The state of pole-cart is represented by continuous values that we need to discretize.

If we discretize these values into small state-space, then the agent gets trained faster, but with the caveat of risking the convergence to the optimal policy.

We use the following helper function to discretize the state-space of the pole-cart environment:

```
# discretize the value to a state space
def discretize(val,bounds,n_states):
    discrete_val = 0
    if val <= bounds[0]:
        discrete_val = 0
    elif val >= bounds[1]:
        discrete_val = n_states-1
    else:
        discrete_val = int(round( (n_states-1) *
                                  ((val-bounds[0])/
                                   (bounds[1]-bounds[0]))
                                ))
    return discrete_val

def discretize_state(vals,s_bounds,n_s):
    discrete_vals = []
    for i in range(len(n_s)):
        discrete_vals.append(discretize(vals[i],s_bounds[i],n_s[i]))
    return np.array(discrete_vals,dtype=np.int)
```

We discretize the space into 10 units for each of the observation dimensions. You may want to try out different discretization spaces. After the discretization, we find the upper and lower bounds of the observations, and change the bounds of velocity and angular velocity to be between -1 and +1, instead of -Inf and +Inf. The code is as follows:

```
env = gym.make('CartPole-v0')
n_a = env.action_space.n
# number of discrete states for each observation dimension
n_s = np.array([10,10,10,10])   # position, velocity, angle, angular
velocity
s_bounds = np.array(list(zip(env.observation_space.low,
env.observation_space.high)))
# the velocity and angular velocity bounds are
# too high so we bound between -1, +1
```

```
s_bounds[1] = (-1.0,1.0)
s_bounds[3] = (-1.0,1.0)
```

Q-Learning with Q-Table

You may follow the code for this section in `ch-13b.ipynb`. Since our discretised space is of the dimensions [10,10,10,10], our Q-Table is of [10,10,10,10,2] dimensions:

```
# create a Q-Table of shape (10,10,10,10, 2) representing S X A -> R
q_table = np.zeros(shape = np.append(n_s,n_a))
```

We define a Q-Table policy that exploits or explores based on the `exploration_rate`:

```
def policy_q_table(state, env):
    # Exploration strategy - Select a random action
    if np.random.random() < explore_rate:
        action = env.action_space.sample()
    # Exploitation strategy - Select the action with the highest q
    else:
        action = np.argmax(q_table[tuple(state)])
    return action
```

Define the `episode()` function that runs a single episode as follows:

1. Start with initializing the variables and the first state:

    ```
    obs = env.reset()
    state_prev = discretize_state(obs,s_bounds,n_s)

    episode_reward = 0
    done = False
    t = 0
    ```

2. Select the action and observe the next state:

    ```
    action = policy(state_prev, env)
    obs, reward, done, info = env.step(action)
    state_new = discretize_state(obs,s_bounds,n_s)
    ```

3. Update the Q-Table:

```
best_q = np.amax(q_table[tuple(state_new)])
bellman_q = reward + discount_rate * best_q
indices = tuple(np.append(state_prev,action))
q_table[indices] += learning_rate*( bellman_q -
q_table[indices])
```

4. Set the next state as the previous state and add the rewards to the episode's rewards:

```
state_prev = state_new
episode_reward += reward
```

The `experiment()` function calls the episode function and accumulates the rewards for reporting. You may want to modify the function to check for consecutive wins and other logic specific to your play or games:

```
# collect observations and rewards for each episode
def experiment(env, policy, n_episodes,r_max=0, t_max=0):
    rewards=np.empty(shape=[n_episodes])
    for i in range(n_episodes):
        val = episode(env, policy, r_max, t_max)
        rewards[i]=val
    print('Policy:{}, Min reward:{}, Max reward:{}, Average reward:{}'
      .format(policy.__name__,
              np.min(rewards),
              np.max(rewards),
              np.mean(rewards)))
```

Now, all we have to do is define the parameters, such as `learning_rate`, `discount_rate`, and `explore_rate`, and run the `experiment()` function as follows:

```
learning_rate = 0.8
discount_rate = 0.9
explore_rate = 0.2
n_episodes = 1000
experiment(env, policy_q_table, n_episodes)
```

For 1000 episodes, the Q-Table-based policy's maximum reward is 180 based on our simple implementation:

```
Policy:policy_q_table, Min reward:8.0, Max reward:180.0, Average
reward:17.592
```

Our implementation of the algorithm is very simple to explain. However, you can modify the code to set the explore rate high initially and then decay as the time-steps pass. Similarly, you can also implement the decay logic for the learning and discount rates. Let us see if we can get a higher reward with fewer episodes as our Q function learns faster.

Q-Learning with Q-Network or Deep Q Network (DQN)

In the DQN, we replace the Q-Table with a neural network (Q-Network) that will learn to respond with the optimal action as we train it continuously with the explored states and their Q-Values. Thus, for training the network we need a place to store the game memory:

1. Implement the game memory using a deque of size 1000:

```
memory = deque(maxlen=1000)
```

2. Next, build a simple hidden layer neural network model, `q_nn`:

```
from keras.models import Sequential
from keras.layers import Dense
model = Sequential()
model.add(Dense(8,input_dim=4, activation='relu'))
model.add(Dense(2, activation='linear'))
model.compile(loss='mse',optimizer='adam')
model.summary()
q_nn = model
```

The Q-Network looks like this:

```
_________________________________________________________________
Layer (type)                 Output Shape              Param #
=================================================================
dense_1 (Dense)              (None, 8)                 40
_________________________________________________________________
dense_2 (Dense)              (None, 2)                 18
=================================================================
```

```
Total params: 58
Trainable params: 58
Non-trainable params: 0
_________________________________________________________________
```

The `episode()` function that executes one episode of the game, incorporates the following changes for the Q-Network-based algorithm:

1. After generating the next state, add the states, action, and rewards to the game memory:

    ```
    action = policy(state_prev, env)
    obs, reward, done, info = env.step(action)
    state_next = discretize_state(obs,s_bounds,n_s)
    # add the state_prev, action, reward, state_new, done to
    memory
    memory.append([state_prev,action,reward,state_next,done])
    ```

2. Generate and update the `q_values` with the maximum future rewards using the bellman function:

    ```
    states = np.array([x[0] for x in memory])
    states_next = np.array([np.zeros(4) if x[4] else x[3] for x in
    memory])
    q_values = q_nn.predict(states)
    q_values_next = q_nn.predict(states_next)

    for i in range(len(memory)):
        state_prev,action,reward,state_next,done = memory[i]
        if done:
            q_values[i,action] = reward
        else:
            best_q = np.amax(q_values_next[i])
            bellman_q = reward + discount_rate * best_q
            q_values[i,action] = bellman_q
    ```

3. Train the `q_nn` with the states and the `q_values` we received from memory:

    ```
    q_nn.fit(states,q_values,epochs=1,batch_size=50,verbose=0)
    ```

The process of saving gameplay in memory and using it to train the model is also known as **memory replay** in deep reinforcement learning literature. Let us run our DQN-based gameplay as follows:

```
learning_rate = 0.8
discount_rate = 0.9
explore_rate = 0.2
n_episodes = 100
experiment(env, policy_q_nn, n_episodes)
```

We get a max reward of 150 that you can improve upon with hyper-parameter tuning, network tuning, and by using rate decay for the discount rate and explore rate:

```
Policy:policy_q_nn, Min reward:8.0, Max reward:150.0, Average
reward:41.27
```

We calculated and trained the model in every step; you may want to explore changing it to training after the episode. Also, you can change the code to discard the memory replay and retraining the model for the episodes that return smaller rewards. However, implement this option with caution as it may slow down your learning as initial gameplay would generate smaller rewards more often.

Summary

In this chapter, we learned how to implement reinforcement learning algorithms in Keras. For the sake of keeping the examples simple, we used Keras; you can implement the same networks and models with TensorFlow as well. We only used a one-layer MLP, as our example game was very simple, but for complex examples, you may end up using complex CNN, RNN, or Sequence to Sequence models.

We also learned about OpenAI Gym, a framework that provides an environment to simulate many popular games in order to implement and practice the reinforcement learning algorithms. We touched on deep reinforcement learning concepts, and we encourage you to explore books specifically written about reinforcement learning to learn deeply about the theories and concepts.

Reinforcement Learning is an advanced technique that you will find is often used for solving complex problems. In the next chapter, we shall learn another family of advanced deep learning techniques: Generative Adversarial Networks.

16

Generative Adversarial Networks

Generative models are trained to generate more data similar to the one they are trained on, and adversarial models are trained to distinguish the real versus fake data by providing adversarial examples.

The **Generative Adversarial Networks** (**GAN**) combine the features of both the models. The GANs have two components:

- A generative model that learns how to generate similar data
- A discriminative model that learns how to distinguish between the real and generated data (from the generative model)

GANs have been successfully applied to various complex problems such as:

- Generating photo-realistic resolution images from low-resolution images
- Synthesizing images from the text
- Style transfer
- Completing the incomplete images and videos

In this chapter, we shall study the following topics for learning how to implement GANs in TensorFlow and Keras:

- Generative Adversarial Networks
- Simple GAN in TensorFlow
- Simple GAN in Keras
- Deep Convolutional GAN with TensorFlow and Keras

Generative Adversarial Networks 101

As shown in the following diagram, the Generative Adversarial Networks, popularly known as GANs, have two models working in sync to learn and train on complex data such as images, videos or audio files:

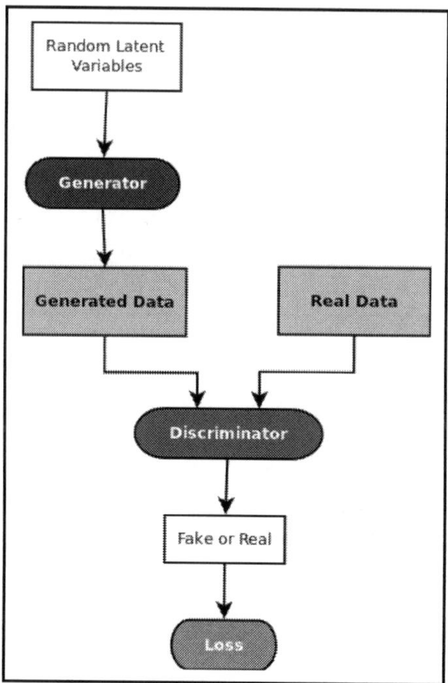

Intuitively, the generator model generates data starting from random noise but slowly learns how to generate more realistic data. The generator output and the real data is fed into the discriminator that learns how to differentiate fake data from real data.

Thus, both generator and discriminator play an adversarial game where the generator tries to fool the discriminator by generating as real data as possible, and the discriminator tries not to be fooled by identifying fake data from real data, thus the discriminator tries to minimize the classification loss. Both the models are trained in a lockstep fashion.

Mathematically, the generative model $G(z)$ learns the probability $p(z)$ distribution such that the discriminator $D(G(z), x)$ is unable to identify between the probability distributions, $p(z)$ and $p(x)$. The objective function of the GAN can be described by the following equation describing the value function *V*, (from `https://papers.nips.cc/paper/5423-generative-adversarial-nets.pdf`):

$$\min_G \max_D V(D,G) = E_{x \sim p_{data}(x)}[logD(x)] + E_{z \sim p_z(z)}[log(1 - D(G(z)))]$$

The seminal tutorial at NIPS 2016 on GANs by Ian Goodfellow can be found at thc following link: `https://arxiv.org/pdf/1701.00160.pdf`.

This description represents a simple GAN (also known as a vanilla GAN in literature), first introduced by Goodfellow in the seminal paper available at this link: `https://arxiv.org/abs/1406.2661`. Since then, there has been tremendous research in deriving different architectures based on GANs and applying them to different application areas.

For example, in conditional GANs the generator and the discriminator networks are provided with the labels such that the objective function of the conditional GAN can be described by the following equation describing the value function *V*:

$$\min_G \max_D V(D,G) = E_{x \sim p_{data}(x)}[logD(x)] + E_{z \sim p_z(z)}[log(1 - D(G(z,y),y))]$$

>

The original paper describing the conditional GANs is located at the following link: `https://arxiv.org/abs/1411.1784`.

Several other derivatives and their originating papers used in applications, such as Text to Image, Image Synthesis, Image Tagging, Style Transfer, and Image Transfer and so on are listed in the following table:

GAN Derivative	Originating Paper	Demonstrated Application
StackGAN	`https://arxiv.org/abs/1710.10916`	Text to Image
StackGAN++	`https://arxiv.org/abs/1612.03242`	Photo-realistic Image Synthesis
DCGAN	`https://arxiv.org/abs/1511.06434`	Image Synthesis
HR-DCGAN	`https://arxiv.org/abs/1711.06491`	High-Resolution Image Synthesis
Conditonal GAN	`https://arxiv.org/abs/1411.1784`	Image Tagging
InfoGAN	`https://arxiv.org/abs/1606.03657`	Style Identification

GAN Derivative	Originating Paper	Demonstrated Application
Wasserstein GAN	`https://arxiv.org/abs/1701.07875` `https://arxiv.org/abs/1704.00028`	Image Generation
Coupled GAN	`https://arxiv.org/abs/1606.07536`	Image Transformation, Domain Adaptation
BE GAN	`https://arxiv.org/abs/1703.10717`	Image Generation
DiscoGAN	`https://arxiv.org/abs/1703.05192`	Style Transfer
CycleGAN	`https://arxiv.org/abs/1703.10593`	Style Transfer

Let us practice creating a simple GAN using the MNIST dataset. For this exercise, we shall normalize the MNIST dataset to lie between [-1,+1], using the following function:

```
def norm(x):
    return (x-0.5)/0.5
```

We also define the random noise with 256 dimensions that would be used to test the generator models:

```
n_z = 256
z_test = np.random.uniform(-1.0,1.0,size=[8,n_z])
```

The function to display the generated images that would be used in all the examples in this chapter:

```
def display_images(images):
    for i in range(images.shape[0]):
        plt.subplot(1, 8, i + 1)
        plt.imshow(images[i])
        plt.axis('off')
    plt.tight_layout()
    plt.show()
```

Best practices for building and training GANs

For the dataset we selected for this demonstration, the discriminator was becoming very good at classifying the real and fake images, and therefore not providing much of the feedback in terms of gradients to the generator. Hence we had to make the discriminator weak with the following best practices:

- The learning rate of the discriminator is kept much higher than the learning rate of the generator.
- The optimizer for the discriminator is `GradientDescent` and the optimizer for the generator is `Adam`.
- The discriminator has dropout regularization while the generator does not.
- The discriminator has fewer layers and fewer neurons as compared to the generator.
- The output of the generator is `tanh` while the output of the discriminator is sigmoid.
- In the Keras model, we use a value of 0.9 instead of 1.0 for labels of real data and we use 0.1 instead of 0.0 for labels of fake data, in order to introduce a little bit of noise in the labels

You are welcome to explore and try other best practices.

Simple GAN with TensorFlow

You can follow along with the code in the Jupyter notebook `ch-14a_SimpleGAN`.

For building the GAN with TensorFlow, we build three networks, two discriminator models, and one generator model with the following steps:

1. Start by adding the hyper-parameters for defining the network:

```
# graph hyperparameters
g_learning_rate = 0.00001
d_learning_rate = 0.01
n_x = 784  # number of pixels in the MNIST image
```

```
# number of hidden layers for generator and discriminator
g_n_layers = 3
d_n_layers = 1
# neurons in each hidden layer
g_n_neurons = [256, 512, 1024]
d_n_neurons = [256]

# define parameter ditionary
d_params = {}
g_params = {}

activation = tf.nn.leaky_relu
w_initializer = tf.glorot_uniform_initializer
b_initializer = tf.zeros_initializer
```

2. Next, define the generator network:

```
z_p = tf.placeholder(dtype=tf.float32, name='z_p',
        shape=[None, n_z])
layer = z_p

# add generator network weights, biases and layers
with tf.variable_scope('g'):
    for i in range(0, g_n_layers):
        w_name = 'w_{0:04d}'.format(i)
        g_params[w_name] = tf.get_variable(
            name=w_name,
            shape=[n_z if i == 0 else g_n_neurons[i - 1],
                   g_n_neurons[i]],
            initializer=w_initializer())
        b_name = 'b_{0:04d}'.format(i)
        g_params[b_name] = tf.get_variable(
            name=b_name, shape=[g_n_neurons[i]],
            initializer=b_initializer())
        layer = activation(
            tf.matmul(layer, g_params[w_name]) +
g_params[b_name])
    # output (logit) layer
    i = g_n_layers
    w_name = 'w_{0:04d}'.format(i)
    g_params[w_name] = tf.get_variable(
        name=w_name,
        shape=[g_n_neurons[i - 1], n_x],
        initializer=w_initializer())
    b_name = 'b_{0:04d}'.format(i)
    g_params[b_name] = tf.get_variable(
        name=b_name, shape=[n_x], initializer=b_initializer())
    g_logit = tf.matmul(layer, g_params[w_name]) +
```

```
g_params[b_name]
        g_model = tf.nn.tanh(g_logit)
```

3. Next, define the weights and biases for the two discriminator networks that we shall build:

```
with tf.variable_scope('d'):
    for i in range(0, d_n_layers):
        w_name = 'w_{0:04d}'.format(i)
        d_params[w_name] = tf.get_variable(
            name=w_name,
            shape=[n_x if i == 0 else d_n_neurons[i - 1],
                   d_n_neurons[i]],
            initializer=w_initializer())

        b_name = 'b_{0:04d}'.format(i)
        d_params[b_name] = tf.get_variable(
            name=b_name, shape=[d_n_neurons[i]],
            initializer=b_initializer())

    #output (logit) layer
    i = d_n_layers
    w_name = 'w_{0:04d}'.format(i)
    d_params[w_name] = tf.get_variable(
        name=w_name, shape=[d_n_neurons[i - 1], 1],
        initializer=w_initializer())

    b_name = 'b_{0:04d}'.format(i)
    d_params[b_name] = tf.get_variable(
        name=b_name, shape=[1], initializer=b_initializer())
```

4. Now using these parameters, build the discriminator that takes the real images as input and outputs the classification:

```
# define discriminator_real

# input real images
x_p = tf.placeholder(dtype=tf.float32, name='x_p',
        shape=[None, n_x])

layer = x_p

with tf.variable_scope('d'):
    for i in range(0, d_n_layers):
        w_name = 'w_{0:04d}'.format(i)
        b_name = 'b_{0:04d}'.format(i)

        layer = activation(
```

```
            tf.matmul(layer, d_params[w_name]) +
d_params[b_name])
        layer = tf.nn.dropout(layer,0.7)
    #output (logit) layer
    i = d_n_layers
    w_name = 'w_{0:04d}'.format(i)
    b_name = 'b_{0:04d}'.format(i)
    d_logit_real = tf.matmul(layer,
        d_params[w_name]) + d_params[b_name]
    d_model_real = tf.nn.sigmoid(d_logit_real)
```

5. Next, build another discriminator network, with the same parameters, but providing the output of generator as input:

```
# define discriminator_fake

# input generated fake images
z = g_model
layer = z

with tf.variable_scope('d'):
    for i in range(0, d_n_layers):
        w_name = 'w_{0:04d}'.format(i)
        b_name = 'b_{0:04d}'.format(i)
        layer = activation(
            tf.matmul(layer, d_params[w_name]) +
d_params[b_name])
        layer = tf.nn.dropout(layer,0.7)
    #output (logit) layer
    i = d_n_layers
    w_name = 'w_{0:04d}'.format(i)
    b_name = 'b_{0:04d}'.format(i)
    d_logit_fake = tf.matmul(layer,
        d_params[w_name]) + d_params[b_name]
    d_model_fake = tf.nn.sigmoid(d_logit_fake)
```

6. Now that we have the three networks built, the connection between them is made using the loss, optimizer and training functions. While training the generator, we only train the generator's parameters and while training the discriminator, we only train the discriminator's parameters. We specify this using the `var_list` parameter to the optimizer's `minimize()` function. Here is the complete code for defining the loss, optimizer and training function for both kinds of network:

```
g_loss = -tf.reduce_mean(tf.log(d_model_fake))
d_loss = -tf.reduce_mean(tf.log(d_model_real) + tf.log(1 -
d_model_fake))
```

```
g_optimizer = tf.train.AdamOptimizer(g_learning_rate)
d_optimizer =
tf.train.GradientDescentOptimizer(d_learning_rate)

g_train_op = g_optimizer.minimize(g_loss,
                var_list=list(g_params.values()))
d_train_op = d_optimizer.minimize(d_loss,
                var_list=list(d_params.values()))
```

7. Now that we have defined the models, we have to train the models. The training is done as per the following algorithm:

```
For each epoch:
  For each batch:
    get real images x_batch
    generate noise z_batch
    train discriminator using z_batch and x_batch
    generate noise z_batch
    train generator using z_batch
```

The complete code for training from the notebook is as follows:

```
n_epochs = 400
batch_size = 100
n_batches = int(mnist.train.num_examples / batch_size)
n_epochs_print = 50

with tf.Session() as tfs:
    tfs.run(tf.global_variables_initializer())
    for epoch in range(n_epochs):
        epoch_d_loss = 0.0
        epoch_g_loss = 0.0
        for batch in range(n_batches):
            x_batch, _ = mnist.train.next_batch(batch_size)
            x_batch = norm(x_batch)
            z_batch =
np.random.uniform(-1.0,1.0,size=[batch_size,n_z])
            feed_dict = {x_p: x_batch,z_p: z_batch}
            _,batch_d_loss = tfs.run([d_train_op,d_loss],
                                    feed_dict=feed_dict)
            z_batch =
np.random.uniform(-1.0,1.0,size=[batch_size,n_z])
            feed_dict={z_p: z_batch}
            _,batch_g_loss = tfs.run([g_train_op,g_loss],
                                    feed_dict=feed_dict)
            epoch_d_loss += batch_d_loss
            epoch_g_loss += batch_g_loss
        if epoch%n_epochs_print == 0:
```

```
            average_d_loss = epoch_d_loss / n_batches
            average_g_loss = epoch_g_loss / n_batches
            print('epoch: {0:04d}   d_loss = {1:0.6f}  g_loss = 
{2:0.6f}'
                  .format(epoch,average_d_loss,average_g_loss))
            # predict images using generator model trained
            x_pred = tfs.run(g_model,feed_dict={z_p:z_test})
            display_images(x_pred.reshape(-1,pixel_size,pixel_size))
```

We printed the generated images every 50 epochs:

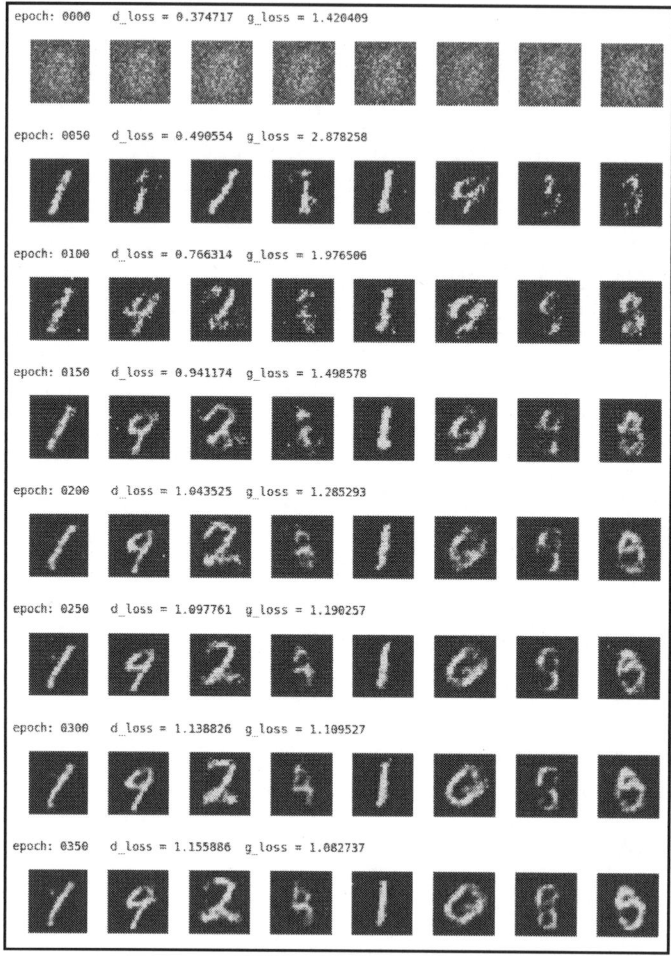

As we can see the generator was producing just noise in epoch 0, but by epoch 350, it got trained to produce much better shapes of handwritten digits. You can try experimenting with epochs, regularization, network architecture and other hyper-parameters to see if you can produce even faster and better results.

Simple GAN with Keras

You can follow along with the code in the Jupyter notebook `ch-14a_SimpleGAN`.

Now let us implement the same model in Keras:

1. The hyper-parameter definitions remain the same as the last section:

```
# graph hyperparameters
g_learning_rate = 0.00001
d_learning_rate = 0.01
n_x = 784  # number of pixels in the MNIST image
# number of hidden layers for generator and discriminator
g_n_layers = 3
d_n_layers = 1
# neurons in each hidden layer
g_n_neurons = [256, 512, 1024]
d_n_neurons = [256]
```

2. Next, define the generator network:

```
# define generator

g_model = Sequential()
g_model.add(Dense(units=g_n_neurons[0],
                  input_shape=(n_z,),
                  name='g_0'))
g_model.add(LeakyReLU())
for i in range(1,g_n_layers):
    g_model.add(Dense(units=g_n_neurons[i],
                      name='g_{}'.format(i)
                     ))
    g_model.add(LeakyReLU())
g_model.add(Dense(units=n_x, activation='tanh',name='g_out'))
print('Generator:')
g_model.summary()
```

```
g_model.compile(loss='binary_crossentropy',
optimizer=keras.optimizers.Adam(lr=g_learning_rate)
            )
```

This is what the generator model looks like:

```
Generator:
_________________________________________________________________
___
Layer (type)                 Output Shape              Param #
=================================================================
===
g_0 (Dense)                  (None, 256)               65792
_________________________________________________________________
___
leaky_re_lu_1 (LeakyReLU)    (None, 256)               0
_________________________________________________________________
___
g_1 (Dense)                  (None, 512)               131584
_________________________________________________________________
___
leaky_re_lu_2 (LeakyReLU)    (None, 512)               0
_________________________________________________________________
___
g_2 (Dense)                  (None, 1024)              525312
_________________________________________________________________
___
leaky_re_lu_3 (LeakyReLU)    (None, 1024)              0
_________________________________________________________________
___
g_out (Dense)                (None, 784)               803600
=================================================================
===
Total params: 1,526,288
Trainable params: 1,526,288
Non-trainable params: 0
_________________________________________________________________
___
```

3. In the Keras example, we do not define two discriminator networks as we defined in the TensorFlow example. Instead, we define one discriminator network and then stitch the generator and discriminator network into the GAN network. The GAN network is then used to train the generator parameters only, and the discriminator network is used to train the discriminator parameters:

```
# define discriminator
```

```
d_model = Sequential()
d_model.add(Dense(units=d_n_neurons[0],
                  input_shape=(n_x,),
                  name='d_0'
                 ))
d_model.add(LeakyReLU())
d_model.add(Dropout(0.3))
for i in range(1,d_n_layers):
    d_model.add(Dense(units=d_n_neurons[i],
                      name='d_{}'.format(i)
                     ))
    d_model.add(LeakyReLU())
    d_model.add(Dropout(0.3))
d_model.add(Dense(units=1, activation='sigmoid',name='d_out'))
print('Discriminator:')
d_model.summary()
d_model.compile(loss='binary_crossentropy',
optimizer=keras.optimizers.SGD(lr=d_learning_rate)
             )
```

This is what the discriminator models look:

```
Discriminator:
_________________________________________________________________
___
Layer (type)                 Output Shape              Param #
=================================================================
===
d_0 (Dense)                  (None, 256)               200960
_________________________________________________________________
___
leaky_re_lu_4 (LeakyReLU)    (None, 256)               0
_________________________________________________________________
___
dropout_1 (Dropout)          (None, 256)               0
_________________________________________________________________
___
d_out (Dense)                (None, 1)                 257
=================================================================
===
Total params: 201,217
Trainable params: 201,217
Non-trainable params: 0
_________________________________________________________________
___
```

4. Next, define the GAN Network, and turn the trainable property of the discriminator model to `false`, since GAN would only be used to train the generator:

```
# define GAN network
d_model.trainable=False
z_in = Input(shape=(n_z,),name='z_in')
x_in = g_model(z_in)
gan_out = d_model(x_in)

gan_model = Model(inputs=z_in,outputs=gan_out,name='gan')
print('GAN:')
gan_model.summary()
gan_model.compile(loss='binary_crossentropy',
optimizer=keras.optimizers.Adam(lr=g_learning_rate)
             )
```

This is what the GAN model looks:

```
GAN:
_________________________________________________________________
___
Layer (type)                 Output Shape              Param #
=================================================================
===
z_in (InputLayer)            (None, 256)               0
_________________________________________________________________
___
sequential_1 (Sequential)    (None, 784)               1526288
_________________________________________________________________
___
sequential_2 (Sequential)    (None, 1)                 201217
=================================================================
===
Total params: 1,727,505
Trainable params: 1,526,288
Non-trainable params: 201,217
_________________________________________________________________
___
```

5. Great, now that we have defined the three models, we have to train the models. The training is as per the following algorithm:

```
For each epoch:
  For each batch:
    get real images x_batch
    generate noise z_batch
    generate images g_batch using generator model
```

```
    combine g_batch and x_batch into x_in and create labels
y_out

    set discriminator model as trainable
    train discriminator using x_in and y_out
    generate noise z_batch
    set x_in = z_batch and labels y_out = 1
    set discriminator model as non-trainable
    train gan model using x_in and y_out,
        (effectively training generator model)
```

For setting the labels, we apply the labels as 0.9 and 0.1 for real and fake images respectively. Generally, it is suggested that you use label smoothing by picking a random value from 0.0 to 0.3 for fake data and 0.8 to 1.0 for real data.

Here is the complete code for training from the notebook:

```
n_epochs = 400
batch_size = 100
n_batches = int(mnist.train.num_examples / batch_size)
n_epochs_print = 50

for epoch in range(n_epochs+1):
    epoch_d_loss = 0.0
    epoch_g_loss = 0.0
    for batch in range(n_batches):
        x_batch, _ = mnist.train.next_batch(batch_size)
        x_batch = norm(x_batch)
        z_batch = np.random.uniform(-1.0,1.0,size=[batch_size,n_z])
        g_batch = g_model.predict(z_batch)
        x_in = np.concatenate([x_batch,g_batch])
        y_out = np.ones(batch_size*2)
        y_out[:batch_size]=0.9
        y_out[batch_size:]=0.1
        d_model.trainable=True
        batch_d_loss = d_model.train_on_batch(x_in,y_out)

        z_batch = np.random.uniform(-1.0,1.0,size=[batch_size,n_z])
        x_in=z_batch
        y_out = np.ones(batch_size)
        d_model.trainable=False
        batch_g_loss = gan_model.train_on_batch(x_in,y_out)
        epoch_d_loss += batch_d_loss
        epoch_g_loss += batch_g_loss
    if epoch%n_epochs_print == 0:
        average_d_loss = epoch_d_loss / n_batches
        average_g_loss = epoch_g_loss / n_batches
        print('epoch: {0:04d}   d_loss = {1:0.6f}  g_loss = {2:0.6f}'
```

```
        .format(epoch,average_d_loss,average_g_loss))
    # predict images using generator model trained
    x_pred = g_model.predict(z_test)
    display_images(x_pred.reshape(-1,pixel_size,pixel_size))
```

We printed the results every 50 epochs, up to 350 epochs:

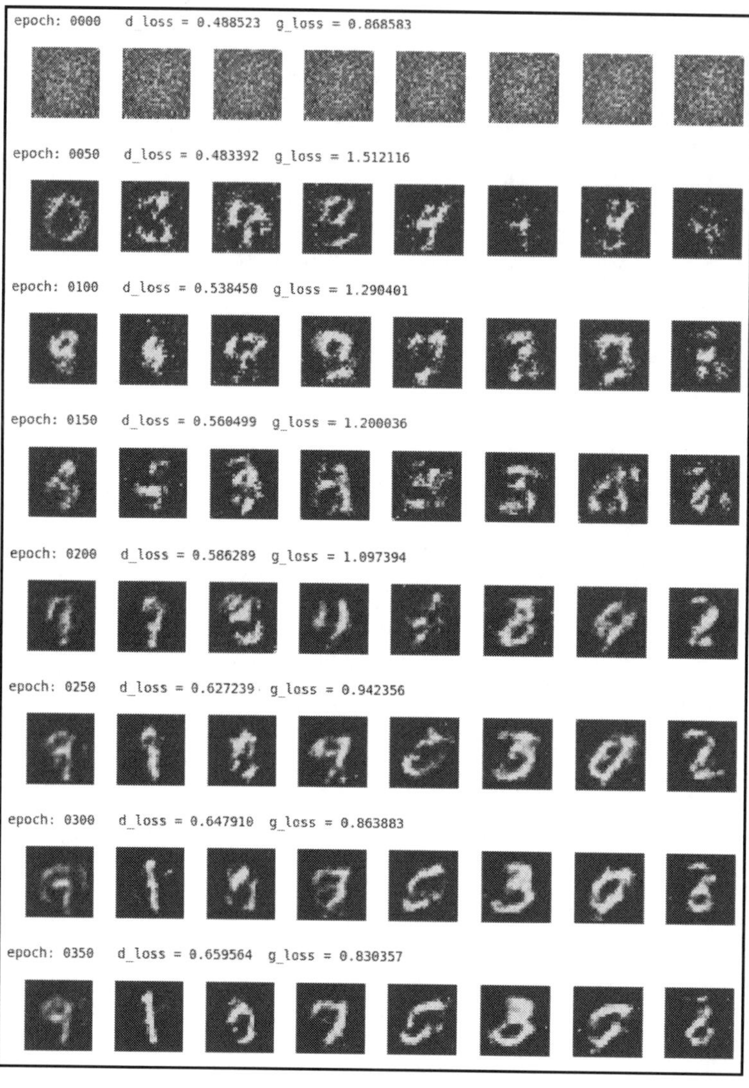

The model slowly learns to generate good quality images of handwritten digits from the random noise.

There are so many variations of the GANs that it will take another book to cover all the different kinds of GANs. However, the implementation techniques are almost similar to what we have shown here.

Deep Convolutional GAN with TensorFlow and Keras

You can follow along with the code in the Jupyter notebook `ch-14b_DCGAN`.

In DCGAN, both the discriminator and generator are implemented using a Deep Convolutional Network:

1. In this example, we decided to implement the generator as the following network:

```
Generator:
_________________________________________________________________
Layer (type)                 Output Shape              Param #
=================================================================
g_in (Dense)                 (None, 3200)              822400
_________________________________________________________________
g_in_act (Activation)        (None, 3200)              0
_________________________________________________________________
g_in_reshape (Reshape)       (None, 5, 5, 128)         0
_________________________________________________________________
g_0_up2d (UpSampling2D)      (None, 10, 10, 128)       0
_________________________________________________________________
g_0_conv2d (Conv2D)          (None, 10, 10, 64)        204864
_________________________________________________________________
g_0_act (Activation)         (None, 10, 10, 64)        0
```

```
________________________________________________________________
___
g_1_up2d (UpSampling2D)       (None, 20, 20, 64)        0
________________________________________________________________
___
g_1_conv2d (Conv2D)           (None, 20, 20, 32)        51232
________________________________________________________________
___
g_1_act (Activation)          (None, 20, 20, 32)        0
________________________________________________________________
___
g_2_up2d (UpSampling2D)       (None, 40, 40, 32)        0
________________________________________________________________
___
g_2_conv2d (Conv2D)           (None, 40, 40, 16)        12816
________________________________________________________________
___
g_2_act (Activation)          (None, 40, 40, 16)        0
________________________________________________________________
___
g_out_flatten (Flatten)       (None, 25600)             0
________________________________________________________________
___
g_out (Dense)                 (None, 784)
20071184
================================================================
===
Total params: 21,162,496
Trainable params: 21,162,496
Non-trainable params: 0
```

2. The generator is a stronger network having three convolutional layers followed by tanh activation. We define the discriminator network as follows:

```
Discriminator:
________________________________________________________________
___
Layer (type)                  Output Shape              Param #
================================================================
===
d_0_reshape (Reshape)         (None, 28, 28, 1)         0
________________________________________________________________
___
d_0_conv2d (Conv2D)           (None, 28, 28, 64)        1664
________________________________________________________________
___
d_0_act (Activation)          (None, 28, 28, 64)        0
```

```
________________________________________________________________
___
d_0_maxpool (MaxPooling2D)   (None, 14, 14, 64)        0
________________________________________________________________
___
d_out_flatten (Flatten)      (None, 12544)             0
________________________________________________________________
___
d_out (Dense)                (None, 1)                 12545
================================================================
===
Total params: 14,209
Trainable params: 14,209
Non-trainable params: 0
________________________________________________________________
___
```

3. The GAN network is composed of the discriminator and generator as demonstrated previously:

```
GAN:
________________________________________________________________
___
Layer (type)                 Output Shape              Param #
================================================================
===
z_in (InputLayer)            (None, 256)               0
________________________________________________________________
___
g (Sequential)               (None, 784)
21162496
________________________________________________________________
___
d (Sequential)               (None, 1)                 14209
================================================================
===
Total params: 21,176,705
Trainable params: 21,162,496
Non-trainable params: 14,209
________________________________________________________________
___
```

When we run this model for 400 epochs, we get the following output:

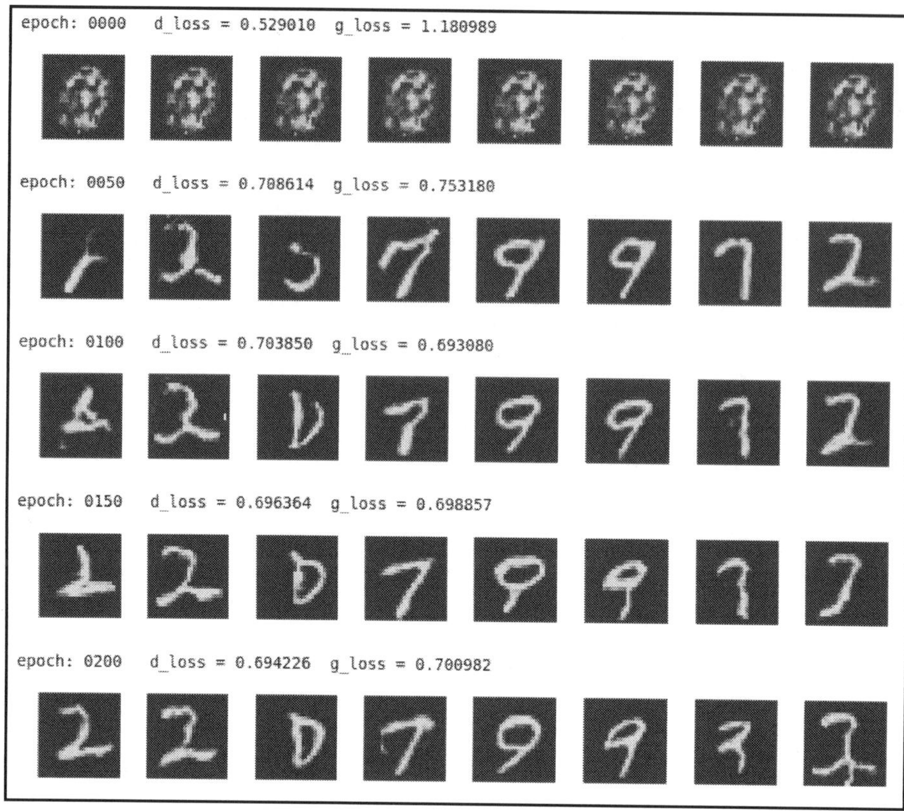

As you can see, the DCGAN is able to generate high-quality digits starting from epoch 100 itself. The DGCAN has been used for style transfer, generation of images and titles and for image algebra, namely taking parts of one image and adding that to parts of another image. The complete code for MNIST DCGAN is provided in the notebook `ch-14b_DCGAN`.

Summary

In this chapter, we learned about Generative Adversarial Networks. We built a simple GAN in TensorFlow and Keras and applied it to generate images from the MNIST dataset. We also learned that many different derivatives of GANs are being introduced continuously, such as DCGAN, SRGAN, StackGAN, and CycleGAN, to name a few. We also built a DCGAN where the generator and discriminator consisted of convolutional networks. You are encouraged to read and experiment with different derivatives to see which models fit the problems they are trying to solve.

In the next chapter, we shall learn how to build and deploy models in distributed clusters with TensorFlow clusters and multiple compute devices such as multiple GPUs.

17
Distributed Models with TensorFlow Clusters

Previously we learned how to run TensorFlow models at scale in production using Kubernetes, Docker and TensorFlow serving. TensorFlow serving is not the only way to run TensorFlow models at scale. TensorFlow provides another mechanism to not only run but also train the models on different nodes and different devices on multiple nodes or the same node. In this chapter, we shall learn how to distribute the TensorFlow models to run on multiple devices across multiple nodes.

In this chapter, we shall cover the following topics:

- Strategies for distributed execution
- TensorFlow clusters
- Data parallel models
- Asynchronous and synchronous updates to distributed models

Strategies for distributed execution

For distributing the training of the single model across multiple devices or nodes, there are the following strategies:

- **Model Parallel:** Divide the model into multiple subgraphs and place the separate graphs on different nodes or devices. The subgraphs perform their computation and exchange the variables as required.

- **Data Parallel:** Divide the data into batches and run the same model on multiple nodes or devices, combining the parameters on a master node. Thus the worker nodes train the model on batches of data and send the parameter updates to the master node, also known as the parameter server.

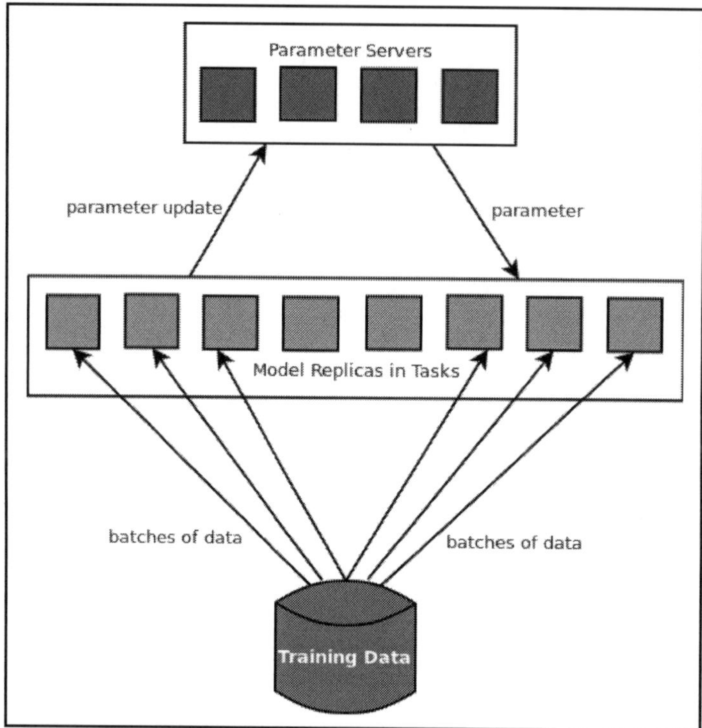

The preceding diagram shows the data parallel approach where the model replicas read the partitions of data in batches and send the parameter updates to the parameter servers, and parameter servers send the updated parameters back to the model replicas for the next batched computation of updates.

In TensorFlow, there are two ways to implement replicating the model on multiple nodes/devices under the data parallel strategy:

- **In-Graph Replication**: In this approach, there is a single client task that owns the model parameters and assigns the model calculations to multiple worker tasks.

- **Between-Graph Replication**: In this approach, each client task connects to its own worker in order to assign the model calculation, but all workers update the same shared model. In this model, TensorFlow automatically assigns one worker to be the chief worker so that the model parameters are initialized only once by the chief worker.

Within both these approaches, the parameters on the parameter server(s) can be updated in two different ways:

- **Synchronous Update**: In a synchronous update, the parameter server(s) wait to receive the updates from all the workers before updating the gradients. The parameter server aggregates the updates, for example by calculating the mean of all the aggregates and applying them to the parameters. After the update, the parameters are sent to all the workers simultaneously. The disadvantage of this method is that one slow worker may slow down the updates for everyone.
- **Asynchronous Update**: In an asynchronous update, the workers send the updates to parameter server(s) as they are ready, and then the parameter server applies the updates as it receives them and sends them back. The disadvantage of this method is that by the time the worker calculates the parameters and sends the updates back, the parameters could have been updated several times by other workers. This problem can be alleviated by several methods such as lowering the batch size or lowering the learning rate. It is a surprise that the asynchronous method even works, but in reality, they do work !!!

TensorFlow clusters

A TensorFlow (TF) *cluster* is one mechanism that implements the distributed strategies that we have just discussed. At the logical level, a TF cluster runs one or more *jobs*, and each *job* consists of one or more *tasks*. Thus a job is just a logical grouping of the tasks. At the process level, each task runs as a TF server. At the machine level, each physical machine or node can run more than one task by running more than one server, one server per task. The *client* creates the graph on different servers and starts the execution of the graph on one server by calling the remote session.

As an example, the following diagram depicts two clients connected to two jobs named `m1`:

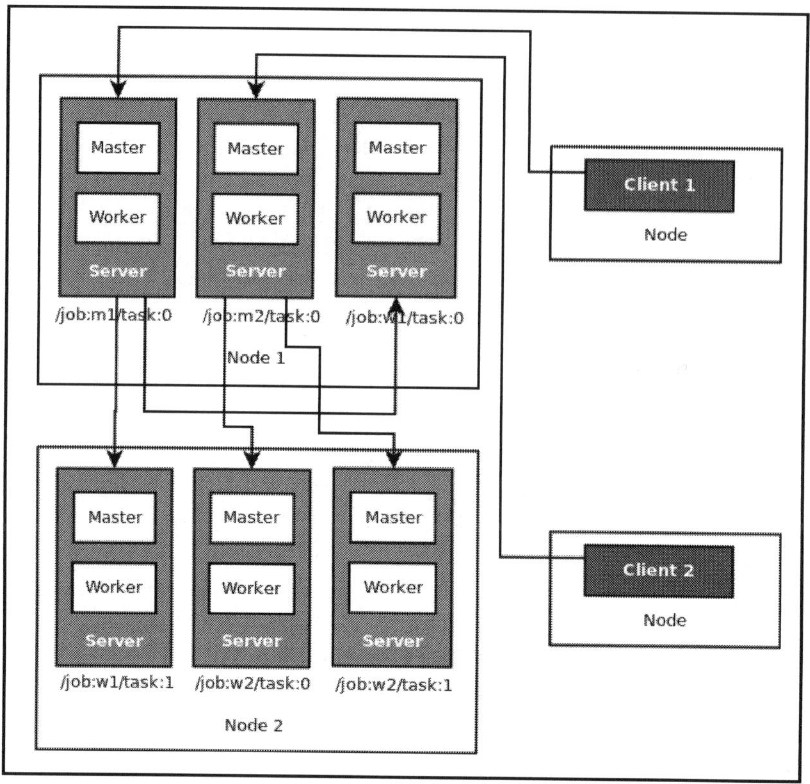

The two nodes are running three tasks each, and the job `w1` is spread across two nodes while the other jobs are contained within the nodes.

A TF server is implemented as two processes: master and worker. The master coordinates the computation with other tasks and the worker is the one actually running the computation. At a higher level, you do not have to worry about the internals of the TF server. For the purpose of our explanation and examples, we will only refer to TF tasks.

To create and train a model in data parallel fashion, use the following steps:

1. Define the cluster specifications
2. Create a server to host a task
3. Define the variable nodes to be assigned to parameter server tasks

4. Define the operation nodes to be replicated on all worker tasks
5. Create a remote session
6. Train the model in the remote session
7. Use the model for prediction

Defining cluster specification

In order to create a cluster, first, define a cluster specification. The cluster specification generally consists of two jobs: `ps` to create parameter server tasks and `worker` to create worker tasks. The `worker` and `ps` jobs contain the list of physical nodes where their respective tasks are running. As an example:

```
clusterSpec = tf.train.ClusterSpec({
  'ps': [
              'master0.neurasights.com:2222',  # /job:ps/task:0
              'master1.neurasights.com:2222'   # /job:ps/task:1
        ]
  'worker': [
              'worker0.neurasights.com:2222',  # /job:worker/task:0
              'worker1.neurasights.com:2222',  # /job:worker/task:1
              'worker0.neurasights.com:2223',  # /job:worker/task:2
              'worker1.neurasights.com:2223'   # /job:worker/task:3
            ]
          })
```

This specification creates two jobs, with two tasks in job `ps` spread across two physical nodes and four tasks in job `worker` spread across two physical nodes.

In our example code, we create all the tasks on a localhost, on different ports:

```
ps = [
        'localhost:9001',  # /job:ps/task:0
     ]
workers = [
        'localhost:9002',  # /job:worker/task:0
        'localhost:9003',  # /job:worker/task:1
        'localhost:9004',  # /job:worker/task:2
        ]
clusterSpec = tf.train.ClusterSpec({'ps': ps, 'worker': workers})
```

As you can see in the comments in the code, the tasks are identified with `/job:<job name>/task:<task index>`.

Create the server instances

Since the cluster contains one server instance per task, on every physical node, start the servers by passing them the cluster specification, their own job name and task index. The servers use the cluster specification to figure out what other nodes are involved in the computation.

```
server = tf.train.Server(clusterSpec, job_name="ps", task_index=0)
server = tf.train.Server(clusterSpec, job_name="worker", task_index=0)
server = tf.train.Server(clusterSpec, job_name="worker", task_index=1)
server = tf.train.Server(clusterSpec, job_name="worker", task_index=2)
```

In our example code, we have a single Python file that will run on all the physical machines, containing the following:

```
server = tf.train.Server(clusterSpec,
                         job_name=FLAGS.job_name,
                         task_index=FLAGS.task_index,
                         config=config
                         )
```

In this code, the `job_name` and the `task_index` are taken from the parameters passed at the command line. The package, `tf.flags` is a fancy parser that gives you access to the command-line arguments. The Python file is executed as follows, on every physical node (or in a separate terminal on the same node if you are using a localhost only):

```
# the model should be run in each physical node
# using the appropriate arguments
$ python3 model.py --job_name='ps' --task_index=0
$ python3 model.py --job_name='worker' --task_index=0
$ python3 model.py --job_name='worker' --task_index=1
$ python3 model.py --job_name='worker' --task_index=2
```

For even greater flexibility to run the code on any cluster, you can also pass the list of machines running parameter servers and workers through the command line: `-ps='localhost:9001' --worker='localhost:9002,localhost:9003,localhost:9004'`. You will need to parse them and set them appropriately in the cluster specifications dictionary.

To ensure that our parameter server only uses CPU and our worker tasks use GPU, we use the configuration object:

```
config = tf.ConfigProto()
config.allow_soft_placement = True

if FLAGS.job_name=='ps':
    #print(config.device_count['GPU'])
    config.device_count['GPU']=0
    server = tf.train.Server(clusterSpec,
                             job_name=FLAGS.job_name,
                             task_index=FLAGS.task_index,
                             config=config
                             )
    server.join()
    sys.exit('0')
elif FLAGS.job_name=='worker':
    config.gpu_options.per_process_gpu_memory_fraction = 0.2
    server = tf.train.Server(clusterSpec,
                             job_name=FLAGS.job_name,
                             task_index=FLAGS.task_index,
                             config=config
```

The parameter server is made to wait with `server.join()` while the worker tasks execute the training of the model and exit.

This is what our GPU looks like when all the four servers are running:

```
+-----------------------------------------------------------------------------+
| NVIDIA-SMI 384.90                 Driver Version: 384.90                    |
|-------------------------------+----------------------+----------------------+
| GPU  Name        Persistence-M| Bus-Id        Disp.A | Volatile Uncorr. ECC |
| Fan  Temp  Perf  Pwr:Usage/Cap|         Memory-Usage | GPU-Util  Compute M. |
|===============================+======================+======================|
|   0  Quadro P5000        Off  | 00000000:01:00.0 Off |                  N/A |
| N/A   58C    P0    34W /  N/A |  10372MiB / 16273MiB |     32%      Default |
+-------------------------------+----------------------+----------------------+

+-----------------------------------------------------------------------------+
| Processes:                                                       GPU Memory |
|  GPU       PID   Type   Process name                             Usage      |
|=============================================================================|
|    0      1505      C   python3                                       93MiB |
|    0     29841      C   python3                                     3423MiB |
|    0     29853      C   python3                                     3423MiB |
|    0     29862      C   python3                                     3423MiB |
+-----------------------------------------------------------------------------+
```

Define the parameter and operations across servers and devices

You can use the `tf.device()` function, to place the parameters on the `ps` tasks and the compute nodes of the graphs on the `worker` tasks.

Note that you can also place the graph nodes on specific devices by adding the device string to the task string as follows: `/job:<job name>/task:<task index>/device:<device type>:<device index>`.

For our demonstration example, we use the TensorFlow function `tf.train.replica_device_setter()` to place the variables and operations.

1. First, we define the worker device to be the current worker:

```
worker_device='/job:worker/task:{}'.format(FLAGS.task_index)
```

2. Next, define a device function using the `replica_device_setter`, passing the cluster specifications and current worker device. The `replica_device_setter` function figures out the parameter servers from the cluster specification, and if there are more than one parameter servers, then it distributes the parameters among them in a round robin fashion by default. The parameter placement strategy can be changed to a user-defined function or prebuilt strategies in the `tf.contrib` package.

```
device_func = tf.train.replica_device_setter(
    worker_device=worker_device,cluster=clusterSpec)
```

3. Finally, we create the graph inside the `tf.device(device_func)` block and train it. The creation and training of the graph is different for synchronous updates and asynchronous updates, hence we cover these in two separate subsections.

Define and train the graph for asynchronous updates

As discussed previously, and shown in the diagram here, in asynchronous updates all the worker tasks send the parameter updates when they are ready, and the parameter server updates the parameters and sends back the parameters. There is no synchronization or waiting or aggregation of parameter updates:

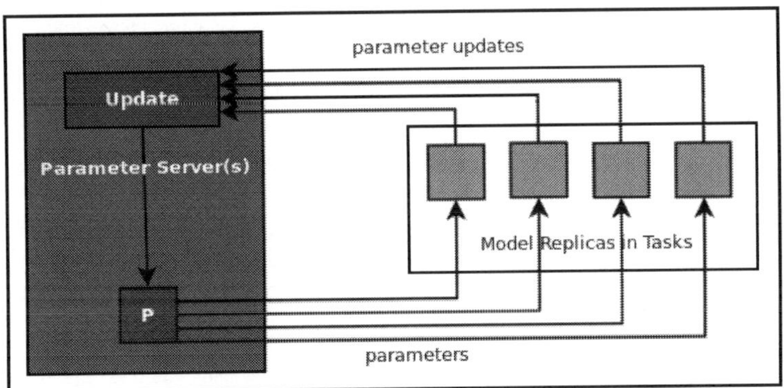

The full code for this example is in `ch-15_mnist_dist_async.py`. You are encouraged to modify and explore the code with your own datasets.

For asynchronous updates, the graph is created and trained with the following steps:

1. The definition of the graph is done within the `with` block:

```
with tf.device(device_func):
```

2. Create a global step variable using the inbuilt TensorFlow function:

```
global_step = tf.train.get_or_create_global_step()
```

3. This variable can also be defined as:

```
tf.Variable(0,name='global_step',trainable=False)
```

4. Define the datasets, parameters, and hyper-parameters as usual:

```
x_test = mnist.test.images
y_test = mnist.test.labels
n_outputs = 10  # 0-9 digits
n_inputs = 784  # total pixels
learning_rate = 0.01
n_epochs = 50
batch_size = 100
n_batches = int(mnist.train.num_examples/batch_size)
n_epochs_print=10
```

5. Define the placeholders, weights, biases, logits, cross-entropy, loss op, train op, accuracy as usual:

```
# input images
x_p = tf.placeholder(dtype=tf.float32,
                     name='x_p',
                     shape=[None, n_inputs])
# target output
y_p = tf.placeholder(dtype=tf.float32,
                     name='y_p',
                     shape=[None, n_outputs])
w = tf.Variable(tf.random_normal([n_inputs, n_outputs],
                                  name='w'
                                  )
                )
b = tf.Variable(tf.random_normal([n_outputs],
                                  name='b'
                                  )
                )
logits = tf.matmul(x_p,w) + b

entropy_op =
tf.nn.softmax_cross_entropy_with_logits(labels=y_p,
logits=logits
                                                      )
loss_op = tf.reduce_mean(entropy_op)

optimizer = tf.train.GradientDescentOptimizer(learning_rate)
train_op = optimizer.minimize(loss_op,global_step=global_step)

correct_pred = tf.equal(tf.argmax(logits, 1), tf.argmax(y_p,
1))
accuracy_op = tf.reduce_mean(tf.cast(correct_pred,
tf.float32))
```

These definitions will change when we learn how to build the synchronous update.

6. TensorFlow provides a supervisor class that helps in creating sessions for training and is very useful in a distributed training setting. Create a supervisor object as follows:

```
init_op = tf.global_variables_initializer
sv = tf.train.Supervisor(is_chief=is_chief,
                         init_op = init_op(),
                         global_step=global_step)
```

7. Use the supervisor object to create a session and run the training under this session block as usual:

```
with sv.prepare_or_wait_for_session(server.target) as mts:
    lstep = 0

    for epoch in range(n_epochs):
        for batch in range(n_batches):
            x_batch, y_batch =
mnist.train.next_batch(batch_size)
            feed_dict={x_p:x_batch,y_p:y_batch}
_,loss,gstep=mts.run([train_op,loss_op,global_step],
                               feed_dict=feed_dict)
            lstep +=1
        if (epoch+1)%n_epochs_print==0:
            print('worker={},epoch={},global_step={}, \
                   local_step={},loss={}'.
format(FLAGS.task_index,epoch,gstep,lstep,loss))
    feed_dict={x_p:x_test,y_p:y_test}
    accuracy = mts.run(accuracy_op, feed_dict=feed_dict)
    print('worker={}, final accuracy = {}'
        .format(FLAGS.task_index,accuracy))
```

On starting the parameter server, we get the following output:

```
$ python3 ch-15_mnist_dist_async.py --job_name='ps' --task_index=0
I tensorflow/core/common_runtime/gpu/gpu_device.cc:1030] Found device
0 with properties:
   name: Quadro P5000 major: 6 minor: 1 memoryClockRate(GHz): 1.506
pciBusID: 0000:01:00.0
totalMemory: 15.89GiB freeMemory: 15.79GiB
I tensorflow/core/common_runtime/gpu/gpu_device.cc:1120] Creating
TensorFlow device (/device:GPU:0) -> (device: 0, name: Quadro P5000,
pci bus id: 0000:01:00.0, compute capability: 6.1)
E1213 16:50:14.023235178   27224 ev_epoll1_linux.c:1051]     grpc
epoll fd: 23
```

```
I tensorflow/core/distributed_runtime/rpc/grpc_channel.cc:215]
Initialize GrpcChannelCache for job ps -> {0 -> localhost:9001}
I tensorflow/core/distributed_runtime/rpc/grpc_channel.cc:215]
Initialize GrpcChannelCache for job worker -> {0 -> localhost:9002, 1
-> localhost:9003, 2 -> localhost:9004}
I tensorflow/core/distributed_runtime/rpc/grpc_server_lib.cc:324]
Started server with target: grpc://localhost:9001
```

On starting the worker tasks we get the following three outputs:

The output from worker 1:

```
$ python3 ch-15_mnist_dist_async.py --job_name='worker' --task_index=0
I tensorflow/core/common_runtime/gpu/gpu_device.cc:1030] Found device
0 with properties:
    name: Quadro P5000 major: 6 minor: 1 memoryClockRate(GHz): 1.506
pciBusID: 0000:01:00.0
totalMemory: 15.89GiB freeMemory: 9.16GiB
I tensorflow/core/common_runtime/gpu/gpu_device.cc:1120] Creating
TensorFlow device (/device:GPU:0) -> (device: 0, name: Quadro P5000,
pci bus id: 0000:01:00.0, compute capability: 6.1)
E1213 16:50:37.516609689   27507 ev_epoll1_linux.c:1051]     grpc
epoll fd: 23
I tensorflow/core/distributed_runtime/rpc/grpc_channel.cc:215]
Initialize GrpcChannelCache for job ps -> {0 -> localhost:9001}
I tensorflow/core/distributed_runtime/rpc/grpc_channel.cc:215]
Initialize GrpcChannelCache for job worker -> {0 -> localhost:9002, 1
-> localhost:9003, 2 -> localhost:9004}
I tensorflow/core/distributed_runtime/rpc/grpc_server_lib.cc:324]
Started server with target: grpc://localhost:9002
I tensorflow/core/distributed_runtime/master_session.cc:1004] Start
master session 1421824c3df413b5 with config: gpu_options {
per_process_gpu_memory_fraction: 0.2 } allow_soft_placement: true
worker=0,epoch=9,global_step=10896, local_step=5500, loss =
1.2575616836547852
worker=0,epoch=19,global_step=22453, local_step=11000, loss =
0.7158586382865906
worker=0,epoch=29,global_step=39019, local_step=16500, loss =
0.43712112307548523
worker=0,epoch=39,global_step=55513, local_step=22000, loss =
0.3935799300670624
worker=0,epoch=49,global_step=72002, local_step=27500, loss =
0.3877961337566376
worker=0, final accuracy = 0.8865000009536743
```

The output from worker 2:

```
$ python3 ch-15_mnist_dist_async.py --job_name='worker' --task_index=1
I tensorflow/core/common_runtime/gpu/gpu_device.cc:1030] Found device
0 with properties:
   name: Quadro P5000 major: 6 minor: 1 memoryClockRate(GHz): 1.506
pciBusID: 0000:01:00.0
totalMemory: 15.89GiB freeMemory: 12.43GiB
I tensorflow/core/common_runtime/gpu/gpu_device.cc:1120] Creating
TensorFlow device (/device:GPU:0) -> (device: 0, name: Quadro P5000,
pci bus id: 0000:01:00.0, compute capability: 6.1)
E1213 16:50:36.684334877   27461 ev_epoll1_linux.c:1051]     grpc
epoll fd: 23
I tensorflow/core/distributed_runtime/rpc/grpc_channel.cc:215]
Initialize GrpcChannelCache for job ps -> {0 -> localhost:9001}
I tensorflow/core/distributed_runtime/rpc/grpc_channel.cc:215]
Initialize GrpcChannelCache for job worker -> {0 -> localhost:9002, 1
-> localhost:9003, 2 -> localhost:9004}
I tensorflow/core/distributed_runtime/rpc/grpc_server_lib.cc:324]
Started server with target: grpc://localhost:9003
I tensorflow/core/distributed_runtime/master_session.cc:1004] Start
master session 2bd8a136213a1fce with config: gpu_options {
per_process_gpu_memory_fraction: 0.2 } allow_soft_placement: true
worker=1,epoch=9,global_step=11085, local_step=5500, loss =
0.6955764889717102
worker=1,epoch=19,global_step=22728, local_step=11000, loss =
0.5891970992088318
worker=1,epoch=29,global_step=39074, local_step=16500, loss =
0.4183048903942108
worker=1,epoch=39,global_step=55599, local_step=22000, loss =
0.32243454456329346
worker=1,epoch=49,global_step=72105, local_step=27500, loss =
0.5384714007377625
worker=1, final accuracy = 0.8866000175476074
```

The output from worker 3:

```
$ python3 ch-15_mnist_dist_async.py --job_name='worker' --task_index=2
I tensorflow/core/common_runtime/gpu/gpu_device.cc:1030] Found device
0 with properties:
   name: Quadro P5000 major: 6 minor: 1 memoryClockRate(GHz): 1.506
pciBusID: 0000:01:00.0
totalMemory: 15.89GiB freeMemory: 15.70GiB
I tensorflow/core/common_runtime/gpu/gpu_device.cc:1120] Creating
TensorFlow device (/device:GPU:0) -> (device: 0, name: Quadro P5000,
pci bus id: 0000:01:00.0, compute capability: 6.1)
E1213 16:50:35.568349791   27449 ev_epoll1_linux.c:1051]     grpc
epoll fd: 23
```

```
I tensorflow/core/distributed_runtime/rpc/grpc_channel.cc:215]
Initialize GrpcChannelCache for job ps -> {0 -> localhost:9001}
I tensorflow/core/distributed_runtime/rpc/grpc_channel.cc:215]
Initialize GrpcChannelCache for job worker -> {0 -> localhost:9002, 1
-> localhost:9003, 2 -> localhost:9004}
I tensorflow/core/distributed_runtime/rpc/grpc_server_lib.cc:324]
Started server with target: grpc://The full code for this example is
in ch-15_mnist_dist_sync.py. You are encouraged to modify and explore
the code with your own datasets.localhost:9004
I tensorflow/core/distributed_runtime/master_session.cc:1004] Start
master session cb0749c9f5fc163e with config: gpu_options {
per_process_gpu_memory_fraction: 0.2 } allow_soft_placement: true
I tensorflow/core/distributed_runtime/master_session.cc:1004] Start
master session 55bf9a2b9718a571 with config: gpu_options {
per_process_gpu_memory_fraction: 0.2 } allow_soft_placement: true
worker=2,epoch=9,global_step=37367, local_step=5500, loss =
0.8077645301818848
worker=2,epoch=19,global_step=53859, local_step=11000, loss =
0.26333487033843994
worker=2,epoch=29,global_step=70299, local_step=16500, loss =
0.6506651043891907
worker=2,epoch=39,global_step=76999, local_step=22000, loss =
0.20321622490882874
worker=2,epoch=49,global_step=82499, local_step=27500, loss =
0.4170967936515808
worker=2, final accuracy = 0.8894000053405762
```

We printed the global step and local step. The global step indicates the count of steps across all the worker tasks while the local step is a count within that worker task, that is why local tasks count up to 27,500 and are the same for every epoch for every worker, but since workers are doing the global steps at their own pace, the number of global steps has no symmetry or pattern across epochs or across workers. Also, we see that the final accuracy is different for each worker, since each worker executed the final accuracy at a different time, with different parameters available at that time.

Define and train the graph for synchronous updates

As discussed before, and depicted in the diagram here, in synchronous updates, the tasks send their updates to the parameter server(s), and ps tasks wait for all the updates to be received, aggregate them, and then update the parameters. The worker tasks wait for the updates before proceeding to the next iteration of computing parameter updates:

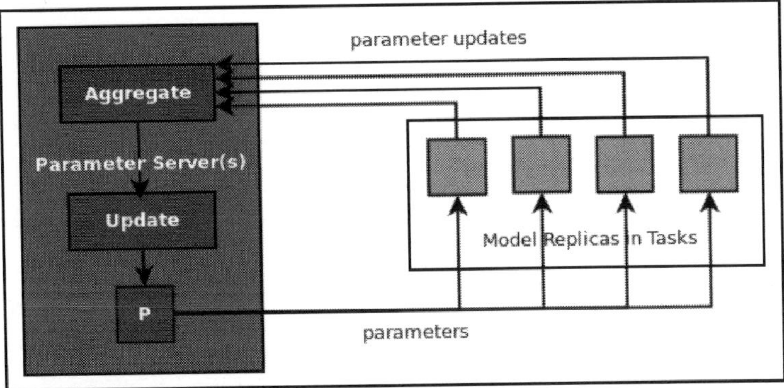

The full code for this example is in `ch-15_mnist_dist_sync.py`. You are encouraged to modify and explore the code with your own datasets.

For synchronous updates, the following modifications need to be made to the code:

1. The optimizer needs to be wrapped in SyncReplicaOptimizer. Thus, after defining the optimizer, add the following code:

```
# SYNC: next line added for making it sync update
optimizer = tf.train.SyncReplicasOptimizer(optimizer,
    replicas_to_aggregate=len(workers),
    total_num_replicas=len(workers),
    )
```

2. This should be followed by adding the training operation as before:

```
train_op = optimizer.minimize(loss_op,global_step=global_step)
```

3. Next, add the initialization function definitions, specific to the synchronous update method:

```
if is_chief:
    local_init_op = optimizer.chief_init_op()
else:
    local_init_op = optimizer.local_step_init_op()
chief_queue_runner = optimizer.get_chief_queue_runner()
init_token_op = optimizer.get_init_tokens_op()
```

4. The supervisor object is also created differently with two additional initialization functions:

```
# SYNC: sv is initialized differently for sync update
sv = tf.train.Supervisor(is_chief=is_chief,
    init_op = tf.global_variables_initializer(),
    local_init_op = local_init_op,
    ready_for_local_init_op =
optimizer.ready_for_local_init_op,
    global_step=global_step)
```

5. Finally, within the session block for training, we initialize the sync variables and start the queue runners if it is the chief worker task:

```
# SYNC: if block added to make it sync update
if is_chief:
    mts.run(init_token_op)
    sv.start_queue_runners(mts, [chief_queue_runner])
```

The rest of the code remains the same as an asynchronous update.

The TensorFlow libraries and functions for supporting distributed training are under continuous development. Hence, be on the lookout for new functionality added or function signatures changed. At the timing of writing of this book, we used TensorFlow 1.4.

Summary

In this chapter, we learned how to distribute the training of our models across multiple machines and devices, using TensorFlow clusters. We also learned model parallel and data parallel strategies for the distributed execution of TensorFlow code.

The parameter updates can be shared with synchronous or asynchronous updates to parameter servers. We learned how to implement code for synchronous and asynchronous parameter updates. With the skills learned in this chapter, you will be able to build and train very large models with very large datasets.

18
Debugging TensorFlow Models

As we learned in this book, TensorFlow programs are used to build and train models that can be used for prediction in various kinds of tasks. When training the model, you build the computation graph, run the graph for training, and evaluate the graph for predictions. These tasks repeat until you are satisfied with the quality of the model, and then save the graph along with the learned parameters. In production, the graph is built or restored from a file and populated with the parameters.

Building deep learning models is a complex art and the TensorFlow API and its ecosystem are equally complex. When we build and train models in TensorFlow, sometimes we get different kinds of errors, or the models do not work as expected. As an example, how often do you see yourself getting stuck in one or more of the following situations:

- Getting NaN in loss and metrics output
- The loss or some other metric doesn't improve even after several iterations

In such situations, we would need to debug the code written using the TensorFlow API.

To fix the code so that it works, one could use the debugger or other methods and tools provided by the platform, such as the Python debugger (`pdb`) in Python and the GNU debugger (`gdb`) in Linux OS. The TensorFlow API also provides some additional support to fix the code when things go wrong.

In this chapter, we shall learn the additional tools and techniques available in TensorFlow to assist in debugging:

- Fetching tensor values with `tf.Session.run()`
- Printing tensor values with `tf.Print()`

- Asserting on conditions with `tf.Assert()`
- Debugging with the TensorFlow debugger (`tfdbg`)

Fetching tensor values with tf.Session.run()

You can fetch the tensor values you want to print with `tf.Session.run()`. The values are returned as a NumPy array and can be printed or logged with Python statements. This is the simplest and easiest approach, with the biggest drawback being that the computation graph executes all the dependent paths, starting from the fetched tensor, and if those paths include the training operations, then it advances one step or one epoch.

Therefore, most of the time you would not call `tf.Session.run()` to fetch tensors in the middle of the graph, but you would execute the whole graph and fetch all the tensors, the ones you need to debug along with the ones you do not need to debug.

The function `tf.Session.partial_run()` is also available for situations where you may want to execute part of the graph, but it is a highly experimental API and not ready for production use.

Printing tensor values with tf.Print()

Another option to print values for debugging purposes is to use `tf.Print()`. You can wrap a tensor in `tf.Print()` to print its values in the standard error console when the path containing the `tf.Print()` node is executed. The `tf.Print()` function has the following signature:

```
tf.Print(
     input_,
     data,
     message=None,
     first_n=None,
     summarize=None,
     name=None
    )
```

The arguments to this function are as follows:

- `input_` is a tensor that gets returned from the function without anything being done to it
- `data` is the list of tensors that get printed
- `message` is a string that gets printed as a prefix to the printed output
- `first_n` represents the number of steps to print the output; if this value is negative then the value is always printed whenever the path is executed
- `summarize` represents the number of elements to print from the tensor; by default, only three elements are printed

You can follow along with the code in the Jupyter notebook `ch-18_TensorFlow_Debugging`.

Let us modify the MNIST MLP model we created earlier to add the print statement:

```
model = tf.Print(input_=model,
                 data=[tf.argmax(model,1)],
                 message='y_hat=',
                 summarize=10,
                 first_n=5
                 )
```

When we run the code, we get the following in Jupyter's console:

```
I tensorflow/core/kernels/logging_ops.cc:79] y_hat=[0 0 0 7 0 0 0 0 0
0...]
I tensorflow/core/kernels/logging_ops.cc:79] y_hat=[0 7 7 1 8 7 2 7 7
0...]
I tensorflow/core/kernels/logging_ops.cc:79] y_hat=[4 8 0 6 1 8 1 0 7
0...]
I tensorflow/core/kernels/logging_ops.cc:79] y_hat=[0 0 1 0 0 0 0 5 7
5...]
I tensorflow/core/kernels/logging_ops.cc:79] y_hat=[9 2 2 8 8 6 6 1 7
7...]
```

The only disadvantage of using `tf.Print()` is that the function provides limited formatting functionality.

Asserting on conditions with tf.Assert()

Yet another way to debug TensorFlow models is to insert conditional asserts. The `tf.Assert()` function takes a condition, and if the condition is false, it then prints the lists of given tensors and throws `tf.errors.InvalidArgumentError`.

1. The `tf.Assert()` function has the following signature:

```
tf.Assert(
    condition,
    data,
    summarize=None,
    name=None
)
```

2. An assert operation does not fall in the path of the graph like the `tf.Print()` function. To make sure that the `tf.Assert()` operation gets executed, we need to add it to the dependencies. For example, let us define an assertion to check that all the inputs are positive:

```
assert_op =
tf.Assert(tf.reduce_all(tf.greater_equal(x,0)),[x])
```

3. Add`assert_op` to the dependencies at the time of defining the model, as follows:

```
with tf.control_dependencies([assert_op]):
    # x is input layer
    layer = x
    # add hidden layers
    for i in range(num_layers):
        layer = tf.nn.relu(tf.matmul(layer, w[i]) + b[i])
    # add output layer
    layer = tf.matmul(layer, w[num_layers]) + b[num_layers]
```

4. To test this code, we introduce an impurity after epoch 5, as follows:

```
if epoch > 5:
    X_batch = np.copy(X_batch)
    X_batch[0,0]=-2
```

5. The code runs fine for five epochs and then throws the error:

```
epoch: 0000   loss = 6.975991
epoch: 0001   loss = 2.246228
epoch: 0002   loss = 1.924571
epoch: 0003   loss = 1.745509
epoch: 0004   loss = 1.616791
epoch: 0005   loss = 1.520804

--------------------------------------------------------
---
InvalidArgumentError            Traceback (most recent call
last)
...
InvalidArgumentError: assertion failed: [[-2 0 0]...]
...
```

Apart from the `tf.Assert()` function, which can take any valid conditional expression, TensorFlow provides the following assertion operations that check for specific conditions and have a simple syntax:

- `assert_equal`
- `assert_greater`
- `assert_greater_equal`
- `assert_integer`
- `assert_less`
- `assert_less_equal`
- `assert_negative`
- `assert_none_equal`
- `assert_non_negative`
- `assert_non_positive`
- `assert_positive`
- `assert_proper_iterable`
- `assert_rank`
- `assert_rank_at_least`
- `assert_rank_in`
- `assert_same_float_dtype`
- `assert_scalar`
- `assert_type`
- `assert_variables_initialized`

As an example, the previously mentioned example assert operation can also be written as follows:

```
assert_op = tf.assert_greater_equal(x,0)
```

Debugging with the TensorFlow debugger (tfdbg)

The TensorFlow debugger (`tfdbg`) works the same way at a high level as other popular debuggers, such as `pdb` and `gdb`. To use a debugger, the process is generally as follows:

1. Set the breakpoints in the code at locations where you want to break and inspect the variables
2. Run the code in debug mode
3. When the code breaks at a breakpoint, inspect it and then move on to next step

Some debuggers also allow you to interactively watch the variables while the code is executing, not just at the breakpoint:

1. In order to use `tfdbg`, first import the required modules and wrap the session inside a debugger wrapper:

```
from tensorflow.python import debug as tfd

with tfd.LocalCLIDebugWrapperSession(tf.Session()) as tfs:
```

2. Next, attach a filter to the session object. Attaching a filter is the same as setting a breakpoint in other debuggers. For example, the following code attaches a `tfdbg.has_inf_or_nan` filter which breaks if any of the intermediate tensors have `nan` or `inf` values:

```
tfs.add_tensor_filter('has_inf_or_nan_filter',
tfd.has_inf_or_nan)
```

3. Now when the code executes the `tfs.run()`, the debugger will start a debugger interface in the console where you can run various debugger commands to watch the tensor values.
4. We have provided the code for trying out `tfdbg` in the `ch-18_mnist_tfdbg.py` file. We see the `tfdbg` console when we execute the code file with `python3`:</li>

```
python3 ch-18_mnist_tfdbg.py
```

```
--- run-start: run #1: 1 fetch (init); 0 feeds ---
| <-- --> | run_info
| run | invoke_stepper | exit |

TTTTTT FFFF DDD  BBBB   GGG
  TT   F    D  D B   B G
  TT   FFF  D  D BBBB  G  GG
  TT   F    D  D B   B G   G
  TT   F    DDD  BBBB   GGG

======================================
Session.run() call #1:

Fetch(es):
  init

Feed dict:
  (Empty)
======================================

Select one of the following commands to proceed ---->
  run:
    Execute the run() call with debug tensor-watching
  run -n:
    Execute the run() call without debug tensor-watching
  run -t <T>:
    Execute run() calls (T - 1) times without debugging, then execute run() once more with debugging and drop back to the CLI
  run -f <filter_name>:
    Keep executing run() calls until a dumped tensor passes a given, registered filter (conditional breakpoint mode)
    Registered filter(s):
        * has_inf_or_nan
  invoke_stepper:
    Use the node-stepper interface, which allows you to interactively step through nodes involved in the graph run() call and inspect/modify their values

For more details, see help..

--- Scroll (PgDn): 0.00% ---
tfdbg>
```

5. Give the command `run -f has_inf_or_nan` at the `tfdbg>` prompt. The code breaks after the first epoch, because we populated the data with the `np.inf` value:

```
--- run-end: run #552: 2 fetches; 2 feeds -----------------------------------------
| <-- --> | lt -f has_inf_or_nan
| list_tensors | node_info | print_tensor | list_inputs | list_outputs | run_info | help |
54 dumped tensor(s) passing filter "has_inf_or_nan":

t (ms)    Size (B) Op type                        Tensor name
[2.590]   306.49k  Switch                         Assert/AssertGuard/Assert/Switch_1:1
[3.053]   6.43k    MatMul                         MatMul:0
[3.318]   6.42k    Add                            add:0
[3.537]   6.42k    Relu                           Relu:0
[3.771]   12.68k   MatMul                         MatMul_1:0
[4.153]   12.68k   Add                            add_1:0
[4.411]   12.68k   Relu                           Relu_1:0
[4.600]   4.09k    MatMul                         MatMul_2:0
[4.875]   4.08k    Add                            add_2:0
[5.408]   4.08k    Print                          Print:0
[6.072]   4.09k    Reshape                        Reshape:0
[6.403]   4.13k    SoftmaxCrossEntropyWithLogits  SoftmaxCrossEntropyWithLogits:1
[6.410]   624      SoftmaxCrossEntropyWithLogits  SoftmaxCrossEntropyWithLogits:0
[6.810]   584      Reshape                        Reshape_2:0
[7.009]   172      Mean                           Mean:0
[8.235]   4.17k    Mul                            gradients/SoftmaxCrossEntropyWithLogits_grad/mul:0
[8.367]   4.13k    Reshape                        gradients/Reshape_grad/Reshape:0
[8.586]   256      Sum                            gradients/add_2_grad/Sum_1:0
[8.590]   4.12k    Sum                            gradients/add_2_grad/Sum:0
[8.754]   4.13k    Reshape                        gradients/add_2_grad/Reshape:0
[8.905]   264      Reshape                        gradients/add_2_grad/Reshape_1:0
[9.023]   4.16k    Identity                       gradients/add_2_grad/tuple/control_dependency:0
[9.211]   298      Identity                       gradients/add_2_grad/tuple/control_dependency_1:0
[9.221]   12.72k   MatMul                         gradients/MatMul_2_grad/MatMul:0
[9.345]   1.48k    MatMul                         gradients/MatMul_2_grad/MatMul_1:0
[9.492]   12.76k   Identity                       gradients/MatMul_2_grad/tuple/control_dependency:0
[9.495]   1.51k    Identity                       gradients/MatMul_2_grad/tuple/control_dependency_1:0
[9.504]   302      ApplyGradientDescent           GradientDescent/update_b_out/ApplyGradientDescent:0
[9.668]   1.51k    ApplyGradientDescent           GradientDescent/update_w_out/ApplyGradientDescent:0
[9.719]   12.72k   ReluGrad                       gradients/Relu_1_grad/ReluGrad:0
[9.949]   12.71k   Sum                            gradients/add_1_grad/Sum:0
[9.956]   346      Sum                            gradients/add_1_grad/Sum_1:0
[10.101]  354      Reshape                        gradients/add_1_grad/Reshape_1:0
[10.121]  12.72k   Reshape                        gradients/add_1_grad/Reshape:0
[10.280]  12.75k   Identity                       gradients/add_1_grad/tuple/control_dependency:0
[10.280]  388      Identity                       gradients/add_1_grad/tuple/control_dependency_1:0
[10.564]  394      ApplyGradientDescent           GradientDescent/update_b_0001/ApplyGradientDescent:0
[10.612]  6.47k    MatMul                         gradients/MatMul_1_grad/MatMul:0
[10.618]  2.23k    MatMul                         gradients/MatMul_1_grad/MatMul_1:0
[10.812]  2.26k    Identity                       gradients/MatMul_1_grad/tuple/control_dependency_1:0
[10.822]  6.51k    Identity                       gradients/MatMul_1_grad/tuple/control_dependency:0
[11.028]  6.47k    ReluGrad                       gradients/Relu_grad/ReluGrad:0
[11.034]  2.26k    ApplyGradientDescent           GradientDescent/update_w_0001/ApplyGradientDescent:0
[11.247]  276      Sum                            gradients/add_grad/Sum_1:0
[11.254]  6.46k    Sum                            gradients/add_grad/Sum:0
[11.399]  6.47k    Reshape                        gradients/add_grad/Reshape:0
[11.406]  284      Reshape                        gradients/add_grad/Reshape_1:0
[11.563]  6.50k    Identity                       gradients/add_grad/tuple/control_dependency:0
[11.565]  318      Identity                       gradients/add_grad/tuple/control_dependency_1:0
--- Scroll (PgDn): 0.00% ----------------------------------------------------------
tfdbg>
```

6. Now you can use the `tfdbg` console or the clickable interface to inspect the values of various tensors. For example, we look at the values of one of the gradients:

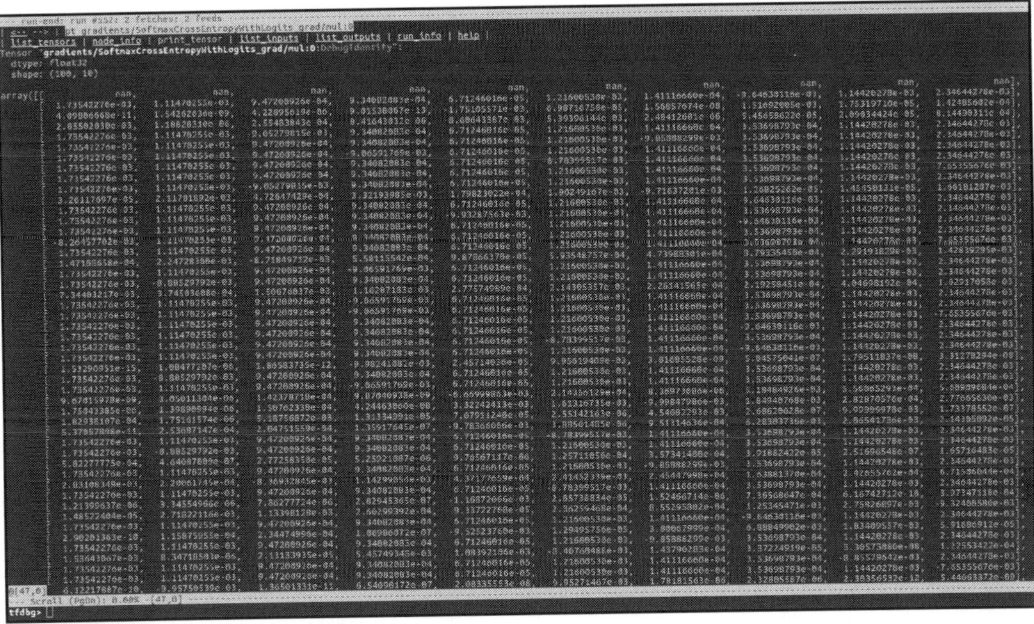

You can find more information about using the `tfdbg` console and inspecting the variables at the following link: `https://www.tensorflow.org/programmers_guide/debugger`.

Summary

In this chapter, we learned how to debug the code for building and training models in TensorFlow. We learned that we can fetch the tensors as NumPy arrays using `tf.Session.run()`. We can also print the values of tensors by adding `tf.Print()` operations in the computation graph. We also learned how to raise errors when certain conditions fail to hold during execution with `tf.Assert()` and other `tf.assert_*` operations. We closed the chapter with an introduction to the TensorFlow debugger (`tfdbg`) for setting breakpoints and watching the values of tensors like we would do for debugging the code in the Python debugger (`pdb`) or the GNU debugger (`gdb`).

This chapter brings our journey to a new milestone. We do not expect that the journey ends here, but we believe that the journey just got started and you will further expand and apply the knowledge and skills gained in this book.

We are keenly looking forward to hearing your experiences, feedback, and suggestions.

19
Tensor Processing Units

A **Tensor Processing Unit** (**TPU**) is an **application-specific integrated circuit** (**ASIC**) that implements hardware circuits optimized for the computation requirements of deep neural networks. A TPU is based on a **Complex Instruction Set Computer** (**CISC**) instruction set that implements high-level instructions for running complex tasks for training deep neural networks. The heart of the TPU architecture resides in the systolic arrays that optimize the matrix operations.

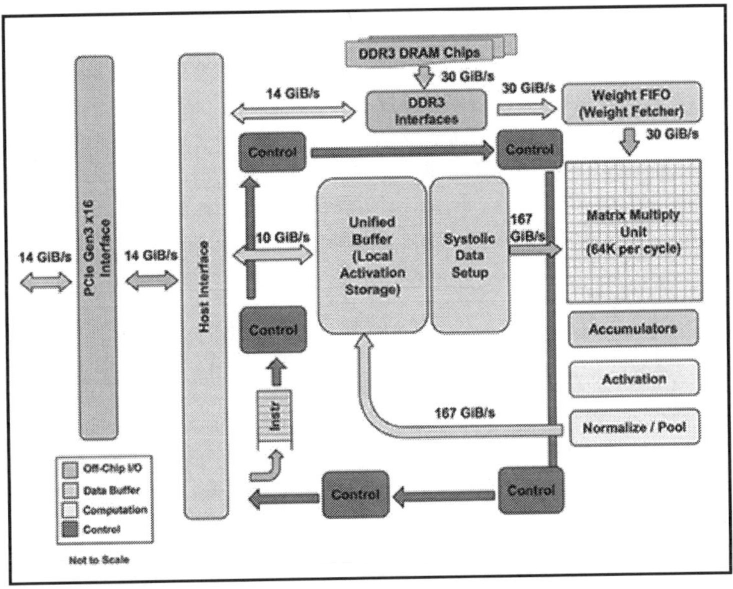

The Architecture of TPU

Image from: https://cloud.google.com/blog/big-data/2017/05/images/149454602921110/tpu-15.png

TensorFlow provides a compiler and software stack that translates the API calls from TensorFlow graphs into TPU instructions. The following block diagram depicts the architecture of TensorFlow models running on top of the TPU stack:

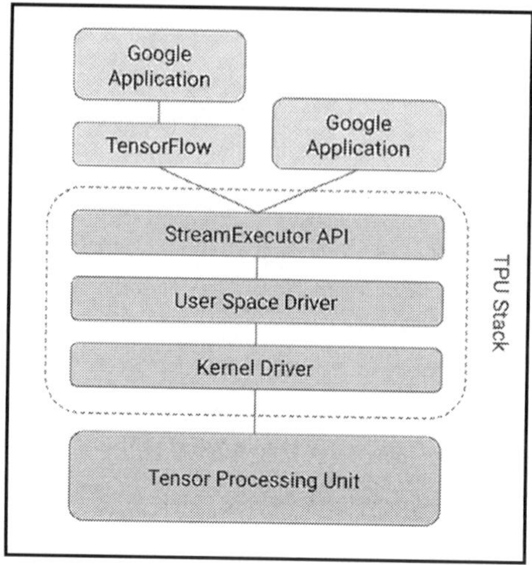

Image from: https://cloud.google.com/blog/big-data/2017/05/images/149454602921110/tpu-2.png

For more information on the TPU architecture, read the blog at the following link: `https://cloud.google.com/blog/big-data/2017/05/an-in-depth-look-at-googles-first-tensor-processing-unit-tpu`.

The TensorFlow API for the TPU resides in the `tf.contrib.tpu` module. For building the models on the TPU, the following three TPU-specific TensorFlow modules are used:

- `tpu_config`: The `tpu_config` module allows you to create the configuration object that contains information about the host that would be running the model.
- `tpu_estimator`: The `tpu_estimator` module encapsulates the estimator in the `TPUEstimator` class. To run the estimator on the TPU, we create an object of this class.
- `tpu_optimizer`: The `tpu_optimizer` module wraps the optimizer. For example, in the following sample code we wrap the SGD optimizer in the `CrossShardOptimizer` class from the `tpu_optimizer` module.

As an example, the following code builds the CNN model for the MNIST dataset on the TPU with the TF Estimator API:

The following code is adapted from https://github.com/tensorflow/tpu-demos/blob/master/cloud_tpu/models/mnist/mnist.py.

```
import tensorflow as tf

from tensorflow.contrib.tpu.python.tpu import tpu_config
from tensorflow.contrib.tpu.python.tpu import tpu_estimator
from tensorflow.contrib.tpu.python.tpu import tpu_optimizer

learning_rate = 0.01
batch_size = 128

def metric_fn(labels, logits):
    predictions = tf.argmax(logits, 1)
    return {
        "accuracy": tf.metrics.precision(
            labels=labels, predictions=predictions),
    }

def model_fn(features, labels, mode):
    if mode == tf.estimator.ModeKeys.PREDICT:
        raise RuntimeError("mode {} is not supported
yet".format(mode))

    input_layer = tf.reshape(features, [-1, 28, 28, 1])
    conv1 = tf.layers.conv2d(
        inputs=input_layer,
        filters=32,
        kernel_size=[5, 5],
        padding="same",
        activation=tf.nn.relu)
    pool1 = tf.layers.max_pooling2d(inputs=conv1, pool_size=[2, 2],
                                    strides=2)
    conv2 = tf.layers.conv2d(
        inputs=pool1,
        filters=64,
        kernel_size=[5, 5],
        padding="same",
        activation=tf.nn.relu)
    pool2 = tf.layers.max_pooling2d(inputs=conv2, pool_size=[2, 2],
                                    strides=2)
    pool2_flat = tf.reshape(pool2, [-1, 7 * 7 * 64])
```

```
    dense = tf.layers.dense(inputs=pool2_flat, units=128,
                            activation=tf.nn.relu)
    dropout = tf.layers.dropout(
        inputs=dense, rate=0.4,
        training=mode == tf.estimator.ModeKeys.TRAIN)
    logits = tf.layers.dense(inputs=dropout, units=10)
    onehot_labels = tf.one_hot(indices=tf.cast(labels, tf.int32),
depth=10)

    loss = tf.losses.softmax_cross_entropy(
        onehot_labels=onehot_labels, logits=logits)

    if mode == tf.estimator.ModeKeys.EVAL:
        return tpu_estimator.TPUEstimatorSpec(
            mode=mode,
            loss=loss,
            eval_metrics=(metric_fn, [labels, logits]))

    # Train.
    decaying_learning_rate = tf.train.exponential_decay(learning_rate,
tf.train.get_global_step(),
                                                        100000,0.96)

    optimizer = tpu_optimizer.CrossShardOptimizer(
            tf.train.GradientDescentOptimizer(
                learning_rate=decaying_learning_rate))

    train_op = optimizer.minimize(loss,
            global_step=tf.train.get_global_step())
    return tpu_estimator.TPUEstimatorSpec(mode=mode,
            loss=loss, train_op=train_op)

def get_input_fn(filename):
    def input_fn(params):
        batch_size = params["batch_size"]

        def parser(serialized_example):
            features = tf.parse_single_example(
                serialized_example,
                features={
                    "image_raw": tf.FixedLenFeature([], tf.string),
                    "label": tf.FixedLenFeature([], tf.int64),
                })
            image = tf.decode_raw(features["image_raw"], tf.uint8)
            image.set_shape([28 * 28])
            image = tf.cast(image, tf.float32) * (1. / 255) - 0.5
            label = tf.cast(features["label"], tf.int32)
            return image, label
```

```
        dataset = tf.data.TFRecordDataset(
            filename, buffer_size=FLAGS.dataset_reader_buffer_size)
        dataset = dataset.map(parser).cache().repeat()
        dataset = dataset.apply(
            tf.contrib.data.batch_and_drop_remainder(batch_size))
        images, labels = dataset.make_one_shot_iterator().get_next()
        return images, labels
    return input_fn

# TPU config

master = 'local' #URL of the TPU instance
model dir = '/home/armando/models/mnist'
n_iterations = 50  # number of iterations per TPU training loop
n_shards = 8   # number of TPU chips

run_config = tpu_config.RunConfig(
        master=master,
        evaluation_master=master,
        model_dir=model_dir,
        session_config=tf.ConfigProto(
            allow_soft_placement=True,
            log_device_placement=True
        ),
        tpu_config=tpu_config.TPUConfig(n_iterations,
                                        n_shards
        )
    )

estimator = tpu_estimator.TPUEstimator(
    model_fn=model_fn,
    use_tpu=True,
    train_batch_size=batch_size,
    eval_batch_size=batch_size,
    config=run_config)

train_file = '/home/armando/datasets/mnist/train' # input data file
train_steps = 1000 # number of steps to train for

estimator.train(input_fn=get_input_fn(train_file),
                max_steps=train_steps
                )
```

```
eval_file = '/home/armando/datasets/mnist/test' # test data file
eval_steps = 10

estimator.evaluate(input_fn=get_input_fn(eval_file),
                   steps=eval_steps
                   )
```

More examples of building models on a TPU can be found at the following link: `https://github.com/tensorflow/tpu-demos`.

20
Getting Started

Computer vision is the science of understanding or manipulating images and videos. Computer vision has a lot of applications, including autonomous driving, industrial inspection, and augmented reality. The use of deep learning for computer vision can be categorized into multiple categories: classification, detection, segmentation, and generation, both in images and videos. In this book, you will learn how to train deep learning models for computer vision applications and deploy them on multiple platforms. We will use **TensorFlow**, a popular python library for deep learning throughout this book for the examples. In this chapter, we will cover the following topics:

- The basics and vocabulary of deep learning
- How deep learning meets computer vision?
- Setting up the development environment that will be used for the examples covered in this book
- Getting a feel for TensorFlow, along with its powerful tools, such as TensorBoard and TensorFlow Serving

Understanding deep learning

Computer vision as a field has a long history. With the emergence of deep learning, computer vision has proven to be useful for various applications. Deep learning is a collection of techniques from **artificial neural network** (**ANN**), which is a branch of machine learning. ANNs are modelled on the human brain; there are nodes linked to each other that pass information to each other. In the following sections, we will discuss in detail how deep learning works by understanding the commonly used basic terms.

Perceptron

An artificial neuron or perceptron takes several inputs and performs a weighted summation to produce an output. The weight of the perceptron is determined during the training process and is based on the training data. The following is a diagram of the perceptron:

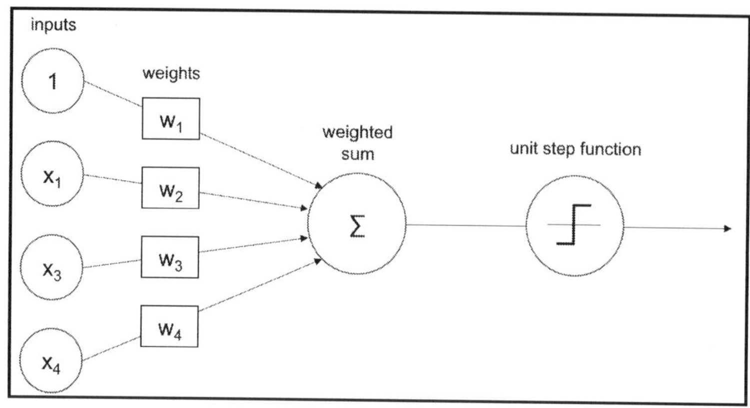

The inputs are weighted and summed as shown in the preceding image. The sum is then passed through a unit step function, in this case, for a binary classification problem. A perceptron can only learn simple functions by learning the weights from examples. The process of learning the weights is called training. The training on a perceptron can be done through gradient-based methods which are explained in a later section. The output of the perceptron can be passed through an `activation` function or `transfer` function, which will be explained in the next section.

Activation functions

The `activation` functions make **neural nets** nonlinear. An activation function decides whether a perceptron should fire or not. During training activation, functions play an important role in adjusting the gradients. An `activation` function such as sigmoid, shown in the next section, attenuates the values with higher magnitudes. This nonlinear behaviour of the `activation` function gives the deep nets to learn complex functions. Most of the `activation` functions are continuous and differential functions, except rectified unit at 0. A continuous function has small changes in output for every small change in input. A differential function has a derivative existing at every point in the domain.

In order to train a neural network, the function has to be differentiable. Following are a few `activation` functions.

Don't worry if you don't understand the terms like continuous and differentiable in detail. It will become clearer over the chapters.

Sigmoid

Sigmoid can be considered a smoothened step function and hence differentiable. Sigmoid is useful for converting any value to probabilities and can be used for binary classification. The sigmoid maps input to a value in the range of 0 to 1, as shown in the following graph:

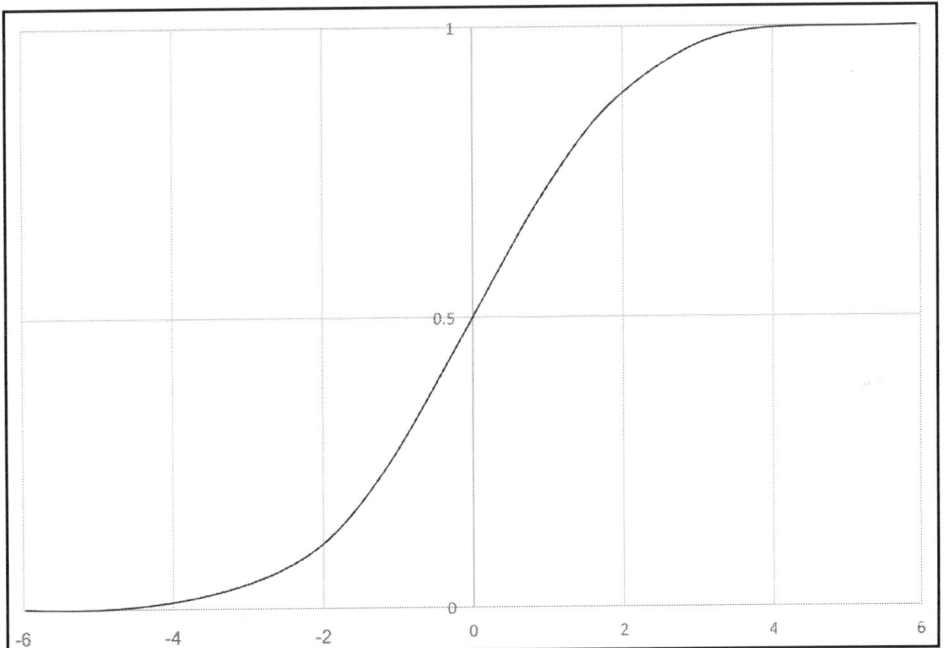

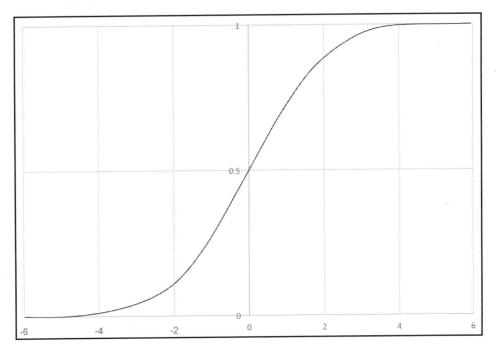

The change in *Y* values with respect to *X* is going to be small, and hence, there will be vanishing gradients. After some learning, the change may be small. Another activation function called `tanh`, explained in next section, is a scaled version of sigmoid and avoids the problem of a vanishing gradient.

The hyperbolic tangent function

The hyperbolic tangent function, or `tanh`, is the scaled version of sigmoid. Like sigmoid, it is smooth and differentiable. The `tanh` maps input to a value in the range of -1 to 1, as shown in the following graph:

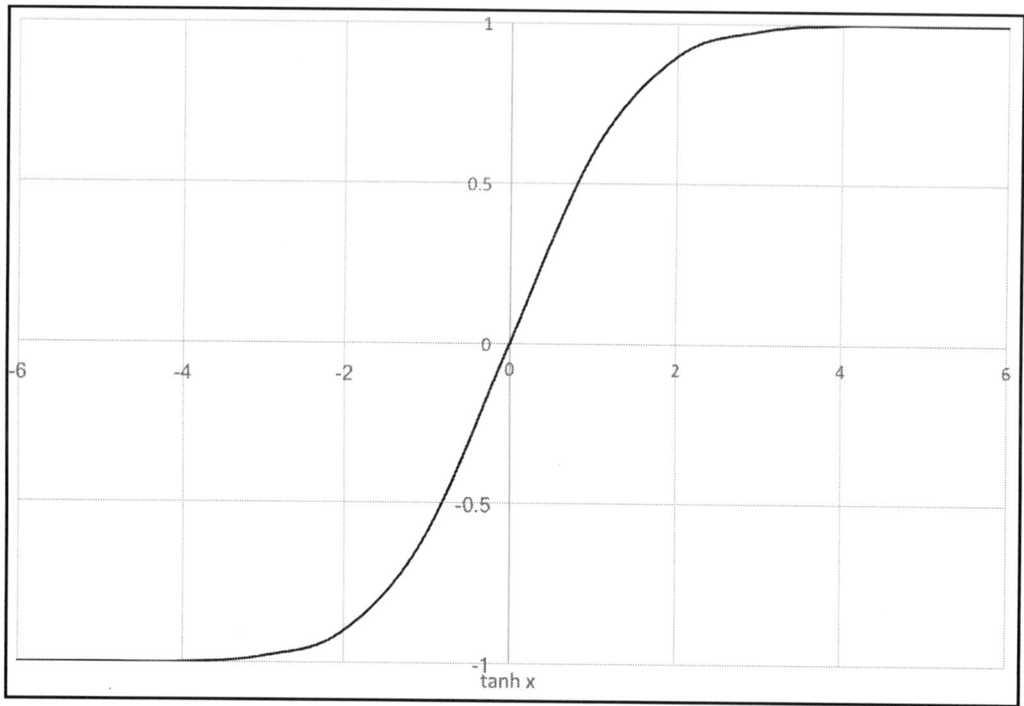

The gradients are more stable than sigmoid and hence have fewer vanishing gradient problems. Both sigmoid and `tanh` fire all the time, making the ANN really heavy. The **Rectified Linear Unit** (**ReLU**) activation function, explained in the next section, avoids this pitfall by not firing at times.

The Rectified Linear Unit (ReLU)

ReLu can let big numbers pass through. This makes a few neurons stale and they don't fire. This increases the sparsity, and hence, it is good. The `ReLU` maps input x to max $(0, x)$, that is, they map negative inputs to 0, and positive inputs are output without any change as shown in the following graph:

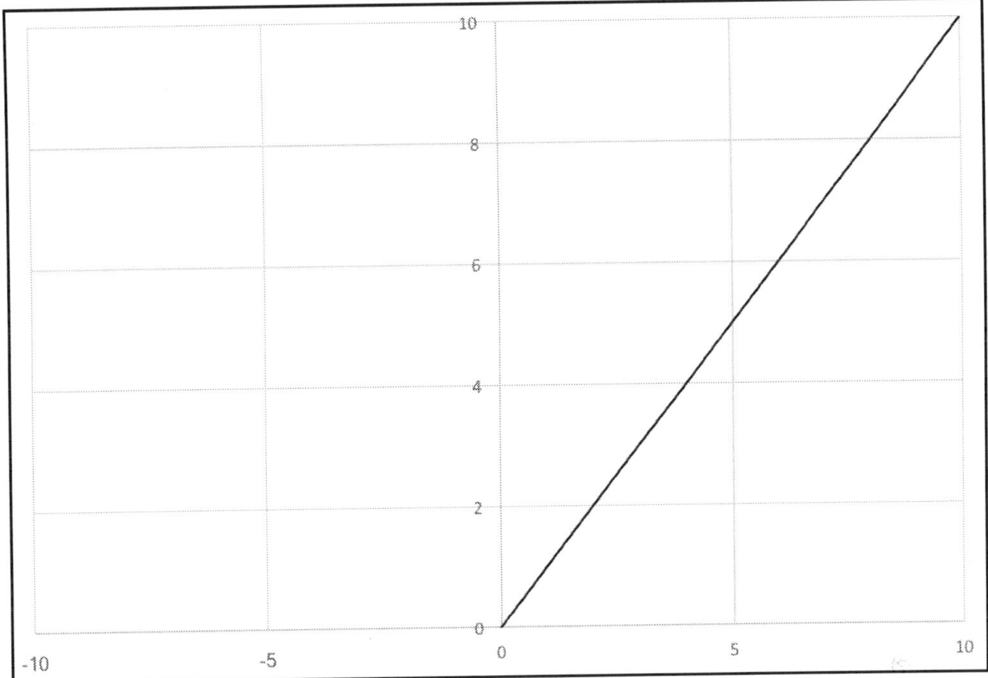

Because ReLU doesn't fire all the time, it can be trained faster. Since the function is simple, it is computationally the least expensive. Choosing the `activation` function is very dependent on the application. Nevertheless, ReLU works well for a large range of problems. In the next section, you will learn how to stack several perceptrons together that can learn more complex functions than perceptron.

Artificial neural network (ANN)

ANN is a collection of perceptrons and `activation` functions. The perceptrons are connected to form hidden layers or units. The hidden units form the nonlinear basis that maps the input layers to output layers in a lower-dimensional space, which is also called artificial neural networks. ANN is a map from input to output. The map is computed by weighted addition of the inputs with biases. The values of weight and bias values along with the architecture are called `model`.

The training process determines the values of these weights and biases. The model values are initialized with random values during the beginning of the training. The error is computed using a loss function by contrasting it with the ground truth. Based on the loss computed, the weights are tuned at every step. The training is stopped when the error cannot be further reduced. The training process learns the features during the training. The features are a better representation than the raw images. The following is a diagram of an artificial neural network, or multi-layer perceptron:

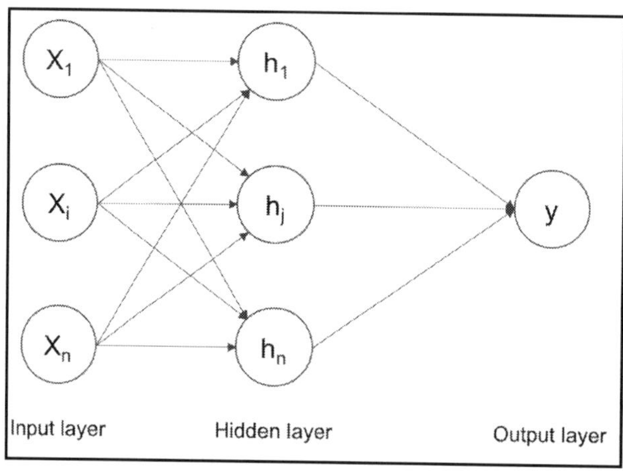

Several inputs of *x* are passed through a hidden layer of perceptrons and summed to the output. The universal approximation theorem suggests that such a neural network can approximate any function. The hidden layer can also be called a dense layer. Every layer can have one of the `activation` functions described in the previous section. The number of hidden layers and perceptrons can be chosen based on the problem. There are a few more things that make this multilayer perceptron work for multi-class classification problems. A multi-class classification problem tries to discriminate more than ten categories. We will explore those terms in the following sections.

One-hot encoding

One-hot encoding is a way to represent the target variables or classes in case of a classification problem. The target variables can be converted from the string labels to one-hot encoded vectors. A one-hot vector is filled with *1* at the index of the target class but with *0* everywhere else. For example, if the target classes are cat and dog, they can be represented by [*1*, *0*] and [*0*, *1*], respectively. For 1,000 classes, one-hot vectors will be of size 1,000 integers with all zeros but *1*. It makes no assumptions about the similarity of target variables. With the combination of one-hot encoding with softmax explained in the following section, multi-class classification becomes possible in ANN.

Softmax

Softmax is a way of forcing the neural networks to output the sum of 1. Thereby, the output values of the `softmax` function can be considered as part of a probability distribution. This is useful in multi-class classification problems. Softmax is a kind of `activation` function with the speciality of output summing to 1. It converts the outputs to probabilities by dividing the output by summation of all the other values. The Euclidean distance can be computed between softmax probabilities and one-hot encoding for optimization. But the cross-entropy explained in the next section is a better cost function to optimize.

Cross-entropy

Cross-entropy compares the distance between the outputs of softmax and one-hot encoding. Cross-entropy is a loss function for which error has to be minimized. Neural networks estimate the probability of the given data to every class. The probability has to be maximized to the correct target label. Cross-entropy is the summation of negative logarithmic probabilities. Logarithmic value is used for numerical stability. Maximizing a function is equivalent to minimizing the negative of the same function. In the next section, we will see the following regularization methods to avoid the overfitting of ANN:

- Dropout
- Batch normalization
- L1 and L2 normalization

Dropout

Dropout is an effective way of regularizing neural networks to avoid the overfitting of ANN. During training, the dropout layer cripples the neural network by removing hidden units stochastically as shown in the following image:

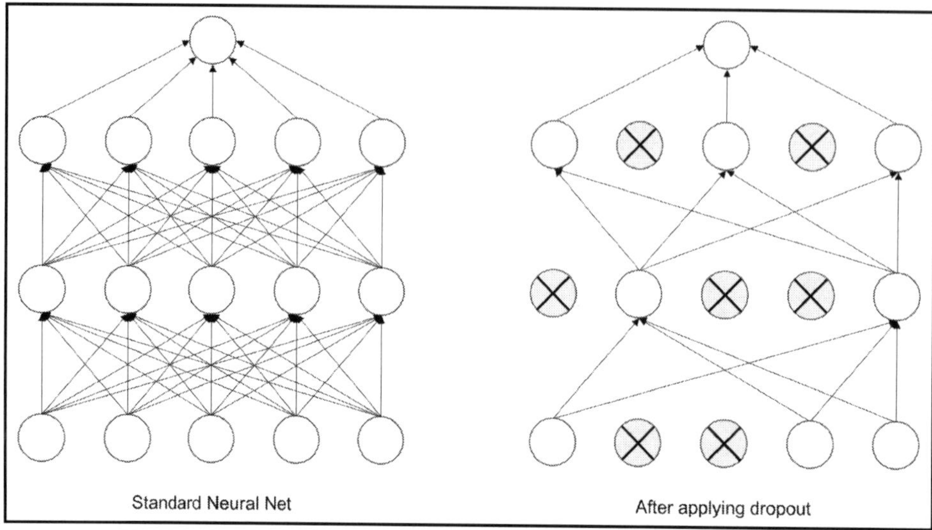

Note how the neurons are randomly trained. Dropout is also an efficient way of combining several neural networks. For each training case, we randomly select a few hidden units so that we end up with different architectures for each case. This is an extreme case of bagging and model averaging. Dropout layer should not be used during the inference as it is not necessary.

Batch normalization

Batch normalization, or batch-norm, increase the stability and performance of neural network training. It normalizes the output from a layer with zero mean and a standard deviation of 1. This reduces overfitting and makes the network train faster. It is very useful in training complex neural networks.

L1 and L2 regularization

L1 penalizes the absolute value of the weight and tends to make the weights zero. L2 penalizes the squared value of the weight and tends to make the weight smaller during the training. Both the regularizes assume that models with smaller weights are better.

Training neural networks

Training ANN is tricky as it contains several parameters to optimize. The procedure of updating the weights is called backpropagation. The procedure to minimize the error is called optimization. We will cover both of them in detail in the next sections.

Backpropagation

A backpropagation algorithm is commonly used for training artificial neural networks. The weights are updated from backward based on the error calculated as shown in the following image:

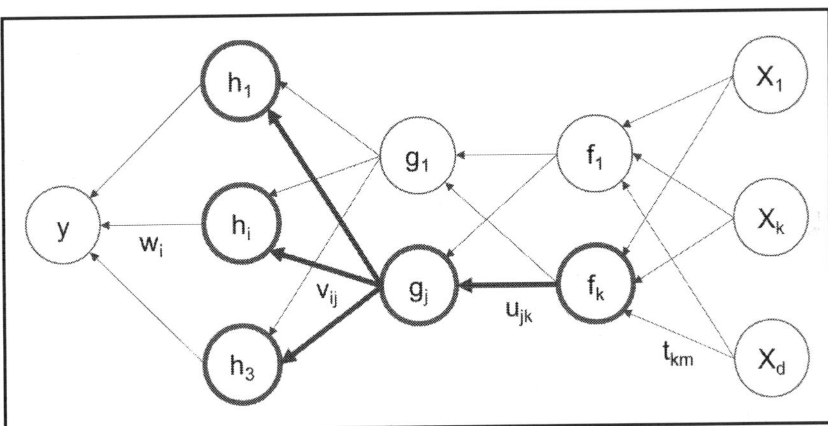

After calculating the error, gradient descent can be used to calculate the weight updating, as explained in the next section.

Gradient descent

The gradient descent algorithm performs multidimensional optimization. The objective is to reach the global maximum. Gradient descent is a popular optimization technique used in many machine-learning models. It is used to improve or optimize the model prediction. One implementation of gradient descent is called the **stochastic gradient descent** (**SGD**) and is becoming more popular (explained in the next section) in neural networks. Optimization involves calculating the error value and changing the weights to achieve that minimal error. The direction of finding the minimum is the negative of the gradient of the `loss` function. The gradient descent procedure is qualitatively shown in the following figure:

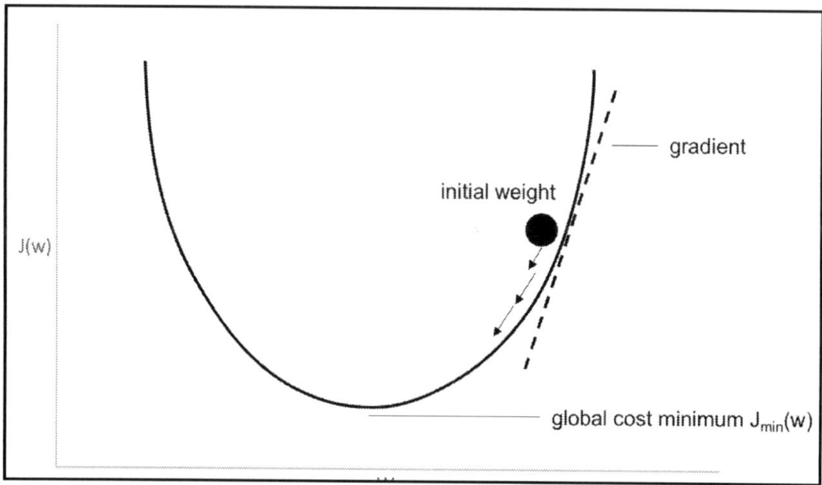

The learning rate determines how big each step should be. Note that the ANN with nonlinear activations will have local minima. SGD works better in practice for optimizing non-convex cost functions.

Stochastic gradient descent

SGD is the same as gradient descent, except that it is used for only partial data to train every time. The parameter is called mini-batch size. Theoretically, even one example can be used for training. In practice, it is better to experiment with various numbers. In the next section, we will discuss convolutional neural networks that work better on image data than the standard ANN.

Visit `https://yihui.name/animation/example/grad-desc/` to see a great visualization of gradient descent on convex and non-convex surfaces.

Playing with TensorFlow playground

TensorFlow playground is an interactive visualization of neural networks. Visit `http://playground.tensorflow.org/`, play by changing the parameters to see how the previously mentioned terms work together. Here is a screenshot of the playground:

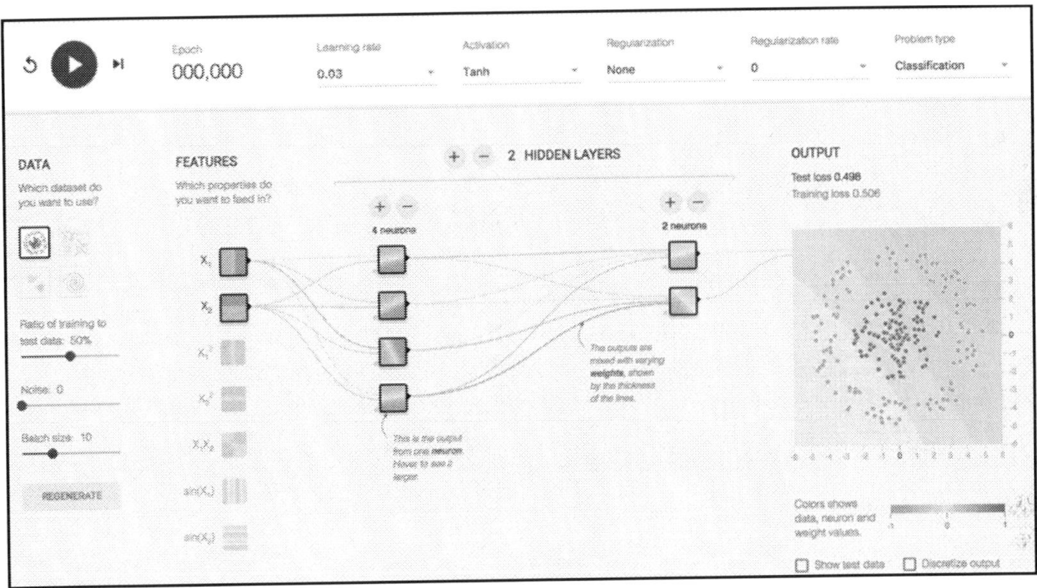

Dashboard in the TensorFlow playground

As shown previously, the reader can change learning rate, activation, regularization, hidden units, and layers to see how it affects the training process. You can spend some time adjusting the parameters to get the intuition of how neural networks for various kinds of data.

Convolutional neural network

Convolutional neural networks (CNN) are similar to the neural networks described in the previous sections. CNNs have weights, biases, and outputs through a nonlinear activation. Regular neural networks take inputs and the neurons fully connected to the next layers. Neurons within the same layer don't share any connections. If we use regular neural networks for images, they will be very large in size due to a huge number of neurons, resulting in overfitting. We cannot use this for images, as images are large in size. Increase the model size as it requires a huge number of neurons. An image can be considered a volume with dimensions of height, width, and depth. Depth is the channel of an image, which is red, blue, and green. The neurons of a CNN are arranged in a volumetric fashion to take advantage of the volume. Each of the layers transforms the input volume to an output volume as shown in the following image:

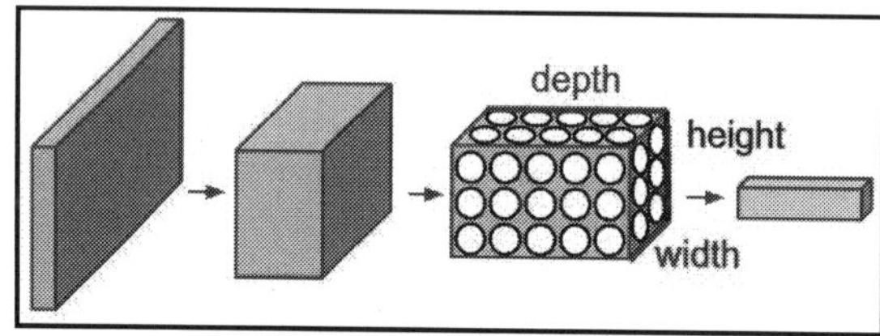

Convolution neural network filters encode by transformation. The learned filters detect features or patterns in images. The deeper the layer, the more abstract the pattern is. Some analyses have shown that these layers have the ability to detect edges, corners, and patterns. The learnable parameters in CNN layers are less than the dense layer described in the previous section.

Kernel

Kernel is the parameter convolution layer used to convolve the image. The convolution operation is shown in the following figure:

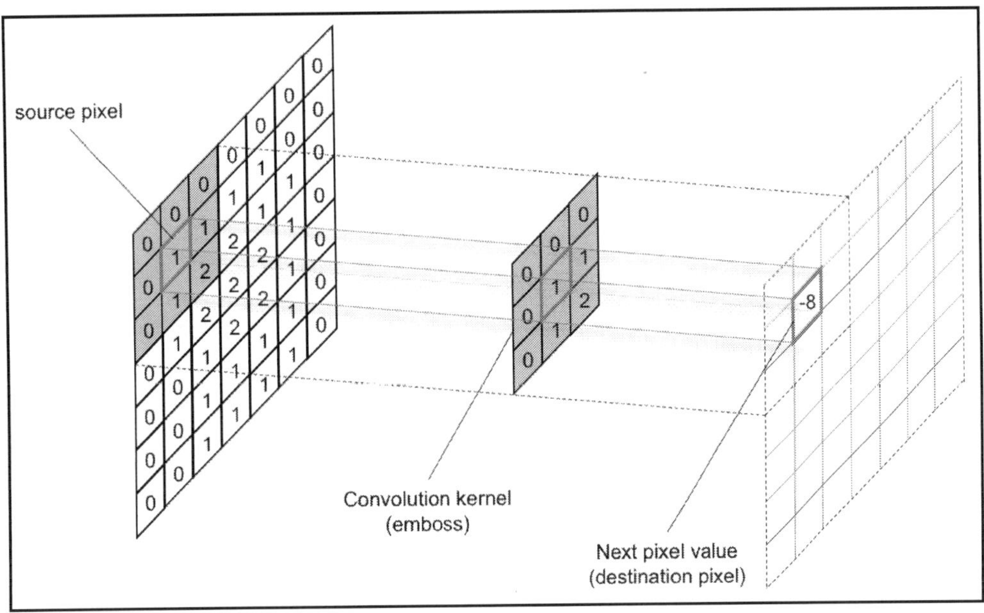

The kernel has two parameters, called stride and size. The size can be any dimension of a rectangle. Stride is the number of pixels moved every time. A stride of length 1 produces an image of almost the same size, and a stride of length 2 produces half the size. Padding the image will help in achieving the same size of the input.

Max pooling

Pooling layers are placed between convolution layers. Pooling layers reduce the size of the image across layers by sampling. The sampling is done by selecting the maximum value in a window. Average pooling averages over the window. Pooling also acts as a regularization technique to avoid overfitting. Pooling is carried out on all the channels of features. Pooling can also be performed with various strides.

The size of the window is a measure of the receptive field of CNN. The following figure shows an example of max pooling:

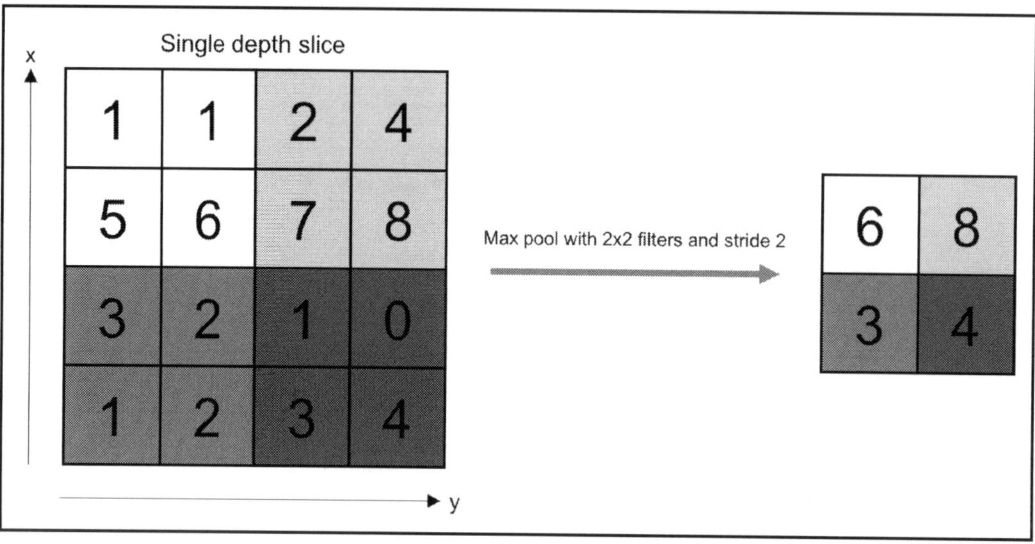

CNN is the single most important component of any deep learning model for computer vision. It won't be an exaggeration to state that it will be impossible for any computer to have vision without a CNN. In the next sections, we will discuss a couple of advanced layers that can be used for a few applications.

Visit `https://www.youtube.com/watch?v=jajksuQW4mc` for a great visualization of a CNN and max-pooling operation.

Recurrent neural networks (RNN)

Recurrent neural networks (**RNN**) can model sequential information. They do not assume that the data points are intensive. They perform the same task from the output of the previous data of a series of sequence data. This can also be thought of as memory. RNN cannot remember from longer sequences or time. It is unfolded during the training process, as shown in the following image:

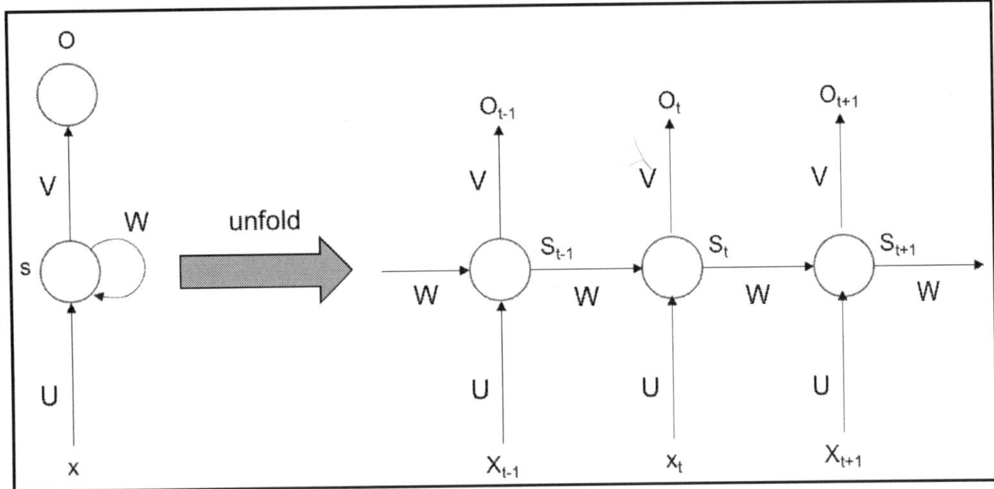

As shown in the preceding figure, the step is unfolded and trained each time. During backpropagation, the gradients can vanish over time. To overcome this problem, Long short-term memory can be used to remember over a longer time period.

Long short-term memory (LSTM)

Long short-term memory (**LSTM**) can store information for longer periods of time, and hence, it is efficient in capturing long-term efficiencies. The following figure illustrates how an LSTM cell is designed:

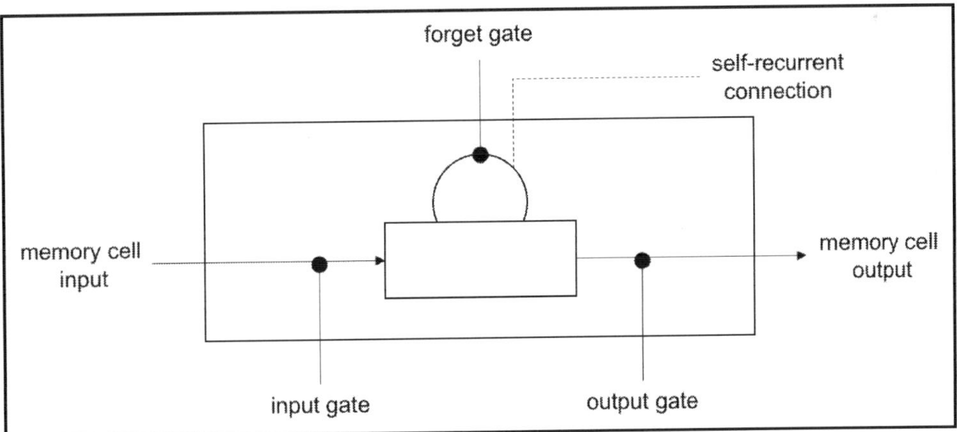

LSTM has several gates: forget, input, and output. Forget gate maintains the information previous state. The input gate updates the current state using the input. The output gate decides the information be passed to the next state. The ability to forget and retain only the important things enables LSTM to remember over a longer time period. You have learned the deep learning vocabulary that will be used throughout the book. In the next section, we will see how deep learning can be used in the context of computer vision.

Deep learning for computer vision

Computer vision enables the properties of human vision on a computer. A computer could be in the form of a smartphone, drones, CCTV, MRI scanner, and so on, with various sensors for perception. The sensor produces images in a digital form that has to be interpreted by the computer. The basic building block of such interpretation or intelligence is explained in the next section. The different problems that arise in computer vision can be effectively solved using deep learning techniques.

Classification

Image classification is the task of labelling the whole image with an object or concept with confidence. The applications include gender classification given an image of a person's face, identifying the type of pet, tagging photos, and so on. The following is an output of such a classification task:

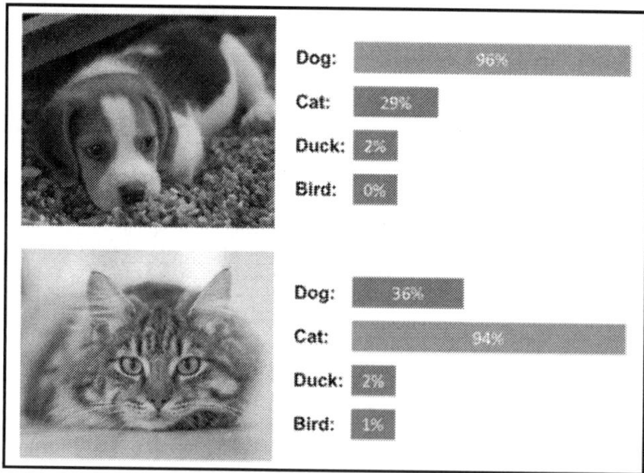

The Chapter 21, *Image Classification*, covers in detail the methods that can be used for classification tasks and in Chapter 22, *Image Retrieval*, we use the classification models for visualization of deep learning models and retrieve similar images.

Detection or localization and segmentation

Detection or localization is a task that finds an object in an image and localizes the object with a bounding box. This task has many applications, such as finding pedestrians and signboards for self-driving vehicles. The following image is an illustration of detection:

Segmentation is the task of doing pixel-wise classification. This gives a fine separation of objects. It is useful for processing medical images and satellite imagery. More examples and explanations can be found in Chapter 23, *Object Detection* and Chapter 24, *Semantic Segmentation*.

Similarity learning

Similarity learning is the process of learning how two images are similar. A score can be computed between two images based on the semantic meaning as shown in the following image:

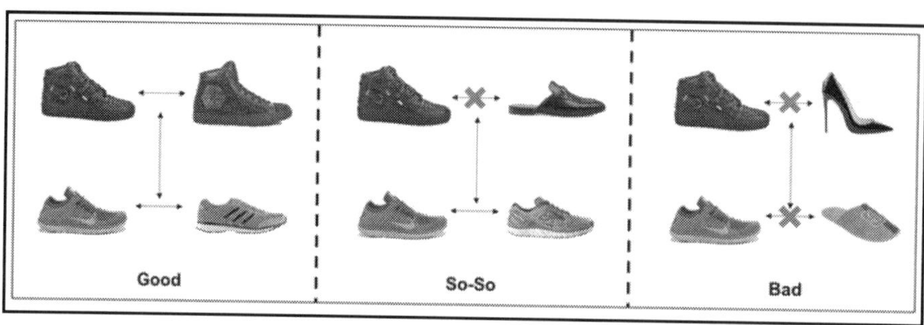

There are several applications of this, from finding similar products to performing the facial identification. `Chapter 25`, *Similarity learning*, deals with similarity learning techniques.

Image captioning

Image captioning is the task of describing the image with text as shown [below] here:

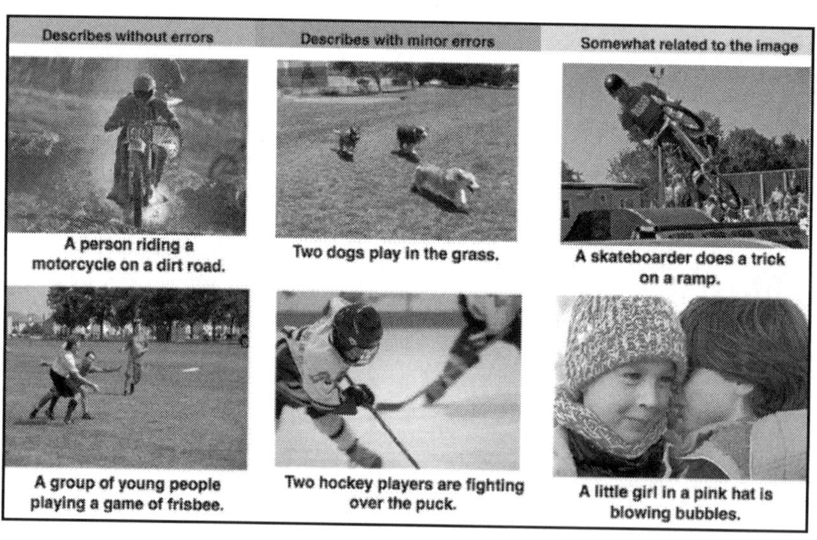

Reproduced with permission from Vinyals et al.

Image Captioning is a unique case where techniques of **natural language processing** (**NLP**) and computer vision have to be combined.

Generative models

Generative models are very interesting as they generate images. The following is an example of style transfer application where an image is generated with the content of that image and style of other images:

Reproduced with permission from Gatys et al.

Images can be generated for other purposes such as new training examples, super-resolution images, and so on.

Video analysis

Video analysis processes a video as a whole, as opposed to images as in previous cases. It has several applications, such as sports tracking, intrusion detection, and surveillance cameras. The new dimension of temporal data gives rise to lots of interesting applications. In the next section, we will see how to set up the development environment.

Development environment setup

In this section, we will set up the programming environment that will be useful for following the examples in the rest of the book. Readers may have the following choices of Operating Systems:

- **Development Operating Systems(OS)** such as Mac, Ubuntu, or Windows
- **Deployment Operating Systems** such as Mac, Windows, Android, iOs, or Ubuntu installed in Cloud platform such as **Amazon Web Services** (**AWS**), **Google Cloud Platform** (**GCP**), Azure, Tegra, Raspberry Pi

Irrespective of the platforms, all the code developed in this book should run without any issues. In this chapter, we will cover the installation procedures for the development environment.

Hardware and Operating Systems - OS

For the development environment, you need to have a lot of computing power as training is significantly computationally expensive. Mac users are rather limited to computing power. Windows and Ubuntu users can beef up their development environment with more processors and **General Purpose - Graphics Processing Unit (GP-GPU)**, which will be explained in the next section.

General Purpose - Graphics Processing Unit (GP-GPU)

GP-GPUs are special hardware that speeds up the training process of training deep learning models. The GP-GPUs supplied by NVIDIA company are very popular for deep learning training and deployment as it has well-matured software and community support. Readers can set up a machine with such a GP-GPU for faster training. There are plenty of choices available, and the reader can choose one based on budget. It is also important to choose the RAM, CPU, and hard disk corresponding to the power of the GP-GPU. After the installation of the hardware, the following drivers and libraries have to be installed. Readers who are using Mac, or using Windows/Ubuntu without a GP-GPU, can skip the installation.

The following are the libraries that are required for setting up the environment:

- **Computer Unified Device Architecture** (**CUDA**)
- **CUDA Deep Neural Network** (**CUDNN**)

Computer Unified Device Architecture - CUDA

CUDA is the API layer provided by NVIDIA, using the parallel nature of the GPU. When this is installed, drivers for the hardware are also installed. First, download the `CUDA` library from the NVIDIA-portal: `https://developer.nvidia.com/cuda-downloads`.

Go through the instructions on the page, download the driver, and follow the installation instructions. Here is the screenshot of Ubuntu CUDA and the installation instructions:

Select Target Platform

Click on the green buttons that describe your target platform. Only supported platforms will be shown.

Operating System	Windows · **Linux** · Mac OSX
Architecture	**x86_64** · ppc64le
Distribution	Fedora · OpenSUSE · RHEL · CentOS · SLES · **Ubuntu**
Version	17.04 · **16.04**
Installer Type	runfile (local) · deb (local) · **deb (network)** · cluster (local)

Download Installer for Linux Ubuntu 16.04 x86_64

The base installer is available for download below.

> Base Installer Download (2.8 KB)

Installation Instructions:

1. `sudo dpkg -i cuda-repo-ubuntu1604_9.0.176-1_amd64.deb`
2. `sudo apt-key adv --fetch-keys https://developer.download.nvidia.com/compute/cuda/repos/ubuntu1604/x86_64/7fa2af80.pub`
3. `sudo apt-get update`
4. `sudo apt-get install cuda`

Other installation options are available in the form of meta-packages. For example, to install all the library packages, replace "cuda" with the "cuda-libraries-9-0" meta package. For more information on all the available meta packages click here.

The CUDA Toolkit contains Open-Source Software. The source code can be found here.
The checksums for the installer and patches can be found in Installer Checksums.
For further information, see the Installation Guide for Linux and the CUDA Quick Start Guide.

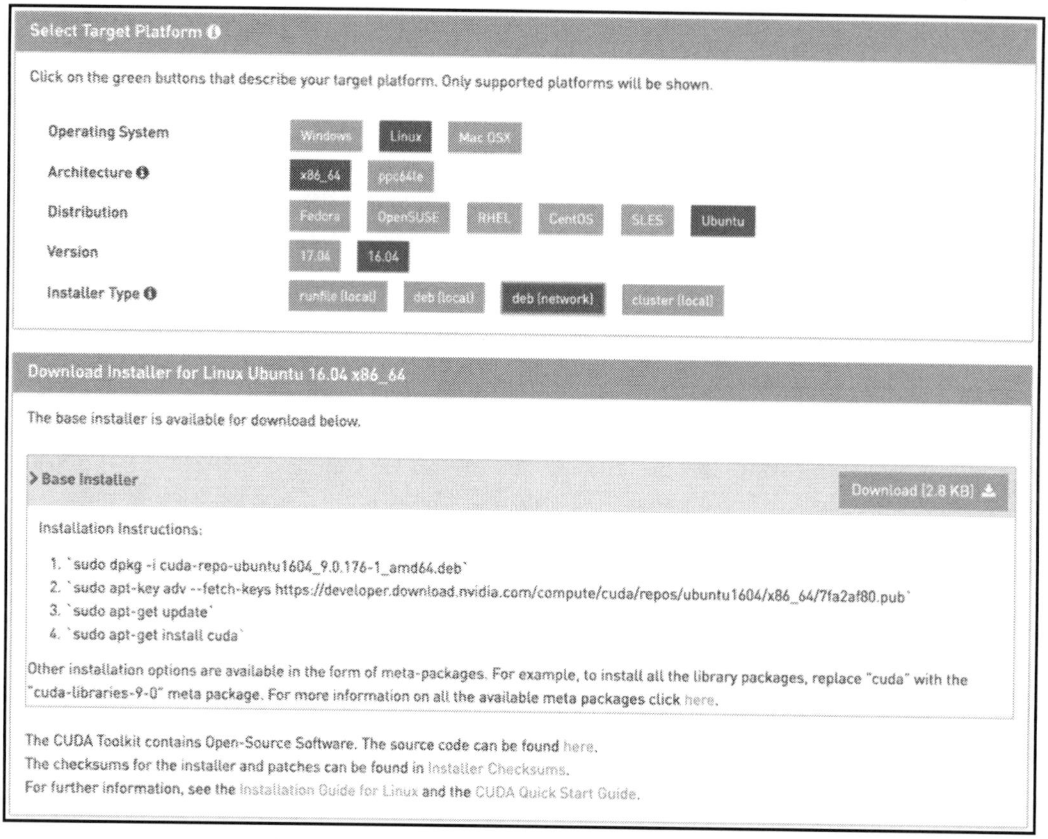

These commands would have installed the `cuda-drivers` and the other CUDA APIs required.

You can check whether the drivers are properly installed by typing `nvidia-smi` in the command prompt.

CUDA Deep Neural Network - CUDNN

The `CUDNN` library provides primitives for deep learning algorithms. Since this package is provided by NVIDIA, it is highly optimized for their hardware and runs faster. Several standard routines for deep learning are provided in this package. These packages are used by famous deep learning libraries such as `tensorflow`, `caffe`, and so on. In the next section, instructions are provided for installing `CUDNN`. You can download `CUDNN` from the NVIDIA portal at `https://developer.nvidia.com/rdp/cudnn-download`.

User account is required (free signup).

Copy the relevant files to the `CUDA` folders, making them faster to run on GPUs. We will not use `CUDA` and `CUDNN` libraries directly. Tensorflow uses these to work on GP-GPU with optimized routines.

Installing software packages

There are several libraries required for trained deep learning models. We will install the following libraries and see the reason for selecting the following packages over the competing packages:

- Python and other dependencies
- OpenCV
- TensorFlow
- Keras

Python

Python is the de-facto choice for any data science application. It has the largest community and support ecosystem of libraries. TensorFlow API for Python is the most complete, and hence, Python is the natural language of choice. Python has two versions—Python2.x and Python3.x. In this book, we will discuss Python3.x. There are several reasons for this choice:

- Python 2.x development will be stopped by 2020, and hence, Python3.x is the future of Python

- Python 3.x avoids many design flaws in the original implementation
- Contrary to popular belief, Python3.x has as many supporting libraries for data science as Python 2.x.

We will use Python version 3 throughout this book. Go to `https://www.python.org/downloads/` and download version 3 according to the OS. Install Python by following the steps given in the download link. After installing Python, **pip3** has to be installed for easy installation of Python packages. Then install the several Python packages by entering the following command, so that you can install `OpenCV` and `tensorflow` later:

```
sudo pip3 install numpy scipy scikit-learn pillow h5py
```

The description of the preceding installed packages is given as follows:

- `numpy` is a highly-optimized numerical computation package. It has a powerful N-dimensional package array object, and the matrix operations of `numpy` library are highly optimized for speed. An image can be stored as a 3-dimensional `numpy` object.
- `scipy` has several routines for scientific and engineering calculations. We will use some optimization packages later in the book.
- `scikit-learn` is a machine-learning library from which we will use many helper functions.
- `Ppillow` is useful for image loading and basic operations.
- `H5py` package is a Pythonic interface to the HDF5 binary data format. This is the format to store models trained using Keras.

Open Computer Vision - OpenCV

The `OpenCV` is a famous computer vision library. There are several image processing routines available in this library that can be of great use. Following is the step of installing OpenCV in Ubuntu.

```
sudo apt-get install python-opencv
```

Similar steps can be found for other OSes at `https://opencv.org/`. It is cross-platform and optimized for CPU-intensive applications. It has interfaces for several programming languages and is supported by Windows, Ubuntu, and Mac.

The TensorFlow library

The `tensorflow` is an open source library for the development and deployment of deep learning models. TensorFlow uses computational graphs for data flow and numerical computations. In other words, data, or tensor, flows through the graph, thus the name `tensorflow`. The graph has nodes that enable any numerical computation and, hence, are suitable for deep learning operations. It provides a single API for all kinds of platforms and hardware. TensorFlow handles all the complexity of scaling and optimization at the backend. It was originally developed for research at Google. It is the most famous deep learning library, with a large community and comes with tools for visualization and deployment in production.

Installing TensorFlow

Install `tensorflow` using pip3 for the CPU using the following command:

```
sudo pip3 install tensorflow
```

If you are using GPU hardware and have installed `CUDA` and `CUDNN`, install the GPU version of the `tensorflow` with the following command:

```
sudo pip3 install tensorflow-gpu
```

Now the `tensorflow` is installed and ready for use. We will try out a couple of examples to understand how TensorFlow works.

TensorFlow example to print Hello, TensorFlow

We will do an example using TensorFlow directly in the Python shell. In this example, we will print **Hello, TensorFlow** using TensorFlow.

1. Invoke Python from your shell by typing the following in the command prompt:

   ```
   python3
   ```

2. Import the `tensorflow` library by entering the following command:

   ```
   >>> import tensorflow as tf
   ```

3. Next, define a constant with the string `Hello, TensorFlow`. This is different from the usual Python assignment operations as the value is not yet initialized:

```
>>> hello = tf.constant('Hello, TensorFlow!')
```

4. Create a session to initialize the computational graph, and give a name to the session:

```
>>> session = tf.Session()
```

The session can be run with the variable `hello` as the parameter.

5. Now the graph executes and returns that particular variable that is printed:

```
>>> print(session.run(hello))
```

It should print the following:

```
Hello, TensorFlow!
```

Let us look at one more example to understand how the session and graph work.

Visit `https://github.com/rajacheers/DeepLearningForComputerVision` to get the code for all the examples presented in the book. The code will be organised according to chapters. You can raise issues and get help in the repository.

TensorFlow example for adding two numbers

Here is another simple example of how TensorFlow is used to add two numbers.

1. Create a Python file and import `tensorflow` using the following code:

```
import tensorflow as tf
```

The preceding import will be necessary for all the latter examples. It is assumed that the reader has imported the library for all the examples. A `placeholder` can be defined in the following manner. The placeholders are not loaded when assigned. Here, a variable is defined as a `placeholder` with a type of `float32`. A `placeholder` is an empty declaration and can take values when a session is run.

2. Now we define a `placeholder` as shown in the following code:

```
x = tf.placeholder(tf.float32)
y = tf.placeholder(tf.float32)
```

3. Now the sum operation of the placeholders can be defined as a usual addition. Here, the operation is not executed but just defined using the following code:

```
z = x + y
```

4. The session can be created as shown in the previous example. The graph is ready for executing the computations when defined as shown below:

```
session = tf.Session()
```

5. Define the value of the `placeholder` in a dictionary format:

```
values = {x: 5.0, y: 4.0}
```

6. Run the session with variable `c` and the values. The graph feeds the values to appropriate placeholders and gets the value back for variable `c`:

```
result = session.run([z], values)
print(result)
```

This program should print [9.0] as the result of the addition.

It's understandable that this is not the best way to add two numbers. This example is to understand how tensors and operations are defined in TensorFlow. Imagine how difficult it will be to use a trillion numbers and add them. TensorFlow enables that scale with ease with the same APIs. In the next section, we will see how to install and use TensorBoard and TensorFlow serving.

TensorBoard

TensorBoard is a suite of visualization tools for training deep learning-based models with TensorFlow. The following data can be visualized in TensorBoard:

- **Graphs**: Computation graphs, device placements, and tensor details
- **Scalars**: Metrics such as loss, accuracy over iterations
- **Images**: Used to see the images with corresponding labels

- **Audio**: Used to listen to audio from training or a generated one
- **Distribution**: Used to see the distribution of some scalar
- **Histograms**: Includes histogram of weights and biases
- **Projector**: Helps visualize the data in 3-dimensional space
- **Text**: Prints the training text data
- **Profile**: Sees the hardware resources utilized for training

Tensorboard is installed along with TensorFlow. Go to the python3 prompt and type the following command, similar to the previous example, to start using Tensorboard:

```
x = tf.placeholder(tf.float32, name='x')
y = tf.placeholder(tf.float32, name='y')
z = tf.add(x, y, name='sum')
```

Note that an argument name has been provided as an extra parameter to placeholders and operations. These are names that can be seen when we visualize the graph. Now we can write the graph to a specific folder with the following command in TensorBoard:

```
session = tf.Session()
summary_writer = tf.summary.FileWriter('/tmp/1', session.graph)
```

This command writes the graph to disk to a particular folder given in the argument. Now Tensorboard can be invoked with the following command:

```
tensorboard --logdir=/tmp/1
```

Any directory can be passed as an argument for the `logdir` option where the files are stored. Go to a browser and paste the following URL to start the visualization to access the TensorBoard:

```
http://localhost:6006/
```

The browser should display something like this:

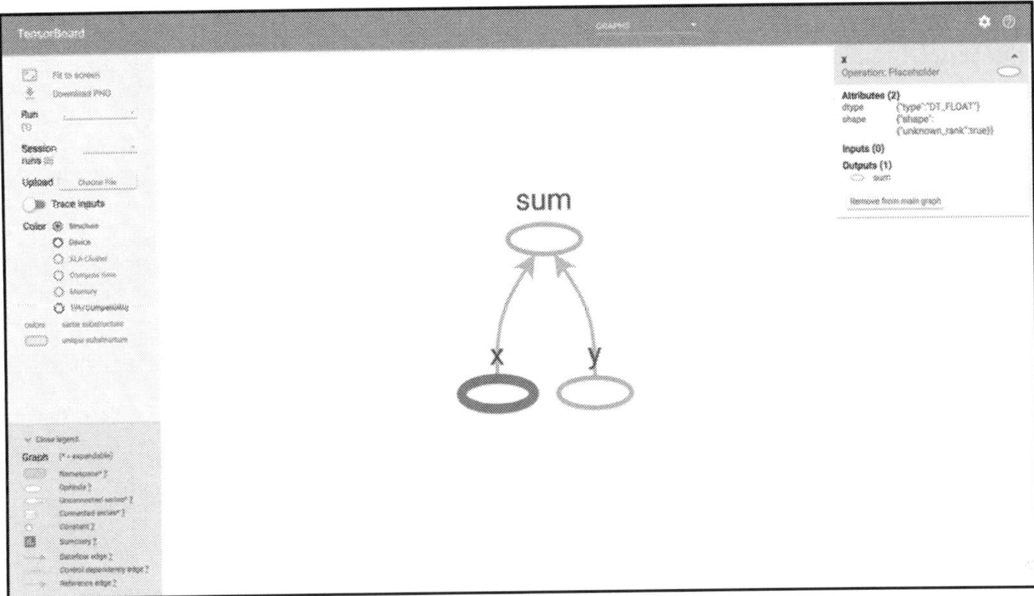

The TensorBoard visualization in the browser window

The graph of addition is displayed with the names given for the placeholders. When we click on them, we can see all the particulars of the tensor for that operation on the right side. Make yourself familiar with the tabs and options. There are several parts in this window. We will learn about them in different chapters. TensorBoard is one the best distinguishing tools in TensorFlow, which makes it better than any other deep learning framework.

The TensorFlow Serving tool

TensorFlow Serving is a tool in TensorFlow developed for deployment environments that are flexible, providing high latency and throughput environments. Any deep learning model trained with TensorFlow can be deployed with serving. Install the Serving by running the following command:

```
sudo apt-get install tensorflow-model-server
```

Step-by-step instructions on how to use serving will be described in `Chapter 22`, *Image Retrieval*. Note that the Serving is easy to install only in Ubuntu; for other OSes, please refer to `https://www.tensorflow.org/serving/setup`. The following figure illustrates how TensorFlow Serving and TensorFlow interact in production environments:

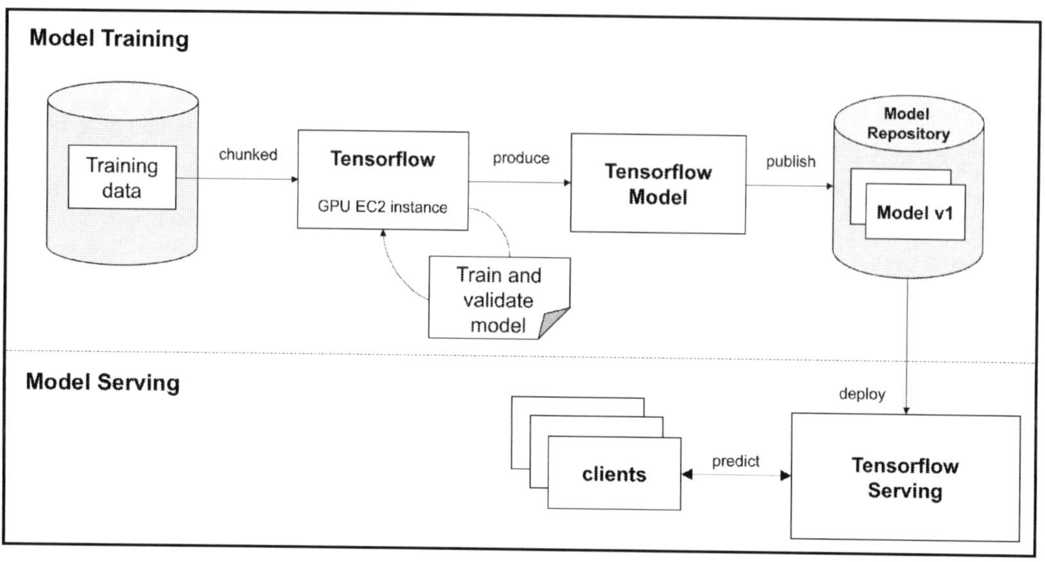

Many models can be produced by the training process, and Serving takes care of switching them seamlessly without any downtime. TensorFlow Serving is not required for all the following chapters, except for `Chapter 22`, *Image Retrieval*.

The Keras library

`Keras` is an open source library for deep learning written in Python. It provides an easy interface to use TensorFlow as a backend. Keras can also be used with Theano, deep learning 4j, or CNTK as its backend. Keras is designed for easy and fast experimentation by focusing on friendliness, modularity, and extensibility. It is a self-contained framework and runs seamlessly between CPU and GPU. Keras can be installed separately or used within TensorFlow itself using the `tf.keras` API. In this book, we will use the `tf.keras` API. We have seen the steps to install the required libraries for the development environment. Having CUDA, CUDNN, OpenCV, TensorFlow, and Keras installed and running smoothly is vital for the following chapters.

Summary

In this chapter, we have covered the basics of deep learning. The vocabulary introduced in this chapter will be used throughout this book, hence, you can refer back to this chapter often. The applications of computer vision are also shown with examples. Installations of all the software packages for various platforms for the development environment were also covered.

In the next chapter, we will look at how to improve the accuracy using a bigger model and other techniques such as augmentation, and fine-tuning. Then, we will see several advanced models proposed by several people around the world, achieving the best accuracy in competitions.

21
Image Classification

Image classification is the task of classifying a whole image as a single label. For example, an image classification task could label an image as a dog or a cat, given an image is either a dog or a cat. In this chapter, we will see how to use TensorFlow to build such an image classification model and also learn the techniques to improve the accuracy.

We will cover the following topics in this chapter:

- The bigger deep learning models
- Training a model for cats versus dogs
- Developing real-world applications

The bigger deep learning models

We will go through several model definitions that have achieved state-of-the-art results in the ImageNet competitions. We will look at them individually on the following topics.

The AlexNet model

AlexNet is the first publication that started a wide interest in deep learning for computer vision. Krizhevsky et al. (`https://papers.nips.cc/paper/4824-imagenet-classification-with-deep-convolutional-neural-networks.pdf`) proposed AlexNet and it has been a pioneer and influential in this field. This model won the ImageNet 2013 challenge. The error rate was 15.4%, which was significantly better than the next. The model was relatively a simple architecture with five convolution layers. The challenge was to classify 1,000 categories of objects. The image and data had 15 million annotated images with over 22,000 categories. Out of them, only a 1,000 categories are used for the competition. AlexNet used ReLU as the activation function and found it was training several times faster than other activation functions. The architecture of the model is shown here:

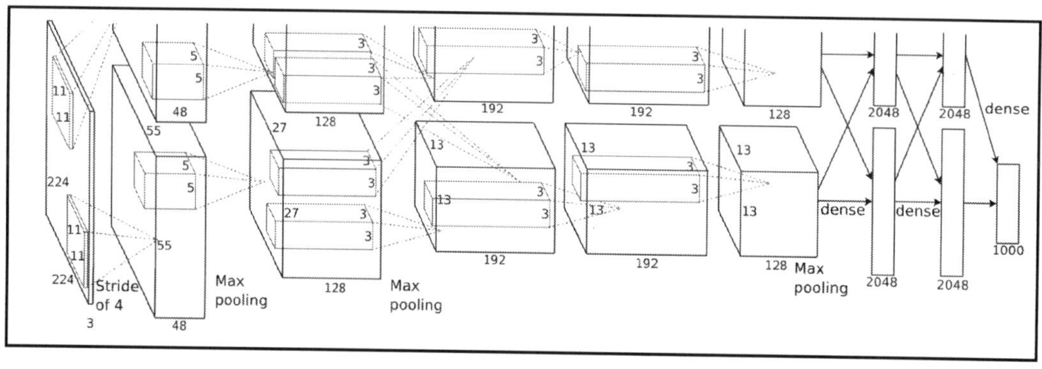

Reproduced with permission from Krizhevsky et al.

The paper also used data augmentation techniques such as image translations, horizontal flips, and random cropping. The dropout layer prevents overfitting. The model used vanilla **Stochastic Gradient Descent** (**SGD**) for training. The parameters of SGD are chosen carefully for training. The learning rate changes over a fixed set of training iterations. The momentum and weight decay take fixed values for training. There is a concept called **Local Response Normalization** (**LRN**) introduced in this paper. The LRN layers normalize every pixel across the filters to avoid huge activation in a particular filter.

This layer is not used anymore as recent research suggests that there is not much improvement because of LRN. AlexNet has 60 million parameters in total.

The VGG-16 model

The **VGG** model stands for the **Visual Geometry Group** from Oxford. The model was very simple and had a greater depth than AlexNet. The paper had two models with 16 and 19 layers depth. All the CNN layers were using 3 by 3 filters with stride and a pad of size 1 and a max pooling size of 2 with stride 2. This resulted in a decrease in the number of parameters. Though the size is decreasing because of max pooling, the number of filters is increasing with layers. The architecture of the 16-layer deep model is as follows:

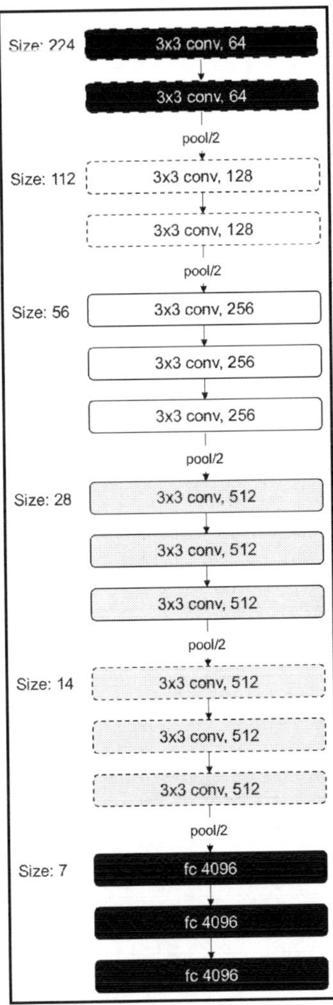

This model has 138 million parameters and is the largest of all the models described here. But the uniformity of parameters is quite good. The characteristic is such that, as deep as the network gets, the smaller the image is with an increased number of filters. One of the data augmentation techniques used was scale jittering. Scale jittering is an augmentation technique where a side with random size is considered to vary the scales.

The Google Inception-V3 model

Inception-V3 was proposed by Szegedy et al. (`https://arxiv.org/pdf/1409.4842.pdf`) and introduced the concept of inception that has a better way of generalization. This was the architecture that won the ImageNet competition in 2014. It is geared towards efficiency for speed and size. It has 12 times lesser parameters than AlexNet. Inception is the micro-architecture on which a macro-architecture is built. Each hidden layer has a higher-level representation of the image. At each layer, we have an option of using pooling or other layers. Instead of using one type of kernel, inception uses several kernels. An average pooling is followed by various size convolutions and then they are concatenated.

The kernel parameters can be learned based on the data. Using several kernels, the model can detect small features as well as higher abstractions. The 1 x 1 convolution will reduce the feature and, hence, computations. This takes less RAM during inference. The following is the inception module in its simplest form where there are options of convolutions with various kernel sizes and pooling:

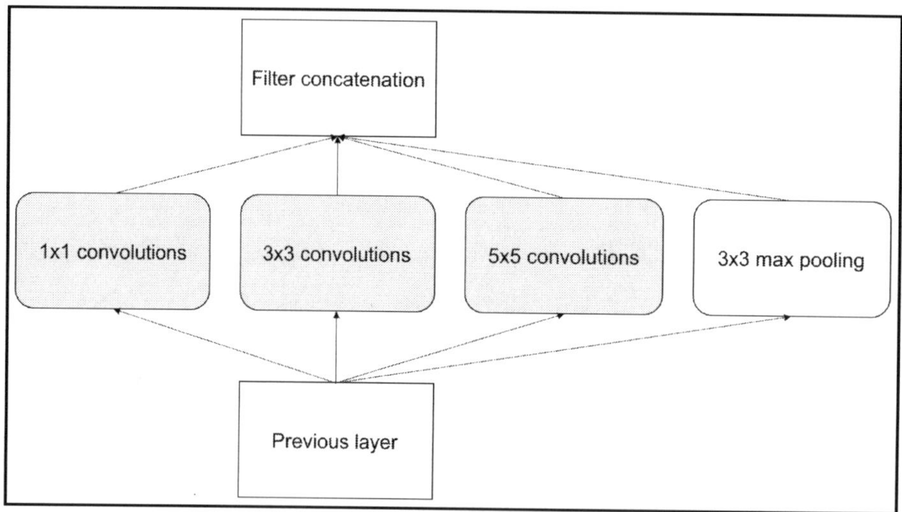

Notice that operations are happening in parallel, as opposed to AlexNet or VGG. The output volume is huge, and hence, 1 x 1 filters are introduced for dimensionality reduction. When the reduced dimensions are added to the architecture it becomes as follows:

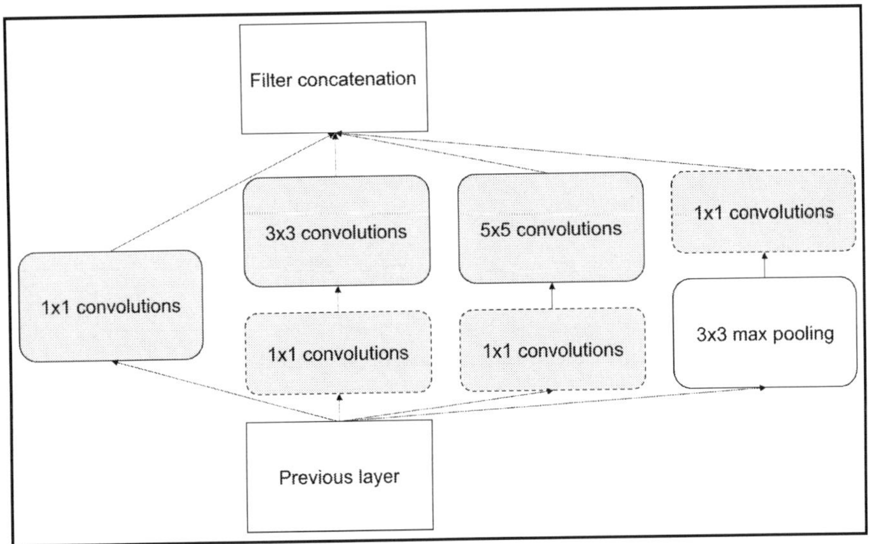

The whole architecture of the model is as follows with all the bells and whistles:

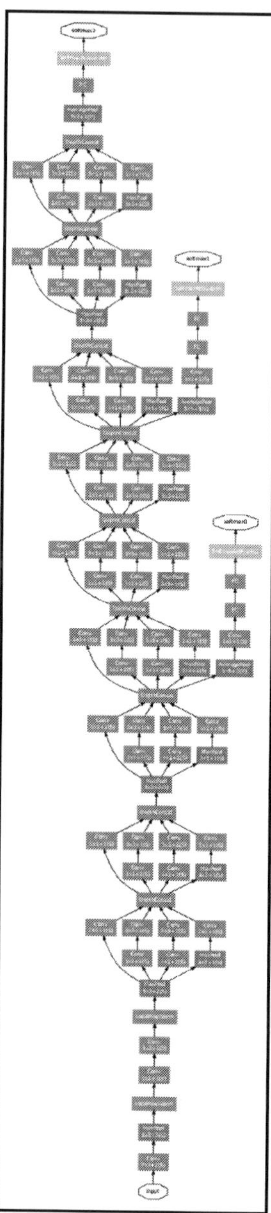

Figure illustrating the Google Inception V3 model architecture [Reproduced with permission from Szegedy et al.]

There are nine inception modules with a total of 100 layers and they achieve good performance.

The Microsoft ResNet-50 model

ResNet was proposed by He et al. (`https://arxiv.org/pdf/1512.03385.pdf`) and won the ImageNet competition in 2015. This method showed that deeper networks can be trained. The deeper the network, the more saturated the accuracy becomes. It's not even due to overfitting or due to the presence of a high number of parameters, but due to a reduction in the training error. This is due to the inability to backpropagate the gradients. This can be overcome by sending the gradients directly to the deeper layers with a residual block as follows:

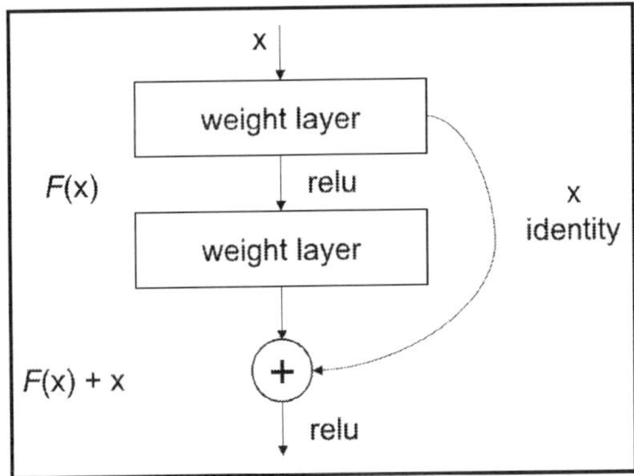

Every two layers are connected forming a residual block. You can see that the training is passed between the layers. By this technique, the backpropagation can carry the error to earlier layers.

The model definitions can be used from `https://github.com/tensorflow/tensorflow/tree/r1.4/tensorflow/python/keras/_impl/keras/applications`. Every layer in the model is defined and pre-trained weights on the `ImageNet` dataset are available.

The SqueezeNet model

The **SqueezeNet** model was introduced by Iandola et al. (`https://arxiv.org/pdf/1602.07360.pdf`), to reduce the model size and the number of parameters.

The network was made smaller by replacing 3 x 3 filters with 1 x 1 filters as shown here:

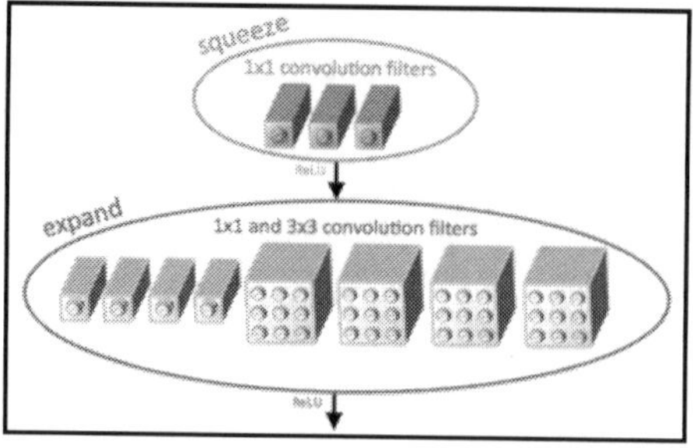

Reproduced with permission from Iandola et al.

The number of inputs of the 3 x 3 filters has also reduced downsampling of the layers when happening at the higher level, providing large activation maps:

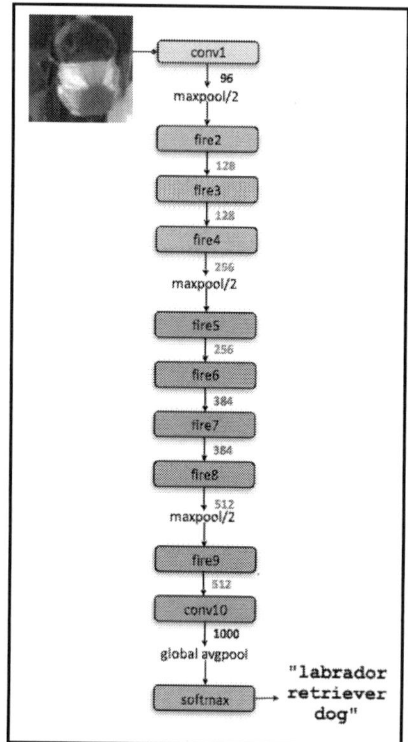

Reproduced with permission from Iandola et al.

Spatial transformer networks

The **spatial transformer networks** proposed by Jaderberg et al. (`https://arxiv.org/pdf/1506.02025.pdf`) try to transform the image before passing to the CNN. This is different from other networks because it tries to modify the image before convolution. This network learns the parameters to transform the image. The parameters are learned for an **affine transformation**. By applying an affine transformation, **spatial invariance** is achieved. In the previous networks, spatial invariance was achieved by max-pooling layers. The placement of spatial transformer networks is shown as follows:

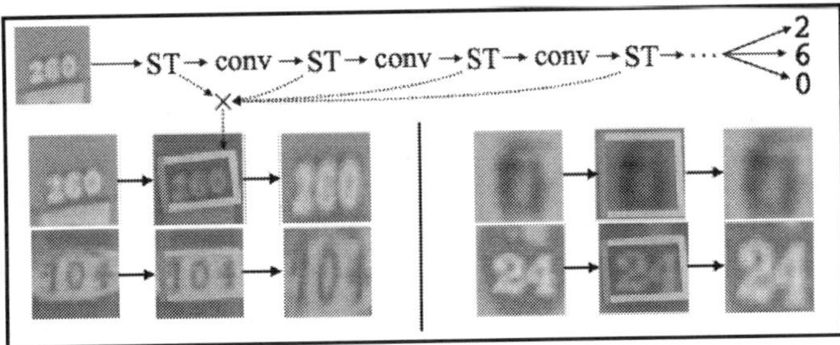

Reproduced with permission from Jaderberg et al.

The DenseNet model

DenseNet is an extension of ResNet proposed by Huang et al. (`https://arxiv.org/pdf/1608.06993.pdf`). In ResNet blocks, the previous layer is merged into the future layer by summation. In DenseNet, the previous layer is merged into the future layer by concatenation. DenseNet connects all the layers to the previous layers and the current layer to the following layers.

In the following diagram, it can be seen how the feature maps are supplied as input to the other layers:

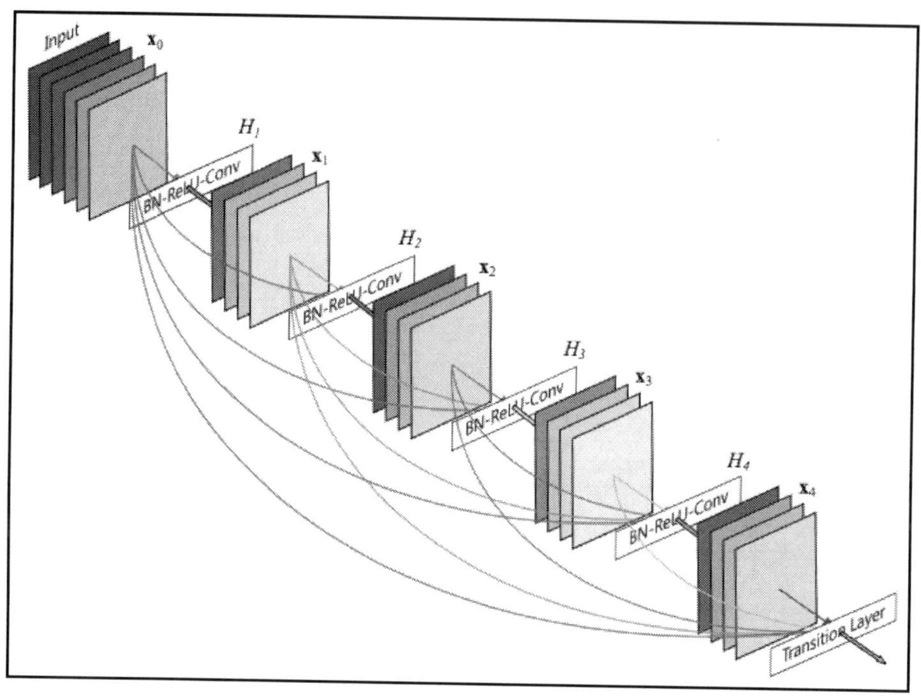

Reproduced with permission from Huang et al.

This way, it provides several advantages such as smoother gradients, feature transformation and so on. This also reduces the number of parameters:

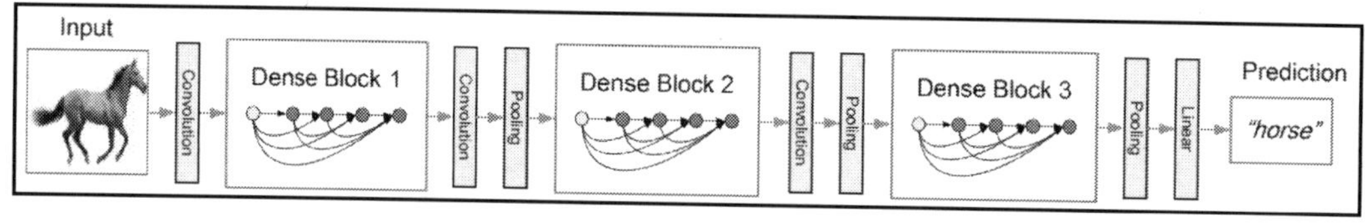

Reproduced with permission from Huang et al.

We have covered all the latest algorithms for the image classification task. Any of the architectures can be used for an image classification task. In the next section, we will see how to train a model to predict pets, using these advanced architectures and improve the accuracy.

Training a model for cats versus dogs

In this section, we will prepare and train a model for predicting cats versus dogs and understand some techniques which increase the accuracy. Most of the image classification problems come into this paradigm. Techniques covered in this section, such as augmentation and transfer learning, are useful for several problems.

Preparing the data

For the purpose of classification, we will download the data from **kaggle** and store in an appropriate format. Sign up and log in to `www.kaggle.com` and go to `https://www.kaggle.com/c/dogs-vs-cats/data`. Download the `train.zip` and `test1.zip` files from that page. The `train.zip` file contains 25,000 images of pet data. We will use only a portion of the data to train a model. Readers with more computing power, such as a **Graphics Processing Unit** (**GPU**), can use more data than suggested. Run the following script to rearrange the images and create the necessary folders:

```
import os
import shutil

work_dir = '' # give your correct directory
image_names = sorted(os.listdir(os.path.join(work_dir, 'train')))


def copy_files(prefix_str, range_start, range_end, target_dir):
    image_paths = [os.path.join(work_dir, 'train', prefix_str + '.' +
str(i) + '.jpg')
                   for i in range(range_start, range_end)]
    dest_dir = os.path.join(work_dir, 'data', target_dir, prefix_str)
    os.makedirs(dest_dir)
    for image_path in image_paths:
        shutil.copy(image_path, dest_dir)


copy_files('dog', 0, 1000, 'train')
copy_files('cat', 0, 1000, 'train')
copy_files('dog', 1000, 1400, 'test')
copy_files('cat', 1000, 1400, 'test')
```

For our experiments, we will use only 1,000 images of cats and dogs. So, copy images 0–999 from the downloaded folder to the newly created `train` folder under `cats`. Similarly, copy 1,000–1,400 to `data/test/cat`, 10–999 in `train/dogs` and 1,000–1,400 in `data/test/dog` so that we have 1,000 training examples for each class and 400 validation examples for each class.

Benchmarking with simple CNN

Let's run the previous `simple_cnn` model on this dataset and see how it performs. This model's performance will be the basic benchmark against which we judge other techniques. We will define a few variables for data loading and training, as shown here:

```
image_height, image_width = 150, 150
train_dir = os.path.join(work_dir, 'train')
test_dir = os.path.join(work_dir, 'test')
no_classes = 2
no_validation = 800
epochs = 2
batch_size = 200
no_train = 2000
no_test = 800
input_shape = (image_height, image_width, 3)
epoch_steps = no_train // batch_size
test_steps = no_test // batch_size
```

This constant is used for the techniques discussed in this section of training a model for predicting cats and dogs. Here, we are using 2,800 images to train and test which is reasonable for a personal computer's RAM. But this is not sustainable for bigger datasets. It's better if we load only a batch of images at a time for training and testing. For this purpose, a `tf.keras` has a class called `ImageDataGenerator` that reads images whenever necessary. It is assumed that a `simple_cnn` model is imported from the previous section. The following is an example of using a generator for loading the images:

```
generator_train =
tf.keras.preprocessing.image.ImageDataGenerator(rescale=1. / 255)
generator_test =
tf.keras.preprocessing.image.ImageDataGenerator(rescale=1. / 255)
```

This definition also rescales the images when it is loaded. Next, we can read the images from the directory using the `flow_from_directory` method as follows:

```
train_images = generator_train.flow_from_directory(
    train_dir,
    batch_size=batch_size,
    target_size=(image_width, image_height))

test_images = generator_test.flow_from_directory(
    test_dir,
    batch_size=batch_size,
    target_size=(image_width, image_height))
```

The directory to load the images, size of batches and target size for the images are passed as an argument. This method performs the rescaling and passes the data in batches for fitting the model. This generator can be directly used for fitting the model. The method `fit_generator` of the model can be used as follows:

```
simple_cnn_model.fit_generator(
    train_images,
    steps_per_epoch=epoch_steps,
    epochs=epochs,
    validation_data=test_images,
    validation_steps=test_steps)
```

This model fits the data from the generator of training images. The number of epochs is defined from training, and validation data is passed for getting the performance of the model overtraining. This `fit_generator` enables parallel processing of data and model training. The CPU performs the rescaling while the GPU can perform the model training. This gives the high efficiency of computing resources. After 50 epochs, this model should give an accuracy of 60%. Next, we will see how to augment the dataset to get an improved performance.

Augmenting the dataset

Data augmentation gives ways to increase the size of the dataset. Data augmentation introduces noise during training, producing robustness in the model to various inputs. This technique is useful in scenarios when the dataset is small and can be combined and used with other techniques. Next, we will see the different types of augmentation.

Augmentation techniques

There are various ways to augment the images as described as follows:

- **Flipping**: The image is mirrored or flipped in a horizontal or vertical direction
- **Random Cropping**: Random portions are cropped, hence the model can deal with occlusions
- **Shearing**: The images are deformed to affect the shape of the objects
- **Zooming**: Zoomed portions of images are trained to deal with varying scales of images
- **Rotation**: The objects are rotated to deal with various degrees of change in objects
- **Whitening**: The whitening is done by a Principal Component Analysis that preserves only the important data
- **Normalization**: Normalizes the pixels by standardizing the mean and variance
- **Channel shifting**: The color channels are shifted to make the model robust to color changes caused by various artifacts

All these techniques are implemented in `ImageDataGenerator` to increase the dataset size. The following is a modified version of `generator_train` with some augmentation techniques discussed previously:

```
generator_train = tf.keras.preprocessing.image.ImageDataGenerator(
    rescale=1. / 255,
    horizontal_flip=True,
    zoom_range=0.3,
    shear_range=0.3,)
```

Replacing the `generator_train` in the preceding code will increase the accuracy to 90%. Change the parameters of augmentation and notice the changes. We will discuss a technique called transfer learning in the following section, which helps in training bigger models with fewer data.

Transfer learning or fine-tuning of a model

Transfer learning is the process of learning from a pre-trained model that was trained on a larger dataset. Training a model with random initialization often takes time and energy to get the result. Initializing the model with a pre-trained model gives faster convergence, saving time and energy. These models that are pre-trained are often trained with carefully chosen hyperparameters.

Either the several layers of the pre-trained model can be used without any modification, or can be bit trained to adapt to the changes. In this section, we will learn how to fine-tune or transfer learning for a model that was trained on the `ImageNet` dataset with millions of classes.

Training on bottleneck features

The models that are covered in the previous sections are simple and hence, may yield less accuracy. Complex models should be built from them. They cannot be built from scratch. Hence, bottleneck features are extracted and the classifier is trained on them. Bottleneck features are the features that are produced by complex architectures training several million images. The images are done with a forward pass and the pre-final layer features are stored. From these, a simple logistic classifier is trained for classification. Extract the bottleneck layers as follows:

```
generator = tf.keras.preprocessing.image.ImageDataGenerator(rescale=1.
/ 255)

model = tf.keras.applications.VGG16(include_top=False)

train_images = generator.flow_from_directory(
    train_dir,
    batch_size=batch_size,
    target_size=(image_width, image_height),
    class_mode=None,
    shuffle=False
)
train_bottleneck_features = model.predict_generator(train_images,
epoch_steps)

test_images = generator.flow_from_directory(
    test_dir,
    batch_size=batch_size,
    target_size=(image_width, image_height),
    class_mode=None,
    shuffle=False
```

```
)

test_bottleneck_features = model.predict_generator(test_images,
test_steps)
```

The VGG model is taken and used to predict the images. The labels are assigned as follows:

```
train_labels = np.array([0] * int(no_train / 2) + [1] * int(no_train /
2))
test_labels = np.array([0] * int(no_test / 2) + [1] * int(no_test /
2))
```

A sequential model with a couple of layers is built, compiled, and trained with the bottleneck features and can be implemented using the code given as follows:

```
model = tf.keras.models.Sequential()
model.add(tf.keras.layers.Flatten(input_shape=train_bottleneck_feature
s.shape[1:]))
model.add(tf.keras.layers.Dense(1024, activation='relu'))
model.add(tf.keras.layers.Dropout(0.3))
model.add(tf.keras.layers.Dense(1, activation='softmax'))
model.compile(loss=tf.keras.losses.categorical_crossentropy,
              optimizer=tf.keras.optimizers.Adam(),
              metrics=['accuracy'])
```

These bottleneck features are trained with the model using the code shown as follows:

```
model.fit(
    train_bottleneck_features,
    train_labels,
    batch_size=batch_size,
    epochs=epochs,
    validation_data=(test_bottleneck_features, test_labels))
```

This gives a different approach to training the model and is useful when the training data is low. This is often a faster method to train a model. Only the final activations of the pre-trained model are used to adapt to the new task. This idea can be extended to fine-tune several layers as shown next:

Fine-tuning several layers in deep learning

A pre-trained model can be loaded and only a few layers can be trained. This approach works better when the given problem is very different from the images that the model is trained upon. **Fine-tuning** is a common practice in deep learning. This gives advantages when the dataset is smaller. The optimization also can be obtained faster.

Training a deep network on a small dataset results in overfitting. This kind of overfitting can also be avoided using the fine-tuning procedure. The model trained on a bigger dataset should be also similar, as we are hoping that the activations and features are similar to the smaller dataset. You can start with the stored weights path as show below:

```
top_model_weights_path = 'fc_model.h5'
```

Load the **Visual Geometry Group** (**VGG**) model and set the initial layers to be non-trainable. The VGG model will be covered in detail in the following section. For now, consider VGG as a big deep learning model that works well on image data. Replace the fully connected layers with new trainable layers using the code given as follows:

```
model = tf.keras.applications.VGG16(include_top=False)
```

A small two-layer feedforward network can be built on top of the VGG model with usually hidden units, activations, and dropout as follows:

```
model_fine_tune = tf.keras.models.Sequential()
model_fine_tune.add(tf.keras.layers.Flatten(input_shape=model.output_s
hape))
model_fine_tune.add(tf.keras.layers.Dense(256, activation='relu'))
model_fine_tune.add(tf.keras.layers.Dropout(0.5))
model_fine_tune.add(tf.keras.layers.Dense(no_classes,
activation='softmax'))
```

The top model has also to be loaded with weights that are already fully trained. The top model can then be added to the convolutional base:

```
model_fine_tune.load_weights(top_model_weights_path)
model.add(model_fine_tune)
```

We can set the top 25 layers to be non-trainable up to the last convolution block so that their weights will be not be updated. Only the rest of the layers will be updated:

```
for vgg_layer in model.layers[:25]:
    vgg_layer.trainable = False
```

Compile the model with the gradient descent optimizer at a slow learning rate with a magnitude of order of 4:

```
model.compile(loss='binary_crossentropy',
              optimizer=tf.keras.optimizers.SGD(lr=1e-4,
momentum=0.9),
              metrics=['accuracy'])
```

We can combine the augmentation techniques that were covered earlier with shear, zoom, and flip. The generator can be added with flow from the directory with both the train and validation datasets. Now the model can be fine-tuned combined with data augmentation. This way of training gives a better accuracy than all the previous methods. The following is a guide for transfer learning:

Data Size	**Similar Dataset**	**Different Dataset**
Smaller data	Fine-tune the output layers	Fine-tune the deeper layer
Bigger data	Fine-tune the whole model	Train from scratch

Depending on the data size, the number of layers to fine-tune can be determined. The less data there is, the lesser the number of layers to fine-tune. We have seen how to improve the accuracy of the model using transfer learning techniques.

Developing real-world applications

Recognizing cats and dogs is a cool problem but less likely a problem of importance. Real-world applications of image classification used in products may be different. You may have different data, targets, and so on. In this section, you will learn the tips and tricks to tackle such different settings. The factors that should be considered when approaching a new problem are as follows:

- The number of targets. Is it a 10 class problem or 10,000 class problem?
- How vast is the intra-class variance? For example, does the different type of cats have to be identified under one class label?

- How vast is the inter-class variance? For example, do the different cats have to be identified?
- How big is the data?
- How balanced is the data?
- Is there already a model that is trained with a lot of images?
- What is the requisite for deployment inference time and model size? Is it 50 milliseconds on an iPhone or 10 milliseconds on Google Cloud Platform? How much RAM can be consumed to store the model?

Try to answer these questions when approaching an image classification problem. Based on the answers, you can design the training architecture and improve the accuracy as described in the next section.

Choosing the right model

There are a lot of options for architectures. Based on the flexibility of deployment, you can choose the model. Remember that convolution is smaller and slower, but dense layers are bigger and faster. There is a trade-off between size, runtime, and accuracy. It is advisable to test out all the architectures before the final decision. Some models may work better than others, based on the application. You can reduce the input size to make the inference faster. Architectures can be selected based on the metrics as described in the following section.

Tackling the underfitting and overfitting scenarios

The model may be sometimes too big or too small for the problem. This could be classified as underfitting or overfitting, respectively. Underfitting happens when the model is too small and can be measured when training accuracy is less. Overfitting happens when the model is too big and there is a large gap between training and testing accuracies. Underfitting can be solved by the following methods:

- Getting more data
- Trying out a bigger model
- If the data is small, try transfer learning techniques or do data augmentation

Overfitting can be solved by the following methods:

- Regularizing using techniques such as dropout and batch normalization
- Augmenting the dataset

Always watch out for loss. The loss should be decreasing over iterations. If the loss is not decreasing, it signals that training has stopped. One solution is to try out a different optimizer. Class imbalance can be dealt with by weighting the loss function. Always use **TensorBoard** to watch the summaries. It is difficult to estimate how much data is needed. This section is the best lesson on training any deep learning models. Next, we will cover some application-specific guidance.

Gender and age detection from face

Applications may require gender and age detection from a face. The face image can be obtained by face detectors. The cropped images of faces can be supplied as training data, and the similar cropped face should be given for inference. Based on the required inference time, OpenCV, or CNN face detectors can be selected. For training, Inception or ResNet can be used. If the required inference time is much less because it is a video, it's better to use three convolutions followed by two fully connected layers. Note that there is usually a huge class imbalance in age datasets, hence using a different metric like precision and recall will be helpful.

Fine-tuning apparel models

Fine-tuning of apparel models is a good choice. Having multiple softmax layers that classify attributes will be useful here. The attributes could be a pattern, color, and so on.

Brand safety

Training bottleneck layers with **Support Vector Machine** (**SVM**) is a good option as the images can be quite different among classes. This is typically used for content moderation to help avoid images that are explicit. You have learned how to approach new problems in image classification.

Summary

In this chapter, we discussed state-of-the-art architectures with some specific applications. Several ways to increase the accuracy such as data augmentation, training on bottleneck layers, and fine-tuning a pre-trained model were also covered. Tips and tricks to train models for new models were also presented.

In the next chapter, we will see how to visualize the deep learning models. We will also deploy the trained models in this chapter for inference. We will also see how to use the trained layers for the application of an image search through an application. Then, we will understand the concept of autoencoders and use it for the dimensionality of features.

22
Image Retrieval

Deep learning can also be called **representation learning** because the features or representations in the model are learned during training. The **visual features** generated during the training process in the hidden layers can be used for computing a distance metric. These models learn how to detect edges, patterns, and so on at various layers, depending on the classification task. In this chapter, we will look at the following:

- How to extract features from a model that was trained for classification
- How to use TensorFlow Serving for faster inference in production systems
- How to compute similarity between a query image and the set of targets using those features
- Using the classification model for ranking
- How to increase the speed of the retrieval system
- Looking at the architecture of the system as a whole
- Learning a compact descriptor when the target images are too many, using autoencoder
- Training a denoising autoencoder

Understanding visual features

Deep learning models are often criticized for not being interpretable. A neural network-based model is often considered to be like a black box because it's difficult for humans to reason out the working of a deep learning model. The transformations of an image over layers by deep learning models are non-linear due to activation functions, so cannot be visualized easily. There are methods that have been developed to tackle the criticism of the non-interpretability by visualizing the layers of the deep network. In this section, we will look at the attempts to visualize the deep layers in an effort to understand how a model works.

Visualization can be done using the activation and gradient of the model. The activation can be visualized using the following techniques:

- **Nearest neighbour**: A layer activation of an image can be taken and the nearest images of that activation can be seen together.
- **Dimensionality reduction**: The dimension of the activation can be reduced by **principal component analysis (PCA)** or **t-Distributed Stochastic Neighbor Embedding (t-SNE)** for visualizing in two or three dimensions. PCA reduces the dimension by projecting the values in the direction of maximum variance. t-SNE reduces the dimension by mapping the closest points to three dimensions. The use of dimensionality reduction and its techniques are out of the scope of this book. You are advised to refer to basic machine learning material to learn more about dimensionality reduction.

Wikipedia is a good source for understanding dimensionality reduction techniques. Here are a few links that you can refer to:

- `https://en.wikipedia.org/wiki/Dimensionality_reduction`
- `https://en.wikipedia.org/wiki/Principal_component_analysis`
- `https://en.wikipedia.org/wiki/T-distributed_stochastic_neighbor_embedding`
- `https://en.wikipedia.org/wiki/Locality-sensitive_hashing`

- **Maximal patches**: One neuron is activated and the corresponding patch with maximum activation is captured.
- **Occlusion**: The images are occluded (obstructed) at various positions and the activation is shown as heat maps to understand what portions of the images are important.

In the following sections, we will see how to implement the visualization of these features.

Visualizing activation of deep learning models

Any model architecture can be visualized with the filters of any layer. Only the initial layers are comprehensible using the technique. The last layer is useful for the nearest neighbor approach. The `ImageNet` dataset, when arranged with nearest neighbors, looks as follows:

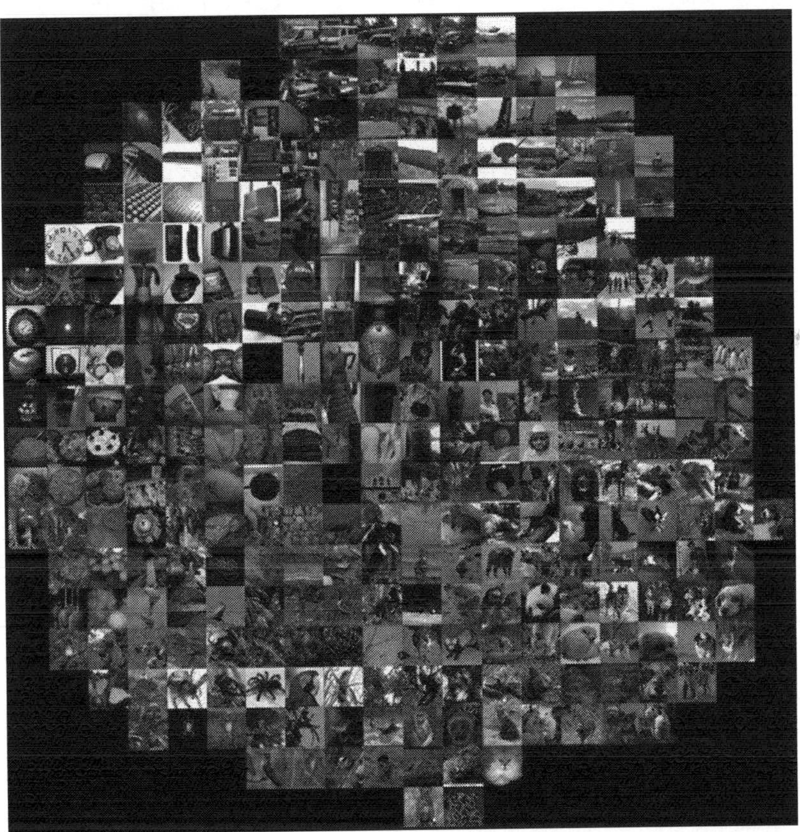

Looking at this image, you can see that the same objects appear together. One of the interesting things is that the animals such as the dog, monkey, and cheetah appear together though they are not trained under one label. Nearest neighbour visualization of the images is useful when objects are similar and hence, we can understand the model's predictions. This last layer can also be visualized by dimensionality reduction techniques, such as principal component analysis and t-SNE. We will see the implementation for visualization using dimensionality reduction in the next section.

Embedding visualization

The embedding layer, which is the pre-final layer, can be visualized in two or three dimensions using TensorBoard. The code snippets in this section are assumed to come after the convolution neural network model trained in the image classification chapter. First, we need a metadata file that is a tab separated file. Every line of the metadata file should have the labels of the images that are going to be visualized. A new variable is required for storing the embedding that is defined between session creation and initialization, as shown in the following code:

```
no_embedding_data = 1000
embedding_variable = tf.Variable(tf.stack(
    mnist.test.images[:no_embedding_data], axis=0), trainable=False)
```

We will take MNIST test data and create a metadata file for visualization, as shown here:

```
metadata_path = '/tmp/train/metadata.tsv'

with open(metadata_path, 'w') as metadata_file:
 for i in range(no_embedding_data):
 metadata_file.write('{}\n'.format(
 np.nonzero(mnist.test.labels[::1])[1:][0][i]))
```

The embedding variable should be made non-trainable by setting the parameter as shown in the preceding code. Next, the projector config has to be defined. It has to have a `tensor_name` which is the embedding variable name, the path to the metadata file, and a sprite image. A sprite image is one image with small images to denote the labels to be visualized with the embeddings. Here is the code for the definition of the projection of the embedding:

```
from tensorflow.contrib.tensorboard.plugins import projector
projector_config = projector.ProjectorConfig()
embedding_projection = projector_config.embeddings.add()
embedding_projection.tensor_name = embedding_variable.name
embedding_projection.metadata_path = metadata_path
```

```
embedding_projection.sprite.image_path = os.path.join(work_dir +
'/mnist_10k_sprite.png')
embedding_projection.sprite.single_image_dim.extend([28, 28])
```

The sprite image dimension has to be specified. Then the projector can be used to visualize the embedding with the summary writer and the configuration, as shown in the following code:

```
projector.visualize_embeddings(train_summary_writer, projector_config)
tf.train.Saver().save(session, '/tmp/train/model.ckpt', global_step=1)
```

Then the model is saved with the session. Then go to TensorBoard to see the following visualization:

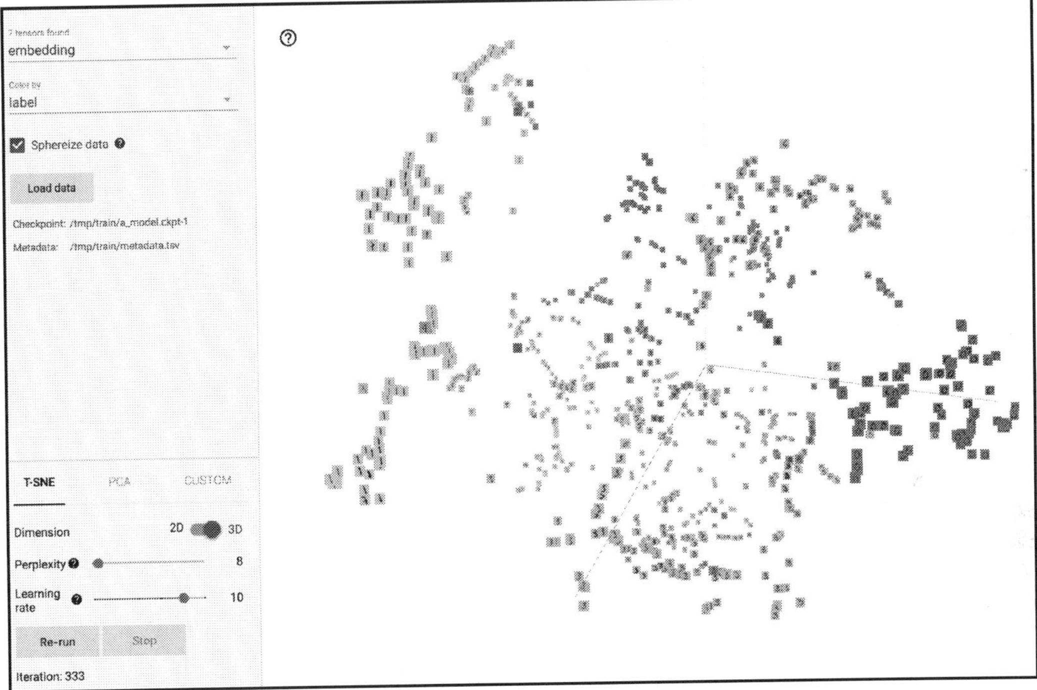

TensorBoard illustrating the output of the code

You have to select the **T-SNE** and **color by** buttons, as shown in the screenshot, to get similar visualization. You can see how digits appear together. This visualization is very useful for the inspection of data and the embedding's that are trained. This is yet another powerful feature of TensorBoard. In the next section, we will implement guided backpropagation for visualization.

Guided backpropagation

The visualization of features directly can be less informative. Hence, we use the training procedure of backpropagation to activate the filters for better visualization. Since we pick what neurons are to be activated for backpropagation, it is called guided backpropagation. In this section, we will implement the guided backpropagation to visualize the features.

We will define the size and load the VGG model, as shown here:

```
image_width, image_height = 128, 128
vgg_model = tf.keras.applications.vgg16.VGG16(include_top=False)
```

The layers are made of a dictionary with layer names as keys, and the layer from the model with weights as the key value for ease of access. Now we will take a first convolution layer from the fifth block, `block5_conv1` for computing the visualization. The input and output are defined here:

```
input_image = vgg_model.input
vgg_layer_dict = dict([(vgg_layer.name, vgg_layer) for vgg_layer in
vgg_model.layers[1:]])
vgg_layer_output = vgg_layer_dict['block5_conv1'].output
```

We have to define the loss function. The loss function will maximize the activation of a particular layer. This is a gradient ascent process rather than the usual gradient descent as we are trying to maximize the loss function. For gradient ascent, it's important to smoothen the gradient. So we smoothen the gradient in this case by normalizing the pixel gradients. This loss function converges rather quickly.

The output of the image should be normalized to visualize it back, gradient ascent is used in an optimization process to get the maxima of a function. Now we can start the gradient ascent optimization by defining the evaluator and gradients, as shown next. Now the loss function has to be defined and gradients have to be computed. The iterator computes the loss and gradient values over iterations as shown:

```
filters = []
for filter_idx in range(20):
```

```
    loss = tf.keras.backend.mean(vgg_layer_output[:, :, :,
filter_idx])
    gradients = tf.keras.backend.gradients(loss, input_image)[0]
    gradient_mean_square =
tf.keras.backend.mean(tf.keras.backend.square(gradients))
    gradients /= (tf.keras.backend.sqrt(gradient_mean_square) + 1e-5)
    evaluator = tf.keras.backend.function([input_image], [loss,
gradients])
```

The input is a random grey image with some noise added to it. A random image is generated and scaling is done, as shown here.

```
    gradient_ascent_step = 1.
    input_image_data = np.random.random((1, image_width, image_height,
3))
    input_image_data = (input_image_data - 0.5) * 20 + 128
```

The optimization of the loss function is started now, and for some filters, the loss values may be 0 which should be ignored, as shown here:

```
    for i in range(20):
        loss_value, gradient_values = evaluator([input_image_data])
        input_image_data += gradient_values * gradient_ascent_step
        # print('Loss :', loss_value)
        if loss_value <= 0.:
            break
```

After this optimization, normalization is done with mean subtraction and adjusting the standard deviation. Then, the filters can be scaled back and clipped to their gradient values, as shown here:

```
    if loss_value > 0:
        filter = input_image_data[0]
        filter -= filter.mean()
        filter /= (filter.std() + 1e-5)
        filter *= 0.1
        filter += 0.5
        filter = np.clip(filter, 0, 1)
        filter *= 255
        filter = np.clip(filter, 0, 255).astype('uint8')
        filters.append((filter, loss_value))
```

These filters are randomly picked and are visualized here:

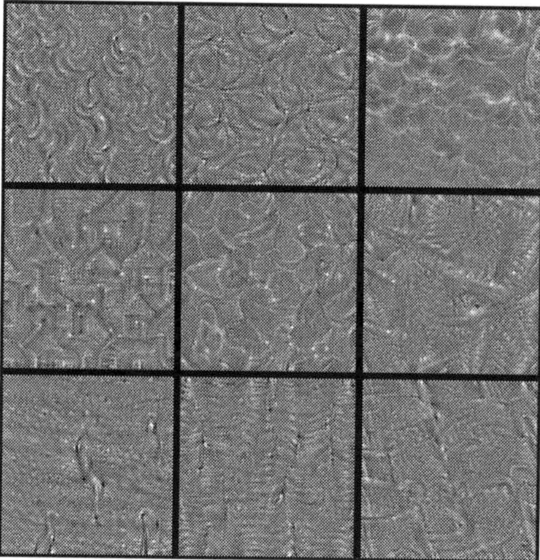

The code to stitch the images and produce an output as shown is available along with the code bundles. The visualization becomes complicated over later layers because the receptive field of the convents becomes bigger. Some filters look similar but only rotated. The hierarchy of visualization can be clearly seen in this case as shown by Zeiler et al. (`https://arxiv.org/pdf/1412.6572.pdf`). Direct visualization of different layers is shown in the following image:

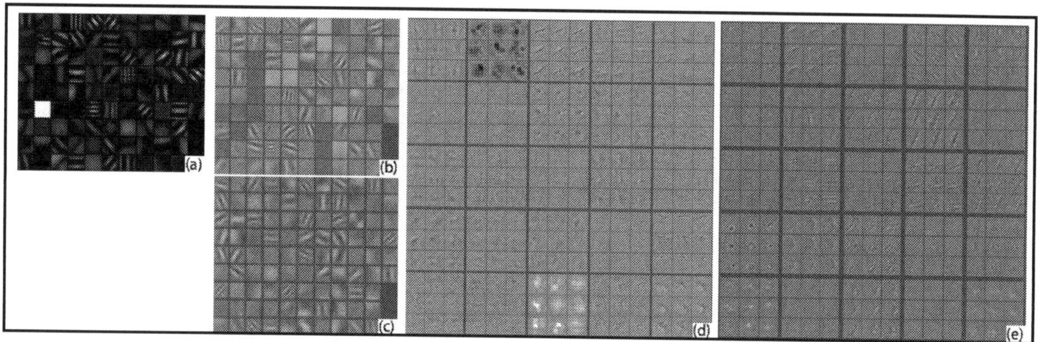

Reproduced with permission from Zeiler et al.

The first two layers look like edge and corner detectors. Gabor-like filters only appear in the third layer. Gabor filters are linear and traditionally used for texture analysis. We have seen the visualization of features directly and by guided backpropagation. Next, we will see how to implement DeepDream for visualization.

The DeepDream

The neuron activations can be amplified at some layer in the network rather than synthesizing the image. This concept of amplifying the original image to see the effect of features is called **DeepDream**. The steps for creating the DeepDream are:

1. Take an image and pick a layer from CNN.
2. Take the activations at a particular layer.
3. Modify the gradient such that the gradient and activations are equal.
4. Compute the gradients of the image and backpropagate.
5. The image has to be jittered and normalized using regularization.
6. The pixel values should be clipped.
7. Multi-scale processing of the image is done for the effect of fractal.

Let's start by importing the relevant packages:

```
import os
import numpy as np
import PIL.Image
import urllib.request
from tensorflow.python.platform import gfile
import zipfile
```

The inception model is pre-trained on the `Imagenet` dataset and the model files provided by Google. We can download that model and use it for this example. The ZIP archive of the model files are downloaded and extracted in a folder, as shown here:

```
model_url =
'https://storage.googleapis.com/download.tensorflow.org/models/incepti
on5h.zip'

file_name = model_url.split('/')[-1]

file_path = os.path.join(work_dir, file_name)

if not os.path.exists(file_path):
    file_path, _ = urllib.request.urlretrieve(model_url, file_path)
```

```
zip_handle = zipfile.ZipFile(file_path, 'r')
zip_handle.extractall(work_dir)
zip_handle.close()
```

These commands should have created three new files in the working directory. This pre-trained model can be loaded into the session, as shown here:

```
graph = tf.Graph()
session = tf.InteractiveSession(graph=graph)
model_path = os.path.join(work_dir, 'tensorflow_inception_graph.pb')
with gfile.FastGFile(model_path, 'rb') as f:
    graph_defnition = tf.GraphDef()
    graph_defnition.ParseFromString(f.read())
```

A session is started with the initialization of a graph. Then the graph definition of the model downloaded is loaded into the memory. The `ImageNet` mean has to be subtracted from the input as shown next, as a preprocessing step. The preprocessed image is then fed to the graph as shown:

```
input_placeholder = tf.placeholder(np.float32, name='input')
imagenet_mean_value = 117.0
preprocessed_input = tf.expand_dims(input_placeholder-
imagenet_mean_value, 0)
tf.import_graph_def(graph_defnition, {'input': preprocessed_input})
```

Now the session and graph are ready for inference. A `resize_image` function will be required with bilinear interpolation. A `resize` function method can be added that resizes the image with a TensorFlow session, as shown here:

```
def resize_image(image, size):
    resize_placeholder = tf.placeholder(tf.float32)
    resize_placeholder_expanded = tf.expand_dims(resize_placeholder,
0)
    resized_image =
tf.image.resize_bilinear(resize_placeholder_expanded, size)[0, :, :,
:]
    return session.run(resized_image, feed_dict={resize_placeholder:
image})
```

An image from the working directory can be loaded into the memory and converted to float value, as shown here:

```
image_name = 'mountain.jpg'
image = PIL.Image.open(image_name)
image = np.float32(image)
```

The image that is loaded is shown here, for your reference:

The number of octaves, size, and scale of the scale space are defined here:

```
no_octave = 4
scale = 1.4
window_size = 51
```

These values work well for the example shown here and hence, require tuning for other images based on their size. A layer can be selected for dreaming and the average mean of that layer will be the `objective` function, as shown here:

```
score = tf.reduce_mean(objective_fn)
gradients = tf.gradients(score, input_placeholder)[0]
```

The gradient of the images is computed for optimization. The octave images can be computed by resizing the image to various scales and finding the difference, as shown:

```
octave_images = []
for i in range(no_octave - 1):
    image_height_width = image.shape[:2]
    scaled_image = resize_image(image,
np.int32(np.float32(image_height_width) / scale))
    image_difference = image - resize_image(scaled_image,
```

```
image_height_width)
    image = scaled_image
    octave_images.append(image_difference)
```

Now the optimization can be run using all the octave images. The window is slid across the image, computing the gradients activation to create the dream, as shown here:

```
for octave_idx in range(no_octave):
    if octave_idx > 0:
        image_difference = octave_images[-octave_idx]
        image = resize_image(image, image_difference.shape[:2]) +
image_difference

    for i in range(10):
        image_heigth, image_width = image.shape[:2]
        sx, sy = np.random.randint(window_size, size=2)
        shifted_image = np.roll(np.roll(image, sx, 1), sy, 0)
        gradient_values = np.zeros_like(image)

        for y in range(0, max(image_heigth - window_size // 2,
window_size), window_size):
            for x in range(0, max(image_width - window_size // 2,
window_size), window_size):
                sub = shifted_image[y:y + window_size, x:x +
window_size]
                gradient_windows = session.run(gradients,
{input_placeholder: sub})
                gradient_values[y:y + window_size, x:x + window_size]
= gradient_windows

        gradient_windows = np.roll(np.roll(gradient_values, -sx, 1), -
sy, 0)
        image += gradient_windows * (1.5 /
(np.abs(gradient_windows).mean() + 1e-7))
```

Now the optimization to create the DeepDream is completed and can be saved as shown, by clipping the values:

```
image /= 255.0
image = np.uint8(np.clip(image, 0, 1) * 255)
PIL.Image.fromarray(image).save('dream_' + image_name, 'jpeg')
```

In this section, we have seen the procedure to create the DeepDream. The result is shown here:

As we can see, dog slugs are activated everywhere. You can try various other layers and see the results. These results can be used for artistic purposes. Similarly, other layers can be activated to produce different artifacts. In the next section, we will see some adversarial examples that can fool deep learning models.

Adversarial examples

The image classification algorithms have reached human-level accuracy on several datasets. But they can be easily fooled by adversarial examples. Adversarial examples are synthetic images that fool a model to produce the outcome that is needed. Take any image and choose a random target class that is incorrect. This image can be modified with noise until the network is fooled as show by Goodfellow et al. (`https://arxiv.org/pdf/1412.6572.pdf`). An example of an adversarial attack on the model is shown here:

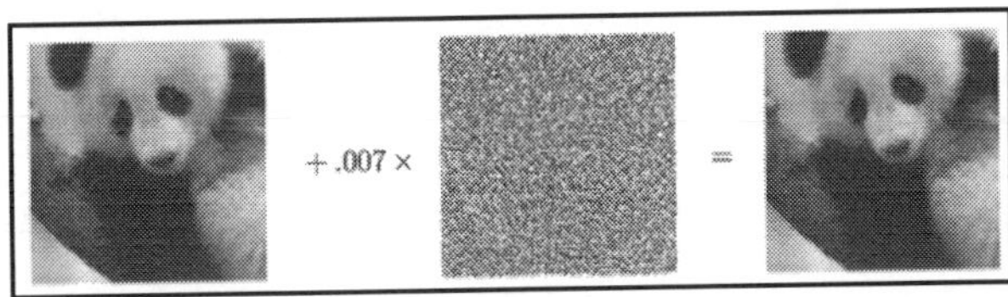

Reproduced with permission from Goodfellow et al.

In this figure, an image is shown on the left with 58% confidence of a particular label. The left image, when combined with noise which is shown in the middle, forms the image on the right side. For a human, the image with noise stills looks the same. But the image with noise is predicted with a different label with 97% confidence. High confidence is assigned to a particular example, despite the image having a very different object. This is a problem with deep learning models and hence, you should understand where this is applicable:

- The adversarial example can even be generated without the access to the models. You can train your own model, generate an adversarial example and can still fool a different model.
- This occurs rarely in practice but it becomes a true problem when someone tries to fool a system for spamming or crashing.
- All machine learning models are susceptible to this problem, not just deep learning models.

You should understand the consequences of deploying a deep learning model on a safety critical system, considering the adversarial examples. In the next section, we will see how to utilize TensorFlow Serving to get a faster inference.

Model inference

Any new data can be passed to the model to get the results. This process of getting the classification results or features from an image is termed as **inference**. Training and inference usually happen on different computers and at different times. We will learn about storing the model, running the inference, and using TensorFlow Serving as the server with good latency and throughput.

Exporting a model

The model after training has to be exported and saved. The weights, biases, and the graph are stored for inference. We will train an MNIST model and store it. Start with defining the constants that are required, using the following code:

```
work_dir = '/tmp'
model_version = 9
training_iteration = 1000
input_size = 784
no_classes = 10
```

```
batch_size = 100
total_batches = 200
```

The `model_version` can be an integer to specify which model we want to export for serving. The `feature config` is stored as a dictionary with placeholder names and their corresponding datatype. The prediction classes and their labels should be mapped. The identity placeholder can be used with the API:

```
tf_example = tf.parse_example(tf.placeholder(tf.string,
name='tf_example'),
                              {'x': tf.FixedLenFeature(shape=[784],
dtype=tf.float32), })
x_input = tf.identity(tf_example['x'], name='x')
```

A simple classifier can be defined with weights, biases, logits, and an optimizer, using the following code:

```
y_input = tf.placeholder(tf.float32, shape=[None, no_classes])
weights = tf.Variable(tf.random_normal([input_size, no_classes]))
bias = tf.Variable(tf.random_normal([no_classes]))
logits = tf.matmul(x_input, weights) + bias
softmax_cross_entropy =
tf.nn.softmax_cross_entropy_with_logits(labels=y_input, logits=logits)
loss_operation = tf.reduce_mean(softmax_cross_entropy)
optimiser =
tf.train.GradientDescentOptimizer(0.5).minimize(loss_operation)
```

Train the model as shown in the following code:

```
mnist = input_data.read_data_sets('MNIST_data', one_hot=True)
for batch_no in range(total_batches):
    mnist_batch = mnist.train.next_batch(batch_size)
    _, loss_value = session.run([optimiser, loss_operation],
feed_dict={
        x_input: mnist_batch[0],
        y_input: mnist_batch[1]
    })
    print(loss_value)
```

Define the prediction signature, and export the model. Save the model to a persistent storage so that it can be used for inference at a later point in time. This exports the data by deserialization and stores it in a format that can be understood by different systems. Multiple graphs with different variables and placeholders can be used for exporting. It also supports `signature_defs` and assets. The `signature_defs` have the inputs and outputs specified because input and output will be accessed from the external clients. Assets are non-graph components that will be utilized for the inference, such as vocabulary and so on.

The classification signature uses access to the classification API of TensorFlow. An input is compulsory and there are two optional outputs (prediction classes and prediction probabilities), with at least one being compulsory. The prediction signature offers flexibility with the number of inputs and outputs. Multiple outputs can be defined and explicitly queried from the client side. The `signature_def` is shown here:

```
signature_def = (
      tf.saved_model.signature_def_utils.build_signature_def(
          inputs={'x':
tf.saved_model.utils.build_tensor_info(x_input)},
          outputs={'y':
tf.saved_model.utils.build_tensor_info(y_input)},
          method_name="tensorflow/serving/predict"))
```

Finally, add the metagraph and variables to the builder with the prediction signature:

```
model_path = os.path.join(work_dir, str(model_version))
saved_model_builder =
tf.saved_model.builder.SavedModelBuilder(model_path)
saved_model_builder.add_meta_graph_and_variables(
      session, [tf.saved_model.tag_constants.SERVING],
      signature_def_map={
          'prediction': signature_def
      },
      legacy_init_op=tf.group(tf.tables_initializer(),
name='legacy_init_op'))
saved_model_builder.save()
```

The builder is saved and ready to be consumed by the server. The shown example is applicable to any model and can be used for exporting. In the next section, we will serve and query the exported model.

Serving the trained model

The model that is exported in the previous section can be served via TensorFlow Serving using the following command:

```
tensorflow_model_server --port=9000 --model_name=mnist --
model_base_path=/tmp/mnist_model/
```

The `model_base_path` points to the directory of the exported model. The server can now be tested with the client. Note that this is not an HTTP server, and hence, a client as shown here, is needed instead of an HTTP client. Import the required libraries:

```
from grpc.beta import implementations
import numpy
import tensorflow as tf
from tensorflow.examples.tutorials.mnist import input_data
from tensorflow_serving.apis import predict_pb2
from tensorflow_serving.apis import prediction_service_pb2
```

Add the constants for concurrency, the number of tests, and working directory. A class is defined for counting the results returned. A **Remote Procedure Call (RPC)** callback is defined with a counter for counting the predictions, as shown here:

```
concurrency = 1
num_tests = 100
host = ''
port = 8000
work_dir = '/tmp'


def _create_rpc_callback():
  def _callback(result):
      response = numpy.array(
        result.result().outputs['y'].float_val)
      prediction = numpy.argmax(response)
      print(prediction)
  return _callback
```

Modify the `host` and `port` according to your requirements. The `_callback` method defines the steps required when the response comes back from the server. In this case, the maximum of the probabilities is computed. Run the inference by calling the server:

```
test_data_set = mnist.test
test_image = mnist.test.images[0]

predict_request = predict_pb2.PredictRequest()
predict_request.model_spec.name = 'mnist'
predict_request.model_spec.signature_name = 'prediction'

predict_channel = implementations.insecure_channel(host, int(port))
predict_stub =
prediction_service_pb2.beta_create_PredictionService_stub(predict_chan
nel)
```

```
predict_request.inputs['x'].CopyFrom(
    tf.contrib.util.make_tensor_proto(test_image, shape=[1,
test_image.size]))
result = predict_stub.Predict.future(predict_request, 3.0)
result.add_done_callback(
    _create_rpc_callback())
```

Call the inference repeatedly to gauge the accuracy, latency, and throughput. The inference error rate should be around 90%, and the concurrency should be great. The export and client methods can be used together for any model to obtain the results and features from the model. In the next section, we will build the retrieval pipeline.

Content-based image retrieval

The technique of **Content-based Image Retrieval** (**CBIR**) takes a query image as the input and ranks images from a database of target images, producing the output. CBIR is an image to image search engine with a specific goal. A database of target images is required for retrieval. The target images with the minimum distance from the query image are returned. We can use the image directly for similarity, but the problems are as follows:

- The image is of huge dimensions
- There is a lot of redundancy in pixels
- A pixel doesn't carry the semantic information

So, we train a model for object classification and use the features from the model for retrieval. Then we pass the query image and database of targets through the same model to get the features. The models can also be called **encoders** as they encode the information about the images for the particular task. Encoders should be able to capture global and local features. We can use the models that we studied in the image classification chapter, trained for a classification task. The searching of the image may take a lot of time, as a brute-force or linear scan is slow. Hence, some methods for faster retrieval are required. Here are some methods for faster matching:

- **Locality sensitive hashing** (**LSH**): LSH projects the features to their subspace and can give a candidate a list and do a fine-feature ranking later. This is also a dimensionality reduction technique such as PCA and t-SNE which we covered earlier in the chapter. This has feature buckets in lower dimensions.

- **Multi-index hashing**: This method hashes the features and it is like pigeonhole fitting making it faster. It uses hamming distance to make the computation faster. Hamming distance is nothing but the number of location differences of the numbers when expressed in binary.

These methods are faster, need lesser memory, with the trade-off being accuracy. These methods also don't capture the semantic difference. The matches results can be re-ranked to get better results based on the query. Re-ranking can improve the results by reordering the returned target images. Re-ranking may use one of the following techniques:

- **Geometric verification**: This method matches the geometries and target images with only similar geometries returned.
- **Query expansion**: This expands the list of target images and searches them exhaustively.
- **Relevance feedback**: This method gets the feedback from the use and returns the results. Based on the user input, the re-ranking will be done.

These techniques are well developed for text and can be used for images. In this chapter, we will focus on extracting features and use them for CBIR. In the next section, we will learn how to do model inference.

Building the retrieval pipeline

The sequence of steps to get the best matches from target images for a query image is called the **retrieval pipeline**. The retrieval pipeline has multiple steps or components. The features of the image database have to be extracted offline and stored in a database. For every query image, the feature has to be extracted and similarity has to be computed across all of the target images. Then the images can be ranked for final output. The retrieval pipeline is shown here:

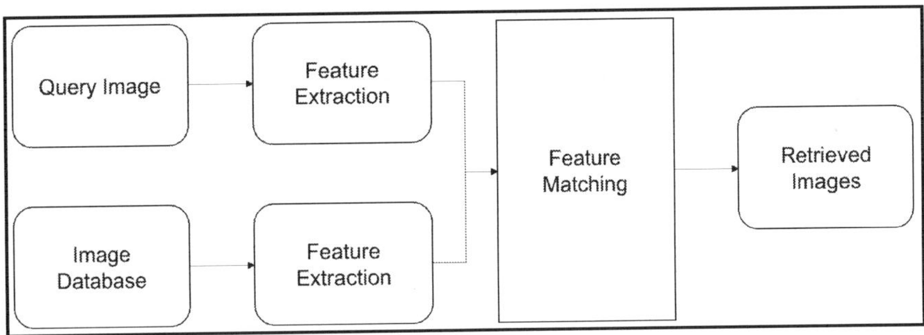

The feature extraction step has to be fast, for which TensorFlow Serving can be used. You can choose which features to use depending on the application. For example, initial layers can be used when texture-based matching is required, later layers can be used when it has to be matched at an object level. In the next section, we will see how to extract features from a pre-trained inception model.

Extracting bottleneck features for an image

Bottleneck features are the values computed in the pre-classification layer. In this section, we will see how to extract the bottleneck features from a pre-trained model using TensorFlow. Let's start by importing the required libraries, using the following code:

```
import os
import urllib.request
from tensorflow.python.platform import gfile
import tarfile
```

Then, we need to download the pre-trained model with the graph definition and its weights. TensorFlow has trained a model on the `ImageNet` dataset using inception architecture and provided the model. We will download this model and unzip it into a local folder, using the following code:

```
model_url =
'http://download.tensorflow.org/models/image/imagenet/inception-2015-1
2-05.tgz'
file_name = model_url.split('/')[-1]
file_path = os.path.join(work_dir, file_name)

if not os.path.exists(file_path):
    file_path, _ = urllib.request.urlretrieve(model_url, file_path)
tarfile.open(file_path, 'r:gz').extractall(work_dir)
```

This created a folder and downloaded the model, only when it does not exist. If the code is executed repeatedly, the model won't be downloaded every time. The graph is stored in a **Protocol Buffers (protobuf)** format in a file. This has to be read as a string and passed to the `tf.GraphDef()` object to bring it into memory:

```
model_path = os.path.join(work_dir, 'classify_image_graph_def.pb')
with gfile.FastGFile(model_path, 'rb') as f:
    graph_defnition = tf.GraphDef()
    graph_defnition.ParseFromString(f.read())
```

In the inception model, the bottleneck layer is named `pool_3/_reshape:0`, and the layer is of 2,048 dimensions. The input placeholder name is `DecodeJpeg/contents:0`, and the resize tensor name is `ResizeBilinear:0`. We can import the graph definition using `tf.import_graph_def` with the required return tensors for further operations:

```
bottleneck, image, resized_input = (
    tf.import_graph_def(
        graph_defnition,
        name='',
        return_elements=['pool_3/_reshape:0',
                         'DecodeJpeg/contents:0',
                         'ResizeBilinear:0'])
)
```

Take a query and target image and load it in the memory. The `gfile` function provides a faster way to load the image into the memory.

```
query_image_path = os.path.join(work_dir, 'cat.1000.jpg')
query_image = gfile.FastGFile(query_image_path, 'rb').read()
target_image_path = os.path.join(work_dir, 'cat.1001.jpg')
target_image = gfile.FastGFile(target_image_path, 'rb').read()
```

Let us define a function that extracts the bottleneck feature from an image, using the `session` and image:

```
def get_bottleneck_data(session, image_data):
    bottleneck_data = session.run(bottleneck, {image: image_data})
    bottleneck_data = np.squeeze(bottleneck_data)
    return bottleneck_data
```

Initiate the session, and pass the image to run the forward inference to get the bottleneck values from the pre-trained model:

```
query_feature = get_bottleneck_data(session, query_image)
print(query_feature)
target_feature = get_bottleneck_data(session, target_image)
print(target_feature)
```

Running the above code should print as shown here:

```
[ 0.55705792 0.36785451 1.06618118 ..., 0.6011821 0.36407694
  0.0996572 ]
[ 0.30421323 0.0926369 0.26213276 ..., 0.72273785 0.30847171
  0.08719242]
```

This procedure of computing the features can be scaled for more target images. Using the values, the similarity can be computed between the query image and target database as described in the following section.

Computing similarity between query image and target database

NumPy's `linalg.norm` is useful for computing the **Euclidean distance**. The similarity between the query image and target database can be computed between the images by calculating the Euclidean distances between the features as shown here:

```
dist = np.linalg.norm(np.asarray(query_feature) -
np.asarray(target_feature))
print(dist)
```

Running this command should print the following:

```
16.9965
```

This is the metric that can be used for similarity calculation. The smaller the Euclidean distance between the query and the target image is, the more similar the images are. Hence, computing the Euclidean distance is a measurement of similarity. Using the features for computing the Euclidean distance is based on the assumption that the features are learned during the training of the model. Scaling this computation for millions of images is not efficient. In a production system, it is expected to return the results in milliseconds. In the next section, we will see how to make this retrieval efficient.

Efficient retrieval

The retrieval can be slow because it's a brute-force method. Matching can be made faster using approximate nearest neighbor. The curse of dimensionality also kicks in, as shown in the following figure:

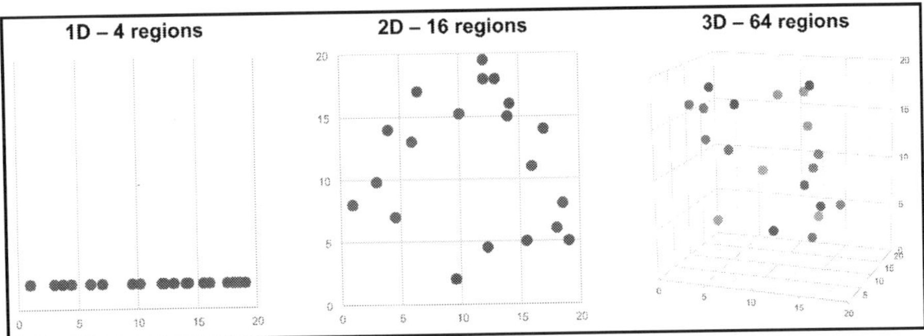

With every increasing dimension, complexity increases as the complexity from two dimensions to three dimensions. The computation of the distance also becomes slower. To make the distance search faster, we will discuss an approximate method in the next section.

Matching faster using approximate nearest neighbour

Approximate nearest neighbour oh yeah (ANNOY) is a method for faster nearest neighbour search. ANNOY builds trees by random projections. The tree structure makes it easier to find the closest matches. You can create an `ANNOYIndex` for faster retrieval as shown here:

```
def create_annoy(target_features):
    t = AnnoyIndex(layer_dimension)
    for idx, target_feature in enumerate(target_features):
        t.add_item(idx, target_feature)
    t.build(10)
    t.save(os.path.join(work_dir, 'annoy.ann'))

create_annoy(target_features)
```

The dimension of the features is required for creating the index. Then the items are added to the index and the tree is built. The bigger the number of trees, the more accurate the results will be with a trade-off of time and space complexity. The index can be created and loaded into the memory. The ANNOY can be queried as shown here:

```
annoy_index = AnnoyIndex(10)
annoy_index.load(os.path.join(work_dir, 'annoy.ann'))
matches = annoy_index.get_nns_by_vector(query_feature, 20)
```

The list of matches can be used to retrieve the image details. The index of the items will be returned.

Visit `https://github.com/spotify/annoy` for a complete implementation of `ANNOY` and its benchmark comparison against other approximate nearest neighbour algorithms, in terms of accuracy and speed.

Advantages of ANNOY

There are many reasons for using ANNOY. The main advantages are listed as follows:

- Has a memory-mapped data structure, hence, less intensive on RAM. The same file can be shared among multiple processes due to this.
- Multiple distances such as Manhattan, Cosine, or Euclidean can be used for computing the similarity between the query image and target database.

Autoencoders of raw images

An autoencoder is an unsupervised algorithm for generating efficient encodings. The input layer and the target output is typically the same. The layers between decrease and increase in the following fashion:

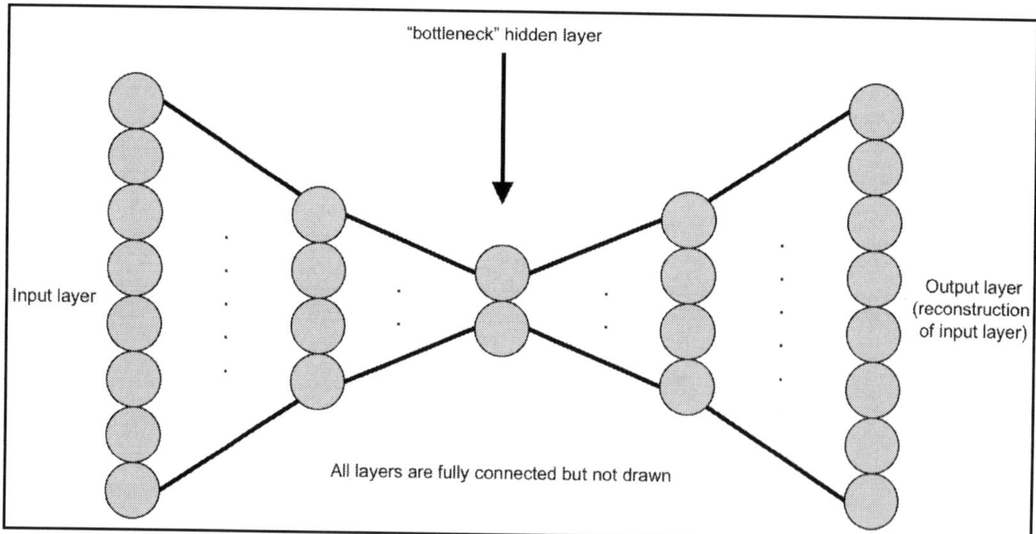

The **bottleneck** layer is the middle layer with a reduced dimension. The left side of the bottleneck layer is called **encoder** and the right side is called **decoder**. An encoder typically reduces the dimension of the data and a decoder increases the dimensions. This combination of encoder and decoder is called an autoencoder. The whole network is trained with reconstruction error. Theoretically, the bottleneck layer can be stored and the original data can be reconstructed by the decoder network. This reduces the dimensions and can be programmed easily, as shown next. Define a convolution, deconvolution, and fully connected layer, using the following code:

```
def fully_connected_layer(input_layer, units):
    return tf.layers.dense(
        input_layer,
        units=units,
        activation=tf.nn.relu
    )


def convolution_layer(input_layer, filter_size):
    return  tf.layers.conv2d(
        input_layer,
        filters=filter_size,
kernel_initializer=tf.contrib.layers.xavier_initializer_conv2d(),
        kernel_size=3,
        strides=2
    )


def deconvolution_layer(input_layer, filter_size,
activation=tf.nn.relu):
    return tf.layers.conv2d_transpose(
        input_layer,
        filters=filter_size,
kernel_initializer=tf.contrib.layers.xavier_initializer_conv2d(),
        kernel_size=3,
        activation=activation,
        strides=2
    )
```

Define the converging encoder with five layers of convolution, as shown in the following code:

```
input_layer = tf.placeholder(tf.float32, [None, 128, 128, 3])
convolution_layer_1 = convolution_layer(input_layer, 1024)
convolution_layer_2 = convolution_layer(convolution_layer_1, 512)
convolution_layer_3 = convolution_layer(convolution_layer_2, 256)
convolution_layer_4 = convolution_layer(convolution_layer_3, 128)
convolution_layer_5 = convolution_layer(convolution_layer_4, 32)
```

Compute the bottleneck layer by flattening the fifth convolution layer. The bottleneck layer is again reshaped back fit a convolution layer, as shown here:

```
convolution_layer_5_flattened = tf.layers.flatten(convolution_layer_5)
bottleneck_layer =
fully_connected_layer(convolution_layer_5_flattened, 16)
c5_shape = convolution_layer_5.get_shape().as_list()
c5f_flat_shape =
convolution_layer_5_flattened.get_shape().as_list()[1]
fully_connected = fully_connected_layer(bottleneck_layer,
c5f_flat_shape)
fully_connected = tf.reshape(fully_connected,
                             [-1, c5_shape[1], c5_shape[2],
c5_shape[3]])
```

Compute the diverging or decoder part that can reconstruct the image, as shown in the following code:

```
deconvolution_layer_1 = deconvolution_layer(fully_connected, 128)
deconvolution_layer_2 = deconvolution_layer(deconvolution_layer_1,
256)
deconvolution_layer_3 = deconvolution_layer(deconvolution_layer_2,
512)
deconvolution_layer_4 = deconvolution_layer(deconvolution_layer_3,
1024)
deconvolution_layer_5 = deconvolution_layer(deconvolution_layer_4, 3,
                                            activation=tf.nn.tanh)
```

This network is trained and it quickly converges. The bottleneck layer can be stored when passed with image features. This helps in decreasing the size of the database, which can be used for retrieval. Only the encoder part is needed for indexing the features. Autoencoder is a lossy compression algorithm. It is different from other compression algorithms because it learns the compression pattern from the data. Hence, an autoencoder model is specific to the data. An autoencoder could be combined with t-SNE for a better visualization. The bottleneck layers learned by the autoencoder might not be useful for other tasks. The size of the bottleneck layer can be larger than previous layers. In such a case of diverging and converging connections are sparse autoencoders. In the next section, we will learn another application of autoencoders.

Denoising using autoencoders

Autoencoders can also be used for image denoising. Denoising is the process of removing noise from the image. A denoising encoder can be trained in an unsupervised manner. The noise can be introduced in a normal image and the autoencoder is trained against the original images. Later, the full autoencoder can be used to produce noise-free images. In this section, we will see step-by-step instructions to denoise MNIST images. Import the required libraries and define the placeholders as shown:

```
x_input = tf.placeholder(tf.float32, shape=[None, input_size])
y_input = tf.placeholder(tf.float32, shape=[None, input_size])
```

Both `x_input` and `y_input` are of the same shape as they should be in an autoencoder. Then, define a dense layer as shown here, with the default activation as the `tanh` activation function. The method, `add_variable_summary` is imported from the image classification chapter example. The definition of the dense layer is shown here:

```
def dense_layer(input_layer, units, activation=tf.nn.tanh):
    layer = tf.layers.dense(
        inputs=input_layer,
        units=units,
        activation=activation
    )
    add_variable_summary(layer, 'dense')
    return layer
```

Next, the autoencoder layers can be defined. This autoencoder has only fully connected layers. The encoder part has three layers of reducing dimensions. The decoder part has three layers of increasing dimensions. Both the encoder and decoder are symmetrical as shown here:

```
layer_1 = dense_layer(x_input, 500)
layer_2 = dense_layer(layer_1, 250)
layer_3 = dense_layer(layer_2, 50)
layer_4 = dense_layer(layer_3, 250)
layer_5 = dense_layer(layer_4, 500)
layer_6 = dense_layer(layer_5, 784)
```

The dimensions of the hidden layers are arbitrarily chosen. Next, the `loss` and `optimiser` are defined. Here we use sigmoid instead of softmax as classification, as shown here:

```
with tf.name_scope('loss'):
    softmax_cross_entropy = tf.nn.sigmoid_cross_entropy_with_logits(
        labels=y_input, logits=layer_6)
    loss_operation = tf.reduce_mean(softmax_cross_entropy,
name='loss')
    tf.summary.scalar('loss', loss_operation)

with tf.name_scope('optimiser'):
    optimiser = tf.train.AdamOptimizer().minimize(loss_operation)
```

TensorBoard offers another kind of summary called `image`, which is useful for visualizing the images. We will take the input, `layer_6` and reshape it to add it to the summary, as shown here:

```
x_input_reshaped = tf.reshape(x_input, [-1, 28, 28, 1])
tf.summary.image("noisy_images", x_input_reshaped)

y_input_reshaped = tf.reshape(y_input, [-1, 28, 28, 1])
tf.summary.image("original_images", y_input_reshaped)

layer_6_reshaped = tf.reshape(layer_6, [-1, 28, 28, 1])
tf.summary.image("reconstructed_images", layer_6_reshaped)
```

The number of images is restricted to three by default and can be changed. This is to restrict it from writing all the images to the summary folder. Next, all the summaries are merged and the graph is added to the summary writer as shown:

```
merged_summary_operation = tf.summary.merge_all()
train_summary_writer = tf.summary.FileWriter('/tmp/train',
session.graph)
```

A normal random noise can be added to the image and fed as the input tensors. After the noise is added, the extra values are clipped. The target will be the original images themselves. The addition of noise and training procedure is shown here:

```
for batch_no in range(total_batches):
    mnist_batch = mnist_data.train.next_batch(batch_size)
    train_images, _ = mnist_batch[0], mnist_batch[1]
    train_images_noise = train_images + 0.2 *
np.random.normal(size=train_images.shape)
    train_images_noise = np.clip(train_images_noise, 0., 1.)
    _, merged_summary = session.run([optimiser,
merged_summary_operation],
```

```
                                    feed_dict={
        x_input: train_images_noise,
        y_input: train_images,
    })
    train_summary_writer.add_summary(merged_summary, batch_no)
```

When this training is started, the results can be seen in TensorBoard. The loss is shown here:

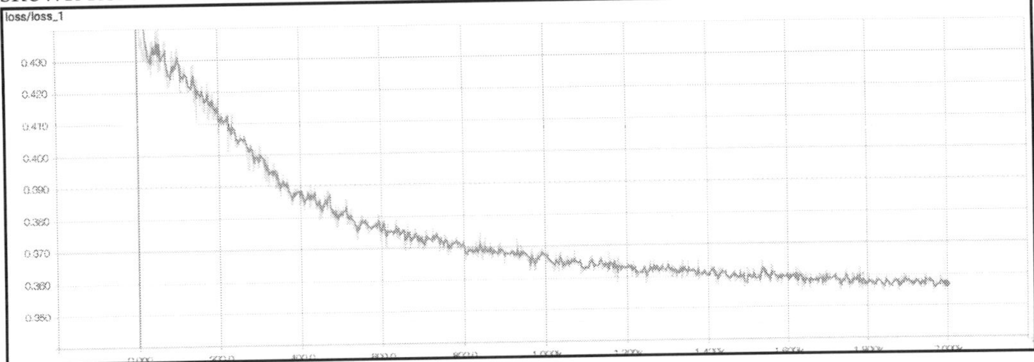

Tensorboard illustrating the output plot

The loss steadily decreases and will keep decreasing slowly over the iterations. This shows how autoencoders converge quickly. Next, three digits are displayed from the original images:

Here are the same images with noise added:

You will notice that there is significant noise and this is given as an input. Next, are the reconstructed images of the same numbers with the denoising autoencoder:

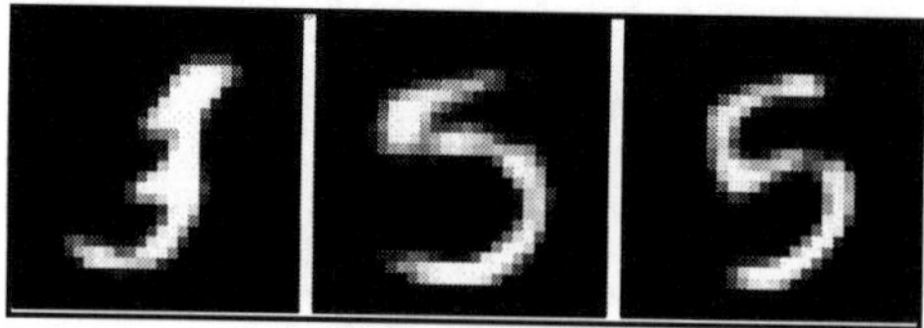

You will notice that the denoising autoencoder has done a fantastic job of removing the noise. You can run this on test images and can see the quality is maintained. For more complex datasets, you can use the convolutional neural net for better results. This example shows the power of deep learning of computer vision, given that this is trained in an unsupervised manner.

Summary

In this chapter, you have learned how to extract features from an image and use them for CBIR. You also learned how to use TensorFlow Serving to get the inference of image features. We saw how to utilize approximate nearest neighbour or faster matching rather than a linear scan. You understood how hashing may still improve the results. The idea of autoencoders was introduced, and we saw how to train smaller feature vectors for search. An example of image denoising using an autoencoder was also shown. We saw the possibility of using a bit-based comparison that can scale this up to billions of images.

In the next chapter, we will see how to train models for object detection problems. We will leverage open source models to get good accuracy and understand all the algorithms behind them. At the end, we will use all the ideas to train a pedestrian detection model.

23
Object Detection

Object detection is the act of finding the location of an object in an image. In this chapter, we will learn the techniques of object detection and implement pedestrian detection by understanding the following topics:

- Basics and the difference between localization and detection
- Various datasets and their descriptions
- Algorithms used for object localization and detection
- TensorFlow API for object detection
- Training new object detection models
- Pedestrian detection on a moving car with YOLO algorithm

Detecting objects in an image

Object detection had an explosion concerning both applications and research in recent years. Object detection is a problem of importance in computer vision. Similar to image classification tasks, deeper networks have shown better performance in detection. At present, the accuracy of these techniques is excellent. Hence it used in many applications.

Image classification labels the image as a whole. Finding the position of the object in addition to labeling the object is called **object localization**. Typically, the position of the object is defined by rectangular coordinates. Finding multiple objects in the image with rectangular coordinates is called detection. Here is an example of object detection:

The image shows four objects with bounding boxes. We will learn algorithms that can perform the task of finding the boxes. The applications are enormous in robot vision, such as self-driving cars and industrial objects. We can summarize localization and detection tasks to the following points:

- Localization detects one object in an image within a label
- Detection finds all the objects within the image along with the labels

The difference is the number of objects. In detection, there are a variable number of objects. This small difference makes a big difference when designing the architectures for the deep learning model concerning localization or detection. Next, we will see various datasets available for the tasks.

Exploring the datasets

The datasets available for object localization and detection are many. In this section, we will explore the datasets that are used by the research community to evaluate the algorithms. There are datasets with a varying number of objects, ranging from 20 to 200 annotated in these datasets, which makes object detection hard. Some datasets have too many objects in one image compared to other datasets with just one object per image. Next, we will see the datasets in detail.

ImageNet dataset

ImageNet has data for evaluating classification, localization, and detection tasks. Similar to classification data, there are 1,000 classes for localization tasks. The accuracy is calculated based on the top five detections. There will be at least one bounding box in all the images. There are 200 objects for detection problems with 470,000 images, with an average of 1.1 objects per image.

PASCAL VOC challenge

The PASCAL VOC challenge ran from 2005 to 2012. This challenge was considered the benchmark for object detection techniques. There are 20 classes in the dataset. The dataset has 11,530 images for training and validations with 27,450 annotations for regions of interest. The following are the twenty classes present in the dataset:

- Person: Person
- Animal: Bird, cat, cow, dog, horse, sheep
- Vehicle: Airplane, bicycle, boat, bus, car, motorbike, train
- Indoor: Bottle, chair, dining table, potted plant, sofa, tv/monitor

You can download the dataset from `http://host.robots.ox.ac.uk/pascal/VOC/voc2012/VOCtrainval_11-May-2012.tar`. There is an average of 2.4 objects per image.

COCO object detection challenge

The **Common Objects in Context** (**COCO**) dataset has 200,000 images with more than 500,000 object annotations in 80 categories. It is the most extensive publicly available object detection database. The following image has the list of objects present in the dataset:

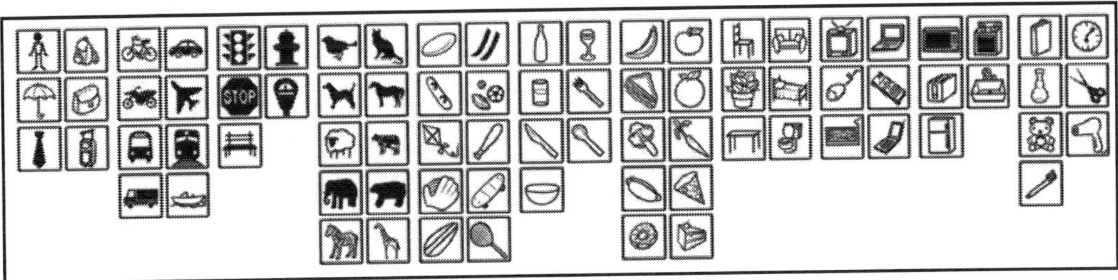

The average number of objects is 7.2 per image. These are the famous datasets for the object detection challenge. Next, we will learn how to evaluate the algorithms against these datasets.

Evaluating datasets using metrics

Metrics are essential for understanding in the context of a deep learning task. The metrics of object detection and localization are peculiar because of human annotation. The human may have annotated a box that is called **ground-truth**. The ground-truth need not be the absolute truth. Moreover, the boxes can be a few pixels different from human to human. Hence it becomes harder for the algorithm to detect the exact bounding box drawn by humans. **Intersection over Union** (**IoU**) is used to evaluate the localization task. **Mean Precision Average** (**mAP**) is used to evaluate the detection task. We will see the descriptions of the metrics in the next sections.

Intersection over Union

The IoU is the ratio of the overlapping area of **ground truth** and predicted area to the total area. Here is a visual explanation of the metric:

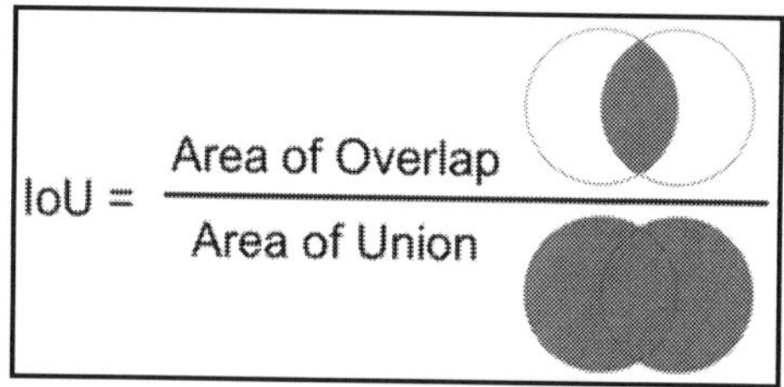

The two squares represent the bounding boxes of ground truth and predictions. The IoU is calculated as a ratio of the area of overlap to the area of the union. Here is the script to compute the IoU is given ground truth and prediction bounding boxes:

```
def calculate_iou(gt_bb, pred_bb):
    '''
    :param gt_bb: ground truth bounding box
    :param pred_bb: predicted bounding box
    '''
    gt_bb = tf.stack([
        gt_bb[:, :, :, :, 0] - gt_bb[:, :, :, :, 2] / 2.0,
        gt_bb[:, :, :, :, 1] - gt_bb[:, :, :, :, 3] / 2.0,
        gt_bb[:, :, :, :, 0] + gt_bb[:, :, :, :, 2] / 2.0,
        gt_bb[:, :, :, :, 1] + gt_bb[:, :, :, :, 3] / 2.0])
```

```
    gt_bb = tf.transpose(gt_bb, [1, 2, 3, 4, 0])
    pred_bb = tf.stack([
        pred_bb[:, :, :, :, 0] - pred_bb[:, :, :, :, 2] / 2.0,
        pred_bb[:, :, :, :, 1] - pred_bb[:, :, :, :, 3] / 2.0,
        pred_bb[:, :, :, :, 0] + pred_bb[:, :, :, :, 2] / 2.0,
        pred_bb[:, :, :, :, 1] + pred_bb[:, :, :, :, 3] / 2.0])
    pred_bb = tf.transpose(pred_bb, [1, 2, 3, 4, 0])
    area = tf.maximum(
        0.0,
        tf.minimum(gt_bb[:, :, :, :, 2:], pred_bb[:, :, :, :, 2:]) -
        tf.maximum(gt_bb[:, :, :, :, :2], pred_bb[:, :, :, :, :2]))
    intersection_area= area[:, :, :, :, 0] * area[:, :, :, :, 1]
    gt_bb_area = (gt_bb[:, :, :, :, 2] - gt_bb[:, :, :, :, 0]) * \
                 (gt_bb[:, :, :, :, 3] - gt_bb[:, :, :, :, 1])
    pred_bb_area = (pred_bb[:, :, :, :, 2] - pred_bb[:, :, :, :, 0]) *
\
                   (pred_bb[:, :, :, :, 3] - pred_bb[:, :, :, :, 1])
    union_area = tf.maximum(gt_bb_area + pred_bb_area -
intersection_area, 1e-10)
    iou = tf.clip_by_value(intersection_area / union_area, 0.0, 1.0)
    return iou
```

The ground truth and predicted bounding boxes are stacked together. Then the area is calculated while handling the case of negative area. The negative area could occur when bounding box coordinates are incorrect. The right side coordinates of the box many occur left to the left coordinates. Since the structure of the bounding box is not preserved, the negative area is bound to occur. The union and intersection areas are computed followed by a final IoU calculation which is the ratio of the overlapping area of **ground truth** and predicted area to the total area. The IoU calculation can be coupled with algorithms to train localization problems.

The mean average precision

The mAP is used for evaluating detection algorithms. The mAP metric is the product of precision and recall of the detected bounding boxes. The mAP value ranges from 0 to 100. The higher the number, the better it is. The mAP can be computed by calculating **average precision** (**AP**) separately for each class, then the average over the class. A detection is considered a true positive only if the mAP is above 0.5. All detections from the test images can be combined by drawing a draw precision/recall curve for each class. The final area under the curve can be used for the comparison of algorithms. The mAP is a good measure of the sensitivity of the network while not raising many false alarms. We have learned the evaluating algorithms for the datasets. Next, we will look at algorithms for a localization task.

Localizing algorithms

Localization algorithms are an extension of the materials learned in `Chapter 21`, *Image Classification* and `Chapter 22`, *Image Retrieval*. In image classification, an image is passed through several layers of a CNN (convolutional neural network). The final layer of CNN outputs the probabilistic value, belonging to each of the labels. This can be extended to localize the objects. We will see these ideas in the following sections.

Localizing objects using sliding windows

An intuitive way of localization is to predict several cropped portions of an image with an object. The cropping of the images can be done by moving a window across the image and predicting for every window. The method of moving a smaller window than the image and cropping the image according to window size is called a **sliding window**. A prediction can be made for every cropped window of the image which is called sliding window object detection.

The prediction can be done by the deep learning model trained for image classification problems with closely-cropped images. Close cropping means that only one object will be found in the whole image. The movement of the window has to be uniform across the image. Each portion of the image is passed through the model to find the classification. There are two problems with this approach.

- It can only find objects that are the same size as the window. The sliding window will miss an object if the object size is bigger than the window size. To overcome this, we will use the concept of **scale space**.
- Another problem is that moving the window over pixels may lead to missing a few objects. Moving the window over every pixel will result in a lot of extra computation hence it will slow down the system. To avoid this, we will incorporate a trick in the convolutional layers.

We will cover both these techniques in the next section.

The scale-space concept

The scale-space is the concept of using images that are of various sizes. An image is reduced to smaller size, hence bigger objects can be detected with the same-sized window. An image can be resized to some sizes with decreasing sizes. The resizing of images by removing alternative pixels or interpolation may leave some artefacts. Hence the image is smoothened and resized iteratively. The images that are obtained by smoothening and resizing are scale space.

The window is slide on every single scale for the localization of objects. Running multiple scales is equivalent to running the image with a bigger window. The computational complexity of running on multiple scales is high. Localization can be sped up by moving faster with a trade-off for accuracy. The complexity makes the solution not usable in production. The idea of the sliding window could be made efficient with a fully convolutional implementation of sliding windows.

Training a fully connected layer as a convolution layer

The problem with the sliding window is the computational complexity. The complexity is because predictions are made for every window. Deep learning features have been computed for every window for overlapping regions. This computation of features for overlapping regions in cropped windows can be reduced. The solution is to use a fully convolutional net which computes the feature only once. For understanding a fully convolutional net, let's first see how to convert a fully connected layer to a `convolution_layer`. The kernel is changed to the same size, with the same number of filters as the number of neurons. It can be repeated for other layers too. Changing the kernel size is an easier way to convert a fully connected layer to a `convolution_layer`:

```
convolution_layer_1 = convolution_layer(x_input_reshape, 64)
pooling_layer_1 = pooling_layer(convolution_layer_1)
convolution_layer_2 = convolution_layer(pooling_layer_1, 128)
pooling_layer_2 = pooling_layer(convolution_layer_2)
dense_layer_bottleneck = convolution_layer(pooling_layer_2, 1024, [5,
5])
logits = convolution_layer(dense_layer_bottleneck, no_classes, [1, 1])
logits = tf.reshape(logits, [-1, 10])
```

The dense layers are expressed as convolution layers. This idea is powerful and useful in various scenarios. We will extend this idea to express sliding window as a full convolution network.

Convolution implementation of sliding window

In this technique, instead of sliding, the final target is made into some targets required as depth and a number of boxes as the window. Sermanet et al. (https://arxiv.org/pdf/1312.6229.pdf) used fully convolution implementation to overcome this problem of the sliding window. Here is an illustration of such convolution implementation, of the sliding window:

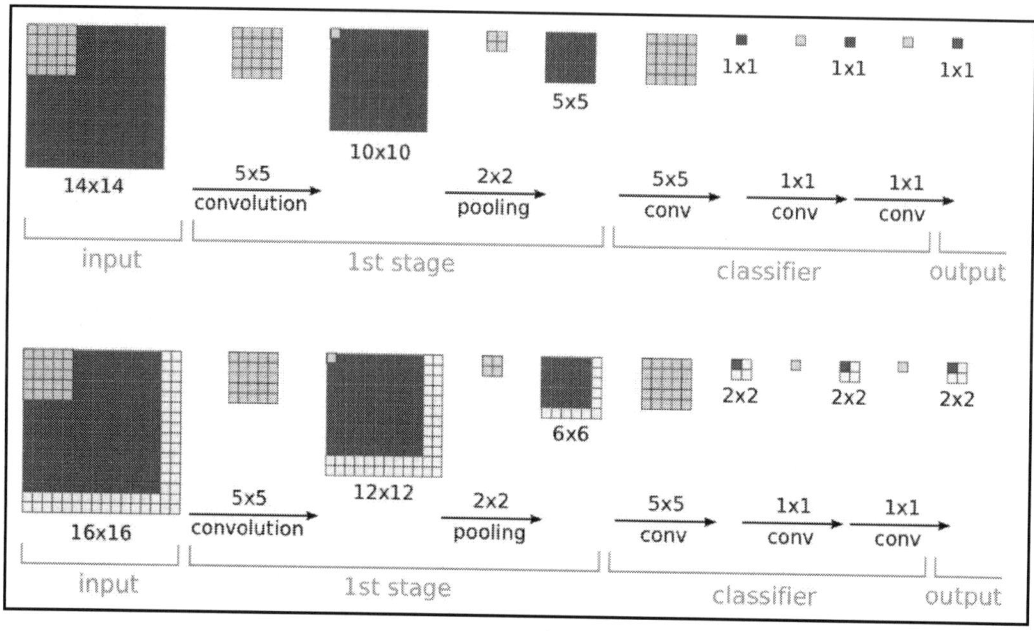

Reproduced with permission from Sermanet et al.

In the upper part of the example, normal classification is represented as a fully convolutional layer. In the lower part of the illustration, the same kernel is applied to a bigger image producing **2x2** at the end instead of 1. The final layer denotes four of the output of those bounding boxes. Having a volume for prediction improves efficiency, but the boxes still have a problem with accurate positioning. So the sliding window is not necessary, hence it solves the complexity. The aspect ratio is always changing and has to be seen at multiple scales. The bounding boxes produced by the fully convolutional method are not very accurate. The extra computations are done only for the extra region. As you can imagine, the boxes are rather restricted to the number of boxes that are trained with. Next, we will see a method to detect the bounding box positions more accurately.

Thinking about localization as a regression problem

One fundamental way to think about localization is modeling the problem as a regression problem. The bounding box is four numbers and hence can be predicted in a direct manner with a setting for regression. We will also need to predict the label, which is a classification problem.

There are different parameterizations available to define the bounding boxes. There are four numbers usually for the bounding box. One of the representations is the center of the coordinates with the height and width of the bounding box. A pre-trained model can be used by removing the fully connected layer and replacing it with a regression encoder. The regression has to be regularized with the L2 loss which performs poorly with an outlier. The L1 loss is better than L1. Swapping regression with a smoothened version of regularization is better. Fine-tuning the model gives a good accuracy, whereas training the whole network gives only a marginal performance improvement. It's a trade-off between training time and accuracy. Next, we will see different applications of regression using convolutional networks.

Applying regression to other problems

Regressing image coordinates is applicable to several other applications, such as **pose detection** and **fiducial point detection**. Pose detection is the act of finding joint locations in a human, as shown here:

In the preceding image, multiple locations such as head, neck, shoulders, ankles, and hands were detected. This can be extended to all human parts. The regression we learned could be used for this application. Here is an example of fiducial point detection:

Fiducial points are landmarks on the face with respect to the location of the eyes, nose, and lips. Finding these landmarks are vital for face-based augmented reality applications. There are some more landmarks available in the face and will be covered in detail in `Chapter 25`, *Similarity Learning*, in the context of face recognition.

Combining regression with the sliding window

The classification score is computed for every window in the sliding window approach or the fully convolutional approach to know what object is present in that window. Instead of predicting the classification score for every window to detect an object, each window itself can be predicted with a classification score. Combining all the ideas such as sliding window, scale-space, full convolution, and regression give superior results than any individual approach. The following are the top five localization error rates on the `ImageNet` dataset achieved by various networks using the regression approach:

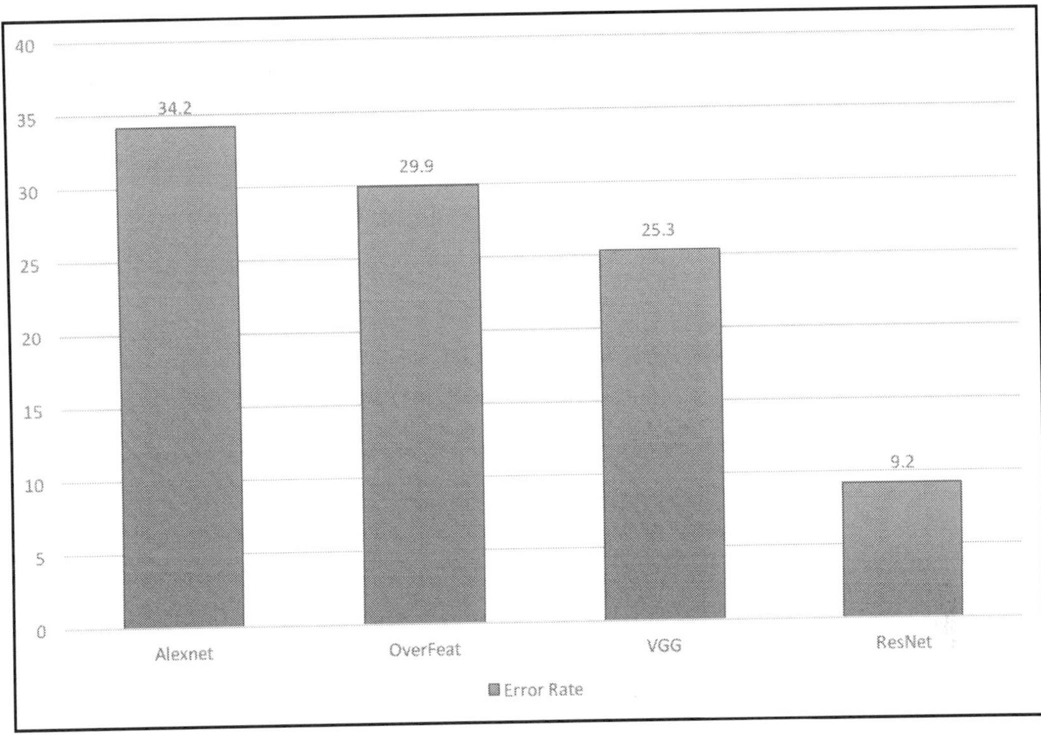

The preceding graph shows that the deeper the network, the better the results. For AlexNet, localization methods were not described in the paper. The OverFeat used multi-scale convolutional regression with box merging. VGG used localization but with fewer scales and location. These gains are attributed to deep features. The ResNet uses a different localization method and much deeper features.

The regression encoder and classification encoder function independently. Hence there is a possibility of predicting an incorrect label for a bounding box. This problem can be overcome by attaching the regression encoder at different layers. This method could also be used for multiple objects hence solving the object detection problem. Given an image, find all instances in that. It's hard to treat detection as regression because the number of outputs are variable. One image may have two objects and another may have three or more. In the next section, we will see the algorithms dealing with detection problems more effectively.

Detecting objects

There are several variants of object detection algorithms. A few algorithms that come with the object detection API are discussed here.

Regions of the convolutional neural network (R-CNN)

The first work in this series was regions for CNNs proposed by Girshick et al.(`https://arxiv.org/pdf/1311.2524.pdf`) . It proposes a few boxes and checks whether any of the boxes correspond to the ground truth. **Selective search** was used for these region proposals. Selective search proposes the regions by grouping the color/texture of windows of various sizes. The selective search looks for blob-like structures. It starts with a pixel and produces a blob at a higher scale. It produces around 2,000 region proposals. This region proposal is less when compared to all the sliding windows possible.

The proposals are resized and passed through a standard CNN architecture such as Alexnet/VGG/Inception/ResNet. The last layer of the CNN is trained with an SVM identifying the object with a no-object class. The boxes are further improved by tightening the boxes around the images. A linear regression model to predict a closer bounding box is trained with object region proposals. The architecture of R-CNN is shown here:

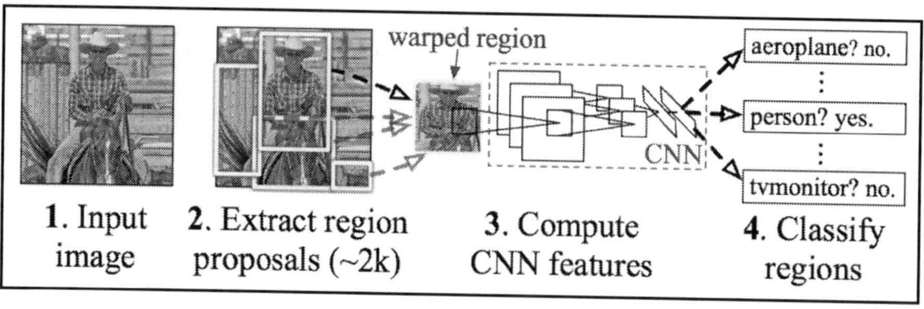

Reproduced with permission from Girshick et al.

The encoder can be a pre-trained model of a standard deep learning model. The features are computed for all the regions from the training data. The features are stored and then the SVM is trained. Next, the bounding boxes are trained with the normalized coordinates. There may be some proposals outside the image coordinates and hence it is normalized for training and inference.

The disadvantages of this method are:

- Several proposals are formed by selective search and hence many inferences have to be computed, usually around 2,000
- There are three classifiers that have to be trained, which increases the number of parameters
- There is no end-to-end training

Fast R-CNN

The Fast R-CNN proposed by Girshick et al. (`https://arxiv.org/pdf/1504.08083.pdf`)method runs CNN inference only once and hence reduces computations. The output of the CNN is used to propose the networks and select the bounding box. It introduced a technique called **Region of Interest pooling**. The Region of Interest pooling takes the CNN features and pools them together according to the regions. The features obtained after the inference using CNN is pooled and regions are selected, as shown in the following image:

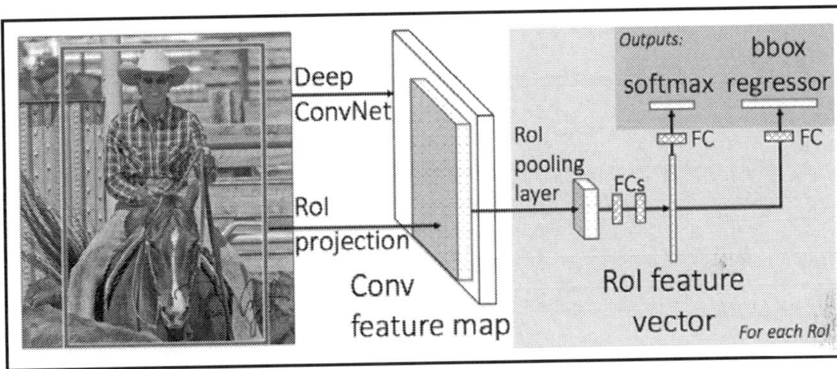

Reproduced with permission from Girshick et al.

This way, an end-to-end training is performed, avoiding multiple classifiers. Note that the SVM is replaced by the softmax layer and the box regressor is replaced by bounding box regressors. The disadvantage that still remains is the selective search, which takes some time.

Faster R-CNN

Faster R-CNN is proposed by Ren et al. (https://arxiv.org/pdf/1506.01497.pdf). The difference between Faster R-CNN and the Fast R-CNN method is that the Faster R-CNN uses CNN features of architecture such as VGG and Inception for proposals instead of selective search. The CNN features are further passed through the region proposal network. A sliding window is passed through features with potential bounding boxes and scores as the output, as well as a few aspect ratios that are intuitive, the model outputs bounding box and score:

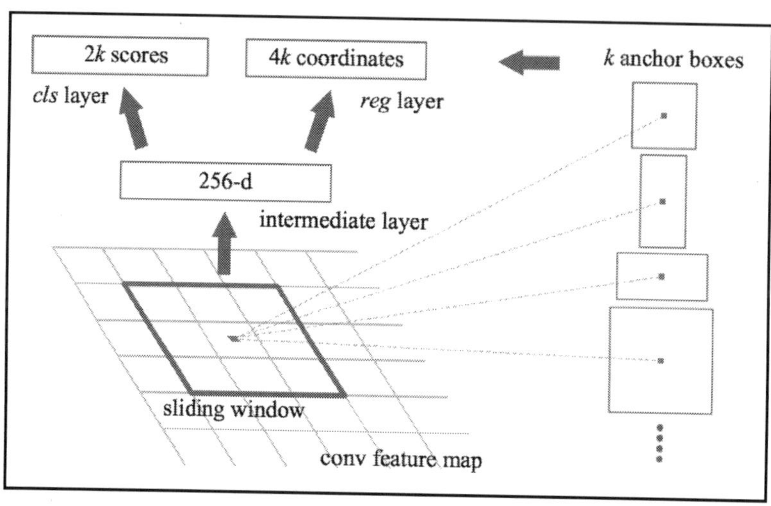

Reproduced with permission from Ren et al.

Faster R-CNN is faster than Fast R-CNN as it saves computation by computing the feature only once.

Single shot multi-box detector

SSD (Single shot multi-box) is proposed by is the fastest of all the methods. This method simultaneously predicts the object and finds the bounding box. During training, there might be a lot of negatives and hence hard-negative mining the class imbalance. The output from CNN has various sizes of features. These are passed to a 3x3 convolutional filter to predict bounding box.

This step predicts the object and bounding box:

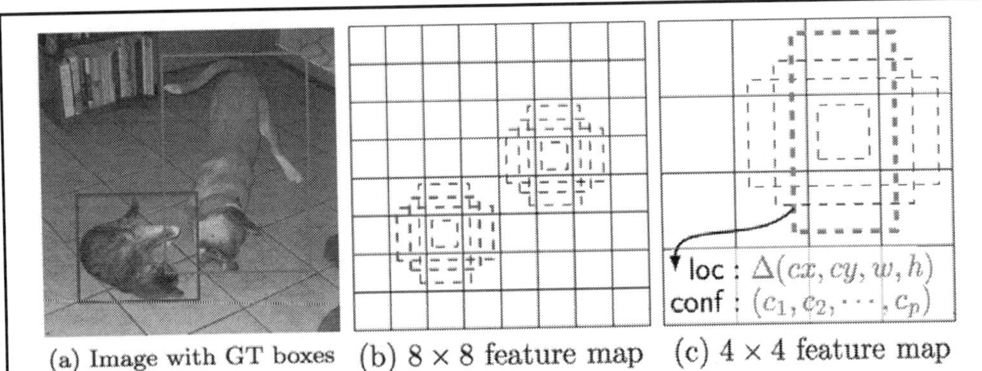

(a) Image with GT boxes (b) 8 × 8 feature map (c) 4 × 4 feature map

Reproduced with permission from Liu et al.

These are the algorithms available for object detection and we will learn how to implement them in the following section.

Object detection API

Google released pre-trained models with various algorithms trained on the `COCO` dataset for public use. The API is built on top of TensorFlow and intended for constructing, training, and deploying object detection models. The APIs support both object detection and localization tasks. The availability of pre-trained models enables the fine-tuning of new data and hence making the training faster. These different models have trade-offs between speed and accuracy.

Installation and setup

Install the Protocol Buffers **(protobuf)** compiler with the following commands. Create a directory for protobuf and download the library directly:

```
mkdir protoc_3.3
cd protoc_3.3
wget https://github.com/google/protobuf/releases/download/v3.3.0/
protoc-3.3.0-linux-x86_64.zip
```

Change the permission of the folder and extract the contents, as shown here:

```
chmod 775 protoc-3.3.0-linux-x86_64.zip
unzip protoc-3.3.0-linux-x86_64.zip
```

Protocol Buffers (protobuf) is Google's language-neutral, platform-neutral, extensible mechanism for serializing structured data. It serves the use of XML but is much simpler and faster. The models are usually exported to this format in TensorFlow. One can define the data structure once but can be read or written in a variety of languages. Then run the following command to compile the protobufs. Move back to the working folder and clone the repo from `https://github.com/tensorflow/models.git` and move them to the following folder:

```
git clone https://github.com/tensorflow/models.git
```

Now, move the model to the research folder, using the following code:

```
cd models/research/
~/protoc_3.3/bin/protoc object_detection/protos/*.proto --python_out=.
```

The TensorFlow object detection API uses protobufs for exporting model weights and the training parameters. The TensorFlow, models, research, and slim directories should be appended to `PYTHONPATH` by the following command:

```
export PYTHONPATH=.:./slim/
```

Adding to the python path with the preceding command works only one time. For the next, this command has to be run again. The installation can be tested by running the following code:

```
python object_detection/builders/model_builder_test.py
```

The output of this code is given here:

```
Ran 7 tests in 0.022s

OK
```

More information about the installation can be obtained from `https://github.com/tensorflow/models/blob/master/research/object_detection/g3doc/installation.md`. Now the installation is complete and tested.

Pre-trained models

There are several models that are pre-trained and made available. All these models are trained on the COCO dataset and can be used for detecting the objects that are available in the COCO dataset such as humans and cars. These models are also useful for transfer learning for a new task such as traffic sign detection. A table of pre-trained models is shown here with relative speed and mAP on the COCO dataset. Various algorithms are trained with different CNN and are depicted in the names:

Model name	Speed	COCO mAP
ssd_mobilenet_v1_coco	fast	21
ssd_inception_v2_coco	fast	24
rfcn_resnet101_coco	medium	30
faster_rcnn_resnet101_coco	medium	32
faster_rcnn_inception_resnet_v2_atrous_coco	slow	37

Based on the requirement, you can choose from the model. Download the SSD model trained on Mobilenet and extract it as shown here by going to the working directory:

```
mkdir Chapter04 && cd Chapter04
wget
http://download.tensorflow.org/models/object_detection/ssd_mobilenet_v
1_coco_11_06_2017.tar.gz
tar -xzvf ssd_mobilenet_v1_coco_11_06_2017.tar.gz
```

There will be various files in the Chapter04 folder, which are listed here:

- The is the proto-definition of the graph—graph.pbtxt
- The weights of the graph frozen and can be used for inference—frozen_inference_graph.pb
- Checkpoint files
    - model.ckpt.data-00000-of-00001
    - model.ckpt.meta
    - model.ckpt.index

This model will be used in the next section for detection tasks.

Re-training object detection models

The same API lets us retrain a model for our custom dataset. Training of custom data involves the preparation of a dataset, selecting the algorithm, and performing fine-tuning. The whole pipeline can be passed as a parameter to the training script. The training data has to be converted to TensorFlow records. TensorFlow records is a file format provided by Google to make the reading of data faster than regular files. Now, we will go through the steps of training.

Data preparation for the Pet dataset

The Oxford-IIIT `Pet` dataset is used for this example. Download the image and annotations with these commands from the `Chapter04` directory.

```
wget http://www.robots.ox.ac.uk/~vgg/data/pets/data/images.tar.gz
wget http://www.robots.ox.ac.uk/~vgg/data/pets/data/annotations.tar.gz
```

Extract the image and annotations as shown here:

```
tar -xvf images.tar.gz
tar -xvf annotations.tar.gz
```

Create the `pet_tf` record file to create the dataset in the `tf` records, as they are the required input for the object detection trainer. The `label_map` for the `Pet` dataset can be found at `object_detection/data/pet_label_map.pbtxt`. Move to the `research` folder and run the following command:

```
python object_detection/create_pet_tf_record.py \
    --label_map_path=object_detection/data/pet_label_map.pbtxt \
    --data_dir=~/chapter4/. \
    --output_dir=~/chapter4/.
```

You can see two `.record` files in the research directory named `pet_train.record` and `pet_val.record`.

Object detection training pipeline

The training protobuf has to be configured for training. The following five things are important in this process:

- The model configuration with the type of model
- The `train_config` for standard training parameters

- The `eval_config` for the metrics that have to be reported
- The `train_input_` config for the dataset
- The `eval_input_` config for the evaluation dataset

We will use the config file from `https://github.com/tensorflow/models/blob/master/research/object_detection/samples/configs/ssd_mobilenet_v1_pets.config`. Download it to the `Chapter04` folder by running the following command. Open the `config` file and edit the following lines:

```
fine_tune_checkpoint:
"~/Chapter04/ssd_mobilenet_v1_coco_11_06_2017/model.ckpt"

train_input_reader: {
  tf_record_input_reader {
    input_path: "~/Chapter04/pet_train.record"
  }
  label_map_path:
"~/model/research/object_detection/data/pet_label_map.pbtxt"
}

eval_input_reader: {
  tf_record_input_reader {
    input_path: "~/Chapter04/pet_val.record"
  }
  label_map_path:
"~/model/research/object_detection/data/pet_label_map.pbtxt"
}
```

Save the `config` file. There are various parameters in the file that affect the accuracy of the model.

Training the model

Now the API, data and config files are ready for re-training. The training can be triggered by the following command:

```
PYTHONPATH=.:./slim/. python object_detection/train.py \
    --logtostderr \
    --pipeline_config_path=~/chapter4/ssd_mobilenet_v1_pets.config \
    --train_dir=~/Chapter04
```

The training will start with a loss of around 140 and will keep decreasing. The training will run forever and has to be killed manually by using the *Ctrl* + *C* command. The checkpoints created during the training can be used for inference later.

Monitoring loss and accuracy using TensorBoard

The training loss and accuracy can be monitored using TensorBoard. Run the TensorBoard using the following command:

```
tensorboard --logdir=/home/ubuntu/Chapter04
```

Both training and evaluation can be visualized in the TensorBoard.

Training a pedestrian detection for a self-driving car

The dataset for training a pedestrian object detection can be found at `http://pascal.inrialpes.fr/data/human/`. The steps to detecting pedestrians can be found at `https://github.com/diegocavalca/machine-learning/blob/master/supervisioned/object.detection_tensorflow/simple.detection.ipynb`. The dataset for training a Sign Detector can be downloaded from `http://www.vision.ee.ethz.ch/~timofter/traffic_signs/` and `http://btsd.ethz.ch/shareddata/`. In the case of a self-driving car, there would be four classes in an image for labeling: pedestrian, car, motorcycle, and background. The background class has to be detected when none of the classes is present. An assumption in training a deep learning classification model is that at least one of the objects will be present in the image. By adding the `background` class, we are overcoming the problem. The neural network can also produce a bounding box of the object from the label.

The YOLO object detection algorithm

A recent algorithm for object detection is **You look only once** (**YOLO**). The image is divided into multiple grids. Each grid cell of the image runs the same algorithm. Let's start the implementation by defining layers with initializers:

```
def pooling_layer(input_layer, pool_size=[2, 2], strides=2,
padding='valid'):
    layer = tf.layers.max_pooling2d(
        inputs=input_layer,
        pool_size=pool_size,
        strides=strides,
        padding=padding
    )
    add_variable_summary(layer, 'pooling')
    return layer
```

```
def convolution_layer(input_layer, filters, kernel_size=[3, 3],
padding='valid',
                      activation=tf.nn.leaky_relu):
    layer = tf.layers.conv2d(
        inputs=input_layer,
        filters=filters,
        kernel_size=kernel_size,
        activation=activation,
        padding=padding,
        weights_initializer=tf.truncated_normal_initializer(0.0,
0.01),
        weights_regularizer=tf.l2_regularizer(0.0005)
    )
    add_variable_summary(layer, 'convolution')
    return layer

def dense_layer(input_layer, units, activation=tf.nn.leaky_relu):
    layer = tf.layers.dense(
        inputs=input_layer,
        units=units,
        activation=activation,
        weights_initializer=tf.truncated_normal_initializer(0.0,
0.01),
        weights_regularizer=tf.l2_regularizer(0.0005)
    )
    add_variable_summary(layer, 'dense')
    return layer
```

It can be noticed that the activation layer is `leaky_relu` and the weights are initialized with truncated normal distribution. These modified layers can be used for building the model. The model is created as follows:

```
yolo = tf.pad(images, np.array([[0, 0], [3, 3], [3, 3], [0, 0]]),
name='pad_1')
yolo = convolution_layer(yolo, 64, 7, 2)
yolo = pooling_layer(yolo, [2, 2], 2, 'same')
yolo = convolution_layer(yolo, 192, 3)
yolo = pooling_layer(yolo, 2, 'same')
yolo = convolution_layer(yolo, 128, 1)
yolo = convolution_layer(yolo, 256, 3)
yolo = convolution_layer(yolo, 256, 1)
yolo = convolution_layer(yolo, 512, 3)
yolo = pooling_layer(yolo, 2, 'same')
yolo = convolution_layer(yolo, 256, 1)
yolo = convolution_layer(yolo, 512, 3)
yolo = convolution_layer(yolo, 256, 1)
yolo = convolution_layer(yolo, 512, 3)
yolo = convolution_layer(yolo, 256, 1)
```

```
yolo = convolution_layer(yolo, 512, 3)
yolo = convolution_layer(yolo, 256, 1)
yolo = convolution_layer(yolo, 512, 3)
yolo = convolution_layer(yolo, 512, 1)
yolo = convolution_layer(yolo, 1024, 3)
yolo = pooling_layer(yolo, 2)
yolo = convolution_layer(yolo, 512, 1)
yolo = convolution_layer(yolo, 1024, 3)
yolo = convolution_layer(yolo, 512, 1)
yolo = convolution_layer(yolo, 1024, 3)
yolo = convolution_layer(yolo, 1024, 3)
yolo = tf.pad(yolo, np.array([[0, 0], [1, 1], [1, 1], [0, 0]]))
yolo = convolution_layer(yolo, 1024, 3, 2)
yolo = convolution_layer(yolo, 1024, 3)
yolo = convolution_layer(yolo, 1024, 3)
yolo = tf.transpose(yolo, [0, 3, 1, 2])
yolo = tf.layers.flatten(yolo)
yolo = dense_layer(yolo, 512)
yolo = dense_layer(yolo, 4096)

dropout_bool = tf.placeholder(tf.bool)
yolo = tf.layers.dropout(
        inputs=yolo,
        rate=0.4,
        training=dropout_bool
    )
yolo = dense_layer(yolo, output_size, None)
```

Several convolution layers are stacked, producing the YOLO network. This network is utilized for creating the object detection algorithm for real-time detection.

Summary

In this chapter, we have learned the difference between object localization and detection tasks. Several datasets and evaluation criteria were discussed. Various approaches to localization problems and algorithms, such as variants of R-CNN and SSD models for detection, were discussed. The implementation of detection in open-source repositories was covered. We trained a model for pedestrian detection using the techniques. We also learned about various trade-offs in training such models.

In the next chapter, we will learn about semantic segmentation algorithms. We will use the knowledge to implement the segmentation algorithms for medical imaging and satellite imagery problems.

24
Semantic Segmentation

In this chapter, we will learn about various semantic segmentation techniques and train models for the same. Segmentation is a pixel-wise classification task. The ideas to solve segmentation problem is an extension to object detection problems. Segmentation is highly useful in applications such medical and satellite image understanding.

The following topics will be covered in the chapter:

- Learning the difference between semantic segmentation and instance segmentation
- Segmentation datasets and metrics
- Algorithms for semantic segmentation
- Application of segmentation to medical and satellite images
- Algorithms for instance segmentation

Predicting pixels

Image classification is the task of predicting labels or categories. Object detection is the task of predicting a list of several deep learning-based algorithms with its corresponding bounding box. The bounding box may have objects other than the detected object inside it. In some applications, labeling every pixel to a label is important rather than bounding box which may have multiple objects. **Semantic segmentation** is the task of predicting pixel-wise labels.

Here is an example of an image and its corresponding semantic segmentation:

As shown in the image, an input image is predicted with labels for every pixel. The labels could be the sky, tree, person, mountain, and bridge. Rather than assigning a label to the whole image, labels are assigned to each pixel. Semantic segmentation labels pixels independently. You will notice that every people is not distinguished. All the persons in the image are labeled in the same way.

Here is an example where every instance of the same label is distinguished:

This task of segmenting every instance with a pixel-wise label is called **instance segmentation**. Instance segmentation can be thought of as an extension of object detection with pixel-level labels. The applications of semantic segmentation and instance segmentation are enormous, and a few of the applications are provided in the next sections.

Diagnosing medical images

A medical image can be diagnosed with segmentation techniques. Modern medical imaging techniques such as **Magnetic Resonance Imaging** (**MRI**), **Computed Tomography** (**CT**), and **Retinopathy** create high-quality images. The images generated by such techniques can be segmented into various regions to detect tumours from brain scans or spots from retina scans. Some devices provide volumetric images which can also be analyzed by segmentation. Segmenting the video for robot surgery enables the doctors to see the regions carefully in robot-assisted surgeries. We will see how to segment medical images later in the chapter.

Understanding the earth from satellite imagery

Satellite images have become abundant recently. The images captured by satellite provide a high-resolution view of the total surface of the earth. By analyzing the satellite imagery, we can understand several things about earth such as:

- Measuring the rate of construction in a country related to economic growth
- Measuring the oil tanks
- Planning and organizing the traffic
- Calculating the deforestation and its effects
- Helping wildlife preservation by counting animals and tracking their movements
- Discovering archaeological sites
- Mapping the damaged regions due to a natural disaster

There are more applications possible with satellite imagery. For most of these problems mentioned, the solution starts with the segmentation of satellite images. We will see how to segment satellite images later in the chapter.

Enabling robots to see

Segmenting the scenes is crucial for robots to see and interact with the world around. Industrial and home robots have to handle the objects. The handling becomes possible once the vision to the robots is stridden according to the objects. There are a few more applications worth mentioning:

- Industrial inspection of tools for segmenting the defects
- Color diagnostics of the fashion industry; an image can be segmented with various fashion objects and use them for color parsing
- Distinguish foreground from background to apply portrait effects

In the next section, we will learn a few public datasets for evaluating segmentation algorithms.

Datasets

The `PASCAL` and `COCO` datasets that were mentioned in `Chapter 23`, *Object Detection*, can be used for the segmentation task as well. The annotations are different as they are labelled pixel-wise. New algorithms are usually benchmarked against the `COCO` dataset. `COCO` also has stuff datasets such as grass, wall, and sky. The pixel accuracy property can be used as a metric for evaluating algorithms.

Apart from those mentioned, there are several other datasets in the areas of medical imaging and satellite imagery. The links to a few of them are provided here for your reference:

- `http://www.cs.bu.edu/~betke/BiomedicalImageSegmentation`
- `https://www.kaggle.com/c/intel-mobileodt-cervical-cancer-screening/data`
- `https://www.kaggle.com/c/diabetic-retinopathy-detection`
- `https://grand-challenge.org/all_challenges`
- `http://www.via.cornell.edu/databases`
- `https://www.kaggle.com/c/dstl-satellite-imagery-feature-detection`
- `https://aws.amazon.com/public-datasets/spacenet`
- `https://www.iarpa.gov/challenges/fmow.html`
- `https://www.kaggle.com/c/planet-understanding-the-amazon-from-space`

Creating training data for segmentation tasks is expensive. There are online tools available for annotating your dataset. The **LabelMe** mobile application provided by **MIT University** is good for annotating and can be downloaded from `http://labelme.csail.mit.edu/Release3.0`.

Algorithms for semantic segmentation

There are several deep learning-based algorithms that were proposed to solve image segmentation tasks. A sliding window approach can be applied at a pixel level for segmentation. A sliding window approach takes an image and breaks the image into smaller crops. Every crop of the image is classified for a label. This approach is expensive and inefficient because it doesn't reuse the shared features between the overlapping patches. In the following sections, we will discuss a few algorithms that can overcome this problem.

The Fully Convolutional Network

The **Fully Convolutional Network** (**FCN**) introduced the idea of an end-to-end convolutional network. Any standard CNN architecture can be used for FCN by removing the fully connected layers, and the implementation of the same was shown in `Chapter 23`, *Object Detection*. The fully connected layers are replaced by a convolution layer. The depth is higher in the final layers and the size is smaller. Hence, 1D convolution can be performed to reach the desired number of labels. But for segmentation, the spatial dimension has to be preserved. Hence, the full convolution network is constructed without a max pooling, as shown here:

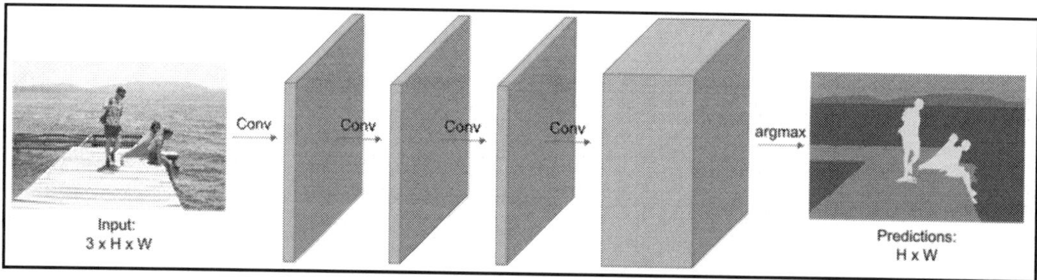

The loss for this network is computed by averaging the cross-entropy loss of every pixel and mini-batch. The final layer has a depth equal to the number of classes. FCN is similar to object detection except that the spatial dimension is preserved. The output produced by the architecture will be coarse as some pixels may be mispredicted. The computation is high and in the next section, we will see how to address this issue.

The SegNet architecture

The **SegNet** has an encoder and decoder approach. The encode has various convolution layers and decoder has various deconvolution layers. SegNet improved the coarse outputs produced by FCN. Because of this, it is less intensive on memory. When the features are reduced in dimensions, it is upsampled again to the image size by deconvolution, reversing the convolution effects. Deconvolution learns the parameters for upsampling. The output of such architecture will be coarse due to the loss of information in pooling layers.

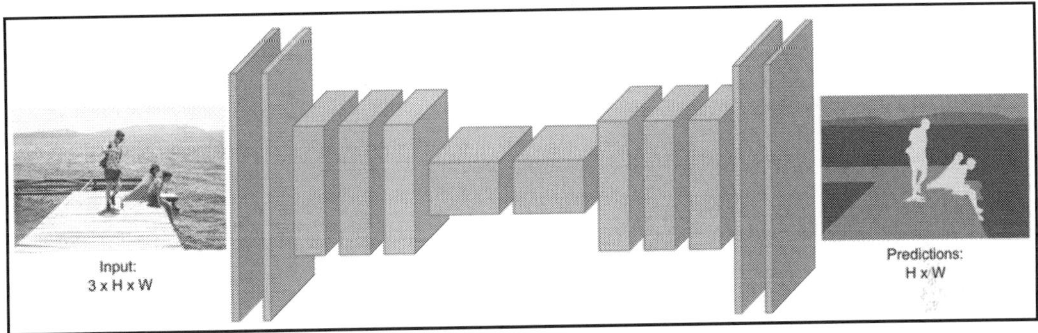

Now, let's learn the few new concepts called upsampling, atrous convolution, and transpose convolution that will help us in understanding this network better.

Upsampling the layers by pooling

In `Chapter 20`, *Getting Started*, we discussed max pooling. Max pooling is a sampling strategy that picks the maximum value from a window. This could be reversed for upsampling. Each value can be surrounded with zeros to upsample the layer, as shown here:

1	2
3	4

→

1	0	2	0
0	0	0	0
3	0	4	0
0	0	0	0

The zeros are added at the same locations which are the numbers that are upsampled. Un-pooling can be improved by remembering the locations of downsampling and using it for upsampling, as shown here:

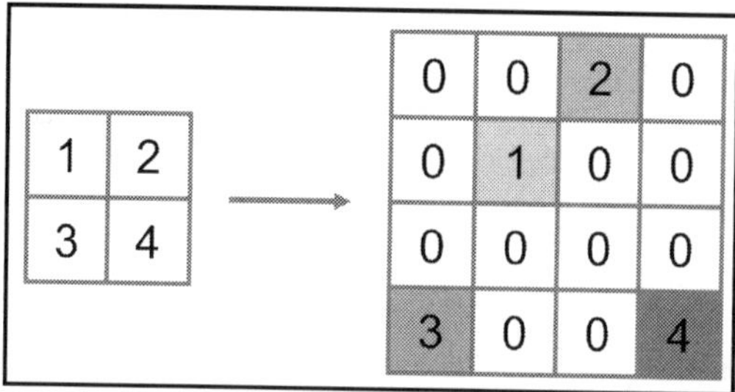

Index-wise, upsampling yields better results than appending zeros. This upsampling the layers by pooling is not learned and works as it is. Next, we will see how we can upsample and downsample with learnable parameters.

Sampling the layers by convolution

The layers can be upsampled or downsampled directly using convolution. The stride used for convolution can be increased to cause downsampling as shown here:

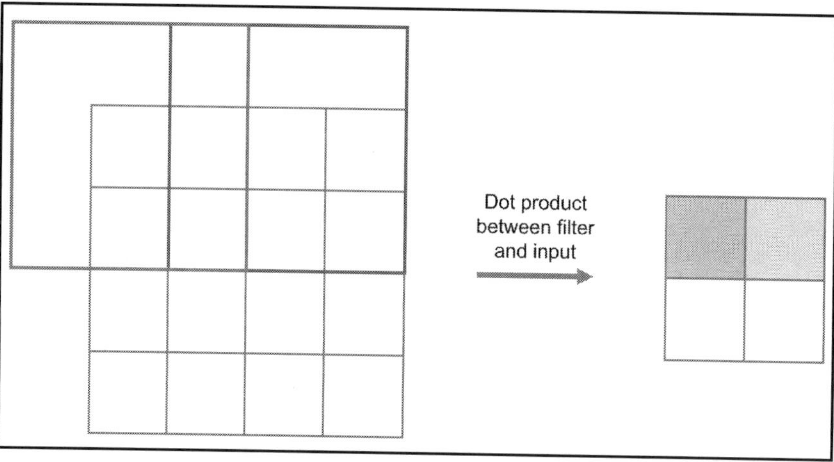

Downsampling by convolution is called **atrous convolution** or **dilated convolution** or **strided convolution**. Similarly, it can be reversed to upsample by learning a kernel as shown here:

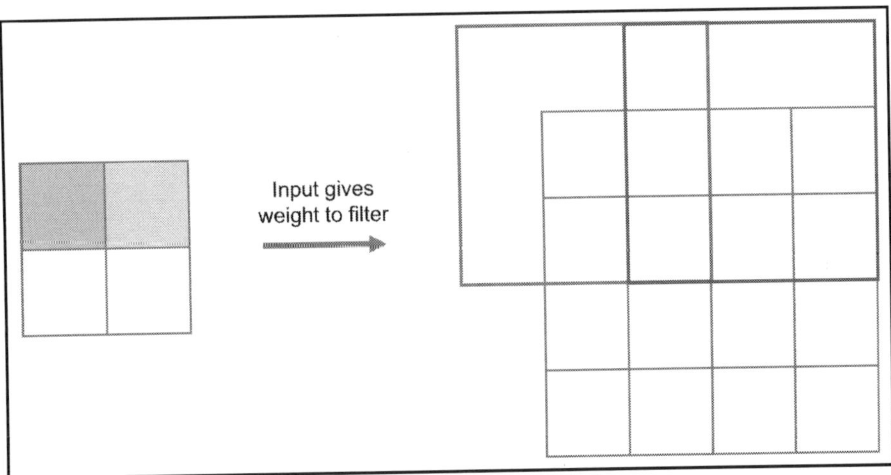

Upsampling directly using a convolution can be termed as **transposed convolution**. Some other synonyms are **deconvolution** or **fractionally strided convolution** or **up-convolution**. Now the process of upsampling is understood. Here is a code snippet that describes the previous algorithm:

```
input_height = 360
input_width = 480
kernel = 3
filter_size = 64
pad = 1
pool_size = 2
```

After the input is taken, it follows the usual convolutional neural net with decreasing size, which can be termed as an encoder. The following code can be used for defining the encoder:

```
model = tf.keras.models.Sequential()
model.add(tf.keras.layers.Layer(input_shape=(3, input_height,
input_width)))

# encoder
model.add(tf.keras.layers.ZeroPadding2D(padding=(pad, pad)))
model.add(tf.keras.layers.Conv2D(filter_size, kernel, kernel,
                                 border_mode='valid'))
model.add(tf.keras.layers.BatchNormalization())
model.add(tf.keras.layers.Activation('relu'))
model.add(tf.keras.layers.MaxPooling2D(pool_size=(pool_size,
pool_size)))

model.add(tf.keras.layers.ZeroPadding2D(padding=(pad, pad)))
model.add(tf.keras.layers.Conv2D(128, kernel, kernel,
border_mode='valid'))
model.add(tf.keras.layers.BatchNormalization())
model.add(tf.keras.layers.Activation('relu'))
model.add(tf.keras.layers.MaxPooling2D(pool_size=(pool_size,
pool_size)))

model.add(tf.keras.layers.ZeroPadding2D(padding=(pad, pad)))
model.add(tf.keras.layers.Conv2D(256, kernel, kernel,
border_mode='valid'))
model.add(tf.keras.layers.BatchNormalization())
model.add(tf.keras.layers.Activation('relu'))
model.add(tf.keras.layers.MaxPooling2D(pool_size=(pool_size,
pool_size)))

model.add(tf.keras.layers.ZeroPadding2D(padding=(pad, pad)))
model.add(tf.keras.layers.Conv2D(512, kernel, kernel,
border_mode='valid'))
model.add(tf.keras.layers.BatchNormalization())
model.add(tf.keras.layers.Activation('relu'))
```

The output of the encoder can be fed to the decoder with increasing size, using the following code:

```
# decoder
model.add(tf.keras.layers.ZeroPadding2D(padding=(pad, pad)))
model.add(tf.keras.layers.Conv2D(512, kernel, kernel,
border_mode='valid'))
model.add(tf.keras.layers.BatchNormalization())
```

```
model.add(tf.keras.layers.UpSampling2D(size=(pool_size, pool_size)))
model.add(tf.keras.layers.ZeroPadding2D(padding=(pad, pad)))
model.add(tf.keras.layers.Conv2D(256, kernel, kernel,
border_mode='valid'))
model.add(tf.keras.layers.BatchNormalization())

model.add(tf.keras.layers.UpSampling2D(size=(pool_size, pool_size)))
model.add(tf.keras.layers.ZeroPadding2D(padding=(pad, pad)))
model.add(tf.keras.layers.Conv2D(128, kernel, kernel,
border_mode='valid'))
model.add(tf.keras.layers.BatchNormalization())

model.add(tf.keras.layers.UpSampling2D(size=(pool_size, pool_size)))
model.add(tf.keras.layers.ZeroPadding2D(padding=(pad, pad)))
model.add(tf.keras.layers.Conv2D(filter_size, kernel, kernel,
border_mode='valid'))
model.add(tf.keras.layers.BatchNormalization())

model.add(tf.keras.layers.Conv2D(nClasses, 1, 1, border_mode='valid',
))
```

The decoded image is of the same size as the input, and the whole model can be trained, using the following code:

```
model.outputHeight = model.output_shape[-2]
model.outputWidth = model.output_shape[-1]

model.add(tf.keras.layers.Reshape((nClasses, model.output_shape[-2] *
model.output_shape[-1]),
                   input_shape=(nClasses, model.output_shape[-2],
model.output_shape[-1])))

model.add(tf.keras.layers.Permute((2, 1)))
model.add(tf.keras.layers.Activation('softmax'))

model.compile(loss="categorical_crossentropy",
optimizer=tf.keras.optimizers.Adam, metrics=['accuracy'])
```

This way of encoding and decoding an image overcomes the shortcomings of FCN-based models. Next, we will see a different concept with dilated convolutions.

Skipping connections for better training

The coarseness of segmentation output can be limited by skip architecture, and higher resolutions can be obtained. Another alternative way is to scale up the last three layers and average them as shown here:

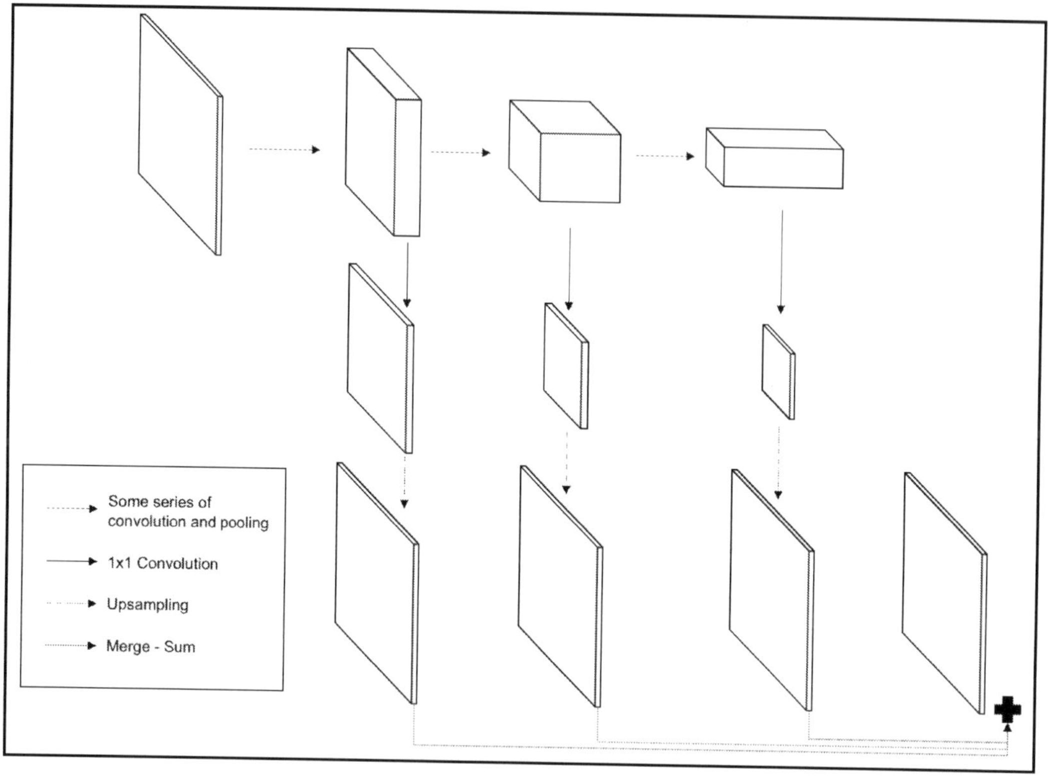

This algorithm is utilized for an example of satellite imagery in a later section.

Dilated convolutions

The pixel-wise classification and image classification are structurally different. Hence, pooling layers that decrease information will produce coarse segmentation. But remember, pooling is essential for having a wider view and allows sampling. A new idea called **dilated convolution** was introduced to solve this problem for less-lossy sampling while having a wider view. The dilated convolution is essentially convolution by skipping every pixel in the window as shown here:

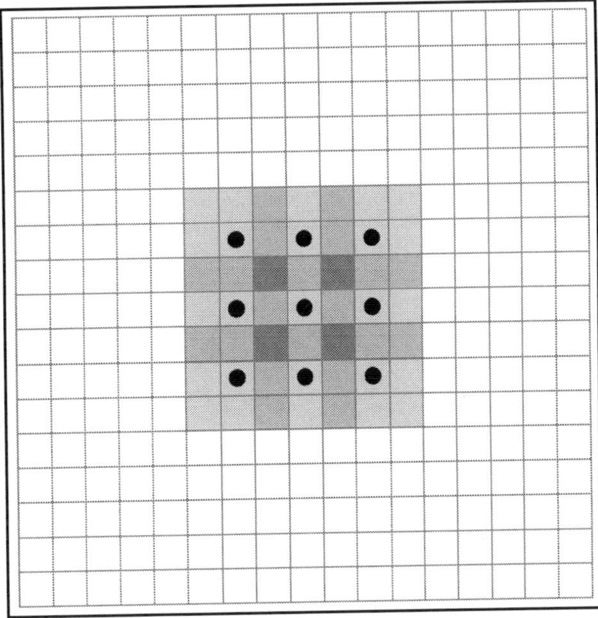

The dilation distance varies from layer to layer. The output of such a segmentation result is upscaled for a finer resolution. A separate network is trained for multi-scale aggregation.

DeepLab

DeepLab proposed by Chen et al. (`https://arxiv.org/pdf/1606.00915.pdf`) performs convolutions on multiple scales and uses the features from various scales to obtain a score map. The score map is then interpolated and passed through a **conditional random field** (**CRF**) for final segmentation. This scale processing of images can be either performed by processing images of various sizes with its own CNN or parallel convolutions with varying level of dilated convolutions.

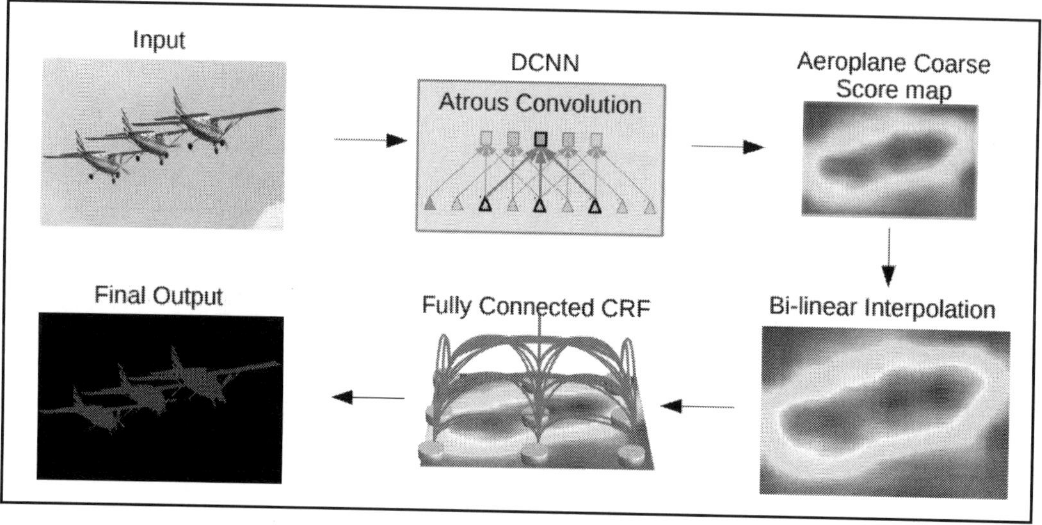

Reproduced with permission from Chen et al.

RefiNet

Dilated convolutions need bigger input and hence, are memory intensive. This presents computational problems when using high-resolution pictures. Reid et al. (`https://arxiv.org/pdf/1611.06612.pdf`) prosed a method called RefiNet to overcome this problem which is shown below:

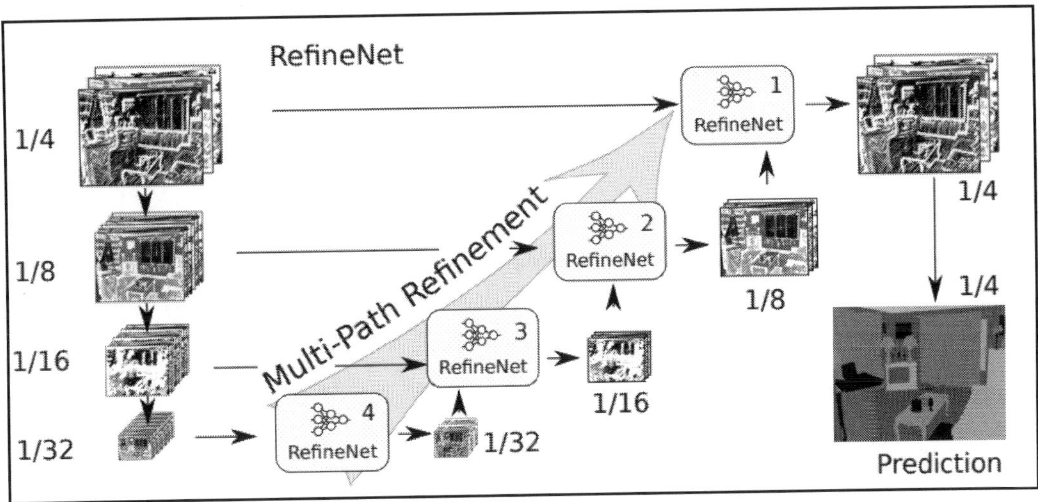

Reproduced with permission from Reid et al.

RefiNet uses an encoder followed by a decoder. Encoder outputs of CNN. The decoder concatenates the features of various sizes:

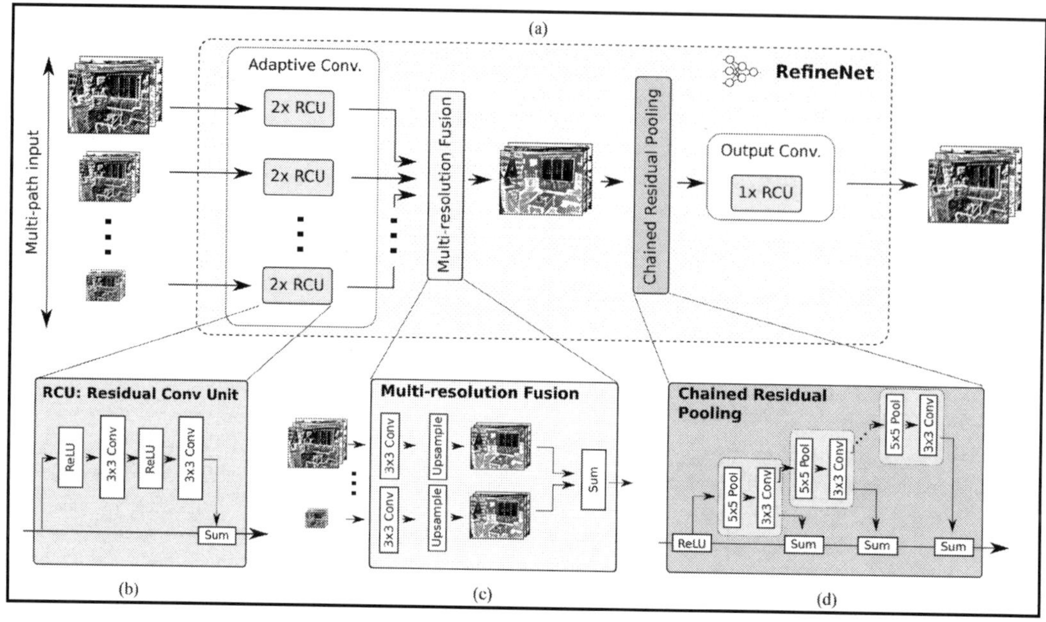

Reproduced with permission from Reid et al.

The concatenation is done upscaling the low dimensional feature.

PSPnet

Global content is utilized in PSPnet introduced by Zhoa et al. (https://arxiv.org/pdf/1612.01105.pdf) by increasing the kernel size of pooling layers. The pooling is carried in a pyramid fashion. The pyramid covers various portions and sizes of the images simultaneously. There is a loss in-between the architecture which enables moderate supervision.

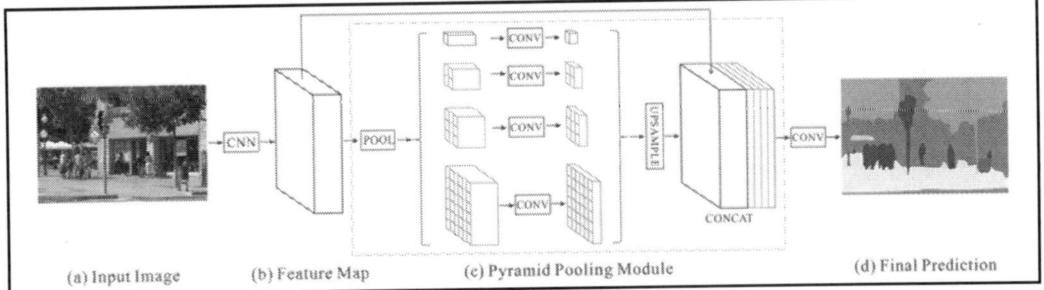

Reproduced with permission from Zhao et al.

Large kernel matters

Peng et al. (`https://arxiv.org/pdf/1703.02719.pdf`) showcased the importance of large kernels. Large kernels have bigger receptive fields than small kernels. The computational complexity of these large kernels can be used to overcome with an approximate smaller kernel. There is a boundary refinement network at the end.

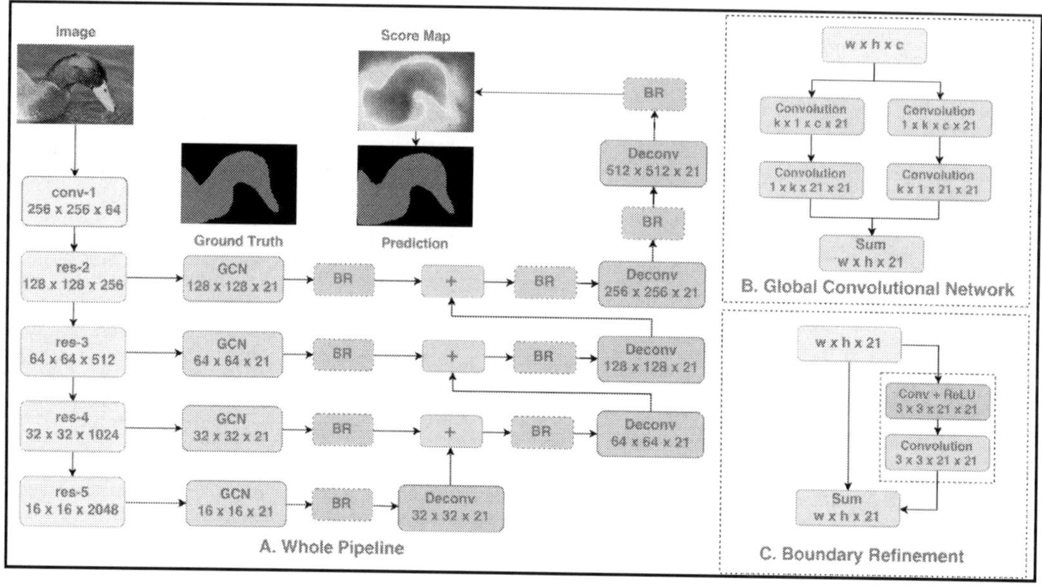

Reproduced with permission from Peng et al.

DeepLab v3

Batch normalization is used in the paper proposed by Chen et al. (`https://arxiv.org/pdf/1706.05587.pdf`) to improve the performance. The multi-scale of the feature is encoded in a cascaded fashion to improve the performance:

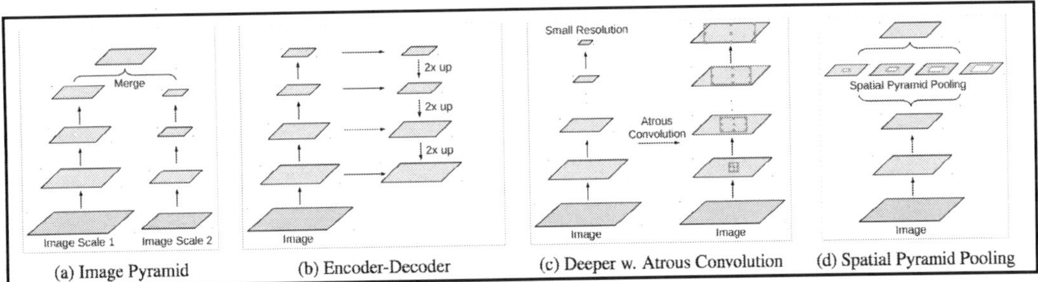

Reproduced with permission from Chen et al.

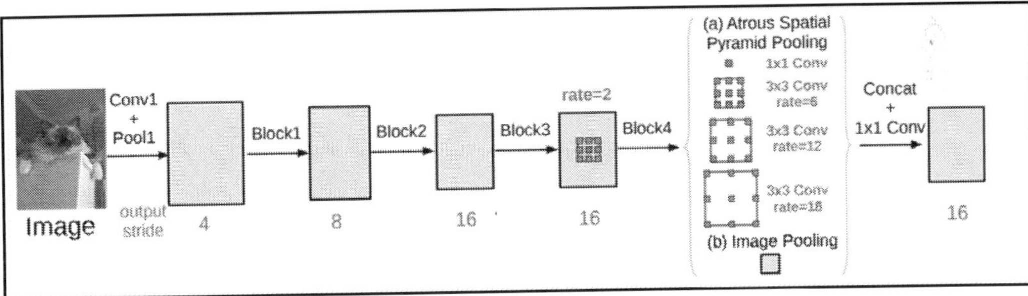

Reproduced with permission from Chen et al.

We have seen several architectures improve the accuracy of image segmentation using deep learning. Next, we will see an application in medical imaging.

Ultra-nerve segmentation

The Kaggler is an organization that conducts competitions on predictive modelling and analytics. The Kagglers were once challenged to segment nerve structures from ultrasound images of the neck. The data regarding the same can be downloaded from `https://www.kaggle.com/c/ultrasound-nerve-segmentation`. The UNET model proposed by Ronneberger et al. (`https://arxiv.org/pdf/1505.04597.pdf`) resembles an autoencoder but with convolutions instead of a fully connected layer. There is an encoding part with the convolution of decreasing dimensions and a decoder part with increasing dimensions as shown here:

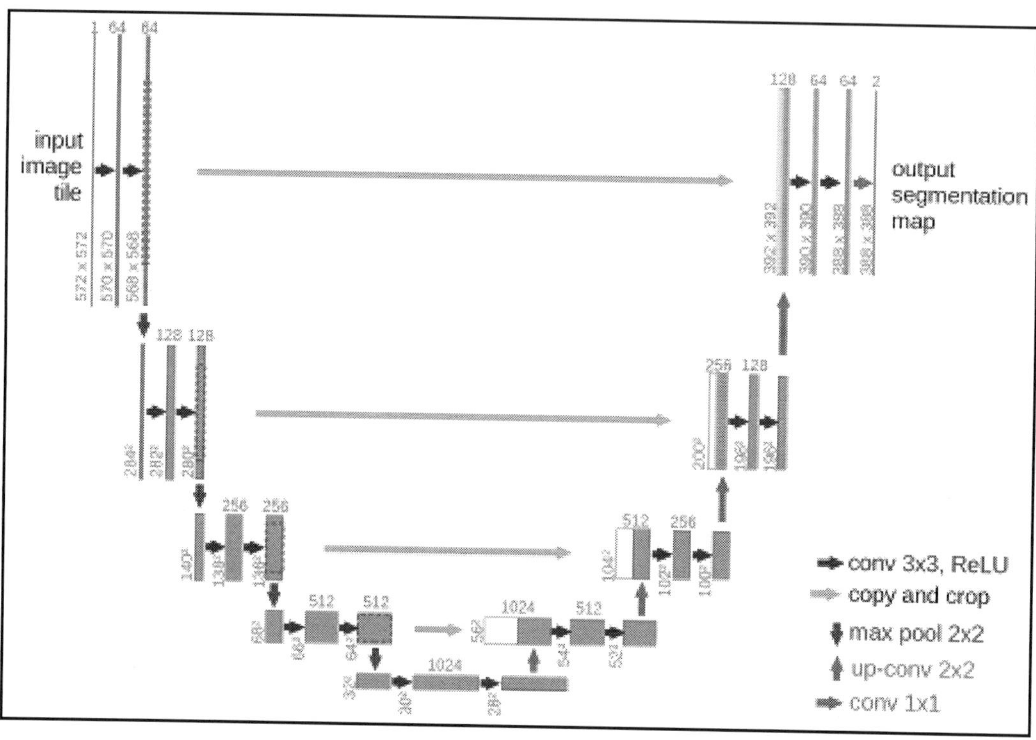

Figure illustrating the architecture of the UNET model [Reproduced with permission from Ronneberger et al.]

The convolutions of the similar sized encoder and decoder part are learning by skip connections. The output of the model is a mask that ranges between 0 and 1. Let's start by importing the functions, with the help of the following code:

```
import os
from skimage.transform import resize
from skimage.io import imsave
import numpy as np
from data import load_train_data, load_test_data
```

After all the imports, we will now define the sizes, using the following code:

```
image_height, image_width = 96, 96
smoothness = 1.0
work_dir = ''
```

Now we will define the `dice_coefficient` and its loss function. The `dice_coefficient` is also the metric in this case:

```
def dice_coefficient(y1, y2):
    y1 = tf.flatten(y1)
    y2 = tf.flatten(y2)
    return (2. * tf.sum(y1 * y2) + smoothness) / (tf.sum(y1) +
tf.sum(y2) + smoothness)


def dice_coefficient_loss(y1, y2):
    return -dice_coefficient(y1, y2)
```

The UNET model can be defined as follows:

```
def preprocess(imgs):
    imgs_p = np.ndarray((imgs.shape[0], image_height, image_width),
dtype=np.uint8)
    for i in range(imgs.shape[0]):
        imgs_p[i] = resize(imgs[i], (image_width, image_height),
preserve_range=True)
    imgs_p = imgs_p[..., np.newaxis]
    return imgs_p


def covolution_layer(filters, kernel=(3,3), activation='relu',
input_shape=None):
    if input_shape is None:
        return tf.keras.layers.Conv2D(
            filters=filters,
            kernel=kernel,
            activation=activation)
```

```
        else:
            return tf.keras.layers.Conv2D(
                filters=filters,
                kernel=kernel,
                activation=activation,
                input_shape=input_shape)


def concatenated_de_convolution_layer(filters):
    return tf.keras.layers.concatenate([
        tf.keras.layers.Conv2DTranspose(
            filters=filters,
            kernel=(2, 2),
            strides=(2, 2),
            padding='same'
        )],
        axis=3
    )
```

All the layers are concatenated and used, as shown in the following code:

```
unet = tf.keras.models.Sequential()
inputs = tf.keras.layers.Input((image_height, image_width, 1))
input_shape = (image_height, image_width, 1)
unet.add(covolution_layer(32, input_shape=input_shape))
unet.add(covolution_layer(32))
unet.add(pooling_layer())

unet.add(covolution_layer(64))
unet.add(covolution_layer(64))
unet.add(pooling_layer())

unet.add(covolution_layer(128))
unet.add(covolution_layer(128))
unet.add(pooling_layer())

unet.add(covolution_layer(256))
unet.add(covolution_layer(256))
unet.add(pooling_layer())

unet.add(covolution_layer(512))
unet.add(covolution_layer(512))
```

The layers are concatenated, and deconvolution layers are used:

```
unet.add(concatenated_de_convolution_layer(256))
unet.add(covolution_layer(256))
unet.add(covolution_layer(256))

unet.add(concatenated_de_convolution_layer(128))
unet.add(covolution_layer(128))
unet.add(covolution_layer(128))

unet.add(concatenated_de_convolution_layer(64))
unet.add(covolution_layer(64))
unet.add(covolution_layer(64))

unet.add(concatenated_de_convolution_layer(32))
unet.add(covolution_layer(32))
unet.add(covolution_layer(32))

unet.add(covolution_layer(1, kernel=(1, 1), activation='sigmoid'))

unet.compile(optimizer=tf.keras.optimizers.Adam(lr=1e-5),
             loss=dice_coefficient_loss,
             metrics=[dice_coefficient])
```

Next, the model can be trained with images, by making use of the following code:

```
x_train, y_train_mask = load_train_data()

x_train = preprocess(x_train)
y_train_mask = preprocess(y_train_mask)

x_train = x_train.astype('float32')
mean = np.mean(x_train)
std = np.std(x_train)

x_train -= mean
x_train /= std

y_train_mask = y_train_mask.astype('float32')
y_train_mask /= 255.

unet.fit(x_train, y_train_mask, batch_size=32, epochs=20, verbose=1,
shuffle=True,
          validation_split=0.2)

x_test, y_test_mask = load_test_data()
x_test = preprocess(x_test)
```

```
x_test = x_test.astype('float32')
x_test -= mean
x_test /= std

y_test_pred = unet.predict(x_test, verbose=1)

for image, image_id in zip(y_test_pred, y_test_mask):
    image = (image[:, :, 0] * 255.).astype(np.uint8)
    imsave(os.path.join(work_dir, str(image_id) + '.png'), image)
```

The image can be pre-processed and used. Now the training and testing of the images can happen. When the model is trained, the segmentation produces good results, as shown here:

We have trained a model that can segment medical images. This algorithm can be used in several use cases. In the next section, we will see how to segment satellite images.

Segmenting satellite images

In this section, we will use a dataset provided by the **International Society for Photogrammetry and Remote Sensing** (**ISPRS**). The dataset contains satellite images of Potsdam, Germany with 5 cm resolution. These images come with an additional data of infrared and height contours of the images. There are six labels associated with the images, which are:

- Building
- Vegetation
- Trees
- Cabs
- Clutter
- Impervious

A total of 38 images are provided with 6,000 x 6,000 patches. Please go to the page, `http://www2.isprs.org/commissions/comm3/wg4/data-request-form2.html` and fill in the form. After that, select the following options on the form:

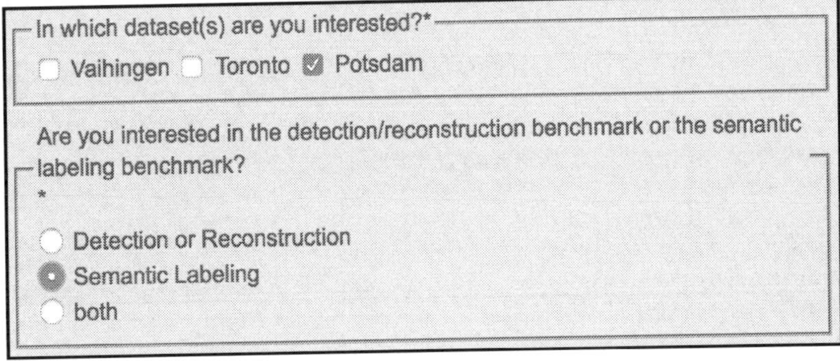

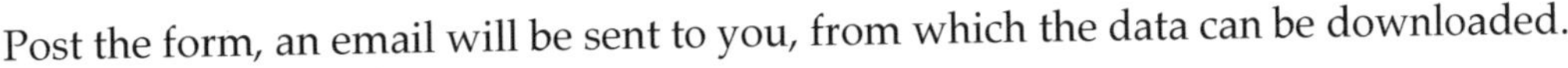
Post the form, an email will be sent to you, from which the data can be downloaded.

Modeling FCN for segmentation

Import the libraries and get the shape of the input. The number of labels is defined as 6:

```
from .resnet50 import ResNet50
nb_labels = 6

img_height, img_width, _ = input_shape
input_tensor = tf.keras.layers.Input(shape=input_shape)
weights = 'imagenet'
```

A `ResNet` model pre-trained on ImageNet will be used as the base model. The following code can be used to define the base model using `ResNet`:

```
resnet50_model = ResNet50(
    include_top=False, weights='imagenet', input_tensor=input_tensor)
```

Now we will use the following code to take the final three layers from the `ResNet`:

```
final_32 = resnet50_model.get_layer('final_32').output
final_16 = resnet50_model.get_layer('final_16').output
final_x8 = resnet50_model.get_layer('final_x8').output
```

Each skip connection has to be compressed to match the channel that is equal to the number of labels:

```
c32 = tf.keras.layers.Conv2D(nb_labels, (1, 1))(final_32)
c16 = tf.keras.layers.Conv2D(nb_labels, (1, 1))(final_16)
c8 = tf.keras.layers.Conv2D(nb_labels, (1, 1))(final_x8)
```

The output of the compressed skip connection can be resized using bilinear interpolation. The interpolation can be implemented by using a `Lambda` layer that can compute TensorFlow operation. The following code snippet can be used for interpolation using the lambda layer:

```
def resize_bilinear(images):
    return tf.image.resize_bilinear(images, [img_height, img_width])


r32 = tf.keras.layers.Lambda(resize_bilinear)(c32)
r16 = tf.keras.layers.Lambda(resize_bilinear)(c16)
r8 = tf.keras.layers.Lambda(resize_bilinear)(c8)
```

The three layers we have defined can be merged by adding the three values, using the following code:

```
m = tf.keras.layers.Add()([r32, r16, r8])
```

The probabilities of the model can be applied using softmax activation. The model is resized before and after applying softmax:

```
x = tf.keras.ayers.Reshape((img_height * img_width, nb_labels))(m)
x = tf.keras.layers.Activation('img_height')(x)
x = tf.keras.layers.Reshape((img_height, img_width, nb_labels))(x)

fcn_model = tf.keras.models.Model(input=input_tensor, output=x)
```

A simple FCN layer has been defined and when trained, it gives the following result:

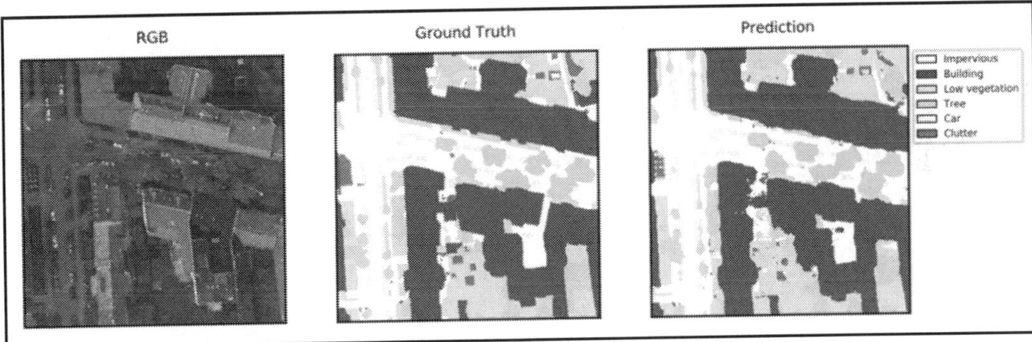

You can see that the prediction of the six labels is reasonable. Next, we will learn about segmenting instances.

Segmenting instances

While analyzing an image, our interest will only be drawn to certain instances in the image. So, it was compelled to segment these instances from the remainder of the image. This process of separating the required information from the rest is widely known as **segmenting instances**. During this process, the input image is first taken, then the bounding box will be localized with the objects and at last, a pixel-wise mask will be predicted for each of the class. For each of the objects, pixel-level accuracy is calculated. There are several algorithms for segmenting instances. One of the recent algorithms is the **Mask RCNN** algorithm proposed by He at al. (`https://arxiv.org/pdf/1703.06870.pdf`). The following figure portrays the architecture of Mask R-CNN:

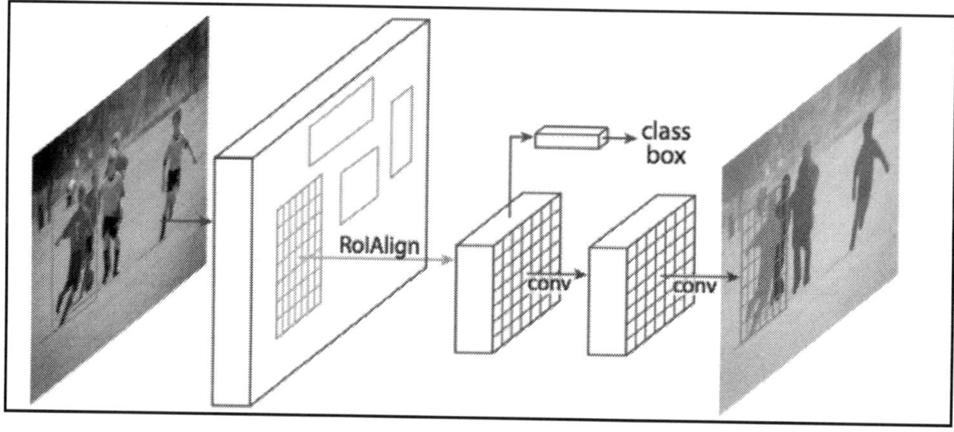

Reproduced with permission from He et al.

The architecture looks similar to the R-CNN with an addition of segmentation. It is a multi-stage network with end-to-end training. The region proposals are learned. The network is split into two, one for detection and the other for a classification score. The results are excellent, as shown here:

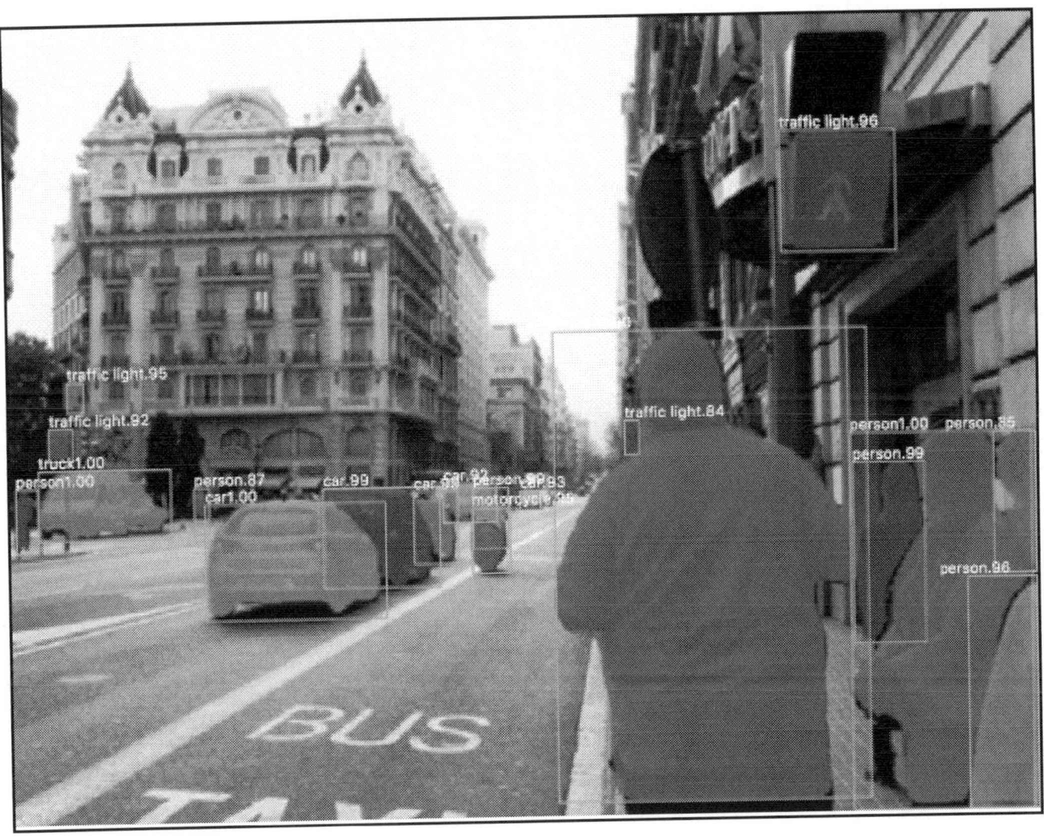

Figure illustrating the segmenting instances process. Note that the objects are detected accurately and are segmented accordingly Reproduced with permission from He et al.

The same network can also predict the poses of people. The two tasks of segmentation and detection are processed in parallel.

Summary

In this chapter, we have learned about the various segmentation algorithms. We also saw the datasets and metrics that are used for benchmarking. We applied the techniques learned to segment satellite and medical images. In the end, we touched upon the Mask R-CNN algorithm for instance segmentation.

In the next chapter, we will learn about similarity learning. Similarity learning models learn a comparison mechanism between two images. It is useful for several applications such as face recognition. We will learn several model architectures that can be used for similarity learning.

25
Similarity Learning

In this chapter, we will learn about similarity learning and learn various loss functions used in similarity learning. Similarity learning us useful when the dataset is small per class. We will understand different datasets available for face analysis and build a model for face recognition, landmark detection. We will cover the following topics in this chapter:

- Different algorithms for similarity learning
- Various loss functions used for similarity learning
- A variety of scenarios in which such models can be used
- The complete process of face recognition

Algorithms for similarity learning

Similarity learning is the process of training a metric to compute the similarity between two entities. This could also be termed as metric learning, as the similarity is learned. A metric could be Euclidean or or some other custom distance function. Entities could be any data such as an image, video, text or tables. To compute a metric, a vector representation of the image is required. This representation can be the features computed by a CNN as described in `Chapter 22`, *Image Retrieval*. The CNN that was learned for object classification can be used as the vector to compute the metric. The feature vector obtained for image classification would not be the best representation of the task at hand. In similarity learning, we find out about CNNs that generate features trained for a similarity learning task. Some applications of similarity learning are given here:

- Face verification for biometrics to compare two faces
- Visual search of real-world objects to find similar products online
- Visual recommendation of products that are similar in some attributes

In this chapter, we will learn about face verification in detail. So let's start with the algorithms that are available for similarity learning.

Siamese networks

A Siamese network, as the name suggests, is a neural network model where the network is trained to distinguish between two inputs. A Siamese network can train a CNN to produced an embedding by two encoders. Each encoder is fed with one of the images in either a positive or a negative pair. A Siamese network requires less data than the other deep learning algorithms. Siamese networks were originally introduced for comparing signatures. A Siamese network is shown in the following image; the weights are shared between the networks:

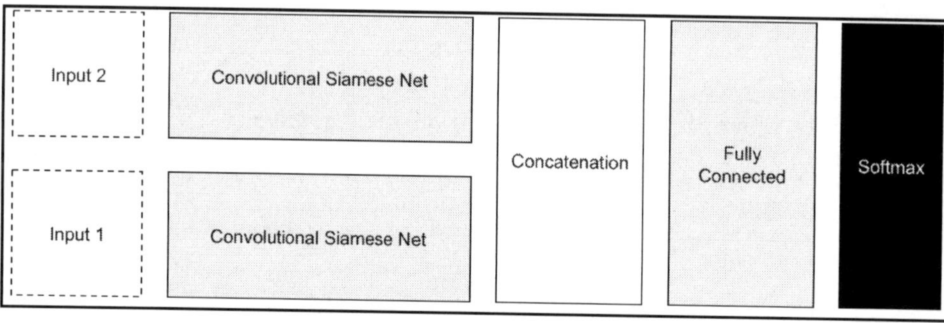

The other use of Siamese networks is one-shot learning. **One-shot learning** is the technique of learning with just one example. In this case, an image can be shown and it can tell whether they are similar. For most of the similarity learning tasks, a pair of positive and negative pairs are required to train. Such datasets can be formed with any dataset that is available for classification tasks, assuming that they are Euclidean distances. The main difference between these algorithms and algorithms in previous chapters is that these encoders try to differentiate one from another.

Contrastive loss

Contrastive loss differentiates images by similarity. The feature or latent layer is compared using a similarity metric and trained with the target for a similarity score. In the case of a positive pair, the target would be 0, as both inputs are the same. For negative pairs, the distance between the pair of latent is a maximum of 0 in the case of cosine distance or regularised Euclidean distance. The loss can be defined by a `contrastive_loss`, which is explained in the following code:

```
def contrastive_loss(model_1, model_2, label, margin=0.1):
    distance = tf.reduce_sum(tf.square(model_1 - model_2), 1)
    loss = label * tf.square(
        tf.maximum(0., margin - tf.sqrt(distance))) + (1 - label) *
distance
    loss = 0.5 * tf.reduce_mean(loss)
    return loss
```

Two model's distances are compared and loss is computed. Now, we will define and train a Siamese network. For a Siamese network, we will need two models that are same. Next, let's define a function for a simple CNN with a given input, with the help of the following code:

```
def get_model(input_):
    input_reshape = tf.reshape(input_, [-1, 28, 28, 1],
                               name='input_reshape')
    convolution_layer_1 = convolution_layer(input_reshape, 64)
    pooling_layer_1 = pooling_layer(convolution_layer_1)
    convolution_layer_2 = convolution_layer(pooling_layer_1, 128)
    pooling_layer_2 = pooling_layer(convolution_layer_2)
    flattened_pool = tf.reshape(pooling_layer_2, [-1, 5 * 5 * 128],
                              name='flattened_pool')
    dense_layer_bottleneck = dense_layer(flattened_pool, 1024)
    return dense_layer_bottleneck
```

The model defined will be used twice to define the encoders necessary for Siamese networks. Next, placeholders for both the models are defined. For every pair, the similarity of the inputs is also fed as input. The models defined are the same. The models can also be defined so that the weights are shared. Two models for the left and right side are defined here:

```
left_input = tf.placeholder(tf.float32, shape=[None, input_size])
right_input = tf.placeholder(tf.float32, shape=[None, input_size])
y_input = tf.placeholder(tf.float32, shape=[None, no_classes])
left_bottleneck = get_model(left_input)
right_bottleneck = get_model(right_input)
```

The bottleneck layers are taken from the models and are concatenated. This is crucial for similarity learning problems. Any number of models can be created, and the final layers can be concatenated, as shown here:

```
dense_layer_bottleneck = tf.concat([left_bottleneck,
right_bottleneck], 1)
```

Next, a dropout layer is added with logits computed out of the concatenated layer. Then the procedure is similar to any other network, as shown here:

```
dropout_bool = tf.placeholder(tf.bool)
dropout_layer = tf.layers.dropout(
        inputs=dense_layer_bottleneck,
        rate=0.4,
        training=dropout_bool
    )
logits = dense_layer(dropout_layer, no_classes)

with tf.name_scope('loss'):
    softmax_cross_entropy = tf.nn.softmax_cross_entropy_with_logits(
        labels=y_input, logits=logits)
    loss_operation = tf.reduce_mean(softmax_cross_entropy,
name='loss')
    tf.summary.scalar('loss', loss_operation)

with tf.name_scope('optimiser'):
    optimiser = tf.train.AdamOptimizer().minimize(loss_operation)

with tf.name_scope('accuracy'):
    with tf.name_scope('correct_prediction'):
        predictions = tf.argmax(logits, 1)
        correct_predictions = tf.equal(predictions, tf.argmax(y_input,
1))
    with tf.name_scope('accuracy'):
        accuracy_operation = tf.reduce_mean(
            tf.cast(correct_predictions, tf.float32))
tf.summary.scalar('accuracy', accuracy_operation)

session = tf.Session()
session.run(tf.global_variables_initializer())

merged_summary_operation = tf.summary.merge_all()
train_summary_writer = tf.summary.FileWriter('/tmp/train',
session.graph)
test_summary_writer = tf.summary.FileWriter('/tmp/test')

test_images, test_labels = mnist_data.test.images,
mnist_data.test.labels
```

The data has to be fed separately for left and right models as shown:

```
for batch_no in range(total_batches):
    mnist_batch = mnist_data.train.next_batch(batch_size)
    train_images, train_labels = mnist_batch[0], mnist_batch[1]
    _, merged_summary = session.run([optimiser,
merged_summary_operation],
                                    feed_dict={
        left_input: train_images,
        right_input: train_images,
        y_input: train_labels,
        dropout_bool: True
    })
    train_summary_writer.add_summary(merged_summary, batch_no)
    if batch_no % 10 == 0:
        merged_summary, _ = session.run([merged_summary_operation,
                                         accuracy_operation],
 feed_dict={
            left_input: test_images,
            right_input: test_images,
            y_input: test_labels,
            dropout_bool: False
        })
        test_summary_writer.add_summary(merged_summary, batch_no)
```

We have seen how to define a Siamese network. Two encoders are defined, and the latent space is concatenated to form the loss of training. The left and right models are fed with data separately. Next, we will see how similarity learning can be performed within a single network.

FaceNet

The FaceNet model proposed by Schroff et al. (`https://arxiv.org/pdf/1503.03832.pdf`) solves the face verification problem. It learns one deep CNN, then transforms a face image to an embedding. The embedding can be used to compare faces to see how similar they are and can be used in the following three ways:

- **Face verification** considers two faces and it is decides whether they are similar or not. Face verification can be done by computing the distance metric.
- **Face recognition** is a classification problem for labelling a face with a name. The embedding vector can be used for training the final labels.

- **Face Clustering** groups similar faces together like how photo applications cluster photos of the same person together. A clustering algorithm such as K-means is used to group faces.

The following image shows the FaceNet architecture:

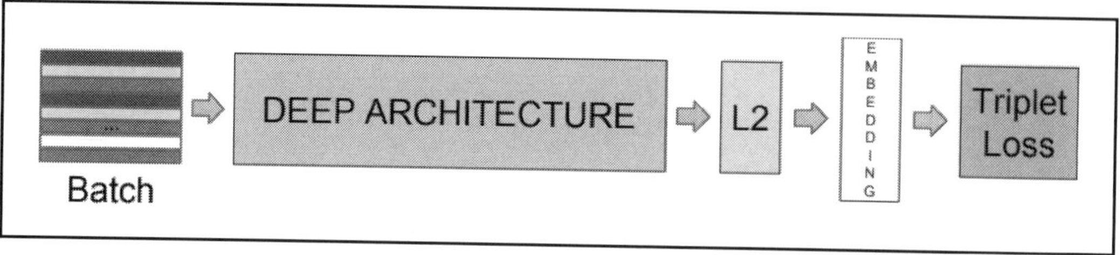

Reproduced with permission from Schroff et al.

FaceNet takes a batch of face images and trains them. In that batch, there will be a few positive pairs. While computing the loss, the positive pairs and closest few negative pairs are considered. Mining selective pairs enable smooth training. If all the negatives are pushed away all the time, the training is not stable. Comparing three data points is called **triplet loss**. The images are considered with a positive and negative match while computing the loss. The negatives are pushed only by a certain margin. Triplet loss is explained in detail here.

Triplet loss

The triplet loss learns the score vectors for the images. The score vectors of face descriptors can be used to verify the faces in Euclidean space. The triplet loss is similar to metric learning in the sense of learning a projection so that the inputs can be distinguished. These projections or descriptors or score vectors are a compact representation, hence can be considered as a dimensionality reduction technique. A triplet consists of an anchor, and positive and negative faces. An anchor can be any face, and positive faces are the images of the same person. The negative image may come from another person. It's obvious that there will be a lot of negative faces for a given anchor.

By selecting negatives that are currently closer to the anchor, its harder for the encoder to distinguish the faces, thereby making it learn better. This process is termed as **hard negative mining**. The closer negatives can be obtained with a threshold in Euclidean space. The following image depicts the triplet loss model:

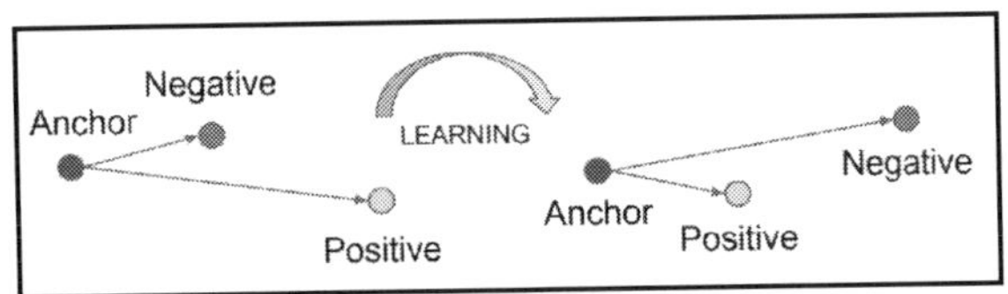

Reproduced with permission from Schroff et al.

The loss computation in TensorFlow is shown here:

```
def triplet_loss(anchor_face, positive_face, negative_face, margin):
    def get_distance(x, y):
        return tf.reduce_sum(tf.square(tf.subtract(x, y)), 1)

    positive_distance = get_distance(anchor_face, positive_face)
    negative_distance = get_distance(anchor_face, negative_face)
    total_distance = tf.add(tf.subtract(positive_distance,
negative_distance), margin)
    return tf.reduce_mean(tf.maximum(total_distance, 0.0), 0)
```

The mining of the triplets is a difficult task. Every point has to be compared with others to get the proper anchor and positive pairs. The mining of the triplets is shown here:

```
def mine_triplets(anchor, targets, negative_samples):
    distances = cdist(anchor, targets, 'cosine')
    distances = cdist(anchor, targets, 'cosine').tolist()
    QnQ_duplicated = [
        [target_index for target_index, dist in enumerate(QnQ_dist) if
dist == QnQ_dist[query_index]]
        for query_index, QnQ_dist in enumerate(distances)]
    for i, QnT_dist in enumerate(QnT_dists):
        for j in QnQ_duplicated[i]:
            QnT_dist.itemset(j, np.inf)

    QnT_dists_topk = QnT_dists.argsort(axis=1)[:, :negative_samples]
    top_k_index = np.array([np.insert(QnT_dist, 0, i) for i, QnT_dist
in enumerate(QnT_dists_topk)])
    return top_k_index
```

This could make the training slower on a GPU machine as the distance computation happens in CPU. The FaceNet model is a state of the art method in training similarity models for faces.

The DeepNet model

The DeepNet model is used for learning the embedding of faces for face verification tasks such as FaceNet. This improves on the method of FaceNet discussed in the previous section. It takes multiple crops of the same face and passes through several encoders to get a better embedding. This has achieved a better accuracy than FaceNet but takes more time for processing. The face crops are made in the same regions and passed through its respective encoders. Then all the layers are concatenated for training against the triplet loss.

DeepRank

DeepRank proposed by Wang et al. (`https://users.eecs.northwestern.edu/~jwa368/pdfs/deep_ranking.pdf`) is used to rank images based on similarity. Images are passed through different models as shown here:

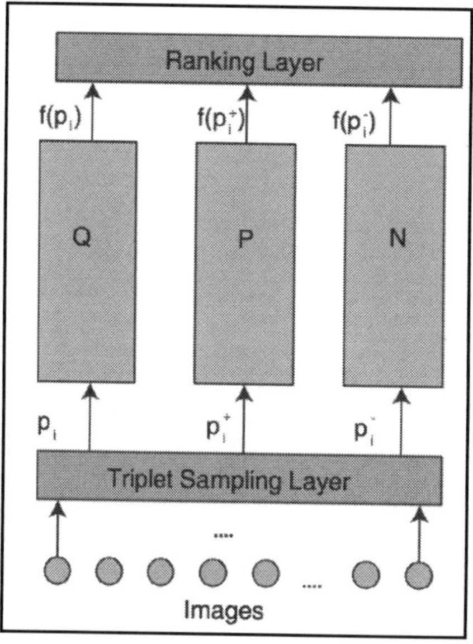

Reproduced with permission from Wang et al.

The triplet loss is computed here as well and backpropagation is done more smoothly. Then the image can be converted to a linear embedding for ranking purposes, as shown:

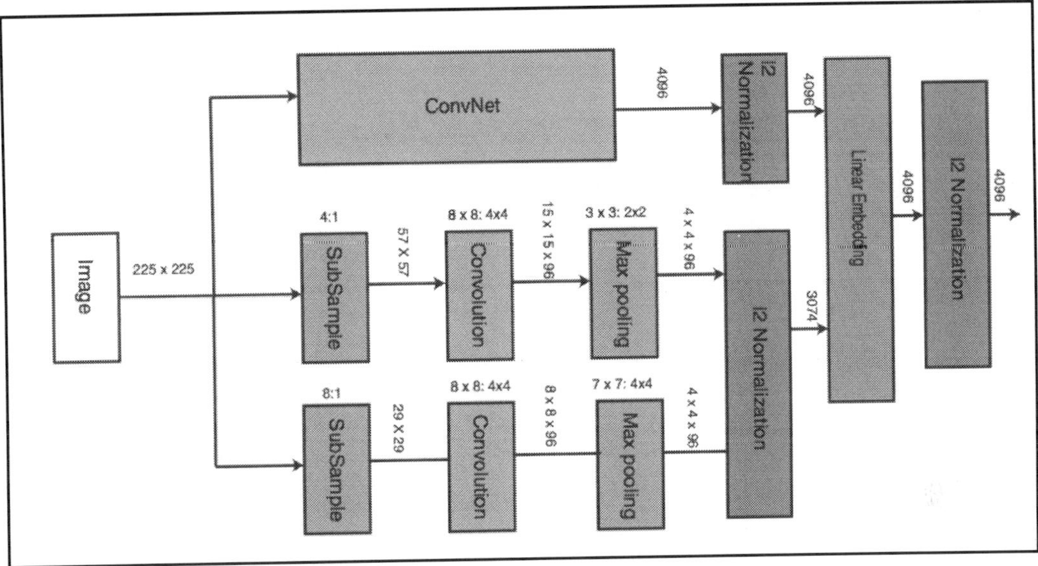

Reproduced with permission from Wang et al.

This algorithm is highly useful for ranking purposes.

Visual recommendation systems

Visual recommendation systems are excellent for getting recommendations for a given image. Recommendation models provide images with similar properties. From the following model proposed by Shankar et al. (`https://arxiv.org/pdf/1703.02344.pdf`) you can learn the embedding for images that are similar and it also provides recommendations:

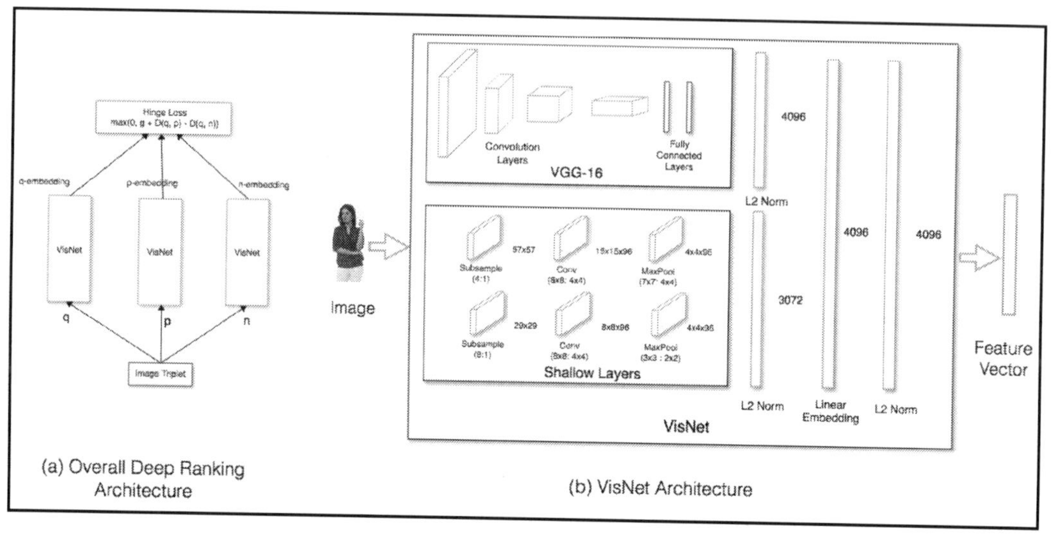

Figure (a) Shows the deep ranking architecture and (b) Shows the VisNet architecture [Reproduced with permission from Shankar et al]

These are some of the algorithms that are used for similarity learning. In the next section, we will see how to apply these techniques to faces.

Human face analysis

The human face can be analyzed in multiple ways using computer vision. There are several factors that are to be considered for this, which are listed here:

- **Face detection**: Finding the bounding box of location of faces
- **Facial landmark detection**: Finding the spatial points of facial features such as nose, mouth and so on

- **Face alignment**: Transforming the face into a frontal face for further analysis
- **Attribute recognition**: Finding attributes such as gender, smiling and so on
- **Emotion analysis**: Analysing the emotions of persons
- **Face verification**: Finding whether two images belong to the same person
- **Face recognition**: Finding an identity for the face
- **Face clustering**: Grouping the faces of the same person together

Let's learn about the datasets and implementation of these tasks in detail, in the following sections.

Face detection

Face detection is similar to the object detection, that we discussed in `Chapter 23`, *Object Detection*. The locations of the faces have to be detected from the image. A dataset called **Face Detection Data Set and Benchmark** (**FDDB**) can be downloaded from `http://vis-www.cs.umass.edu/fddb/`. It has 2,845 images with 5,171 faces. Another dataset called **wider face** can be downloaded from `http://mmlab.ie.cuhk.edu.hk/projects/WIDERFace/`proposed by Yang et al. It has 32,203 images with 393,703 faces. Here is a sample of images from the wider face dataset:

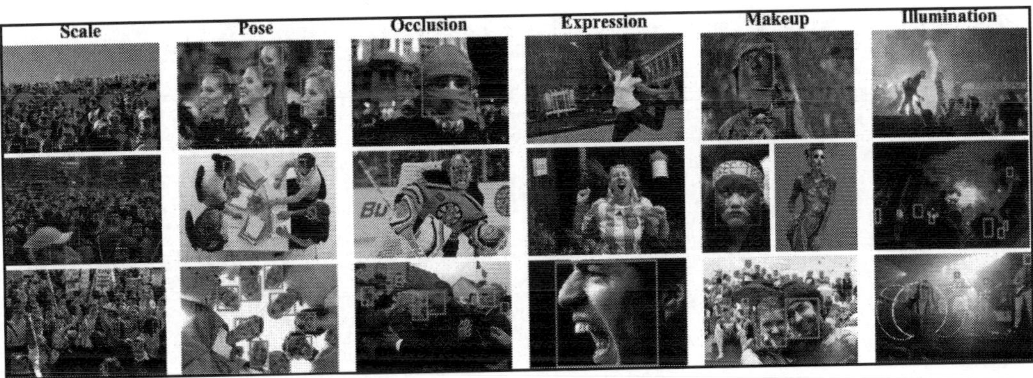

Proposed by Yang et al. and reproduced from http://mmlab.ie.cuhk.edu.hk/projects/WIDERFace/support/intro.jpg

The dataset has a good variation of scale, pose, occlusion, expression, makeup, and illumination. Another dataset called **Multi-Attribute Labelled Faces** (**MALF**) has 5,250 images with 11,931 faces. MALF can be accessed from the link `http://www.cbsr.ia.ac.cn/faceevaluation/`. The same techniques used in object detection can be applied for face detection as well.

Face landmarks and attributes

Face landmarks are the spatial points in a human face. The spatial points correspond to locations of various facial features such as eyes, eyebrows, nose, mouth, and chin. The number of points may vary from 5 to 78 depending on the annotation. Face landmarks are also referred to as **fiducial-points**, **facial key points**, or **face pose**. The face landmarks have many applications as listed here:

- Alignment of faces for better face verification or face recognition
- To track faces in a video
- Facial expressions or emotions can be measured
- Helpful for diagnosis of medical conditions

Next, we will see some databases that have the annotation for fiducial points.

The Multi-Task Facial Landmark (MTFL) dataset

The `MTFL` dataset is proposed by Zhang et al. and is annotated with five facial landmarks along with gender, smiling, glasses and head pose annotations. There are 12,995 faces present in the database. `MTFL` can be downloaded from `http://mmlab.ie.cuhk.edu.hk/projects/TCDCN/data/MTFL.zip`.

Here is a sample of the images present in `MTFL`:

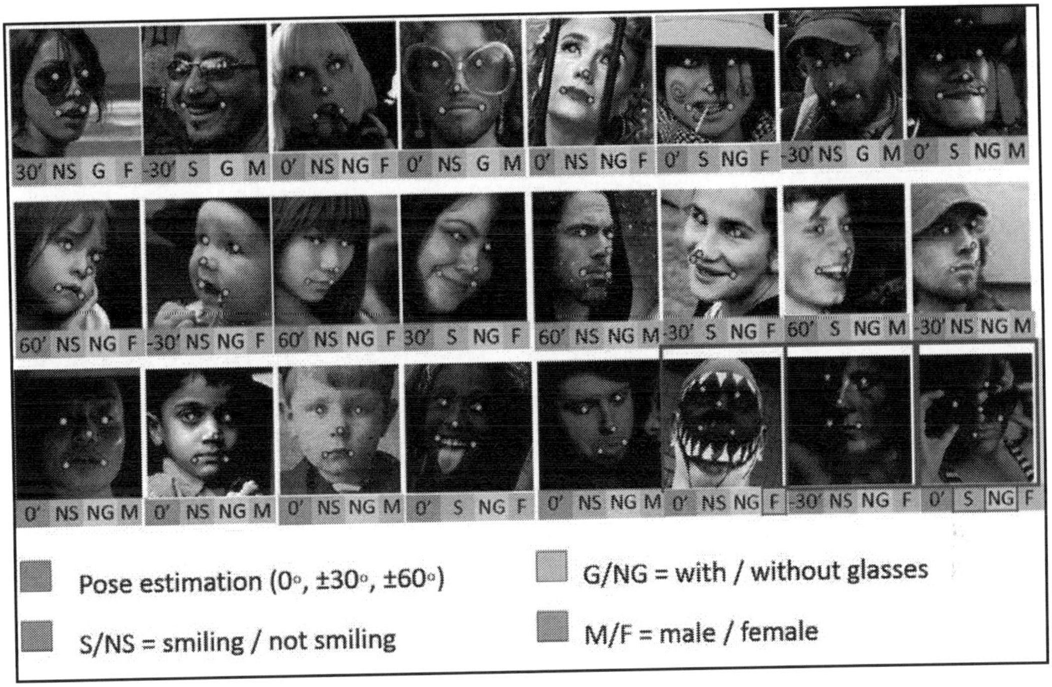

Proposed by Zhang et al. and reproduced from http://mmlab.ie.cuhk.edu.hk/projects/TCDCN/img/1.jpg

There are a lot of variations in the faces with respect to age, illumination, emotions and so on. **Head pose** is the angle of face direction, denoted in degrees. Glasses, smiling, gender attributes, and so on are annotated with binary labels.

The Kaggle keypoint dataset

The Kaggle keypoint dataset is annotated with 15 facial landmarks. There are 8,832 images present in the dataset. It can be downloaded from the link `https://www.kaggle.com/c/facial-keypoints-detection/data`. The images are 96 pixels by 96 pixels in size.

The Multi-Attribute Facial Landmark (MAFL) dataset

The `MAFL` dataset proposed by Zhang et al. is annotated with 5 facial landmarks with 40 different facial attributes. There are 20,000 faces present in the database. `MAFL` can be downloaded from `https://github.com/zhzhanp/TCDCN-face-alignment`. Here is a sample of the images present in `MAFL`:

Proposed by Liu et al. and reproduced from http://mmlab.ie.cuhk.edu.hk/projects/celeba/overview.png

The attributes of annotation include pointy-nose, bands, moustache, wavy hair, wearing a hat and so on. These images are included in the `CelebA` dataset as well, which will be discussed in detail later.

Learning the facial key points

As discussed in the earlier topics, there are a few parameters that are to be defined while calculating the key facial points. We will use the following code to define these parameters:

```
image_size = 40
no_landmark = 10
no_gender_classes = 2
no_smile_classes = 2
no_glasses_classes = 2
no_headpose_classes = 5
batch_size = 100
total_batches = 300
```

Next, allow a few placeholders for the various inputs.

```
image_input = tf.placeholder(tf.float32, shape=[None, image_size,
image_size])
landmark_input = tf.placeholder(tf.float32, shape=[None, no_landmark])
gender_input = tf.placeholder(tf.float32, shape=[None,
no_gender_classes])
smile_input = tf.placeholder(tf.float32, shape=[None,
no_smile_classes])
glasses_input = tf.placeholder(tf.float32, shape=[None,
no_glasses_classes])
headpose_input = tf.placeholder(tf.float32, shape=[None,
no_headpose_classes])
```

Next, construct the main model with four convolution layers, as shown in the following code:

```
image_input_reshape = tf.reshape(image_input, [-1, image_size,
image_size, 1],
                                 name='input_reshape')

convolution_layer_1 = convolution_layer(image_input_reshape, 16)
pooling_layer_1 = pooling_layer(convolution_layer_1)
convolution_layer_2 = convolution_layer(pooling_layer_1, 48)
pooling_layer_2 = pooling_layer(convolution_layer_2)
convolution_layer_3 = convolution_layer(pooling_layer_2, 64)
pooling_layer_3 = pooling_layer(convolution_layer_3)
convolution_layer_4 = convolution_layer(pooling_layer_3, 64)
flattened_pool = tf.reshape(convolution_layer_4, [-1, 5 * 5 * 64],
                            name='flattened_pool')
dense_layer_bottleneck = dense_layer(flattened_pool, 1024)
dropout_bool = tf.placeholder(tf.bool)
dropout_layer = tf.layers.dropout(
```

```
            inputs=dense_layer_bottleneck,
            rate=0.4,
            training=dropout_bool
    )
```

Next, we will create a branch of logits for all the different tasks, by making use of the following code:

```
landmark_logits = dense_layer(dropout_layer, 10)
smile_logits = dense_layer(dropout_layer, 2)
glass_logits = dense_layer(dropout_layer, 2)
gender_logits = dense_layer(dropout_layer, 2)
headpose_logits = dense_layer(dropout_layer, 5)
```

The loss is computed individually for all the facial features, as shown in the following code:

```
landmark_loss = 0.5 * tf.reduce_mean(
    tf.square(landmark_input, landmark_logits))

gender_loss = tf.reduce_mean(
    tf.nn.softmax_cross_entropy_with_logits(
        labels=gender_input, logits=gender_logits))

smile_loss = tf.reduce_mean(
    tf.nn.softmax_cross_entropy_with_logits(
        labels=smile_input, logits=smile_logits))

glass_loss = tf.reduce_mean(
    tf.nn.softmax_cross_entropy_with_logits(
        labels=glasses_input, logits=glass_logits))

headpose_loss = tf.reduce_mean(
    tf.nn.softmax_cross_entropy_with_logits(
        labels=headpose_input, logits=headpose_logits))

loss_operation = landmark_loss + gender_loss + \
                 smile_loss + glass_loss + headpose_loss
```

Now, we will initialize the optimizer and start the training, as shown in the following code:

```
optimiser = tf.train.AdamOptimizer().minimize(loss_operation)
session = tf.Session()
session.run(tf.initialize_all_variables())
fiducial_test_data = fiducial_data.test

for batch_no in range(total_batches):
```

```
fiducial_data_batch = fiducial_data.train.next_batch(batch_size)
loss, _landmark_loss, _ = session.run(
    [loss_operation, landmark_loss, optimiser],
    feed_dict={
        image_input: fiducial_data_batch.images,
        landmark_input: fiducial_data_batch.landmarks,
        gender_input: fiducial_data_batch.gender,
        smile_input: fiducial_data_batch.smile,
        glasses_input: fiducial_data_batch.glasses,
        headpose_input: fiducial_data_batch.pose,
        dropout_bool: True
})
if batch_no % 10 == 0:
    loss, _landmark_loss, _ = session.run(
        [loss_operation, landmark_loss],
        feed_dict={
            image_input: fiducial_test_data.images,
            landmark_input: fiducial_test_data.landmarks,
            gender_input: fiducial_test_data.gender,
            smile_input: fiducial_test_data.smile,
            glasses_input: fiducial_test_data.glasses,
            headpose_input: fiducial_test_data.pose,
            dropout_bool: False
        })
```

This process can be used to detect the facial features as well as landmarks.

Face recognition

The **face recognition** or **facial recognition** is the process of identifying a personage from a digital image or a video. Let's learn about the datasets available for face recognition in the next sections.

The labeled faces in the wild (LFW) dataset

The `LFW` dataset contains 13,233 faces with 5,749 unique people and is considered as the standard dataset to evaluate face verification datasets. An accuracy metric can be used to assess the algorithms. The dataset can be accessed in the link `http://vis-www.cs.umass.edu/lfw/`.

The YouTube faces dataset

The YouTube `faces` dataset contains 3,425 video clips with 1,595 unique people. The videos are collected from YouTube. The dataset has at least two videos per person. This dataset is considered as a standard dataset for face verification in videos. The dataset can be accessed in the link `https://www.cs.tau.ac.il/~wolf/ytfaces/`.

The CelebFaces Attributes dataset (CelebA)

The `CelebA` dataset is annotated with identities of people along with 5 facial landmarks and 40 attributes. There are 10,177 unique people with 202,599 face images in the database. It is one of the large datasets available for face verification, detection, landmark and attributes recognition problems. The images have good variations of faces with diverse annotations. The dataset can be accessed in the link `http://mmlab.ie.cuhk.edu.hk/projects/CelebA.html`.

CASIA web face database

The `CASIA` dataset is annotated with 10,575 unique people with 494,414 images in total. The dataset can be obtained from `http://www.cbsr.ia.ac.cn/english/CASIA-WebFace-Database.html`. This is the second largest public dataset available for face verification and recognition problems.

The VGGFace2 dataset

The `VGGFace2` dataset proposed by Cao et al. is annotated with 9,131 unique people with 3.31 million images. The dataset can be obtained from `http://www.robots.ox.ac.uk/~vgg/data/vgg_face2/`. The variation includes age, ethnicity, pose, profession, and illumination. This is the largest dataset available for face verification.

Here is a sample of the images present in the dataset:

Proposed by Cao et al. and reproduced from http://www.robots.ox.ac.uk/~vgg/data/vgg_face2/web_page_img.png

The minimum, mean, and maximum number of images per unique person are 87, 362.6, and 843 respectively.

Computing the similarity between faces

The computing of face similarities is a multi-step problem. The faces have to be detected, followed by finding the fiducial points. The faces can be aligned with the fiducial points. The aligned face can be used for comparison. As I have mentioned earlier, face detection is similar to object detection. So, in order to find the similarities between faces, we will first import the required libraries and also the `facenet` library, with the help of the following code:

```
from scipy import misc
import tensorflow as tf
import numpy as np
import os
import facenet
print facenet
from facenet import load_model, prewhiten
import align.detect_face
```

The images can be loaded and aligned as shown:

```
def load_and_align_data(image_paths, image_size=160, margin=44,
gpu_memory_fraction=1.0):
    minsize = 20
    threshold = [0.6, 0.7, 0.7]
    factor = 0.709

    print('Creating networks and loading parameters')
    with tf.Graph().as_default():
        gpu_options =
tf.GPUOptions(per_process_gpu_memory_fraction=gpu_memory_fraction)
        sess =
tf.Session(config=tf.ConfigProto(gpu_options=gpu_options,
log_device_placement=False))
        with sess.as_default():
            pnet, rnet, onet = align.detect_face.create_mtcnn(sess,
None)

    nrof_samples = len(image_paths)
    img_list = [None] * nrof_samples
    for i in range(nrof_samples):
        img = misc.imread(os.path.expanduser(image_paths[i]),
mode='RGB')
        img_size = np.asarray(img.shape)[0:2]
        bounding_boxes, _ = align.detect_face.detect_face(img,
minsize, pnet, rnet, onet, threshold, factor)
        det = np.squeeze(bounding_boxes[0, 0:4])
        bb = np.zeros(4, dtype=np.int32)
        bb[0] = np.maximum(det[0] - margin / 2, 0)
        bb[1] = np.maximum(det[1] - margin / 2, 0)
        bb[2] = np.minimum(det[2] + margin / 2, img_size[1])
        bb[3] = np.minimum(det[3] + margin / 2, img_size[0])
        cropped = img[bb[1]:bb[3], bb[0]:bb[2], :]
        aligned = misc.imresize(cropped, (image_size, image_size),
interp='bilinear')
        prewhitened = prewhiten(aligned)
        img_list[i] = prewhitened
    images = np.stack(img_list)
    return images
```

Now we will process the image paths to get the embeddings. The code for the same is given here:

```
def get_face_embeddings(image_paths, model='/20170512-110547/'):
    images = load_and_align_data(image_paths)
    with tf.Graph().as_default():
            with tf.Session() as sess:
                load_model(model)
                images_placeholder =
tf.get_default_graph().get_tensor_by_name("input:0")
                embeddings =
tf.get_default_graph().get_tensor_by_name("embeddings:0")
                phase_train_placeholder =
tf.get_default_graph().get_tensor_by_name("phase_train:0")
                feed_dict = {images_placeholder: images,
phase_train_placeholder: False}
                emb = sess.run(embeddings, feed_dict=feed_dict)

    return emb
```

Now we will compute the distance between the embeddings using the following code:

```
def compute_distance(embedding_1, embedding_2):
    dist = np.sqrt(np.sum(np.square(np.subtract(embedding_1,
embedding_2))))
    return dist
```

This function will compute the **Euclidean** distance between the embeddings.

Finding the optimum threshold

Using the preceding functions, the accuracy of this system can be calculated. The following code can be used for calculating the optimum threshold:

```
import sys
import argparse
import os
import re
from sklearn.metrics import classification_report
from sklearn.metrics import accuracy_score
```

Now, the image paths are obtained from the folder, using the following code:

```
def get_image_paths(image_directory):
    image_names = sorted(os.listdir(image_directory))
    image_paths = [os.path.join(image_directory, image_name) for
image_name in image_names]
    return image_paths
```

The distances of the images are obtained when embeddings are passed, as shown in the following code:

```
def get_labels_distances(image_paths, embeddings):
    target_labels, distances = [], []
    for image_path_1, embedding_1 in zip(image_paths, embeddings):
        for image_path_2, embedding_2 in zip(image_paths, embeddings):
            if (re.sub(r'\d+', '', image_path_1)).lower() ==
(re.sub(r'\d+', '', image_path_2)).lower():
                target_labels.append(1)
            else:
                target_labels.append(0)
            distances.append(compute_distance(embedding_1,
embedding_2)) # Replace distance metric here
    return target_labels, distances
```

The threshold is varied as shown in the following code and various metrics are printed accordingly:

```
def print_metrics(target_labels, distances):
    accuracies = []
    for threshold in range(50, 150, 1):
        threshold = threshold/100.
        predicted_labels = [1 if dist <= threshold else 0 for dist in
distances]
        print("Threshold", threshold)
        print(classification_report(target_labels, predicted_labels,
target_names=['Different', 'Same']))
        accuracy = accuracy_score(target_labels, predicted_labels)
        print('Accuracy: ', accuracy)
        accuracies.append(accuracy)
    print(max(accuracies))
```

Now, the image paths are passed to the embeddings, with the help of the following code:

```
def main(args):
    image_paths = get_image_paths(args.image_directory)
    embeddings = get_face_embeddings(image_paths)  # Replace your
embedding calculation here
    target_labels, distances = get_labels_distances(image_paths,
embeddings)
    print_metrics(target_labels, distances)
```

Finally, the directory of the images is passed as the main argument to these methods, as shown in the following code:

```
if __name__ == '__main__':
    parser = argparse.ArgumentParser()
    parser.add_argument('image_directory', type=str, help='Directory
containing the images to be compared')
    parsed_arguments = parser.parse_args(sys.argv[1:])
    main(parsed_arguments)
```

In this example, we have taken a pre-trained model and used it to construct a face verification method. ;

Face clustering

Face clustering is the process of grouping images of the same person together for albums. The embeddings of faces can be extracted, and a clustering algorithm such as K-means can be used to club the faces of the same person together. TensorFlow provides an API called `tf.contrib.learn.KmeansClustering` for the K-means algorithm. The K-means algorithm groups the data points together. With the help of this K-means algorithm, the embeddings of an album can be extracted and the faces of individuals can be found together, or in other words, clustered together.

Summary

In this chapter, we covered the basics of similarity learning. We studied algorithms such as metric learning, Siamese networks, and FaceNet. We also covered loss functions such as contrastive loss and triplet loss. Two different domains, ranking and recommendation, were also covered. Finally, the step-by-step walkthrough of face identification was covered by understanding several steps including detection, fiducial points detections, and similarity scoring.

Other Books You May Enjoy

If you enjoyed this book, you may be interested in these other books by Packt:

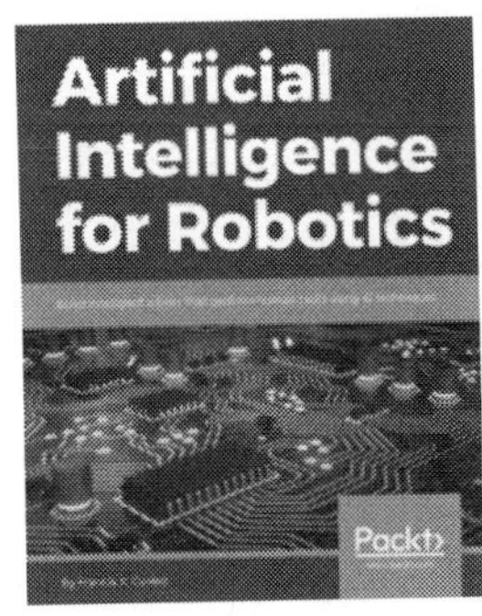

Artificial Intelligence for Robotics
Francis X. Govers

ISBN: 9781788835442

- Get started with robotics and artificial intelligence
- Apply simulation techniques to give your robot an artificial personality
- Understand object recognition using neural networks and supervised learning techniques
- Pick up objects using genetic algorithms for manipulation
- Teach your robot to listen using NLP via an expert system
- Use machine learning and computer vision to teach your robot how to avoid obstacles
- Understand path planning, decision trees, and search algorithms in order to enhance your robot

Hands-On Chatbot Development with Alexa Skills and Amazon Lex
Sam Williams

ISBN: 9781788993487

- Create a development environment using Alexa Skills Kit, AWS CLI, and Node.js
- Build Alexa Skills and Lex chatbots from scratch
- Gain access to third-party APIs from your Alexa Skills and Lex chatbots
- Use AWS services such as Amazon S3 and DynamoDB to enhance the abilities of your Alexa Skills and Amazon Lex chatbots
- Publish a Lex chatbot to Facebook Messenger, Twilio SMS, and Slack
- Create a custom website for your Lex chatbots
- Develop your own skills for Alexa-enabled devices such as the Echo

Leave a review - let other readers know what you think

Please share your thoughts on this book with others by leaving a review on the site that you bought it from. If you purchased the book from Amazon, please leave us an honest review on this book's Amazon page. This is vital so that other potential readers can see and use your unbiased opinion to make purchasing decisions, we can understand what our customers think about our products, and our authors can see your feedback on the title that they have worked with Packt to create. It will only take a few minutes of your time, but is valuable to other potential customers, our authors, and Packt. Thank you!

Index

A

D

E

F

G

H

I

K

L

M

N

O

S

T

U

V

W

Y

Z

Made in the USA
Columbia, SC
10 November 2022

70768295R00417